The Eighth Fact Extraction and VERification Workshop (FEVER 2025)

Vienna, Austria
31 July 2025

ISBN: 979-8-3313-2407-0

Printed from e-media with permission by:

Curran Associates, Inc.
57 Morehouse Lane
Red Hook, NY 12571

Some format issues inherent in the e-media version may also appear in this print version.

Printed with permission by Curran Associates, Inc. (2025)

For permission requests, please contact the Association for Computational Linguistics at the address below.

Association for Computational Linguistics
209 N. Eighth Street
Stroudsburg, Pennsylvania 18360

Phone: 1-570-476-8006
Fax: 1-570-476-0860

acl@aclweb.org

Additional copies of this publication are available from:

Curran Associates, Inc.
57 Morehouse Lane
Red Hook, NY 12571 USA
Phone: 845-758-0400
Fax: 845-758-2633
Email: curran@proceedings.com
Web: www.proceedings.com

FEVER 2025

The Eighth Fact Extraction and VERification Workshop

Proceedings of the Workshop

July 31, 2025

The FEVER organizers gratefully acknowledge the support from the following sponsors.

Supported by

Google

Introduction

With billions of individual pages on the web providing information on almost every conceivable topic, we should have the ability to collect facts that answer almost every conceivable question. However, only a small fraction of this information is contained in structured sources such as Wikidata; we are therefore limited by our ability to transform free-form text to structured knowledge. There is, however, another problem that has become the focus of a lot of recent research and media coverage: false information coming from unreliable sources.

To ensure accuracy, any content must be verified. However, the volume of information precludes human moderators from doing so. Hence, it is paramount to research automated means to verify accuracy and consistency of information published online and the downstream systems (such as Question Answering, Search and Digital Personal Assistants) which rely on it.

The eighth edition of the FEVER workshop collocated with ACL 2025 aims to continue promoting ongoing research in above area, following on from the first seven collocated with EMNLP 2018, EMNLP 2019, ACL 2020, EMNLP 2021, ACL 2022, EACL 2023, EMNLP 2024, and four shared tasks in 2018, 2019, 2021, and 2024. This year's workshop consists of 3 oral and 14 poster presentations of accepted papers (64% overall acceptance rate), 3 poster presentations from ACL Findings papers, and presentations from 5 invited speakers. FEVER 2025 also hosts the second AVeriTeC shared task on open-weights, reproducible and efficient fact verification systems of real-world claims. The annotation of the new shared task test set was conducted by a donation from Google. The workshop is held in hybrid mode with in-person and virtual poster sessions, live-streamed panel discussion, oral presentations, and invited talks.

The organisers would like to thank the authors of all submitted papers, the reviewers, the panelists, and the invited speakers for their efforts, and we are looking forward to next year's edition.

Best wishes,
The FEVER organisers

Organizing Committee

Workshop Organisers

Mubashara Akhtar, King's College London
Rami Aly, University of Cambridge
Rui Cao, University of Cambridge
Yulong Chen, University of Cambridge
Christos Christodoulopoulos, Amazon
Oana Cocarascu, King's College London
Zhenyun Deng, University of Cambridge
Zifeng Ding, University of Cambridge
Zhijiang Guo, Hong Kong University of Science and Technology
Arpit Mittal, Meta
Michael Schlichtkrull, Queen Mary University of London
James Thorne, KAIST AI
Andreas Vlachos, University of Cambridge
Chenxi Whitehouse, Meta

Program Committee

Program Committee

Mahmud Elahi Akhter, Queen Mary, University of London
Iqra Ali, Queen Mary, University of London
Anab Maulana Barik
Andrew Bell, New York University
Rui Cao, University of Cambridge and Singapore Management University
Jenny Chim, Queen Mary, University of London and Queen Mary University London
Zifeng Ding, University of Cambridge
Roksana Goworek, Queen Mary University of London
Kriti Goyal, Apple
Lovisa Hagström, Chalmers University of Technology
Spencer Hong, National University of Singapore
Maeve Hutchinson, City University
Saidah Zahrotul Jannah, Universitas Airlangga and Nara Institute of Science and Technology
Myunghoon Kang, Korea University
Pride Kavumba, SB Intuitions
David Kletz, IDSIA
Guneet Singh Kohli, Queen Mary, University of London and GreyOrange
Gaurav Kumar, Moveworks
Pietro Lesci, University of Cambridge
Irene Li, University of Tokyo
Christopher Malon, NEC Laboratories America
Kunwoo Park, Soongsil University
Heesoo Park, Dunamu
Parth Patwa, Amazon and University of California, Los Angeles
Dominik Stammbach, Princeton University
Herbert Ullrich, Czech Technical University
Juraj Vladika, Technische Universität München
Moy Yuan, University of Cambridge
Linda Zeng, The Harker School, San Jose and University of California, Santa Cruz
Yuji Zhang, University of Illinois at Urbana-Champaign
Dongzhuoran Zhou, University of Oslo
Yuxiang Zhou, Queen Mary, University of London

Invited Speakers

Christo Buschek, BuzzFeed
Pepa Atanasova, University of Copenhagen
Oana Maria Camburu, Imperial College London
Leyang Cui, Tencent
Michiel Bakker, Massachusetts Institute of Technology

Table of Contents

Program

Thursday, July 31, 2025

09:00 - 09:05 *Opening*

09:05 - 09:50 *Keynote Talk: Christo Buschek*

09:50 - 10:10 *Shared Task Overview*

The 2nd Automated Verification of Textual Claims (AVeriTeC) Shared Task: Open-weights, Reproducible and Efficient Systems
Mubashara Akhtar, Rami Aly, Yulong Chen, Zhenyun Deng, Michael Schlichtkrull, Chenxi Whitehouse and Andreas Vlachos

10:10 - 10:30 *Contributed Shared Task Talks*

AIC CTU@FEVER 8: On-premise fact checking through long context RAG
Herbert Ullrich and Jan Drchal

Exploring Semantic Filtering Heuristics For Efficient Claim Verification
Max Upravitelev, Premtim Sahitaj, Arthur Hilbert, Veronika Solopova, Jing Yang, Nils Feldhus, Tatiana Anikina, Simon Ostermann and Vera Schmitt

10:30 - 11:00 *Morning Break*

11:00 - 12:00 *Poster session*

Automated Claim–Evidence Extraction for Political Discourse Analysis: A Large Language Model Approach to Rodong Sinmun Editorials
Gyuri Choi and Hansaem Kim

Language Model Re-rankers are Fooled by Lexical Similarities
Lovisa Hagström, Ercong Nie, Ruben Halifa, Helmut Schmid, Richard Johansson and Alexander Junge

Portuguese Automated Fact-checking: Information Retrieval with Claim extraction
Juliana Gomes, Eduardo Garcia and Arlindo Rodrigues Galvão Filho

Multilingual Symptom Detection on Social Media: Enhancing Health-related Fact-checking with LLMs
Saidah Zahrotul Jannah, Elyanah Aco, Shaowen Peng, Shoko Wakamiya and Eiji Aramaki

Thursday, July 31, 2025 (continued)

When Scale Meets Diversity: Evaluating Language Models on Fine-Grained Multilingual Claim Verification
Hanna Shcharbakova, Tatiana Anikina, Natalia Skachkova and Josef Van Genabith

Less Can be More: An Empirical Evaluation of Small and Large Language Models for Sentence-level Claim Detection
Andrew Bell

RAG based Question Answering of Korean Laws and Precedents
Kiho Seo and Takehito Utsuro

FACT5: A Novel Benchmark and Pipeline for Nuanced Fact-Checking of Complex Statements
Shayan Chowdhury, Sunny Fang and Smaranda Muresan

Correcting Hallucinations in News Summaries: Exploration of Self-Correcting LLM Methods with External Knowledge
Juraj Vladika, Ihsan Soydemir and Florian Matthes

The Law of Knowledge Overshadowing: Towards Understanding, Predicting, and Preventing LLM Hallucination
Yuji Zhang, Sha Li, Cheng Qian, Jiateng Liu, Pengfei Yu, Chi Han, Yi R. Fung, Kathleen McKeown, ChengXiang Zhai, Manling Li and Heng Ji

GQC: LLM-Based Grouped QA Consolidation for Open-Domain Fact Verification at AVeriTeC
Dongzhuoran Zhou, Roxana Pop, Yuqicheng Zhu and Evgeny Kharlamov

(Fact) Check Your Bias
Eivind Morris Bakke and Nora Winger Heggelund

EMULATE: A Multi-Agent Framework for Determining the Veracity of Atomic Claims by Emulating Human Actions
Spencer Hong, Meng Luo and Xinyi Wan

SemQA: Evaluating Evidence with Question Embeddings and Answer Entailment for Fact Verification
Kjetil Indrehus, Caroline Vannebo and Roxana Pop

Team HUMANE at AVeriTeC 2025: HerO 2 for Efficient Fact Verification
Yejun Yoon, Jaeyoon Jung, Seunghyun Yoon and Kunwoo Park

Thursday, July 31, 2025 (continued)

Exploring Semantic Filtering Heuristics For Efficient Claim Verification
Max Upravitelev, Premtim Sahitaj, Arthur Hilbert, Veronika Solopova, Jing Yang, Nils Feldhus, Tatiana Anikina, Simon Ostermann and Vera Schmitt

OldJoe at AVeriTeC: In-context learning for fact-checking
Farah Ftouhi, Russel Dsouza, Lance Calvin Lim Gamboa, Asim Abbas, Mubashir Ali, Yue Feng, Mark G. Lee and Venelin Kovatchev

SANCTUARY: An Efficient Evidence-based Automated Fact Checking System
Arbaaz Dharmavaram and Saqib Hakak

Fathom: A Fast and Modular RAG Pipeline for Fact-Checking
Farrukh Bin Rashid and Saqib Hakak

Graph-of-Thoughts for Fact-Checking with Large Language Models
Sascha Rolinger and Jin Liu

AIC CTU@FEVER 8: On-premise fact checking through long context RAG
Herbert Ullrich and Jan Drchal

12:00 - 12:45 *Keynote Talk: Pepa Atanasova*

12:45 - 14:00 *Lunch Break*

14:00 - 14:45 *Keynote Talk: Oana Maria Camburu*

14:45 - 15:30 *Keynote Talk: Leyang Cui*

15:30 - 16:00 *Afternoon Break*

16:00 - 16:30 *Contributed Workshop Talks*

When Scale Meets Diversity: Evaluating Language Models on Fine-Grained Multilingual Claim Verification
Hanna Shcharbakova, Tatiana Anikina, Natalia Skachkova and Josef Van Genabith

Thursday, July 31, 2025 (continued)

	FACT5: A Novel Benchmark and Pipeline for Nuanced Fact-Checking of Complex Statements Shayan Chowdhury, Sunny Fang and Smaranda Muresan
	The Law of Knowledge Overshadowing: Towards Understanding, Predicting, and Preventing LLM Hallucination Yuji Zhang, Sha Li, Cheng Qian, Jiateng Liu, Pengfei Yu, Chi Han, Yi R. Fung, Kathleen McKeown, ChengXiang Zhai, Manling Li and Heng Ji
16:30 - 17:15	*Keynote Talk: Michiel Bakker*
17:15 - 17:30	*Closing Remarks*

Automated Claim–Evidence Extraction for Political Discourse Analysis: A Large Language Model Approach to *Rodong Sinmun* Editorials

Gyuri Choi, Hansaem Kim*
Interdisciplinary Graduate Program of Linguistics and Informatics, Yonsei University
{gyuri1345, khss}@yonsei.ac.kr

Abstract

This study investigates the feasibility of automating political discourse analysis using large language models (LLMs), with a focus on 87 editorials from *Rodong Sinmun*, North Korea's official newspaper. We introduce a structured analytical framework that integrates Chain-of-Thought prompting for claim–evidence extraction and a GPT-4o–based automated evaluation system (G-Eval). Experimental results demonstrate that LLMs possess emerging discourse-level reasoning capabilities, showing notably improved alignment with expert analyses under one-shot prompting conditions. However, the models often reproduced ideological rhetoric uncritically or generated interpretive hallucinations, highlighting the risks of fully automated analysis. To address these issues, we propose a Hybrid Human-in-the-Loop evaluation framework that combines expert judgment with automated scoring. This study presents a novel approach to analyzing politically sensitive texts and offers empirical insights into the quantitative assessment of ideological discourse, underscoring the scalability and potential of automation-driven methodologies.

1 Introduction

Editorials in *Rodong Sinmun*, North Korea's official newspaper, function both as journalistic reports and instruments of political discourse that aid in the internalization and justification of the state's ideology and policies. As noted in Baek(2023), these editorials are structured more around persuasion than formal argumentation, with topics and supporting grounds intricately intertwined. Consequently, the discursive structure of these texts is difficult to discern without familiarity with the North Korean language and culture. Traditional rule-based information extraction and keyword-centric analytical approaches have shown limitations in capturing the indirect and ideologically laden nature of these texts, leading to a predominance of qualitative analyses. In South Korea, several studies (Lee, 1997; Kim, 2003; Jin, 2013; Kim and Cho, 2022) have examined *Rodong Sinmun* to investigate shifts in North Korean political policy, but these have also relied primarily on qualitative methods. This study presents the first framework designed to automatically extract and evaluate the core claims and supporting arguments of North Korean editorials by leveraging the step-by-step reasoning capabilities of large language models and automated evaluation metrics for text generation quality. By comparing the automated output with human analyses, we assess both the potential and interpretive risks of automation and propose a structure-based analytical method that extends beyond traditional qualitative approaches.

2 Related Work

LLMs have shown strong performance across various NLP tasks, including information extraction and automatic evaluation. However, their application to complex texts involving rhetoric, emotion, and ideology—such as political discourse—remains limited. In information extraction, Liu et al. (2024) used few-shot prompting to identify executable directives in emergency planning documents, and Xu et al. (2024) proposed ChatUIE, a unified framework for named entity recognition, relation extraction, and event extraction, addressing task imbalance and consistency. Yet, these methods are primarily designed for technical or practical texts, with limited applicability to political content. The "LLM-as-a-judge" paradigm has emerged as an alternative to human evaluation. For instance, Afzal et al. (2024) introduced G-Eval to assess responses from a RAG-based HR chatbot,

Proceedings of the Eighth Fact Extraction and VERification Workshop (FEVER), pages 1–17
July 31, 2025 ©2025 Association for Computational Linguistics

showing high alignment with human judgments. Le Mens and Gallego (2025) found that LLMs can infer ideological positions in political texts with expert-level consistency. However, Stureborg et al. (2024) highlighted that evaluation results can vary significantly depending on prompt design, criteria, and temperature settings, indicating the need for more robust and systematic evaluation protocols.

Concerns over LLMs' political bias have also been raised. Yang et al. (2024) demonstrated that responses vary by model origin, size, and training time, while Kronlund-Drouault (2024) argued that model alignment may reflect dominant capitalist ideologies.

In sum, although progress has been made in information extraction, evaluation automation, and bias detection, integrated approaches for inferring and evaluating claim–evidence structures in political discourse remain underexplored. While Gao and Feng (2025) attempted stance analysis in journalistic texts, this study extends such methods to political texts, experimentally examining the combination of structural inference and automatic evaluation as a means of analyzing political rhetoric as a mode of governance.

3 System Architecture & Methodology

This section outlines the architecture and implementation of our LLM-based system for analyzing political discourse. We focus on 87 editorials from *Rodong Sinmun*, the official newspaper of North Korea, aiming to automatically extract political messages and quantitatively evaluate them based on criteria such as coherence, factuality, and relevance.

Based on pilot experiments regarding North Korea–related content and potential bias, GPT-4o demonstrated relatively stable performance in both understanding and restrained expression. As a result, all automated evaluations in this study were conducted using GPT-4o.

The evaluation consists of three main components:

(1) Logical coherence between the identified claim and its supporting evidence.

(2) Response quality, which include accuracy, relevance, and logical consistency.

(3) Hallucination rate, which detects external insertions or excessive rhetorical language beyond the source text.

Following the automated assessment, a subset of outputs was manually reviewed by human evaluators to verify the validity of the evaluations and identify common error types.

The overall system pipeline is summarized in Figure 1.

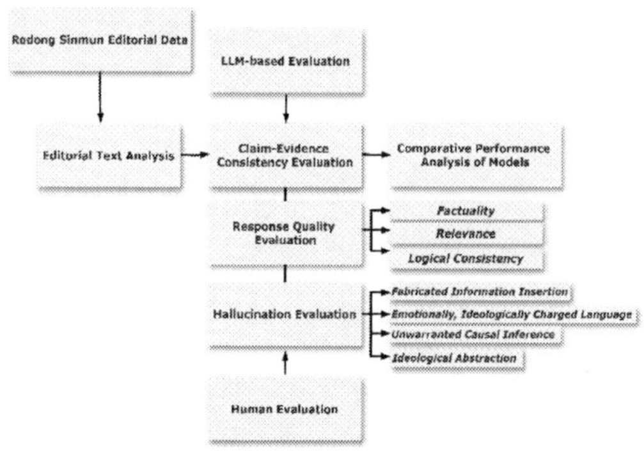

Figure 1: Structured Evaluation Pipeline for Analyzing Claim–Evidence Relations in Political Editorials. The pipeline systematically evaluates extracted claim–evidence pairs across coherence, response quality, and hallucination dimensions.

3.1 Prompt Design and Response Structure

To address the repetitive narrative structure and symbolic rhetoric typical of *Rodong Sinmun* editorials, we designed prompts that explicitly elicit chain-of-thought (CoT) reasoning. Inspired by Baek (2023), our CoT-based analysis prompt guides the model through three sequential steps:

(1) Identifying the main argument.

(2) Citing supporting evidence.

(3) Interpreting the underlying political objective.

This structure is intended to help the model uncover the implicit logic embedded in ideologically charged discourse.

> You are an expert analyst specializing in political propaganda and editorial discourse. The following editorial text covers multiple domains—including politics, economics, and society—and embeds a specific political goal or ideological message.
>
> Please analyze the editorial by following the Chain-of-Thought (CoT) procedure below to uncover its political strategy and messaging intent:
>
> Step 1. Specify the editorial's metadata, including the title, publication date, and source.

Step 2. Read the entire editorial carefully and identify the central argument that is emphasized repeatedly or serves as the core theme. Step 3. Provide at least one direct quotation from the editorial that supports the identified argument. Step 4. Interpret the political objective or strategic message the editorial seeks to convey. Step 5. Synthesize your analysis in a clear and concise summary using the format below:

Table 1: Example of Chain-of-Thought Prompt Design for Political Editorial Analysis.

The model is instructed to produce responses in a fixed format, as shown below Table 2.

◆ Summary of Key Themes • Evidence [Provide justification based on a direct quote from the editorial or the editorial's title.] • Interpretation of Political Strategy or Message [Analyze and explain the intended political objective or strategic messaging embedded in the editorial.]

Table 2: Prompt Design for Output Format Standardization in Editorial Analysis.

To elicit structured reasoning from the model, the response format was designed to guide it beyond simple summarization by prompting it to autonomously construct a logical connection between the central claim and supporting evidence within the editorial. This allowed the model to demonstrate discourse-level analytical capabilities.

The experiment was designed to evaluate the language models' capacity for structured inference, using two prompting conditions: zero-shot and one-shot. The zero-shot setting assessed the model's ability to autonomously infer rhetorical structure without guidance, while the one-shot condition tested whether the model could reproduce a structured response based on a single expert-provided example. Only one demonstration was used in the one-shot setting; variations across examples or prompt sensitivity were not examined within the scope of this study. The number of shots was deliberately restricted to maintain experimental control, and multi-shot prompts were excluded due to potential risks of overfitting.

3.2 G-Eval–Based Automated Evaluation Framework

Model outputs were quantitatively assessed using the G-Eval framework. We adopted three evaluation dimensions tailored to claim–evidence extraction tasks: (1) Coherence, (2) Response Quality, and (3) Hallucination. All scores were generated automatically on a scale from 1-5 using GPT-4o.

The Coherence dimension evaluates the logical connection and inferential validity between the model-generated claim and the cited evidence from the original text. Rather than surface-level similarity, this metric focuses on semantic reasoning, aligning with prior research emphasizing structure-aware evaluation in discourse tasks (Yin and Roth, 2018).

The Response Quality dimension can be further subdivided into accuracy, relevance, and logical consistency. These subdimensions measure factual alignment with the source, reflection of the central theme, and the internal coherence of the generated response, respectively. This multidimensional approach mitigates the limitations of single-metric evaluation (Zhong et al., 2022).

The Hallucination dimension identifies instances where the model introduces unsupported content, rhetorical exaggerations, or ideologically skewed interpretations. This is particularly critical in the context of political discourse, as highlighted in recent work on hallucination in NLG systems (Ji et al., 2023). We assessed four types of hallucination: factual insertion, emotional overstatement, logical leap, and thematic generalization.

Detailed scoring guidelines for each category are provided in Appendix A.

4 Dataset & Models

This study analyzes the complete set of *Rodong Sinmun* editorials published in 2021, which consist of 87 articles in total. All texts were collected in their original Korean form. The editorials span a variety of topics, including politics, diplomacy, and economics. Each editorial was individually processed by the model for discourse-level analysis.

Four LLMs were selected for comparison: GPT-o3 Mini (OpenAI, 2024), Claude 3.7(Anthropic, 2024), Gemini 2.0 (Google, 2025), and EXAONE 7.8B (Research LG et al., 2025). The selection was based on general-purpose capability and adaptation to the Korean language. In particular, EXAONE 7.8B, although smaller in scale than the other models, was included under the hypothesis that its linguistic alignment would offer advantages in interpreting the unique rhetorical patterns and ideological expressions found in *Rodong Sinmun*.

This setup aims to explore how differences in language adaptation affect the models' performance in political discourse analysis. Detailed model characteristics and configurations are summarized in Table 3.

Model	Key Characteristics
GPT-o3 Mini	Lightweight and fast; responsive to structured reasoning and chain-of-thought prompts.
Claude 3.7-Sonnet	Emphasizes consistency over complex reasoning; supports reflective and pragmatic generation.
Gemini 2.0-Flash	Optimized for long form processing and summarization; handles large context windows and multimodal input.
EXAONE 7.8B	Korean-specialized; includes CoT reasoning capabilities; excels in Korean style and vocabulary adaptation.

Table 3: Key Characteristics of Language Models Used in Political Editorial Analysis

The evaluation relied on GPT-4o (OpenAI), to serve as an automated judge to assess the outputs of each model. Scoring was performed along three dimensions: logical coherence between claims and evidence, overall response quality (accuracy, relevance, consistency), and hallucination detection.

4.1 Ground-Truth

To validate model outputs and ensure the external reliability of the evaluation results, we employed expert-written analytical reports [1]from the Korea Institute for National Security Strategy (KINSS). These reports were manually curated by specialists in North Korean politics, military affairs, and inter-Korean relations, providing in-depth qualitative interpretations of the political messages and rhetorical structures of each editorial. An example of individual editorial analysis is provided in Appendix B.

Using these expert analyses as reference, we conducted a secondary human review on a randomly sampled subset of model outputs following the automated evaluation. This step was intended to complement the AI-based scoring by enhancing the precision and trustworthiness of the results, through human verification.

[1] https://www.inss.re.kr/publication/bbs/nk_list.do

5 Results & Analysis

This section presents the quantitative results of model responses to *Rodong Sinmun* editorials, as evaluated using GPT-4o. Detailed scoring criteria are provided in Appendix A.

Overall, the models failed to detect certain strategic rhetorical features such as the de-mystification of the Supreme Leader and exhibited limitations in integrating complex or contradictory issues into a coherent interpretation. However, in the 1-shot condition, model outputs showed greater structural and interpretive alignment with human analysis compared to the 0-shot condition, suggesting that prompt-based guidance positively influences discourse reasoning.

Based on these findings, we provide a comparative analysis in the following sections of how each model responds to political discourse, examining their capabilities in interpreting, structuring, and evaluating ideologically driven texts.

5.1 Analysis of Claim–Evidence Coherence

To assess the models' actual reasoning capabilities, we focused on the logical coherence between the claims and their corresponding evidence within each editorial. This metric goes beyond surface-level response quality and aims to evaluate whether the model can accurately identify and connect semantic units through a valid inferential structure. It serves as a core indicator of the model's ability to engage in discourse-level reasoning. The coherence metric result from which model are summarized in the table below.

Model	0-shot	1-shot
GPT-o3 Mini	4.99	**5.00**
Claude 3.7	4.99	4.95
Gemini 2.0	4.95	4.99
EXAONE 7.8B	4.95	4.80

Table 4: Average Scores for Claim–Evidence Coherence Evaluation.

GPT-o3 Mini demonstrated the most consistent performance across all prompt settings, achieving coherence scores close to the maximum (5.0). It reliably identified core claims, presented corresponding evidence in concrete terms, and explicitly established sentence-level logical connections.

Claude 3.7 also received favorable evaluations, particularly under the 1-shot condition, where its performance closely approached that of GPT-o3 Mini. However, approximately 4.6% of its responses were rated at level 3, as the supporting evidence tended to be explanatory rather than directly aligned with the central claim—indicating a relative weakness in evidential precision.

Gemini 2.0 consistently maintained a Claim–Evidence–Summary structure, demonstrating strength in formal coherence. Nevertheless, in approximately 1.1% of cases involving abstract topics, the evidence lacked sufficient specificity, leading to slightly weaker logical linkage. Although this had minimal impact on the overall average, it suggests a marginal decline in performance for more abstract editorial content.

EXAONE 7.8B exhibited relatively natural performance in identifying claims. However, in approximately 12.6% of its responses, relevant evidence was either missing or only weakly connected. This was particularly evident when the model overly fixated on the emotional and symbolic rhetoric of *Rodong Sinmun* editorials, repeatedly failing to shift toward logic-based analysis.

Overall, GPT-o3 Mini outperformed the other models in both structural explicitness and logical stability. Claude 3.7 showed strong consistency but lacked fine-grained alignment between claims and evidence. Gemini 2.0 offered solid structural scaffolding but weaker inferential integration, while EXAONE 7.8B showed a tendency to prioritize rhetorical affect over semantic reasoning. These findings suggest a persistent gap between surface-level fluency and genuine semantic inference in large language models. The Claim–Evidence coherence evaluation thus serves as a meaningful metric for quantifying this gap and may prove valuable for assessing LLM applicability in downstream NLP tasks involving reasoning over political discourse.

5.2 Response Quality Analysis

In this section, we quantitatively evaluate the response quality of each language model based on three sub-criteria: accuracy, relevance, and logical consistency. Each response was scored on a 5-point scale using the automated evaluation framework. The results are summarized as follows:

Model	Accuracy	Relevance	Logical Consistency
GPT-o3 Mini	4.94/ 4.85	4.98/ 4.96	5.00/ 5.00
Claude 3.7	4.90/ 4.75	4.90/ 4.95	5.00/ 4.96
Gemini 2.0	4.80/ 4.72	4.85/ 4.84	4.84/ 4.83
EXAONE 7.8B	4.31/ 3.86	4.84/ 4.20	4.82/ 4.33

Table 5: Average Scores for Response Quality Evaluation(0shot/1shot)

GPT-o3 Mini consistently achieved near-perfect scores across all categories, demonstrating the highest overall response quality. It reliably identified key arguments, maintained factually grounded and logically coherent reasoning, and exhibited stable performance regardless of prompt configuration.

Claude 3.7 also performed well, particularly in logical consistency and structured response construction. While 1-shot prompting improved its overall output quality, it occasionally introduced unsupported information or omitted critical details, resulting in slightly lower accuracy.

Gemini 2.0 excelled in structural composition, frequently utilizing repetitive rhetorical formats and summarization strategies. It was particularly effective in sequentially presenting leadership-oriented messages or policy narratives. However, its propensity to generalize topics or incorporate information not grounded in the source text resulted in a marked decline in accuracy.

EXAONE 7.8B showed consistently low response quality, with the weakest performance particularly in the 1-shot accuracy setting. Its outputs frequently included off-topic content and exhibited abrupt logical transitions. Performance gains remained minimal even with increased shot counts. For example, despite prompts designed to highlight Kim Jong Il's achievements in party-building and to signal the emergence of

Kimjongunism[2], the model often focused instead on Kim Jong Un's own contributions or produced analyses unrelated to the intended theme, indicating a lack of output reliability.

Category	Content
Editorial Title	Editorial on the 24th Anniversary of Kim Jong Il's Appointment as General Secretary (Oct 8, 1994)
Ground Truth	Emphasizes that the foundation of Party-building lies in Kim Jong Il's ideology and theory. Calls for the thorough establishment of the monolithic ideological system throughout the Party. Commemorates Kim Jong Il's leadership and achievements.
EXAONE 7.8B Output	Focuses on Kim Jong Un's Party-building achievements and reinforcement of socialism. Emphasizes organized Party operations in absolute obedience to Kim Jong Un. Highlights self-reliance and internal mobilization to solve funding and production issues.
Reasons for evaluation	*Accuracy score: 1* The AI misinterprets the editorial, which is intended to commemorate Kim Jong Il's legacy in Party-building and ideological leadership. While Kim Jong Un is briefly referenced in the original, EXAONE 7.8B places undue emphasis on his role, effectively shifting the main theme away from Kim Jong Il. This indicates a failure to distinguish symbolic continuity from thematic centrality in North Korean political discourse.

Table 6: A Case of Accuracy Error in EXAONE 7.8B's Interpretation of North Korean Political Discourse

In summary, GPT-o3 Mini provided consistently high-quality responses across all metrics. Claude 3.7 offered structurally sound outputs but lacked precision in content. Gemini 2.0 demonstrated strong formatting ability but limited inferential accuracy. EXAONE 7.8B struggled most with factual precision, though its Korean specialization suggests potential for future domain-specific tuning.

These findings highlight the partial success of CoT-based structuring while underscoring the persistent challenge of achieving fine-grained semantic inference. They suggest that although LLMs can simulate aspects of discourse analysis, their application to politically charged texts remains constrained.

In particular, despite its relatively low accuracy, EXAONE 7.8B demonstrated sensitivity to Korean rhetorical structures, indicating its potential as a domain-specific model. This points to the possibility of future performance improvements through model scaling and targeted fine-tuning.

Furthermore, human annotators were able to engage in deeper contextual interpretation. For instance, they inferred that the editorial commemorating Kim Jong Il's appointment as General Secretary was strategically framed to reflect Kim Jong Un's recent title change at the 8th Party Congress. In contrast, LLMs restricted their responses to the immediate content of the editorial, failing to account for broader historical or institutional context.

5.3 Analysis of Hallucination Types

In our evaluation, hallucination was assessed using a single composite score (1–5) per response, rather than assigning separate scores for each hallucination type. The rubric defines four representative types—factual insertion, emotional or ideological embellishment, causal overreach, and thematic abstraction—not as independent evaluation axes, but as qualitative indicators that guided holistic judgment. This approach was adopted to reflect the entangled nature of hallucination in political discourse, where multiple error types often co-occur or reinforce one another in a single output.

[2] "Kim Jong-un-ism" was made known to the outside world through a report released by South Korea's National Intelligence Service on October 28, 2021. Although it has not been officially adopted as North Korea's state ideology, it has been used internally to establish Kim Jong-un's independent leadership system. This can be interpreted as an attempt to construct a new ideological framework following Kim Il-sung-ism and Kim Jong-il-ism.

Model	0-shot	1-shot
GPT-o3 Mini	4.52	4.21
Claude 3.7	4.75	4.52
Gemini 2.0	4.92	4.92
EXAONE 7.8B	4.47	4.57

Table 7: Average Scores for Hallucination Detection Evaluation.

GPT-o3 Mini recorded the lowest hallucination score '4.21' under the 1-shot condition, indicating the most factually grounded output among all models. The hallucination rate decreased under the few-shot setting, and the responses remained stable and centered on verifiable content.

Claude 3.7 produced structurally consistent outputs but frequently included emotionally charged phrases in leader-centric or mobilization-themed editorials. The uncritical reproduction of ideological rhetoric contributed to slightly elevated hallucination scores of '4.75' in the 0-shot condition, and '4.52' in 1-shot condition. Gemini 2.0 recorded the highest hallucination score of '4.92' across both 0-shot and 1-shot settings. Although its outputs exhibited structural consistency, they frequently employed symbolic or ideologically charged language that compromised factual grounding. Such hallucinations appeared to be systematically embedded in its output patterns.

Category	Content
Editorial Title	Let Us Thoroughly Implement the Tasks Set Forth in the First Year of the Five-Year Plan, Upholding the Spirit of the 2nd Plenary Meeting of the 8th Central Committee of the WPK *(Feb 14, 2021)*
Ground Truth	The editorial calls for the full implementation of the first-year tasks of the new Five-Year Plan, as set forth by the 2nd Plenary Meeting of the 8th Party Central Committee, which was held just a month after the 8th Party Congress.
Gemini2.0 Output	Describes the editorial as emphasizing unconditional obedience to the Party's decisions, framing it as a typical example of North Korean propaganda.
Reasons for evaluation	The editorial's call for practical implementation of Party decisions is reduced to a narrative of "unconditional obedience," reflecting interpretive bias. This reframes the text's original policy- and action-oriented message as ideological compliance, resulting in a distortion of its core intent.

Table 8: Case of Hallucination Induced by Ideological Framing in Gemini2.0's Interpretation of a North Korean Editorial

EXAONE 7.8B exhibited an increase in hallucination scores despite the addition of more shots, with the score rising from '4.47' in the 0-shot condition to '4.57' in the 1-shot setting. The model showed a marked tendency to overreact to North Korean rhetorical expressions—such as "great," "absolute," and "historic"—frequently producing formulaic constructions, overly generalized summaries, and nonfactual content. Although the outputs were linguistically fluent, they consistently demonstrated low semantic precision.

Category	Content
Model Output	The editorial was interpreted as emphasizing the strengthening of North Korea's political-ideological capabilities and the continued advancement of socialism, in response to Kim Jong Un's *historic* policy speech.
Reasons for evaluation	*Hallucination score: 5* The term *"historic"* was not used in the source text to glorify Kim Jong Un's speech. The model introduces a value-laden interpretation that is absent from the original, resulting in semantic distortion.

Table 9: Example of Hallucination in EXAONE 7.8B's Output: Overreaction to Rhetorical Expressions

Overall, GPT-o3 Mini exhibited the lowest hallucination frequency and highest factual alignment, with few-shot prompting further reducing rhetorical deviation. Claude maintained structural stability but was prone to rhetorical interference. Gemini demonstrated a distinctive tendency to produce outputs in which hallucinations were structurally embedded, driven by interpretive framing that distorted the intended meaning. EXAONE 7.8B tended to prioritize rhetorical surface features—such as "great" and "absolute"—over semantic fidelity, frequently leading to repeated factual inaccuracies. These findings suggest that hallucination in political discourse is not merely a factual error but a higher-order generation failure where rhetorical form distorts intended meaning. The uncritical reproduction of ideological content by LLMs, especially in texts like North Korean editorials, demonstrates how hallucination can emerge as a structural phenomenon. This highlights the need for heightened model accountability when applying LLMs to politically sensitive discourse tasks.

5.4 Reliability of Automated Evaluation and Overall Model Interpretability

In this section, we compare the automated evaluation results generated by GPT-4o (G-Eval) with human assessments based on approximately 30% of the dataset. The goal is to analyze the alignment and reliability of the automated scoring system. The evaluation criteria were consistent across both approaches: claim–evidence coherence, response quality, and hallucination severity. The average Pearson correlation coefficients are reported below.

Dimension	0-shot Avg.	1-shot Avg.
Accuracy	0.64	0.78
Relevance	0.59	0.75
Logical Consistency	0.73	0.64
Coherence	0.55	0.60
Hallucination	0.65	0.77

Table 10: Average Spearman correlation coefficients between model predictions and human judgments across evaluation dimensions in 0-shot and 1-shot settings. Most correlations are statistically significant ($p < 0.05$), indicating meaningful alignment between model and human evaluations.

As shown in the table, GPT-4o generally produced judgments that were well aligned with those of human evaluators, exhibiting high correlation across all evaluation criteria. In particular, correlation coefficients improved across most dimensions under the 1-shot prompt setting, suggesting that example-based prompting helped the model better internalize evaluation criteria and align more closely with human judgments.

However, for logical consistency, the 1-shot setting resulted in a lower correlation compared to 0-shot. This may indicate that the model became overly dependent on the prompt example, simplifying its reasoning process.

In addition, while G-Eval showed generally strong correlations with human raters, its score distribution tended to be skewed toward the higher end. For instance, in the coherence dimension, several responses received scores of 4.0 or above from the automatic evaluator, despite containing clear logical inconsistencies or stylistic issues. This pattern suggests that the model applies the scoring rubric conservatively and is relatively reluctant to assign lower scores. It indicates that GPT-4o tends to make more lenient judgments than human evaluators. While G-Eval achieves a reasonable degree of quantitative reliability, these findings underscore the need for calibrated interpretation when relying on its absolute scores.

When comparing the performance across models, clear differences emerged. While all models demonstrated a baseline capacity for structured generation and output stability, their ability to interpret political discourse varied significantly. GPT-o3 Mini and Claude 3.7 responded stably to the rhetorical structure and stylistic patterns of *Rodong Sinmun* editorials, maintaining thematic flow and coherent response composition. In contrast, EXAONE 7.8B and Gemini 2.0 frequently overreacted to political symbolism and emotional rhetoric, resulting in repeated hallucinations and semantic distortion.

These findings suggest that beyond surface-level fluency, LLMs still face structural limitations in interpreting the ideological abstraction and rhetorical complexity inherent in political discourse. This study empirically delineates the boundary between what LLMs can and cannot do in the context of political discourse analysis and underscores the need for a Hybrid Human-in-the-Loop framework where human interpretation complements, rather than simply post-processes, automated outputs.

6 Conclusion

This study empirically examined the potential for automating political discourse analysis by applying LLMs and an automated evaluation framework to North Korea's *Rodong Sinmun* editorials. Unlike traditional approaches to political text analysis that rely primarily on rule-based methods or qualitative interpretation, this research proposed a structure-based framework that automatically extracts Claim–Evidence structures through CoT-based prompting and quantitatively evaluates the generated responses using the G-Eval framework. This approach offers a scalable and systematic methodological alternative that maintains the interpretive depth of qualitative analysis while ensuring the consistency and reproducibility of automation.

Experimental results show that LLMs can produce responses with a reasonable level of coherence and logical linkage. In particular, under the 1-shot condition, model outputs demonstrated high alignment with expert evaluations. The study also revealed differences in rhetorical structure interpretation across models and quantified tendencies in hallucination generation. These findings suggest that LLMs can serve not only as generative tools but also as potential instruments for analyzing and structuring ideological discourse.

At the same time, the models tended to reproduce or overinterpret political symbolism and emotional rhetoric without critical reasoning. This often manifested as exaggerated ideological framing or uncritical mimicry of rhetorical forms, revealing interpretive risks inherent in politically sensitive text generation.

G-Eval, the GPT-4o-based automatic evaluation system, achieved a fair degree of correlation with human assessments but failed to fully capture subtle contextual errors or rhetorical distortions. This highlights that automatic evaluation may also reflect model-internal biases, and excessive reliance on a single model could undermine both reliability and interpretive precision. Accordingly, a Hybrid Human-in-the-Loop framework that complements automatic scoring with expert judgment is proposed as a necessary strategy for high-fidelity political discourse analysis.

This study's methodology is distinguished from prior CoT prompting approaches by its design innovation. The prompt structure not only extracted claims and evidence but also guided higher-order inference by incorporating a political objective interpretation step. Evaluation criteria were also tailored to political discourse, including coherence, ideological consistency, and rhetorical hallucination. The experimental design aligned prompt construction, response generation, automatic scoring, and human reference evaluation in a tightly structured sequence, making it a well-organized empirical attempt to assess both the capabilities and limitations of LLM-based analysis.

As a pioneering study, this work demonstrates the viability of quantifying rhetorical structures in political texts and empirically evaluates the promise and constraints of automatic scoring systems. Future research may extend this framework to various languages and genres of political discourse, thereby further validating the generalizability and real-world applicability of LLM-based analytical methods.

7 Limitations

This study represents an empirical attempt to automate political discourse analysis, but it also has several limitations.

First, the evaluation of generated responses was conducted by a single expert, which may introduce subjective bias. The classification of hallucination errors also relied solely on GPT-4o's automated judgment, lacking inter-rater agreement measures or explicit annotation guidelines.

Second, the prompt was designed as a fixed five-step structure, but no ablation study was conducted to assess the contribution of each step. In addition, the one-shot prompt relied on a single demonstration, and its sensitivity to prompt selection was not systematically evaluated. Third, while hallucination scores were calculated as composite values across four error types, the individual frequency and influence of each type were not analyzed. This limits the ability to make fine-grained comparisons of model-specific error patterns.

Lastly, the analysis focused on *Rodong Sinmun* editorials from a specific period, meaning the temporal scalability and cross-genre generalizability of the proposed methodology remain untested.

These limitations highlight the need for further research to improve the precision of automated systems and to capture the multilayered nature of political discourse. Future work could include ablation analyses of prompt components, few-shot designs with diverse examples, the development of annotation protocols with multiple evaluators, and the application of this framework across genres and languages to enhance both the robustness and scalability of automated political text analysis.

References

Baek, Seungjoo (2023). Analyzing the textual organization of North Korean Rodong Sinmun editorials. The Journal of Language & Literature, 94, 85-118. 10.15565/jll.2023.3.93.85

Lee Hang-Dong (1997). A Study on North Korea's Policy Change - With an Content Analysis of the Editorials in the Ro-Dong Sinmun. Korean Political Science Review, 31(4), 131-160.

Kim Yong Hyeon. (2003). A study on the political change in North Korea through the analysis of Rodong Shinmun: 1945-1950. NORTH KOREAN STUDIES REVIEW, 7(1), 107-127.

Heegwan chin. (2013). The Relations of Japan-North Korea and Chongryon Policy of North Korea: Through the analysis of Rodong Shinmun (1946-2010). The Korean Journal of Unification Affairs, 25(1), 361-396.

Kim. Jeong-ho, & Cho. Yunyoung (2022). North Korea"s Political-Economic Changes Under the Five-Year Economic Development Plan: Kim Jong-Un Regime"s rising ruling tasks and challenges on the 「Rodong Newspaper」. Journal of Peace Studies, 23(1), 155-178.

Liu, Z., Liu, Y., Zhang, Z., Di, L., Wei, F., & Wang, Y. (2024, February). Method for extracting power emergency plan information based on LLM Prompt Learning. In Proc. of SPIE Vol (Vol. 13080, pp. 130800G-1).

Xu, J., Sun, M., Zhang, Z., & Zhou, J. (2024). ChatUIE: Exploring Chat-based Unified Information Extraction using Large Language Models. arXiv preprint arXiv:2403.05132. https://arxiv.org/abs/2403.05132

Afzal, A., Kowsik, A., Fani, R., & Matthes, F. (2024). Towards Optimizing and Evaluating a Retrieval Augmented QA Chatbot using LLMs with Human in the Loop. arXiv preprint arXiv:2407.05925.

Le Mens, G., & Gallego, A. (2025). Positioning Political Texts with Large Language Models by Asking and Averaging. Political Analysis, 1–9. https://doi.org/10.1017/pan.2024.29

Stureborg, R., Alikaniotis, D., & Suhara, Y. (2024). Large language models are inconsistent and biased evaluators. arXiv preprint arXiv:2405.01724.

Yang, K., Li, H., Chu, Y., Lin, Y., Peng, T. Q., & Liu, H. (2024). Unpacking Political Bias in Large Language Models: Insights Across Topic Polarization. arXiv preprint arXiv:2412.16746.

Kronlund-Drouault, P. (2024). Propaganda is all you need. arXiv preprint arXiv:2410.01810.

Gao, Q., & Feng, D. W. (2025). Deploying large language models for discourse studies: An exploration of automated analysis of media attitudes. PLOS ONE, 20(1), e0313932. https://doi.org/10.1371/journal.pone.0313932

Wenpeng Yin and Dan Roth. 2018. TwoWingOS: A Two-Wing Optimization Strategy for Evidential Claim Verification. In Proceedings of the 2018 Conference on Empirical Methods in Natural Language Processing, pages 105–114, Brussels, Belgium. Association for Computational Linguistics.

Zhong, M., Liu, Y., Yin, D., Mao, Y., Jiao, Y., Liu, P., ... & Han, J. (2022). Towards a unified multi-dimensional evaluator for text generation. arXiv preprint arXiv:2210.07197.

Ji, Z., Lee, N., Frieske, R., Yu, T., Su, D., Xu, Y., ... & Fung, P. (2023). Survey of hallucination in natural language generation. ACM computing surveys, 55(12), 1-38.

OpenAI. (2024, April 17). Introducing the OpenAI o3 mini models. OpenAI. https://openai.com/index/openai-o3-mini/

Anthropic. (2024, June 20). Claude 3.5 Sonnet: faster, smarter, more accessible. Anthropic. https://www.anthropic.com/news/claude-3-7-sonnet

Google. (2025, February 15). Gemini model updates: February 2025. Google Blog. https://blog.google/technology/google-deepmind/gemini-model-updates-february-2025/

Research, L. G., Bae, K., Choi, E., Choi, K., Choi, S. J., Choi, Y., ... & Yun, H. (2025). EXAONE Deep: Reasoning Enhanced Language Models. arXiv preprint arXiv:2503.12524. Appendices

Ministry of Unification. 2021. North Korea Knowledge Dictionary. Seoul: Ministry of Unification.

A Appendix: Evaluation Criteria

1. Claim–Evidence Coherence Evaluation Criteria

Score	Description	Example	Evaluation Rationale
5	The supporting evidence clearly aligns with the claim, and the overall logical structure and meaning flow are consistent and coherent.	- The editorial calls for honoring Kim Jong Il's immortal revolutionary achievements on the occasion of Gwangmyeongseong Day, and for implementing the decisions of the 8th Party Congress to advance socialism. - Emphasis is placed on advancing socialism through the ideological and leadership continuity between Kim Jong Il and Kim Jong Un. - Citations from classical works like *Socialism is a Science* reinforce ideological legitimacy. - Statements such as "Respected Comrade Kim Jong Un is fulfilling the patriotic and strong nation-building aspirations of the great General" reinforce leadership succession. - The Party Congress is framed as a concrete political and economic action plan.	The claim and supporting evidence are organically connected, coherently linking theoretical legitimacy, leadership succession, and actionable goals. Logical structure and persuasive force are both strong.
4	The supporting evidence includes partial contradictions or tension with the claim, slightly weakening the legitimacy of the response.	- The editorial reaffirms Kim Jong Il's achievements while emphasizing the importance of implementing the 8th Party Congress decisions. - Citations of Kim Jong Il's ideological works are presented, but also suggest a gap with current realities. - Leadership succession is emphasized yet focus fluctuates between Kim Jong Il and Kim Jong Un. - References to the Party Congress include future goals, but also allude to unresolved challenges.	The response emphasizes socialist continuity, but the evidence introduces interpretive tension: theoretical-practical gaps, dual leadership focus, and incomplete outcomes. This weakens coherence and justification.
3	The relationship between the claim and evidence is unclear, and the justification lacks sufficient detail, making judgment difficult.	- The editorial commemorates Kim Jong Il's achievements and vaguely connects them to future direction. - Kim Jong Un's leadership is highlighted, with Kim Jong Il's ideology only symbolically mentioned.	While evidence exists, it lacks sufficient clarity or strength to justify the claim. Semantic links between ideological succession and practical content are weak or vague.

		- Citations like "Socialism is a Science" are disconnected from concrete policy. - The Party Congress is mentioned, but without detail or evaluative substance.	
2	The evidence includes both support and implicit contradiction, leading to interpretive ambiguity.	- The editorial commemorates Kim Jong Il while centering current leadership on Kim Jong Un. - Kim Jong Un's leadership is emphasized as the practical driver of socialism, while Kim Jong Il's ideology remains symbolic. - Party Congress content is referenced, but with limited mention of implementation or results.	The response expresses dual emphasis but lacks cohesion. It does not clearly justify the original ideological claim, and contradictory focus on past vs. present undermines consistency.
1	The response relies on irrelevant, fragmented, or selectively cited content that artificially supports the claim.	- The editorial introduces Kim Jong Un's international standing and recent achievements, rather than substantiating the ideological continuity from Kim Jong Il. - Citations from Kim Jong Il's works are missing or peripheral. - Party Congress goals are sidelined in favor of recent military or technological advancements.	The claim of ideological succession is not substantively supported. The response introduces unrelated topics (e.g., foreign evaluation, defense) and lacks logical justification.

Table A 1. Scoring Criteria for Claim–Evidence Coherence

2. Response Quality Evaluation Criteria

To evaluate the quality of model-generated responses, we adopt a three-dimensional framework comprising:

- **Accuracy**: The degree to which the response faithfully reflects factual content presented in the original editorial.
- **Relevance**: The extent to which the response directly captures the core themes, ideological messages, and strategic intent of the source text.
- **Logical Consistency**: The internal coherence of the response, including the logical progression of ideas, structural clarity, and stability of the narrative.

Each dimension is scored on scale from 1-5, with detailed scoring rubrics are provided in Tables **A2-**1~3.

Score	Description	Example	Rationale
5	The response fully and precisely matches the facts in the source text.	- The editorial commemorates Gwangmyeongseong Day by glorifying the revolutionary legacy of Kim Jong Il and calls for implementing the 8th Party Congress decisions to achieve new victories in socialism.	The response accurately reflects all key elements of the editorial—textual citations, leadership references, and policy phrases—without distortion or exaggeration. It

		- The model highlights Kim Jong Il's ideological contributions, the leadership of Kim Jong Un, and their joint role in advancing North Korean-style socialism. - Citations from classic texts such as *"Socialism is Science"* and *"Our Socialism Centered on the Masses Is Invincible"* are used to emphasize ideological legitimacy. - The response reflects Kim Jong Un's role in realizing Kim Jong Il's patriotic vision and the Party's five-year plan goals.	faithfully reproduces the core message.
4	Most information is accurate, but some details are slightly exaggerated or inaccurate.	- The editorial emphasizes Kim Jong Il's legacy while highlighting the importance of completing a ten-year national economic development strategy from the 8th Party Congress. - The model blends Kim Jong Il's classical thought with Kim Jong Un's pragmatic economic policies, focusing on self-reliance and science-based development. - However, the editorial actually refers to a five-year plan, not a ten-year strategy.	Although the overall context is preserved, certain terms (e.g., mislabeling "five-year plan" as "ten-year strategy") and emphasis (e.g., focus shifting from Kim Jong Il to Kim Jong Un) reduce factual precision.
3	Some factual inaccuracies exist, but the main idea is generally retained.	- The editorial commemorates both Kim Jong Il's revolutionary legacy and Kim Il Sung's anti-Japanese struggle. - The model emphasizes Juche ideology and identifies military buildup and foreign policy independence as Kim Jong Un's main agenda. - Kim Il Sung is referenced more than Kim Jong Il, whose writings are underrepresented. - The economic and ideological themes of the actual editorial are not sufficiently addressed.	Although the response touches on socialist legitimacy, the main message—emphasizing Kim Jong Il's leadership and the 8th Party Congress—is diluted by unrelated content. Core intent is partially retained but weakened.
2	Frequent factual errors lead to confusion in conveying the core message.	- The editorial is framed around Kim Jong Un's 10th year in power, emphasizing defense strategy and self-reliant military buildup. - Kim Jong Il's legacy and Gwangmyeongseong Day's ideological significance are omitted.	The key theme—celebrating Kim Jong Il's accomplishments—is missing. The focus is shifted to unrelated topics (e.g., military policy), causing thematic distortion and confusion.
1	The response is largely fabricated or factually inconsistent.	- Gwangmyeongseong Day is described as Kim Jong Un's birthday. - The editorial is said to focus on capitalist reforms and reconciliation with the U.S., citing a fictional quote from Kim Jong Un: "True socialism is	The description entirely contradicts the actual editorial. Key terms, individuals, and messages are either fabricated or misrepresented. Factual and

		impossible without the inflow of capital and technology."	contextual integrity is severely compromised.

Table A 2-1. Scoring Rubric for Accuracy

Score	Description	Example	Rationale
5	The response accurately captures the editorial's core themes.	- The editorial commemorates Gwangmyeongseong Day by honoring Kim Jong Il's revolutionary legacy and calls for implementing the 8th Party Congress decisions to achieve new socialist victories. - The model emphasizes the ideological centrality of Kim Jong Il's contributions and Kim Jong Un's leadership, citing key texts and Party goals.	The response reflects all key elements: the holiday's significance, leadership succession, and ideological continuity. Topic alignment and internal structure are coherent and consistent.
4	Minor divergence occurs as the response includes peripheral information.	- The editorial commemorates Kim Jong Il but focuses on Kim Jong Un's recent economic policies and leadership philosophy. - While ideological continuity is mentioned, emphasis shifts to economic achievements. - References to the 8th Party Congress are included but secondary.	While the response remains within the broader thematic scope, the main focus leans toward peripheral content. Core themes are partially reflected but slightly diluted.
3	Only part of the main theme is captured; secondary content dominates.	- The editorial highlights Kim Jong Un's governance and international strategy under sanctions. - Kim Jong Il is referenced symbolically, and policy content focuses on foreign relations. - The 8th Party Congress is framed as a diplomatic rather than ideological initiative.	The response emphasizes a different priority (e.g., foreign strategy), only lightly touching on the intended ideological focus of the editorial. Central themes are marginally addressed.
2	The response misinterprets the topic or lacks clear connection to the source.	- The editorial discusses Kim Jong Un's military leadership and weapons development as key to the nation's future. - Gwangmyeongseong Day is mentioned symbolically but disconnected from its ideological context.	The response shifts away from the intended subject—Kim Jong Il's legacy—and misrepresents the thematic core. Ideological continuity is largely absent.
1	The response is entirely unrelated to the editorial's main themes.	- The editorial focuses on North Korea's youth policy and university education reform. - No mention is made of Kim Jong Il, Kim Jong Un, or the 8th Party Congress.	The response bears no thematic connection to the original editorial. It discusses unrelated content, making the response irrelevant.

Table A2-2 Scoring Rubric for Relevance

Score	Description	Example	Rationale
5	The response is logically coherent and maintains a consistent tone and structure throughout.	- The editorial commemorates Gwangmyeongseong Day, celebrates Kim Jong Il's revolutionary legacy, and emphasizes implementing the 8th Party Congress decisions. - The narrative connects Kim Jong Il's ideological works to Kim Jong Un's leadership and the Party's five-year plan, presenting them as a unified framework. - The overall discourse links past ideology with present execution, achieving both ideological and practical persuasiveness.	The flow from Kim Jong Il's thought → Kim Jong Un's leadership → Party policy is clear and cohesive. Paragraph transitions are smooth, and the logical structure is firm and well-developed.
4	The overall tone is consistent, but minor gaps or ambiguities in logical flow appear.	- The editorial underscores Kim Jong Il's thought and ties it to Kim Jong Un's leadership and the importance of implementing Party decisions. - However, the final connection to economic self-reliance is slightly abrupt.	The response generally maintains consistency, but certain thematic transitions (e.g., ideological → economic emphasis) are underdeveloped or weakly linked.
3	There are some logical issues, but the overall flow is intact.	- The editorial highlights Kim Jong Il's legacy, justifies Kim Jong Un's socialist path, and introduces the 8th Party Congress. - However, unrelated themes such as youth enthusiasm and national defense appear toward the end.	While the initial structure is coherent, the later introduction of unrelated themes weakens cohesion. The response contains logical fragmentation but retains general structure.
2	The logical flow is frequently broken, with unclear transitions or inconsistent development.	- The editorial references Kim Jong Il's achievements, then abruptly shifts to Kim Jong Un's diplomacy and traditional cultural restoration. - Connections between ideological and policy narratives are unclear.	The narrative lacks smooth transitions, and the logical linkage between ideas is weak or missing. Shifts in topic reduce persuasiveness and structural integrity.
1	The response is logically unstable and lacks consistent structure.	- The editorial commemorates North Korea–China friendship, Kim Il Sung's anti-Japanese resistance, and Kim Jong Un's inter-Korean diplomacy. - The discourse shifts to sports diplomacy and peaceful socialism, suggesting reinterpretation of Kim Jong Il's life. - These themes are unrelated to the editorial's original purpose.	The response mixes unrelated topics without a coherent central thread. The lack of logical progression or consistent focus severely undermines credibility.

Table A2-3. Scoring Rubric for Logical Consistency

3. Hallucination

Hallucination is assessed based on the presence of factual inaccuracies, emotionally or ideologically exaggerated rhetoric, speculative causal inferences, or abstraction that distorts the original intent of the editorial. Four primary types are considered:

- **Factual Insertion:** Mentions of people, policies, or events not found in the source.
- **Ideological/Emotional Embellishment:** Rhetorical flourishes or glorifying language absent from the original text.
- **Causal Overreach:** Speculative or ideologically motivated inference not supported by the editorial.
- **Thematic Abstraction:** Specific claims reduced to vague ideological values.

Score	Description	Example	Rationale
5	The response is heavily distorted with pervasive embellishment, ideological exaggeration, or speculative interpretation that severely undermines the factual structure.	- Gwangmyeongseong Day is described as honoring "the greatest thinker in human civilization," and Kim Jong Il's philosophy is said to guide global politics for the next 1,000 years. - Kim Jong Un is claimed to have "defeated all imperialist powers," and the 8th Party Congress is described as "humanity's final revolutionary blueprint."	A combination of extreme exaggeration, ideological inflation, and factual fabrication severely undermines the editorial's meaning. This is a prototypical example of Level 5 hallucination.
4	Multiple sentences include ideological overreach or speculative narratives that diverge from the editorial's meaning.	- The editorial declares Kim Jong Il's thought a "universal ideological guide for humanity," and predicts global socialist unification under Kim Jong Un's leadership. - It frames the 8th Party Congress as a final confrontation to end capitalism.	Phrases like "global unification" and "end of capitalism" are ideologically motivated hallucinations not supported by the editorial. Interpretation diverges significantly from the source.
3	Promotional rhetoric or emotional expressions limit the clarity of factual content.	- The editorial says the people are "engraving in their hearts the legendary love and genius leadership of the General." - Kim Jong Un is portrayed as upholding "the red banner of Juche socialism with blood and sweat."	Phrases such as "genius leadership" and "red banner" introduce sentimentality that dilutes factual clarity. While the intent remains, persuasive value declines due to rhetorical overload.
2	Minor flowery or rhetorical expressions are added, but the meaning and facts remain intact.	- Gwangmyeongseong Day is called a "sacred day" to commemorate Kim Jong Il's immortal thought. - The editorial praises Kim Jong Un's leadership in achieving a socialist powerhouse.	Although phrases like "sacred day" and "immortal thought" are embellishments, they don't distort the factual core or argument. Rhetoric is present but minimally invasive.
1	No hallucinations observed; the response is	- The editorial commemorates Kim Jong Il's revolutionary	The response is factual, concise, and objective.

factually grounded and faithful to the source.	achievements and affirms new socialist victories under Kim Jong Un's leadership. - Citations from Kim Jong Il's writings support the legitimacy of socialism, and the Party's five-year plan is emphasized.	There is no exaggeration, distortion, or ideological inflation—making it a reliable and hallucination-free summary.

Table A3. Scoring Rubric for Hallucination

B Appendix: Analysis Report on *Rodong Sinmun* Editorial

"Let Us Internalize the Juche Ideology as Our Worldview and Philosophy of Life" (May 7 Editorial)

❍ **These editorial urges readers to thoroughly embody the Juche ideology as both a worldview and a philosophy of life, applying it comprehensively to work and daily life.**

❍ **Juche is framed as "the eternal guiding ideology of our revolution," with emphasis placed on the roles of Kim Il-sung, Kim Jong-il, and Kim Jong-un:**
– Kim Il-sung is credited with founding the ideology, Kim Jong-il with its systematization and theoretical development, and Kim Jong-un with its succession and further advancement.
– Notably, the editorial highlights Juche ideology instead of the officially codified Kimilsung–Kimjongilism stated in the Party Charter, suggesting a renewed focus on internal strength and subjective power.

❍ **The editorial elaborates on what it means to internalize Juche as a worldview and philosophy of life:**
– Taking it as the starting point for all thought and action, and treating it as an absolute standard in life and struggle
– A necessary condition for preserving ideological purity and unity within the revolutionary ranks
– A key requirement for significantly strengthening internal power and achieving new victories in the revolution
– The fundamental guarantee for fully carrying through and completing the revolution

❍ **It also outlines the tasks required to internalize Juche ideology:**
– **Deep understanding of its significance**:
∆ Recognizing that Juche is the sole guiding ideology for our era and future
∆ Studying and fully internalizing its principles, legitimacy, scientific basis, and vitality
∆ Arming oneself with the proud history and revolutionary traditions
∆ Engaging in systematic and comprehensive study of the classical works of Kim Il-sung, Kim Jong-il, and Kim Jong-un
– **Integrating ideological study with revolutionary practice**:
∆ Grasping the truth and traction of Juche through the tangible superiority of socialism in our style
∆ Engraving the Party's line and policies, which embody Juche, onto one's consciousness
∆ Creating more socialist wealth through struggles aimed at comprehensive development of socialism in our style
– **Enhancing the roles of Party and working people's organizations**

Table B: Structured Expert Interpretation of One of the *Rodong Sinmun* Editorials Published in May 2021

Language Model Re-rankers are Fooled by Lexical Similarities

Lovisa Hagström[1,2] Ercong Nie[3,4] Ruben Halifa[5]
Helmut Schmid[3] Richard Johansson[1,2] Alexander Junge[5]
[1]Chalmers University of Technology [2]University of Gothenburg
[3]LMU Munich [4]Munich Center for Machine Learning [5]amass technologies
lovhag@chalmers.se

Abstract

Language model (LM) re-rankers are used to refine retrieval results for retrieval-augmented generation (RAG). They are more expensive than lexical matching methods like BM25 but assumed to better process semantic information and the relations between the query and the retrieved answers. To understand whether LM re-rankers always live up to this assumption, we evaluate 6 different LM re-rankers on the NQ, LitQA2 and DRUID datasets. Our results show that LM re-rankers struggle to outperform a simple BM25 baseline on DRUID. Leveraging a novel separation metric based on BM25 scores, we explain and identify re-ranker errors stemming from lexical dissimilarities. We also investigate different methods to improve LM re-ranker performance and find these methods mainly useful for the more popular NQ dataset. Taken together, our work identifies and explains weaknesses of LM re-rankers and points to the need for more adversarial and realistic datasets for their evaluation.

1 Introduction

Retrieval-augmented generation (RAG) is used to alleviate problems arising from imperfect parametric knowledge of language models (LMs) (Gao et al., 2024; Vu et al., 2024). However, the efficiency of RAG hinges on the retrieval of useful information (Wang et al., 2024b). To this end, LM re-rankers are increasingly used to provide more accurate retrieval results for RAG, superseding simpler methods based on keyword matching, such as BM25 (see Figure 1). While there are many benchmark results for LM re-rankers (Thakur et al., 2021; Petroni et al., 2021), little is known about when the computationally expensive LM re-rankers are worth the cost and whether they always can be expected to outperform simpler methods.

In this paper, we evaluate LM re-rankers to better understand when they work well and when they fail to outperform less expensive alternatives.[1] The contributions of this paper are as follows:

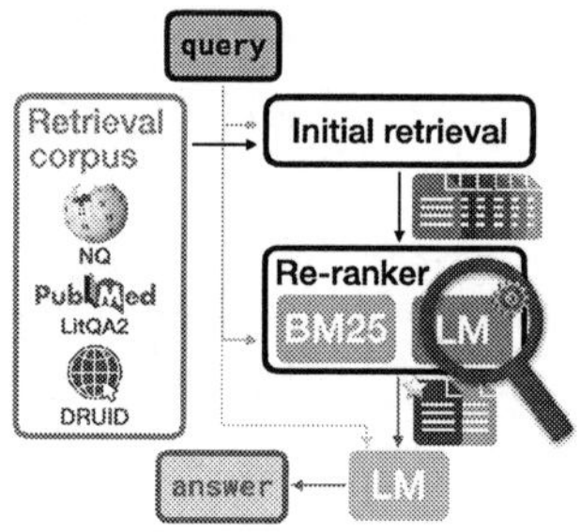

Figure 1: An overview of a RAG pipeline.

- We evaluate 6 LM re-rankers on the NQ, LitQA2 and DRUID datasets to compare re-ranker performance for scenarios of varying aspects of difficulty and domain. NQ is focused on generic QA, LitQA2 on scientific information extraction and DRUID on claim verification.
- We explain variations in LM re-ranker performance using passage-query similarities, leveraging BM25 scores and our novel separation metric D_S. All LM re-rankers underperform on samples corresponding to low D_S values and we tie these to high rates of *distractors* (non-gold passages with high lexical similarity to the query) and *lack of document context*.
- We evaluate a set of methods for improving LM re-ranker performance, such as adding contextual information. Our results show that while most methods work well on NQ, they are less effective for LitQA2 and DRUID.

Taken together, our paper identifies and measures novel aspects of difficulty for LM re-rankers; *distractors* and *lack of contextual information*. These aspects are likely to occur in real-world scenarios relying on e.g. information retrieval from the

[1]Our code is available at https://github.com/lovhag/rerankers-and-lexical-similarities.

Proceedings of the Eighth Fact Extraction and VERification Workshop (FEVER), pages 18–33
July 31, 2025

web, such as in a fact-checking setting. Our work points to the need of more adversarial and real-world aligned evaluation datasets to better understand and address LM re-ranker deficiencies.

2 Related Work

The goal of using a re-ranker in an information retrieval context is to refine the outputs of an initial retrieval step based on a lexicographical or semantic database search. LM-based re-rankers are more expensive to run compared to simpler methods based on lexical matching, like BM25, but are expected to increase the performance of the overall retrieval system thanks to their semantic understanding (Glass et al., 2022; Li et al., 2023). Sun et al. (2023) also showed how standard LLMs, like GPT-4, can be used as re-rankers.

Two popular benchmarks for re-rankers are the BEIR and KILT benchmarks by Thakur et al. (2021); Petroni et al. (2021). Compared to our work, these benchmarks focus on high-level re-ranker performance and do not consider fine-grained aspects of difficulty for re-rankers.

Similarly to our work, Sturua et al. (2024) identify and investigate fine-grained aspects of difficulty for their `jina` models, of which one is *misleading syntactic similarities*. This describes the case when passages with high syntactic similarity to the query are favoured over gold documents with lower syntactic overlap. Henceforth referred to as *distractors*. Wang et al. (2024a) instead consider an aspect of difficulty related to *missing document context*, for which a re-ranker may fail to identify a gold passage if its identification hinges on knowing that the passage comes from a relevant document or webpage. By prepending page titles to passages they were able to alleviate this issue on NQ.

In contrast to these works, we expand on the analysis of distractors and missing document context to include multiple SOTA re-rankers, datasets from diverse domains and better tuned metrics. We also tie these aspects of difficulty to a more fundamental question of whether LM re-rankers are fooled by lexical similarities. To measure this, we develop a new metric which allows us to identify problematic samples.

3 Method

This section describes the re-rankers, datasets, metrics and alleviation methods investigated.

3.1 Re-rankers

We evaluate a wide cohort of LM re-rankers to enable comprehensive comparisons between different model types and sizes. Three closed-source LM re-rankers are evaluated: the industrial grade re-ranker Cohere[2] (`Cohere`), a re-ranker based on GPT-4o (`GPT-4o`) and a lightweight re-ranker based on GPT-4o mini (`GPT-4o m`) (Sun et al., 2023) (Appendix E).[3]

We also evaluate three open-source re-rankers from Hugging Face: the large-scale LM re-ranker `bge-reranker-v2-gemma` (`BGE`), the lightweight re-ranker `jina-reranker-v1-turbo-en` (`Jina turbo`) and `jina-reranker-v2-base-multilingual` (`Jina base`), a larger re-ranker from the same model family. As a baseline, we consider BM25 scores, leveraging lexical matching, similar to TF-IDF (Lù, 2024). See Appendix D to get a rough estimate of the runtime of each re-ranker.

3.2 Evaluation datasets

We evaluate the re-rankers on three datasets representative of different domains and aspects of difficulty: NQ, LitQA2 and DRUID. All datasets have already undergone an initial retrieval step and are thus suitable for the evaluation of re-rankers. Natural Questions (NQ) is a popular dataset for re-ranker evaluations with passages from Wikipedia pages (Kwiatkowski et al., 2019). LitQA2 measures the ability of a system to extract information from scientific literature (Laurent et al., 2024), containing a high rate of domain-specific biomedical language. LitQA2 can be expected to test the robustness to domain-shifts of LM re-rankers. DRUID (Dataset of Retrieved Unreliable, Insufficient and Difficult-to-understand contexts) contains fact-checked claims and corresponding potential evidence automatically retrieved from the web (Hagström et al., 2024). It can be expected to contain more noisy passages and to test the capability of re-rankers to identify relevant information for fact-checking. More details and examples can be found in Appendix C.

3.3 Evaluation metrics

We mainly use Precision@1 (P@1) for our re-ranker evaluations to accommodate the small num-

[2]`rerank-english-v3.0` from `https://docs.cohere.com/v2/docs/models#rerank`

[3]`gpt-4o-2024-08-06` and `gpt-4o-mini-2024-07-18`.

ber of passages available in DRUID.[4] To understand when LM re-rankers fail to outperform simpler methods, we also compare to alignment with BM25 relevance scores, as follows.

$$\Delta\text{P@1}(R) = \text{P@1}(R) - \text{P@1}_{\text{BM25}}(R) \quad (1)$$

Given re-ranker predictions R, $\text{P@1}(R)$ denotes the score measured when document relevance is given by gold labels (default) and $\text{P@1}_{\text{BM25}}(R)$ when relevance is given by BM25 scores. Leveraging this metric, we can investigate whether re-rankers align with gold labels over BM25 scores, which corresponds to positive ΔP@1 values. Negative ΔP@1 values correspond to when the re-ranker predictions align more with BM25 scores over gold labels.

3.4 Gold from similar separation metric

To better understand why and when re-rankers fail to identify gold passages in a document, we define a *gold-from-similar separation metric* D_S for a given text similarity measure S. Given a query q, a set of passages $\mathbf{p} = \{p_1, ..., p_n\}$ and corresponding gold labels $\mathbf{y}$ indicating whether a passage p_i is gold ($y_i = 1$) or not ($y_i = 0$), we compute the metric D_S by subtracting the maximal similarity of the non-gold standard passages from the maximal similarity of the gold standard passages:

$$D_S(q, \mathbf{p}, \mathbf{y}) = \max_{i:\, y_i=1} S(q, p_i) - \max_{i:\, y_i=0} S(q, p_i) \quad (2)$$

This metric indicates whether the most similar gold standard passage is more or less similar to the query than the most similar non-gold standard passage.

We assume there to exist at least one gold passage per (q, $\mathbf{p}$) sample. The similarity measure S can be any measure of choice that takes two documents as input. A larger value of S should signify greater similarity between the two documents.

3.5 Alleviation methods

We investigate two known methods previously shown to improve re-ranker performance: prepending page titles (`Prepend titles`) (Wang et al., 2024a) and incorporating contextual information generated by GPT-4o mini (`Incorporate context`).[5] Prepending titles is quite straightforward for NQ and LitQA2, while the more noisy webpage text in DRUID yields low-quality titles, with missing values and inaccuracies. The DRUID samples also lack complete contexts, barring the `Incorporate context` method. We instead experiment with adjusting the re-ranker prompt to better suit the fact-checking setting represented by DRUID (`Prompt`) (Appendix F).

4 Results

The zero-shot performance of the re-rankers considered in this paper are shown in Table 1. Additional results can be found in Appendix G. Based on these results, we reach the following conclusions.

Re-ranker	NQ	LitQA2	DRUID
Standard mode			
Cohere	0.65 (0.13)	0.76 (0.08)	0.68 (−0.21)
BGE	0.68 (0.17)	0.78 (0.10)	0.73 (−0.15)
Jina turbo	0.56 (0.08)	0.61 (0.03)	0.69 (−0.20)
Jina base	0.68 (0.15)	0.65 (0.06)	0.65 (−0.20)
GPT-4o m	0.83 (0.37)	0.51 (0.10)	0.72 (−0.10)
GPT-4o	**0.85** (0.40)	0.50 (0.10)	0.73 (−0.10)
BM25	0.46	0.67	0.66
Prepend titles			
Cohere	0.77 (0.23)	0.79 (0.09)	0.71 (−0.17)
BGE	0.76 (0.23)	**0.80** (0.10)	0.74 (−0.14)
Jina turbo	0.69 (0.16)	0.66 (0.02)	0.71 (−0.17)
Jina base	0.78 (0.24)	0.77 (0.07)	0.69 (−0.18)
GPT-4o m	**0.85** (0.34)	0.50 (0.08)	0.72 (−0.08)
GPT-4o	**0.85** (0.36)	0.51 (0.07)	0.74 (−0.06)
BM25	0.50	0.70	0.68
Incorporate context			*Prompt*
Cohere	0.72 (0.24)	0.69 (0.06)	0.69 (−0.18)
BGE	0.72 (0.26)	0.70 (0.05)	0.77 (−0.06)
Jina turbo	0.62 (0.15)	0.60 (−0.04)	0.72 (−0.17)
Jina base	0.74 (0.27)	0.63 (0.09)	0.72 (−0.14)
GPT-4o m	0.80 (0.37)	0.47 (0.12)	0.79 (−0.02)
GPT-4o	0.81 (0.38)	0.46 (0.11)	**0.83** (0.05)
BM25	0.44	0.58	0.68

Table 1: P@1 of all re-rankers. Values in (parenthesis) indicate ΔP@1 (Equation (1)). Values in **bold** indicate top scores.

LitQA2 is generally easier and NQ generally more difficult. The majority of the LM re-rankers perform best on LitQA2, followed by DRUID and NQ. The only exceptions are the Jina models and GPT-4o models. The GPT-4o models likely struggle on LitQA2 due to token limitations.

Large LM re-rankers struggle to outperform a BM25 baseline on DRUID. The best-performing re-ranker (BGE) outperforms the BM25 baseline by 10% on DRUID. This is smaller than the 46% on NQ (for GPT-4o) and 15% on LitQA2 (for BGE).

[4] Metrics are defined by TREC in https://trec.nist.gov/pubs/trec16/appendices/measures.pdf.

[5] https://www.anthropic.com/news/contextual-retrieval

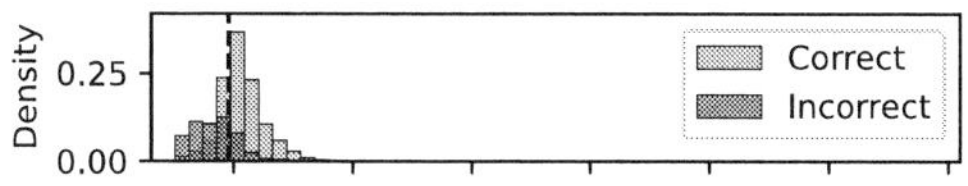

(a) NQ

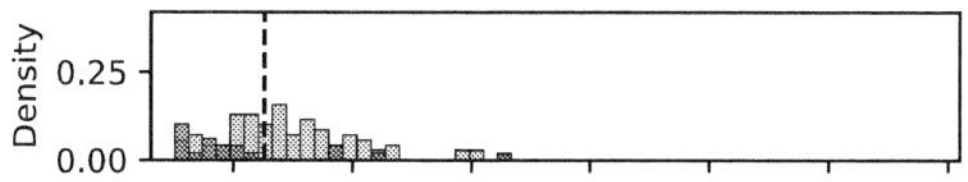

(b) LitQA2

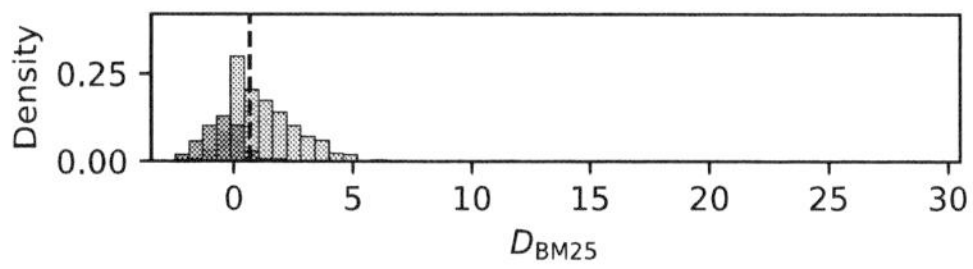

(c) DRUID

Figure 2: Distribution of D_{BM25} (Equation (2)) for NQ, LitQA2 and DRUID. Correctness is based on P@1 of the BGE re-ranker. The dashed vertical lines indicate the mean values.

We also note that the smaller Jina LM re-rankers clearly outperform the BM25 baseline on NQ while they perform worse than or equal to BM25 on LitQA2 and DRUID.

LM re-rankers align more with BM25 scores than gold labels on DRUID. The ΔP@1 values are negative for all LM re-rankers on DRUID in Table 1, indicating that the re-rankers align more with BM25 scores than gold labels on DRUID.

We note that while DRUID is *easier* compared to NQ with respect to LM re-ranker accuracy, it is *harder* with respect to how LM re-rankers struggle to outperform simpler methods like BM25. We hypothesise that DRUID provides a greater challenge in this sense as it contains passages from the web and popular claims that may have seen frequent discussion, increasing the rate of distractors.

4.1 Query-passage similarities

To understand why LM re-rankers struggle to outperform BM25 on DRUID, we apply our separation metric D_S to the passages in NQ, LitQA2 and DRUID and make comparisons to re-ranker precision. D_{BM25} results are found in Figure 2 (results for other similarity metrics can be found in Appendix G). A summary of the distribution and corresponding re-ranker performance can be found in Table 7. To better understand the re-ranker performance on DRUID we also partition the dataset by D_{BM25} value and report the re-ranker scores in Table 8. Our conclusion is as follows.

LM re-rankers struggle to identify gold samples with markedly low BM25 scores. The results in Figure 2 show that LM re-rankers are generally good at identifying gold samples if they are sufficiently similar to the query. However, if the gold passage is too dissimilar to the query (corresponding to low D_{BM25} values), the LM re-rankers are prone to make mistakes.

We see how NQ and DRUID pose a greater challenge by including gold passages that are relatively dissimilar to the query. An inspection of some samples with low D_{BM25} scores in Appendix H reveals a high rate of distractors and gold passages lacking document context. LitQA2 samples, on the other hand, have generally high D_{BM25} values and we hypothesise this makes the dataset easier for LM re-rankers. Seemingly, the domain-specific queries and passages of LitQA2 are less of a challenge compared to the lexical dissimilarities between gold passage and query in the other datasets.

4.2 Alleviation methods

The results from the investigations described in Section 3.5 can be found in Table 1. We reach the following conclusions.

Prepending page titles yields the greatest effects on NQ. Prepending page titles to the passages yields performance improvements for large LM re-rankers on NQ and unchanged performance on LitQA2 and DRUID. For LitQA2, this could be caused by the more distracting details from the scientific paper titles (Wang et al., 2024a). For DRUID it likely stems from the noisy webpage titles. Seemingly, the method of prepending page titles is more suitable for nicely formatted datasets, such as NQ. We also observe that the method of incorporating contexts is inferior to prepending page titles.

Adjusting the prompt yields significantly improved results for GPT-4o on DRUID. Table 1 shows how GPT-4o benefits the most from an adjusted prompt, indicating significance of prompt for the performance of LLMs as re-rankers.

5 Conclusion

Our paper identifies and explores an important weakness of LM re-rankers: they struggle to identify gold samples with markedly low BM25 scores. We hypothesise that real-world datasets like DRUID, with passages from the web, contain more distractors, resulting in gold samples with low BM25 scores. However, most current datasets for re-ranker evaluation fail to capture this aspect of difficulty and methods for improving LM re-ranker performance are less effective for the noisier LitQA2 and DRUID samples. Our work points to the need of more adversarial and real-world aligned datasets to better understand LM re-rankers and their weaknesses in realistic settings.

Limitations

The datasets used in this study were not specifically designed to measure the preference of re-ranking models for similar over gold passages. A dataset specifically curated for this purpose, potentially complemented by synthetically generated samples, would allow a deeper analysis of our research questions. We leave this for future work.

Our work only investigated a subset of the alleviation methods that exist for improving re-ranker performance. For example, there are also methods focused on adapting chunk sizes, and methods avoiding chunking all together. It would be interesting to also expand our analysis to incorporate additional alleviation methods.

Ethical Considerations

There are no major ethical concerns related to our work on LM re-ranker performance. The datasets used and methods investigated are not associated with any ethical concerns.

Acknowledgments

This work was supported by the Wallenberg AI, Autonomous Systems and Software Program (WASP) funded by the Knut and Alice Wallenberg Foundation. The computations were enabled by resources provided by the National Academic Infrastructure for Supercomputing in Sweden (NAISS) at Alvis partially funded by the Swedish Research Council through grant agreement no. 2022-06725. The work was also supported by compute credits from a Cohere For AI Research Grant.

References

Yunfan Gao, Yun Xiong, Xinyu Gao, Kangxiang Jia, Jinliu Pan, Yuxi Bi, Yi Dai, Jiawei Sun, Meng Wang, and Haofen Wang. 2024. Retrieval-augmented generation for large language models: A survey. *Preprint*, arXiv:2312.10997.

Michael Glass, Gaetano Rossiello, Md Faisal Mahbub Chowdhury, Ankita Naik, Pengshan Cai, and Alfio Gliozzo. 2022. Re2G: Retrieve, rerank, generate. In *Proceedings of the 2022 Conference of the North American Chapter of the Association for Computational Linguistics: Human Language Technologies*, pages 2701–2715, Seattle, United States. Association for Computational Linguistics.

Lovisa Hagström, Sara Vera Marjanović, Haeun Yu, Arnav Arora, Christina Lioma, Maria Maistro, Pepa Atanasova, and Isabelle Augenstein. 2024. A reality check on context utilisation for retrieval-augmented generation. *Preprint*, arXiv:2412.17031.

Tom Kwiatkowski, Jennimaria Palomaki, Olivia Redfield, Michael Collins, Ankur Parikh, Chris Alberti, Danielle Epstein, Illia Polosukhin, Jacob Devlin, Kenton Lee, Kristina Toutanova, Llion Jones, Matthew Kelcey, Ming-Wei Chang, Andrew M. Dai, Jakob Uszkoreit, Quoc Le, and Slav Petrov. 2019. Natural questions: A benchmark for question answering research. *Transactions of the Association for Computational Linguistics*, 7:452–466.

Jon M. Laurent, Joseph D. Janizek, Michael Ruzo, Michaela M. Hinks, Michael J. Hammerling, Siddharth Narayanan, Manvitha Ponnapati, Andrew D. White, and Samuel G. Rodriques. 2024. Lab-bench: Measuring capabilities of language models for biology research. *Preprint*, arXiv:2407.10362.

Chaofan Li, Zheng Liu, Shitao Xiao, and Yingxia Shao. 2023. Making large language models a better foundation for dense retrieval. *Preprint*, arXiv:2312.15503.

Xing Han Lù. 2024. Bm25s: Orders of magnitude faster lexical search via eager sparse scoring. *Preprint*, arXiv:2407.03618.

Fabio Petroni, Aleksandra Piktus, Angela Fan, Patrick Lewis, Majid Yazdani, Nicola De Cao, James Thorne, Yacine Jernite, Vladimir Karpukhin, Jean Maillard, Vassilis Plachouras, Tim Rocktäschel, and Sebastian Riedel. 2021. KILT: a benchmark for knowledge intensive language tasks. In *Proceedings of the 2021 Conference of the North American Chapter of the Association for Computational Linguistics: Human Language Technologies*, pages 2523–2544, Online. Association for Computational Linguistics.

Saba Sturua, Isabelle Mohr, Mohammad Kalim Akram, Michael Günther, Bo Wang, Markus Krimmel, Feng Wang, Georgios Mastrapas, Andreas Koukounas, Nan Wang, et al. 2024. jina-embeddings-v3: Multilingual embeddings with task lora. *arXiv preprint arXiv:2409.10173*.

Weiwei Sun, Lingyong Yan, Xinyu Ma, Shuaiqiang Wang, Pengjie Ren, Zhumin Chen, Dawei Yin, and Zhaochun Ren. 2023. Is ChatGPT good at search? investigating large language models as re-ranking agents. In *Proceedings of the 2023 Conference on Empirical Methods in Natural Language Processing*, pages 14918–14937, Singapore. Association for Computational Linguistics.

Nandan Thakur, Nils Reimers, Andreas Rücklé, Abhishek Srivastava, and Iryna Gurevych. 2021. BEIR: A heterogeneous benchmark for zero-shot evaluation of information retrieval models. In *Thirty-fifth Conference on Neural Information Processing Systems Datasets and Benchmarks Track (Round 2)*.

Tu Vu, Mohit Iyyer, Xuezhi Wang, Noah Constant, Jerry Wei, Jason Wei, Chris Tar, Yun-Hsuan Sung, Denny Zhou, Quoc Le, and Thang Luong. 2024. FreshLLMs: Refreshing large language models with search engine augmentation. In *Findings of the Association for Computational Linguistics: ACL 2024*, pages 13697–13720, Bangkok, Thailand. Association for Computational Linguistics.

Kexin Wang, Nils Reimers, and Iryna Gurevych. 2024a. DAPR: A benchmark on document-aware passage retrieval. In *Proceedings of the 62nd Annual Meeting of the Association for Computational Linguistics (Volume 1: Long Papers)*, pages 4313–4330, Bangkok, Thailand. Association for Computational Linguistics.

Xiaohua Wang, Zhenghua Wang, Xuan Gao, Feiran Zhang, Yixin Wu, Zhibo Xu, Tianyuan Shi, Zhengyuan Wang, Shizheng Li, Qi Qian, Ruicheng Yin, Changze Lv, Xiaoqing Zheng, and Xuanjing Huang. 2024b. Searching for best practices in retrieval-augmented generation. In *Proceedings of the 2024 Conference on Empirical Methods in Natural Language Processing*, pages 17716–17736, Miami, Florida, USA. Association for Computational Linguistics.

A Computational resources

All open-source re-rankers are evaluated without fine-tuning on one T4, V100 or A100 Nvidia GPU per evaluation. The choice of GPU type depended on the model size (see Table 6 for detailed information on what GPU type was used for what model). The closed-source models were accessed via APIs so it is unclear as to exactly what GPU devices were involved. The total computational budget for the evaluations was about 50 GPU hours.

B Use of AI assistants

AI assistants like Copilot and ChatGPT were intermittently used to generate template code and rephrase sentences in the paper, etc. However, no complete paper sections or code scripts have been generated by an AI assistant. All generated text content has been inspected and verified by the authors. ChatGPT was also used and evaluated as a re-ranker in this work.

C Evaluation datasets

The evaluation datasets are described in further detail below. High-level statistics for the datasets can be found in Table 2 and examples of samples from each dataset can be found in Tables 3 to 5. From each dataset we extract a set of *questions*, corresponding *passages* to choose between and corresponding *gold labels* indicating whether a passage contains the answer to the given question or not.

Dataset	#samples	#passages/sample			#gold
		mean	min	max	/sample
NQ	3,759	16	4	244	1
LitQA2	124	145	33	359	1
DRUID	875	4	2	5	2

Table 2: Statistics for the evaluation datasets. Exactly one gold passage is found per sample for NQ and LitQA2. DRUID samples may contain more than one gold passage.

C.1 Natural Questions

Natural Questions (NQ) by Kwiatkowski et al. (2019) is a popular dataset for re-ranker evaluations that contains real search engine queries and corresponding Wikipedia pages with the gold passage annotated. The gold passage annotators were instructed to identify the first paragraph on the Wikipedia page that contains the answer to the query, which means that there may be multiple unidentified gold passages for each query. To avoid issues stemming from this, we only retain all passages up to and including the gold passage as the retrieval corpora.

Chunking approach The chunking is based on html elements, for which each passage is made out of one html element (e.g. a table <Table> or paragraph <P>), similarly to the approach used by the NQ authors to annotate gold passages. These passages are then matched to the annotated gold labels based on token indices.

C.2 LitQA2

LitQA2 by Laurent et al. (2024) measures the ability of a system to extract information from scientific literature. The dataset contains a high rate of domain-specific biomedical language compared to the more generic queries of NQ and can be expected to test the robustness to domain-shifts of LM re-rankers. The dataset consists of multiple-choice questions that are intended to be only answerable based on the full text, not on the abstract, of a given paper and nowhere else in the literature. PubMedCentral[6] was used to scrape the full articles. Only

[6]https://pmc.ncbi.nlm.nih.gov

Question	Passages	Gold labels
when did hyderabad became a part of india?	"<H1> Hyderabad state (1948–56) </H1>"	0
	"Jump to: navigation, search This article is about a State of the Indian Union 1948–1956 . For other uses, see Hyderabad (disambiguation)."	0
	"<Table> <Tr> <Td colspan=3> Hyderabad State (1948 - 1956) </Td> </Tr> <Tr> <Td colspan=3> State of India </Td> </Tr> <Tr> <Td colspan=3> <Table> <Tr> <Td> \u2190 </Td> <Td> 1948–1956 </Td> <Td> \u2192 </Td> </Tr> </Table> </Td> </Tr> <Tr> <Td colspan=3> 1956 map of Southern India showing Hyderabad state in yellowish green . After the States reorganisation in 1956, regions west of the red and blue lines merged with Bombay and Mysore states respectively and the remaining part (Telangana) was merged with Andhra state to form Andhra Pradesh . </Td> </Tr> <Tr> <Td colspan=2> History </Td> <Td> </Td> </Tr> <Tr> <Td> </Td> <Td> Hyderabad State formed from Hyderabad Princely State </Td> <Td> 1948 </Td> </Tr> <Tr> <Td> </Td> <Td> Reorganized and renamed Andhra Pradesh </Td> <Td> 1956 </Td> </Tr> <Tr> <Td colspan=3> States of India since 1947 </Td> </Tr> </Table>"	0
	"Hyderabad state until 1956"	0
	"<P> Hyderabad State was a state in Independent India, formed after the accession of the princely state of Hyderabad into the Indian Union on 24 November 1949 . It existed from 1948 to 1956 . </P>"	1

Table 3: Data sample from NQ.

124 out of 200 samples were retained from this dataset as some articles were unavailable. We decided to include the dataset in the analysis despite the small sample size as this is the only high-quality dataset that enables evaluations of re-rankers for the biomedical domain.

Chunking approach The chunking is based on newlines, for which each passage is made out by a new paragraph. Passages can then be matched to the manually extracted gold passage via fuzzy matching, to get the gold labels for each passage.

C.3 DRUID

DRUID (Dataset of Retrieved Unreliable, Insufficient and Difficult-to-understand contexts) by Hagström et al. (2024) contains fact-checked claims and corresponding potential evidence pieces retrieved from the web. Each evidence piece has been annotated for whether it contains sufficient information to conclude whether the corresponding claim is true or false. The claims from the dataset are used as questions to the re-rankers and the collected DRUID passages corresponding to the given claim make out the passages for the query. Passages with sufficient information to reach a fact-check verdict, i.e. marked as 'refuting' or 'supporting', are considered gold and each sample corresponds to at least two potential passages from different webpages, of which at least one has to be gold and at least one not gold. The Cohere re-ranker was used for the automated retrieval of evidence pieces so the samples in DRUID can be expected to be more adversarial in the sense that they already have been pre-selected by a LM re-ranker (and then manually annotated for quality).

Chunking approach The passages have already been chunked in a previous automated retrieval pipeline by the DRUID authors. Each passage is based on text snippets from a webpage, for which multiple snippets may have been extracted across the same webpage.

Question	Passages	Gold labels
Neonatal male mice injected with NIF, a glycoprotein produced by a canine hookworm, show a significant reduction in microglial phagocytic capacity and engulfment of which neurotransmitter transporter? (A) VGlut2, (B) VGlut1, (C) VGlut3, (D) GAT1, (E) GAT2, (F) GAT3, or (G) not enough info?	"The incidences of neurodevelopmental disorders (NDDs) have been increasing in recent decades, suggesting a role for non-genetic environmental factors. Furthermore, sex is a significant risk factor for these disorders, with a strong male bias."	0
	"Air pollutant exposure during pregnancy or the first year of life is one of the most consistent environmental risk factors for NDDs. However, the associations of single environmental agents with NDDs have been relatively weak, and thus causality has been difficult to determine. Non-chemical stressors such as limited resources or social support of the mother can increase the vulnerability of the fetus to toxic exposures, which could explain why certain populations are disproportionately affected. In fact, neighborhood quality is a significant modifier of air pollution risk, suggesting that environmental and social stressors synergize to increase vulnerability to pollutant exposure, but how these exposures alter fetal brain development and affect offspring behavior is largely unknown."	0
	"Inflammatory events during pregnancy, such as maternal infection with bacteria or viruses, lead to maternal immune activation (MIA), which is linked to NDDs in offspring. Recent transcriptome-wide studies in postmortem brains of individuals diagnosed with an NDD have identified expression modules with enrichment of genes involved in neuroinflammatory function, with a particular dysregulation of microglial genes. Microglia are the primary immunocompetent cells of the brain and are exquisitely sensitive to perturbations of homeostasis and thus may be poised to act as immediate responders to environmental insults. Microglia are also essential regulators of activity-dependent synaptic remodeling during development, in which they prune inappropriate/weak synapses while sparing appropriate/strong connections. Importantly, transcriptome studies have found that immune changes co-occur with gene enrichment modules affecting synaptic function, suggesting the possibility that neuroimmune changes during development could lead to aberrant synapse development by altering microglial function."	0
	"A recent analysis found that MIA was more common in male children with ASD than female children, suggesting that a sex difference in response to maternal inflammation may be one mechanism that underlies increased male vulnerability. Furthermore, we and others have found sex differences in microglial development, maturation, and function, including an increased relative expression of microglial genes in male brains, compared with females. Interestingly, the microglial genes enriched in male brains are also implicated in ASD. Together these data point to a mechanism by which sexually dimorphic microglial responses to prenatal stressors could lead to aberrant brain development, primarily in males."	0
	[...]	
	"In this experiment, WT neonatal male mice received bilateral microinjections of PBS or NIF (200 ng) into the ACC at P7, and brain tissue was collected 24 h later (Figure 7A). To confirm the effects of NIF on microglial phagocytic capacity, we quantified changes in the microglial lysosomal volume of CD68 (Figure 7B). As expected, microglia from animals microinjected with NIF had a significant reduction in the phagocytic index (50%) and a significant decrease in the total lysosomal content within each microglia (Figures 7C and 7D). To determine whether this reduction in CD68 impaired microglial interactions with VGlut2 synapses, we once again performed Imaris reconstructions and quantified the volume of VGlut2 within microglia (Figure 7E). Microglia from NIF-treated animals are significantly smaller (25%) than PBS control animals (Figure 7F); furthermore, this size reduction is accompanied by a significant decrease in the volume of internalized VGlut2 in microglia cells (Figure 7G). Last, we quantified the co-localization of VGlut2 and PSD95 and found that NIF-injected animals had about a 20% increase in VGlut2+ synapses (Figure 7H). Thus, NIF injections at P7 effectively reduce microglial phagocytic capacity and engulfment of VGlut2, which induces an abnormal increase in VGlut2 synapse density."	1
	[...]	

Table 4: Data sample from LitQA2. "[...]" indicates that we are skipping across passages in the sample to save space.

Question	Passages	Source	Gold labels	DRUID labels
WikiLeaks has published the 1st list of black money holders in Swiss banks.	"WikiLeaks has never published the list of Indians who have stashed their money in Swiss banks. Hence, the claim stands FALSE."	`https://factly.in/wikileaks-list-of-black-money-holders-in-swiss-bank-is-a-fake-one/`	1	refutes
	"Various posts on social media claim that WikiLeaks has released the "first list" of black money holders in Swiss Bank. The post is going viral on all social media platforms. DigitEye Team also received the message on its Whatsapp fact-checking number. The list contains 24 names \u2014 Sonia Gandhi, A Raja, Rahul Gandhi, Sharad Pawar, P Chidambaram to name a few. All the money listed next to the names are figures in dollars. The first name on the alleged list is Congress leader Sonia Gandhi who it claimed to be holding more than $56 billion. The numbers are not in chronological order and neither the names are in any set order. According to the alleged list, the lowest amount is held by P Chidambaram. [...] WikiLeaks has not published any report on the same on its website. The latest report was published in October 2019. WikiLeaks took to Twitter and tweeted about a similar list of Indian black money holders. In the 2011 tweet, it clarified that such list "never appeared on WikiLeaks"."	`https://digiteye.in/viral-list-of-black-money-holding-accounts-in-swiss-bank-is-fake/`	1	refutes
	"INDIA/SWIZERLAND– Black money trail: 2nd list of Indian Swiss accounts to be shared [...] TNN I Sep 14, 2011, 11.11AM IST http://timesofindia.indiatimes.com/india/Black-money-trail-2nd-list-of-Indian-Swiss-accounts-to-be-shared/articleshow/9977871.cms NEW DELHI: A second list containing names of Indians, who have stashed black money in Swiss banks, will be shared by the Germans, Times Now reported."	`https://wikileaks.org/gifiles/docs/70/703306_india-swizerland-black-money-trail-2nd-list-of-indian-swiss.html`	0	insufficient
	"(See attached file: List of Black Money Holders from Wiki"	`https://groups.google.com/g/yeida/c/V2gxTIXY-sQ`	0	insufficient

Table 5: Data sample from DRUID. "[...]" inside a passage does not indicate additional information included to the re-ranker, it simply indicates that the passage was retrieved as snippets from a webpage, for which there is additional page content between the snippets.

D Runtime comparison

To exemplify the difference in efficiency between different re-rankers, we compare runtimes of the investigated re-rankers in Table 6. Unfortunately, the models could not be run on the same devices due to space and other practical reasons.

Re-ranker	Runtime [mins]	Device
Cohere	15	*Cohere API*
BGE	42	A100:1
Jina turbo	3	V100:1
Jina base	80	T4:1
GPT-4o m	145	*OpenAI API*
GPT-4o	135	*Azure API*
BM25	0.5	MacBook Pro

Table 6: Runtimes of the different re-rankers for getting scores corresponding to all samples from NQ (no prepended titles or context) on their corresponding devices. The MacBook Pro device is using a 2.3 GHz Quad-Core Intel Core i7.

E Implementation details of RankGPT

LLMs demonstrate strong capabilities in understanding long texts and handling complex tasks, making them suitable for use as re-rankers in passage re-ranking tasks. Building on the prompting strategies proposed by Sun et al. (2023), we explore the use of LLM-based re-rankers, specifically leveraging two advanced OpenAI models: GPT-4o (`gpt-4o-2024-08-06`) and GPT-4o mini (`gpt-4o-mini-2024-07-18`). As illustrated in Figure 3, the re-ranking process with LLMs is facilitated via prompting. Specifically, a set of text chunks, each assigned a unique identifier (e.g., `[1]`,`[2]`) is provided as input to the LLM. The model is then instructed to reorder the chunks in descending order of relevance to a given query. The output is a ranked list of identifiers in a format such as `[3] > [4] > [1] > [2]`. Notably, this approach directly generates a ranking without calculating intermediate relevance scores.

For datasets such as `NQ` and `DRUID`, we apply this direct permutation generation strategy without modification. However, for the `LitQA2` dataset, the samples of which contain a significantly larger number of candidate chunks (an average of 145 per query), the token limitations of LLMs pose a challenge. To address this, we employ the sliding window strategy, following Sun et al. (2023). This method processes the chunks iteratively, using a sliding window size w and a step size s, to re-rank the chunks in a back-to-first order. In our experiments on `LitQA2`, we set the window size to 20 and the step size to 2. However, we note that the GPT-4o re-ranker performance suffers on LitQA2 in spite of these adaptations.

F Adjusted prompt for DRUID

The prompts used for the prompt adjustment investigations for DRUID are as follows:

- Default prompt: "<claim>"
- Adjusted prompt: "Is the following claim accurate?\nClaimant: <claimant>\nClaim: <claim>"

Here, "<claim>" and "<claimant>" are replaced by the corresponding values in DRUID. This prompt is tuned to adapt re-rankers to the fact-checking setting, as opposed to a QA setting. The results for these prompts can be found in Table 1 and Figure 4.

G Additional re-ranker results

Additional results corresponding to Table 1 can be found in Figures 5 and 6. We also report additional D_{BM25} results in Tables 7 and 8.

Dataset	**Partition**	**% of data**	**P@1**
NQ	$D_{\text{BM25}} < -0.5$	32	0.31
	$-0.5 \leq D_{\text{BM25}}$	68	0.85
LitQA2	$D_{\text{BM25}} < -0.5$	31	0.47
	$-0.5 \leq D_{\text{BM25}}$	69	0.92
DRUID	$D_{\text{BM25}} < -0.5$	20	0.24
	$-0.5 \leq D_{\text{BM25}}$	80	0.85

Table 7: Re-ranker accuracy on the different datasets partitioned by D_{BM25} values. P@1 is reported for `bge-reranker-v2-gemma`.

	DRUID	
Re-ranker	$D_{\text{BM25}} < 0.5$	$0.5 \leq D_{\text{BM25}}$
Cohere	0.10 (−0.78)	0.83 (−0.07)
BGE	0.24 (−0.56)	0.85 (−0.05)
Jina turbo	0.13 (−0.72)	0.83 (−0.07)
Jina base	0.18 (−0.64)	0.77 (−0.09)
GPT-4o m	0.34 (−0.41)	0.82 (−0.02)
GPT-4o	0.32 (−0.40)	0.83 (−0.02)
BM25	0.00	0.83

Table 8: Re-ranker zero-shot alignment with gold measured using P@1 on DRUID partitioned by D_{BM25} values. Values in parenthesis indicate ΔP@1 (Equation (1)).

Additional separation results for the similarity measures Jaccard similarity (D_{JS}) and BERT score

system:
You are RankGPT, an intelligent assistant that can rank passages based on their relevancy to the query.

user:
I will provide you with `{{num}}` passages, each indicated by number identifier []. Rank them based on their relevance to query: `{{query}}`.

assistant:
Okay, please provide the passages.

user:
[1] `{{passage_1}}`

assistant:
Received passage [1]

user:
[2] `{{passage_2}}`

assistant:
Received passage [2]

(more passages) ...

user
Search Query: `{{query}}`.
Rank the `{{num}}` passages above based on their relevance to the search query. The passages should be listed in descending order using identifiers, and the most relevant passages should be listed first, and the output format should be [] > [], e.g., [1] > [2]. Only response the ranking results, do not say any word or explain.

Figure 3: Prompt template for `GPT-4o` and `GPT-4o-mini` as re-rankers (Sun et al., 2023).

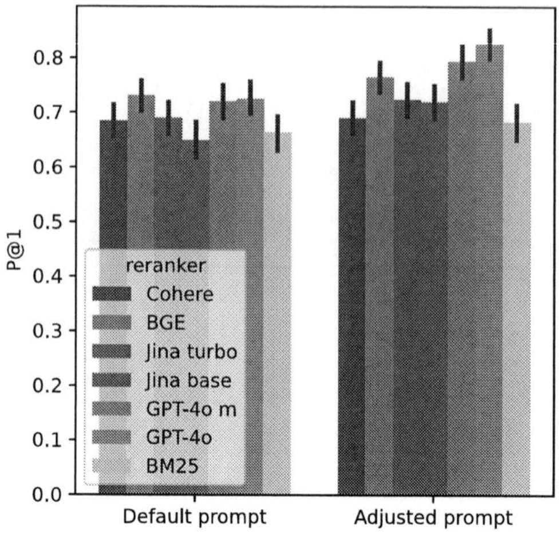

Figure 4: Re-ranker zero-shot alignment with gold labels on DRUID for different prompts.

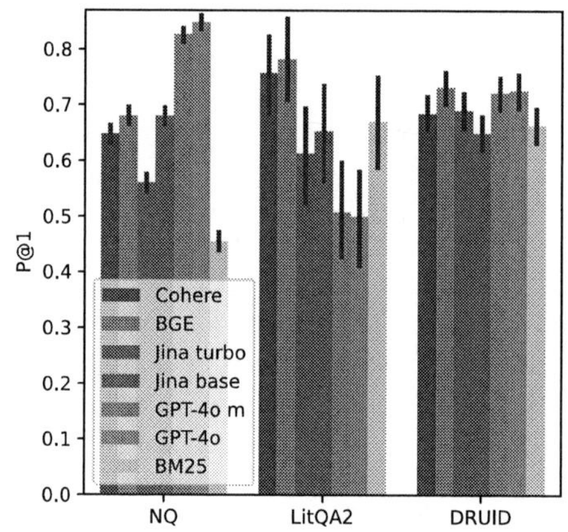

Figure 5: Re-ranker zero-shot alignment with gold labels for different datasets. The error bars indicate 95% confidence intervals.

(D_{BERT}) can be found in Figures 7 and 8. D_{BM25} scores with correctness evaluated based on GPT-4o and Jina base scores can be found in Figures 9 and 10.

H Samples with different separation values

Tables 9 to 11 contain samples from NQ, LitQA2 and DRUID with corresponding D_{BM25} values.

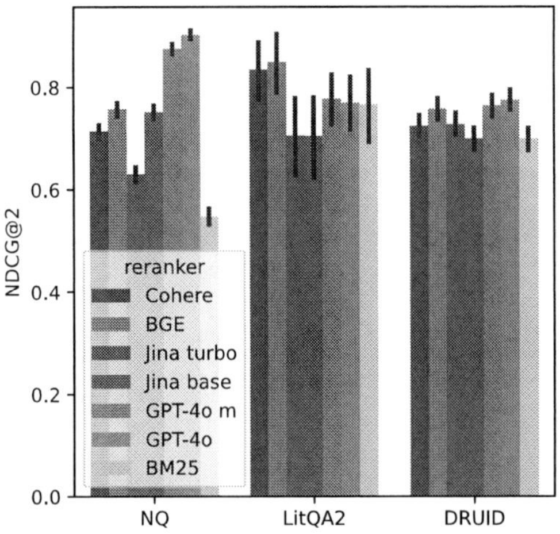

Figure 6: Re-ranker zero-shot alignment with gold labels for different datasets. The error bars indicate 95% confidence intervals.

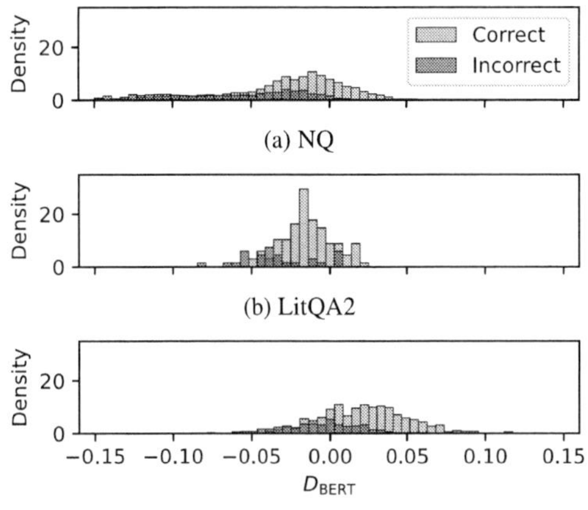

(a) NQ

(b) LitQA2

(c) DRUID

Figure 8: D_{BERT} (Equation (2)) on NQ, LitQA2 and DRUID. Correctness is based on P@1 for `bge-reranker-v2-gemma`.

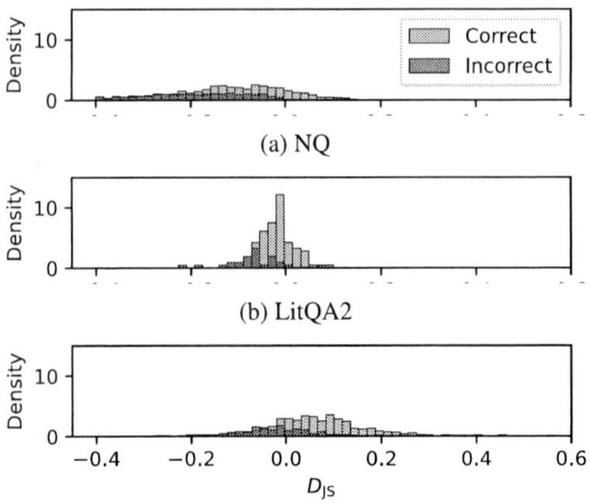

(a) NQ

(b) LitQA2

(c) DRUID

Figure 7: D_{JS} (Equation (2)) on NQ, LitQA2 and DRUID. Correctness is based on P@1 for `bge-reranker-v2-gemma`.

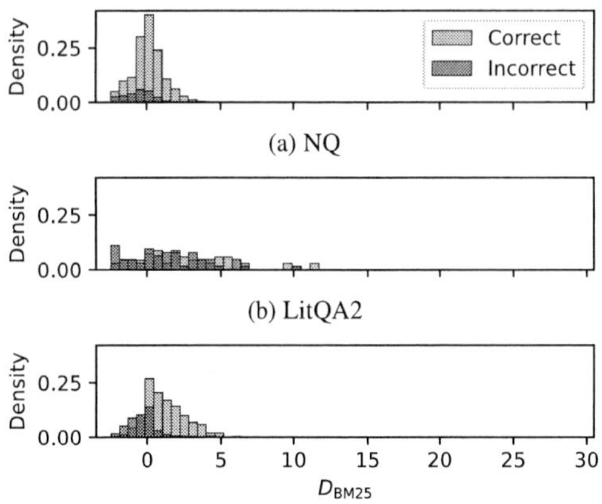

(a) NQ

(b) LitQA2

(c) DRUID

Figure 9: D_{BM25} (Equation (2)) on NQ, LitQA2 and DRUID. Correctness is based on P@1 for GPT-4o.

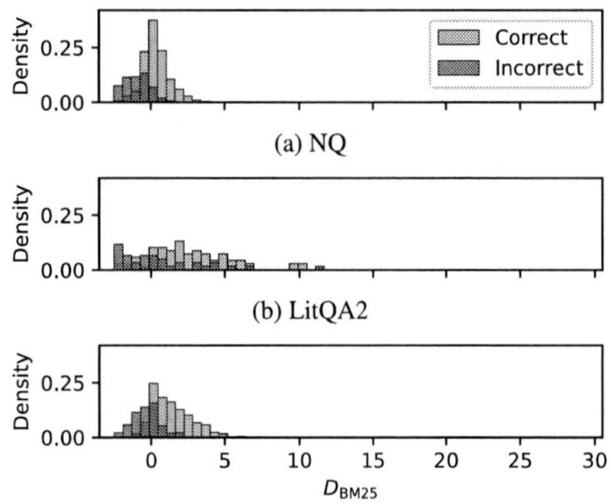

(a) NQ

(b) LitQA2

(c) DRUID

Figure 10: D_{BM25} (Equation (2)) on NQ, LitQA2 and DRUID. Correctness is based on P@1 for `jina-reranker-v2-base-multilingual`.

D_{BM25}	Question	Gold passage	Most similar passage
-4.92	who won the academy award for best original musical score?	<Table> <Tr> <Th> Year </Th> <Th> Film </Th> <Th> Nominees </Th> </Tr> <Tr> <Td> (83rd) </Td> </Tr> <Tr> <Td> The Social Network </Td> <Td> Trent Reznor & Atticus Ross </Td> </Tr> <Tr> <Td> How to Train Your Dragon </Td> <Td> John Powell </Td> </Tr> <Tr> <Td> Inception </Td> <Td> Hans Zimmer </Td> </Tr> <Tr> <Td> The King's Speech </Td> <Td> Alexandre Desplat </Td> </Tr> <Tr> <Td> 127 Hours </Td> <Td> A.R. Rahman </Td> </Tr> <Tr> <Td> 2011 (84th) </Td> </Tr> <Tr> <Td> The Artist </Td> <Td> Ludovic Bource </Td> </Tr> <Tr> <Td> The Adventures of Tintin </Td> <Td> John Williams </Td> </Tr> <Tr> <Td> Hugo </Td> <Td> Howard Shore </Td> </Tr> <Tr> <Td> Tinker Tailor Soldier Spy </Td> <Td> Alberto Iglesias </Td> </Tr> <Tr> <Td> War Horse </Td> <Td> John Williams </Td> </Tr> <Tr> <Td> 2012 (85th) </Td> </Tr> <Tr> <Td> Life of Pi </Td> <Td> Mychael Danna </Td> </Tr> <Tr> <Td> Anna Karenina </Td> <Td> Dario Marianelli </Td> </Tr> <Tr> <Td> Argo </Td> <Td> Alexandre Desplat </Td> </Tr> ... </Td> </Tr> </Table>	<P> The Academy began awarding movies for their scores in 1935 . The category was originally called Best Scoring . At the time, winners and nominees were a mix of original scores and adaptations of pre-existing material . Following the controversial win of Charles Previn for One Hundred Men and a Girl in 1938, a film without a credited composer that featured pre-existing classical music, the Academy added a Best Original Score category in 1939 . In 1942, the distinction between the two Scoring categories changed slightly as they were renamed to Best Music Score of a Dramatic Picture and Best Scoring of a Musical Picture . This marked the first time the category was split into separate genres, a distinction that technically still lasts today, although there haven't been enough submissions for the musical category to be activated since 1985 . From 1942 to 1985, musical scores had their own category, with the exception of 1958, 1981 and 1982 . During that time, both categories had many name changes: </P>
-3.68	tumhi ho bandhu sakha tumhi cast real name?	<Ul> <Li> Chandni Bhagwanani as Sanjana Ajay Pethewala </Li> <Li> Sreejita De as Shreya Bhushan Pethewala </Li> <Li> Kabeer K as Ajay Pethewala </Li> <Li> Neil Bhatt as Bhushan Trilokchand Pethewala </Li> <Li> Dimple Jhangiani as Avni Pethawala </Li> <Li> Lavina Tandon as Shaina </Li> ... </Ul>	<P> The show began with the working title Pethawala before being named Tum Hi Ho Bandhu Sakha Tumhi . The show ended due to low trp ratings . </P>
-0.33	when did the movie karate kid come out?	<P> Jaden Christopher Syre Smith (born July 8, 1998) is an American actor, rapper, singer and songwriter . He is the son of Jada Pinkett Smith and Will Smith . Jaden Smith's first movie role was with his father in the 2006 film The Pursuit of Happyness . He also acted in the 2008 remake of The Day the Earth Stood Still and the 2010 remake of The Karate Kid, and was in the 2013 film After Earth with his father . </P>	[same as gold]
5.84	who said i think there is a world market for maybe five computers?	<P> Although Watson is well known for his alleged 1943 statement, "I think there is a world market for maybe five computers," there is scant evidence he said it . Author Kevin Maney tried to find the origin of the quote, but has been unable to locate any speeches or documents of Watson's that contain this, nor are the words present in any contemporary articles about IBM . One of the very first attributions may be found in The Experts Speak, a book written by Christopher Cerf and Victor S. Navasky in 1984, however Cerf and Navasky just quote from a book written by Morgan and Langford, Facts and Fallacies . Another early article source (May 15, 1985) is a column by Neil Morgan, a San Diego Evening Tribune writer who wrote: "Forrest Shumway, chairman of The Signal Cos., doesn't make predictions . His role model is Tom Watson, then IBM chairman, who said in 1958:' I think there is a world market for about five computers ."' The earliest known citation on the Internet is from 1986 on Usenet in the signature of a poster from Convex Computer Corporation as "' I think there is a world market for about five computers'–Remark attributed to Thomas J. Watson (Chairman of the Board of International Business Machines), 1943". All these early quotes are questioned by Eric Weiss, an editor of the Annals of the History of Computing in ACS letters in 1985 . </P>	[same as gold]

Table 9: Examples of samples from NQ with relatively high and low D_{BM25} values. Passages lacking document context are marked in purple. Passages containing distractors are marked in green with the distracting terms in **bold**.

D_{BM25}	Question	Gold passage	Most similar passage
-5.97	How long do mouse neurons survive following CRISPR inactivation of HSPA5? (A) 14 days, (B) 3 days, (C) 5 days, (D) 10 days, (E) 28 days, or (F) not enough info?	We selected Hspa5, a top hit that was not previously identified as a hit in iPSC-derived neurons, for individual validation. In mouse embryonic fibroblasts expressing CRISPRi machinery, we confirmed that an sgRNA targeting Hspa5 (sgHspa5) suppresses expression of the endogenous Hspa5 transcript (Fig. 5a). In primary neurons cultured from conditional CRISPRi mice, AAVs delivering sgHspa5 led to marked Cre-dependent neuronal death within 2 weeks of expression (Fig. 5b,c). Furthermore, injection of this sgRNA into neonatal mice led to a severe motor phenotype after approximately 2 weeks in mice co-expressing hSyn1-Cre, but not the sgRNA alone (Supplementary Videos 1 and 2), and the brains from mice with sgHspa5 + hSyn1-Cre were markedly smaller in size relative to sgHspa5-only littermates (Fig. 5d). This confirms the capability of our platform to uncover neuron-essential genes.	For **mouse** primary **neurons** transduced with AAV, live imaging was performed every other day using an ImageXpress Micro Confocal HT.ai High-Content Imaging System (Molecular Devices). The imaging chamber was warmed to 37°C and equilibrated with 5% CO2. The system used an Andor Zyla 4.5 camera with a Plan Apo ×10/0.45NA objective lens, an 89 North LDI laser illumination unit, 10-500 ms exposure time, 1×1 binning, and 10% laser intensity using 405-nm, 475-nm, and 555-nm lasers, running MetaXpress (version 6.7.1.157). Resulting images were imported into Cell Profiler (version 4.2.1)28 and analyzed using a custom pipeline. hSyn1-Cre-GFP+ nuclei were segmented using the 'IdentifyPrimaryObjects' module, with expected diameter 8-40 pixels, using an Adaptive threshold (size 50) and the Minimum Cross-Entropy method, with a 1.5 smoothing scale, 1.0 correction factor, and lower- and upper-bound threshold at 0.435 and 1, respectively. Segmented objects were exported, and counted in each field, then summed across all fields within a well to calculate the number of objects per well (n=29 fields per well, n=4 wells per condition), using a custom R script. This was repeated for each timepoint. Data was normalized to fluorescent intensity at **day** 8 (as before that day, fluorescence intensity increased linearly with time in all channels as cells manufactured fluorescent proteins) and percentage change was calculated for each well from **day** 8, for subsequent timepoints through **day** 16.
11.62	Based on whole genome bisulfite sequencing data (WGBS) from publicly available datasets (the ROADMAP epigenome project and the ENCODE data portal), what is the relationship between DNA methylation patterns between introns and exons (after excluding consideration of the first intron and first exon)? (A) There are no significant differences, (B) Introns have more DNA methylation, (C) Exons have more DNA methylation, (D) Neither introns nor exons can be methylated, (E) only areas very close to the transcription start site, or (F) not enough info?	Further, we considered a possible association between these gradients in DNA methylation, and the mutation risk in comparing exonic versus intronic DNA, in light of reports of subtly different mutation rates and subtly different DNA methylation in exons versus introns . We checked the DNA methylation level of exons and introns, separately for each exon/intron in sequence, for a representative gene set (middle tertile of genes by length, and middle tertile in expression level). While methylation in the first exon was substantially lower compared to the first intron, consistent with the exon's more 5' positioning, the DNA methylation levels across the subsequent introns and exons were highly similar (Supplementary Figure S7). Thus, in human WGBS data, after accounting for 5' gene end hypomethylation, we see no notably different DNA methylation in the exonic versus intronic loci, and if there are any differences between introns and exons in mutation rates, these do not stem from different DNA methylation.	[same as gold]

Table 10: Examples of samples from LitQA2 with relatively high and low D_{BM25} values. Passages lacking document context are marked in purple. Passages containing distractors are marked in green with the distracting terms in **bold**.

D_{BM25}	Question	Gold passage	Most similar passage
-4.71	"Before the pandemic, just over 40,000 were on continuing UI claims. Now, there are well over 100,000 on state or federal UI benefits."	Department of Workforce Development datashows that in the week ending on March 7, 2020, there were 41,015 unemployment claims statewide. For the week of May 22, 202, there were 127,745 claims.	Lisa Subeck stated on February 16, 2024 in X, formerly Twitter: "The United States is an outlier, one of only about half a dozen countries, without any guarantee of paid leave for new parents and/or other health care needs." Tim Kaine stated on March 15, 2022 in a tweet.: "Virginia women are paid 80 cents for every dollar paid to Virginia men." Mandela Barnes stated on May 23, 2021 in Twitter: "It's been over 50 years since minimum (wage) and inflation parted ways, then over a decade since the federal minimum went up at all." Glenn Grothman stated on June 8, 2021 in Twitter: "We have a record 9.3 million job openings in the U.S." Mark Born stated on June 2, 2021 in Twitter: **"Before the pandemic, just over 40,000 were on continuing UI claims.** Mandela Barnes stated on May 23, 2021 in Twitter: "Since 1978, CEO compensation rose over 1,000% and only 11.9% for average workers." Joe Biden stated on April 15, 2020 in comments at a virtual town hall meeting: "Until this week, they [OSHA] weren't even enforcing these guidelines [for coronavirus]. [...] Mark Born stated on June 2, 2021 in Twitter: **"Before the pandemic, just over 40,000 were on continuing UI claims.**
-3.59	Claims that President George Washington once said, "Government is not reason; it is not eloquence; it is force. Like fire, it is a dangerous servant and a fearful master."	There is no record of Washington ever making this statement.	FACT CHECK: Did George Washington Call Government **'A Dangerous Servant And A Fearful Master'**? An image shared on Facebook claims that President George Washington once said, **"Government is not reason; it is not eloquence; it is force.** [...] According to the website Quote Investigator, the depiction of government as **"a dangerous servant and a fearful master"** is reminiscent of a centuries-old saying about water and fire. "Water is a very good seruaunt, but it is a cruell mayster," reads an excerpt from 1562.
3.88	The Police Service of Northern Ireland (PSNI) are to pilot a Snapchat social media platform initiative to monitor social mitigation compliance in Northern Ireland.	The PSNI have no plans to introduce any monitoring scheme on any social media platform. Complaints about social mitigation compliance can be registered on the PSNI website. A claim was published on social media, that the Police Service of Northern Ireland (PSNI) is "to roll out a new 'Snap-fish' pilot scheme" on the Snapchat social media platform "to help catch individuals not adhering to social distancing, social bubbles and gathering more than six people" (often referred to as "social mitigation compliance"). [...] "The Police Service of Northern Ireland has no plans to introduce a 'snap-fish' scheme ... nor indeed any new social media platforms around the enforcement of COVID-19 restrictions."	[same as gold]
5.88	Families of the deceased persons to be given an assistance of 4 lakh rupees, up from 2.5 lakh rupees.	Is assistance of Rs. 4 lakh being provided for families of deceased persons? The third claim is that 'families of the deceased persons to be given an assistance of 4 lakh rupees, up from 2.5 lakh rupees'. It is true that the revised norms of assistance from the SDRF increase the assistance per deceased persons to Rs. 4 lakh from the existing Rs. 1.5 lakh per person. It has to be noted that is not for farmers alone, but for any deceased person during a notified natural disaster.	[same as gold]

Table 11: Examples of samples from DRUID with relatively high and low D_{BM25} values. Passages lacking document context are marked in purple. Passages containing distractors are marked in green with the distracting terms marked in **bold**.

Portuguese Automated Fact-checking: Information Retrieval with Claim Extraction

Juliana Gomes, Eduardo Garcia, Arlindo Rodrigues Galvão Filho

Advanced Knowledge Center for Immersive Technologies - AKCIT
Institute of Informatics, Federal University of Goiás
Correspondence: juliana.resplande@discente.ufg.br

Abstract

Current Portuguese Automated Fact-Checking (AFC) research often relies on datasets lacking integrated external evidence crucial for comprehensive verification. This study addresses this gap by systematically enriching Portuguese misinformation datasets. We retrieve web evidence by simulating user information-seeking behavior, guided by core claims extracted using Large Language Models (LLMs). Additionally, we apply a semi-automated validation framework to enhance dataset reliability.

Our analysis reveals that inherent dataset characteristics impact data properties, evidence retrieval, and AFC model performance. While enrichment generally improves detection, its efficacy varies, influenced by challenges such as self-reinforcing online misinformation and API limitations. This work contributes enriched datasets, associating original texts with retrieved evidence and LLM-extracted claims, to foster future evidence-based fact-checking research.

The code and enriched data for this study is available at `https://github.com/ju-resplande/pt_afc`.

1 Introduction

News fact-checking agencies, such as Agência Lupa and Boatos.org in Brazil, manually investigate the veracity of claims (Faustini and Covões, 2019; Couto et al., 2021). However, the speed at which viral messages spread surpasses the capacity of investigative journalists to verify the accuracy of the information.

This inherent limitation has spurred the development of Automated Fact-Checking (AFC) systems, which aim to verify claims by leveraging external knowledge sources through techniques from Information Retrieval (IR) and Natural Language Processing (NLP) (Guo et al., 2022).

Despite advances in AFC, a significant gap persists within the Portuguese language context. Our investigation reveals that existing approaches and datasets for misinformation detection in Portuguese predominantly focus on intrinsic content analysis, such as writing style or bias (Monteiro et al., 2018), rather than incorporating the crucial step of external evidence verification.

This work aims to directly address this lacuna. Our objective is to develop, apply, and analyze a methodology for enriching existing Portuguese-language misinformation datasets with relevant external evidence retrieved through web search mechanisms. This process mimics how users might seek corroborating information online. To guide the search effectively, especially when initial queries yield suboptimal results, we employ Large Language Models (LLMs) to extract the main claim from each news item, which then serves as an optimized query.

The key contributions of this work are: (i) A comparative analysis of Portuguese-language misinformation-related datasets, detailing their characteristics, including domains, sources, and data collection methodologies (top-down vs. bottom-up (Hangloo and Arora, 2022)); (ii) A semi-automatic data validation process, addressing near-duplicates, instances referencing the same URL, and cross-verification using the Google FactCheck Claim Search API; (iii) A methodology for enriching Portuguese misinformation datasets with external evidence retrieved via web search, guided by LLM-based claim extraction, alongside an experimental evaluation of this enrichment's impact on the performance of misinformation detection models.

2 Related work

Large Language Models (LLMs), such as Gemini and ChatGPT, are increasingly central to fact-checking. They offer a cost-effective alternative to manual methods like crowdsourcing or expert

Proceedings of the Eighth Fact Extraction and VERification Workshop (FEVER), pages 34–53
July 31, 2025 ©2025 Association for Computational Linguistics

review (Ali et al., 2022; Aimeur et al., 2023), with performance often comparable to human crowd-sourcers (Maia and da Silva, 2024; Ni et al., 2024). A key advantage of LLMs is their proficiency in zero-shot or few-shot learning and their ability to generate explanations, frequently without the need for supervised fine-tuning (Gangi Reddy et al., 2022; Chen and Shu, 2024). This marks a notable distinction from smaller language model architectures (SLMs), which typically require substantial supervised training for specific tasks (Qiu and Jin, 2024).

In automated fact-checking pipelines (Guo et al., 2022), LLMs are employed at various stages. These include claim identification (extracting main claims (Kotitsas et al., 2024; Ni et al., 2024), multiple claims (Tang et al., 2024), or generating search queries (Cho et al., 2022)), claim verification (the detection task itself) (Tan et al., 2023; Choi and Ferrara, 2024), and the generation of justifications for verification outcomes (Kim et al., 2024; Zeng and Gao, 2024).

While prior work has utilized LLMs for claim extraction (Kotitsas et al., 2024; Ni et al., 2024) or for zero-shot classification of claims (Tan et al., 2023; Choi and Ferrara, 2024), our research distinctly focuses on enriching existing Portuguese datasets. We achieve this by retrieving web-based evidence, where the search process is triggered by main claims extracted from the news items using LLMs.

Numerous Portuguese-language datasets for misinformation detection exist (Monteiro et al., 2018; Moreno and Bressan, 2019; Vargas et al., 2023; Nielsen and McConville, 2022). However, a significant challenge is that few of these datasets provide directly accessible external evidence. Many only offer tweet identifiers or indirect references, which hinders the direct use of evidence for verification (Cordeiro and Pinheiro, 2019; da Silva et al., 2020; Shahi and Nandini, 2020). Our work aims to address this critical gap by systematically augmenting these resources with verifiable, web-retrieved evidence.

3 Methods

The core of our methodology involves enriching misinformation datasets with external evidence. This process, depicted in Figure 1, begins with an input text from a selected misinformation dataset. If an initial web search for this text (or a query derived from it) yields results with strong lexical correspondence to the query, claim extraction is bypassed. Otherwise, an LLM extracts the main claim from the text, and this extracted claim is used for a subsequent, more targeted web search. Each component is detailed below.

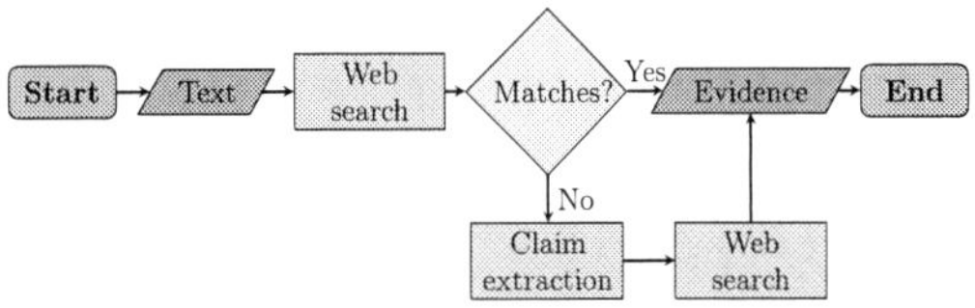

Figure 1: Flowchart for evidence retrieval from an input text. The web search was conducted using Google Custom Search Engine (CSE), and claim extraction was performed by Gemini 1.5 Flash.

3.1 Dataset Selection

We selected datasets for public availability, a minimum of 1000 examples, and a peer-reviewed publication. We excluded those solely comprising fact-checking reports (not original misleading content). Table 1 details the three selected datasets:

Fake.br (Monteiro et al., 2018). Relevant for its canonical status in Portuguese misinformation research, this dataset consists of news articles from web pages, covering general domains, collected between 2016 and 2018. It uses a bottom-up collection approach, directly gathering content from these web pages (Hangloo and Arora, 2022).

COVID19.BR (Martins et al., 2021; de Sá et al., 2021). Contains messages from the WhatsApp platform from 236 public groups, focusing on the health topic (COVID-19), collected between April and June 2020. It also follows a bottom-up collection approach.

MuMiN-PT (Nielsen and McConville, 2022) is a Portuguese corpus of X (formerly Twitter) posts from general domains (2020-2022). It provide a crucial methodological contrast to the others, having been collected using a top-down approach (Hangloo and Arora, 2022) by finding posts corresponding to claims verified by fact-checkers. It is a subset of the multilingual MuMiN corpus, extracted with Lingua (Stahl, 2023).

3.2 Dataset Validation and Cleaning

To ensure the quality and integrity of our datasets, we implemented a rigorous semi-automatic validation and cleaning pipeline. This multi-stage process combined automated scripts with targeted manual

Dataset	Domain	Source	Collection Approach	Size per label	Temporal Coverage	Fact-Checking Sources
Fake.BR (Monteiro et al., 2018)	General	News Websites	Bottom-up	3,600 true 3,600 fake	2016–2018	estadao.com.br folha.uol.com.br g1.globo.com
COVID19.BR (Martins et al., 2021)	Health	WhatsApp	Bottom-up	1,987 true 912 fake	2020	boatos.org lupa.uol.com.br
MuMiN-PT (Nielsen and McConville, 2022)	General	Twitter (now X)	Top-down	1,339 fake 65 true	2020–2022	afp.com/pt aosfatos.org projetocomprova.com.br observador.pt oglobo.globo.com piaui.folha.uol.com.br uol.com.br

Table 1: Characteristics of datasets enriched with external verification evidence in this study. Collection approaches follow the classification by Hangloo and Arora (2022), where **top-down** involves collecting posts for known, long-standing rumors (often starting from fact-checking websites), and **bottom-up** involves gathering all relevant posts from a given time frame to identify emerging misinformation. While original publications list verification sources, they typically do not provide the specific evidence snippets used for fact-checking each item.

review by one of the authors to identify and rectify issues ranging from formatting errors to label inconsistencies. The primary steps in our pipeline were as follows:

1. **Automated Initial Filtering:** Removal of exact duplicates and entries with fewer than 15 tokens after removing emojis, URLs, stopwords, and punctuation[1].
2. **Language Filtering:** Automatic Portuguese detection via Lingua (Stahl, 2023), followed by manual verification and exclusion of non-Portuguese examples.
3. **Contradictory Duplicate Removal:** Manual review of near-duplicate pairs that were automatically identified via MinHash LSH (Section 4.1.1) with inconsistent labels. The conflicting instances were subsequently removed to maintain dataset integrity.
4. **External Label Verification:** Manual review of instances where a dataset's label potentially conflicted with results from the Google FactCheck Claim Search API. The original labels were corrected when the external evidence provided a clear refutation or confirmation.
5. **URL Reference Removal:** Manual review of instances that referenced the exact same URL within their text but possessed differing veracity labels. The conflicting instances were subsequently removed to maintain dataset integrity.
6. **Random Inspection:** Manual check of a random subset from each dataset for overall quality.
7. **Specific Treatment for Fake.br:** (a) Removed near-duplicates from the same source URL, as the source in this corpus is a URL; (b) Examples lacking full text were removed from the original authors' normalized set [2]; (c) Maintained pair integrity by removing items whose pair was previously excluded.

The number of instances corrected or removed at each stage is quantified in Table 2. For a detailed breakdown of case counts and illustrative examples, please see Appendix A.

Validation Stage	COVID19.BR	Fake.br	MuMiN-PT
Initial Automated Filtering	804	1	0
Language Filtering	8	0	11801
Contradiction Resolution	20	0	0
External Label Verification	23	0	4
Subset Inspection	88	0	0
Fake.br Specific Treatment	0	61	0

Table 2: Number of examples corrected or removed in the corpora during the semi-automatic validation workflow.

As a final preprocessing step, all explicitly mentioned URLs were removed from the original texts to mitigate potential biases from URL domains, as shown in Appendix B.

3.3 LLM-based Claim Extraction

For claim extraction, we utilized the Gemini 1.5 Flash model. To simulate a user's initial scan of a text for its core assertion, we provided the LLM with up to the first 75 words of the news item or message.

[1] using cl100k_base tokenizer from https://github.com/openai/tiktoken

[2] https://github.com/roneysco/Fake.br-Corpus/issues/7

We experimented with variations on a small data subset. We opted for single main claim extraction, excluding multi-claim splitting to avoid generating multiple queries per input item. The final prompt used is shown in Figure 2. This zero-shot prompt proved effective for our goal of generating concise search queries, without requiring specific role instructions or few-shot examples.

> What is the main fact presented in the text?
> 1. Extract a passage of up to 20 words from the following text.
> 2. Return only the claim, without any title or preamble.
>
> Text: `[INPUT TEXT]`
> Claim:

Figure 2: Prompt template used with Gemini 1.5 Flash for main claim extraction.

3.4 Evidence Retrieval via Web Search

Our evidence retrieval process involves up to two stages of web searching.

Initial Web Search Strategy. The initial input text (from the dataset) is queried using the Google Custom Search Engine (CSE) API[3]. Query parameters for CSE were `gl=pt-BR` (geographical restriction to Brazil), and `lr=lang_pt` (language restriction to Portuguese).

To simulate how a user might create a concise search query, we developed a set of empirically-determined heuristics. The logic was designed to quickly extract the core assertion from a given text. For short texts of 20 words or less, the entire text was used as the query. For longer texts, we first extracted the initial sentence. If this sentence was long enough to likely contain the main claim (7 words or more), it became the query. However, if the first sentence was too brief (fewer than 7 words), the query was then formed by taking the longer of either the full first paragraph or the first 20 words of the text. Emojis and specific Unicode quote characters were removed from queries.

Correspondence Check. The lexical containment of the query (excluding stopwords) within CSE snippets is assessed. The proportion of the query's non-stopword terms found in the snippet is calculated. Empirically, if $\geq$80% of the query's non-stopwords are present in the snippet, claim extraction is bypassed.

[3] `https://developers.google.com/custom-search/v1/reference/rest/v1/cse/list`

FactCheck API Search. The input text is also searched using the Google FactCheck Claim Search API[4] with parameters `languageCode=pt-BR`, and `pageSize=5`. The same query preprocessing from CSE search was applied.

Claim-based Fallback Search. If the initial CSE search is unsuccessful, a claim is extracted, and the claim initiates a second search using both CSE and FactCheck Claim Search APIs with original parameters.

If a CSE result links to a page indexed by Google FactCheck, a `ClaimReview` schema might be present in the CSE result's metadata. While this schema typically does not include the veracity label itself directly in the CSE metadata, we store the first such linked result if found via CSE.

4 Cleaned and Enriched Data Analysis

4.1 Cleaned Dataset

After applying the validation and cleaning steps from Section 3.2, we analyzed the remaining data. Table 3 shows statistics for the cleaned datasets.

Stats.	MuMiN-PT		Fake.br		COVID19.BR	
	fake	true	fake	true	fake	true
count	1339	65	3580	3580	848	1139
% URL	0.3%	0.0%	1.0%	0.7%	28.9%	56.5%
# words	18.9	16.3	181.4	183.1	167.7	111.1
word len (chars)	5.0	4.9	4.8	5.0	4.9	6.6
# sents	1.4	1.4	10.4	9.0	10.9	5.8
# words/ sent	14.5	12.3	18.6	22.1	19.2	22.9

Table 3: Cleaned dataset statistics: overall size and word/sentence counts per label.

Table 3 summarizes the textual statistics. The average text length varies significantly, reflecting the source platform: posts on X (MuMiN-PT) are the shortest, followed by WhatsApp messages (COVID19.BR), and web news articles (Fake.br). The average word length, however, was remarkably stable across datasets and labels, hovering around 4.8-5.0 characters.

In terms of labels, MuMiN-PT does not show variation in word and sentence statistics between true and false labels, possibly due to the low character limit imposed on X. Fake.br's true news is

[4] `https://developers.google.com/fact-check/tools/api#the-google-factcheck-claim-search-api`

typically longer, so its original paper (Monteiro et al., 2018) normalized text length by truncation for fair classification. This work uses this normalized version (see Section 3.1). Conversely, in COVID19.BR, fake texts are longer and more variable, which its authors attribute to different writing styles (Martins et al., 2021).

COVID19.BR leads in link count (889 examples, 44.7%), likely because WhatsApp environments foster more link sharing than websites or X. True news in both COVID19.BR and Fake.br feature more links. MuMiN-PT, as expected for X posts, has virtually no links.

4.1.1 Near-Duplicates Analysis

Near-duplicate detection used the Akin library[5] (v0.1.0) with MinHash LSH (char 5-grams, 128 hash bits, 50 bands, Jaccard threshold 0.7, seed=3).

COVID19.BR had the most (271 examples, 13.6% of cleaned data), likely due to easy sharing of short, similar messages on WhatsApp. Fake.br had the fewest (6 examples, 0.08%), while MuMiN-PT had 28 (2.0%). In Fake.br, near-duplicates were all true news articles, often minor updates republished by the same outlet (see Appendix C). Conversely, near-duplicates in MuMiN-PT (all examples) and COVID19.BR (186 examples) were predominantly false. This pattern, especially the volume in COVID19.BR, likely reflects viral misinformation spread via short, easily shared messages on WhatsApp

4.1.2 Observed Data Limitations

Beyond near-duplicates, we noted other challenges:

Topic Temporality: Misinformation topics and associated vocabulary are volatile and time-dependent. Evidence found today might not reflect the context when the claim first appeared.

Label Temporality: The truthfulness of a claim can change over time (e.g., "Mask use is mandatory in Goiás" depends on the specific date).

Degrees of Veracity: Fact-checking employs a spectrum of veracity labels beyond a simple true/false dichotomy, such as "misleading," "partly false," and "unproven" (Wang, 2017; Hangloo and Arora, 2022; Couto et al., 2021).

Claim Verifiability: Some texts express personal experiences or uncheckable anecdotes (e.g., "I want to stay quietly at home. Today a gentleman with coronavirus passed away here." from COVID19.BR).

URL Dependence: Analyzing text without linked content misses crucial verification data. Additionally, URL domains can act as strong veracity heuristics due to varying frequencies in true/false claims (Appendix B).

4.2 Claim Extraction Outcomes

Per Section 3, Gemini 1.5 Flash extracted claims when the initial CSE search failed to find strong correspondence, which was for 94.0% (1,868/1,987) of COVID19.BR, 80.1% (5,738/7,160) of Fake.BR, and 70.7% (992/1,404) of MuMiN-PT examples.

The lower need for extraction in MuMiN-PT might relate to its bottom-up construction (starting from verified claims, potentially leading to posts that closely match searchable claims) and the concise nature of posts on X. Conversely, Fake.BR often required extraction, possibly because full news articles are less likely to directly match concise search results without summarizing the core claim. COVID19.BR (WhatsApp messages) frequently required extraction, perhaps due to conversational context or less structured claims.

Analysis of the successfully extracted claims (using the prompt in Figure 2) showed an average length of 11-12 words per claim, with an average word length of 4.9 characters, consistent across the corpora. Appendix E shows examples of the full enrichment process.

4.3 Search Engine Results Analysis

The top three domains found in the Google CSE results (combining results from both initial searches and searches using extracted claims) were consistent across searches for all three datasets: Brazilian government sites ('gov.br'), Globo (major media network), and the BBC. Brazilian government sites accounted for 34.0% of results for COVID19.BR, 25.0% for Fake.BR, and 23.1% for MuMiN-PT. Globo represented 3.9%, 11.0%, and 7.0% respectively, while the BBC appeared in 2.8%, 3.7%, and 3.7% of results for the same datasets.

Table 4 presents the domains corresponding to fact-checking search results. These results refer to instances where a CSE search result links to a page containing a `ClaimReview` schema, as indicated in the CSE result's metadata. However, this metadata from CSE typically does not include the actual veracity label (e.g., true, false) of the claim.

In particular, the domains `e-farsas.com`, `sbt.com.br`, and `sapo.pt` noted in our search results (Table 4) do not appear as source agencies

[5] https://github.com/justinbt1/Akin/tree/v0.1.0

Domain	COVID19.BR	Fake.br	MuMiN-PT
afp.com	8	10	154
uol.com.br	5	11	95
observador.pt	4	4	80
estadao.com.br	4	17	11
e-farsas.com	0	1	8
sbt.com.br	3	5	0
globo.com	0	0	7
projetocomprova.com.br	0	0	7
sapo.pt	0	1	0

Table 4: Count of fact-checking agency domains found within CSE search results containing `ClaimReview` metadata. Parent domains aggregate related subdomains (e.g., `uol.com.br` includes `lupa.uol.com.br`).

in Table 1. Alternatively, `boatos.org` is indicated as a source agency there but is absent from our CSE-retrieved `ClaimReview` findings.

Some CSE results from agency domains included publication dates. Figure 3 plots these dates. Results associated with COVID19.BR peaked in 2020, and MuMiN-PT results clustered in 2020-2022, aligning well with their collection periods (Table 1). Fake.br results showed a broader date distribution, often more recent than the original 2016-2018 collection period.

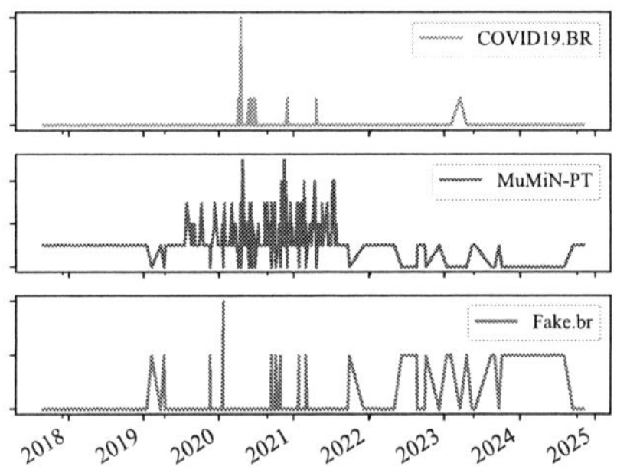

Figure 3: Publication dates of agency results from the CSE search that included `ClaimReview` metadata.

The Google FactCheck Claim Search API yielded results in 58.8% of MuMiN-PT, 5.0% of COVID19.BR, and 0.9% of Fake.br cases. The high rate for MuMiN-PT is expected, as Google FactCheck Claim Search was involved in its creation process. The low rate for Fake.br might be due to its age and website source (less likely indexed by the ClaimReview schema compared to social media or recent news). COVID19.BR's rate is intermediate, reflecting its WhatsApp origin and timing during the pandemic.

The FactCheck API directly provides the veracity label assigned by the reviewing organization. Table 5 summarizes the labels found across 986 claims retrieved successfully via this API for all datasets combined. The labels predominantly indicate falsity or related categories. Only 11 claims were explicitly labeled "true". This supports the observation that fact-checking efforts predominantly target content perceived as problematic or false.

Compared to the CSE results with `ClaimReview` metadata (Table 4), the direct FactCheck API query retrieved results from `boatos.org` but not from `e-farsas.com` or `sbt.com.br`.

The label distribution generally aligns with findings by Couto et al. (2021), although direct comparison is limited by differences in data collection scope and time period.

4.4 Evidence Patterns from Search Results

Analysis of CSE and FactCheck API search results revealed distinct evidence patterns for true/false claims:

For TRUE claims:

T1: Corroboration: Links to original/reliable sources confirming the information (Appendix E, T1 Ex.).

T2: Absence of Explicit Confirmation: Fact-checkers rarely explicitly confirmed true claims via CSE/API (as they primarily debunk, Table 5).

For FALSE claims:

F1: Direct Debunk: Reputable articles/fact-checks directly refute the claim (Appendix E, F1 Ex.).

F2: Misinformation Reinforcement: Results often surface the same misinformation from unreliable sources, amplifying it (Appendix E, F2 Ex.).

F3: Academic Recognition as Misinformation: Scholarly articles identify the claim as known misinformation (Appendix E, F3 Ex.).

While T1/F1 provide clear veracity signals, F2 can propagate misinformation, and F3 offers meta-evidence of falsity. (Examples: Appendix E). While T1 and F1 offer clear veracity signals, F2 can propagate misinformation. F3 provides unique meta-evidence of a claim's dubious nature. Illustrative examples are in Appendix E.

5 Experimental Strategy and Setup

To assess the impact of our data enrichment, we established the following experimental configurations, which were applied to the COVID19.BR and Fake.BR datasets. While MuMiN-PT was invalu-

Fact-checking Source	Total Claims Retrieved	Assigned Veracity Labels (Count)
aosfatos.org	283	**false (246)**, distorted (29), not quite so (2), unsustainable (2), exaggerated (2), contradictory (2)
uol.com.br	150	**false (130), misleading (10)**, unsustainable (7), distorted (2), satire (1)
observador.pt	147	**wrong (124), misleading (23)**
lupa.uol.br	114	**false (100)**, true (5), true but (5), exaggerated (2), under review (1), too early to tell (1)
boatos.org	99	**false (99)**
afp.com/pt	71	**false (48), misleading (17)**, unverified (2), true (1), no evidence (1), out of context (1), lacks context (1)
estadao.com.br/estadao-verifica	47	**misleading (25), false (20)**, out of context (2)
projetocomprova.com.br	45	**false (24), misleading (21)**
g1.globo.com/fato-ou-fake	11	**fake (11)**
bol.uol.com.br	2	**false (2)**
folha.uol.com.br	2	**misleading (1), false (1)**
piaui.folha.uol.com.br	2	**false (2)**

Table 5: Veracity labels assigned by fact-checking agencies as retrieved via the Google FactCheck Claim Search API across all datasets. The most frequent labels, primarily indicating falsity or deception, are highlighted in bold. These results were used to guide our manual "External Label Verification" step (Section 3.2), where conflicts with an original dataset's binary label prompted a review. Appendix A.4 details which labels were considered evidence for FAKE NEWS or TRUE.

able for the preceding comparative analyses of data characteristics and evidence retrieval patterns (Sections 4.1 to 4.4), it was excluded from classification experiments due to severe class imbalance (Table 3).

1. **Validated-only Data (Baseline):** Datasets after our full semi-automatic validation workflow (Section 3.2). This configuration serves as the baseline to measure the impact of enrichment.
2. **Validated and Enriched Data:** Validated datasets supplemented with external web search evidence, evaluated under two conditions:
   (a) **Complete Enrichment:** Using the first Google API CSE search result as context.
   (b) **Filtered Enrichment (No Social Media):** Excluding social media results (e.g., Twitter/X, Facebook) from CSE searches.

For comparability, both COVID19.BR and Fake.br used a standardized 80/10/10 train/validation/test split. For Fake.br, news pairs from the original dataset were kept together within each partition to ensure methodological consistency.

Model performance per data configuration was measured via: 1) supervised fine-tuning of the Portuguese SLM Bertimbau base (Souza et al., 2020), and 2) few-shot learning with the Gemini 1.5 Flash LLM (Reid et al., 2024).

5.1 Evaluation Environment

For few-shot learning, the prompt for each test instance included the same set of 15 randomly selected examples from the training set. All experiments were run 3 times to be averaged, but the result between each experiment was the same. Figure 4 presents the base prompt used for inference by the model.

> The following are texts from messages and news in Portuguese. Your task is to classify each text as containing FAKE NEWS or as being TRUE.
> To assist in the classification, extra context will also be provided, corresponding to a Google search for the terms of the text to be classified.
> Respond **only** with one of the following *tags*: "FAKE NEWS" or "TRUE".

Figure 4: Base prompt for misinformation detection. The underlined section is included when external context (retrieved evidence) is incorporated.

Fine-tuning experiments used PyTorch with SimpleTransformers (Rajapakse et al., 2024) on NVIDIA V100 (32GB VRAM) or A100 (80GB VRAM) GPUs. Runs typically required 8-12 GB VRAM, varying with data configuration and batch size. Hyperparameter grid search details are in Appendix F. Best hyperparameters were chosen via validation F1-score.

6 Experimental Results and Discussion

This section presents misinformation detection results for fine-tuned Bertimbau base and few-shot Gemini 1.5 Flash, comparing performance on validated-only data against data enriched with external evidence (Table 6).

The introduction of external evidence through enrichment generally led to performance gains over the validated-only baseline, although the impact varied by dataset and model. For COVID19.BR, complete enrichment improved the F1-macro score for both Bertimbau (+1.0) and Gemini (+2.4).

The introduction of external evidence through enrichment generally led to performance gains over the validated-only baseline, though the impact varied. On COVID19.BR, it improved the F1-macro score for both Bertimbau (+1.0) and Gemini (+2.4). In contrast, on Fake.BR, enrichment provided a modest improvement for Bertimbau (+0.3) but degraded performance for Gemini, a result potentially explained by temporally mismatched evidence for this older dataset (Figure 3).

A notable result is Bertimbau's near-perfect performance on the canonical Fake.br dataset, a score suggesting the dataset may be 'saturated' for modern models. The original corpus authors (Monteiro et al., 2018; Silva et al., 2020) explain this by noting significant, systematic differences between the classes: true news was sourced from professional journalistic outlets while fake news came from amateur sites, resulting in disparate writing quality and style. Although we use a length-normalized version of the dataset, these other strong intrinsic signals likely contribute to the exceptionally high baseline performance, making it difficult to measure the marginal impact of our evidence enrichment. This underlines the importance of evaluating on more varied datasets like COVID19.BR, which proved to be a more challenging benchmark for assessing the value of external evidence.

Filtering social media from enriched data (Filtered vs. Complete) generally reduced performance for Bertimbau on both datasets and for Gemini on COVID19.BR. This suggests that the excluded social media content contained relevant signals for the models.

Overall, the fine-tuned Bertimbau base model consistently outperformed the few-shot Gemini 1.5 Flash across all configurations and datasets, which is expected given its supervised training on a larger volume of task-specific data.

7 Conclusion

Our analysis included three distinct datasets: the canonical Fake.br, the topic-specific COVID19.BR, and the bottom-up collected MuMiN-PT. While Fake.br and MuMiN-PT presented limitations for our final classification task, they were instrumental, alongside COVID19.BR, for our broader investigation. Fake.br, while foundational, exhibited signs of saturation, with models reaching near-perfect accuracy, making it a less sensitive benchmark for measuring evidence enrichment. MuMiN-PT was excluded from classification entirely due to severe class imbalance. This left COVID19.BR as our primary dataset for evaluating the impact of enrichment, as it provided a more challenging and less saturated baseline. Nevertheless, the inclusion of all three was invaluable for a comprehensive comparative analysis: they provided contrasting examples of collection methodologies (top-down vs. bottom-up), domains (general vs. health), and highlighted challenges such as temporal evidence misalignment (most prominent in the older Fake.br) and the varying effectiveness of evidence retrieval APIs across different data sources.

While a validation pipeline improved dataset reliability by removing various issues, models trained on the cleaned data sometimes performed slightly worse. This suggests the cleaning process, despite enhancing quality, might remove useful heuristic signals, thereby increasing the task's intrinsic difficulty before external contextual evidence is applied.

A qualitative analysis of the retrieved evidence revealed significant variability in the usefulness of recovered content for fact-checking purposes. While true claims often found corroboration through reliable news sources and official statements, false claims presented more complex evidence patterns. The ideal evidence for false claims consisted of direct refutations from established fact-checking organizations, but such explicit debunking was not consistently available through our search methodology. Crucially, the retrieved evidence cannot be uniformly considered golden evidence for automated verification. Our analysis identified several quality issues: (1) the self-reinforcing nature of online misinformation; (2) varying coverage by the Google FactCheck Claim Search API; and (3) temporal misalignment between claims and available evidence, particularly affecting older datasets like Fake.BR. These findings highlight

Model	Processing	COVID19.BR		Fake.br	
		Accuracy	F1-macro	Accuracy	F1-macro
Bertimbau base (Souza et al., 2020)	Validated-only	81.1	81.4	98.9	98.9
	+Enriched (Complete)	**82.1**	**82.4**	**99.2**	**99.2**
	+Enriched (Filtered)	77.9	78.3	98.7	98.8
Gemini 1.5 Flash (Reid et al., 2024)	Validated-only	76.9	76.9	**81.0**	**80.4**
	+Enriched (Complete)	**79.3**	**79.3**	77.6	76.7
	+Enriched (Filtered)	79.0	78.9	78.1	77.2

Table 6: Accuracy and F1-Macro results for Bertimbau base (fine-tuned) and Gemini 1.5 Flash (few-shot) on the test set. Performance is compared between validated-only data (baseline) and validated data enriched with external evidence. The best scores for each model and dataset are in bold.

that evidence retrieval quality significantly impacts the potential effectiveness of evidence-based fact-checking systems.

Fine-tuned Bertimbau (SLM) consistently outperformed few-shot Gemini 1.5 Flash (LLM). While external web content enrichment generally improved performance over validated-only data (notably for COVID19.BR), its benefits varied. Efficacy depended on search quality, claim extraction accuracy, API coverage, and temporal alignment of claims and evidence.

The enriched datasets generated in this study, which associate original claims with retrieved web evidence snippets and LLM-extracted main claims, offer valuable resources for future research. Potential applications include developing more sophisticated evidence-based fact-checking models, exploring stance detection between claims and evidence, and investigating the temporal dynamics of misinformation and its verification.

Our findings underscore that robust misinformation detection likely requires a hybrid approach, combining sophisticated textual analysis with a critical and nuanced evaluation of external evidence.

Limitations

The inherited binary veracity labels (true/false) do not capture the full veracity spectrum (e.g., "misleading") used by fact-checkers (Hangloo and Arora, 2022; Wang, 2017), although our FactCheck API retrieval offered some nuance (Table 5). Some claims, such as personal anecdotes or opinions, are inherently unverifiable via external web evidence. Furthermore, the temporality of claims and evidence remains a challenge, as current evidence may not reflect past contexts.

A core limitation of our work is the absence of semantic verification between claims and retrieved evidence; no explicit stance detection or Natural Language Inference (NLI) was performed to determine if evidence supports or refutes a claim. Additionally, the quality of the LLM-based claim extraction itself was not directly evaluated against a human-annotated ground truth, which is a key methodological limitation. Our claim extraction focused on a single main claim per text, while texts with multiple claims would require more advanced splitting techniques (Tang et al., 2024; Vargas et al., 2023). Results from claim extraction (Gemini 1.5 Flash) and evidence retrieval (Google Search API) are dependent on these specific LLMs and APIs and might vary with alternatives.

Furthermore, our study relied on Google's Search APIs for evidence retrieval. A valuable direction for future work would be to compare this approach against a broader range of state-of-the-art information retrieval techniques. This could include employing dense retrieval models or more advanced query expansion strategies to assess how different retrieval methods impact the quality of the evidence found and, consequently, the performance of the fact-checking model.

The lack of a fixed random seed for the Gemini API version used limits exact reproducibility of claim extraction. Finally, evidence retrieval analyzed search snippets and metadata, not in-depth content of full URLs, potentially missing richer contextual information.

Ethics Statement

The authors have reviewed and commit to upholding the ACL Code of Ethics. We have considered the ethical implications of our research, data usage, and potential applications throughout this work. Our research focuses on the Fact Extraction and VERification (FEVER) task, specifically by enriching Portuguese-language misinformation datasets with external evidence.

Data Handling and Potential Biases: The datasets used in this study (Fake.BR, COVID19.BR, MuMiN-PT) are publicly available. Our semi-automated validation process (Section 3.2) aimed to improve data quality and consistency. However, we acknowledge that these datasets may contain inherent biases stemming from their original collection methodologies (e.g., source, topic selection as described in Table 1), temporal context, and the nature of misinformation itself, which often includes sensitive or controversial topics. While our cleaning process addresses some structural issues (e.g., near-duplicates, label inconsistencies), it does not eliminate all potential underlying biases in the data. The texts themselves, being misinformation, can contain harmful or offensive content; our work analyzes this existing data and does not generate new harmful content. To prevent models from relying on superficial source-based heuristics, URLs were removed from texts before classification experiments, as discussed in Appendix B. We acknowledge this methodological choice may be misplaced for real-world applications. In practice, links often provide essential context for fact-checking, and developing models that learn to evaluate source trustworthiness could prove more beneficial and realistic than simply removing this information. This represents a trade-off between controlled experimental conditions and ecological validity that should be reconsidered in future work.

Models and Algorithmic Bias: We utilize Large Language Models (Gemini 1.5 Flash) for claim extraction (Section 3.3) and web search APIs (Google Custom Search Engine, Google FactCheck Claim Search API) for evidence retrieval (Section 3). We recognize that both LLMs and search engine results can exhibit biases (e.g., reflecting dominant viewpoints, perpetuating stereotypes, or being influenced by algorithmic filtering) and are not infallible. Our analysis (e.g., Pattern F2, Section 4.4, Appendix E) shows that search can sometimes reinforce misinformation. The performance and fairness of Automated Fact-Checking (AFC) systems heavily depend on the quality and representativeness of the data and the underlying models. The lack of a fixed random seed for the Gemini API version used, as mentioned in Section 7, presents a limitation for exact reproducibility of claim extraction.

Potential for Misuse and Mitigation Strategies: Automated Fact-Checking systems, if inaccurate or misused, could inadvertently lead to the mislabeling of information, potentially suppressing legitimate speech or failing to identify harmful misinformation. Our work aims to improve the robustness of AFC by focusing on evidence-based verification. By making our enriched datasets and Python code publicly available upon publication (as stated in the Abstract and Conclusion), we aim to foster transparency, reproducibility, and further research into more reliable and fair fact-checking systems for the Portuguese language.

Scope and Limitations: This work operates primarily with binary veracity labels (true/false) inherited from the source datasets, which is a simplification of the nuanced reality of information veracity, as discussed in Sections 4.1.2 and 7. Some claims are inherently difficult to verify through automated web searches (e.g., personal opinions, unverifiable anecdotes). The temporality of claims and evidence also poses a challenge (Section 4.1.2), as the truthfulness or relevance of information can change over time. Our evidence retrieval is based on search snippets and metadata, not full-page analysis for all results, which is a limitation in depth.

Broader Impact: The intended broader impact of this research is to contribute to the development of more effective tools for combating misinformation in Portuguese, a significant societal challenge. By providing enriched, evidence-linked datasets (associating original texts with retrieved evidence and LLM-extracted claims, as mentioned in the Abstract and Conclusion), we hope to facilitate advancements in evidence-aware AFC systems. We believe that responsible development and deployment of such technologies are crucial for a well-informed public discourse.

Acknowledgments

This work has been fully funded by the project Computational Techniques for Multimodal Data Security and Privacy supported by Advanced Knowledge Center in Immersive Technologies (AKCIT), with financial resources from the PPI IoT/Manufatura 4.0 / PPI HardwareBR of the MCTI grant number 057/2023, signed with EMBRAPII.

References

Zahra Abbasiantaeb and Mohammad Aliannejadi. 2024. Generate then retrieve: Conversational response retrieval using llms as answer and query generators. *Preprint*, arXiv:2403.19302.

Esma Aimeur, Sabrine Amri, and Gilles Brassard. 2023. Fake news, disinformation and misinformation in social media: a review. *Social Network Analysis and Mining*, 13(1):30.

Ihsan Ali, Mohamad Nizam Bin Ayub, Palaiahnakote Shivakumara, and Nurul Fazmidar Binti Mohd Noor. 2022. Fake news detection techniques on social media: A survey. *Wireless Communications and Mobile Computing*, 2022.

Gilmara Joanol Arndt, Milena Tarcisa Trindade, Juliana de Oliveira Alves, and Raquel de Barros Pinto Miguel. 2021. Quem é de direita toma cloroquina, quem é de esquerda toma... vacina. *Revista Psicología Política*, 21(51):608–626.

Andréa Barbieri. 2021. Tem dúvida? não compartilhe! o uso de fake news por professores de língua portuguesa do ensino fundamental ii com o propósito de desenvolver habilidades em educação midiática com seus alunos. Dissertação (mestrado), Universidade Tuiuti do Paraná, Curitiba, 10. Orientadora: Mônica Cristine Fort.

Suelen Mazza Batista. 2020. Onde os fatos não têm vez: uma análise foucaultiana das fake news relativas à cultura. Dissertação (mestrado em administração), Universidade Federal de Pernambuco, Recife, 2. Orientador: Sérgio Carvalho Benício de Mello.

Marcia Borin da Cunha and Beatriz Tilschneider Garcia Rosa. 2022. Fake science: proposta de análise. *Góndola, Enseñanza y Aprendizaje de las Ciencias*, 17(3):520–538.

Francisco Frank Dourado Capistrano. 2022. Fake news sobre a covid-19 nas aulas de química: uma abordagem didática na monitoria das práticas de ensino. Trabalho de conclusão de curso (licenciatura em química), Universidade Federal do Pará, Ananindeua, 8. Orientadora: Janes Kened Rodrigues dos Santos.

Canyu Chen and Kai Shu. 2024. Combating misinformation in the age of llms: Opportunities and challenges. *AI Magazine*, 45(3):354–368.

Sukmin Cho, Soyeong Jeong, Wonsuk Yang, and Jong Park. 2022. Query generation with external knowledge for dense retrieval. In *Proceedings of Deep Learning Inside Out (DeeLIO 2022): The 3rd Workshop on Knowledge Extraction and Integration for Deep Learning Architectures*, pages 22–32, Dublin, Ireland and Online. Association for Computational Linguistics.

Eun Cheol Choi and Emilio Ferrara. 2024. Automated claim matching with large language models: Empowering fact-checkers in the fight against misinformation. In *Companion Proceedings of the ACM on Web Conference 2024*, WWW '24, page 1441–1449, New York, NY, USA. Association for Computing Machinery.

Paulo Roberto Cordeiro and Vladia Pinheiro. 2019. Um corpus de notıcias falsas do twitter e verificaçao automática de rumores em lıngua portuguesa. In *Proceedings of the Symposium in Information and Human Language Technology*, pages 219–228.

Joao MM Couto, Breno Pimenta, Igor M de Araújo, Samuel Assis, Julio CS Reis, Ana Paula C da Silva, Jussara M Almeida, and Fabrício Benevenuto. 2021. Central de fatos: Um repositório de checagens de fatos. In *Anais do III Dataset Showcase Workshop*, pages 128–137. SBC.

Flávio Roberto Matias da Silva, Paulo Márcio Souza Freire, Marcelo Pereira de Souza, Gustavo de A. B. Plenamente, and Ronaldo Ribeiro Goldschmidt. 2020. Fakenewssetgen: A process to build datasets that support comparison among fake news detection methods. In *Proceedings of the Brazilian Symposium on Multimedia and the Web*, WebMedia '20, page 241–248, New York, NY, USA. Association for Computing Machinery.

Ulisses Matheus Braga de Freitas Melo. 2022. Feita sob medida: a estrutura de uma notícia falsa e seu papel no convencimento do eleitor. Dissertação (mestrado em ciência política), Universidade Federal de Pernambuco, Recife, 2. Orientador: Sérgio Carvalho Benício de Mello.

Mônica Chaves de Melo. 2019. A pauta da desinformação: "fake news" e categorizações de pertencimento nas eleições presidenciais brasileiras de 2018. Dissertação (mestrado), Pontifícia Universidade Católica do Rio de Janeiro, 4. Orientadora: Adriana Andrade Braga.

Mônica Chaves de Melo. 2021. *A pauta da desinformação: as ideias por trás das "fake news" nas eleições de 2018*, 1 edition. Fafich/Selo PPG-COM/UFMG, Belo Horizonte.

Ivandro Claudino de Sá. 2021. Digital lighthouse: a platform for monitoring misinformation in whatsapp public groups. Dissertação (mestrado), Universidade Federal do Ceará. Orientação: Prof. Dr. José Maria da Silva Monteiro Filho.

Ivandro Claudino de Sá, José Monteiro, José Franco da Silva, Leonardo Medeiros, Pedro Mourão, and Lucas Carneiro da Cunha. 2021. Digital lighthouse: A platform for monitoring public groups in whatsapp. In *Proceedings of the 23rd International Conference on Enterprise Information Systems - Volume 1: ICEIS,*, pages 297–304. INSTICC, SciTePress.

Jacob Devlin, Ming-Wei Chang, Kenton Lee, and Kristina Toutanova. 2019. BERT: Pre-training of deep bidirectional transformers for language understanding. In *Proceedings of the 2019 Conference of the North American Chapter of the Association for*

Computational Linguistics: Human Language Technologies, Volume 1 (Long and Short Papers), pages 4171–4186, Minneapolis, Minnesota. Association for Computational Linguistics.

Jia Ding, Yongjun Hu, and Huiyou Chang. 2020. Bert-based mental model, a better fake news detector. In *Proceedings of the 2020 6th International Conference on Computing and Artificial Intelligence*, ICCAI '20, page 396–400, New York, NY, USA. Association for Computing Machinery.

Felipe dos Santos Gusmão. 2023. Estudo comparativo de modelos de classificação textual aplicados na classificação de fake news. Trabalho de conclusão de curso (bacharelado em engenharia da computação), Universidade Federal do Amazonas, Manaus, 6. Orientador: José Luiz de Souza Pio.

Salma El Anigri, Mohammed Majid Himmi, and Abdelhak Mahmoudi. 2021. How bert's dropout fine-tuning affects text classification? In *Business Intelligence*, pages 130–139, Cham. Springer International Publishing.

Pedro Faustini and Thiago Covões. 2019. Fake news detection using one-class classification. In *2019 8th Brazilian Conference on Intelligent Systems (BRACIS)*, pages 592–597.

Revanth Gangi Reddy, Sai Chetan Chinthakindi, Yi R. Fung, Kevin Small, and Heng Ji. 2022. A zero-shot claim detection framework using question answering. In *Proceedings of the 29th International Conference on Computational Linguistics*, pages 6927–6933, Gyeongju, Republic of Korea. International Committee on Computational Linguistics.

Daniel Grießhaber, Johannes Maucher, and Ngoc Thang Vu. 2020. Fine-tuning BERT for low-resource natural language understanding via active learning. In *Proceedings of the 28th International Conference on Computational Linguistics*, pages 1158–1171, Barcelona, Spain (Online). International Committee on Computational Linguistics.

Zhijiang Guo, Michael Schlichtkrull, and Andreas Vlachos. 2022. A survey on automated fact-checking. *Transactions of the Association for Computational Linguistics*, 10:178–206.

Sakshini Hangloo and Bhavna Arora. 2022. Combating multimodal fake news on social media: methods, datasets, and future perspective. *Multimedia Systems*, 28(6):2391–2422.

Arthur Ituassu, Sergio Lifschitz, Letícia Capone, and Vivian Mannheimer. 2019. De donald trump a jair bolsonaro: democracia e comunicação política digital nas eleições de 2016, nos estados unidos, e 2018, no brasil. In *Anais do 8º Congresso da Associação Brasileira de Pesquisadores em Comunicação e Política*, Brasília. Universidade de Brasília, Associação Brasileira de Pesquisadores em Comunicação e Política - Compolítica.

Ryo Kamoi, Tanya Goyal, Juan Diego Rodriguez, and Greg Durrett. 2023. WiCE: Real-world entailment for claims in Wikipedia. In *Proceedings of the 2023 Conference on Empirical Methods in Natural Language Processing*, pages 7561–7583, Singapore. Association for Computational Linguistics.

Kyungha Kim, Sangyun Lee, Kung-Hsiang Huang, Hou Pong Chan, Manling Li, and Heng Ji. 2024. Can llms produce faithful explanations for fact-checking? towards faithful explainable fact-checking via multi-agent debate. *Preprint*, arXiv:2402.07401.

Sotiris Kotitsas, Panagiotis Kounoudis, Eleni Koutli, and Haris Papageorgiou. 2024. Leveraging fine-tuned large language models with LoRA for effective claim, claimer, and claim object detection. In *Proceedings of the 18th Conference of the European Chapter of the Association for Computational Linguistics (Volume 1: Long Papers)*, pages 2540–2554, St. Julian's, Malta. Association for Computational Linguistics.

Eulália Vera Lúcia Fraga Leurquin and Chloé Leurquin. 2021. Fake news, desinformação e necessidade de formar leitores críticos. *Scripta*, 25(54):265–295.

Arthur Guimarães Lima. 2019. A propagação de fake news e seus impactos: um estudo sobre a onda conservadora na política ocidental contemporânea. Trabalho de conclusão de curso (bacharelado em comunicação social com habilitação em relações públicas), Universidade de São Paulo, São Paulo. Orientador: Luiz Alberto de Farias.

Guilherme Lima, Marcos Calazans, and Luciana MASSI. 2021. Mensagens falsas sobre o novo coronavírus: legitimidade e manipulação na luta de classes. *Chasqui. Revista Latinoamericana de Comunicación*, 1(147):259–280.

Yinhan Liu, Myle Ott, Naman Goyal, Jingfei Du, Mandar Joshi, Danqi Chen, Omer Levy, Mike Lewis, Luke Zettlemoyer, and Veselin Stoyanov. 2019. Roberta: A robustly optimized bert pretraining approach. *Preprint*, arXiv:1907.11692.

Dyonnatan Maia and Nádia Félix Felipe da Silva. 2024. Enhancing stance detection in low-resource Brazilian Portuguese using corpus expansion generated by GPT-3.5. In *Proceedings of the 16th International Conference on Computational Processing of Portuguese - Vol. 1*, pages 503–508, Santiago de Compostela, Galicia/Spain. Association for Computational Lingustics.

Antônio Diogo Forte Martins, Lucas Cabral, Pedro Jorge Chaves Mourao, Ivandro Claudino de Sá, José Maria Monteiro, and Javam Machado. 2021. Covid19.br: A dataset of misinformation about covid-19 in brazilian portuguese whatsapp messages. In *Anais do III Dataset Showcase Workshop*, pages 138–147. SBC.

Rafael A. Monteiro, Roney L. S. Santos, Thiago A. S. Pardo, Tiago A. de Almeida, Evandro E. S. Ruiz, and Oto A. Vale. 2018. Contributions to the study of fake news in portuguese: New corpus and automatic detection results. In *Computational Processing of the Portuguese Language*, pages 324–334. Springer International Publishing.

João Moreno and Graça Bressan. 2019. Factck.br: A new dataset to study fake news. In *Proceedings of the 25th Brazillian Symposium on Multimedia and the Web*, WebMedia '19, page 525–527, New York, NY, USA. Association for Computing Machinery.

Jaqueline Gonçalves do Nascimento. 2021. Disseminação de desinformação sobre a covid-19 em um núcleo familiar: um estudo de caso. Trabalho de conclusão de curso (bacharelado em biblioteconomia), Universidade Federal do Ceará, Fortaleza. Orientador: Antonio Wagner Chacon Silva.

Jingwei Ni, Minjing Shi, Dominik Stammbach, Mrinmaya Sachan, Elliott Ash, and Markus Leippold. 2024. Afacta: Assisting the annotation of factual claim detection with reliable llm annotators. *Preprint*, arXiv:2402.11073.

Dan S Nielsen and Ryan McConville. 2022. Mumin: A large-scale multilingual multimodal fact-checked misinformation social network dataset. In *Proceedings of the 45th International ACM SIGIR Conference on Research and Development in Information Retrieval*, pages 3141–3153.

Gabriel Nogueira. 2021. Br fake news detection. `https://github.com/Talendar/br_fake_news_detection`. Accessed on 2/2/2025.

Luiza Prevedel Pereira and Juliano Desiderato Antonio. 2023. É verdade ou fake news? estratégicas linguísticas de manipulação em textos que promovem a desinformação. *Revista USP*, (138):27–38.

Yunjian Qiu and Yan Jin. 2024. Chatgpt and finetuned bert: A comparative study for developing intelligent design support systems. *Intelligent Systems with Applications*, 21:200308.

Miguel Quessada. 2022. Desinformação e esquerda brasileira: o discurso por trás das fake news. Dissertação (mestrado), Universidade Federal de São Carlos, São Carlos, 2. Orientador: Thales Haddad Novaes de Andrade.

Vanessa Daiane Contente Quintanilha. 2021. Combatendo as fake news sobre o sars-cov-2: o revisor como fact-checker. Dissertação (mestrado), Universidade Nova, 9. Orientadora: Matilde Gonçalves.

Thilina C. Rajapakse, Andrew Yates, and Maarten de Rijke. 2024. Simple transformers: Open-source for all. In *Proceedings of the 2024 Annual International ACM SIGIR Conference on Research and Development in Information Retrieval in the Asia Pacific Region*, SIGIR-AP 2024, pages 209–215.

Machel Reid, Nikolay Savinov, Denis Teplyashin, Dmitry Lepikhin, Timothy Lillicrap, Jean-baptiste Alayrac, Radu Soricut, Angeliki Lazaridou, Orhan Firat, Julian Schrittwieser, et al. 2024. Gemini 1.5: Unlocking multimodal understanding across millions of tokens of context. *arXiv preprint arXiv:2403.05530*.

Márcio Moretto Ribeiro and Pablo Ortellado. 2018. O que são e como lidar com as notícias falsas. *Sur - Revista Internacional de Direitos Humanos*, 15(27):71–83.

Guilherme Yukio Sakurai. 2019. Processamento de linguagem natural - detecção de fake news. Trabalho de conclusão de curso (bacharelado em ciência da computação), Universidade Estadual de Londrina, Londrina. Orientador: Sérgio Montazzolli Silva.

Mirella Gadelha Santos. 2020. DetecÇÃo de fake news: Um comparativo entre os modelos de aprendizado supervisionado passive agressive e multinomial naive bayes. Trabalho de conclusão de curso (bacharelado em sistemas de informação, Centro Universitário Christus - Unichristus, Fortaleza, 8. Orientador: Daniel Nascimento Teixeira.

Alessandro Scirè, Karim Ghonim, and Roberto Navigli. 2024. FENICE: Factuality evaluation of summarization based on natural language inference and claim extraction. In *Findings of the Association for Computational Linguistics: ACL 2024*, pages 14148–14161, Bangkok, Thailand. Association for Computational Linguistics.

Gautam Kishore Shahi and Durgesh Nandini. 2020. *FakeCovid- A Multilingual Cross-domain Fact Check News Dataset for COVID-19*. ICWSM.

Renato M. Silva, Roney L.S. Santos, Tiago A. Almeida, and Thiago A.S. Pardo. 2020. Towards automatically filtering fake news in portuguese. *Expert Systems with Applications*, 146:113199.

Fábio José dos Santos Sousa. 2022. Transferência de conhecimento para detecção automática de fake news com aprendizagem profunda. Trabalho de conclusão de curso (bacharelado em ciência da computação), Universidade Federal do Ceará, Cratéus. Orientador: Livio Antonio de Melo Freire.

Fábio Souza, Rodrigo Nogueira, and Roberto Lotufo. 2020. Bertimbau: Pretrained bert models for brazilian portuguese. In *Intelligent Systems*, pages 403–417, Cham. Springer International Publishing.

Peter M Stahl. 2023. Lingua-py. `https://github.com/pemistahl/lingua-py`. Acessed on 4/3/2024.

Xin Tan, Bowei Zou, and Ai Ti Aw. 2023. Evidence-based interpretable open-domain fact-checking with large language models. *Preprint*, arXiv:2312.05834.

Liyan Tang, Philippe Laban, and Greg Durrett. 2024. MiniCheck: Efficient fact-checking of LLMs on grounding documents. In *Proceedings of the 2024*

Conference on Empirical Methods in Natural Language Processing, pages 8818–8847, Miami, Florida, USA. Association for Computational Linguistics.

Francielle Vargas, Kokil Jaidka, Thiago Pardo, and Fabrício Benevenuto. 2023. Predicting sentence-level factuality of news and bias of media outlets. In *Proceedings of the 14th International Conference on Recent Advances in Natural Language Processing*, pages 1197–1206, Varna, Bulgaria. INCOMA Ltd., Shoumen, Bulgaria.

William Yang Wang. 2017. "liar, liar pants on fire": A new benchmark dataset for fake news detection. In *Proceedings of the 55th Annual Meeting of the Association for Computational Linguistics (Volume 2: Short Papers)*, pages 422–426, Vancouver, Canada. Association for Computational Linguistics.

Yuxia Wang, Revanth Gangi Reddy, Zain Muhammad Mujahid, Arnav Arora, Aleksandr Rubashevskii, Jiahui Geng, Osama Mohammed Afzal, Liangming Pan, Nadav Borenstein, Aditya Pillai, Isabelle Augenstein, Iryna Gurevych, and Preslav Nakov. 2024. Factcheck-bench: Fine-grained evaluation benchmark for automatic fact-checkers. In *Findings of the Association for Computational Linguistics: EMNLP 2024*, pages 14199–14230, Miami, Florida, USA. Association for Computational Linguistics.

Fengzhu Zeng and Wei Gao. 2024. JustiLM: Few-shot justification generation for explainable fact-checking of real-world claims. *Transactions of the Association for Computational Linguistics*, 12:334–354.

A Illustrative Examples of the Semi-automatic Validation Workflow

This appendix provides concrete examples to illustrate the different stages of the semi-automatic validation workflow described in Section 3.2.

It is important to note that the removal of URLs from texts, mentioned as a general step to avoid domain bias, was performed after the validation steps exemplified here that might depend on the presence of these URLs (such as URL-based contradiction resolution or Fake.br-specific filtering by source URL). The examples below show the texts before this final URL removal, but with other specific validation processes being illustrated.

A.1 Initial Automated Filtering

This stage removed examples that did not meet basic content or format criteria. Figure 5 illustrates three types of removal in this phase: texts composed solely of a URL, texts considered excessively short after tokenization and removal of *stopwords*, and exact duplicates within the same corpus.

Text composed only of a URL (COVID19.BR) - Removed

```
https://fanoticias.com.br/covid-19-jovem
-sobre-os-efeitos-parecia-furar-meu-peito/
,
```

Text with few relevant tokens (COVID19.BR) - Removed

hahaha looks like corona.hahaha

Exact Duplicate (Fake.br) - Example `true_0069` removed

Suplicy will participate in Doria's web program this Thursday
Councilman Eduardo Suplicy (PT-SP) will participate this Thursday (10), at 8:30 PM, in the program "Olho no Olho" (Eye to Eye), broadcast on Mayor João Doria's (PSDB-SP) social media.
Doria has already hosted allies and personalities on the show such as singer Lobão, presenter José Luiz Datena, former basketball player Oscar, singer Roger from Ultraje a Rigor, and journalist Joice Hasselman.
At the beginning of his term, the tucano (PSDB member) spared criticism of his predecessor Fernando Haddad (PT-SP), but in recent months, he has accused the former mayor of leaving a R$ 7 billion deficit in the city hall. Haddad denies this and says he left the city's accounts in order.
Suplicy, in turn, is one of the critical voices against Doria in the City Council.

Figure 5: English-translated examples of removals performed in the initial automated filtering stage.

A.2 Language Filtering

Examples identified as not being primarily in Portuguese were removed. The Lingua tool was used for automatic detection, followed by manual verification in ambiguous cases. Figure 6 shows examples removed for being in English and Spanish.

A.3 Contradiction Resolution

This stage addressed label inconsistencies between semantically very similar examples or those that referenced the same source. Figure 7 illustrates a case of near-identical texts in the COVID19.BR corpus that had conflicting veracity labels (true vs. false). After manual analysis, based on context and external sources when available, both conflicting examples were removed.

A.4 External Label Verification

The Google FactCheck API was used to identify potential labeling errors in the original data. When an API result was found, we performed a manual review by one of the authors if the retrieved verac-

Example in English (COVID19.BR) - Removed

German state minister kills himself as coronavirus hits economy
- `https://www.aljazeera.com/news/2020/03/german-state-minister-kills-coronavirus-hits-economy-200329165242615.html`

Example in Spanish (MuMiN) - Removed

Vídeo de fraude en las urnas de Flint (Michigan) durante las elecciones de Estados Unidos

Figure 6: Examples filtered for not being in Portuguese.

Near-Duplicate Text A (COVID19.BR) - Original Label: False

Amidst the severe CORONAVIRUS crisis, the National Congress refused to give up the money allocated to the electoral fund to aid in combating the pandemic. As always, these bloodsuckers show they only care about their own interests. Let's sign the petition for the closure of the National Congress!
👉 `https://peticaopublica.org/fechamento-congresso-nacional/`

Excerpt considered true (COVID19.BR)

Amidst the severe CORONAVIRUS crisis, the National Congress refused to give up the money allocated to the electoral fund to aid in combating the pandemic. As always, these bloodsuckers show they only care about their own interests. Let's sign the petition for the closure of the National Congress!
`https://peticaopublica.org/fechamento-congresso-nacional/`

Figure 7: Example of a pair of near-duplicate texts in the COVID19.BR corpus that had contradictory veracity labels. Manual resolution was necessary to determine the correct label or remove the pair.

ity label conflicted with the original binary label. During this review, retrieved labels that clearly indicated falsity—specifically "false," "fake," "misleading," and "wrong" (highlighted in Table 5)—were considered strong evidence to check for a potential `FAKE NEWS` mislabel. Conversely, a retrieved label of "true" was used to check for potential `TRUE` mislabels. Nuanced or uncertain labels like "not quite so" or "too early to tell" did not automatically trigger a label change but were considered by the human annotator to inform the final decision for that specific case. Figure 8 demonstrates a case in the MuMiN-PT corpus where the original label (`true`) was corrected to `fake` after external verification and manual analysis confirmed the initial incorrectness.

Example of Label Correction (MuMiN-PT)

Corpus: MuMiN-PT

Original text: The American Medical Association lifted restrictions and began recommending hydroxychloroquine against covid-19

Label: ~~`true`~~ `fake`

Query (Extracted claim): The American Medical Association recommends hydroxychloroquine against covid-19.

CSE Result:

> **Title:** `<b>Hydroxychloroquine</b> is not recommended as early treatment ...`
>
> **Snippet:** `1 day ago <b>...</b> From time to time, the drug <b>hydroxychloroquine</b> is again pointed out as an effective early treatment <b>against Covid</b>-<b>19</b>.`

FactCheck Result:

> **Agency:** Aos Fatos | **Label:** False | **Reviewed claim:** American Medical Association does not recommend hydroxychloroquine ...'

Figure 8: Illustration of the external label verification process. An example from MuMiN-PT had its original label (`true`) corrected to `fake` based on evidence from the Google FactCheck API and subsequent manual confirmation.

A.5 Specific Treatment for Fake.br

The Fake.br corpus has particular characteristics that required additional treatment steps. Figure 9 illustrates the removal of near-duplicate texts that shared the same source URL, a situation specific to this corpus. Additionally, two other specific rules were applied (not illustrated with detailed visual examples for brevity, but described below):

(a) **Removal of incomplete texts:** Examples whose normalized texts (as per 4.1) were identified as truncated or incomplete compared to the original news story (addressed in Issue #7 of the Fake.br repository) were removed.

(b) **Maintenance of pairs:** Given that Fake.br is structured in pairs of news items (true and false about the same event), if one element of the pair was removed by any of the previous validation criteria, the corresponding element was also removed to preserve the integrity of the dataset's paired structure.

Near-Duplicates with Same Source URL (Fake.br) - Example `true_3023` removed

The offenders' paradise To get a third of the deputies' votes, Temer decrees pardon of fines Privatization projects to improve public accounts performance are being undermined in the process of winning a third of the Chamber's votes to spare President Temer from investigation for crimes of criminal organization and obstruction of justice. More so now, after the convicted Waldemar da Costa Neto, aka Boy, was heeded, who demanded the removal of Congonhas airport from the announced package, which would bring in 6 billion in revenue, in exchange for keeping the country's second-largest airport under Infraero's control. It's obvious that the corruption scheme of previous governments is maintained. ...

Figure 9: Example of Fake.br-specific removal: near-duplicate texts (`true_0251` and `true_3023`) originating from the same source URL. One of them (`true_3023`) was removed to reduce redundancy originating from the collection.

B URL Dependency

In the context of *links* in the COVID19.BR dataset, Table 7 shows the most mentioned URL domains in the examples. The domains Gazeta Brasil, bit.ly, Globo, WhatsApp, and JapinaWeb almost always represent true examples. However, the presence of a governmental domain is not, in itself, a guarantee of veracity. Brazilian government domains, such as `gov.br`, can be instrumentalized in misleading contexts, as illustrated by an example from the MuMiN-PT corpus in Figure 10.

Example of Misleading Use of Official URL (MuMiN-PT)

Everyone, you need to register on conectesus to get vaccinated. I suggest doing it now. The site probably won't handle the traffic when the time comes. `https://conectesus-paciente.saude.gov.br/` It's a SUS registration. Those who took the Yellow Fever vaccine in 2018 already have it. Or those who have used SUS in recent years. The application works more or less like those driver's license or voter ID apps.

Figure 10: Example from MuMiN-PT where an official URL is used in a misinformation context. [6]

Mentioned URL Domains	fake	% fake	true	% true	Total
gazetabrasil	0	0.0	259	**100.0**	259
bit.ly	6	6.8	82	**93.2**	88
youtube	47	67.1	23	32.9	70
globo	6	11.3	47	**88.7**	53
facebook	19	38.0	31	62.0	50
dunapress	0	0.0	46	**100.0**	46
twitter	25	56.8	19	43.2	44
whatsapp	1	3.1	31	**96.9**	32
uol	11	37.9	18	62.1	29
conexaopolitica	16	59.3	11	40.7	27
gov.br	6	26.1	17	73.9	23
instagram	5	21.7	18	78.3	23
jornaldacidadeonline	14	63.6	8	36.4	22
japinaweb	0	0.0	21	**100.0**	21
atrombetanews	7	35.0	13	65.0	20

Table 7: Count of the 15 most referenced URL domains in the COVID19.BR corpus, broken down by `fake` and `true` labels (absolute counts and percentages). Domains and their '% true' values are highlighted in bold if over 80% of the mentions for that domain are in examples labeled as true. Brazilian governmental domains were aggregated under "gov.br".

C Near-Duplicate Examples

This appendix provides examples of near-duplicate texts identified during the validation process (Section 3.2).

Figure 11 shows two near-duplicate examples from the Fake.br dataset, both originally labeled 'true'. They report the same event (death of journalist Marcelo Rezende) but were published a few hours apart on the same news site (G1) with minor updates regarding the wake.

Figure 12 shows examples of near-duplicate messages from the COVID19.BR dataset, originally labeled 'false'. These messages promote a non-existent offer of free internet data, varying slightly in the amount offered (10GB vs. 500GB) and the link provided.

D Prompt Patterns Explored

This appendix lists the main types of prompts identified in our literature review (Section 3.3) for claim extraction and related tasks. We experimented with variations based on these patterns before settling on the simpler zero-shot prompt in Figure 2.

- **Simple Claim Detection (Kotitsas et al., 2024):** Basic instruction asking for the main claim.

  What is the main claim of the input?

- **Claim Splitting/Decomposition (Scirè et al., 2024; Kamoi et al., 2023; Tang et al., 2024; Wang et al., 2024):** Instruction to break down a

Marcelo Rezende passed away at 65 in São Paulo. He was a victim of multiple organ failure resulting from cancer, as reported by Hospital Moriah.. The journalist Marcelo Rezende died at 5:45 PM on Saturday (16th) in São Paulo, at 65 years old, victim of multiple organ failure resulting from cancer, according to Hospital Moriah....

(a) English-translation of the original news article posted at `https://web.archive.org/web/20220808194736/https://g1.globo.com/sao-paulo/noticia/morre-aos-65-anos-o-jornalista-marcelo-rezende.ghtml`

The body of Marcelo Rezende will lie in state at the Legislative Assembly this Sunday. He died from multiple organ failure resulting from cancer, as reported by Hospital Moriah.. The body of journalist Marcelo Rezende will lie in state this Sunday (17th) at the São Paulo Legislative Assembly. The burial arrangements have not yet been announced by the family. ...

(b) English-translation of the updated news article at `https://web.archive.org/web/20190208022401/https://g1.globo.com/sao-paulo/noticia/corpo-de-marcelo-rezende-sera-velado-na-assembleia-legislativa-neste-domingo.ghtml`

Figure 11: Two near-duplicate examples (English translations) from the Fake.br dataset ('true' label). The second is an update of the first, published shortly after by the same source (G1). Differences are highlighted.

● Free 500 GB 4G Internet ● Due to the COVID-19 epidemic, we're offering 10 GB of free Internet, valid for 90 days to help you stay home! **Get free Internet access and stay home** 👉
https://bit.ly/10gbytes

● Free 500 GB 4G Internet ● Due to the COVID-19 epidemic, we're offering 500 GB of free Internet, valid for 90 days to help you stay home! **Get free Internet access and stay home** 👉
http://hu5k.com/Covid

● Free 500 GB 4G Internet ● Due to the COVID-19 epidemic, we're offering 500 GB of free Internet, valid for 90 days to help you stay home! **Get free Internet access and stay home** 👉
https://bit.ly/500gbytes

Figure 12: Near-duplicate examples (English translations) of misinformation (*clickbait*) from the COVID19.BR dataset ('false' label). Minor variations in text and URL are highlighted.

sentence into multiple atomic claims. (Not used in our final approach).

> Segment the following sentence into individual facts: [SENTENCE]

- **Role Specification (Kotitsas et al., 2024):** Defining the AI's role to guide its behavior.

  > You are an AI assistant helping fact-checkers identify check-worthy information. Extract the main claim from: [TEXT]

- **Explicit Fact Categories (Ni et al., 2024):** Providing definitions of what constitutes a factual claim.

  > Identify claims mentioning specific actions, quantities, correlations, rules, or predictions in the following text: [TEXT]

- **Query Formulation Analogy (Abbasiantaeb and Aliannejadi, 2024):** Framing the task as generating a search query to verify the text.

  > What would you search on Google to verify this text? Extract the core query: [TEXT]

- **Few-shot Demonstration (Scirè et al., 2024):** Providing input/output examples chinite the prompt.

  > Input: [Example Text 1]
  > Claim: [Example Claim 1]
  > Input: [Actual Text]
  > Claim:

Our final prompt (Figure 2) is closest to the Simple Claim Detection pattern, adding constraints on length and output format.

E Evidence Pattern Examples

This appendix provides concrete examples illustrating the evidence patterns T1, F1, F2, and F3, as discussed in Section 4.4. Each example includes metadata from the original dataset (`dataset`, `label`, original `text` with the query portion underlined), the `query` used for search (either the underlined text or an extracted `claim`), the primary `CSE result` snippet obtained, and any relevant `FactCheck API result`. Translations are provided where necessary.

Pattern T1: Corroboration of True Claims

This pattern involves finding evidence from reliable sources (like news articles) that confirms the factual information in a true claim. The example below (Figure 13) shows a claim extracted from a message about COVID-19 test reliability. The CSE result points to an article from a reputable source (Fiocruz, a Brazilian research institution) discussing the possibility of false negatives, thus corroborating the claim. The FactCheck API returned no results, consistent with pattern T2.

Example of Pattern T1: Corroboration

Dataset: COVID19.BR

Original Text: We've had patients who took COVID-19 tests, including tests at Sabin laboratory that came back negative, but when repeated at Oswaldo Cruz Hospital using rapid tests showed positive results. Remember that nasal swab tests may yield false negatives. Stay alert to avoid false negatives... (truncated)

Original Label: true

Query (Extracted Claim): COVID-19 tests may yield false negatives, even when conducted at reputable laboratories.

CSE Result:

Title: `<b>Covid</b>-<b>19</b>: Fiocruz researcher answers questions about <b>testing</b>...`

Snippet: `Jan 15, 2021 <b>...</b> ... <b>false negatives may</b> occur due to low specificity and analytical sensitivity of the <b>test</b>... ... no <b>laboratory test</b> is perfect and its...`

FactCheck API Result: None

Figure 13: Example illustrating Pattern T1. The search based on the extracted claim found corroborating information from a reliable source. (English translation from COVID19.BR)

Pattern F1: Direct Debunk

This pattern represents the ideal outcome for verifying a false claim, where search results contain a direct refutation from a fact-checking agency or reliable source. Figure 14 shows an example where the CSE search for a claim about coronavirus transmission via parcels returned a result explicitly stating the opposite, effectively debunking the claim. Note that in this specific instance, the FactCheck API did not return a result, but the CSE result itself serves as the debunk.

Pattern F2: Misinformation Reinforcement

This common pattern occurs when searching for a piece of misinformation returns results that simply repeat or amplify the same false claim, often from unreliable sources or social media. Figure

Example of Pattern F1: Direct Debunk

Dataset: MuMiN-PT

Original Text: The new coronavirus can be transmitted through parcels shipped from China.

Original Label: false

Query (Original Text): The new coronavirus can be transmitted through parcels shipped from China.

CSE Result:

Title: `<b>The new coronavirus</b> cannot survive in <b>parcels shipped</b> from ...`

Snippet: `March 4, 2020 <b>...</b> ... <b>coronavirus can be transmitted through parcels shipped</b> by mail from <b>China</b> to other countries. The claim, which served as the basis ...`

Source Type: News/Fact-Check Report

FactCheck API Result: None

Figure 14: Example illustrating Pattern F1. The CSE search using the false claim as a query yielded a result directly refuting it. (English translation from MuMiN-PT)

15 demonstrates this: the CSE search for the false claim about the "Popular Pharmacy" program returned a result from an unreliable source echoing the misinformation. Critically, even though the FactCheck API did find a relevant debunk for this claim, the CSE result exemplifies the F2 pattern, highlighting the challenge where search engines might surface reinforcing content alongside (or instead of) corrective information.

Pattern F3: Academic Recognition as Misinformation

This pattern occurs when searching for a known piece of misinformation yields results pointing to academic literature (papers, theses, articles) that cite or discuss the misinformation as an object of study. While not providing a direct debunk snippet in the same way as F1, these results serve as 'meta-evidence', confirming that the claim is recognized as problematic or false within the research community. Table 8 provides a list of such academic publications encountered during our searches for misinformation examples present in the datasets used. No figure is provided for F3 as the primary evidence is the existence of these academic refer-

Example of Pattern F2: Misinformation Reinforcement

Dataset: Fake.br

Original Text: Temer government will end the popular pharmacy. Who hasn't heard of or even needed the popular pharmacy, right? The system offers the distribution of free medicines for various types of diseases, these resources are available until the month of August 2017 ... (truncated)

Original Label: false

Query (Original Text): Temer government will end the popular pharmacy.

CSE Result:

> **Title:** `<b>Temer Government</b> closes <b>Popular Pharmacy</b> and intends to abolish the SUS ...`
>
> **Snippet:** `Feb 22, 2018 <b>...</b> Are you going to <b>allow</b> it? The Ministry of Health <b>has just closed</b> the 517 <b>popular pharmacies</b> maintained by the federal <b>government</b> in the country.`
>
> **Source Type:** Unreliable Blog/Social Media

FactCheck API Result:

> **Agency:** Lupa - UOL | **Rating:** False | **Claim Reviewed:** Temer does not 'make official the end of the Popular Pharmacy project'

Figure 15: Example illustrating Pattern F2. The CSE search returned a result reinforcing the false claim, despite a debunk existing (found via the FactCheck API). (English translation from Fake.br)

ences rather than a specific search snippet.

F Hyperparameter Details for Bertimbau Fine-tuning

Table 9 presents the hyperparameter grid search space used to fine-tune the base Bertimbau model across each training data configuration. For each configuration and corpus, the best hyperparameters were chosen based on the highest validation F1-score.

Based on prior work with similar models and tasks (Devlin et al., 2019; Liu et al., 2019; Ding et al., 2020; Nogueira, 2021; dos Santos Gusmão, 2023; Souza et al., 2020), we set maximum training epochs to 10. A standard weight decay of 0.01 was used (Devlin et al., 2019; Souza et al., 2020; Liu et al., 2019).

We employed the AdamW optimizer (standard for BERT) with canonical $\beta_1(0.9)$, $\beta_2(0.999)$ (Devlin et al., 2019; Souza et al., 2020; Rajapakse et al., 2024), and SimpleTransformers' default AdamW epsilon ($1e-8$) (Rajapakse et al., 2024). The maximum sequence length was set to the standard 512 tokens.

Task layer dropout rates of 0.1, 0.2, and 0.3 were tested, as higher rates can aid regularization with limited data (El Anigri et al., 2021; Grießhaber et al., 2020). Batch sizes of 8 and 16 were explored, consistent with similar applications (Devlin et al., 2019; Liu et al., 2019; Souza et al., 2020; Ding et al., 2020; Nogueira, 2021; dos Santos Gusmão, 2023).

A learning rate scheduler with linear decay and 6% warmup followed (Liu et al., 2019)'s recommendations. Early stopping based on the validation F1-score (halting if no improvement greater than 0.001 for 3 epochs) prevented overfitting and optimized training time.

Reference	Area	Year	Institution	Publication Medium	Theme
(Ribeiro and Ortellado, 2018)	Social Sciences	2018	USP	Journal	Politics
(de Melo, 2019)	Communication	2019	PUC-RIO	Master's Thesis	Politics
(Sakurai, 2019)	Computer Science	2019	UEL	Final Project	General
(Ituassu et al., 2019)	Communication	2019	PUC-RIO	Conference	Politics
(Santos, 2020)	Computer Science	2020	Unichristus	Final Project	General
(de Melo, 2021)	Communication	2021	PUC-RIO	Book	Politics
(Barbieri, 2021)	Communication	2021	UTP	Master's Thesis	COVID-19
(Quintanilha, 2021)	Linguistics	2021	UNL	Master's Thesis	COVID-19
(Lima et al., 2021)	Communication	2021	UFOP	Journal	COVID-19
(Lima, 2019)	Communication	2021	USP	Final Project	Politics
(Arndt et al., 2021)	Politics	2021	UFSC	Journal	COVID-19
(Leurquin and Leurquin, 2021)	Linguistics	2021	UFC	Journal	COVID-19, Politics
(de Sá, 2021)	Computer Science	2021	UFC	Master's Thesis	COVID-19, Politics
(Nascimento, 2021)	Library Science	2021	UFC	Final Project	COVID-19
(Capistrano, 2022)	Chemistry	2021	UFPA	Final Project	COVID-19
(Batista, 2020)	Administration	2021	UFPE	Master's Thesis	General
(de Freitas Melo, 2022)	Politics	2022	UFPE	Master's Thesis	Politics
(Borin da Cunha and Tilschneider Garcia Rosa, 2022)	Education	2022	Unioeste	Journal	COVID-19, Science
(Sousa, 2022)	Computer Science	2022	UFC	Final Project	General
(Quessada, 2022)	Politics	2022	UFSCAR	Master's Thesis	Politics
(Pereira and Antonio, 2023)	Linguistics	2023	UEM	Journal	General
(dos Santos Gusmão, 2023)	Computer Science	2023	UFAM	Final Project	General

Table 8: Selection of Academic Publications Found in Search Results Discussing Misinformation Examples from the Datasets (Illustrating Pattern F3).

Hyperparameters	**Search space / Value**
Batch size	8, 16
Learning rate	{1e-6, 5e-6, 1e-5, 2.5e-5,5e-5,1e-4}
Task layer dropout	0.1, 0.2, 0.3
Seed	2025
Weight decay	0.01
Max. train epochs	10
Max. Seq. Length	512
Learning rate scheduler	Linear w/ 6% *warmup*
Optimizer	AdamW
AdamW ϵ	1e-8
AdamW β_1	0.9
AdamW β_2	0.999
Early stopping patience	3 epochs
Early stopping threshold (F1-score)	0.001

Table 9: Hyperparameter search space for fine-tuning the base Bertimbau model.

Multilingual Symptom Detection on Social Media: Enhancing Health-related Fact-checking with LLMs

Sa'idah Zahrotul Jannah, Elyanah Aco, Shaowen Peng, Shoko Wakamiya, and **Eiji Aramaki**
Nara Institute of Science and Technology, Japan
saidah.zahrotul_jannah.rw9@naist.ac.jp
elyanah_marie_cariaga.aco.ef1@naist.ac.jp
peng.shaowen@naist.ac.jp
{wakamiya, aramaki}@is.naist.jp

Abstract

Social media has emerged as a valueable source for early pandemic detection, as repeated mentions of symptoms by users may signal the onset of an outbreak. However, to be a reliable system, validation through fact-checking and verification against official health records is essential. Without this step, systems risk spreading misinformation to the public. The effectiveness of these systems also depend on their ability to process data in multiple languages, given the multilingual nature of social media data. Yet, many NLP datasets and disease surveillance system remain heavily English-centric, leading to significant performance gaps for low-resource languages. This issue is especially critical in Southeast Asia, where symptom expression may vary culturally and linguistically. Therefore, this study evaluates the symptom detection capabilities of LLMs in social media posts across multiple languages, models, and symptoms to enhance health-related fact-checking. Our results reveal significant language-based discrepancies, with European languages outperforming under-resourced Southeast Asian languages. Furthermore, we identify symptom-specific challenges, particularly in detecting respiratory illnesses such as influenza, which LLMs tend to overpredict. The overestimation or misclassification of symptom mentions can lead to false alarms or public misinformation when deployed in real-world settings. This underscores the importance of symptom detection as a critical first step in medical fact-checking within early outbreak detection systems.

1 Introduction

Social media can be used for early pandemic detection (Shi et al., 2024). When many users repeatedly mention or complain about a certain symptom, it may indicate the potential onset of an outbreak. Gour et al. (2022) conducted a study on the COVID-19 outbreak and found that social media activity can reflect the state of an outbreak. Specifically, the study revealed that negative tweets posted during a crisis tend to align with the scale of the disease outbreak. However, to ensure the reliability of these detections, it is essential to validate them by fact-checking and verifying against the official health records. This transition from detection to health-related fact-checking and verification forms the foundation for building reliable public health monitoring systems. If a system detects a potential pandemic that does not correspond to official health records, it may contribute to the spread of misinformation to the public.

Nevertheless, the effectiveness of such systems relies on their ability to process data in multiple languages, as social media users come from all over the world. Yet, a comprehensive study on Natural Language Processing (NLP) datasets revealed a significant bias towards English, resulting in better performance than other languages for many tasks (Brown et al., 2020; Yu et al., 2022; Lai et al., 2023). In the field of disease surveillance, most existing epidemiological datasets and detection systems have also been developed primarily in English, with only limited support for other languages (Parekh et al., 2024a).

The performance gap is potentially wider for languages with little labeled or even unlabeled data, such as the majority of languages in Southeast Asia (SEA), a linguistically diverse region home to over 1300 languages (Joshi et al., 2020; Lovenia et al., 2024). These factors also pose a challenge in developing automatic symptom detection due to cultural (Anggoro and Jee, 2021) and linguistic variations (Wang et al., 2010), such as the use of idiomatic expressions and colloquial terms for common symptoms. A notable gap persists in addressing symptom identification and health-related data processing for languages in this region and under-resourced languages as a whole.

Addressing those challenges requires technolo-

Proceedings of the Eighth Fact Extraction and VERification Workshop (FEVER), pages 54–68
July 31, 2025 ©2025 Association for Computational Linguistics

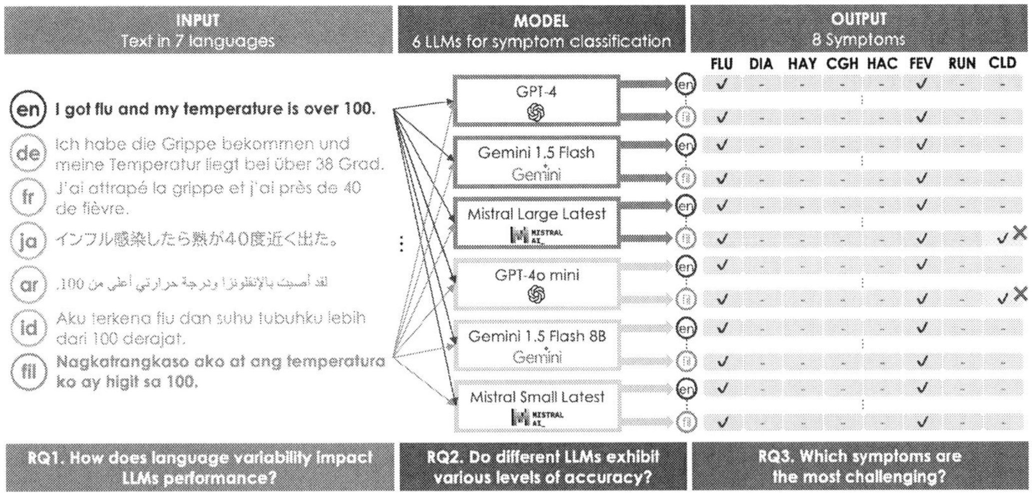

Figure 1: Overview of this study. We evaluate the symptom detection capabilities of LLMs on social media posts across seven languages (English: en, German: de, French: fr, Japanese: ja, Arabic: ar, Indonesian: id, Filipino: fil), six models (large-parameter models, e.g., GPT-4, Gemini 1.5 Flash, and Mistral Large Latest, and small-parameter models, e.g., GPT-4o mini, Gemini 1.5 Flash 8B, and Mistral Small Latest), and eight symptoms (influenza: FLU, diarrhea: DIA, hay fever: HAY, cough: CGH, headache: HAC, fever: FEV, runny nose: RUN, and cold: CLD). On the right side (Output), '✓' and '-' mean positive and negative for a symptom, respectively. Labels with a pink background indicate correct predictions, while labels with a gray background indicate incorrect predictions.

gies that can generalize across diverse linguistic contexts. In this regard, LLMs offer promising capabilities for improving symptom detection system, supporting health-related fact-checking. This study aims to investigate how language variability affects symptom identification using LLMs, highlighting the importance of developing practical systems with multilinguality in building reliable health-related fact-checking and disease surveillance systems. Specifically, the contribution of this paper is by answering the following research questions.

RQ1. How does language variability affect the LLMs performance for detecting symptom mentions that support health-related fact-checking?

RQ2. Do different LLMs exhibit various levels of accuracy when classifying symptoms?

RQ3. Which symptoms are the most challenging for LLMs to detect accurately, potentially impacting factuality assessment?

This study used European (English, German, and French) and Asian (Japanese, Arabic, Indonesian, and Filipino) languages as shown in Figure 1. Using an extended version of the NTCIR-13 MedWeb test dataset, we evaluated two model sizes (large- and small-parameter) from three general LLM providers: OpenAI, Google Gemini, and Mistral AI. Each model performs zero-shot multilabel symptom classification, categorizing posts as positive or negative for eight symptoms including influenza, diarrhea, hay fever, etc.Performance is measured through F1-score (standard NLP evaluation) and Relative Distance (disease-surveillance perspective) to assess estimation bias.

2 Related Work

2.1 Health-related Fact-Checking

Health-related fact-checking often involves addressing misinformation and infodemics. Social media, while being a rapid channel for the spread of misinformation, also serves as a valuable platform to counter false information, particularly during disease outbreaks, by disseminating content grounded in scientific evidence and supported by collaborations with local health authorities (Bayani et al., 2025; Vázquez-Gestal et al., 2024; Purnat et al., 2024). Approaches to fact-checking typically include manual verification, automated claim detection, and evidence retrieval (Sarrouti et al., 2021; Sharifpoor et al., 2025; Vladika et al., 2024).

Existing studies have primarily focused on verifying complete health claims. In contrast, this paper aims to explore symptom mention detection as a critical first step within the broader framework of health-related fact-checking, especially in the context of disease outbreaks.

Accurately identifying symptoms from user-generated content is essential for improving both the speed and reliability of outbreak response. Recent research has demonstrated the potential of social media as an early detection system for pandemics, identifying signs of an outbreak before it is officially declared. Parekh et al. (2024b) conducted research on epidemic prediction using event detection from social media data. Their framework was able to generate warnings 4 to 9 weeks earlier than the official epidemic declaration by the WHO for Monkeypox. The study demonstrated an alignment between the predicted outbreaks and the actual epidemic cases later confirmed by the official sources.

2.2 Multilingual Medical LLMs

Several studies have shown that language and cultural barriers between patients and healthcare providers can lead to unequal health outcomes, such as misdiagnoses, inadequate treatment, and lower patient safety and satisfaction (Ohtani et al., 2015; Schouten et al., 2020; Shamsi et al., 2020). This is especially the case in low-resource settings and for ethnic minorities, where intermediaries such as qualified interpreters and comprehensive translation resources may not easily be available.

The introduction of LLMs has opened up possibilities for addressing these barriers by enabling real-time translation and enhancing diagnostic accuracy, especially when fine-tuned for medical applications. While most medical corpora and language models are primarily in and designed for English, recent advancements have expanded their capability to support multiple languages. Models such as Medical mT5, Apollo, and BiMediX, which were trained on medical datasets for languages other than English, demonstrate higher average performance across different languages compared to commercial models (García-Ferrero et al., 2024; Pieri et al., 2024; Wang et al., 2024). Additionally, multilingual medical benchmarks such as in Qiu et al. (2024) have been developed to evaluate LLMs on tasks such as biomedical academical question-answering and diagnosis assessment.

However, resource constraints and ethical issues can hinder the development of truly inclusive multilingual medical LLMs. Building medical corpora for low-resource languages to train models may require substantial effort, such as collecting and transcribing hand-written health records and building local data dictionaries for medical terminologies (Wahl et al., 2018). Bias and misinformation within training data can be reproduced in LLM-generated content, posing significant risks in medical decision-making and reinforcing health outcome inequities (Omiye et al., 2023; Poulain et al., 2024; Yang et al., 2024).

3 Corpus

The NTCIR-13 MedWeb task test dataset was used and extended for this study. The dataset was crowdsourcing-generated short posts as detailed in Wakamiya et al. (2017). It consists of 640 posts, with no personal identifiers, related to systemic (fever and headache), digestive (diarrhea) and respiratory symptoms (cold, cough, hay fever, influenza, and runny nose).

The posts were labeled as positive or negative for each symptom based on whether the user indicated experiencing that symptom at the time, following the annotation guideline for NTCIR-13 MedWeb task (MedWeb, 2017). As seen in Table 1, only a small number of posts are classified as positive for each symptom. Table 2 shows examples of post labeled for each symptom.

Symptoms	# of Positive label	% of Positive label
Influenza (FLU)	24	3.75%
Diarrhea (DIA)	64	10.00%
Hayfever (HAY)	46	7.19%
Cough (CGH)	80	12.50%
Headache (HAC)	77	12.03%
Fever (FEV)	93	14.53%
Runnynose (RUN)	123	19.22%
Cold (CLD)	90	14.06%

Table 1: Positive label count and percentage per symptom.

Aside from English and Japanese which were included in the original task, the dataset was expanded using human translation service to five different languages: German, French, Modern Standard Arabic, Indonesian, and Filipino. This represents a mix of languages from European (specifically Indo-European) and Asian language families, all of which are considered high-resource except for the SEA languages Indonesian and Filipino (Joshi et al., 2020; Hammarström et al., 2024). These languages exhibit substantial linguistic diversity due to differences in scripts, phonological structures and other linguistic features, which lead to varying levels of complexity in text processing. The use of translation service is to minimize translation bias and to ensure that the symptom expressions were naturally and appropriately conveyed in the target language. The service had experienced some translation tasks related to the author's research previously and complied with the institution's financial procedures. Payment is made according to the agreed terms between the service provider and the authors. We provided the instruction to do the translation and the delivery format as seen in Appendix A.1.

4 Experimental Setup

4.1 Large Language Models

Two models of different parameter sizes (large and small) were chosen from each of three LLM families. The six chosen models are GPT-4 and GPT-4o mini by OpenAI, Gemini 1.5 Flash and Gemini 1.5 Flash 8B by Gemini Team Google, and Mistral Large and Small by Mistral AI. GPT-4, GPT-4o mini, Gemini 1.5 Flash, and Gemini 1.5 Flash 8B are under their respective licenses. Mistral Large is under Mistral Research License while Mistral Small is under Apache 2 License.

Not all models are provided with the parameter size information. OpenAI has not disclosed the exact parameter size of GPT-4 and GPT-4o mini. However, as an advancement of GPT-3, which has 175 billion parameters (Dale, 2021), GPT-4 is believed to have a larger parameter size with its ability to comprehend natural language in more complex and nuanced contexts (OpenAI et al., 2024). Meanwhile, OpenAI has described GPT-4o-mini as its most cost-efficient small model (OpenAI, 2024). The Gemini Team Google has not revealed the parameter size of Gemini 1.5 Flash as well. However, it is known that the model has a larger parameter size than Gemini 1.5 Flash 8B, which, as its name suggests, contains 8 billion parameters (Kilpatrick and Mallick, 2024). In contrast, Mistral AI has announced the parameter sizes for Mistral Large Latest at 123 billion and Mistral Small Latest at 22 billion (Mistral, 2025).

Pretraining data for these models, nor the languages within them, are not publicly released. However, previous studies have demonstrated these LLM families' proficiency on multiple languages, including low-resourced ones. For example, Lovenia et al. (2024) showed that GPT-4 and Mistral LLMs generally matched or outperformed multilingual or language-specific models for various NLP tasks on SEA languages. In Ahuja et al. (2024), larger commercial models such as GPT-4 and Gemini performed better than smaller ones across various multilingual evaluation benchmarks, although the possibility of data contamination in pretraining is not ruled out. Despite this, Zhang et al. (2023) and Jin et al. (2024) found that commercial models consistently perform better on English prompts than their translations in other languages.

Three trials were done for each model, using default model parameters (temperature, maximum tokens, etc.) to perform zero-shot multilabel symptom classification on posts using the following prompt. See Appendix A.2 for the full set of rules, which follow the original NTCIR-13 task.

The prompt used for the study

Instruction:
Determine if the creator of this post is exhibiting symptoms for each of the following: influenza, diarrhea, hay fever, cough, headache, fever, runny nose, cold. For each symptom, only answer either 0 or 1 for negative (no symptoms) or positive (has symptoms) respectively.

Determination of symptoms is carried out based on the following rules:
- Cases where the symptom is expressed directly, including mild symptoms, are considered positive;
- A symptom can be labeled positive with indirect expressions of having a symptom;

...
- Other cases, like symptoms belonging to blog friends, should be labeled as negative since it is difficult to determine their location.

Post:
{A post in one of the seven studied languages.}

Return the result as a JSON object with the symptoms as keys and the values as either 0 or 1.

4.2 Evaluation Methods

In this study, results were evaluated from two perspectives. From the standard NLP perspective, models are evaluated using the average F1-score. From the disease surveillance perspective, we propose a new metric more suitable for capturing model estimation bias. Both metrics are discussed in detail in the following subsections.

4.2.1 NLP Perspective: F1-score

The F1-score is a weighted average between precision, or accuracy of positive predictions, and recall, or ability to capture positive instances. This

Post	Symptom							
	FLU	DIA	HAY	CGH	HAC	FEV	RUN	CLD
I got flu and my temperature is over 100.	✓	-	-	-	-	✓	-	-
It was diarrhea that woke me up in the middle of the night.	-	✓	-	-	-	-	-	-
My wife's allergies are acting up, it seems rough.	-	-	✓	-	-	-	✓	-
It's almost the flu season.	-	-	-	-	-	-	-	-
I think I coughed too much. My stomach muscles hurt.	-	-	-	✓	-	-	-	-
This cold is rough. I've got a headache too, it might not be an ordinary cold. Yikes.	-	-	-	-	✓	-	✓	✓

Table 2: Sample English posts with multi-symptom labels. '✓' and '-' mean positive and negative for a symptom, respectively. A post may be positive for multiple symptoms.

makes it a preferred evaluation metric for machine learning and NLP tasks, especially on imbalanced datasets. We used `scikit-learn` to calculate the F1-score for this evaluation.

4.2.2 Surveillance Perspective: Relative Distance

While the F1-score is commonly used within NLP, it is more common and practical to evaluate disease surveillance models based on how closely the total predicted positive cases match the actual figures (Xiang-Sheng and Zhong, 2015; Samui et al., 2020; Bhatia et al., 2021). We propose a new metric called relative distance (RD) for measuring estimation bias, which reflects a model's tendency to overestimate or underestimate positive predictions. This metric provides added practical relevance for public health applications beyond what standard NLP metrics can offer.

We define RD as the ratio change between predicted and actual positives as described in the following formula:

$$\mathrm{RD} = \frac{(\mathrm{TP} + \mathrm{FP}) - (\mathrm{TP} + \mathrm{FN})}{\mathrm{TP} + \mathrm{FN}} = \frac{\mathrm{FP} - \mathrm{FN}}{\mathrm{TP} + \mathrm{FN}} \quad (1)$$

where TP indicates the number of true positives, FP the number of false positives, and FN the number of false negatives.

In a binary classification task, 0 serves as the gold standard or baseline against which prediction values are compared. A positive RD indicates overestimation of positives while a negative RD indicates underestimation.

5 Results and Discussion

We analyze LLM performance in multilingual symptom prediction across three dimensions: language-based, LLM-based, and symptom-based. The results provide insights into the applicability of LLMs for disease surveillance task, revealing current strengths and remaining challenges for real-world implementation and decision-making.

5.1 NLP Perspective: F1-Score Insights

The distribution of F1-scores across the three dimensions are shown in Figure 2. Appendix A.3 and A.4 provide evaluation details.

5.1.1 Language-based Analysis

Figure 2(a) shows the distribution of F1-scores for each language, where each point corresponds to a specific symptom.

Scores range from moderate to high in all languages. The average F1-scores for English, German, and French are 0.748, 0.730, 0.719 while for Asian languages (Japanese, Arabic, Indonesian, and Filipino) are 0.714, 0.687, 0.685, and 0.656 respectively. The scores showed that LLMs performed better in the three European languages (English, German, and French) than the Asian ones based on average F1-scores, with the mid-resourced Indonesian and Filipino ranking the lowest. Furthermore, a comparison based on language categories as shown in Appendix A.5, European and Asian, reveals a significant difference in mean F1 scores. The average F1 scores for European and Asian languages are 0.73 and 0.68, respectively, with a p-value of 0.0000. Moreover, variability across European languages is also lower than all Asian languages except Japanese.

Vocabulary sharing and cultural nuances between languages may explain these results. Indo-European languages were found to improve model performance on unseen languages in the same family, but the same was not observed on other language families (Yuan et al., 2024). Addition-

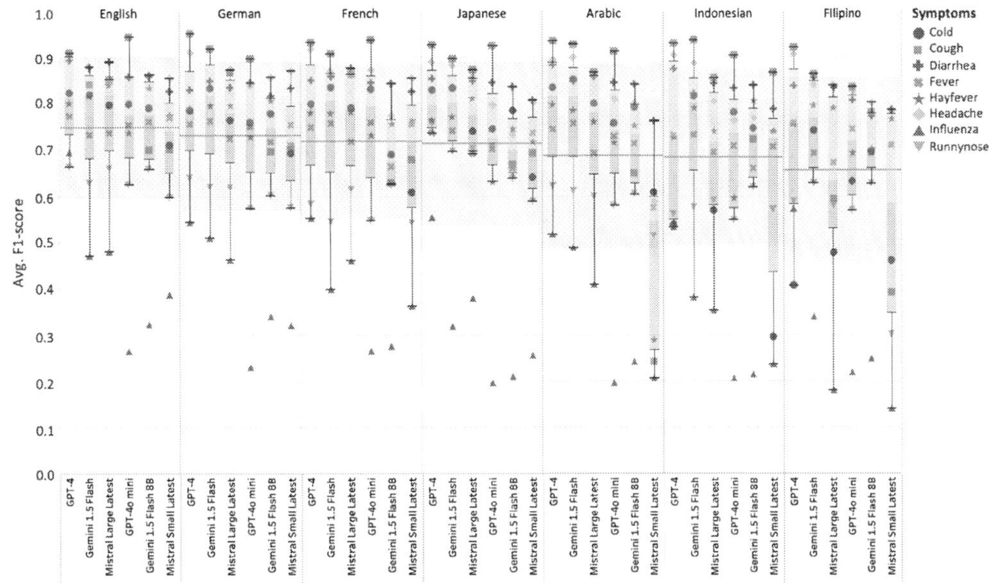

(a) Score distribution per language

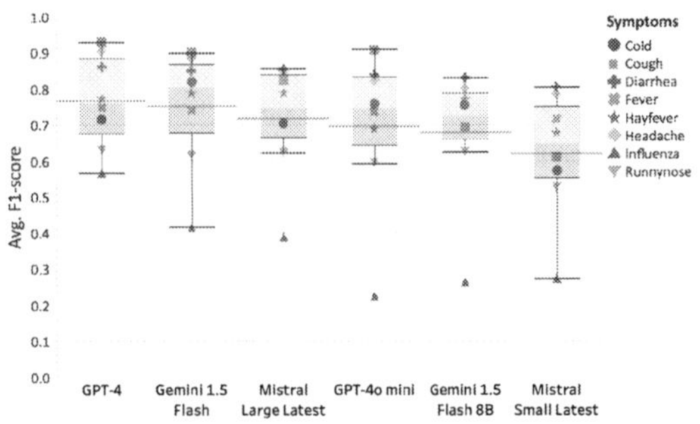

(b) Score distribution per LLM

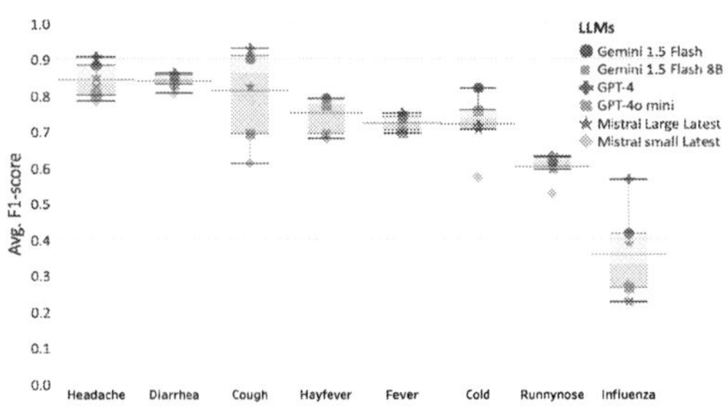

(c) Score distribution per symptom

Figure 2: Comparative performance of LLMs in several perspectives. Horizontal lines within each shaded area represent group averages, while shaded areas denote scores within one standard deviation of this average. From language perspective, (a) suggests that English, German, and French have better performance than Asian languages. In LLMs' view, (b) showing large-parameter models are better. Moreover, in language-based (c) presents that Influenza is harder for LLM to predict accurately.

ally, languages with cultural contexts and idiomatic expressions that differ from those predominantly found in training data had lower and less consistent model performance (Tao et al., 2024).

Numerous outliers with F1-scores below 0.4 are observed for all languages, indicating possible challenges in symptom prediction regardless of language used. The presence of outliers is crucial in real-world applications, where low-performance instances can lead to critical errors, especially in sensitive tasks such as disease symptom detection. The following sections examine model-specific and symptom-specific performance to identify factors contributing to these outliers.

5.1.2 LLM-based Analysis

Figure 2(b) shows the distribution of F1 scores for each LLM, with points representing individual symptoms. Large-parameter models—GPT-4, Gemini 1.5 Flash, and Mistral Large Latest—achieved higher average F1 scores. The average performance of small-parameter models was at least 0.02 lower than their larger counterparts, with the largest gap observed between GPT-4 and Mistral Small Latest. Furthermore, statistical testing (Appendix A.6) confirmed a significant difference between large- and small-models, with mean scores of 0.74 and 0.66 and a p-value of 0.0000.

Outliers were observed in some models, indicating potential challenges in predicting certain symptoms. Additionally, Mistral Small Latest exhibited outlier behavior for certain symptoms in Figure 2(c), suggesting difficulties in accurately identifying those symptoms.

In detailed, as shown in Appendix A.3, Gemini 1.5 Flash has the smallest variance across different languages among the larger parameter models, although it does not reach the higher F1-scores achieved by GPT-4. All models perform better on European languages than Asian ones, and English continues to have the highest F1 scores for most models. The performance difference between European and Asian languages is more pronounced in Mistral LLMs. This may be explained by the number of languages officially supported by each family. Only English, French, Spanish, German, and Italian are officially supported in the Mistral models (Mistral AI, 2024), compared to the 98 supported in OpenAI's speech-to-text Whisper models (Radford et al., 2023) and over 100 supported in Google's Gemini models (Barkley, 2024).

These results highlight two key insights. First, selecting between large- and small-parameter models for complex tasks such as multilingual symptom detection involves a significant trade-off between performance and cost-effectiveness. Second, even large-parameter models can struggle on lower-resourced languages like Indonesian and Filipino. Addressing these challenges is crucial to improving the reliability and applicability of LLMs in disease surveillance.

5.1.3 Symptom-based Analysis

Figure 2(c) shows the distribution of F1-scores for each symptom, with the points representing the models. Respiratory symptoms generally exhibit high variability in scores, with RUN and FLU particularly standing out due to their lower averages compared to other symptoms. Furthermore, a significant difference was observed among digestive, systemic, and respiratory symptoms. Their mean F1 scores were 0.84, 0.78, and 0.62, respectively, with all pairwise p-values below 0.000 (See Appendix A.7).

Outliers in Figure 2(a) and 2(b) were from FLU predictions, which occurred across all languages and most models. Low outliers in multiple languages and models suggest that this symptom poses challenges, leading to sharp drops in performance for these instances.

As detailed in Appendix A.4, symptom scores vary across different languages and language groups. All European languages scored above average and all Asian languages scored below average for HAC and FLU. A similar pattern is observed for RUN except for Japanese. For other symptoms, scores for at least one language fell outside the standard deviation range. Notably, CLD scores for Indonesian and Filipino and were significantly lower than those of other languages, while RUN scores were significantly higher. CGH scores for Arabic and Filipino were also lower, while scores for Indonesian were higher.

Score differences like these may be due to cultural variations in how symptoms are named or described in different languages. Some symptoms may have no direct counterparts in some languages, resulting in the use of catch-all terms that can apply to multiple symptoms depending on the context. In Filipino, then term *sipon* can refer to either having a cold or a runny nose. Additionally, expressions and colloquial terms may instead be used, such as *meler* which can be referred as Runny nose, *meriang* and *masuk angin* in Indonesian which describe feeling unwell, including having a cold (Anggoro and Jee, 2021). This ambiguity makes it challenging for LLMs to identify specific symptoms, especially if pretraining was done primarily on formal texts.

Thus, to address these challenges, expanding training datasets to include informal and colloquial expressions is crucial for enhancing model robustness across diverse linguistic contexts, especially in digital disease surveillance, where social media data often contains local terms used by the public to describe symptoms. Additionally, fine-tuning models for underrepresented languages and cultural contexts can help bridge performance gaps and improve the accuracy of symptom detection across languages.

5.2 Surveillance Perspective: Relative Distance Insights

Table 3 shows that models tend to overestimate or label symptoms as positive for most languages, likely due to the dataset being imbalanced for all symptoms. Even so, RD scores for FLU are much higher than other symptoms for all languages, especially Asian ones. For example, the RD score for FLU in Japanese is 5.019, indicating that the predicted positive labels are five times higher than the actual positive cases. When combined with the low F1-scores for this symptom (Figure 2(c)), this suggests that LLMs are overly cautious by overpre-

Symptom	Language							Average
	English	German	French	Japanese	Arabic	Indonesian	Filipino	
FEV	-0.047	-0.002	0.011	0.084	0.032	0.090	0.038	0.030
RUN	-0.139	-0.005	0.218	-0.023	-0.071	0.113	0.161	0.036
CGH	0.268	0.246	0.257	0.324	0.178	0.173	0.462	0.273
DIA	0.235	0.309	0.290	0.302	0.253	0.323	0.394	0.301
CLD	0.290	0.270	0.491	0.457	0.356	0.075	0.249	0.313
HAC	0.293	0.271	0.301	0.426	0.498	0.470	0.362	0.374
HAY	0.442	0.582	0.568	0.682	0.437	0.564	0.539	0.545
FLU	**2.852**	**3.250**	**3.313**	**5.019**	**4.519**	**4.764**	**3.977**	**3.596**
Average	0.524	0.615	0.684	0.909	0.775	0.821	0.773	0.729

Table 3: Relative distance (RD) scores by language and symptom. Shaded scores are beyond ± 0.2, showing that LLMs overestimate positive cases for most symptoms and languages, while bold numbers presenting the highest overestimation of symptom prediction in each language.

dicting at the cost of performance. On the other hand, RD scores for FEV are close to 0 for all languages, indicating minimal bias for this symptom.

Traditional case-based surveillance systems are generally affected by some degree of underestimation, such as individuals attempting to self-treat their symptoms or institutions underreporting the cases. Final estimates usually have to be adjusted to capture a more accurate picture of disease incidence (Gibbons et al., 2014). Our findings suggest that text-based digital epidemiological systems, especially LLMs which are trained on large amounts of data, may have an advantage over traditional systems in this regard.

However, overestimation can lead to a loss of public trust or factuality in digital epidemiological disease surveillance, especially when underlying algorithms are not replicable or are hard to interpret. The validity of the now-defunct Google Flu Trends, which used search query data for predictions, was questioned after it overestimated peak flu levels during the 2012/2013 epidemic season by nearly double the actual figures (Butler, 2013; Olson et al., 2013). Mitigating overestimation bias by fine-tuning for specific symptoms or languages is recommended when deploying LLM-based surveillance systems.

In summary, there are two insights that can be drawn. First, Overestimation Tendency: LLMs exhibit a tendency to overestimate symptoms. It means that they are inclined to label symptoms as positive. From this observation, there are two key lessons: (1) if an LLM is deployed as a symptom identification and its results indicate a critical or dangerous situation, this may not necessarily reflect the actual case. This highlights that overestimation or misclassification of symptom mentions could lead to false alarms or public misinformation; however (2) if the system identifies a situation as safe, this can be considered reliable and trustworthy. These insights contribute to the practical application of LLM as a symptom identification system. Second, Influenza Detection Challenges: Detecting diseases similar to Influenza, such as COVID-19, using a symptom-based disease surveillance system with LLMs can result in poor performance. One possible contributing factor is the limited capabilities of LLMs in handling multilingual task, particularly in medical-related content in underrepresented languages. This limitation may lead to inaccurate symptom identification which can affect the factual accuracy of detected disease signal.

6 Conclusion

This paper evaluates LLM performance in symptom detection across different languages, LLMs and symptoms as the first crucial steps in health-related fact-checking data. In terms of (1) languages, our experiments show that European languages outperform Asian languages, particularly the SEA languages Indonesian and Filipino. Then, (2) LLMs achieve moderate to high performance overall, but varies significantly across languages and symptoms especially for small parameter models. As for (3) symptoms, respiratory symptoms are notably challenging for LLMs to predict accurately, with influenza being significantly overpredicted across all languages. These findings underscore the potential of LLMs in digital epidemiology, while at the same time highlighting the need to address performance gaps in lower-resourced languages before practical implementation. We acknowledge that commercial LLMs are helpful, but adapting them to the public health field is likely needed for high-risk tasks like disease surveillance which can be explored in the future research. Moreover, symptom detection for medical fact-checking becomes critical to ensure that the early outbreak detection system align with real-world health conditions and are not based on misclassified or incomplete symptom data.

Limitations

This paper evaluates multiple languages, models, and symptoms in assessing LLMs for symptom detection for enhancing medical fact-checking, with a particular focus on the performance of Southeast Asian languages compared to high-resource ones. However, many key Southeast Asian languages remain unaddressed, including highly under-resourced languages such as Khmer, Burmese, and Lao. While this study examines LLM performance in symptom identification across languages, it does not propose new methods to enhance LLM performance. Instead, it aims to highlight the potential applications of LLMs in fact-checking for disease surveillance systems. Additionally, our approach to disease surveillance relies on identifying common symptoms from social media, which may be self-diagnosed by users. The models used also do not incorporate a large language model (LLM) specifically designed for the target language or fine-tuned for languages within the region. Furthermore, as the posts analyzed were translated rather than directly sourced from online platforms, they may not fully capture the linguistic and cultural nuances of how native speakers communicate in their own language online. To address these limitations, future iterations of this study will expand the evaluation by covering more languages and models, providing a more comprehensive assessment of multilingual LLM performance in digital epidemiology.

Ethics Statement

This study is an extension of the NTCIR-13 Task, utilizing its test dataset with the consent from the task organizers. The dataset used was pseudotweets since the tweet data obtained via the Twitter API cannot be publicly shared due to Twitter's developer policy on data redistribution. The dataset, originally in Japanese, was generated through crowdsourcing and subsequently translated into six other languages by human translators to minimize bias in machine translation. Additionally, all resources used in this study comply with their respective licenses. We have authorized API access to the resources, strictly for research purposes, and have fully complied with all terms and conditions. No personally identifiable information (PII) was included, and the research does not involve human subjects requiring IRB approval.

References

Sanchit Ahuja, Divyanshu Aggarwal, Varun Gumma, Ishaan Watts, Ashutosh Sathe, Millicent Ochieng, Rishav Hada, Prachi Jain, Mohamed Ahmed, Kalika Bali, and Sunayana Sitaram. 2024. MEGAVERSE: Benchmarking large language models across languages, modalities, models and tasks. In *Proceedings of the 2024 Conference of the North American Chapter of the Association for Computational Linguistics: Human Language Technologies*, pages 2598–2637.

Florencia K. Anggoro and Benjamin D. Jee. 2021. The substance of cold: Indonesians' use of cold weather theory to explain everyday illnesses. *Frontiers in Psychology*, 12.

Warren Barkley. 2024. New strides in making ai accessible for every enterprise. Accessed: 19 May 2025.

Azadeh Bayani, Alexandre Ayotte, and Jean Noel Nikiema. 2025. Transformer-based tool for automated fact-checking of online health information: Development study. *JMIR Infodemiology*, 5:e56831.

Sangeeta Bhatia, Britta Lassmann, Emily Cohn, Angel N Desai, Malwina Carrion, Moritz U G Kraemer, Mark Herringer, John Brownstein, Larry Madoff, Anne Cori, and Pierre Nouvellet. 2021. Using digital surveillance tools for near real-time mapping of the risk of infectious disease spread. *npj Digital Medicine*, 4(1):73.

Tom Brown, Benjamin Mann, Nick Ryder, Melanie Subbiah, Jared D Kaplan, Prafulla Dhariwal, Arvind Neelakantan, Pranav Shyam, Girish Sastry, Amanda Askell, Sandhini Agarwal, Ariel Herbert-Voss, Gretchen Krueger, Tom Henighan, Rewon Child, Aditya Ramesh, Daniel Ziegler, Jeffrey Wu, Clemens Winter, Chris Hesse, Mark Chen, Eric Sigler, Mateusz Litwin, Scott Gray, Benjamin Chess, Jack Clark, Christopher Berner, Sam McCandlish, Alec Radford, Ilya Sutskever, and Dario Amodei. 2020. Language models are few-shot learners. In *Advances in Neural Information Processing Systems*, volume 33, pages 1877–1901. Curran Associates, Inc.

Declan Butler. 2013. When Google got flu wrong. *Nature*, 494:155–156.

Robert Dale. 2021. Gpt-3: What's it good for? *Natural Language Engineering*, 27(1):113–118.

Iker García-Ferrero, Rodrigo Agerri, Aitziber Atutxa Salazar, Elena Cabrio, Iker de la Iglesia, Alberto Lavelli, Bernardo Magnini, Benjamin Molinet, Johana Ramirez-Romero, German Rigau, Jose Maria Villa-Gonzalez, Serena Villata, and Andrea Zaninello. 2024. MedMT5: An open-source multilingual text-to-text LLM for the medical domain. In *Proceedings of the 2024 Joint International Conference on Computational Linguistics, Language Resources and Evaluation (LREC-COLING 2024)*, pages 11165–11177, Torino, Italia. ELRA and ICCL.

Gemini Team Google. 2024. Gemini 1.5: Unlocking multimodal understanding across millions of tokens of context. *Preprint*, arXiv:2403.05530.

Cheryl L. Gibbons, Marie-Josée J. Mangen, Dietrich Plass, Brooke Russell John Havelaar, Arie H., Piotr Kramarz, Karen L. Peterson, Anke L. Stuurman, Alessandro Cassini, Eric M. Fèvre, and Mirjam EE. Kretzchmar. 2014. Measuring underreporting and under-ascertainment in infectious disease datasets: a comparison of methods. *BMC Public Health*, 14.

Alekh Gour, Shikha Aggarwal, and Subodha Kumar. 2022. Lending ears to unheard voices: An empirical analysis of user-generated content on social media. *Production and Operations Management*, 31(6):2457–2476.

Harald Hammarström, Robert Forkel, Martin Haspelmath, and Sebastian Bank. 2024. Glottolog 5.1. Accessed: 19 May 2025.

Yiqiao Jin, Mohit Chandra, Gaurav Verma, Yibo Hu, Munmun De Choudhury, and Srijan Kumar. 2024. Better to ask in English: Cross-lingual evaluation of large language models for healthcare queries. In *Proceedings of the ACM Web Conference*, pages 2627–2638. Association for Computing Machinery.

Pratik Joshi, Sebastin Santy, Amar Budhiraja, Kalika Bali, and Monojit Chodhury. 2020. The state and fate of linguistic diversity and inclusion in the nlp world. In *Proceedings of the 58th Annual Meeting of the Association for Computational Linguistics*, pages 6282–6293.

Logan Kilpatrick and Shrestha Basu Mallick. 2024. Gemini 1.5 flash-8b is now production ready. Accessed: 19 May 2025.

Viet Dac Lai, Nghia Ngo, Amir Pouran Ben Veyseh, Hieu Man, Franck Dernoncourt, Trung Bui, and Thien Huu Nguyen. 2023. ChatGPT beyond English: Towards a comprehensive evaluation of large language models in multilingual learning. In *Findings of the Association for Computational Linguistics: EMNLP 2023*, pages 13171–13189, Singapore. Association for Computational Linguistics.

Holy Lovenia, Rahmad Mahendra, Salsabil Maulana Akbar, Lester James Validad Miranda, Jennifer Santoso, Elyanah Aco, Akhdan Fadhilah, Jonibek Mansurov, Joseph Marvin Imperial, Onno P. Kampman, Joel Ruben Antony Moniz, Muhammad Ravi Shulthan Habibi, Frederikus Hudi, Jann Railey Montalan, Ryan Ignatius Hadiwijaya, Joanito Agili Lopo, William Nixon, Börje F. Karlsson, James Jaya, Ryandito Diandaru, Yuze Gao, Patrick Amadeus Irawan, Bin Wang, Jan Christian Blaise Cruz, Chenxi Whitehouse, Ivan Halim Parmonangan, Maria Khelli, Wenyu Zhang, Lucky Susanto, Reynard Adha Ryanda, Sonny Lazuardi Hermawan, Dan John Velasco, Muhammad Dehan Al Kautsar, Willy Fitra Hendria, Yasmin Moslem, Noah Flynn, Muhammad Farid Adilazuarda, Haochen Li, Johanes Lee, R. Damanhuri, Shuo Sun, Muhammad Reza Qorib, Amirbek Djanibekov, Wei Qi Leong, Quyet V. Do, Niklas Muennighoff, Tanrada Pansuwan, Ilham Firdausi Putra, Yan Xu, Tai Ngee Chia, Ayu Purwarianti, Sebastian Ruder, William Chandra Tjhi, Peerat Limkonchotiwat, Alham Fikri Aji, Sedrick Keh, Genta Indra Winata, Ruochen Zhang, Fajri Koto, Zheng Xin Yong, and Samuel Cahyawijaya. 2024. SEACrowd: A multilingual multimodal data hub and benchmark suite for Southeast Asian languages. In *Proceedings of the 2024 Conference on Empirical Methods in Natural Language Processing*, pages 5155–5203, Miami, Florida, USA. Association for Computational Linguistics.

MedWeb. 2017. Ntcir-13 medweb annotation corpus guideline. Accessed: 19 May 2025.

Mistral. 2025. Model weights. Accessed: 19 May 2025.

Mistral AI. 2024. Au large. Accessed: 19 May 2025.

Ai Ohtani, Takefumi Suzuki, Hiroyoshi Takeuchi, and Hiroyuki Uchida. 2015. Language barriers and access to psychiatric care: A systematic review. *Psychiatric Services*, 66(8):798–805.

Donald R. Olson, Kevin J. Konty, Marc Paladini, Cecile Viboud, and Lone Simonsen. 2013. Reassessing Google Flu Trends data for detection of seasonal and pandemic influenza: A comparative epidemiological study at three geographic scales. *PLOS Computational Biology*, 9(10).

Jesutofunmi A. Omiye, Jenna C. Lester, Simon Spichak, Veronica Rotemberg, and Roxana Daneshjou. 2023. Large language models propogate race-based medicine. *npj Digital Medicine*, 6(195).

OpenAI. 2024. Gpt-4 technical report. *Preprint*, arXiv:2303.08774.

OpenAI. 2024. Gpt-4o mini: Advancing cost-efficient intelligence. Accessed: 19 May 2025.

OpenAI, Josh Achiam, Steven Adler, Sandhini Agarwal, Lama Ahmad, Ilge Akkaya, Florencia Leoni Aleman, Diogo Almeida, Janko Altenschmidt, Sam Altman, Shyamal Anadkat, Red Avila, Igor Babuschkin,

Suchir Balaji, Valerie Balcom, Paul Baltescu, Haiming Bao, Mohammad Bavarian, Jeff Belgum, Irwan Bello, Jake Berdine, Gabriel Bernadett-Shapiro, Christopher Berner, Lenny Bogdonoff, Oleg Boiko, Madelaine Boyd, Anna-Luisa Brakman, Greg Brockman, Tim Brooks, Miles Brundage, Kevin Button, Trevor Cai, Rosie Campbell, Andrew Cann, Brittany Carey, Chelsea Carlson, Rory Carmichael, Brooke Chan, Che Chang, Fotis Chantzis, Derek Chen, Sully Chen, Ruby Chen, Jason Chen, Mark Chen, Ben Chess, Chester Cho, Casey Chu, Hyung Won Chung, Dave Cummings, Jeremiah Currier, Yunxing Dai, Cory Decareaux, Thomas Degry, Noah Deutsch, Damien Deville, Arka Dhar, David Dohan, Steve Dowling, Sheila Dunning, Adrien Ecoffet, Atty Eleti, Tyna Eloundou, David Farhi, Liam Fedus, Niko Felix, Simón Posada Fishman, Juston Forte, Isabella Fulford, Leo Gao, Elie Georges, Christian Gibson, Vik Goel, Tarun Gogineni, Gabriel Goh, Rapha Gontijo-Lopes, Jonathan Gordon, Morgan Grafstein, Scott Gray, Ryan Greene, Joshua Gross, Shixiang Shane Gu, Yufei Guo, Chris Hallacy, Jesse Han, Jeff Harris, Yuchen He, Mike Heaton, Johannes Heidecke, Chris Hesse, Alan Hickey, Wade Hickey, Peter Hoeschele, Brandon Houghton, Kenny Hsu, Shengli Hu, Xin Hu, Joost Huizinga, Shantanu Jain, Shawn Jain, Joanne Jang, Angela Jiang, Roger Jiang, Haozhun Jin, Denny Jin, Shino Jomoto, Billie Jonn, Heewoo Jun, Tomer Kaftan, Łukasz Kaiser, Ali Kamali, Ingmar Kanitscheider, Nitish Shirish Keskar, Tabarak Khan, Logan Kilpatrick, Jong Wook Kim, Christina Kim, Yongjik Kim, Jan Hendrik Kirchner, Jamie Kiros, Matt Knight, Daniel Kokotajlo, Łukasz Kondraciuk, Andrew Kondrich, Aris Konstantinidis, Kyle Kosic, Gretchen Krueger, Vishal Kuo, Michael Lampe, Ikai Lan, Teddy Lee, Jan Leike, Jade Leung, Daniel Levy, Chak Ming Li, Rachel Lim, Molly Lin, Stephanie Lin, Mateusz Litwin, Theresa Lopez, Ryan Lowe, Patricia Lue, Anna Makanju, Kim Malfacini, Sam Manning, Todor Markov, Yaniv Markovski, Bianca Martin, Katie Mayer, Andrew Mayne, Bob McGrew, Scott Mayer McKinney, Christine McLeavey, Paul McMillan, Jake McNeil, David Medina, Aalok Mehta, Jacob Menick, Luke Metz, Andrey Mishchenko, Pamela Mishkin, Vinnie Monaco, Evan Morikawa, Daniel Mossing, Tong Mu, Mira Murati, Oleg Murk, David Mély, Ashvin Nair, Reiichiro Nakano, Rajeev Nayak, Arvind Neelakantan, Richard Ngo, Hyeonwoo Noh, Long Ouyang, Cullen O'Keefe, Jakub Pachocki, Alex Paino, Joe Palermo, Ashley Pantuliano, Giambattista Parascandolo, Joel Parish, Emy Parparita, Alex Passos, Mikhail Pavlov, Andrew Peng, Adam Perelman, Filipe de Avila Belbute Peres, Michael Petrov, Henrique Ponde de Oliveira Pinto, Michael, Pokorny, Michelle Pokrass, Vitchyr H. Pong, Tolly Powell, Alethea Power, Boris Power, Elizabeth Proehl, Raul Puri, Alec Radford, Jack Rae, Aditya Ramesh, Cameron Raymond, Francis Real, Kendra Rimbach, Carl Ross, Bob Rotsted, Henri Roussez, Nick Ryder, Mario Saltarelli, Ted Sanders, Shibani Santurkar, Girish Sastry, Heather Schmidt, David Schnurr, John Schulman, Daniel Selsam, Kyla Sheppard, Toki Sherbakov, Jessica Shieh, Sarah Shoker, Pranav Shyam, Szymon Sidor, Eric Sigler, Maddie Simens, Jordan Sitkin, Katarina Slama, Ian Sohl, Benjamin Sokolowsky, Yang Song, Natalie Staudacher, Felipe Petroski Such, Natalie Summers, Ilya Sutskever, Jie Tang, Nikolas Tezak, Madeleine B. Thompson, Phil Tillet, Amin Tootoonchian, Elizabeth Tseng, Preston Tuggle, Nick Turley, Jerry Tworek, Juan Felipe Cerón Uribe, Andrea Vallone, Arun Vijayvergiya, Chelsea Voss, Carroll Wainwright, Justin Jay Wang, Alvin Wang, Ben Wang, Jonathan Ward, Jason Wei, CJ Weinmann, Akila Welihinda, Peter Welinder, Jiayi Weng, Lilian Weng, Matt Wiethoff, Dave Willner, Clemens Winter, Samuel Wolrich, Hannah Wong, Lauren Workman, Sherwin Wu, Jeff Wu, Michael Wu, Kai Xiao, Tao Xu, Sarah Yoo, Kevin Yu, Qiming Yuan, Wojciech Zaremba, Rowan Zellers, Chong Zhang, Marvin Zhang, Shengjia Zhao, Tianhao Zheng, Juntang Zhuang, William Zhuk, and Barret Zoph. 2024. Gpt-4 technical report. *Preprint*, arXiv:2303.08774.

Tanmay Parekh, Jeffrey Kwan, Jiarui Yu, Sparsh Johri, Hyosang Ahn, Sreya Muppalla, Kai-Wei Chang, Wei Wang, and Nanyun Peng. 2024a. SPEED++: A multilingual event extraction framework for epidemic prediction and preparedness. In *Proceedings of the 2024 Conference on Empirical Methods in Natural Language Processing*, pages 12936–12965, Miami, Florida, USA. Association for Computational Linguistics.

Tanmay Parekh, Anh Mac, Jiarui Yu, Yuxuan Dong, Syed Shahriar, Bonnie Liu, Eric Yang, Kuan-Hao Huang, Wei Wang, Nanyun Peng, and Kai-Wei Chang. 2024b. Event detection from social media for epidemic prediction. In *Proceedings of the 2024 Conference of the North American Chapter of the Association for Computational Linguistics: Human Language Technologies (Volume 1: Long Papers)*, pages 5758–5783, Mexico City, Mexico. Association for Computational Linguistics.

Sara Pieri, Sahal Shaji Mullappilly, Fahad Shahbaz Khan, Rao Muhammad Anwer, Salman Khan, Timothy Baldwin, and Hisham Cholakkal. 2024. BiMediX: Bilingual medical mixture of experts LLM. In *Findings of the Association for Computational Linguistics: EMNLP 2024*, pages 16984–17002, Miami, Florida, USA. Association for Computational Linguistics.

Raphael Poulain, Hamed Fayyaz, and Rahmatollah Beheshti. 2024. Bias patterns in the application of LLMs for clinical decision support: A comprehensive study. *Preprint*, arXiv:2404.15149.

T Purnat, M Kajimoto, J Kalinic, A Stevanovic, S Mandic-Rajcevic, and E Wilhelm. 2024. How factchecking organizations can partner within public health for a healthier internet. *European Journal of Public Health*, 34.

Pengcheng Qiu, Chaoyi Wu, Xiaoman Zhang, Weixiong Lin, Haicheng Wang, Ya Zhang, Yanfeng Wang, and

Weidi Xie. 2024. Towards building multilingual language model for medicine. *Nature Communications*, 15(1):8384.

Alec Radford, Jong Wook Kim, Tao Xu, Greg Brockman, Christine McLeavey, and Ilya Sutskever. 2023. Robust speech recognition via large-scale weak supervision. JMLR.org.

Piu Samui, Jayanta Mondal, and Subhas Khajanchi. 2020. A mathematical model for covid-19 transmission dynamics with a case study of india. *Chaos, Solitons Fractals*, 140:110173.

Mourad Sarrouti, Asma Ben Abacha, Yassine Mrabet, and Dina Demner-Fushman. 2021. Evidence-based fact-checking of health-related claims. In *Findings of the Association for Computational Linguistics: EMNLP 2021*, pages 3499–3512, Punta Cana, Dominican Republic. Association for Computational Linguistics.

Barbara C. Schouten, Antoon Cox, Gözde Duran, Koen Kerremans, Leyla Köseoğlu Banning, Ali Lahdidioui, Maria van den Muijsenbergh, Sanne Schinkel, Hande Sungur, Jeanine Suurmond, Rena Zendedel, and Demi Krystallidou. 2020. Mitigating language and cultural barriers in healthcare communication: Towards a holistic approach. *Patient Education and Counseling*, 103(12):2604–2608.

Hilal Al Shamsi, Abdullah G. Alumtairi, Sulaiman Al Mashrafi, and Talib Al Kalbani. 2020. Implications of language barriers for healthcare: A systematic review. *Oman medical journal*, 35(2).

Elham Sharifpoor, Maryam Okhovati, Mostafa Ghazizadeh-Ahsaee, and Mina Avaz Beigi. 2025. Classifying and fact-checking health-related information about COVID-19 on Twitter/X using machine learning and deep learning models. *BMC Medical Informatics and Decision Making*, 25(1):73.

Boyang Shi, Weixiang Huang, Yuanyuan Dang, and Wenhui Zhou. 2024. Leveraging social media data for pandemic detection and prediction. *Humanities and Social Sciences Communications*, 11(1):1075.

Yan Tao, Olga Viberg, Ryan S Baker, and René F Kizilcec. 2024. Cultural bias and cultural alignment of large language models. *PNAS Nexus*, 3(9):pgae346.

Juraj Vladika, Phillip Schneider, and Florian Matthes. 2024. HealthFC: Verifying health claims with evidence-based medical fact-checking. In *Proceedings of the 2024 Joint International Conference on Computational Linguistics, Language Resources and Evaluation (LREC-COLING 2024)*, pages 8095–8107, Torino, Italia. ELRA and ICCL.

Montse Vázquez-Gestal, Jesús Pérez-Seoane, and Ana-Belén Fernández-Souto. 2024. Disinformation and health: fact-checking strategies of spanish health public institutions through youtube. *Frontiers in Communication*, Volume 9 - 2024.

Brian Wahl, Aline Cossy-Gantner, Stefan Germann, and Nina R Schwalbe. 2018. Artificiall intelligence (AI) and global health: how can AI contribute to health in resource-poor settings? *BMJ Global Health*, 3(4).

Shoko Wakamiya, Mizuki Morita, Yoshinobu Kano, Tomoko Ohkuma, and Eiji Aramaki. 2017. Overview of the NTCIR-13 MedWeb Task. In *Proceedings of the 13th NTCIR Conference on Evaluation of Information Access Technologies (NTCIR-13)*, pages 40–49.

Xidong Wang, Nuo Chen, Junyin Chen, Yidong Wang, Guorui Zhen, Chunxian Zhang, Xiangbo Wu, Yan Hu, Anningzhe Gao, Xiang Wan, Haizhou Li, and Benyou Wang. 2024. Apollo: A lightweight multilingual medical llm towards democratizing medical ai to 6b people. *Preprint*, arXiv:2403.03640.

Xin Shelley Wang, Charles S. Cleeland, Tito R. Mendoza, Young Ho Yun, Ying Wang, Toru Okuyama, and Valen E. Johnson. 2010. Impact of cultural and linguistic factors on symptom reporting by patients with cancer. *JNCI: Journal of the National Cancer Institute*, 102(10):732–738.

Wang. Xiang-Sheng and Luoyi Zhong. 2015. Ebola outbreak in West Africa: real-time estimaion and multiple-wave prediction. *Mathematical Biosciences and Engineering*, 12(5).

Yifan Yang, Xiaoyu Liu, Qiao Jin, Furong Huang, and Zhiyong Lu. 2024. Unmasking and quantifying racial bias of large language models in medical report generation. *Communications Medicine*, 4(176).

Xinyan Yu, Trina Chatterjee, Akari Asai, Junjie Hu, and Eunsol Choi. 2022. Beyond counting datasets: A survey of multilingual dataset construction and necessary resources. In *Findings of the Association for Computational Linguistics: EMNLP 2022*, pages 3725–3743, Abu Dhabi, United Arab Emirates. Association for Computational Linguistics.

Fei Yuan, Shuai Yuan, Zhiyong Wu, and Lei Li. 2024. How vocabulary sharing facilitates multilingualism in LLaMA? In *Findings of the Association for Computational Linguistics: ACL 2024*, pages 12111–12130, Bangkok, Thailand. Association for Computational Linguistics.

Xiang Zhang, Senyu Li, Bradley Hauer, Ning Shi, and Grzegorz Kondrak. 2023. Don't Trust ChatGPT when your Question is not in English: A Study of Multilingual Abilities and Types of LLMs. In *Proceedings of the 2023 Conference on Empirical Methods in Natural Language Processing*. Association for Computational Linguistics.

A Appendix

A.1 Instruction to the Human Translation Services

Method

The text written in cells B2 to B641 of the attached

Excel file will be translated into the following languages. Text written in cells other than column B will not be translated.
• Indonesian
• Filipino
• Arabic
• German
• French

The target text consisted of 640 sentences with a total of 8,276 words. The manuscript tweet data is available in two files, one written in Japanese and one written in English, with the same content.

Delivery form
Excel data (any data format can be delivered via email attachment or file sharing system) Please create Excel data according to the following procedure.
• Separate files for each language
• Edit only columns A and B, and copy the values from the manuscript to columns C to J.
• Column A (ID)
• Enter the same number + language code as the original
• Example: If the row in column A of a Japanese manuscript with "1921ja" is to be translated into German, the ID of column A in the German Excel file should be "1921de". For language codes, see below `https://mt-auto-minhon-mlt.ucri.jgn-x.jp/content/help/detail.html?q_pid=FAQ_ETC` • Column B (Tweet)
• Enter the translated text.

Delivery Date
Friday, November 29, 2024

A.2 Complete Prompts

Instruction:
Determine if the sender of this Twitter message is exhibiting symptoms for each of the following: influenza, diarrhea, hay fever, cough, headache, fever, runny nose, cold. For each symptom, only answer either 0 or 1 for negative (no symptoms) or positive (has symptoms) respectively. Determination of symptoms is carried out based on the following rules:
• Cases where the symptom is expressed directly including mild symptoms are considered positive;
• A symptom can be labeled positive with indirect expressions of a symptom;
• If a symptom is mentioned but then also dismissed or denied, this information is regarded as positive;
• It is considered positive if someone or the user is still affected with such mild symptoms during recovery. However, if the symptoms are completely gone, it is considered negative;
• A symptom is positive even if the user expresses uncertainty regarding its cause;
• Since it is generally presumed that many patients may overlook symptoms or diseases due to insufficient medical knowledge, even suspicion of symptoms and diseases are recognized and labeled positive;
• Symptoms that disappeared completely are recognized and labeled negative. Note that we regarded and labeled positive when a user took medicine that could cause temporary recovery from a symptom;
• For cases that express expectation or process, indicated with words such as "if," "going," "if it is," etc., these should be labeled as negative;
• If the disease is mentioned merely as a topic rather than someone having it, these tweets should be labeled as negative. These include news, general theories, and advertisements;
• If the disease is mentioned in the context of a joke, these should be labeled as negative;
• The symptoms are only for humans;
• Symptoms are within 24 hours including today;
• The label for symptoms that occurred yesterday are dependent on the disease or symptom;
• Past Symptoms Including Two or More Days Ago considered as negative;
• Recent occurrence and Recurring Symptom that Still Persists considered as positive;
• We regard as a symptom in the vicinity and label positive regardless of living together or not (i.e. family members). We also label positive when a symptom was observed from hearsay;
• As for symptoms of people belonging to a specified group in the vicinity (school, club, etc.), we labeled them positive.
• Other cases, like symptoms belonging to blog friends, should be labeled as negative since it is difficult to determine their location.

Post:
A post in one of the seven studied languages.

Return the result STRICTLY as a JSON object with the symptoms as keys and the values as either

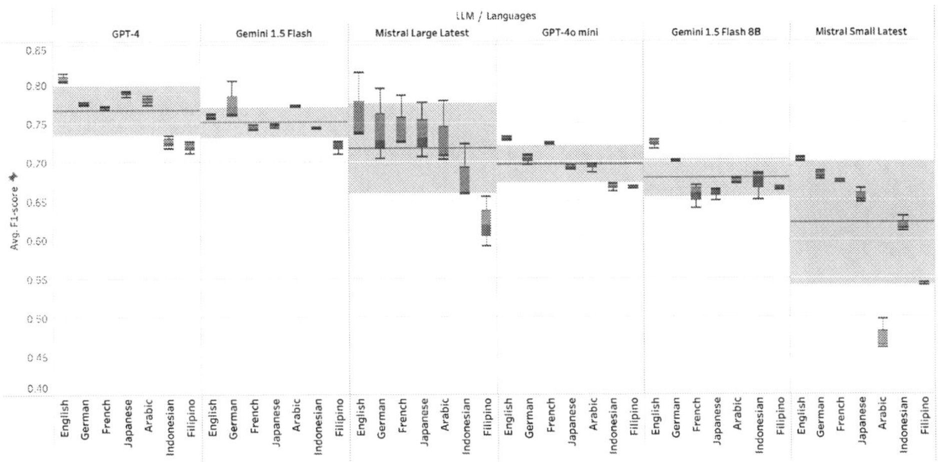

Figure 3: F1-Score Distribution of Each LLM Across Different Language.

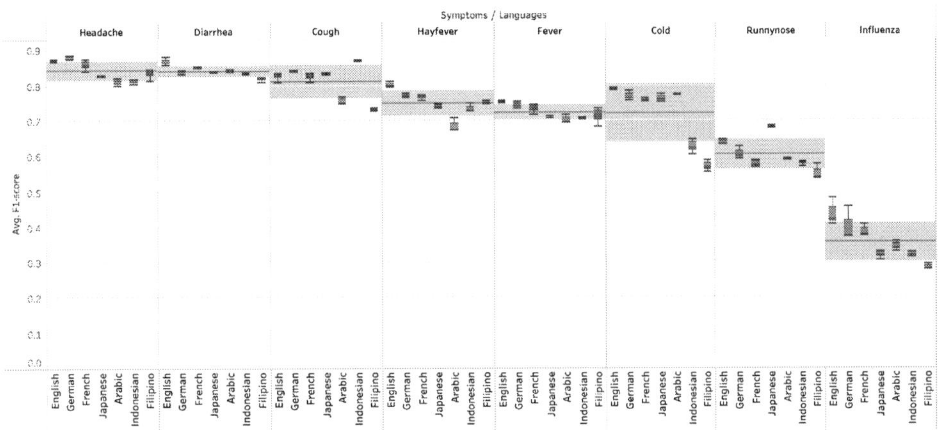

Figure 4: F1-Score Distribution of Each Symptom Across Different Language

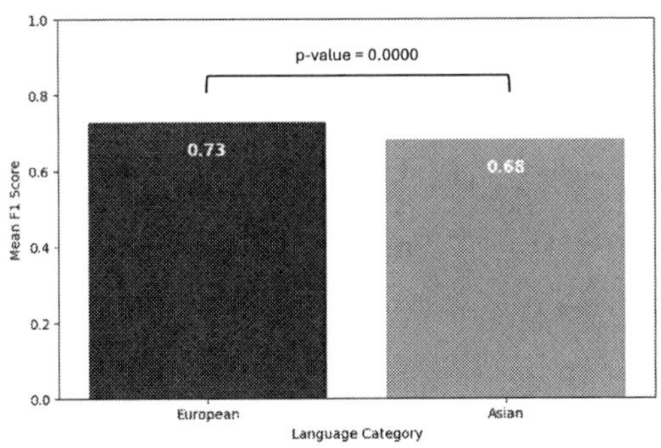

Figure 5: One-way ANOVA Test in Language Category

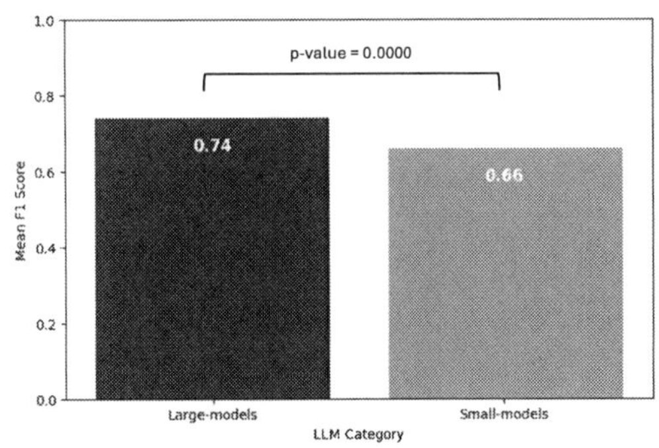

Figure 6: One-way ANOVA Test in LLM Category

0 or 1.

A.3 F1-Score Distribution of Each LLM Across Different Language

Figure 3 illustrates the F1 scores of each LLM across different languages, aiming to analyze per-

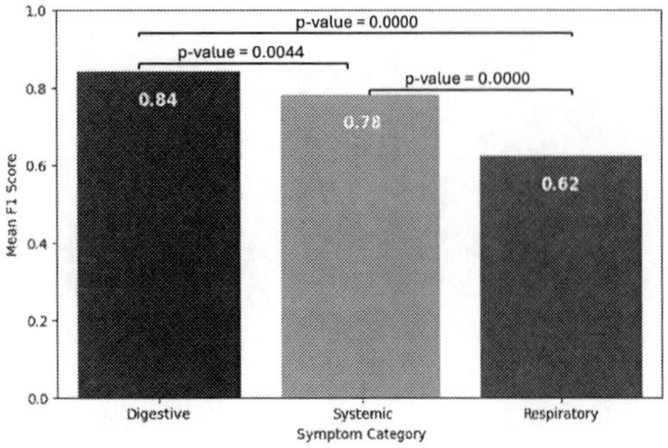

Figure 7: One-way ANOVA Test in Symptom Category

formance variations across languages.

A.4 F1-Score Distribution of Each Symptom Across Different Language

Figure 4 provides the F1-scores of each symptom in various languages, with the goal of examining performance differences across languages.

A.5 Statistical Testing on F1-Score for Language Categories

Figure 5 shows the mean comparison of F1-score for language categories to determine significant statistical differences.

A.6 Statistical Testing on F1-Score for LLM Categories

Statistical testing was presented in Figure 6 to compare average F1-score for LLM categories.

A.7 Statistical Testing on F1-Score for Symptom Categories

The comparison of mean F1 scores across symptoms was analyzed to identify statistically significant differences as presented in Figure 7.

When Scale Meets Diversity: Evaluating Language Models on Fine-Grained Multilingual Claim Verification

Hanna Shcharbakova[1],
hash00004@stud.uni-saarland.de
Tatiana Anikina[2], **Natalia Skachkova**[2], **Josef van Genabith**[1,2]
{tatiana.anikina, natalia.skachkova, josef.van_genabith}@dfki.de

[1]Saarland University
[2]German Research Center for Artificial Intelligence (DFKI)

Abstract

The rapid spread of multilingual misinformation requires robust automated fact verification systems capable of handling fine-grained veracity assessments across diverse languages. While large language models have shown remarkable capabilities across many NLP tasks, their effectiveness for multilingual claim verification with nuanced classification schemes remains understudied. We conduct a comprehensive evaluation of five state-of-the-art language models on the X-Fact dataset, which spans 25 languages with seven distinct veracity categories. Our experiments compare small language models (encoder-based XLM-R and mT5) with recent decoder-only LLMs (Llama 3.1, Qwen 2.5, Mistral Nemo) using both prompting and fine-tuning approaches.[1] Surprisingly, we find that XLM-R (270M parameters) substantially outperforms all tested LLMs (7-12B parameters), achieving 57.7% macro-F1 compared to the best LLM performance of 16.9%. This represents a 15.8% improvement over the previous state-of-the-art (41.9%), establishing new performance benchmarks for multilingual fact verification. Our analysis reveals problematic patterns in LLM behavior, including systematic difficulties in leveraging evidence and pronounced biases toward frequent categories in imbalanced data settings. These findings suggest that for fine-grained multilingual fact verification, smaller specialized models may be more effective than general-purpose large models, with important implications for practical deployment of fact-checking systems.

1 Introduction

The rapid spread of misinformation on the internet has become a critical challenge in today's digital age (Scheufele and Krause, 2019; Fung et al., 2022). With the increasing amount of false information being shared across different languages and platforms, automated fact verification systems have emerged as useful tools for maintaining information reliability.

The field of automated fact verification has seen significant progress in recent years, particularly with the advent of large language models and transformer-based architectures (Guo et al., 2022). However, most of these advancements have been predominantly focused on English-language content (Singhal et al., 2024; Dmonte et al., 2024), creating a significant gap in addressing misinformation in other languages.

Multilingual fact verification presents fundamental challenges for NLP (Dmonte et al., 2024; Wang et al., 2024; Zhang et al., 2024), particularly when employing fine-grained classification schemes that better capture the nuanced nature of truth assessment (Gupta and Srikumar, 2021; Pelrine et al., 2023; Mohtaj et al., 2024). While existing datasets and approaches employ various classification systems, classification beyond binary (*true/false*) and ternary (*true/false/other*) categories remains understudied across multiple languages.

The multi-category nature of this task bears conceptual similarity to Natural Language Inference (NLI) tasks (Poliak et al., 2018), though claim verification differs in its specific objectives. While NLI focuses on determining entailment relationships (*entails, contradicts, neutral*) between premise and hypothesis, our task requires assessing veracity across different distinct truth categories that reflect professional fact-checking standards.

In this work, we examine the performance of diverse model architectures and sizes on multilingual claim verification with fine-grained truth categories. We benchmark language model performance on the X-Fact dataset (Gupta and Srikumar, 2021) spanning multiple languages with seven distinct veracity categories, contrasting encoder-based model XLM-

[1]We consider a large language model (LLM) to be any model with more than 1B parameters, and correspondingly, small language model (SLM) to have less than 1B parameters.

Proceedings of the Eighth Fact Extraction and VERification Workshop (FEVER), pages 69–84
July 31, 2025 ©2025 Association for Computational Linguistics

R base (Conneau et al., 2020), encoder-decoder architecture mT5 base (Xue et al., 2021), and recent decoder-only models Llama 3.1 8B (Dubey et al., 2024), Qwen 2.5 7B (Yang et al., 2024), and Mistral Nemo 12B (Mistral AI Team, 2024).[2] For smaller models, we employ standard fine-tuning, while for larger models, we use both parameter-efficient fine-tuning with LoRA (Hu et al., 2022a) and carefully engineered few-shot prompting approaches. We evaluate models under two conditions: using claims alone and using claims with accompanying evidence text, which allows us to assess both inherent verification capabilities and evidence-augmented reasoning across models using a classification scheme that better reflects the nuanced assessments made by professional fact-checkers.

Our contributions include:

- We conduct comprehensive benchmarking of five state-of-the-art language models on the challenging seven-category multilingual X-Fact dataset, achieving new state-of-the-art results with a 15.8% improvement in macro-F1 score over previous best performance reported by Gupta and Srikumar (2021). We reveal a substantial performance gap between encoder-based and decoder-only architectures despite the latter's greater size and general capabilities.

- We provide analysis of model behaviors and error patterns across architectures, identifying several factors that appear to influence multilingual fact verification performance. These observations may help inform future research on verification approaches for diverse languages.

2 Related Work

2.1 Multilingual Fact Verification Datasets

While a substantial portion of fact verification research has centered on English-language content (Guo et al., 2022; Singhal et al., 2024; Dmonte et al., 2024), several datasets have emerged to address the multilingual dimensions of this challenge. These datasets vary significantly in size, language coverage, and labeling schemes.

Multilingual datasets include FakeCovid (Shahi and Nandini, 2020), covering 5K claims across 40 languages, and MM-COVID (Li et al., 2020), which provides 11K articles in English, Spanish, Portuguese, Hindi, French, and Italian. The Multi-Claim dataset (Pikuliak et al., 2023) contains 28K social media posts in 27 languages that can be leveraged for fact verification tasks. FbMultiLingMisinfo (Barnabò et al., 2022) offers 7K news articles spanning 37 languages, while NewsPolyML (Mohtaj et al., 2024) includes 32K claims across English, German, French, Spanish, and Italian. The X-Fact dataset (Gupta and Srikumar, 2021) provides 31K claims from fact-checking websites in 25 languages across 11 language families.

Labeling approaches range from binary classification (Li et al., 2020; Barnabò et al., 2022) to three-category systems (Nørregaard and Derczynski, 2021; Hu et al., 2022b; Ullrich et al., 2023) and more complex multi-class schemes including 11 categories in FakeCovid (Shahi and Nandini, 2020), 4 in NewsPolyML (Mohtaj et al., 2024), and 7 in X-Fact (Gupta and Srikumar, 2021). The diversity of annotation schemes, while enabling finer-grained veracity assessments, complicates cross-dataset training and evaluation for cross-lingual verification.

2.2 Methods for Fact Verification

The task of claim verification has evolved significantly with various methodological approaches emerging to tackle the complexities of determining claim veracity. Transformer-based architectures (Devlin et al., 2019) brought substantial advancements to fact verification. Gupta and Srikumar (2021) evaluated mBERT-based models on the X-Fact dataset spanning 25 languages with 7-way classification. Their best model achieved an F1 score of 41.9% on the in-domain test set, though performance dropped to 16.2% F1 on out-of-domain and 16.7% F1 on zero-shot test sets, highlighting cross-lingual generalization challenges.

Recent research has explored large language models for fact verification using various approaches. For prompting-based methods, Cao et al. (2023) investigated different prompting strategies for fact-checking, finding that carefully crafted prompts with explicit instructions about expected output formats and task definitions significantly improved performance. Hu et al. (2023) found that increasing few-shot examples beyond a certain threshold provides substantial gains, suggesting a threshold effect. Self-consistency methods

[2]Further details on the specific model versions are provided in Appendix A.

using majority voting from multiple LLM runs improved performance, while self-refinement strategies where models iteratively refine their answers showed gains over standard approaches.

Chain of Thought (CoT) approaches have shown promising results by enabling LLMs to articulate reasoning processes before reaching conclusions (Wei et al., 2022). Hu et al. (2023) found that CoT prompting significantly improved performance across all tested models on English data compared to standard prompting.

Pelrine et al. (2023) compared GPT-4 against traditional approaches across multiple datasets. For binary classification on English LIAR (Wang, 2017), GPT-4 variants outperformed traditional models like ConvBERT (Jiang et al., 2020) and BERT. However, in multi-way classification tasks, performance declined significantly with traditional models like DeBERTa (He et al., 2021) showing better results. The same study demonstrated GPT-4's cross-lingual capabilities on CT-FAN-22 (Shahi et al., 2021), with GPT-4 substantially outperforming RoBERTa-L (Liu et al., 2019) on English multiway classification.

Cekinel et al. (2024) found that fine-tuning LLaMA-2 models (Touvron et al., 2023) on Turkish language data outperformed cross-lingual transfer methods for fact verification. Their fine-tuned model achieved strong performance on binary classification, while cross-lingual prompting with English data showed improvements but proved less effective than language-specific fine-tuning. Mohtaj et al. (2024) evaluated multiple models on the NewsPolyML dataset spanning five European languages with four veracity categories. Interestingly, mBERT achieved the highest performance, suggesting that model size does not necessarily correlate with performance in multilingual fact verification tasks.

3 Dataset

For our experiments, we use the X-Fact dataset (Gupta and Srikumar, 2021). This dataset was selected due to several advantages over other multilingual fact verification resources. X-Fact encompasses a broad range of topics from verified fact-checking websites, making it more representative of real-world misinformation challenges compared to specialized datasets like FakeCovid (Shahi and Nandini, 2020) that focus solely on COVID-19 related claims. Unlike datasets derived from social media platforms such as FbMultiLingMisinfo (Barnabò et al., 2022), X-Fact provides ready-to-use data without requiring access to platform-specific APIs, ensuring reproducibility of research findings.

X-Fact comprises 31,189 claims across 25 languages from 11 language families, including Indo-European, Afro-Asiatic, Austronesian, Kartvelian, Dravidian, and Turkic. The dataset was carefully constructed by identifying reliable fact-checking sources from the International Fact-Checking Network[3] and Duke Reporter's Lab[4], excluding websites that conduct fact-checks in English to avoid overlap with existing datasets. Each claim in X-Fact is accompanied by up to 5 pieces of evidence extracted from fact-checking articles, with an average of 4.75 non-empty evidence pieces per claim. The dataset also includes valuable metadata such as the language of the claim and evidence, the fact-checking site where the claim was derived from, links to the evidence where they were published, claim date, review date, and claimant information. Examples of claims, corresponding evidence, and associated metadata can be found in Appendix B.

To ensure consistent evaluation across different fact-checking standards, the dataset employs a standardized seven-label classification scheme: *true, mostly true, partly true/misleading, mostly false, false, complicated/hard to categorize*, and *other*. This fine-grained approach provides a more nuanced assessment of claim veracity compared to less fine-grained classification schemes used in many other datasets.

The dataset is divided into multiple subsets designed to evaluate different aspects of model performance (see Table 1). The training set contains 19,079 claims across 13 languages, while the development set comprises 2,535 claims spanning 13 languages. For testing, X-Fact provides three separate subsets: an in-domain test set with 3,826 claims from the same languages and sources as the training data; an out-of-domain test set containing 2,368 claims from the same languages but different sources; and a zero-shot test set featuring 3,381 claims from 12 languages not present in the training data. This evaluation framework supports a thorough assessment of models' generalization capabilities across both domains and languages.

The label distribution in the X-Fact exhibits

[3]https://www.poynter.org/ifcn/.

[4]https://reporterslab.org/.

Dataset Subset	# Claims	# Languages
Training	19079	13
Development	2535	13
In-domain	3826	13
Out-of-domain	2368	5
zero-shot	3381	12

Table 1: Overview of the X-Fact dataset subsets.

significant variation across all subsets (see Figure 1). The *false* label dominates the training set with 7,515 instances (39.4%), followed by *partly true/misleading* with 4,359 instances (22.8%). The least represented label is *other* with only 576 instances (1.9%).

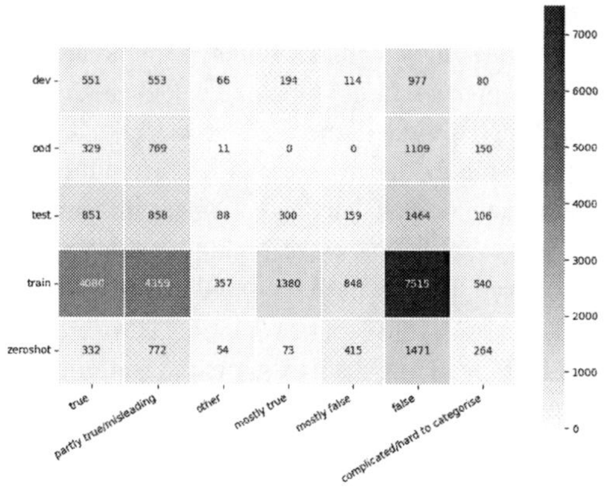

Figure 1: Distribution of data in X-Fact by label across subsets.

The language distribution also shows substantial variation across different subsets (see Figure 2). Portuguese dominates the training set with 5,601 claims (29.4%), followed by Indonesian with 2,231 claims (11.7%) and Arabic with 1,567 claims (8.2%). Serbian has the lowest representation with only 624 claims (3.3%).

These imbalances may potentially impact model learning, particularly for cross-lingual transfer, and present additional challenges for models to learn fine-grained veracity categories.

4 Experiments

4.1 Experimental Setup

Our evaluation focuses on benchmarking different language model architectures on the multilingual fact verification task, using X-Fact's seven-category classification scheme across multiple languages. We evaluate both small language models (SLMs, <1B parameters) and large language models (LLMs, >1B parameters) to determine their relative effectiveness for fine-grained multilingual verification. Table 2 provides an overview of the models evaluated in this study.

We selected these models based on their strong multilingual capabilities and architectural diversity. XLM-R was chosen for its robust pre-training on 100 languages and encoder-only architecture that has proven effective for classification tasks. MT5 represents the encoder-decoder paradigm, offering a different architectural approach while maintaining strong multilingual capabilities across 101 languages. For LLMs, we selected Llama 3.1 8B, Qwen 2.5 7B, and Mistral Nemo 12B to represent state-of-the-art decoder-only architectures with varying degrees of multilingual support.

We prioritized open-source models with moderate parameter sizes to ensure reproducibility and facilitate deployment in resource-constrained environments. This selection allows us to evaluate whether sophisticated reasoning in current LLMs transfers effectively to multilingual fact verification compared to smaller, specialized architectures like XLM-R.

Model	# Par.	# Lang.	Architecture
XLM-R	270 M	100	Encoder-only
mT5	580 M	101	Encoder-decoder
Llama 3.1	8 B	8	Decoder-only
Qwen 2.5	7 B	29	Decoder-only
Mistral Nemo	12 B	11	Decoder-only

Table 2: Models evaluated on multilingual fact verification using the X-Fact dataset. # Par. is the number of parameters and # Lang. is the number of languages supported by each model.

For the SLMs, we performed fine-tuning experiments, while for LLMs, we explored both direct prompting and parameter-efficient fine-tuning using LoRA. The models' implementation details can be found in the Appendix C.

4.2 Small Language Models Experiments

For XLM-R and mT5, we conducted two types of fine-tuning experiments:

- **Full Model Fine-tuning:** We performed complete fine-tuning of the models, allowing all parameters to be updated during training.

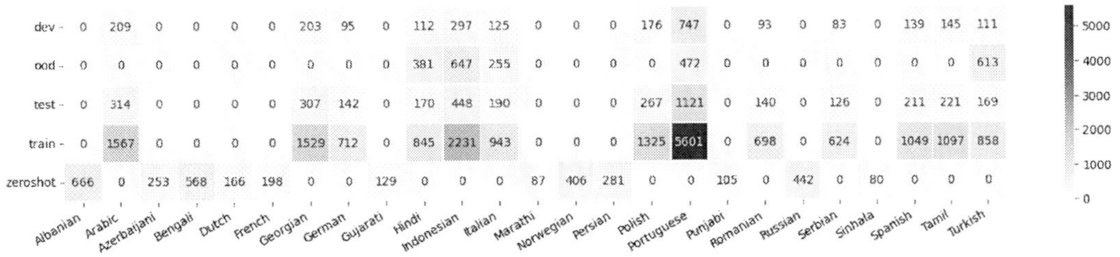

Figure 2: Distribution of data in X-Fact by language across subsets.

- **Classification Head Fine-tuning:** We fine-tuned only the classification head while keeping the base model frozen.

For both approaches, we provided the models with the claim text and evidence as input. We did not conduct experiments using only claim text without evidence, as preliminary experiments confirmed the X-Fact paper's finding that claim-only setups yield worse performance.

4.3 Large Language Models Experiments

For LLMs, we explored both few-shot prompting and parameter-efficient fine-tuning approaches. We evaluated each model in two input configurations: (1) claim-only, providing only the claim text; and (2) claim with evidence, providing both claim and evidence text. Our experimental setup included the following approaches:

- **Few-shot prompting:** We developed 7-shot prompts containing examples for each veracity category to guide prediction without training. Each prompt included clear instructions, category definitions, and was tested in both claim-only and claim+evidence variants.

- **LoRA fine-tuning:** We implemented parameter-efficient fine-tuning using LoRA for both claim-only and claim+evidence configurations.

The optimized prompt template is provided in the Appendix E.

5 Results

5.1 SLMs Performance

Table 3 presents the macro-F1 scores for small language models across three evaluation subsets. XLM-R with full fine-tuning achieves the highest performance with 57.7% macro-F1 on the test set, substantially outperforming the previous state-of-the-art mBERT baseline (41.9%) by 15.8% reported in Gupta and Srikumar (2021). XLM-R also demonstrates superior cross-domain and cross-lingual generalization, maintaining relatively strong performance across all evaluation subsets.

Model	Test	OOD	Zero-shot
mBERT (baseline)	41.9	16.2	16.7
XLM-R frozen	51.4	40.8	41.3
XLM-R	**57.7**	**47.6**	**43.2**
mT5	47.6	22.2	19.2

Table 3: SLMs performance on the X-Fact dataset (macro-F1 scores). XLM-R frozen refers to fine-tuning the classification head only. mBERT performance is derived from (Gupta and Srikumar, 2021).

MT5 reaches 47.6% macro-F1 on the test set but shows poor generalization to out-of-domain (22.2%) and zero-shot (19.2%) scenarios. The performance gap between XLM-R and mT5 widens significantly on these evaluation sets, indicating that XLM-R's encoder-only architecture may be better suited for multilingual fact verification tasks.

5.2 LLMs Performance

Table 4 presents LLMs' results across different configurations. Despite their significantly larger size (7-12B parameters), all LLMs substantially underperform compared to SLMs. The best LLM configuration (Qwen claim-only fine-tuning) achieves only 16.9% macro-F1 on the test set - 40.8% points below XLM-R. For visualizations of models' performance across different evaluation subsets, refer to Appendix D.

Among the LLMs, Qwen 2.5 consistently demonstrates the best performance across most configurations. The model achieves its highest macro-F1 score of 16.9% with claim-only fine-tuning on the test set, compared to 15.9% with claim+evidence fine-tuning and 11.4%-12.7% with

Method	Few-shot				LoRA-based Finetune			
	Claim+Evidence		Claim Only		Claim+Evidence		Claim Only	
	macro	micro	macro	micro	macro	micro	macro	micro
Qwen 2.5								
Test	12.7	24.9	11.4	18.6	15.9	**39.5**	**16.9**	29.6
OOD	13.0	29.6	11.2	27.4	**15.1**	**47.1**	11.1	31.3
Zero-shot	10.9	18.9	12.9	23.9	**15.4**	**35.8**	11.7	24.5
Mistral Nemo								
Test	**14.8**	30.8	8.5	23.4	14.6	**31.9**	10.3	20.2
OOD	**16.1**	**42.6**	9.7	36.6	12.1	34.2	9.6	27.1
Zero-shot	**15.1**	28.7	10.6	**29.6**	12.9	25.7	8.2	15.6
Llama 3.1								
Test	14.0	**32.0**	10.8	18.4	14.3	27.6	**15.5**	30.5
OOD	13.3	**41.2**	8.7	21.2	11.2	27.1	**13.5**	33.2
Zero-shot	**12.9**	**30.1**	8.7	17.6	9.6	17.5	12.1	29.4

Table 4: LLMs performance on the X-Fact dataset (macro-F1 and micro-F1 scores). Bold values indicate the highest macro- and micro-F1 scores for each model-subset combination.

few-shot prompting. LoRA-based fine-tuning consistently improves performance over few-shot inference across all models and configurations, with Qwen 2.5 showing the largest gains.

The impact of adding evidence to claims varies significantly across models and methods. For Qwen 2.5, fine-tuning with claim-only (16.9%) outperforms claim+evidence (15.9%) on the test set, showing a consistent pattern across all evaluation sets. In contrast, Mistral Nemo generally performs better with claim+evidence input in few-shot settings (14.8% vs 8.5% on test set) but shows mixed results with fine-tuning. Llama 3.1 demonstrates the most inconsistent performance across different configurations. While it achieves reasonable performance on the test set (15.5% macro-F1 with claim-only fine-tuning), it shows the largest performance drop on the zero-shot set, with the worst configuration (claim+evidence fine-tuning) falling to 9.6% macro-F1.

LoRA Fine-tuning and Few-shot Prompting. Fine-tuning consistently improves performance over few-shot prompting across all models. Qwen shows the most substantial improvement (from 12.7% in few-shot with claim+evidence setting to to 15.9% in fine-tuning with claim+evidence setting) on the test set. Mistral Nemo shows minimal differences between methods, with some configurations favoring few-shot prompting (16.1% vs 12.1% on out-of-domain with claim+evidence). Llama 3.1 generally benefits from fine-tuning, improving from 10.8% to 15.5% in the claim-only configuration on the test set.

Performance Across Evaluation Subsets. All models show declining performance from test to out-of-domain and zero-shot sets when fine-tuning. Qwen 2.5 maintains stable performance, with the sharpest drop by 5.2% from test to zero-shot. Mistral Nemo shows the least variation, performing best on out-of-domain (16.1%). Llama 3.1 exhibits the largest degradation, dropping from 15.5% on test to 9.6% on zero-shot in comparable configurations. Refer to the Appendix F for visualizations comparing LLMs performance across these evaluation subsets. For a combined view of claim+evidence configurations across all LLMs, refer to Appendix G, which directly compares the macro-F1 scores across evaluation subsets and highlights the best performing method for each model.

Macro vs. Micro F1 Score. The substantial gap between micro- and macro-F1 scores is consistent across all LLMs, with the largest gaps observed in fine-tuning configurations. Qwen 2.5 achieves 39.5% micro-F1 compared to 15.9% macro-F1 in its claim+evidence fine-tuning on the test set, a gap of 23.6%. Similarly, Mistral Nemo shows a 17.2% gap in its claim+evidence fine-tuning configuration on the test set.

Few-shot configurations generally show smaller gaps. For instance, Qwen's few-shot claim+evidence on the test set shows an 12.2% gap, while its fine-tuning equivalent shows a 23.6% gap. This pattern holds across all models where fine-tuning configurations consistently exhibit gaps ranging from 15 to 32 percentage points, while few-shot configurations typically show gaps between 8 to 20 percentage points. The visualizations depicting the performance gaps between macro- and micro-F1 scores across LLMs can be found in Appendix H.

6 Discussion

Our comprehensive evaluation across 25 languages reveals several important findings that advance our understanding of how different architectures handle fine-grained veracity classification across languages.

Performance Gap Between Model Types. The most striking finding is XLM-R's superiority over all tested LLMs, achieving 57.7% macro-F1 compared to the best LLM performance of 16.9% from Qwen 2.5. This performance difference is particularly noteworthy given that LLMs contain many more parameters than XLM-R. XLM-R was pre-trained on 100 languages using a masked language modeling objective that may align well with classification tasks, whereas LLMs use next-token prediction objectives optimized for text generation. These differences in pre-training approaches and objectives may contribute to the observed performance gap.

While our comparison involves different training methodologies (full fine-tuning for SLMs versus LoRA for LLMs), it is important to note that even when comparing more similar approaches, substantial performance gaps persist. Our frozen XLM-R configuration, which only updates the classification head similar to LoRA's parameter-efficient approach, still achieves 51.4% macro-F1 compared to the best LLM performance of 16.9%. This suggests that the performance differences extend beyond training methodology. Future work should include detailed per-label performance analysis to better understand model biases and identify which veracity categories prove most challenging across different architectures.

Evidence Integration Patterns. A clear pattern emerges in how LLMs handle evidence: surprisingly, incorporating additional evidence often does not enhance performance and can even lead to worse results. For instance, Qwen's claim-only fine-tuning (16.9%) outperforms its claim+evidence configuration (15.9%). This pattern persists across all Llama 3.1 configurations, suggesting systematic difficulties in leveraging additional context for verification decisions.

We hypothesize several factors that may contribute to this counterintuitive finding. First, the architectural limitations of decoder-only LLMs may hinder effective evidence integration. Unlike XLM-R's bidirectional attention that allows simultaneous consideration of all evidence elements against all claim components, LLMs' autoregressive attention can only consider previous tokens. This sequential processing creates a tendency to forget or ignore earlier information as sequences become longer, making balanced evidence evaluation more challenging.

Second, our input formatting may have contributed to this issue. While we used clear demarcation between claims and evidence in our prompts (as shown in Appendix E), we did not implement more sophisticated structuring techniques that might have helped LLMs better distinguish and compare these elements. Context window size was treated as a hyperparameter in our experiments, with LLMs tested at both 2048 and 4096 tokens, while SLMs were evaluated with context windows ranging from 256 to 512 tokens. With evidence pieces having median lengths of 25-35 words each and approximately 4.75 pieces per claim on average, the evidence was fully accommodated within the context windows of all models. Therefore, evidence truncation was not a contributing factor to the observed performance patterns.

This finding is particularly significant because evidence-based reasoning is fundamental to reliable fact verification. The fact that simply providing claims yields better results than including supporting evidence indicates that current LLMs may not be effectively utilizing the additional information or may be getting confused by the increased input complexity.

Fine-Grained Classification Challenges. The severe data imbalances in X-Fact likely contributes to the observed performance patterns. The dominance of *false* and *partly true/misleading* categories creates a challenging environment for models to learn effective representations for less frequent but equally important categories. This imbalance effect is aggravated in the seven-category setting, where models must not only distinguish between *true* and *false* but also navigate subtle gradations of partial truth. Furthermore, the language distribution imbalance (Portuguese comprising 29.4% of training data while Serbian represents only 3.3%) likely impacts cross-lingual performance. Models may develop language-specific biases that hinder their ability to generalize across languages, particularly to those underrepresented in the training data.

The substantial disparity between micro- and macro-F1 scores across all LLMs reveals critical limitations in handling nuanced veracity categories. The micro-F1 scores being consistently higher than macro-F1 scores confirms that performance is driven primarily by accuracy on frequent categories, while rare categories remain poorly predicted. This pattern is particularly pronounced in LLMs, suggesting they may be more influenced by biases in the training data than the fine-tuned XLM-R.

Cross-Lingual and Cross-Domain Generalization. Performance degradation across evaluation subsets is consistent across all models but varies in magnitude. XLM-R demonstrates the most robust cross-lingual transfer, while LLMs show steeper drops. The relatively stable performance of XLM-R on unseen languages suggests that its multilingual pre-training provides effective cross-lingual representations for fact verification task. The sharper declines observed in LLMs may indicate that their multilingual capabilities are less robust when faced with languages not well represented in their training data or when transferring across different fact-checking domains.

Even when comparing XLM-R's frozen configuration (which only updates the classification head, similar to LoRA's parameter-efficient approach), we still observe substantial outperformance over LLMs (51.4% vs 16.9% best LLM performance). This suggests that the performance differences may stem not only from the fine-tuning methodology but also from other factors such as architectural advantages of encoder-based models for this specific task or the amount and quality of the pre-training data available in different languages.

7 Conclusion and Future Work

This work presents a comprehensive evaluation of diverse language model architectures (small and large; encoder, encoder-decoder, and decoder-only) on multilingual fact verification using the challenging seven-category X-Fact dataset. Our findings reveal several key insights that advance understanding of how different models handle fine-grained veracity classification across languages.

Fully fine-tuned XLM-R emerges as the clear winner, achieving 57.7% macro-F1 on the test set – a 15.8% improvement over previous state-of-the-art. Despite having significantly fewer parameters, XLM-R substantially outperforms all tested LLMs, with the best LLM (Qwen 2.5) reaching only 16.9% macro-F1. The magnitude of this performance gap persists even when comparing lightweight fine-tuning approaches (e.g., frozen XLM-R with a trained classification head: 51.4% vs best LLM: 16.9%), suggesting that factors beyond training methodology contribute to the observed differences. However, the exact nature of these factors requires further investigation.

Our analysis reveals problematic patterns in LLM behavior, particularly their inability to effectively utilize additional evidence. Models often perform worse when provided with claim-evidence pairs compared to claims alone, indicating systematic challenges in leveraging external information for verification decisions. This limitation is particularly problematic given that evidence-based reasoning is fundamental to reliable fact-checking, though the underlying causes of this behavior need deeper exploration.

The significant disparity between micro- and macro-F1 scores across the models reveals the challenge of handling imbalanced datasets with fine-grained categories. Models tend to learn shortcuts based on frequent categories while struggling with rare but equally important veracity labels. This bias appears more pronounced in LLMs, indicating they may be more vulnerable to dataset imbalances than smaller models that have been carefully fine-tuned.

These findings have important implications for the development of multilingual fact verification systems. While LLMs show promise for many NLP tasks, our results suggest that for fine-grained fact verification across languages, smaller specialized models may provide better performance while requiring fewer computational resources.

8 Limitations

Our study has several limitations that should be considered when interpreting the results.

Training Methodology Differences. Our comparison involves fundamentally different training approaches: XLM-R undergoes full fine-tuning with all parameters being updated, while LLMs utilize LoRA that freezes the majority of the original model parameters. This methodological difference could significantly impact the ability of LLMs to adapt to the specific task requirements and may partially explain the observed performance gaps.

Prompt Engineering Constraints. Our prompt engineering approach may not be equally optimal across all languages in our multilingual evaluation. While we developed carefully engineered 7-shot prompts with examples balanced across the seven veracity categories, our prompt design focused primarily on ensuring representative coverage of each label rather than optimizing for linguistic diversity. This approach may have favored certain languages or language families that were better represented in our example selection. Language-specific prompt optimization could potentially narrow the performance gap, though this would require substantial additional engineering effort for each target language.

Evidence Interpretation Limitations. Given the relatively small performance differences between claim-only and claim+evidence configurations, we cannot definitively conclude that LLMs are incapable of evidence utilization. The limited performance gap may simply reflect the inherent difficulty of the task or limitations in our evaluation approach. It's possible that with more sophisticated prompting strategies, larger datasets, or alternative evidence presentation formats, LLMs might demonstrate improved evidence integration capabilities. The evidence quality in the X-Fact dataset may also play a role, as analysis reveals that search snippets may not always contain sufficient information for accurate verification (Gupta and Srikumar, 2021).

Practical Computing Considerations. Our comparison between fully fine-tuned XLM-R and LoRA-adapted LLMs reflects realistic scenario with limited computational resources. Full fine-tuning of billion-parameter models requires substantial computational resources that are often prohibitive for many researchers. In contrast, parameter-efficient methods like LoRA can be applied with modest computational resources, making them the more practical choice for deploying large models. This comparison addresses a critical question: given realistic computational constraints, which approach provides better performance for multilingual fact verification? Our results demonstrate that a smaller, fully fine-tuned model can significantly outperform much larger models adapted with parameter-efficient methods, suggesting that for specific tasks like multilingual fine-grained verification, specialized smaller models may be preferable to general-purpose large models.

Output Analysis and Reproducibility. To enhance reproducibility and enable further investigation of the observed performance patterns, we make our LLM outputs available in the repository[5], including detailed predictions and model responses. A comprehensive analysis of these outputs, including confusion matrices and detailed error patterns that could reveal potential parsing issues or systematic biases, represents important future work that could provide deeper insights into the substantial performance differences observed between model architectures.

9 Acknowledgments

This project was supported by the German Federal Ministry of Research, Technology and Space (BMFTR) as part of the project TRAILS (01IW24005), which provided funding for Josef van Genabith and Tatiana Anikina. This work was also co-funded by the Erasmus Mundus Masters Programme in Language and Communication Technologies (EU grant no. 2019-1508).

References

Giorgio Barnabò, Federico Siciliano, Carlos Castillo, Stefano Leonardi, Preslav Nakov, Giovanni Da San Martino, and Fabrizio Silvestri. 2022. Fbmultilingmisinfo: Challenging large-scale multilingual benchmark for misinformation detection. In *2022 International Joint Conference on Neural Networks (IJCNN)*, pages 1–8. IEEE.

Han Cao, Lingwei Wei, Mengyang Chen, Wei Zhou, and Songlin Hu. 2023. Are large language models good fact checkers: A preliminary study. *Preprint*, arXiv:2311.17355.

Recep Firat Cekinel, Pinar Karagoz, and Çağrı Çöltekin. 2024. Cross-lingual learning vs. low-resource fine-tuning: A case study with fact-checking in Turkish. In *Proceedings of the 2024 Joint International Conference on Computational Linguistics, Language Resources and Evaluation (LREC-COLING 2024)*, pages 4127–4142, Torino, Italia. ELRA and ICCL.

Alexis Conneau, Kartikay Khandelwal, Naman Goyal, Vishrav Chaudhary, Guillaume Wenzek, Francisco Guzmán, Edouard Grave, Myle Ott, Luke Zettlemoyer, and Veselin Stoyanov. 2020. Unsupervised cross-lingual representation learning at scale. In *Proceedings of the 58th Annual Meeting of the Association for Computational Linguistics*, pages 8440–8451, Online. Association for Computational Linguistics.

[5]https://github.com/Aniezka/xfact-fever.

Michael Han Daniel Han and Unsloth team. 2023. Unsloth.

Jacob Devlin, Ming-Wei Chang, Kenton Lee, and Kristina Toutanova. 2019. BERT: Pre-training of deep bidirectional transformers for language understanding. In *Proceedings of the 2019 Conference of the North American Chapter of the Association for Computational Linguistics: Human Language Technologies, Volume 1 (Long and Short Papers)*, pages 4171–4186, Minneapolis, Minnesota. Association for Computational Linguistics.

Alphaeus Dmonte, Roland Oruche, Marcos Zampieri, Prasad Calyam, and Isabelle Augenstein. 2024. Claim verification in the age of large language models: A survey. *arXiv preprint arXiv:2408.14317*.

Abhimanyu Dubey, Abhinav Jauhri, Abhinav Pandey, Abhishek Kadian, Ahmad Al-Dahle, Aiesha Letman, Akhil Mathur, Alan Schelten, Amy Yang, Angela Fan, and 1 others. 2024. The llama 3 herd of models. *arXiv preprint arXiv:2407.21783*.

Yi R Fung, Kung-Hsiang Huang, Preslav Nakov, and Heng Ji. 2022. The battlefront of combating misinformation and coping with media bias. In *Proceedings of the 28th ACM SIGKDD Conference on Knowledge Discovery and Data Mining*, pages 4790–4791.

Zhijiang Guo, Michael Schlichtkrull, and Andreas Vlachos. 2022. A survey on automated fact-checking. *Transactions of the Association for Computational Linguistics*, 10:178–206.

Ashim Gupta and Vivek Srikumar. 2021. X-fact: A new benchmark dataset for multilingual fact checking. In *Proceedings of the 59th Annual Meeting of the Association for Computational Linguistics and the 11th International Joint Conference on Natural Language Processing (Volume 2: Short Papers)*, pages 675–682, Online. Association for Computational Linguistics.

Pengcheng He, Xiaodong Liu, Jianfeng Gao, and Weizhu Chen. 2021. Deberta: Decoding-enhanced bert with disentangled attention. In *International Conference on Learning Representations*.

Edward J. Hu, Yelong Shen, Phillip Wallis, Zeyuan Allen-Zhu, Yuanzhi Li, Shean Wang, Lu Wang, and Weizhu Chen. 2022a. Lora: Low-rank adaptation of large language models. In *ICLR*. OpenReview.net.

Xuming Hu, Junzhe Chen, Xiaochuan Li, Yufei Guo, Lijie Wen, Philip S. Yu, and Zhijiang Guo. 2023. Do large language models know about facts? *Preprint*, arXiv:2310.05177.

Xuming Hu, Zhijiang Guo, GuanYu Wu, Aiwei Liu, Lijie Wen, and Philip Yu. 2022b. CHEF: A pilot Chinese dataset for evidence-based fact-checking. In *Proceedings of the 2022 Conference of the North American Chapter of the Association for Computational Linguistics: Human Language Technologies*, pages 3362–3376, Seattle, United States. Association for Computational Linguistics.

Zi-Hang Jiang, Weihao Yu, Daquan Zhou, Yunpeng Chen, Jiashi Feng, and Shuicheng Yan. 2020. Convbert: Improving bert with span-based dynamic convolution. In *Advances in Neural Information Processing Systems*, volume 33, pages 12837–12848. Curran Associates, Inc.

Yichuan Li, Bohan Jiang, Kai Shu, and Huan Liu. 2020. Mm-covid: A multilingual and multimodal data repository for combating covid-19 disinformation. *Preprint*, arXiv:2011.04088.

Yinhan Liu, Myle Ott, Naman Goyal, Jingfei Du, Mandar Joshi, Danqi Chen, Omer Levy, Mike Lewis, Luke Zettlemoyer, and Veselin Stoyanov. 2019. Roberta: A robustly optimized bert pretraining approach. *arXiv preprint arXiv:1907.11692*.

Mistral AI Team. 2024. Mistral nemo. `https://mistral.ai/en/news/mistral-nemo`. Accessed: 14-Feb-2025.

Salar Mohtaj, Ata Nizamoglu, Premtim Sahitaj, Vera Schmitt, Charlott Jakob, and Sebastian Möller. 2024. Newspolyml: Multi-lingual european news fake assessment dataset. In *Proceedings of the 3rd ACM International Workshop on Multimedia AI against Disinformation*, MAD '24, page 82–90, New York, NY, USA. Association for Computing Machinery.

Jeppe Nørregaard and Leon Derczynski. 2021. DanFEVER: claim verification dataset for Danish. In *Proceedings of the 23rd Nordic Conference on Computational Linguistics (NoDaLiDa)*, pages 422–428, Reykjavik, Iceland (Online). Linköping University Electronic Press, Sweden.

Kellin Pelrine, Anne Imouza, Camille Thibault, Meilina Reksoprodjo, Caleb Gupta, Joel Christoph, Jean-François Godbout, and Reihaneh Rabbany. 2023. Towards reliable misinformation mitigation: Generalization, uncertainty, and GPT-4. In *Proceedings of the 2023 Conference on Empirical Methods in Natural Language Processing*, pages 6399–6429, Singapore. Association for Computational Linguistics.

Matúš Pikuliak, Ivan Srba, Robert Moro, Timo Hromadka, Timotej Smoleň, Martin Melišek, Ivan Vykopal, Jakub Simko, Juraj Podroužek, and Maria Bielikova. 2023. Multilingual previously fact-checked claim retrieval. In *Proceedings of the 2023 Conference on Empirical Methods in Natural Language Processing*, pages 16477–16500, Singapore. Association for Computational Linguistics.

Adam Poliak, Jason Naradowsky, Aparajita Haldar, Rachel Rudinger, and Benjamin Van Durme. 2018. Hypothesis only baselines in natural language inference. In *Proceedings of the Seventh Joint Conference on Lexical and Computational Semantics*, pages 180–191, New Orleans, Louisiana. Association for Computational Linguistics.

Dietram A Scheufele and Nicole M Krause. 2019. Science audiences, misinformation, and fake news. *Proceedings of the National Academy of Sciences*, 116(16):7662–7669.

Gautam Kishore Shahi and Durgesh Nandini. 2020. *FakeCovid- A Multilingual Cross-domain Fact Check News Dataset for COVID-19*. ICWSM.

Gautam Kishore Shahi, Julia Maria Struß, and Thomas Mandl. 2021. Overview of the clef-2021 checkthat! lab task 3 on fake news detection. *Working Notes of CLEF*.

Aryan Singhal, Thomas Law, Coby Kassner, Ayushman Gupta, Evan Duan, Aviral Damle, and Ryan Luo Li. 2024. Multilingual fact-checking using LLMs. In *Proceedings of the Third Workshop on NLP for Positive Impact*, pages 13–31, Miami, Florida, USA. Association for Computational Linguistics.

Hugo Touvron, Louis Martin, Kevin Stone, Peter Albert, Amjad Almahairi, Yasmine Babaei, Nikolay Bashlykov, Soumya Batra, Prajjwal Bhargava, Shruti Bhosale, Dan Bikel, Lukas Blecher, Cristian Canton Ferrer, Moya Chen, Guillem Cucurull, David Esiobu, Jude Fernandes, Jeremy Fu, Wenyin Fu, and 49 others. 2023. Llama 2: Open foundation and fine-tuned chat models. *Preprint*, arXiv:2307.09288.

Herbert Ullrich, Jan Drchal, Martin Rýpar, Hana Vincourová, and Václav Moravec. 2023. Csfever and ctkfacts: acquiring czech data for fact verification. *Language Resources and Evaluation*, 57(4):1571–1605.

William Yang Wang. 2017. "liar, liar pants on fire": A new benchmark dataset for fake news detection. In *Proceedings of the 55th Annual Meeting of the Association for Computational Linguistics (Volume 2: Short Papers)*, pages 422–426, Vancouver, Canada. Association for Computational Linguistics.

Xinyu Wang, Wenbo Zhang, and Sarah Rajtmajer. 2024. Monolingual and multilingual misinformation detection for low-resource languages: A comprehensive survey. *Preprint*, arXiv:2410.18390.

Jason Wei, Xuezhi Wang, Dale Schuurmans, Maarten Bosma, Brian Ichter, Fei Xia, Ed H. Chi, Quoc V. Le, and Denny Zhou. 2022. Chain-of-thought prompting elicits reasoning in large language models. In *Proceedings of the 36th International Conference on Neural Information Processing Systems*, NIPS '22, Red Hook, NY, USA. Curran Associates Inc.

Linting Xue, Noah Constant, Adam Roberts, Mihir Kale, Rami Al-Rfou, Aditya Siddhant, Aditya Barua, and Colin Raffel. 2021. mT5: A massively multilingual pre-trained text-to-text transformer. In *Proceedings of the 2021 Conference of the North American Chapter of the Association for Computational Linguistics: Human Language Technologies*, pages 483–498, Online. Association for Computational Linguistics.

An Yang, Baosong Yang, Beichen Zhang, Binyuan Hui, Bo Zheng, Bowen Yu, Chengyuan Li, Dayiheng Liu, Fei Huang, Haoran Wei, and 1 others. 2024. Qwen2. 5 technical report. *arXiv preprint arXiv:2412.15115*.

Caiqi Zhang, Zhijiang Guo, and Andreas Vlachos. 2024. Do we need language-specific fact-checking models? the case of Chinese. In *Proceedings of the 2024 Conference on Empirical Methods in Natural Language Processing*, pages 1899–1914, Miami, Florida, USA. Association for Computational Linguistics.

A Model Implementation Details

For our experimental evaluation, we used the following model versions:

XLM-R base. We used *FacebookAI/xlm-roberta-base* (270 million parameters) model from Hugging Face, which has been pre-trained on text in 100 languages. The model was tested in two configurations: (1) with frozen parameters and only the classification head fine-tuned, and (2) with full fine-tuning of all parameters.

mT5 base. We employed the *google/mt5-base* model (580 million parameters) from Hugging Face, which follows an encoder-decoder architecture and has been pre-trained on multilingual text.

Llama 3.1 8B. We used the instruction-tuned version of Llama 3.1 with 8 billion parameters. This model officially supports seven languages: French, German, Hindi, Italian, Portuguese, Spanish, and Thai, in addition to English.

Qwen 2.5 7B. We employed the instruction-tuned Qwen 2.5 model with 7 billion parameters. This model supports 29 languages and has demonstrated strong performance in both English and multilingual tasks.

Mistral Nemo 12B. We used the Mistral Nemo model with 12 billion parameters. This model supports 11 languages: English, French, German, Spanish, Italian, Portuguese, Chinese, Japanese, Korean, Arabic, and Hindi.

All experiments with LLMs were conducted using the Unsloth library (Daniel Han and team, 2023) to efficiently implement and optimize the fine-tuning and inference processes, ensuring faster training times and reduced memory usage without compromising model performance.

B Details on X-Fact

For examples from the X-Fact dataset, please refer to the Figure 3.

C Hyperparameter Details

C.1 Small Language Models

For our small language models (XLM-R and mT5), we employed Bayesian hyperparameter optimization through Weights&Biases, conducting 90 sweeps for the classification head approach and 60

Claim	*Muslimische Gebete sind Pflichtprogramm an katholischer Schule.* Muslim prayers are compulsory in Catholic schools.
Label	Mostly-False (*Grösstenteils Falsch*)
Claimant	Freie Welt
Language	German
Source	`de.correctiv.org`
Claim Date	March 16, 2018
Review Date	March 23, 2018
Claim	*Temos, hoje, a despesa de Previdência Social representando 57% do orçamento.* Today, we have Social Security expenses representing 57% of the budget.
Label	Partly-True (*Exagerado*)
Claimant	Henrique Meirelles
Language	Portuguese (Brazilian)
Source	`pt.piaui.folha.uol.com.br`
Claim Date	None
Review Date	May 2, 2018

Figure 3: Details of the X-Fact dataset. Examples from X-Fact as presented in the original paper by Gupta and Srikumar (2021). For reference, translations are also shown.

sweeps each for the full fine-tuning experiments. We used an AdamW optimizer with a polynomial learning rate scheduler. To prevent overfitting, we implemented early stopping. Table 5 shows the key hyperparameter values for each model variant.

Model	Learning Rate	Batch Size
XLM-R frozen	5.7e-04	8
XLM-R	1.82e-05	6
mT5	2.2e-05	8

Table 5: Key hyperparameter values for SLMs.

C.2 Large Language Models

For large language models, we used parameter-efficient fine-tuning with LoRA. Through systematic experimentation, we identified optimal LoRA configurations with a rank of 16 and adapter alpha of 32. We targeted both attention components (query, key, value, and output projections) and feed-forward layers (gate projections and up/down projections).

Lower rank values (r = 2, 4, 8) and alpha values (8, 16) produced inferior results, while increasing these parameters beyond our chosen values (r > 16, alpha > 32) provided negligible performance gains while substantially increasing memory requirements.

For prompt engineering, we tested various temperature settings and found that temperatures between 0.3 and 0.5 provided the best balance between confident predictions and appropriate uncertainty handling. Lower temperatures led to overly deterministic outputs that failed to capture nuanced veracity judgments, while higher temperatures resulted in inconsistent classifications.

All LLM experiments were conducted using 4-bit quantization to enable efficient processing on GPUs while maintaining performance.

D Performance Comparison across Models

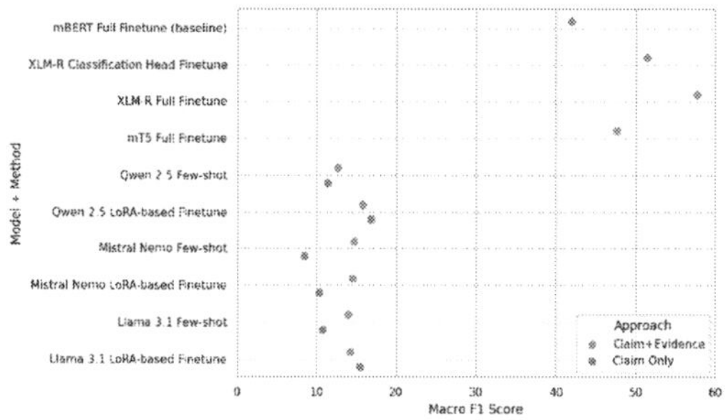

Figure 4: Macro-F1 scores across test subset by model.

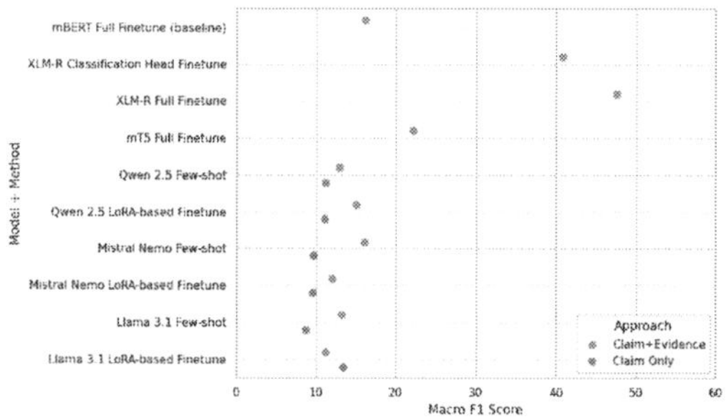

Figure 5: Macro-F1 scores across OOD subset by model.

E Prompt Template

In Figure 7 we provide a prompt template used to instruct LLMs.

F LLMs Performance Comparison Visualizations

In Figure 8 we provide a comparison of macro- and micro F1 scores across LLMs, evaluation subsets, and training methods.

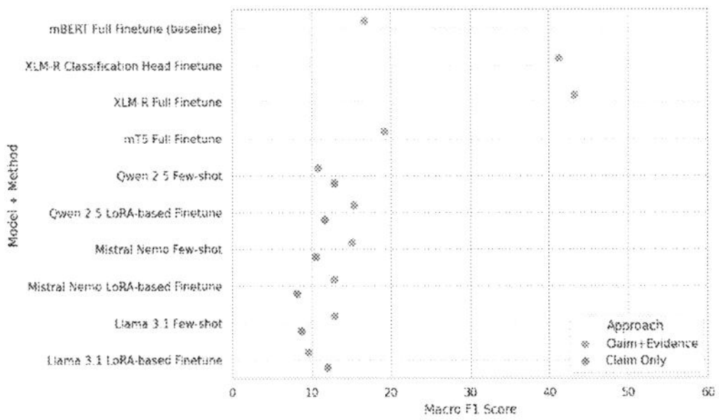

Figure 6: Macro-F1 scores across zero-shot subset by model.

G LLMs Performance Summary Table

In Table 6 we present a combined comparison of macro-F1 scores for all evaluated models using claim+evidence configurations across the three evaluation subsets (Test, OOD, Zero-shot). This table extracts the claim+evidence results from Table 4 and combines them with the small language model performance to facilitate direct performance comparison.

H Micro- and Macro-F1 Scores Comparison across LLMs

In Figure 9 we provide a comparison of average macro- and micro-F1 scores across LLMs for each evaluation subset.

Method	Test	OOD	Zero-shot
mBERT (SLM)	41.9	16.2	16.7
XLM-R frozen (SLM)	51.4	40.8	41.3
XLM-R (SLM)	**57.7**	**47.6**	**43.2**
mT5 (SLM)	47.6	22.2	19.2
Qwen 2.5 Few-shot (LLM)	12.7	13.0	10.9
Qwen 2.5 LoRA (LLM)	**15.9**	**15.1**	**15.4**
Mistral Nemo Few-shot (LLM)	**14.8**	**16.1**	**15.1**
Mistral Nemo LoRA (LLM)	14.6	12.1	12.9
Llama 3.1 Few-shot (LLM)	14.0	**13.3**	**12.9**
Llama 3.1 LoRA (LLM)	**14.3**	11.2	9.6

Table 6: Macro-F1 performance comparison across evaluation subsets for claim+evidence configurations. Bold values indicate the highest macro-F1 score for each LLM model across the two training methods (Few-shot vs LoRA). SLMs results included for reference.

Your task is to evaluate the given claim and evidence, then provide a verdict using one of the following labels: false (completely incorrect), true (completely correct), mostly true (mainly correct with minor issues), mostly false (mainly incorrect with minor true elements), partly true/misleading (mix of true and false elements), complicated/hard to categorise (cannot be verified with given evidence) or other (doesn't fit other categories).

Q: Claim: In Ungheria le tasse sulle imprese sono al 9 per cento e sulle persone fisiche al 15 per cento, e l'Ungheria cresce del 5 per cento.\nEvidence: L'Ungheria, insieme ad altri paesi della Ue (Lussemburgo, Belgio, Olanda, ... Puntando su una tassazione dei redditi di forte vantaggio (9% per le società e 15% per le ... Per bilanciare la bassa imposizione fiscale su imprese e persone fisiche, ... L'Iva è generalmente al 27% anche se esistono aliquote al 18% e al 5%.
A: Label: true
Q: Claim: Das Coronavirus enthält HIV-Anteile, wurde also im Labor erschaffen.\nEvidence: Apr 26, 2020 — Paris - Es klingt wie eine wilde Verschwörungstheorie - und doch hat es der französische Virologe Luc Montagnier bei einer Fernsehdisk. Das Coronavirus enthält HIV-Anteile, wurde also im Labor erschaffen. Feb 6, 2020 — Im Internet kursieren wilde Theorien über den Ursprung des Virus. Dazu tragen auch fragwürdige „Forscher" bei. Schnelle Studien enthalten oft ...
A: Label: false
Q: Claim: "La velocidad promedio de Internet en 2015 era apenas de 4,5 megabits por segundo, hoy la triplicamos".\nEvidence: Mar 5, 2019 — Macri: "La velocidad promedio de Internet en 2015 era apenas de 4,5 megabits por segundo, hoy la triplicamos". ¿Es así? Leé el chequeo acá: ...
A: Label: mostly true
Q: Claim: „Trenutno se radi na popisu državne imovine..\nEvidence: Državna imovina u RH klasificira se, evidentira i vrednuje na neodgovarajući način. • Glavna knjiga Državne riznice ne ... prosinca svake godine provesti sveobuhvatni popis državne imovine kojom ... rad na izradi aplikacijskog rješenja za drugu fazu ISUDIO je u tijeku. (dovršenje se ... trenutno važećem Zakonu):. Poseban ...
A: Label: mostly false
Q: Claim: "ევროპული ღირებულებები" - იტალიის სამაშველო სამსახურებს მიგრანტების ჩაძირული გემების დახმარება აეკრძ...\nEvidence: Oct 4, 2018 — იტალიის სამაშველო სამსახურებს მიგრანტების ჩაძირული გემების დახმარება ულტრა-მემარჯვენე შინაგან საქმეთა ...
A: Label: partly true/misleading
Q: Claim: A evasão do Pronatec foi de 80%.\nEvidence: Palavras-Chave: Políticas públicas; Avaliação; Implementação; Pronatec ... os cursos FIC foi de 618, o que corresponde a 80,26 % do total de vagas ofertadas. ... Outra questão apontada como causa da evasão, foi a dificuldade, por boa parte ...
A: Label: complicated/hard to categorise
Q: Claim: Yoris Raweyai Bantah Terkait Tuntutan Pembubaran Banser.\nEvidence: Aug 25, 2019 — Anggota DPD terpilih Yorrys Raweyai menyebut hanya menerima selebaran tujuh poin tuntutan warga di Sorong, yang salah satunya meminta ...
A: Label: other
Q: *[claim and evidence]*
A: Label:

Figure 7: Prompt template used for LLMs.

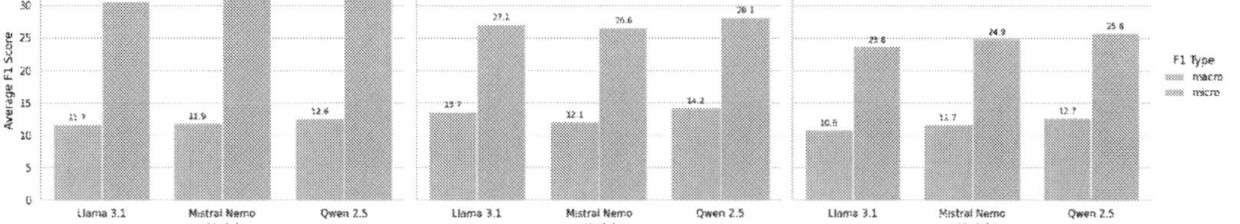

Figure 8: Comparison of macro- and micro F1 scores across LLMs, evaluation subsets, and training methods.

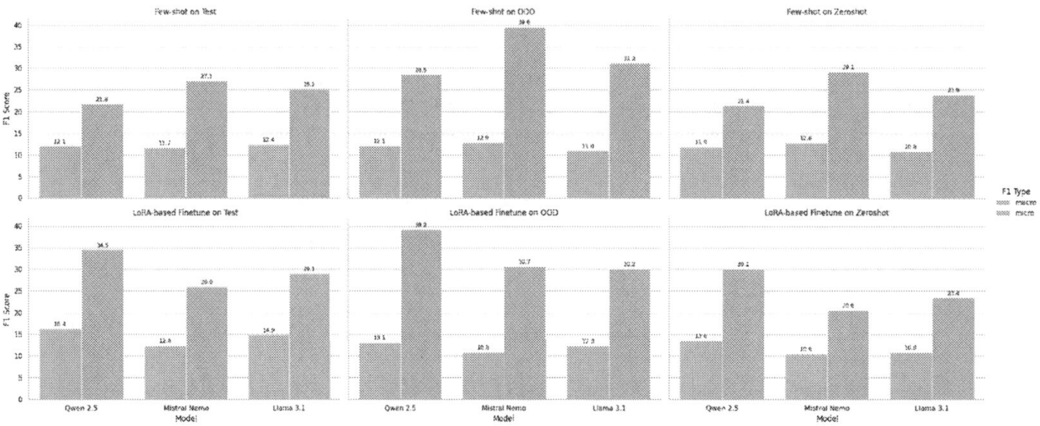

Figure 9: Comparison of average macro- and micro-F1 scores across LLMs for each evaluation subset.

Less Can be More: An Empirical Evaluation of Small and Large Language Models for Sentence-level Claim Detection

Andrew Bell
Verita Research
New York, New York
andrew@veritaresearch.org

Abstract

Sentence-level claim detection is a critical first step in the fact-checking process. While Large Language Models (LLMs) seem well-suited for claim detection, their computational cost poses challenges for real-world deployment. This paper investigates the effectiveness of both small and large pretrained Language Models for the task of claim detection. We conduct a comprehensive empirical evaluation using BERT, ModernBERT, RoBERTa, Llama, and ChatGPT-based models. Our results reveal that smaller models, when finetuned appropriately, can achieve competitive performance with significantly lower computational overhead on *in-domain* tasks. Notably, we also find that BERT-based models transfer poorly on sentence-level claim detection in *out-of-domain* tasks, often over-predicting the positive outcome. We discuss the implications of these findings for practitioners and highlight directions for future research.

1 Introduction

Due to the increasing flow of global information, distinguishing factual content from opinion, speculation, or misinformation through fact-checking has become critically important. A foundational step in the fact-checking process is *sentence-level*[1] *claim detection*, or identifying whether a given sentence contains a factual claim or assertion. Without accurate claim detection, fact-checking efforts risk wasting resources.

Tools and approaches for automatically detecting factual claims from text have been developed in tandem with advances in Natural Language Processing. As of the writing of this paper, approaches using BERT-based models (Ni et al., 2024; Soleimani et al., 2020) are being replaced with those using state-of-the-art Large Language Models (LLMs) (Wang et al., 2024; Metropolitansky and Larson, 2025). Yet, there are inherent disadvantages to using LLMs for sentence-level claim detection: the computational demands of these models — both during training and inference — pose significant barriers to their deployment in real-time or in resource-constrained environments.

To this end, in this short paper, we present an empirical evaluation of the performance of different-sized Language Models on sentence-level claim detection. Specifically, we evaluate BERT, ModernBERT, RoBERTa, Llama, and ChatGPT-based models on a composite dataset constructed from three publicly available, human-curated datasets. we also test the ability of finetuned Language Models to generalize on "out-of-domain" data.

Contributions. First, we conduct experiments evaluating both the *in-domain* (Section 3) and *out-of-domain* (Section 4) performance of six models on sentence-level claim detection tasks. Second, we release four artifacts:[2] a composite dataset of approximately 13,000 sentences containing sentences and a binary label for whether or not the sentence is a claim, a finetuned BERT model, a finetuned ModernBERT model, and a finetuned Llama-3.2-1B-Instruct model. Third, in Section 5, we offer recommendations to practitioners on when it is worthwhile to use BERT-based language models as opposed to LLMs. Fourth, also in Section 5, we identify several research gaps and future research directions.

Findings. This paper finds that smaller, fine-tuned BERT-based models outperform LLMs on *in-domain* sentence-level claim detection tasks, making them a practical choice for resource-constrained settings. However—and perhaps expectedly—LLMs generalize better to *out-of-domain* data *without the need for fine-tuning*. In

[1]Sentence-level claim detection is distinguished from *document-level claim extraction* (Deng et al., 2024).

[2]https://github.com/VeritaResearch/claim-extraction

Proceedings of the Eighth Fact Extraction and VERification Workshop (FEVER), pages 85–90
July 31, 2025

Source	# of records	% positive
Claimbuster (Hassan et al., 2017)	7,976	25.00
PoliClaim Gold (Ni et al., 2024)	1,953	59.09
AVeriTeC (Schlichtkrull et al., 2023)	3,068	100.00
Total	12,997	47.83

Table 1: Composite dataset used for training and testing claim detection models.

some cases, finetuning can even harm LLM performance. Therefore, our results suggest that specialized models are more suitable for narrow domains, while LLMs are more effective for broad, diverse domains.

2 Methods

2.1 Dataset

We construct and release a composite dataset for training and testing sentence-level claim detection models made from three high-quality, publicly available datasets, summarized in Table 1. Importantly, all three of these datasets are *human-curated.* Claimbuster (Hassan et al., 2017) and PoliClaim (Ni et al., 2024) were collected specifically to train and test machine learning models for sentence-level claim detection, and contain sentences from US political speeches and debates. AVeriTeC (Schlichtkrull et al., 2023) contains claims published by over 50 different organizations, including fact-checking organizations like FullFact and Snopes.[3]

For finetuning and evaluation, wedivided this composite dataset into a *training* set (via random sampling of 80% of the samples), and a *testing* set (the remaining 20%). These samples were frozen throughout the finetuning and evaluation procedure, and can be found in the accompanying GitHub repository.[4]

2.2 Models

We evaluated the efficacy of using six models for sentence-level claim extraction, which are listed

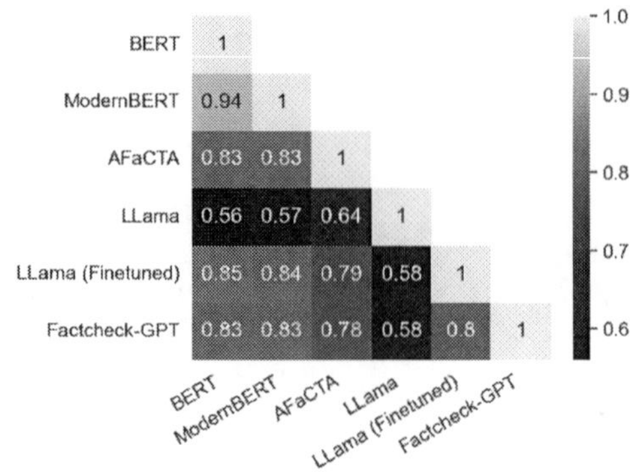

Figure 1: Overlap in positively predicted labels corresponding to Table 2.

in Table 2 (and 3). The first two models were a finetuned BERT model[5] and a finetuned ModernBERT model,[6] an updated version of its namesake (Warner et al., 2024). These models have 110 million and 150 million parameters, respectively. The third model, known as AFaCTA, comes from Ni et al. (2024), and is a fine-tuned RoBERTa model (Zhuang et al., 2021) containing 125 million parameters.[7] The fourth and fifth models were a base Meta-Llama-3.2-1B-Instruct model[8] and a finetuned version of that same model. The sixth model used was Factcheck-GPT (Wang et al., 2024), for which the underlying model is OpenAI's ChatGPT-3.5 Turbo model.[9] The system and user prompts used for Factcheck-GPT and the Llama-3.2-1B-Instruct model can be found in Appendix Section A.

2.3 Finetuning details

As described in Section 2.1, 80% of the composite dataset constructed and released with this work was reserved for finetuning (training). Full parameter finetuning was used for the BERT and ModernBERT models, while LoRA was used to finetune the Llama-3.2-1B-Instruct model. Finetuning was carried out using the Huggingface `Trainer` class, and exact implementation details can be found in the GitHub repository accompanying this work.

[3]The full AVeriTeC dataset contains 4,568 real-world claims, but weonly include the publicly released training dataset which contains 3,068 claims.

[4]https://github.com/VeritaResearch/claim-extraction

[5]https://huggingface.co/google-bert/bert-base-uncased

[6]https://huggingface.co/answerdotai/ModernBERT-base

[7]https://huggingface.co/JingweiNi/roberta-base-afacta

[8]https://huggingface.co/meta-llama/Llama-3.2-1B-Instruct

[9]https://platform.openai.com/docs/models/gpt-3.5-turbo

Table 2: Sentence-level claim detection results (speeches & fact-checks, composite dataset described in Section 2.1).

Model	Accuracy	Precision	Recall	F1 Score
BERT (Finetuned)	**0.917**	**0.918**	0.904	**0.911**
ModernBERT (Finetuned)	0.911	0.907	0.902	0.904
AFaCTA (Ni et al., 2024)	0.831	0.755	**0.945**	0.839
LLama-3.2-1B-Instruct	0.571	0.526	0.816	0.640
LLama-3.2-1B-Instruct (Finetuned)	0.850	0.844	0.834	0.839
Factcheck-GPT (Wang et al., 2024)	0.824	0.802	0.829	0.815

All finetuning was performed on an NVIDIA GTX 4060 Ti with 8GB of VRAM and took 24 hours or less to complete for each model. The training loss can be seen in Figure 2. The BERT and ModernBERT models were trained over 5 epochs which was sufficient for training loss to converge to close to 0. Due to resource constraints, the Llama-3.2-1B-Instruct model was only trained for 30 epochs and training loss was reduced from 2.3932 to 0.8570 (a 64.2% decrease).

3 Results

The performance for all six models on sentence-level claim extraction can be found in Table 2. The best performing model with respect to accuracy, precision, and F1 score was the finetuned BERT model at 91.7%, 91.8%, and 91.1%, respectively. We found that the AFaCTA model had the best recall at 94.5% — although, the model has a relatively low precision. As we will discuss in Section 4, we observed a tendency of BERT-based models to over-predict claims (the positive outcome) when used on "out-of-domain" data.

We observe a significant performance difference between the two "base" LLMs used in our experiments: the Llama-3.2-1B-Instruct model and Factcheck-GPT, which uses OpenAI's ChatGPT-3.5 Turbo model. While the size of ChatGPT-3.5 Turbo is not publicly available, it is believed to be significantly larger than 1B parameters, indicating that larger LLMs may be better suited for claim detection tasks. Significantly, fine-tuning the Llama-3.2-1B-Instruct model results in strong performance improvements: the F1 score increased from 64.0% to 83.9%.

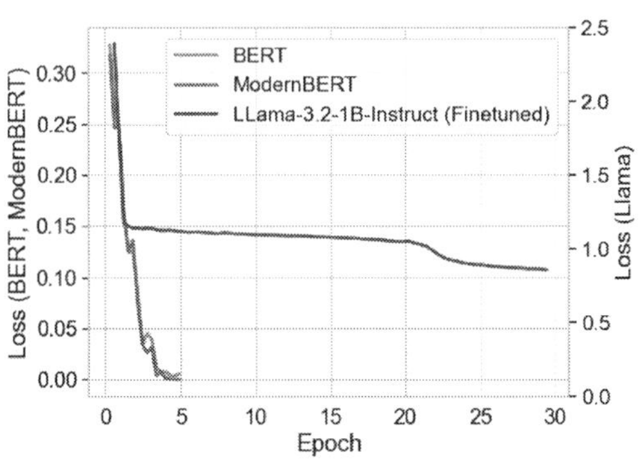

Figure 2: Finetuning training loss.

Figure 1 shows the overlap in positive predictions between the six models. In general, overlap closely follows from similarities between model precisions. Perhaps unsurprisingly, BERT and ModernBERT share 94% of their positively predicted labels, indicating that the two models are likely learning the same underlying semantic structures of claims.

4 Transfer and out-of-domain performance

We also evaluated the performance of the six models on *out-of-domain* claims to test how well performance generalizes. In this short paper use "out-of-domain" to refer to a domain of claims that may have a different underlying semantic structure as compared to the domain a model was trained on.

To carry out this evaluation, we obtained a dataset released by CheckThat[10] containing Tweets posted to X.com in the English language, where each Tweet has a label indicating whether or not it contains verifiable, factual claims (Nakov et al., 2022). The dataset contains 911 human-labeled Tweets, where 63.0% are labeled as claims (the positive outcome). Results for sentence-level claim detection among the six models studied can be seen seen in Table 3. Importantly, Tweets have a different semantic character than political speeches: many examples in CheckThat contain internet

[10] https://gitlab.com/checkthat_lab/clef2022-checkthat-lab/clef2022-checkthat-lab

Table 3: Sentence-level claim detection results on **out-of-domain** samples (Tweets posted to X.com, described in 4). For clarity: we did not re-finetune the BERT, ModernBERT, and Llama-3.2-1B-Instruct model on these out-of-domain samples—models were finetuned using the composite dataset in Table 1 as described in Section 2.1.

Model	Accuracy	Precision	Recall	F1 Score
BERT (Finetuned)	0.633	0.632	0.998	0.774
ModernBERT (Finetuned)	0.637	0.634	**1.000**	0.776
AFaCTA (Ni et al., 2024)	0.633	0.642	0.940	0.763
LLama-3.2-1B-Instruct	0.607	0.663	0.765	0.710
LLama-3.2-1B-Instruct (Finetuned)	0.634	0.633	0.996	0.774
Factcheck-GPT (Wang et al., 2024)	**0.680**	**0.676**	0.944	**0.788**

slang, leet-speak, hashtags and other emojis.

Performance varies *significantly* on out-of-domain samples. In all cases and across all models, F1 scores dropped between 2.7% and 13.7%. Accuracy only increased for the Llama-3.2-1B-Instruct, and otherwise saw similar drops as observed with F1 score. The model with the best accuracy, precision, and F1 score was Factcheck-GPT with 68.0%, 67.6% and 78.7%, respectively. The ModernBERT model had the highest recall at 100.00%.

Importantly, we observe another salient finding: all models reported high recall on out-of-domain samples, yet relatively low precision scores close to the number of positive samples in the dataset (63.0%). This indicates a bias of all models—but particularly by those finetuned on in-domain samples—to over-predict the positive label (*i.e.,* that a sentence is a claim). Perhaps most surprisingly, the finetuned Llama-3.2-1B-Instruct model actually performed *worse* than the non-finetuned base version.

5 Discussion

Takeaways. The findings of this short paper suggest two key takeaways: first, when restricted to in-domain data, **less can be more**. we found that smaller, finetuned BERT-based models outperformed LLMs. This is good news for practitioners who are resource constrained: we found that BERT-based models can easily be finetuned over a small number of epochs (we use 5 in this paper) and with a small GPU having only 8GB of VRAM.

Our second key takeaway is a drawback of using finetuned, BERT-based models for claim detection: LLMs perform better on out-of-domain problems **without finetuning**. In fact, we present one example where finetuning actually *worsened* out-of-domain performance for an LLM. Overall, this finding is consistent with current literature which shows that LLMs perform well on zero- and few-shot learning (Kojima et al., 2022). It's also worth noting that because LLMs are trained on such large and diverse sets of data, the out-of-domain data may actually be "in-domain" for an LLM.

Our takeaway for those building claim detection models can be summarized in the following way: if one is detecting claims in a restricted domain (*e.g.,* political speeches), we recommend training a small, specialized model. However, if one will be detecting claims from an *un*restricted domain, LLMs will likely yield better performance over the long run.

Research gaps. We leave several important research gaps for future researchers working on claim detection: first, what constitutes a *domain* in claim-detection? In this paper, we separate domain by speeches and fact-checks versus Tweets posted to X.com. However, if one adopted a speech-like pattern to writing their Tweets, or wrote the sentences of their speech in the style of Tweets, would domain transfer be possible? One could explore the boundary of domains in claim detection, perhaps relating measures of semantic structures or word distributions to define a domain distance. Second, how many training samples are required to ensure that a claim detection model performs well on a domain (Kocielnik et al., 2023)? Third, is it possible to generalize a BERT or ModernBERT model to multiple domains, and is there a limit to that generalization? These research questions generally drive at fundamental questions of transfer learning in Natural Language Processing (Wang and Chen, 2022).[11]

[11]See the *Transfer Learning for Natural Language Processing* workshop co-located with NeurIPS in 2022 at `https://tl4nlp.github.io/`.

6 Limitations

This short paper has several limitations. First, we only explore two different domains, giving a limited insight on when domain transfer may (or may not) be possible. Instead, this paper only serves as a single "counterexample" demonstrating the difficulty of generalizing BERT-based models tuned for sentence-level claim detection across domains. Second, we only explore two LLM choices in this paper, one which is known to be small (1B parameters) and another which is thought to be very large. Future work could include adding "medium"-sized LLMs (like those with 7B or 8B parameters) and mixture-of-experts type models (Jiang et al., 2024).

References

Zhenyun Deng, Michael Schlichtkrull, and Andreas Vlachos. 2024. Document-level claim extraction and decontextualisation for fact-checking. In *Proceedings of the 62nd Annual Meeting of the Association for Computational Linguistics (Volume 1: Long Papers)*, pages 11943–11954.

Naeemul Hassan, Fatma Arslan, Chengkai Li, and Mark Tremayne. 2017. Toward automated fact-checking: Detecting check-worthy factual claims by claimbuster. In *Proceedings of the 23rd ACM SIGKDD International Conference on Knowledge Discovery and Data Mining*, KDD '17, page 1803–1812, New York, NY, USA. Association for Computing Machinery.

Albert Q Jiang, Alexandre Sablayrolles, Antoine Roux, Arthur Mensch, Blanche Savary, Chris Bamford, Devendra Singh Chaplot, Diego de las Casas, Emma Bou Hanna, Florian Bressand, et al. 2024. Mixtral of experts. *arXiv preprint arXiv:2401.04088*.

Rafal Kocielnik, Sara Kangaslahti, Shrimai Prabhumoye, Meena Hari, Michael Alvarez, and Anima Anandkumar. 2023. Can you label less by using out-of-domain data? active amp; transfer learning with few-shot instructions. In *Proceedings of The 1st Transfer Learning for Natural Language Processing Workshop*, volume 203 of *Proceedings of Machine Learning Research*, pages 22–32. PMLR.

Takeshi Kojima, Shixiang Shane Gu, Machel Reid, Yutaka Matsuo, and Yusuke Iwasawa. 2022. Large language models are zero-shot reasoners. *Advances in neural information processing systems*, 35:22199–22213.

Dasha Metropolitansky and Jonathan Larson. 2025. Towards effective extraction and evaluation of factual claims. *arXiv preprint arXiv:2502.10855*.

Preslav Nakov, Alberto Barrón-Cedeño, Giovanni Da San Martino, Firoj Alam, Julia Maria Struß, Thomas Mandl, Rubén Míguez, Tommaso Caselli, Mucahid Kutlu, Wajdi Zaghouani, et al. 2022. The clef-2022 checkthat! lab on fighting the covid-19 infodemic and fake news detection. In *European conference on information retrieval*, pages 416–428. Springer.

Jingwei Ni, Minjing Shi, Dominik Stammbach, Mrinmaya Sachan, Elliott Ash, and Markus Leippold. 2024. AFaCTA: Assisting the annotation of factual claim detection with reliable LLM annotators. In *Proceedings of the 62nd Annual Meeting of the Association for Computational Linguistics (Volume 1: Long Papers)*, pages 1890–1912, Bangkok, Thailand. Association for Computational Linguistics.

Michael Schlichtkrull, Zhijiang Guo, and Andreas Vlachos. 2023. Averitec: A dataset for real-world claim verification with evidence from the web. In *Advances in Neural Information Processing Systems*, volume 36, pages 65128–65167. Curran Associates, Inc.

Amir Soleimani, Christof Monz, and Marcel Worring. 2020. Bert for evidence retrieval and claim verification. *Advances in Information Retrieval*, 12036:359.

Jindong Wang and Yiqiang Chen. 2022. Transfer learning for natural language processing. In *Introduction to transfer learning: Algorithms and Practice*, pages 275–279. Springer.

Yuxia Wang, Revanth Gangi Reddy, Zain Muhammad Mujahid, Arnav Arora, Aleksandr Rubashevskii, Jiahui Geng, Osama Mohammed Afzal, Liangming Pan, Nadav Borenstein, Aditya Pillai, Isabelle Augenstein, Iryna Gurevych, and Preslav Nakov. 2024. Factcheck-bench: Fine-grained evaluation benchmark for automatic fact-checkers. In *Findings of the Association for Computational Linguistics: EMNLP 2024*, pages 14199–14230, Miami, Florida, USA. Association for Computational Linguistics.

Benjamin Warner, Antoine Chaffin, Benjamin Clavié, Orion Weller, Oskar Hallström, Said Taghadouini, Alexis Gallagher, Raja Biswas, Faisal Ladhak, Tom Aarsen, Nathan Cooper, Griffin Adams, Jeremy Howard, and Iacopo Poli. 2024. Smarter, better, faster, longer: A modern bidirectional encoder for fast, memory efficient, and long context finetuning and inference.

Liu Zhuang, Lin Wayne, Shi Ya, and Zhao Jun. 2021. A robustly optimized BERT pre-training approach with post-training. In *Proceedings of the 20th Chinese National Conference on Computational Linguistics*, pages 1218–1227, Huhhot, China. Chinese Information Processing Society of China.

A Prompts

Factcheck-GPT System Prompt

```
You are a helpful factchecker
    assistant.
```

Factcheck-GPT User Prompt

```
Your task is to identify whether
    texts are checkworthy in the
    context of fact-checking.
Let's define a function named
    checkworthy(input: List[str]).
The return value should be a list
    of strings, where each string
    selects from ["Yes", "No"].
"Yes" means the text is a factual
    checkworthy statement.
"No" means that the text is not
    checkworthy, it might be an
    opinion, a question, or others.
For example, if a user call
    checkworthy(["I think Apple is
    a good company.", "Friends is a
    great TV series.", "Are you
    sure Preslav is a professor in
    MBZUAI?", "The Stanford Prison
    Experiment was conducted in the
    basement of Encina Hall.", "As
    a language model, I can't
    provide these info."])
You should return a python list
    without any other words,
["No", "Yes", "No", "Yes", "No"]
Note that your response will be
    passed to the python
    interpreter, SO NO OTHER WORDS!

checkworthy({texts})
```

Llama-3.2-1B-Instruct System Prompt

```
Only answer with Yes or No
```

Llama-3.2-1B-Instruct User Prompt

```
SENTENCE: {texts}

Is the sentence a factual claim
    that could be verified by a
    factchecker? Yes or No
```

RAG based Question Answering of Korean Laws and Precedents

Kiho Seo
Central Police Academy
Korean National Police Agency
seokiho_@_police.go.kr

Takehito Utsuro
Dept. of Intelligent Interaction Tech.,
Faculty of Engineering, Information and
Systems, University of Tsukuba
utsuro_@_iit.tsukuba.ac.jp

Abstract

We propose a method of improving the performance of question answering based on the interpretation of criminal law regulations in the Korean language by using large language models. In this study, we develop a system that accumulates legislative texts and case precedents related to criminal procedures published on the Internet. The system searches for relevant legal provisions and precedents related to the query under the RAG (Retrieval-Augmented Generation) framework. It generates accurate responses to questions by conducting reasoning through large language models based on these relevant laws and precedents. As an application example of this system, it can be utilized to support decision making in investigations and legal interpretation scenarios within the field of Korean criminal law.

1 Introduction

In recent years, the utilization of Large Language Models (LLMs) (Singh, 2024) in the legal field has been attracting attention, and their potential is particularly expected in legal interpretation and case analysis. In the Korean criminal justice system, as legislative amendments and the accumulation of precedents have led to a continuous increase in legal information that should be referenced, it is not easy for investigators to make prompt and accurate decisions. Here, conventional keyword-based search systems cannot sufficiently consider the context and semantic relevance of legal documents, making it difficult to efficiently acquire knowledge, particularly when educating and training new investigators on the effective use of keyword-based search systems.

Based on this background, this paper aims to model question answering based on criminal procedure-related legal interpretations and case references by utilizing the latest LLM technology. Specifically, we apply the RAG (Retrieval-Augmented Generation) (Lewis et al., 2021) framework to legal provisions and case information published on the Korean legal information website[1]. In the RAG framework, legal and case information is converted into embedding vectors and stored in a searchable database using FAISS[2]. Then, for a given question, the system searches for legal provisions and precedents related to the question, and based on these relevant legal provisions and precedents, generates accurate answers to questions by conducting reasoning through large language models. Through the RAG framework, it is expected to mitigate the hallucination problems of LLMs while improving the quality and efficiency of decision-making in investigations.

However, deploying RAG systems in legal domains carries significant risks, particularly hallucination — generating plausible but incorrect legal advice. Recent incidents have demonstrated that legal AI systems can provide misleading advice to users. Our comprehensive error analysis addresses these concerns by systematically categorizing failure modes in legal response generation, evaluating the reliability of RAG systems when generating applicable statutes, relevant precedents, and legal opinions through prompt engineering.

This paper makes the following key contributions:

- **Hierarchical Document Segmentation**: We develop a comprehensive three-tier hierarchical document segmentation methodology (articles, paragraphs, items) specifically designed for Korean legal texts, enabling fine-grained retrieval and legal reasoning.
- **Domain-Specific Query Expansion**: We propose a custom query expansion technique tailored to Korean legal terminology and multi-

[1] http://www.law.go.kr
[2] https://faiss.ai

Proceedings of the Eighth Fact Extraction and VERification Workshop (FEVER), pages 91–100
July 31, 2025

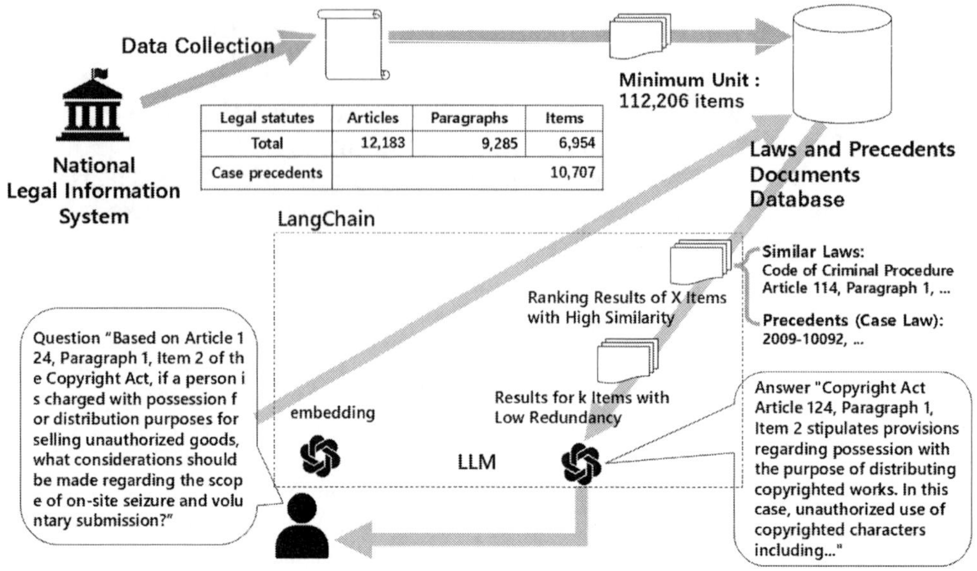

Figure 1: Architecture of the Korean Legal RAG System. The framework integrates (1) data collection from national legal databases, (2) hierarchical document segmentation and embedding, (3) query expansion and MMR-based retrieval, and (4) GPT-4-turbo based answer generation with legal reasoning.

statute queries, allowing more effective retrieval of relevant statutes and precedents for complex legal questions.

- **Systematic Error Analysis**: We conduct the first comprehensive error analysis of RAG systems in the Korean legal domain, identifying precedent selection as the primary challenge (23.7% of errors) while confirming high reliability in legislation application (0.8% error rate).

2 Related Work

In relation to this paper, literature (Hendrycks et al., 2021) publishes a dataset annotated by experts for the task of extracting important sections in legal contracts, and evaluates the performance of various models in the task. Literature (Papaloukas et al., 2021) proposed a model for topic classification of legal texts at various granularities of legal topics. Literature (Niklaus et al., 2021) proposes a multilingual legal judgment prediction benchmark using case precedent data. Literature (Hong et al., 2021) conducts research on information extraction tasks targeting dialogue examples in the legal domain. The literature (Choi et al., 2023) analyzes AI use methods in legal consultations and document preparation by lawyers. Literature (Trozze et al., 2024) describes the results of evaluating the usefulness of large language models as tools for legal interpretation and lawyer support in litigation.

3 Legal Statutes and Judicial Precedent Data

In Korea, the National Legal Information System[3] provides metadata for legal provisions and administrative regulations. In this paper, we use the API of this system to collect and utilize information on legal provisions (articles, paragraphs, items) and case precedents. As a result, as shown in Figure 1 and Table 1, we collected a total of 12,183 articles, 9,285 paragraphs, 6,954 items, and information on 10,707 criminal case precedents from 1975 to 2023. Next, regarding these provisions and precedents, we divided them by articles, paragraphs, and items, and saved them in the searchable database at the smallest unit, resulting in 112,206 minimum items being stored. We collected data from 20 core legal statutes related to criminal procedures. However, we identified 2,419 precedents classified as "Others" that either applied multiple statutes simultaneously or referenced statutes not included in our core 20 due to legal amendments or name changes. These additional legal statutes were included in our database to ensure comprehensive coverage, bringing the total number of statutory provisions

[3]https://open.law.go.kr

to 12,183 articles as shown in Table 1. Also, newly enacted regulations such as "Regulations on Mutual Cooperation between Prosecutors and Judicial Police Officers and General Investigation Rules" did not have corresponding precedents.

3.1 Legal Statutes

Our legal statute collection follows a hierarchical three-tier structure: articles, paragraphs, and items. Each tier serves as an independent searchable unit while maintaining hierarchical relationships.

Article Level: The highest structural unit containing complete legal provisions. For example, Criminal Act Article 43 (Sentence and Loss or Suspension of Qualification) constitutes a single article object with metadata including: title ("Sentence and Loss or Suspension of Qualification"), law name ("Criminal Act"), article number ("43"), enforcement date, and unique identifier ("Criminal_Act_43").

Paragraph Level: Subdivisions within articles marked by circled numbers (①, ②, etc.). For instance, "① A person who has been sentenced to death penalty, imprisonment for life, or imprisonment without prison labor for life shall lose the following qualifications:" forms a paragraph object with law name, article number, paragraph identifier (①), and unique identifier ("Criminal_Act_43_①").

Item Level: The most granular subdivisions within paragraphs, marked by numbers (1, 2, etc.). For example, "1. Qualification to become a public official" creates an item object with item number ("1") and unique identifier ("Criminal_Act_43_①_1").

Hierarchical Relationships: Articles can exist independently, but paragraphs require parent articles. Items can exist under articles with or without intermediate paragraphs. This structure enables both broad contextual searches and precise legal provision retrieval.

3.2 Judicial Precedent Data

The data structure for cases integrates case content and metadata in a unified format. For example, it is structured in formats such as "Case Number: 2023 No. 2102," "Case Name: Violation of the Act on the Control of Narcotics (Psychotropic Substances)," "Summary of Judgment: The description of the facts in the prosecution specifies the facts by clearly indicating the time, place, and method of the crime (omitted)." This structure includes information such as case number, case name, court name, judgment date, and referenced legal provisions, which are centrally managed as metadata. Additionally, the case content includes the case number, referenced legal provisions, and detailed descriptions of the precedent, enabling efficient searching and utilization of case information.

4 Question Answering System Using RAG

In this paper, for prompts in RAG, we use zero-shot and few-shot approaches (with evaluations conducted using 5-shot in this paper), and for embeddings in LLM, we use `text-embedding-ada-002`[4]. For the LLM itself, we use the GPT model `gpt-4-turbo`[5]. Additionally, we implement RAG using LangChain[6] as the platform.

4.1 Self-query Approach

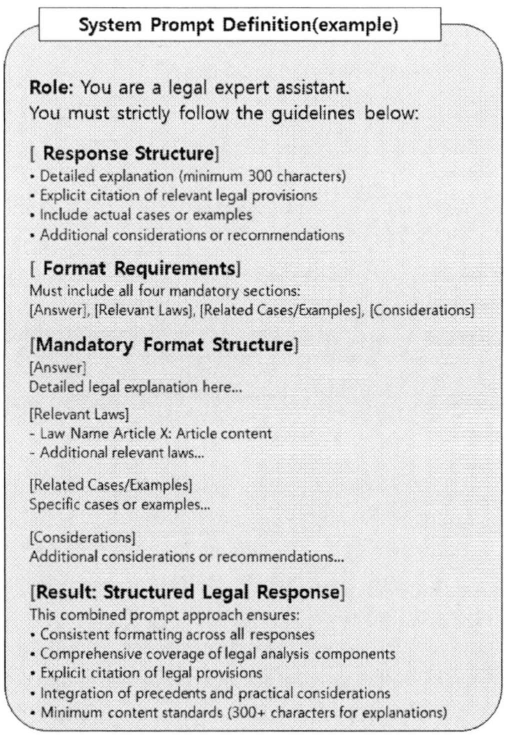

Figure 2: Legal Expert Assistant Prompt System Architecture

[4]https://platform.openai.com/docs/guides/embeddings#embedding-models

[5]https://platform.openai.com/docs/models#gpt-4-turbo-and-gpt-4

[6]https://www.langchain.com/

Legal Statute Name	#Art.	#Para.	#Items	#Cases	Total
Criminal Act	459	312	18	5,276	10,283
Criminal Procedure Act	641	866	150	2,059	
Regulations on Mutual Cooperation between Prosecutors and Judicial Police Officers	87	174	98	0	
Special Act on Telecommunications Financial Fraud Prevention	30	69	83	3	
National Sports Promotion Act	107	251	156	9	
Korea Racing Authority Act	86	121	122	2	
Special Act on Prevention of Insurance Fraud	19	18	6	1	
Act on Prohibition of Improper Solicitation and Receipt	31	72	82	19	
Road Traffic Act	223	474	427	274	
Act on Special Cases for Traffic Accidents	6	8	15	45	
Dishonored Checks Control Act	7	8	3	69	
Attorney-at-Law Act	189	305	150	88	
Specialized Credit Finance Business Act	129	267	242	7	
Special Measures Act on Real Estate Registration	12	21	10	4	
Act on Information Network Utilization and Protection	155	298	326	17	
Act on Punishment of Sexual Violence Crimes	68	192	85	165	
Act on Aggravated Punishment of Economic Crimes	14	35	12	10	
Act on the Punishment of Violence	10	21	14	215	
Act on Protection of Children Against Sexual Abuse	92	226	203	20	
Act on Punishment of Child Abuse Crimes	78	182	85	5	
Others	9,740	5,365	4,667	2,419	
Total	12,183	9,285	6,954	10,707	10,283

Table 1: Number of Articles, Paragraphs, Items, Cases, and Total Incidents by Legal Statute

Method	Response Type	Accuracy
5-shot, with Self Query	Ambiguous	90
	Unambiguous	137
	Total	60.4% (137/227)
5-shot, without Self Query	Ambiguous	87
	Unambiguous	140
	Total	**61.7%** (140/227)
zero-shot, with Self Query	Ambiguous	102
	Unambiguous	125
	Total	55.1% (125/227)
zero-shot, without Self Query	Ambiguous	100
	Unambiguous	127
	Total	55.9% (127/227)

Table 2: Evaluation Results

Query expansion enhances document retrieval by transforming a single query into multiple similar variants in LLMs. This technique generates alternative perspectives while preserving the original intent, allowing RAG models to leverage questions and context as cues for optimal query formulation, thereby improving information retrieval quality.

We developed a custom prompt engineering methodology for query expansion that generates multiple related queries from a single input question. Unlike LangChain's built-in Self Querying[7] API, our approach uses domain-specific prompt templates that explicitly instruct the model to generate follow-up questions addressing key legal elements such as constituent elements of crimes and culpability assessment.

Implementation Details: The system employs a two-stage approach for comprehensive legal analysis. First, the self-querying mechanism processes the original query and generates 3–5 additional related queries using domain-specific prompt templates that address key legal analysis components such as constituent elements, culpability assessment, procedural requirements, and precedent applicability. All generates queries are then used simultaneously for document retrieval, enabling comprehensive coverage of complex legal scenarios that span multiple statutes. Following the retrieval process, the system applies a structured prompt template as shown in Figure 2 to ensure consistent and comprehensive responses. The prompt defines the assistant as a legal expert that must strictly follow specific instructions, requiring responses to include four mandatory sections: [Answer] providing detailed legal explanation(minimum 300 characters), [Relevant Laws] with explicit citation of legal provisions, [Related Cases/Examples] describing specific precedents and examples, and [Considerations] offering additional recommendations. This structured approach ensures that all generated responses maintain consistent formatting and comprehensive coverage of legal analysis components.

Specific Example: When presented with the query "If a person is charged with possession

[7] `https://python.langchain.com/docs/how_to/self_query/`

for distribution purposes for selling unauthorized goods based on Article 124, Paragraph 1, Item 2 of the Copyright Act, what are the considerations for on-site seizure scope and voluntary submission?", our system generates complementary queries including: "What constitutes possession for distribution under copyright law?", "What are the procedural requirements for on-site seizure in intellectual property cases?", and "What precedents exist for voluntary submission in copyright violation cases?"

4.2 Extraction of Similar Documents Using MMR

Furthermore, in this paper, to extract documents relevant to questions, we adopt a method to search for multiple highly relevant documents by using MMR (Maximal Marginal Relevance) (Carbonell and Goldstein, 1998)[8] in LangChain. The formulation of MMR is shown below.

$$\mathrm{MMR} = \begin{aligned} &\underset{D_i \in D \setminus S}{\arg\max} \Big[\lambda \cdot \mathrm{Sim}(D_i\text{fi}Q) \\ &\quad - (1-\lambda) \cdot \max_{D_j \in S} \mathrm{Sim}(D_i\text{fi}D_j)\Big] \end{aligned}$$

- λ: Weight between similarity and diversity($0 \leq \lambda \leq 1$)
- D: Set of all candidate documents for search
- S: Set of already searched documents
- $\mathrm{Sim}(D_i\text{fi}Q)$: Similarity between document D_i and Q
- $\mathrm{Sim}(D_i\text{fi}D_j)$: Similarity between documents D_i and D_j

This method allows for the selection of documents containing more diverse information while avoiding redundancy. For the similarity measure, we use the sum of SBERT[9] and BERTScore[10].

Parameter Optimization: For the main parameters λ (in increments of 0.1), X (number of candidate items to remove redundant results in search results), and k (number of results after removing redundant results in search results), we performed parameter adjustment and evaluation through two-fold cross-validation on 227 evaluation question-answering cases. Our experimental results demonstrated that the optimal performance on the experimental dataset was achieved with parameter values of $X = 10$, $k = 5$, and $\lambda = 0.9$ across zero-shot, few-shot, and self-query approaches.

[8] https://python.langchain.com/docs/how_to/example_selectors_mmr/

[9] https://sbert.net

[10] https://pypi.org/project/bert-score

5 Evaluation

5.1 Overview

For 227 evaluation question-answering cases, the first author manually evaluated the answers generated by the proposed method, classified whether the answers were ambiguous or clear, and then determined whether the answers were correct. The calculated accuracy results are shown in Table 2.

The assistance system utilizes LangChain's MMR retriever to extract five non-redundant case precedents per query. Evaluation against content relevance, legislation application, and precedent references revealed that 51.9% of errors occurred across all three criteria simultaneously. Precedent selection emerged as the primary challenge, with errors involved incorrect precedents only, while legislation application proved most reliable (only 0.8% of errors). Few-shot prompting without self-query achieved the highest accuracy, consistently outperforming Zero-shot approaches, though self-query implementation showed no significant improvement. Testing with 227 real-world cases confirmed performance improvements.

While our approach shows promise compared to traditional keyword-based retrieval methods, this study did not include baseline comparisons with conventional legal search systems. Future work will focus on systematic baseline comparisons to quantify performance improvements, expanding the dataset, developing systems for legislative and precedent updates, and refining precedent selection algorithms.

5.2 Error Analysis

Response accuracy was evaluated against three criteria: content relevance, correctly applied legislation, and appropriately referenced precedents. The analysis revealed that 51.9% of erroneous responses exhibited failures across all three criteria simultaneously, as shown in Figure 3, representing the most significant error category.

Among the remaining errors, those involving incorrectly referenced precedents alone constituted 23.7% of cases as shown in Figure 5. These errors were particularly notable for citing nonexistent case numbers or irrelevant judicial precedents despite providing correct legislative applications. This error pattern was observed in public indecency cases where defendants engaged in masturbation in semi-public spaces such as apartment balconies and hallways. The system correctly identified relevant

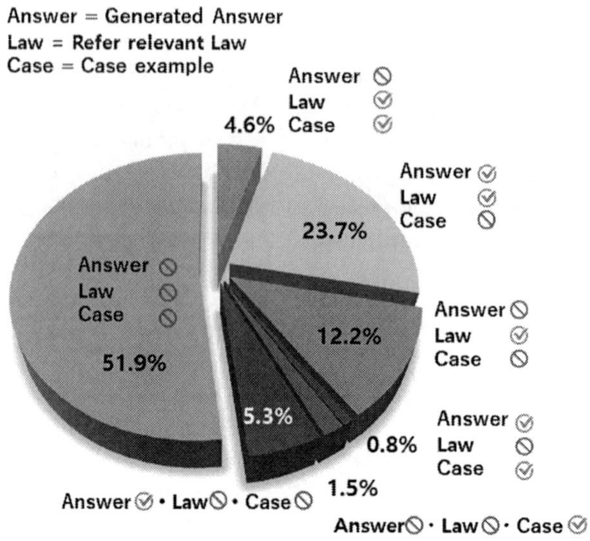

Figure 3: Error Distribution Analysis. Multi-criteria failures (51.9%) represent the largest error category, where responses fail across content relevance, legislation application, and precedent reference simultaneously. Precedent-only errors (23.7%) constitute the second largest category, highlighting precedent selection as a primary challenge.

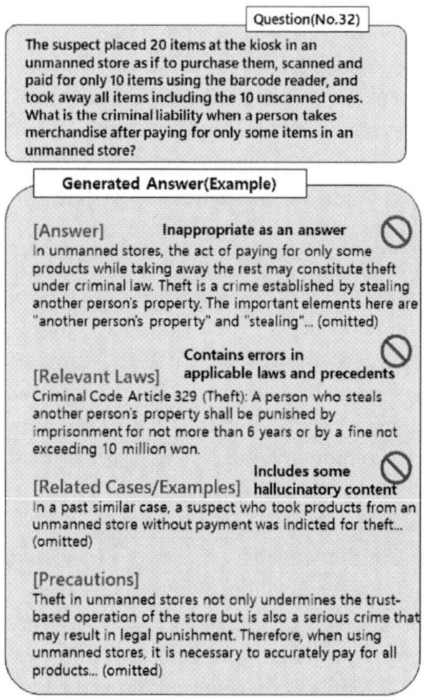

Figure 4: Error category = incorrect answer / irrelevant law / unrelated case-example

statutes but failed to cite appropriate precedential authority, instead referencing non-existent or unrelated case law.

Answer errors combined with precedent misidentification accounted for 12.2% of erroneous responses as shown in Figure 6. In these instances, while the applied legislation was correctly identified, the response content failed to appropriately address the query, and the cited precedents were irrelevant to the question posed. This error pattern was observed in domestic cohabitation disputes involving refusal to vacate shared residences, where the system struggled to provide coherent legal analysis despite correct statutory identification. This error pattern typically occurred in cases involving domestic disputes and housing law.

Less frequent error patterns included cases where content was correct but both legislation and precedents were incorrectly identified (5.3%) as shown in Figure 7. These responses demonstrated accurate understanding of the legal question but failed to properly ground the analysis in relevant legal frameworks. Such errors were observed in cases involving insurance liability and vehicle operation regulations.

Instances where only the response content was inaccurate (4.6%) as shown in Figure 8, represented scenarios where both legislation and precedent citations were correct, but the analysis contained sub-

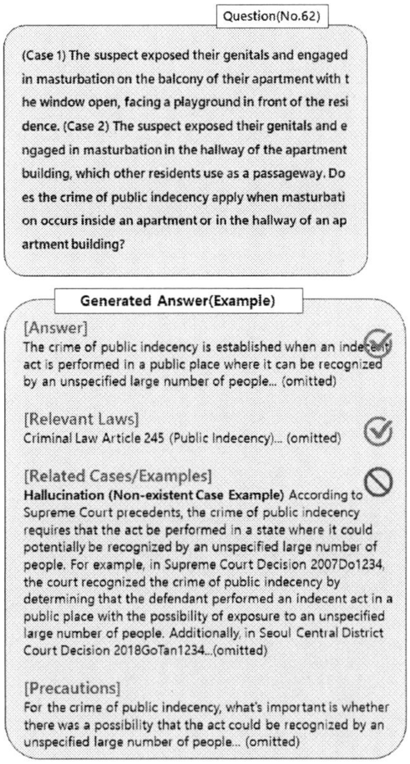

Figure 5: Error category = unrelated case-example only

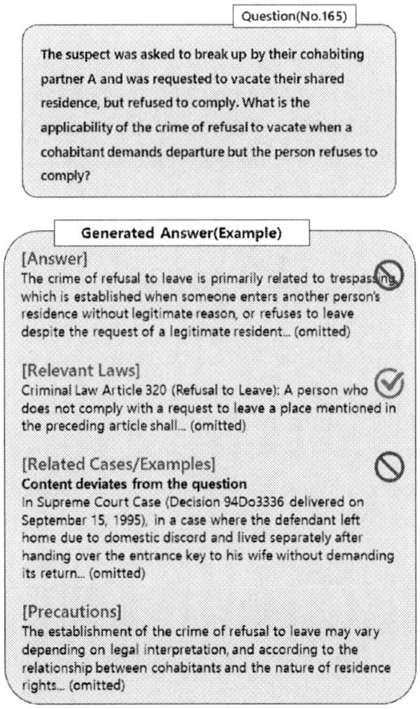

Figure 6: Error category = relevant law only

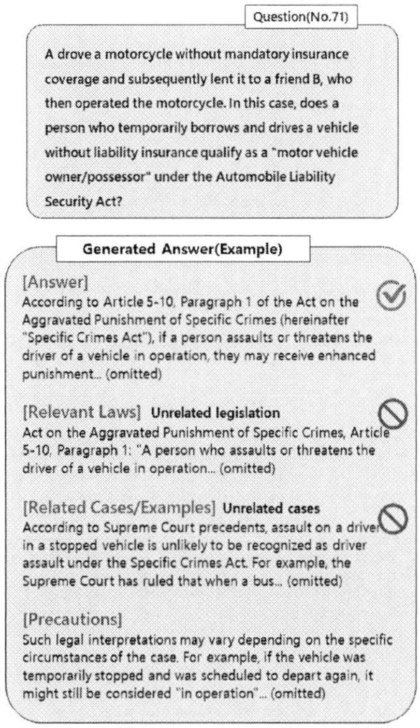

Figure 7: Error category = correct answer only

stantive errors. This pattern was observed in theft cases involving partial payment at unmanned stores, where the system correctly identified relevant laws and precedents but provided flawed legal reasoning. This pattern appeared in cases involving commercial transactions and theft-related offenses.

Scenarios where only precedent selection was accurate (1.5%) as shown in Figure 9,involved responses where both the content and applied legislation were incorrect, yet the system successfully identified relevant case precedents. This pattern was observed in healthcare fraud cases involving identity deception for medical treatment and insurance benefits, where appropriate precedents were cited despite incorrect statutory analysis and flawed reasoning. This rare pattern was observed in cases involving identity fraud and healthcare-related offenses.

The rarest category involved cases where legislation application alone was incorrect (0.8%) as shown in Figure 10. In these instances, both the response content and referenced precedents were appropriate, but the system erroneously cited inappropriate statutory provisions. This pattern occurred in drunk driving cases involving breath test refusal due to physical injury, where the system provided sound analysis and relevant precedents but incorrectly applied statutory measurement refusal provisions. This pattern appeared in cases involving traffic violations and alcohol-related offenses.

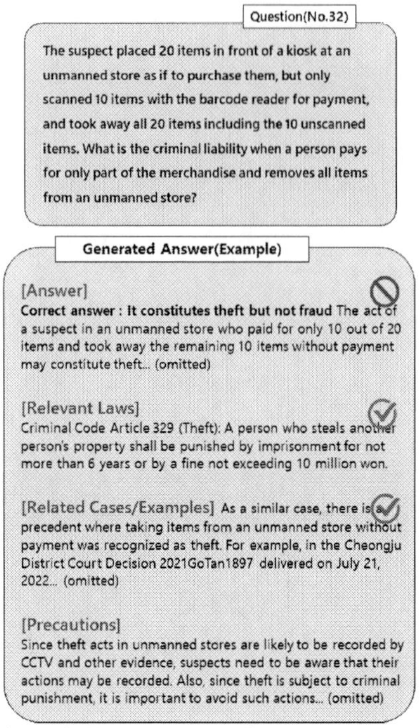

Figure 8: Error category = incorrect answer only

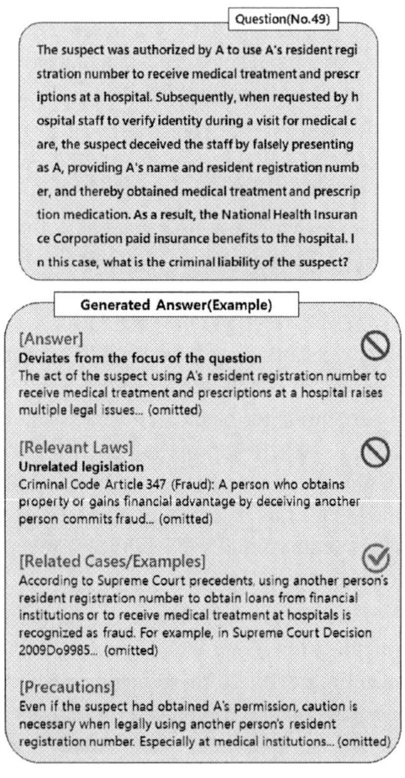

Figure 9: Error category = related case-example only

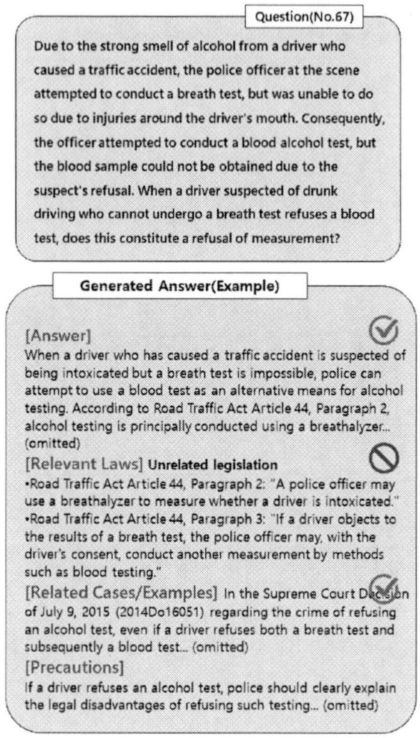

Figure 10: Error category = irrelevant law only

This comprehensive error analysis demonstrates that precedent selection represents the primary challenge affecting system accuracy, while legislation application demonstrates the highest reliability when evaluated as an independent component. The significant proportion of multi-criteria failures suggests potential interdependencies in the system's reasoning process that warrant further investigation. As shown in the error analysis figures (Figures 2-8), the system's performance varies significantly depending on the type of legal question and the complexity of the required legal reasoning, with precedent selection being particularly challenging in cases that involve recent or nuanced legal interpretations.

6 Conclusion

This study demonstrated the effectiveness of a retrieval-augmented generation approach for Korean criminal law question answering. By integrating legislative texts and judicial precedents, the proposed framework enables context-aware legal reasoning. In evaluations on 227 real-world cases, few-shot prompting consistently outperformed zero-shot prompting, achieving an accuracy of 61.7%. Error analysis indicated that precedent selection was the primary source of errors (23.7%), while legislation application remained highly reliable (0.8%). The comprehensive error analysis revealed that 51.9% of failures occurred across multiple criteria simultaneously, highlighting the interconnected nature of legal reasoning components. This finding reveals significant hallucination risks, particularly in precedent citation where the system frequently generated non-existent case references despite correct legislative applications. Future work includes constructing more comprehensive evaluation datasets, addressing temporal dynamics in legal interpretation, and expanding the precedent database to include lower court rulings. The system demonstrates potential for supporting legal education and preliminary case analysis, though deployment in critical legal decision-making contexts requires additional safeguards and human oversight. The 61.7% accuracy rate, while promising, underscores the need for continued research before practical implementation.

7 Limitations

Our study has several limitations that should be acknowledged:

- **Limited Evaluation Dataset**: Our evaluation relied solely on question-answer pairs from legal manuals, lacking the diversity of real-world legal scenarios. A more comprehensive evaluation dataset encompassing varied legal contexts and query types would enable more thorough performance assessment.
- **Temporal Dynamics**: Legal interpretations change over time, affecting which laws and precedents are optimal for a given query. Our current framework lacks version control functionality to account for these temporal changes in legal content, potentially leading to outdated or superseded legal guidance.
- **Dataset Scope**: Our study faces significant limitations in both dataset scope and precedent coverage. The dataset scope is constrained to Korean criminal law cases derived from legal manuals, which may not represent the full spectrum of legal complexity encountered in practice. Additionally, our precedent database contains only Supreme Court cases, omitting lower court rulings that often provide relevant guidance for practical legal questions. This limited precedent coverage excludes district court decisions, appellate court rulings, and specialized court judgments that frequently address nuanced legal issues not covered by Supreme Court precedents. Future work should incorporate comprehensive multi-level court decisions to provide more complete legal coverage and expand dataset scope to include diverse legal domains.
- **Single Evaluator Bias**: The manual evaluation was conducted by a single author, potentially introducing subjective bias in accuracy assessments. Multi-evaluator scoring with inter-annotator agreement measures would strengthen the evaluation's reliability.

References

Jaime Carbonell and Jade Goldstein. 1998. The use of MMR, diversity-based reranking for reordering documents and producing summaries. In *Prof. 21st SIGIR*, page 335–336.

Jonathan H. Choi, Amy Monahan, and Daniel B. Schwarcz. 2023. Lawyering in the age of artificial intelligence. *109 Minnesota Law Review (Forthcoming 2024), Minnesota Legal Studies Research Paper*, pages 1–65.

Dan Hendrycks, Collin Burns, Anya Chen, and Spencer Ball. 2021. CUAD: an expert-annotated NLP dataset for legal contract review. In *Prof. 35th NeurIPS*.

Jenny Hong, Derek Chong, and Christopher Manning. 2021. Learning from limited labels for long legal dialogue. In *Proc. Natural Legal Language Processing Workshop 2021*, pages 190–204.

Patrick Lewis, Ethan Perez, Aleksandra Piktus, Fabio Petroni, Vladimir Karpukhin, Naman Goyal, Heinrich Küttler, Mike Lewis, Wen tau Yih, Tim Rocktäschel, Sebastian Riedel, and Douwe Kiela. 2021. Retrieval-augmented generation for knowledge-intensive NLP tasks. In *Prof. 34th NIPS*, pages 9459 - 9474.

Joel Niklaus, Ilias Chalkidis, and Matthias Stürmer. 2021. Swiss-judgment-prediction: A multilingual legal judgment prediction benchmark. In *Proc. Natural Legal Language Processing Workshop 2021*, page 19–35.

Christos Papaloukas, Ilias Chalkidis, Konstantinos Athinaios, Despina-Athanasia Pantazi, and Manolis Koubarakis. 2021. Multi-granular legal topic classification on Greek legislation. In *Proc. Natural Legal Language Processing Workshop 2021*, page 63–75.

Bhawna Singh. 2024. Introduction to large language models. In *Building Applications with Large Language Models: Techniques, Implementation, and Applications*, pages 1–25. Apress.

Arianna Trozze, Toby Davies, and Bennett Kleinberg. 2024. Large language models in cryptocurrency securities cases: can a GPT model meaningfully assist lawyers? *Artifcial Intelligence and Law*.

FACT5: A Novel Benchmark and Pipeline for Nuanced Fact-Checking of Complex Statements

Shayan Chowdhury[1], Sunny Fang[2], Smaranda Muresan[2]

[1]Department of Computer Science, Columbia University, New York, NY, USA
[2]Department of Computer Science, Barnard College, Columbia University, New York, NY, USA

Abstract

Fact-checking complex statements is integral to combating misinformation, but manual approaches are time-consuming, while automated approaches often oversimplify truthfulness into binary classifications and rely on resource-intensive models. This paper introduces: (i) FACT5, a curated dataset of 150 real-world statements with five ordinal classes of truthfulness, designed to capture the nuanced nature of factual accuracy and (ii) an open-source end-to-end pipeline using large language models (LLMs) that decomposes statements into atomic claims, generates targeted questions, retrieves evidence from the web, and produces justified verdicts. We evaluate our pipeline on FACT5 using MISTRAL-7B-V0.3 and Google's GEMINI-1.5-FLASH. Our findings demonstrate significant improvements over baseline LLM performance, with MISTRAL-7B showing a 71.9% reduction in MSE for pass@3 evaluation. The FACT5 dataset, pipeline implementation, and evaluation framework are anonymized and provided at https://github.com/shayantist/FACT5/, and a demo of the pipeline can be interacted with at https://fact5check.streamlit.app/.

1 Introduction

Traditionally, fact-checking relied on time-consuming and resource-intensive work by human experts (e.g., crowd-sourcing). With the widespread dissemination of mis/disinformation, coupled with growing capabilities of large language models (LLMs), recent work has been exploring how to leverage LLMs for automated fact-checking. Wang et al. (2024) proposed Factcheck-GPT, an approach that uses retrieval-augmented methods to detect and correct factual errors in natural language, including text generated by LLMs, which can be prone to hallucinations. Gou et al. (2023) introduced the CRITIC framework for LLM self-correction, which extends the output through iterations of verification and correction.

When handling claims that require reasoning, existing methods fail to capture the nuances of factuality by relying on binary true/false labels (Vlachos and Riedel, 2014). Factcheck-GPT by Wang et al. (2024) addresses this issue by breaking down complex claims into a series of atomic facts to verify separately, whereas Min et al. (2023) proposed more fine-grained metrics such as FACTSCORE, computing the percentage of atomic facts supported by reliable knowledge sources.

Despite progress, challenges remain, particularly for fact-checking long-form statements that are decomposable and require multi-hop reasoning. Our work addresses these challenges with the following contributions: (i) curated test dataset—named **FACT5**: **F**actual **A**nalysis of **C**omplex **T**ruths (**5**-label)—of 150 statements with a five-class ordinal scale for truthfulness classification, (ii) a comprehensive end-to-end pipeline that supports ranked web-based search, multi-hop reasoning, question-answering, and five-way classification, and (iii) enhanced transparency and explainability through source citations and reasoning at each intermediary step. In addition, we perform an error analysis that provides insights into the types of fallacies present in misleading claims (e.g., hasty generalization, causal oversimplification).

2 Related Work

In recent years, automated fact-checking has gained traction in the journalistic process, from pioneers such as ClaimBuster (Hassan et al., 2017), to novel approaches such as one that leverages a frame-semantic parser (FSP) (Devasier et al., 2025). Guo et al. (2022) comprehensively reviewed the state of fact-checking research as of 2022. A common theme recognizes that simple true/false labels for factuality fall short in capturing factual correctness

Proceedings of the Eighth Fact Extraction and VERification Workshop (FEVER), pages 101–117
July 31, 2025

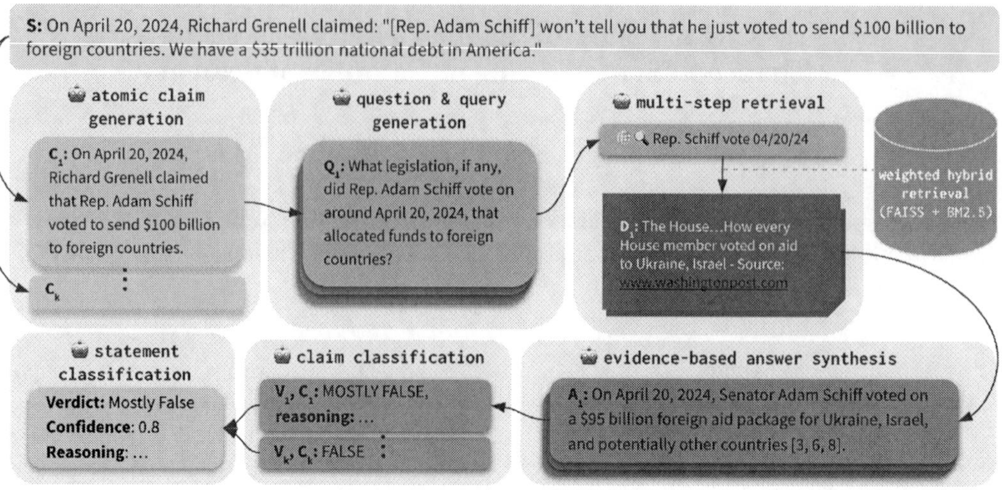

Figure 1: Overview of our proposed pipeline. Each gray box indicates a step detailed in §3.2

in abstractive or complex (e.g., political) settings. Thus, research has developed multi-level typologies or turned to sources such as PolitiFact as potential datasets (Wang, 2017; Ma et al., 2023; Devasier et al., 2025), which informed the design of our evaluation dataset detailed in §3.1. Other benchmarks such as AVERITEC extend slightly the binary labels by adding conflicting evidence/cherry picking (Schlichtkrull et al., 2024). However, challenges remain, as Pagnoni et al. (2021) notes how conventional metrics in natural language processing (NLP), such as METEOR score, fall short in measuring factual correctness of generated reasoning. Factuality classification aside, quality evaluation of textual justifications is an emerging direction for fact-checking (Russo et al., 2023).

Our fact-checking pipeline, detailed in §3.2, is outlined in the following steps: (1) atomic claim generation, (2) question/query generation, (3) retrieval of relevant documents, (4) answer synthesis, (5) claim-wise classification, and (6) overall statement classification and justification. Similar approaches have been seen in past research (Wang et al., 2024; Rothermel et al., 2024; Wei et al., 2024). Other work has focused on investigating intermediary steps, such as atomic claim generation (Gunjal and Durrett, 2024; Wanner et al., 2024a) and found that conducting decomposition and decontextualization in one step yields optimal results (Wanner et al., 2024b), which we incorporated into our pipeline. Steps 2 through 4 are inspired by past work that demonstrates the importance of related information, oftentimes in the form of question-answer pairs, in improving the accuracy of fact-checking (Fan et al., 2020). Furthermore, we focus on using smaller models that can be run on consumer hardware.

3 Methods

3.1 Test Dataset

The need for a new dataset (FACT5) stems from several critical limitations in existing fact-checking datasets. Current datasets predominantly use binary true/false labels, which fail to capture the nuanced nature of factual correctness in complex statements. While AVERITEC represents an important benchmark in fact-checking research, our decision to evaluate primarily on FACT5 was motivated by several key factors, including label granularity and temporal relevance.

Additionally, concerns about data contamination and model memorization necessitate fresh data collection (Balloccu et al., 2024; Carlini et al., 2022). As LLMs may have been trained on existing fact-checking datasets, evaluating their true fact-checking capabilities requires testing on previously unseen claims. Our dataset's temporal range (January 2024 to January 2025) ensures the evaluation of model performance on genuinely novel information rather than memorized training data.

We developed our **FACT5** dataset as an initial benchmark for evaluating nuanced fact-checking capabilities. We began by collecting candidate statements from recognized fact-checking insti-

Sources	Verdicts				
	F	MF	HT	MT	T
PolitiFact	21	24	22	24	20
Snopes	4	0	1	1	4
WaPo	9	3	2	0	0
CNN	8	0	2	2	3
Total	42	27	27	27	27

Table 1: Summary of Dataset
F = FALSE, MF = MOSTLYFALSE, HT = HALFTRUE, MT = MOSTLYTRUE, T = TRUE

tutions, including PolitiFact[1], Snopes.com[2], The Washington Post's Fact Checker Section[3], and CNN's Facts First[4], covering the period from January 10th, 2024, to January 31st, 2025. Following a meticulous manual curation process, we prioritized statements necessitating multi-hop reasoning and ensured consistent mapping of original verdict labels to our five-class ordinal scale, resulting in our final FACTS dataset comprising 150 statements. Future work on expanding the size and scope of this benchmark dataset is in §6. This carefully selected set is intended as a focused resource for testing models on this complex, fine-grained classification task. The distribution of sources is summarized in Table 1.

A key methodological decision was to prioritize sources that provide gold label evaluations alongside fact-check analyses, whose labels can be mapped to PolitiFact's *Truth-O-Meter* labels. This was essential for our classification objective, though it necessarily narrowed the pool of eligible source materials. *Truth-O-Meter* labels are provided in Table 6 in Appendix A.1. Mappings for the labels among data sources are in Appendix A.2, Table 7. A snippet of the dataset can be found in Appendix A.3.

Based on the *Truth-O-Meter*, the five classes used to classify a given statement are TRUE, MOSTLYTRUE, HALFTRUE, MOSTLYFALSE, and FALSE, representing an ordinal scale of factuality. The verdict UNVERIFIABLE is provided as an option for models to explicitly state when there is insufficient evidence to make a verdict. The dataset contains $n = 42$ statements labeled FALSE and $n = 27$ for each of the other four factuality labels, reflecting the real-world importance of identifying falsehoods.

3.2 Fact-Checking Pipeline

This section details each step of our fact-checking pipeline, visualized in Figure1.[5] For prompting, we leverage the `DSPy` library (Khattab et al., 2022, 2023), a framework that optimizes language model outputs via a declarative programming approach, replacing manual prompt engineering. Each step also leverages chain-of-thought (CoT) prompting to elicit improved reasoning capabilities (Wei et al., 2022).

Step 1: Atomic Claim Generation. Given a `statement` from §3.1, the model is prompted to decompose and decontextualize the statements into **`atomic_claims`**, a list of strings. Each claim should not rely on additional context to be understood and should focus on a single idea or concept (Barsalou, 1982; Wang et al., 2024).

Step 2: Question & Query Generation. For each claim in **`atomic_claims`**, the model is prompted to generate two key components: (1) questions that break down the claim into verifiable subcomponents and (2) search queries optimized for retrieving relevant evidence.

Step 3: Multi-Stage Retrieval of Relevant Documents. We implement a custom retrieval-augmented generation (RAG) system (Lewis et al., 2020) that involves fetching information from external sources (i.e., the internet) and a hybrid retrieval approach combining dense and sparse retrieval. For each claim, we iterated through the list of **`questions`** and conducted two sub-steps for each question:

Step 3a: Querying. Using the queries generated for each question from Step 2, we conduct web searches via API calls. We have implemented functionality to use both DuckDuckGo as well as Google Search via Serper's Search Engine Results Page (SERP) API[6], which returns a list of **`search_results`**, each containing the title, a search engine-provided excerpt, and website metadata.

Step 3b: Dense-Sparse Hybrid Retrieval. We first split the **`search_results`** retrieved from the

[1] www.politifact.com
[2] www.snopes.com
[3] www.washingtonpost.com/politics/fact-checker
[4] www.cnn.com/specials/politics/fact-check-politics
[5] For each, see Appendix B for criteria & DSPy signature
[6] https://serper.dev/

web into chunks and processed them for retrieval using a dual-index system as demonstrated in Wang et al. (2021). For dense retrieval, we utilize the `all-MiniLM-L6-v2` pre-trained sentence embedding model (Wang et al., 2020) using the Sentence-Transformers library to calculate vector representations of each text chunk, then store them in a vector database—in this case, Facebook AI Similarity Search (FAISS) (Douze et al., 2024) due to its efficiency and ease of implementation, but any other vector database such as ChromaDB could also be used. Simultaneously, for sparse retrieval, we implement `BM25`, the keyword text-retrieval algorithm using the `BM25Okapi` library for traditional lexical matching. To combine these two retrieval methods, we use a weighted combination ($\alpha * BM25 + (1 - \alpha) * FAISS$) to determine final document relevance, ensuring that the retrieved documents are both semantically and lexically similar to the query, similar to how web search engines work. We then retrieve 10 documents with the highest combined relevance scores to help answer each question in the following step.

Step 4: Evidence-Based Answer Synthesis. For each question, the pipeline synthesizes answers using the relevant evidence. Since each chunk of evidence retrieved retains metadata regarding the source, we can maintain provenance through explicit source attribution and inline citations. Furthermore, the pipeline also tracks the relevance score of each document to the question to help with the synthesis process to weigh the importance of each document in the final answer. This process is then repeated for every single question-answer pair for each claim.

Step 5: Claim-Wise Classification. With a list of question-answer pairs and evidence for each atomic claim, each claim is then evaluated for truthfulness, assigned one of the five ordinal classes or 'UNVERIFIABLE', and accompanied by a justification.

Step 6: Overall Statement Classification. Similar to the claim-wise classification step, the overall statement containing all the claims is then evaluated for truthfulness. The final verdict for the statement is determined by considering the atomic claims—and each of their question-answer pairs, verdicts, and confidence scores from step 5—inter-claim relationships, and the original statement.

Since the truthfulness reasoning of each claim contains information pertinent to determining the overall statement's truthfulness, we harness the reasoning capabilities of the model (Zhang and Gao, 2023). Adopting the same class labels from the claim-wise classification in the previous step, we finally classify the overall statement into one of the six classes (five ordinal plus UNVERIFIABLE).

3.3 Language Models Used & Technical Specifications

Models used for our research include GEMINI-1.5-FLASH and MISTRAL-7B-V0.3. MISTRAL-7B is an open-weight model that utilizes Grouped Query Attention (GQA) and Sliding Window Attention (SWA) to improve performance and lower cost (Jiang et al., 2023). MISTRAL-7B-V0.3, an iteration upon previous versions, features a vocabulary of 32,768 tokens, enhancing the model's language understanding and generation capabilities (Jiang et al., 2024). Google's GEMINI-1.5-FLASH is designed for high-volume, cost-effective applications. It is online-distilled from GEMINI-1.5-PRO, a sparse mixture of experts (MoE) model; its number of parameters is not disclosed but can be reasonably estimated to be somewhere between 8B and 200B (Team et al., 2024).

We chose these two models specifically due to their cost-effectiveness and performance to maximize accessibility and ease of use: MISTRAL-7B is open-source and can be run locally on many consumer-grade hardware, while GEMINI-1.5-FLASH has a "free tier" with limited rate limits but is still a very powerful, versatile, and fast model. We ran our experiments on a MacBook Pro with an M1 Pro processor and 16GB of RAM using Ollama (Ollama, 2024) to leverage MISTRAL-7B for local inference, requiring roughly 3 GPU hours per pass over the FACT5 dataset. In total, we ran 3 passes through the dataset for each model, taking roughly 9 GPU hours for MISTRAL-7B and 2.5 GPU hours for GEMINI-1.5-FLASH. All models were run with a temperature of 0.3 and a maximum context length of 8192 tokens.

4 Evaluation

4.1 Ablation Studies

Beyond the full pipeline (§3.2), we evaluated baseline LLM performance where only the statement itself was provided for factuality prediction. The two main methods tested are as follows:

- **Baseline**: Only the `statement` is given to the model to generate a factuality label.
- **Pipeline**: After iterating through the proposed pipeline (§3.2), the statement, atomic claims, question-answer pairs, and claim assessment are given to the model to generate a factuality label.

If providing relevant information queried from the internet enhances the model's fact-checking capability, it would demonstrate the model's ability to effectively synthesize and reason over external knowledge sources, a desirable trait for reliable automated claim verification systems. The baseline condition provides a basis for comparison to see if the model can answer accurately without external information. Since not all language models have an explicit cutoff date, a fair baseline performance makes it challenging to know if the correct answer stems from memorization.

4.2 Evaluation Metrics

As mentioned in §3.1, our work treats fact-checking as an **ordinal multi-class classification** task. Our evaluation framework first mapped ordinal verdict classes to numerical values (TRUE = 5, MOSTLYTRUE = 4, HALFTRUE = 3, MOSTLYFALSE = 2, FALSE = 1). Crucially, although not in the gold dataset, the label UNVERIFIABLE is a possible output for the LLMs at the classification step, erring on the side of caution when there is insufficient evidence. For ordinality-based metrics, we excluded UNVERIFIABLE verdicts from calculations. This decision was motivated by two key factors: the inherent difficulty of quantifying the 'distance' between an UNVERIFIABLE verdict and ordinal categories, and the fundamentally different nature of UNVERIFIABLE claims, which indicate insufficient evidence rather than a position on the ordinal truth spectrum.

Drawing lessons from Kulal et al. (2019), we employ the pass@k metric when evaluating model outputs. Under this paradigm, we prompted the model k times for each statement. For the ablation study detailed in §4.1, we extracted labels for pass@1 and pass@3. Specifically, for pass@1 evaluation, we considered only the first prediction and excluded UNVERIFIABLE responses, whereas for pass@3 evaluation, we sorted predictions by their Mean Squared Error (MSE) and selected the best non-UNVERIFIABLE prediction if available.

The ordinal nature of classes calls for an evaluation metric that penalizes misclassifications that are "further" away from the gold label. For example, misclassifying FALSE as MOSTLYFALSE should be less penalized than misclassifying it as MOSTLYTRUE. Several studies have investigated the most appropriate way of handling ordinal classification (Cardoso and Sousa, 2011; Sakai, 2021; Amigó et al., 2020). Literature suggests that MSE remains a better metric when the severity of errors weighs more (Gaudette and Japkowicz, 2009). MSE, thus, serves as our primary metric, with lower values indicating better performance.

Another evaluation metric measures the inter-rater agreement between expert fact-checkers (i.e., gold verdict from our dataset) and LLMs. Cohen's *quadratic weighted* κ is well-suited for ordinal multi-class classification (Cohen, 1968; Yilmaz and Demirhan, 2023). Similar to MSE, disagreements farther apart are weighed more with quadratic weights. The metric ranges from -1 to 1, with values closer to 1 indicating better agreement. We conducted listwise deletion (i.e., dropping statements if prediction is UNVERIFIABLE) as suggested in the findings of De Raadt et al. (2019).

Macro-average metrics remain crucial in evaluating multi-class classification performance, although ordinality is not considered. Macro metrics and balanced accuracy consider the overall performance without taking into account class sizes, which is well-suited for our purposes since correctness regardless of class is crucial for fact-checking (Grandini et al., 2020). §5 discusses results in detail.

5 Results

We evaluated model architectures mentioned in §3.3 and §4.1 with metrics detailed in §4.2.

5.1 Comparative Analysis

We observe that both model implementations demonstrate the effectiveness of our pipeline, with MISTRAL-7B demonstrating larger relative MSE reductions over its baseline (55.8% at pass@1 and 71.9% at pass@3) compared to GEMINI-1.5-FLASH (43.7% and 67.1% respectively). The pipeline consistently showed better coverage across both models, particularly with MISTRAL, making verifiable predictions in nearly all cases (147/150 at pass@3). For pass@3, our methodology of selecting the best non-UNVERIFIABLE prediction among the top three responses allowed both systems to improve their performance compared to pass@1, with the pipeline showing particularly strong gains.

The stark difference in improvement percentages between pass@1 and pass@3 reveals an interesting characteristic of our pipeline. While both systems benefit from multiple prediction opportunities, our pipeline shows a more pronounced improvement with additional chances, suggesting that the pipeline maintains a more reliable ranking of alternative verdicts. Even when the first prediction isn't perfect, the correct verdict is more likely to appear in subsequent predictions, suggesting the pipeline's uncertainty estimation is better calibrated, allowing it to generate meaningful alternative verdicts rather than just variations of the same prediction. In turn, the pipeline also enhances the model's ability to reduce UNVERIFIABLE predictions while maintaining or improving accuracy. This suggests that our structured approach helps models make more definitive verdicts without sacrificing reliability.

pass@k	Ablation	GEMINI-1.5-FLASH	MISTRAL-7B-V0.3
1	baseline	0.434	0.232
	pipeline	**0.681**	**0.516**
3	baseline	0.444	0.284
	pipeline	**0.810**	**0.702**

Table 2: Cohen's κ by ablation

GEMINI-1.5-FLASH. As shown in Figure 2, for our implementation with GEMINI-1.5-FLASH, our pipeline demonstrated substantial improvements over the baseline. In pass@1 evaluation, where we considered only the first prediction and excluded UNVERIFIABLE responses, the pipeline achieved an MSE of 1.3 compared to the baseline's 2.3, representing a 43.7% reduction in MSE. As for Cohen's quadratic weighted κ, the pipeline achieved 0.68 compared to the baseline's 0.43 on a [-1,1] scale, showing a 56.9% improvement in κ. The pipeline also maintained better coverage, handling 101 of 150 cases (49 UNVERIFIABLE predictions excluded) compared to the baseline's 89 cases (61 UNVERIFIABLE excluded).

The improvement was even more pronounced in pass@3 evaluation, where we sorted predictions by their MSE and selected the best non-UNVERIFIABLE prediction. Here, the pipeline achieved an MSE of 0.8 compared to the baseline's

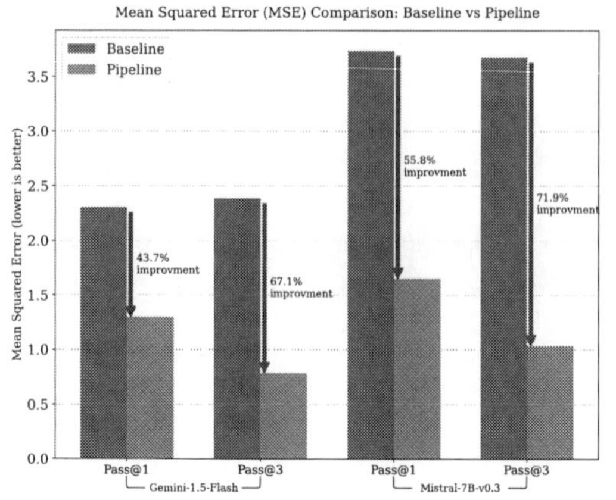

Figure 2: Comparison of Mean Squared Error (MSE), showcasing improvement of pipeline on our multi-class ordinal truthfulness classification task, with sample size (out of 150) as follows (UNVERIFIABLES excluded): GEMINI: pass@1: base: n=89, pipeline: n=101; pass@3: base: n=96, pipeline: n=121 MISTRAL: pass@1: base: n=72, pipeline: n=135; pass@3: base: n=89, pipeline: n=147

2.4, marking a 67.1% reduction in error. Similarly, the pipeline outperformed in terms of Cohen's quadratic weighted κ, showcasing an 82.5% improvement with 0.81 compared to the baseline's 0.44. The pipeline successfully processed 121 cases (excluding 29 cases where all predictions were UNVERIFIABLE) while the baseline handled 96 cases (54 UNVERIFIABLE excluded).

MISTRAL-7B-V0.3. Figure 2 also demonstrates our implementation using Mistral-7B showing even stronger improvements. In pass@1 evaluation, the pipeline achieved an MSE of 1.6 compared to the baseline's 3.7, representing a 55.8% improvement. The pipeline achieved Cohen's quadratic weighted κ of 0.12 compared to the baseline's 0.06, demonstrating a 122.5% improvement. The pipeline also demonstrated significantly better coverage, processing 135 out of 150 cases (15 UNVERIFIABLE excluded) compared to the baseline's 72 cases (78 UNVERIFIABLE excluded).

For pass@3 evaluation, the pipeline achieved an MSE of 1.0 compared to the baseline's 3.7, showing a 71.9% reduction in error. Likewise, the pipeline achieved Cohen's quadratic weighted κ of 0.31 compared to the baseline's 0.09, demonstrating a 147.1% improvement. Moreover, pipeline maintained exceptional coverage with 147 cases (only 3 fully UNVERIFIABLE cases excluded) compared to the baseline's 89 cases (61 UNVERIFI-

Model	Ablation		Acc	Prec	Recall	F1
GEMINI	1	B	0.21	0.24	0.15	0.17
		P	**0.25**	**0.34**	**0.19**	**0.21**
	3	B	0.23	0.29	0.17	0.19
		P	**0.41**	**0.40**	**0.33**	**0.33**
MISTRAL	1	B	0.14	0.18	0.10	0.12
		P	**0.27**	**0.34**	**0.22**	**0.23**
	3	B	0.18	0.22	0.13	0.15
		P	**0.43**	**0.48**	**0.35**	**0.35**

Table 3: Balanced Accuracy and Macro Metrics (Precision, Recall, and F1-score) by LLMs and ablation: pass@k and B = baseline, P = pipeline (our method). Best performance in each group are in bold.

Gold Verdict	Top 3 Predictions		
FALSE (F)	*MF* 0.48	*F* 0.45	*HT* 0.04
MOSTLYFALSE (MF)	*MF* **0.52**	*HT* 0.22	*MT* 0.15
HALFTRUE (HT)	*MT* 0.40	*MF* 0.33	*HT* 0.22
MOSTLYTRUE (MT)	*MT* **0.63**	*HT* 0.26	*MF* 0.11
TRUE (T)	*MT* 0.44	*T* 0.22	*HT* 0.22

Table 4: Top 3 predictions and respective proportions for pass@3 results from MISTRAL-7B-V0.3. Highlighted cells indicate exact match between gold and predicted.

ABLE excluded).

5.2 Performance Analysis

Additional classification metrics—balanced accuracy, macro recall, precision, and F1-scores—are presented in Table 3. While we excluded UNVERIFIABLE predictions from the MSE calculations to avoid distorting distance-based penalties—given that this class does not adhere to the ordinal structure—we included them in the macro calculations as it evaluates classification performance across all classes independently, allowing us to evaluate the models' performance across all possible outcomes.

The results demonstrate that our pipeline consistently outperforms the baseline across all metrics. Notably, the pass@1 pipeline configuration even surpasses the pass@3 baseline for both models.

Notably, MISTRAL-7B-V0.3 achieves the best overall performance among the tested models. This superior performance aligns with our earlier observation in the MSE analysis (Figure 2), where MISTRAL-7B-V0.3 showed a tendency to make fewer UNVERIFIABLE predictions. In the context of these classification metrics, this characteristic suggests that MISTRAL-7B-V0.3 may be more decisive in assigning specific truthfulness categories, potentially contributing to its improved performance across all classes.

To better understand the performance of our pipeline on different classes, we analyzed the distribution of predictions for each right verdict class in our pass@3 evaluation, revealing interesting patterns as shown in Table 4. For FALSE claims, the pipeline shows strong discrimination between FALSE (45%) and MOSTLYFALSE (48%) verdicts, with minimal confusion with more positive verdicts. MOSTLYTRUE claims see the highest confidence predictions, with 63% of cases correctly identified. The pipeline shows some conservative tendency for TRUE claims, more frequently predicting MOSTLYTRUE (44%) than TRUE (22%). However, for HALFTRUE claims, the pipeline is more likely to predict MOSTLYTRUE (40%) than HALFTRUE (22%), and often gets confused with MOSTLYFALSE as well—possibly due to the ambiguity of the verdict itself.

Model	Top misclass.	Top fallacy and count
MISTRAL	F →MF (20)	causal oversimplification (6) hasty generalization(3)
GEMINI	HT →MT (14)	hasty generalization (3) causal oversimplification (3)

Table 5: Top misclassifications and top 2 fallacy counts for pipeline pass @3, excluding unverifiables

While the results of our approach are promising, they are still relatively low even for this harder task of 5-way classification. To further understand the possible sources of misclassifications in our fact-checking pipeline, we conducted an analysis on a subset of misclassified claims to assess whether they contain some types of fallacies. Our approach involved a two-step process: first, we prompted MISTRAL-7B-V0.3 to generate an open-ended fallacy label for each misclassified claim, based on the general definition of fallacy. Subsequently, these open-ended descriptions were categorized into a predefined set of fallacy types using a separate classification model, also using MISTRAL-7B-v0.3, drawing categories sourced from Alhindi et al. (2023). The prompts are detailed in Appendix C. This approach allowed us to identify and quantify fallacies present in claims, potentially explaining the pipeline's difficulties in correct factuality labeling.

Table 5 presents the top two types of misclassifications observed for two different models for the results for pipeline pass@3, using MISTRAL-7B-v0.3 and GEMINI-1.5-FLASH, along with the fallacy most frequently associated with each. We excluded "unverifiable" labels from this analysis for clarity. Pipeline pass@3 is chosen for this analysis, since it is our best performing ablation by MSE and Cohen's κ.

When a claim was fundamentally FALSE, the MISTRAL pipeline frequently identified some falsity but cautioned against a full refutation, labeling it as MOSTLYFALSE, which suggests a challenge in fully debunking complex or subtly flawed false claims. The most prominent fallacies associated with this error are causal oversimplification (6 instances) and hasty generalization (3 instances). This pattern indicates that MISTRAL struggles to refute claims where a simplified or incorrect cause-and-effect relationship is presented, or where broad, unsupported conclusions are drawn from insufficient evidence, which may give rise to some false sense of plausibility to an otherwise false claim, making it difficult for the pipeline to reach a definitive FALSE label.

Interestingly, for GEMINI, the most common error pipeline pass@3 makes is classifying HALFTRUE claims as MOSTLYTRUE, indicating a tendency for GEMINI to be "overly" permissive in its truth assessment. The top associated fallacies in these cases are hasty generalization (3 instances) and causal oversimplification (3 instances). This suggests that when a claim is partially true but then extends that truth to an unwarranted broad conclusion (hasty generalization) or draws an incorrect causal link (causal oversimplification), GEMINI pipeline may tend to prioritize the verifiable true components and fail to penalize the flawed logical step, causing an inflated truth assessment.

6 Conclusion and Future Work

We introduced a challenging benchmark, FACT5, for fine-grained, nuanced fact-checking. By introducing this benchmark, we hope to contribute to the development of more nuanced evaluation frameworks that move beyond binary classification. Our five-class ordinal scale and emphasis on complex, multi-hop reasoning requirements could serve as a foundation for future benchmarks that better capture the complexity of real-world fact-checking scenarios. The dataset's temporal recency and careful source attribution also address important considerations around data contamination and evaluation validity that should be standard features of fact-checking benchmarks moving forward.

The improved performance of our pipeline over the baseline models, particularly with smaller open-source models such as MISTRAL-7B-v0.3 model, is encouraging. Furthermore, the pass@3 performance of our pipeline indicates that it can be used in a semi-automated setting, where the system provides multiple ranked verdicts for human review. The verdict-wise analysis suggests that our system is particularly adept at identifying clearly false information. The additional analysis of the presence of fallacies in claims helps identify the harder cases for current models. While a broader systematic review—ideally with human annotators—is needed, it is important to understand how fallacies can cause models to either understate (e.g., MISTRAL) or inflate (e.g., GEMINI) the factuality of a statement. Further work could potentially add fallacy classification as part of the factuality assessment to understand if it leads to more accurate classifications.

Limitations

While our research advances the automated fact-checking of complex statements using LLMs, some limitations need to be carefully considered.

Dataset Size Limitations Our current evaluation relies on our own curated FACT5 dataset of 150 statements, which represents a relatively small sample size compared to other NLP benchmarks. Though our pipeline shows promising results on the FACT5 dataset, its performance on a broader range of statement types and domains remains to be fully validated. The current evaluation, while thorough, may not capture all edge cases or statement complexities that could arise in real-world fact-checking scenarios. To mitigate these limitations, we focused on high-quality, professionally fact-checked statements, ensured balanced representation across truthfulness categories, selected temporally relevant statements to test model performance on current claims, and incorporated multiple evaluation metrics for a comprehensive performance analysis. Future work could focus on expanding this benchmark dataset while maintaining these quality standards through collaboration with professional fact-checking organizations to access larger pools of verified claims or by potentially exploring semi-automated data collection using web-browsing agents (Costabile et al., 2025) or advanced synthetic data generation methods (Chung et al., 2025; Tang et al., 2024; Li et al., 2023). The FACT5 dataset's recency (2024-2025) presents both advantages and limitations. While it allows testing of models' capabilities on current events, it also means that the dataset might become less relevant over time as the context of these statements changes, or if the training cutoff date for language models gets extended to incorporate more recent web data. This temporal dependency could affect the long-term utility of both the dataset and the evaluation metrics derived from it.

Pipeline Robustness The sequential nature of our pipeline means that errors in early stages (e.g., atomic claim decomposition or question generation) can propagate through the system and affect final verdicts. While our results show strong overall performance, the interdependence of pipeline components could make the system vulnerable to cascading failures, particularly when dealing with especially complex or nuanced statements. For example, the retrieval of top-k results from search engines serves as a fundamental component of our fact-checking pipeline. However, the inherent challenge lies in the lack of a definitive method to ensure the accuracy of the retrieved information. Despite prioritizing reliable sources and performing rigorous post-processing, the inherent accuracy of the information obtained cannot be guaranteed.

Need for Expert Human Evaluation While we conducted a preliminary evaluation with participants lacking specialized knowledge in fact-checking, the results demonstrated limited value. The overwhelming agreement between untrained participants and model outputs suggests that this method may not provide sufficiently discriminative or insightful feedback for our purposes. Consequently, we have chosen to focus our analysis on more informative metrics detailed in §4.2, which are better suited to assess the performance of our five-way classification task for truthfulness. Nonetheless, as noted in Russo et al. (2023), evaluating the quality of model reasoning is also crucial beyond examining the correctness of the model outputs. Therefore, for future work, expert evaluators in journalistic fields or who work as fact-checkers would be necessary for conducting a robust human evaluation.

Challenges in Data Leakage The absence of publicly accessible training data restricts our ability to explore the phenomenon of information memorization by LLMs for fact-checking purposes. Despite efforts to mitigate bias by blacklisting certain sources like PolitiFact, the ubiquity of its work across online content poses a challenge. Even if PolitiFact itself is excluded from the training data, its findings may still indirectly influence other sources used during the retrieval process, potentially impacting the reliability of the fact-checking outcomes.

Political Biases and Logical Fallacies Previous work has exhibited that political leanings can be embedded into LLMs (Feng et al., 2023). Due to the nature of our research, it is possible that LLMs exhibited political biases when determining the factuality of a statement, which could diverge from the nonpartisan nature of fact-checking tasks. A closer look at the results is needed to verify the presence of potential political biases in judging the factuality of statements. It is also important to note that although our model is primarily designed to fact-check complex statements, it is not yet equipped to identify common fallacies that are often deployed in political speeches (e.g., red herring and straw man fallacies).

Ethics Statement

Our work aims to contribute positively to the challenge of combating misinformation by introducing a more nuanced approach to automated fact-checking and by developing tools that can be more accessible. However, we acknowledge several ethical considerations and potential risks associated with the development and deployment of such a system. While our pipeline demonstrates promising capabilities for assisted fact-checking, the deployment of our system could inadvertently contribute to reduced trust in legitimate news when the model makes incorrect classifications. Our pipeline's reliance on web-retrieved data also raises concerns regarding the handling of copyrighted material and user privacy. Furthermore, inherent biases in LLMs, including potential political leanings, might influence factuality assessments, and the current system is not designed to identify all types of logical fallacies, which can be prevalent in misleading statements.

To mitigate these risks, we strongly advocate for human oversight in any practical deployment, especially for sensitive claims. We have designed the pipeline with transparency in mind, including source citation, to aid such oversight. Future development should prioritize robust data minimization practices, clear protocols for copyrighted content, and the integration of privacy-preserving techniques. Continued research into debiasing LLMs and enhancing fallacy detection will also be crucial.

Ultimately, by highlighting these challenges and proposing a more granular approach to fact-checking, we hope to contribute to the development of more responsible and effective AI systems for combating misinformation and supporting critical information consumption.

References

Tariq Alhindi, Tuhin Chakrabarty, Elena Musi, and Smaranda Muresan. 2023. Multitask instruction-based prompting for fallacy recognition. *arXiv preprint arXiv:2301.09992*.

Enrique Amigó, Julio Gonzalo, Stefano Mizzaro, and Jorge Carrillo-de Albornoz. 2020. An effectiveness metric for ordinal classification: Formal properties and experimental results. *arXiv preprint arXiv:2006.01245*.

Simone Balloccu, Patrícia Schmidtová, Mateusz Lango, and Ondřej Dušek. 2024. Leak, cheat, repeat: Data contamination and evaluation malpractices in closed-source llms. In *Proceedings of the 18th Conference of the European Chapter of the Association for Computational Linguistics*. Association for Computational Linguistics.

Lawrence W Barsalou. 1982. Context-independent and context-dependent information in concepts. *Memory & cognition*, 10(1):82–93.

Jaime S Cardoso and Ricardo Sousa. 2011. Measuring the performance of ordinal classification. *International Journal of Pattern Recognition and Artificial Intelligence*, 25(08):1173–1195.

Nicholas Carlini, Daphne Ippolito, Matthew Jagielski, Katherine Lee, Florian Tramer, and Chiyuan Zhang. 2022. Quantifying memorization across neural language models. *arXiv preprint arXiv:2202.07646*.

Yi-Ling Chung, Aurora Cobo, and Pablo Serna. 2025. Beyond translation: Llm-based data generation for multilingual fact-checking.

Jacob Cohen. 1968. Weighted kappa: Nominal scale agreement provision for scaled disagreement or partial credit. *Psychological bulletin*, 70(4):213.

Luigia Costabile, Gian Marco Orlando, Valerio La Gatta, and Vincenzo Moscato. 2025. Assessing the potential of generative agents in crowdsourced fact-checking.

Alexandra De Raadt, Matthijs J Warrens, Roel J Bosker, and Henk AL Kiers. 2019. Kappa coefficients for missing data. *Educational and psychological measurement*, 79(3):558–576.

Jacob Devasier, Rishabh Mediratta, Akshith Putta, and Chengkai Li. 2025. Automatic fact-checking with frame-semantics. *arXiv preprint arXiv:2501.13288*.

Matthijs Douze, Alexandr Guzhva, Chengqi Deng, Jeff Johnson, Gergely Szilvasy, Pierre-Emmanuel Mazaré, Maria Lomeli, Lucas Hosseini, and Hervé Jégou. 2024. The faiss library.

Angela Fan, Aleksandra Piktus, Fabio Petroni, Guillaume Wenzek, Marzieh Saeidi, Andreas Vlachos, Antoine Bordes, and Sebastian Riedel. 2020. Generating fact checking briefs. *arXiv preprint arXiv:2011.05448*.

Shangbin Feng, Chan Young Park, Yuhan Liu, and Yulia Tsvetkov. 2023. From pretraining data to language models to downstream tasks: Tracking the trails of political biases leading to unfair nlp models. *arXiv preprint arXiv:2305.08283*.

Lisa Gaudette and Nathalie Japkowicz. 2009. Evaluation methods for ordinal classification. In *Advances in Artificial Intelligence: 22nd Canadian Conference on Artificial Intelligence, Canadian AI 2009 Kelowna, Canada, May 25-27, 2009 Proceedings 22*, pages 207–210. Springer.

Zhibin Gou, Zhihong Shao, Yeyun Gong, Yelong Shen, Yujiu Yang, Nan Duan, and Weizhu Chen. 2023. Critic: Large language models can self-correct with tool-interactive critiquing. *arXiv preprint arXiv:2305.11738*.

Margherita Grandini, Enrico Bagli, and Giorgio Visani. 2020. Metrics for multi-class classification: an overview. *arXiv preprint arXiv:2008.05756*.

Anisha Gunjal and Greg Durrett. 2024. Molecular facts: Desiderata for decontextualization in llm fact verification. *arXiv preprint arXiv:2406.20079*.

Zhijiang Guo, Michael Schlichtkrull, and Andreas Vlachos. 2022. A survey on automated fact-checking. *Transactions of the Association for Computational Linguistics*, 10:178–206.

Naeemul Hassan, Gensheng Zhang, Fatma Arslan, Josue Caraballo, Damian Jimenez, Siddhant Gawsane, Shohedul Hasan, Minumol Joseph, Aaditya Kulkarni, Anil Kumar Nayak, et al. 2017. Claimbuster: The first-ever end-to-end fact-checking system. *Proceedings of the VLDB Endowment*, 10(12):1945–1948.

Albert Jiang, Alexandre Sablayrolles, Alexis Tacnet, Antoine Roux, Arthur Mensch, Audrey Herblin-Stoop, Baptiste Bout, Baudouin de Monicault, Blanche Savary, Bam4d, Caroline Feldman, Devendra Singh Chaplot, Diego de las Casas, Eleonore Arcelin, Emma Bou Hanna, Etienne Metzger, Gianna Lengyel, Guillaume Bour, Guillaume Lample, Harizo Rajaona, Jean-Malo Delignon, Jia Li, Justus Murke, Louis Martin, Louis Ternon, Lucile Saulnier, Lélio Renard Lavaud, Margaret Jennings, Marie Pellat, Marie Torelli, Marie-Anne Lachaux, Nicolas Schuhl, Patrick von Platen, Pierre Stock, Sandeep Subramanian, Sophia Yang, Szymon Antoniak, Teven Le Scao, Thibaut Lavril, Timothée Lacroix, Théophile Gervet, Thomas Wang, Valera Nemychnikova, William El Sayed, and William Marshall. 2024. Mistral-7b-v0.3.

AQ Jiang, A Sablayrolles, A Mensch, C Bamford, DS Chaplot, D de las Casas, F Bressand, G Lengyel, G Lample, L Saulnier, et al. 2023. Mistral 7b (2023). *arXiv preprint arXiv:2310.06825*.

O. Khattab, K. Santhanam, X. L. Li, D. Hall, P. Liang, C. Potts, and M. Zaharia. 2022. Demonstrate-search-predict: Composing retrieval and language models for knowledge-intensive nlp. *arXiv preprint arXiv:2212.14024*.

O. Khattab, A. Singhvi, P. Maheshwari, Z. Zhang, K. Santhanam, S. Vardhamanan, and C. Potts. 2023. Dspy: Compiling declarative language model calls into self-improving pipelines. *arXiv preprint arXiv:2310.03714*.

Sumith Kulal, Panupong Pasupat, Kartik Chandra, Mina Lee, Oded Padon, Alex Aiken, and Percy S Liang. 2019. Spoc: Search-based pseudocode to code. *Advances in Neural Information Processing Systems*, 32.

Patrick Lewis, Ethan Perez, Aleksandra Piktus, Fabio Petroni, Vladimir Karpukhin, Naman Goyal, Heinrich Küttler, Mike Lewis, Wen-tau Yih, Tim Rocktäschel, et al. 2020. Retrieval-augmented generation for knowledge-intensive nlp tasks. *Advances in Neural Information Processing Systems*, 33:9459–9474.

Zhuoyan Li, Hangxiao Zhu, Zhuoran Lu, and Ming Yin. 2023. Synthetic data generation with large language models for text classification: Potential and limitations.

Huanhuan Ma, Weizhi Xu, Yifan Wei, Liuji Chen, Liang Wang, Qiang Liu, and Shu Wu. 2023. Ex-fever: A dataset for multi-hop explainable fact verification. *arXiv preprint arXiv:2310.09754*.

Sewon Min, Kalpesh Krishna, Xinxi Lyu, Mike Lewis, Wen-tau Yih, Pang Wei Koh, Mohit Iyyer, Luke Zettlemoyer, and Hannaneh Hajishirzi. 2023. Factscore: Fine-grained atomic evaluation of factual precision in long form text generation. *arXiv preprint arXiv:2305.14251*.

Ollama. 2024. Ollama. `https://github.com/ollama/ollama`.

Artidoro Pagnoni, Vidhisha Balachandran, and Yulia Tsvetkov. 2021. Understanding factuality in abstractive summarization with frank: A benchmark for factuality metrics. *arXiv preprint arXiv:2104.13346*.

Mark Rothermel, Tobias Braun, Marcus Rohrbach, and Anna Rohrbach. 2024. Infact: A strong baseline for automated fact-checking. In *Proceedings of the Seventh Fact Extraction and VERification Workshop (FEVER)*, pages 108–112.

Daniel Russo, Serra Sinem Tekiroğlu, and Marco Guerini. 2023. Benchmarking the generation of fact checking explanations. *Transactions of the Association for Computational Linguistics*, 11:1250–1264.

Tetsuya Sakai. 2021. Evaluating evaluation measures for ordinal classification and ordinal quantification. In *Proceedings of the 59th Annual Meeting of the Association for Computational Linguistics and the 11th International Joint Conference on Natural Language Processing (Volume 1: Long Papers)*, pages 2759–2769.

Michael Schlichtkrull, Zhijiang Guo, and Andreas Vlachos. 2024. Averitec: A dataset for real-world claim verification with evidence from the web. *Advances in Neural Information Processing Systems*, 36.

Liyan Tang, Philippe Laban, and Greg Durrett. 2024. Minicheck: Efficient fact-checking of llms on grounding documents.

Gemini Team, Petko Georgiev, Ving Ian Lei, Ryan Burnell, Libin Bai, Anmol Gulati, Garrett Tanzer, Damien Vincent, Zhufeng Pan, Shibo Wang, et al. 2024. Gemini 1.5: Unlocking multimodal understanding across millions of tokens of context. *arXiv preprint arXiv:2403.05530*.

Andreas Vlachos and Sebastian Riedel. 2014. Fact checking: Task definition and dataset construction. In *Proceedings of the ACL 2014 workshop on language technologies and computational social science*, pages 18–22.

Shuai Wang, Shengyao Zhuang, and Guido Zuccon. 2021. Bert-based dense retrievers require interpolation with bm25 for effective passage retrieval. In *Proceedings of the 2021 ACM SIGIR International Conference on Theory of Information Retrieval*, ICTIR '21, page 317–324, New York, NY, USA. Association for Computing Machinery.

Wenhui Wang, Furu Wei, Li Dong, Hangbo Bao, Nan Yang, and Ming Zhou. 2020. Minilm: Deep self-attention distillation for task-agnostic compression of pre-trained transformers.

William Yang Wang. 2017. "liar, liar pants on fire": A new benchmark dataset for fake news detection. *arXiv preprint arXiv:1705.00648*.

Yuxia Wang, Revanth Gangi Reddy, Zain Mujahid, Arnav Arora, Aleksandr Rubashevskii, Jiahui Geng, Osama Mohammed Afzal, Liangming Pan, Nadav Borenstein, Aditya Pillai, et al. 2024. Factcheck-bench: Fine-grained evaluation benchmark for automatic fact-checkers. In *Findings of the Association for Computational Linguistics: EMNLP 2024*, pages 14199–14230.

Miriam Wanner, Seth Ebner, Zhengping Jiang, Mark Dredze, and Benjamin Van Durme. 2024a. A closer look at claim decomposition. *arXiv preprint arXiv:2403.11903*.

Miriam Wanner, Benjamin Van Durme, and Mark Dredze. 2024b. Dndscore: Decontextualization and decomposition for factuality verification in long-form text generation. *arXiv preprint arXiv:2412.13175*.

Jason Wei, Xuezhi Wang, Dale Schuurmans, Maarten Bosma, Fei Xia, Ed Chi, Quoc V Le, Denny Zhou, et al. 2022. Chain-of-thought prompting elicits reasoning in large language models. *Advances in neural information processing systems*, 35:24824–24837.

Jerry Wei, Chengrun Yang, Xinying Song, Yifeng Lu, Nathan Hu, Dustin Tran, Daiyi Peng, Ruibo Liu, Da Huang, Cosmo Du, et al. 2024. Long-form factuality in large language models. *arXiv preprint arXiv:2403.18802*.

Ayfer Ezgi Yilmaz and Haydar Demirhan. 2023. Weighted kappa measures for ordinal multi-class classification performance. *Applied Soft Computing*, 134:110020.

Xuan Zhang and Wei Gao. 2023. Towards llm-based fact verification on news claims with a hierarchical step-by-step prompting method. *Proceedings of the 13th International Joint Conference on Natural Language Processing and the 3rd Conference of the Asia-Pacific Chapter of the Association for Computational Linguistics*.

A FACT5 Pilot Dataset

A.1 Explanation of Ratings

Label	Description
True	The statement is accurate, and there's nothing significant missing.
Mostly True	The statement is accurate but needs clarification or additional information.
Half True	The statement is partially accurate but leaves out important details or takes things out of context.
Mostly False	The statement contains an element of truth but ignores critical facts that would give a different impression.
False	The statement is not accurate.
Pants on Fire	The statement is not accurate and makes a ridiculous claim.

Table 6: Truth-O-Meter rating used by PolitiFact

A.2 Mapping of Fact-checking Metrics

Numeric Label	Our Mapping	Credible Sources		
		PolitiFact	The Fact Checker (WaPo)	Snopes
0	Unverifiable	N/A	No Verdict	Unproven / Unfounded
1	False	Pants on Fire / False	Four Pinocchios	False
2	Mostly False	Mostly False	Three Pinocchios	Mostly False
3	Half True	Half True	Two Pinocchios	Mixture
4	Mostly True	Mostly True	One Pinocchio	Mostly True
5	True	True	The Geppetto Checkmark	True

Table 7: Mappings of Fact-checking Metrics

A.3 Snippet of the Pilot Dataset

verdict	statement_originator	statement	statement_date	factchecker
FALSE	Joe Biden	"Remember in 2020, 55 of the biggest companies in America made 40 billion and paid zero in federal income taxes. [...]"	3/7/2024	CNN
MOSTLY FALSE	Elissa Slotkin	"[...] Mike Rogers 'believes he should make that decision' about whether to end pregnancies."	9/30/2024	PolitiFact
HALF TRUE	Dana Loesch	"Buncombe County 'is still demanding property taxes on homes destroyed by Hurricane Helene [...]'"	1/6/2025	PolitiFact
MOSTLY TRUE	Ron DeSantis	"[Nikki Haley] spent 100% of her money attacking me..."	1/26/2024	CNN
TRUE	David Crowley	"Under [Biden] [...] fastest growth of Black-owned small businesses in more than 30 years."	5/16/2024	PolitiFact

Table 8: Selected Rows and Columns from Pilot Dataset

B Pipeline Details

B.1 Atomic Claim Generation

DSPy signature for claim extraction, which consists of the criteria for each claim.

```
"""Extract specific claims from the given statement.
1. Split the statement into multiple claims, but if the statement is atomic (has
one main claim), keep it as is.
2. If context is included (e.g., time, location, source/speaker who made the
statement, etc.), include the context in each claim to help verify it. Do not
make up a context if it is not present in the text.
3. Consider the source (e.g. name of the speaker, organization, etc.) and date
of the statement if given in the context, and include them in each claim.
4. Each claim should be independent of each other and not refer to other claims.
5. Always extract claims regardless of the content """
```

Output field

```
"""JSON object containing:
{
"claims": [
{
"text": string, }
]
}"""
```

B.2 Question Generation

DSPy signature for question generation

```
"""Break down the given claim derived from the original statement to generate
independent questions and search queries to answer it. Be as specific and concise
as possible, try to minimize the number of questions and search queries while
still being comprehensive to verify the claim."""
```

Output field

```
"""JSON object containing: {
"questions": [
{
"question": string, # question text (e.g. "What was the GDP growth rate during
the Trump administration?")
"search_queries": [string], # independent search queries used to answer the
question, try to be as specific as possible and avoid redundancy, 1-2 queries
is ideal
}
]}"""
```

B.3 Answer Synthesis

DSPy signature for answer synthesis

```
"""Synthesize an answer based on retrieved documents with inline citations."""
```

Output field

```
"""JSON object containing:
{
"text": string, # answer with inline citations where the number in the brackets
is the index of the citation in the citations list (e.g., "The wage gap was
shrinking [1]")
"citations": [{ # list of citations
"snippet": string, # exact quote from source
"source_url": string,
"source_title": string,
"relevance_score": float
}]
}"""
```

C Fallacy Classification Prompt

C.1 Open-ended fallacy detection

DSPy signature for open-ended fallacy detection

```
"""Classify logical fallacies given the statement"""
Input field statement = "Statement to analyze"
```

Output field

1. **fallacy** (str) = "A fallacy or a fallacious argument is one that seems valid but is not. Identify the fallacy in the statement. If no fallacy is present, return 'none'."
2. **confidence** (float) = "0-1 confidence score"
3. **rationale** (str) = "Step-by-step reasoning"

C.2 Fallacy Categorization

Predefined categories, from Alhindi et al. (2023)

```
'ad hominem', 'appeal to emotion', 'hasty generalization', 'irrelevant authority', 'red herring', 'black and white fallacy', 'causal oversimplification', 'doubt', 'exaggeration or minimization', 'appeal to fear/prejudice', 'flag-waving', 'loaded language', 'name calling or labeling', 'reductio ad hitlerum', 'slogans', 'strawman', 'thought-terminating cliches', 'whataboutism', 'ad populum', 'circular reasoning', 'deductive fallacy', 'equivocation', 'fallacy of extension', 'intentional fallacy', 'evading burden of proof', 'cherrypicking', 'post hoc (causal oversimplification)', 'vagueness', 'none'
```

DSPy signature for fallacy categorization

```
"""Categorize an open-ended fallacy description into a predefined list of fallacy types.If the detected fallacy does not clearly fit into any of the predefined categories,classify it as 'Other'."""
```

1. **open_ended_fallacy** (str) = "The name or description of the fallacy detected by an open-ended system (e.g., 'This is an ad hominem because...', or 'Attacking the person instead of the argument', or 'none')."
2. **target_categories** List[str] = A list of predefined fallacy categories to map the detected fallacy into.

Output field

1. **categorized_fallacy**: (str) The category from the target_categories list that best matches the detected fallacy. If the open_ended_fallacy is 'none' or doesn't fit any category, return 'Other' or 'None Detected' as appropriate."
2. **confidence**: (float) "0-1 confidence score for this categorization."
3. **rationale**: (str) = "Step-by-step reasoning for choosing the category, or for choosing 'Other'/'None Detected'."

Correcting Hallucinations in News Summaries: Exploration of Self-Correcting LLM Methods with External Knowledge

Juraj Vladika, Ihsan Soydemir, Florian Matthes
Technical University of Munich
School of Computation, Information and Technology
Department of Computer Science
Garching, Germany
{juraj.vladika, ihsan.soydemir, matthes}@tum.de

Abstract

While large language models (LLMs) have shown remarkable capabilities to generate coherent text, they suffer from the issue of hallucinations – factually inaccurate statements. Among numerous approaches to tackle hallucinations, especially promising are the *self-correcting* methods. They leverage the multi-turn nature of LLMs to iteratively generate verification questions inquiring additional evidence, answer them with internal or external knowledge, and use that to refine the original response with the new corrections. These methods have been explored for encyclopedic generation, but less so for domains like news summarization. In this work, we investigate two state-of-the-art self-correcting systems by applying them to correct hallucinated summaries using evidence from three search engines. We analyze the results and provide insights into systems' performance, revealing interesting practical findings on the benefits of search engine snippets and few-shot prompts, as well as high alignment of G-Eval and human evaluation.

1 Introduction

The advent of Large Language Models (LLMs) has revolutionized the field of Natural Language Processing (NLP), enabling models to perform complex tasks such as summarization and question answering with remarkable fluency (Wang et al., 2023b). While they can produce human-sounding text, LLMs are also prone to generating *hallucinations* – responses that sound convincing but are factually incorrect or misleading (Ji et al., 2023). This limitation poses challenges for their reliability and adoption, especially in critical applications like law, healthcare, and news (Wang et al., 2023a).

While numerous methods to counter hallucinations have been developed in recent years (Tonmoy et al., 2024), many focus on pre-training and fine-tuning. For popular closed models like GPT or Gemini, the *post-hoc correction* methods, which correct the initial response after it has been generated, are quite important. In particular, *self-correcting* methods approach hallucination correction as a step-by-step process where the response is broken into smaller units and iteratively corrected using internal LLM knowledge or external sources (Kamoi et al., 2024; Vladika et al., 2025).

The effectiveness of these methods has been demonstrated for tasks like generating biographies or lists (Min et al., 2023; Chern et al., 2023), but their application to news summarization remains underexplored. News articles are time-sensitive and factually dense, which underscores the need for correct summaries and effective fact-checking (Graves and Amazeen, 2019; Palić et al., 2019).

Furthermore, evidence retrieval is a crucial component of self-correcting systems – many questions are open regarding which search engine to use, which snippets or article chunks to select, and how to best integrate them. Finally, the trade-off between balancing the faithfulness to original text with doing strong corrections is often neglected.

To explore these research gaps, we take two popular multi-step correction systems, CoVE (Dhuliawala et al., 2024) and RARR (Gao et al., 2023), augment them with external search engines, and apply them to correct hallucinated news summaries from the dataset SummEdits (Laban et al., 2023). We compare the performance of different search engines and settings, three LLMs, two retrieval settings, and the influence of prompts, uncovering important considerations for future. We outline main challenges of these systems and provide future steps on how to improve them. Code and data is available in a GitHub repository.[1]

2 Related Work

Hallucinations are a common problem in natural language generation (NLG) tasks, including ab-

[1]https://github.com/jvladika/HalluCorrect

Proceedings of the Eighth Fact Extraction and VERification Workshop (FEVER), pages 118–131
July 31, 2025

stractive text summarization (Ji et al., 2023; Afzal et al., 2023). A survey by Zhang et al. (2023) divides hallucinations into input-conflicting, context-conflicting, and fact-conflicting. The focus of our work lies in fact-conflicting, which are hallucinations where facts in output contradict the world knowledge. While hallucinations can be observed by looking at the uncertainty in model's logits (Varshney et al., 2023), this is only possible for open-source models. In closed models such as ChatGPT, factuality has to be assessed through textual output. This has led to the rise of *fact-checking* mechanisms (Vladika and Matthes, 2023; Wang et al., 2024; Zhang et al., 2025), as well as *self-correcting* LLM techniques (Kamoi et al., 2024).

The multi-step self-correcting LLM methods tend to base the corrections on internal LLM knowledge (Madaan et al., 2023; Kim et al., 2023). For external search, usually only Wikipedia (Gou et al., 2024) or Google search (Wei et al., 2024) is used. It is often applied to tasks like generating biographies. Abstractive summarization of news articles often contains factual errors (Tang et al., 2022). For news summaries, methods such as text infilling with smaller LMs (Balachandran et al., 2022) or entity linking to graphs (Dong et al., 2022) have been explored to correct errors. Application of iterative self-correcting methods to the news domain is still mostly missing.

We augment the two self-correcting methods, CoVe and RARR, to support external search. Our study is among the first to explore this type of methods for news, to evaluate three different search engines, changes in snippets and full-text retrieval, and to compare closed with open base LLMs.

3 Systems

In our study, we use two systems designed to detect and iteratively correct hallucinations, both of which have demonstrated strong results and gained popularity: Chain-of-Verification (CoVe) and Retrofit Attribution using Research and Revision (RARR).

Both systems follow the same workflow: (1) Get Initial Response, (2) Generate Verification Questions (to help self-correct any errors), (3) Answer Questions (using evidence from internal knowledge or search engine), (4) Rewrite Response (with previous answers and any found inconsistencies).

Given the baseline response b, there are k generated follow-up questions $q_1, ..., q_k$, which try to gather more information related to the response b. This is generated using a base LLM and a prompt M_q. Afterward, evidence e for each question q is retrieved from the source s using the method $R(q, s)$, where s can be internal LLM knowledge, gold news article, or external search engine. This collected evidence is used as input with questions to the answering model $M_a(q, e)$, which gives answers $a_1, ..., a_k$. Finally, baseline response and answers are given to the refinement model $M_r(b, a)$, which outputs the final refined response r. All prompts for M are in Appendix C.

The difference between models is in prompts used to generate and answer the questions, and perform the final refinement. Also, CoVe is zero-shot, while RARR is based on few-shot examples.

4 Setup and Experiments

The LLM used in most experiments is *GPT-4o-mini-2024-07-18* (OpenAI, 2024). It was queried through OpenAI API. Any encoder-only models were run on one Nvidia V100 GPU with 16GB VRAM for one computation hour.

4.1 Dataset

SummEdits (Laban et al., 2023) is a benchmark dataset of hallucinated text summaries in many domains. The dataset was constructed by first perturbing named entities and relations in summaries and then passing to humans for annotation on whether the summaries are factual or not. We take the subset *news* (constructed from top Google News 2023 articles), consisting of 819 summaries. While the original intent of benchmark was to evaluate hallucination detection ability of LLMs, we repurpose it for hallucination detection with fact correction.

4.2 Evaluation Methods

Since the dataset provides gold (human-written) summaries, we use them as reference answers.

We measure string dissimilarity using the Levenshtein normalized edit distance (**NED**) (Yujian and Bo, 2007). This metric is not ideal because even one word difference can be a major hallucination. Therefore, we compare the semantic similarity (**Sem.**) between the gold and output summary by embedding them with the model SimCSE (Gao et al., 2021) and calculating the cosine similarity.

NLI Score is a metric that utilizes the concept of natural language inference (NLI), or entailment recognition, by using the reference answer as the hypothesis and the generated answer as the premise.

verification system	evidence source	simple		NLI			G-Eval ↑		
		NED ↓	Sem. ↑	Ent. ↑	Neu.	Con. ↓	Overall	Factual.	Relev.
CoVE	GPT 4o mini	0.51	81	30	28	42	50	45	49
RARR	GPT 4o mini	0.10	94	45	15	40	65	62	70
CoVE	Google (snip.)	0.51	84	41	25	34	56	50	59
CoVE	Bing (snip.)	0.55	81	37	28	35	49	46	51
CoVE	DDG (snip.)	0.54	80	31	28	41	47	42	47
RARR	Google (full)	0.33	91	24	46	**30**	64	51	68
RARR	Bing (full)	0.32	92	28	40	32	63	50	68
RARR	DDG (full)	0.34	91	27	41	32	64	50	68
RARR	Google (snip.)	0.24	93	40	28	32	67	56	72
RARR	Bing (snip.)	**0.14**	**95**	**49**	16	35	**69**	**60**	**73**
RARR	DDG (snip.)	0.25	92	32	28	40	60	49	62
CoVE	gold article	0.49	88	43	39	18	70	63	76
RARR	gold article	0.21	94	47	34	19	75	67	83

Table 1: Results of CoVE and RARR on SummEdits using three different search engines. NED refers to normalized edit distance, Sem. to average cosine semantic similarity, NLI scores to average prediction probability for entailment, neutral, and contradiction. The best score for each metric is in **bold**, while the second best is underlined.

The intuition behind this approach is that a good answer should logically entail the reference answer. Using NLI this way has been done for evaluating the quality of summaries (Mishra et al., 2021; Laban et al., 2022; Steen et al., 2023). Following this approach, we use the model DeBERTa-v3 (He et al., 2023), We use the version fine-tuned on a wide array of NLI datasets, which works well for long text (Laurer et al., 2024). This model predicts three scores (entailment, neutral, contradiction) and we report the average score across the whole dataset.

G-Eval (Liu et al., 2023) is a framework based on LLM prompting with chain-of-thoughts to evaluate the quality of generated texts in a form-filling paradigm. It is one of the most popular "LLM-as-judge" metrics (Zheng et al., 2023), which evaluate the LLM output with an LLM using finely crafted LLM prompts (see Appendix C) and take the numerical output as final score. We evaluate three aspects: relevance, factuality, and overall quality.

Human Evaluation. We perform human evaluation with 25 participants. They were shown 10 gold summaries and refined summaries by RARR and CoVe, and rated for each the overall quality (based on factuality and relevance) from 1 to 10 and the entailment relation for each summary, amounting to 1000 ratings (see more details in Appendix A).

4.3 Search Engines

Google is the world's most widely used search engine. It offers the API service Google Programmable Search Engine, which queries the search engine and returns results as links and snippets. The price is 5 US dollars per 1,000 queries. **Bing** is the flagship search engine from Microsoft. We use it via Bing Web Search API provided by the Azure platform for the price of 10 USD per 1,000 transactions. **DuckDuckGo** is a smaller search engine, aiming to help protect online privacy. While the coverage is lower than the other two engines, its usage through API is completely free. We query it through the Python package *duckduckgo-search*.[2]

We use the search results of these search engines in two settings: chunks from *full articles* and *snippets*. All search engines return results for the query with links to articles included in top results. In the full-article setting, we parse the text from HTML of the article, split into chunks, embed with SimCSE, and use cosine similarity to the query to select top 5 passages. We concatenate these passages and use them as input evidence. In addition to links, all search engines provide snippets that answer the query and highlight the most important part from the respective article. We use the top 5 snippets and concatenate them, using them as input evidence.

5 Results and Discussion

Table 1 shows the average results of all metrics for the two systems on SummEdits. Qualitative insights are found in Tables 2 and 3.

Internal vs. External Knowledge. The first two rows of Tab. 1 used internal LLM knowledge to answer verification question. While this led to moderate performance, results with search engines were higher for both systems – showing the **need for external search** for effective factual error correction.

The last two rows show the baseline of using the original (gold) news article as input evidence. It

[2]https://pypi.org/project/duckduckgo-search/

Gold Summary	The James Webb Space Telescope captured a new image of Pandora's Cluster, a megacluster of galaxies that allowed astronomers to peer into the distant universe and observe never-before-seen details."
Hallucinated Summary (input to system)	The James Webb Space Telescope captured a **old** image of Pandora's Cluster, a megacluster of galaxies that allowed **biologists** to peer into the distant universe and observe never-before-seen details.
CoVe with **Bing** snip.	The James Webb Space Telescope is primarily designed for astronomical observations, **not biological observations.** It is used to study the formation of stars, galaxies, and planetary systems, as well as to investigate the origins of life and the universe. It cannot be used for biological observations. The telescope studies galaxy formation and evolution, star formation and planet formation, planetary systems, and the origins of life. **It did capture an image of Pandora's Cluster.**
CoVe with **Google** snip.	The James Webb Space Telescope is primarily designed for astronomical observations, specifically to study the formation of stars and galaxies, the evolution of galaxies, and the formation of planetary systems. **It is not designed for biological observations.** Therefore, it does not allow biologists to observe never-before-seen details in the distant universe. However, it is ***capable of capturing*** images of Pandora's Cluster.
CoVe with **DDG** snip.	The James Webb Space Telescope is primarily designed for astronomical observations, **not biological observations.** It is used to study the formation of stars, galaxies, and planetary systems, among other astrophysical phenomena. It can observe details in the distant universe and has captured *images of megaclusters of galaxies.*

Table 2: Example of final refined responses from CoVe using the search snippets from three different search engines. All results correctly identified the error with biologists, although only Bing properly reported on the image of Pandora's Cluster being captured.

had the highest G-Eval scores, highlighting the key role of precise evidence for effective corrections.

Choice of Search Engine. As seen in Table 1, Google snippets performed the best for CoVE but Bing outperformed it on RARR for the full-article setting. The highest performance overall was achieved by Bing snippets with RARR, as measured by six different metrics. This shows the promising potential of Bing, which is under-explored in existing studies. DuckDuckGo also achieved decent but lower performance.

Table 2 shows examples of refined responses from CoVe with the three engines. All three engines successfully identified the hallucination involving biologists. Still, they found different extra information that was included in the refined response, with Bing the only one pinpointing the correct telescope discovery. This shows the engines get similar results but Bing usually led to best corrections overall, because for generated queries Bing provided longer and more informative snippets.

Still, the high price of Google and Bing APIs could be a hurdle for large-scale usage. DuckDuckGo achieved adequate performance for $0 and, thus, offers a promising free alternative. Future work could explore additional search filters or filtering of results by trustworthy domains.

Snippets or Full-Article Chunks? When looking at RARR scores of NED, sem. similarity, and G-Eval for snippets and full articles, all are slightly better for the snippets setting. Still, the average NLI scores reveal the full picture – the setting with full articles had high NLI neutral scores. This is because the responses were often refined with irrelevant evidence, whereas the snippet setting produced responses that had a higher NLI-entailment score. The contradiction scores were similar in both. This shows that **snippets** are usually more **on point and related to the actual search query**, while using the **full articles** can lead to selecting **noisy or irrelevant passages from articles**.

Another interesting finding is the general similarity of overall scores, including NLI scores, for the setting with full articles – this shows that all three search engines mostly found the same articles among its top results and then the similarity function selected same passages from those articles.

Zero-shot or Few-shot? Table 3 shows an instance from SummEdits with the gold, hallucinated, and refined summaries by both systems. Both used Bing as the search engine and, thus, both managed to correct factual errors in the input summary (e.g., *struggling* instead of *thriving*). Still, it is evident that RARR returned a summary close in form to the input summary, whereas CoVe augmented the summary with additional information found on Bing.

This difference in length is the consequence of the fact that RARR uses six examples in its few-shot prompt, while CoVe does not use any examples. CoVe also sometimes returned summaries similar to the input summary with minimal changes,

Gold Summary	The founder of the troubled digital start-up Ozy Media has been arrested on fraud charges as part of a scheme to prop up the financially struggling company.
Hallucinated Summary (input to system)	The founder of the **triumphant** digital start-up Ozy Media has been arrested for fraud charges as part of a scheme to **sell** the financially **thriving** company Ozy Media.
RARR (Bing snip.)	The founder of the **ailing** digital start-up Ozy Media has been arrested on fraud charges as part of a plan to **support** the financially **struggling** company.
CoVe (Bing snip.)	The CEO of Ozy Media, Carlos Watson, has been arrested on fraud charges. Ozy Media is facing financial **struggles** and there is a scheme in place to **prop up** the company. However, there is no information or news updates regarding the CEO's arrest. The current status of Ozy Media is that it has shut down, and its CEO has been accused of deceiving potential investors. The company's chairman, Marc Lasry, has stepped down.

Table 3: Example of an instance from SummEdits with final outputs of CoVE and RARR, both based on Bing search snippets. The RARR correction was a lot more concise, while CoVe was more informative and detailed.

however it often returned a lot longer summaries. Long summaries do not necessarily imply hallucinations, but can be summaries with additional context for readers. This points to the fact that **few-shot** prompts are better if the end goal is to **preserve the faithfulness to the original draft**, while **zero-shot** relaxed prompts are better when **adding additional context and making bold edits is preferred**. The few-shot examples are general-domain, so the findings are not just for news.

Open LLMs. We also ran experiments with LLaMa 3.1 (70B), results are in Table 7. For RARR, it had on average weaker scores than GPT 4o-mini, but came quite close, confirming the recent trend of open models closing the gap to closed competitors. For CoVe, which does not have few-shot examples, it generated a lot longer final refined responses than GPT, with lots of detailed explanations. This led to increased G-Eval (Overall & Relevance) and NLI metrics, since these metrics favor information-heavy summaries, but the G-Eval factuality score heavily decreased and summaries were too complex. We additionally ran Mixtral 8x7B with internal knowledge, but it underperformed compared to both Llama and GPT. Future work could explore more open LLMs and evaluate user-centric text quality aspects like readability.

5.1 Human Evaluation

The mean human scores for quality of 10 examples with Bing snippets for 25 participants were **0.68** for RARR and **0.54** for CoVe, showing **users preferred RARR** refinements. The mean G-Eval score for these 10 examples were **0.65** and **0.52**, respectively. This shows an impressively **high alignment of humans with G-Eval** (Pearson correlation coefficient 0.87, p<1%), with the average difference of 3%. Our custom prompts for factuality and relevancy have a high potential for future use, and this positions G-Eval as a promising metric to use when human annotations are not available due to time and costs. For NLI, the alignment was decent but less apparent – DeBERTa overpredicted the neutral class, while human annotators favored the entailment class. Ideally, the DeBERTa-NLI model should be fine-tuned on examples focusing on hallucination detection. More details on human evaluation are in Appendix A.

6 Conclusion and Future Work

In this study, we explored the impact of different evidence sources and search engines on the performance of two SotA systems for post-hoc hallucination correction, CoVe and RARR, for news summaries. Our detailed results show that zero-shot correction systems like CoVe yield more expressive and bold corrections that change the style, while few-shot systems like RARR optimize for faithfulness to the original text and this was favored by humans in evaluation. Additionally, G-Eval metric was highly aligned with humans. We also found that Bing's search snippets led to most informative corrections, followed closely by Google, but DuckDuckGo can be a viable alternative due to its free API and decent performance. We envision future work focusing on enhancing retrieval with structured queries and assessing evidence reliability.

Limitations

An important limitation lies in the fact that all modules of the iterative self-correcting systems rely on using LLMs, which comes with its own set of challenges. The generated follow-up questions are not always perfect or precise, the generated answers from snippets can be off-point, and the final refinement of responses can be too excessive. Future work could explore how to incorporate more controllable generation or structured and rule-based techniques for correcting the output.

Another limitation comes from the high complexity of the system and reliance on calls to external APIs, including LLM APIs and search engine APIs. This can inevitably lead to slow processing speed of these systems when compared to approaches that use smaller encoder-only models or rule-based techniques. Still, we were forced to rely on API calls to LLMs due to our hardware resource limitations. Other lines of work could explore how to better incorporate open and local models into the workflow, for better accountability and faster processing time.

Finally, our work deals only with the news domain, which could limit the generalizability of findings to other domains and use cases.

References

Anum Afzal, Juraj Vladika, Daniel Braun, and Florian Matthes. 2023. Challenges in domain-specific abstractive summarization and how to overcome them. In *15th International Conference on Agents and Artificial Intelligence, ICAART 2023*, pages 682–689. SCITEPRESS.

Vidhisha Balachandran, Hannaneh Hajishirzi, William Cohen, and Yulia Tsvetkov. 2022. Correcting diverse factual errors in abstractive summarization via post-editing and language model infilling. In *Proceedings of the 2022 Conference on Empirical Methods in Natural Language Processing*, pages 9818–9830, Abu Dhabi, United Arab Emirates. Association for Computational Linguistics.

I-Chun Chern, Steffi Chern, Shiqi Chen, Weizhe Yuan, Kehua Feng, Chunting Zhou, Junxian He, Graham Neubig, and Pengfei Liu. 2023. Factool: Factuality detection in generative ai – a tool augmented framework for multi-task and multi-domain scenarios. *Preprint*, arXiv:2307.13528.

Shehzaad Dhuliawala, Mojtaba Komeili, Jing Xu, Roberta Raileanu, Xian Li, Asli Celikyilmaz, and Jason Weston. 2024. Chain-of-verification reduces hallucination in large language models. In *Findings of the Association for Computational Linguistics: ACL 2024*, pages 3563–3578, Bangkok, Thailand. Association for Computational Linguistics.

Yue Dong, John Wieting, and Pat Verga. 2022. Faithful to the document or to the world? mitigating hallucinations via entity-linked knowledge in abstractive summarization. In *Findings of the Association for Computational Linguistics: EMNLP 2022*, pages 1067–1082, Abu Dhabi, United Arab Emirates. Association for Computational Linguistics.

Luyu Gao, Zhuyun Dai, Panupong Pasupat, Anthony Chen, Arun Tejasvi Chaganty, Yicheng Fan, Vincent Zhao, Ni Lao, Hongrae Lee, Da-Cheng Juan, and Kelvin Guu. 2023. RARR: Researching and revising what language models say, using language models. In *Proceedings of the 61st Annual Meeting of the Association for Computational Linguistics (Volume 1: Long Papers)*, pages 16477–16508, Toronto, Canada. Association for Computational Linguistics.

Tianyu Gao, Xingcheng Yao, and Danqi Chen. 2021. SimCSE: Simple contrastive learning of sentence embeddings. In *Proceedings of the 2021 Conference on Empirical Methods in Natural Language Processing*, pages 6894–6910, Online and Punta Cana, Dominican Republic. Association for Computational Linguistics.

Zhibin Gou, Zhihong Shao, Yeyun Gong, yelong shen, Yujiu Yang, Nan Duan, and Weizhu Chen. 2024. CRITIC: Large language models can self-correct with tool-interactive critiquing. In *The Twelfth International Conference on Learning Representations*.

Lucas Graves and Michelle A. Amazeen. 2019. Fact-checking as idea and practice in journalism. *Oxford Research Encyclopedia of Communication*.

Pengcheng He, Jianfeng Gao, and Weizhu Chen. 2023. DeBERTav3: Improving deBERTa using ELECTRA-style pre-training with gradient-disentangled embedding sharing. In *The Eleventh International Conference on Learning Representations*.

Ziwei Ji, Nayeon Lee, Rita Frieske, Tiezheng Yu, Dan Su, Yan Xu, Etsuko Ishii, Ye Jin Bang, Andrea Madotto, and Pascale Fung. 2023. Survey of hallucination in natural language generation. *ACM Comput. Surv.*, 55(12).

Albert Q. Jiang, Alexandre Sablayrolles, Antoine Roux, Arthur Mensch, Blanche Savary, Chris Bamford, Devendra Singh Chaplot, Diego de las Casas, Emma Bou Hanna, Florian Bressand, Gianna Lengyel, Guillaume Bour, Guillaume Lample, Lélio Renard Lavaud, Lucile Saulnier, Marie-Anne Lachaux, Pierre Stock, Sandeep Subramanian, Sophia Yang, Szymon Antoniak, Teven Le Scao, Théophile Gervet, Thibaut Lavril, Thomas Wang, Timothée Lacroix, and William El Sayed. 2024. Mixtral of experts. *Preprint*, arXiv:2401.04088.

Ryo Kamoi, Yusen Zhang, Nan Zhang, Jiawei Han, and Rui Zhang. 2024. When can LLMs actually correct their own mistakes? a critical survey of self-correction of LLMs. *Transactions of the Association for Computational Linguistics*, 12:1417–1440.

Geunwoo Kim, Pierre Baldi, and Stephen Marcus McAleer. 2023. Language models can solve computer tasks. In *Thirty-seventh Conference on Neural Information Processing Systems*.

Philippe Laban, Wojciech Kryscinski, Divyansh Agarwal, Alexander Fabbri, Caiming Xiong, Shafiq Joty, and Chien-Sheng Wu. 2023. SummEdits: Measuring LLM ability at factual reasoning through the lens of summarization. In *Proceedings of the 2023 Conference on Empirical Methods in Natural Language Processing*, pages 9662–9676, Singapore. Association for Computational Linguistics.

Philippe Laban, Tobias Schnabel, Paul N. Bennett, and Marti A. Hearst. 2022. SummaC: Re-visiting NLI-based models for inconsistency detection in summarization. *Transactions of the Association for Computational Linguistics*, 10:163–177.

Moritz Laurer, Wouter Van Atteveldt, Andreu Casas, and Kasper Welbers. 2024. Less annotating, more classifying: Addressing the data scarcity issue of supervised machine learning with deep transfer learning and bert-nli. *Political Analysis*, 32(1):84–100.

Yang Liu, Dan Iter, Yichong Xu, Shuohang Wang, Ruochen Xu, and Chenguang Zhu. 2023. G-eval: NLG evaluation using gpt-4 with better human alignment. In *Proceedings of the 2023 Conference on Empirical Methods in Natural Language Processing*, pages 2511–2522, Singapore. Association for Computational Linguistics.

AI @ Meta Llama Team. 2024. The llama 3 herd of models. *Preprint*, arXiv:2407.21783.

Aman Madaan, Niket Tandon, Prakhar Gupta, Skyler Hallinan, Luyu Gao, Sarah Wiegreffe, Uri Alon, Nouha Dziri, Shrimai Prabhumoye, Yiming Yang, Shashank Gupta, Bodhisattwa Prasad Majumder, Katherine Hermann, Sean Welleck, Amir Yazdanbakhsh, and Peter Clark. 2023. Self-refine: Iterative refinement with self-feedback. In *Thirty-seventh Conference on Neural Information Processing Systems*.

Sewon Min, Kalpesh Krishna, Xinxi Lyu, Mike Lewis, Wen-tau Yih, Pang Koh, Mohit Iyyer, Luke Zettlemoyer, and Hannaneh Hajishirzi. 2023. FActScore: Fine-grained atomic evaluation of factual precision in long form text generation. In *Proceedings of the 2023 Conference on Empirical Methods in Natural Language Processing*, pages 12076–12100, Singapore. Association for Computational Linguistics.

Anshuman Mishra, Dhruvesh Patel, Aparna Vijayakumar, Xiang Lorraine Li, Pavan Kapanipathi, and Kartik Talamadupula. 2021. Looking beyond sentence-level natural language inference for question answering and text summarization. In *Proceedings of the 2021 Conference of the North American Chapter of the Association for Computational Linguistics: Human Language Technologies*, pages 1322–1336, Online. Association for Computational Linguistics.

OpenAI. 2024. Gpt-4 technical report. *Preprint*, arXiv:2303.08774.

Niko Palić, Juraj Vladika, Dominik Čubelić, Ivan Lovrenčić, Maja Buljan, and Jan Šnajder. 2019. Takelab at semeval-2019 task 4: Hyperpartisan news detection. In *Proceedings of the 13th international workshop on semantic evaluation*, pages 995–998.

Julius Steen, Juri Opitz, Anette Frank, and Katja Markert. 2023. With a little push, NLI models can robustly and efficiently predict faithfulness. In *Proceedings of the 61st Annual Meeting of the Association for Computational Linguistics (Volume 2: Short Papers)*, pages 914–924, Toronto, Canada. Association for Computational Linguistics.

Liyan Tang, Tanya Goyal, Alexander R Fabbri, Philippe Laban, Jiacheng Xu, Semih Yavuz, Wojciech Kryściński, Justin F Rousseau, and Greg Durrett. 2022. Understanding factual errors in summarization: Errors, summarizers, datasets, error detectors. *arXiv preprint arXiv:2205.12854*.

S. M Towhidul Islam Tonmoy, S M Mehedi Zaman, Vinija Jain, Anku Rani, Vipula Rawte, Aman Chadha, and Amitava Das. 2024. A comprehensive survey of hallucination mitigation techniques in large language models. *Preprint*, arXiv:2401.01313.

Neeraj Varshney, Wenlin Yao, Hongming Zhang, Jianshu Chen, and Dong Yu. 2023. A stitch in time saves nine: Detecting and mitigating hallucinations of llms by validating low-confidence generation. *Preprint*, arXiv:2307.03987.

Juraj Vladika, Ivana Hacajova, and Florian Matthes. 2025. Step-by-step fact verification system for medical claims with explainable reasoning. In *Proceedings of the 2025 Conference of the Nations of the Americas Chapter of the Association for Computational Linguistics: Human Language Technologies (Volume 2: Short Papers)*, pages 805–816, Albuquerque, New Mexico. Association for Computational Linguistics.

Juraj Vladika and Florian Matthes. 2023. Scientific fact-checking: A survey of resources and approaches. In *Findings of the Association for Computational Linguistics: ACL 2023*, pages 6215–6230, Toronto, Canada. Association for Computational Linguistics.

Boxin Wang, Weixin Chen, Hengzhi Pei, Chulin Xie, Mintong Kang, Chenhui Zhang, Chejian Xu, Zidi Xiong, Ritik Dutta, Rylan Schaeffer, Sang T. Truong, Simran Arora, Mantas Mazeika, Dan Hendrycks, Zinan Lin, Yu Cheng, Sanmi Koyejo, Dawn Song, and Bo Li. 2023a. Decodingtrust: A comprehensive assessment of trustworthiness in GPT models. In *Thirty-seventh Conference on Neural Information Processing Systems Datasets and Benchmarks Track*.

Haifeng Wang, Jiwei Li, Hua Wu, Eduard Hovy, and Yu Sun. 2023b. Pre-trained language models and their applications. *Engineering*, 25:51–65.

Yuxia Wang, Revanth Gangi Reddy, Zain Muhammad Mujahid, Arnav Arora, Aleksandr Rubashevskii, Jiahui Geng, Osama Mohammed Afzal, Liangming Pan, Nadav Borenstein, Aditya Pillai, Isabelle Augenstein, Iryna Gurevych, and Preslav Nakov. 2024. Factcheck-bench: Fine-grained evaluation benchmark for automatic fact-checkers. In *Findings of the Association for Computational Linguistics: EMNLP*

2024, pages 14199–14230, Miami, Florida, USA. Association for Computational Linguistics.

Jerry Wei, Chengrun Yang, Xinying Song, Yifeng Lu, Nathan Zixia Hu, Jie Huang, Dustin Tran, Daiyi Peng, Ruibo Liu, Da Huang, Cosmo Du, and Quoc V Le. 2024. Long-form factuality in large language models. In *The Thirty-eighth Annual Conference on Neural Information Processing Systems*.

Li Yujian and Liu Bo. 2007. A normalized levenshtein distance metric. *IEEE transactions on pattern analysis and machine intelligence*, 29(6):1091–1095.

Jiawei Zhang, Chejian Xu, Yu Gai, Freddy Lecue, Shuang Yang, Dawn Song, and Bo Li. 2025. Knowhalu: Hallucination detection via multi-form knowledge based factual checking. In *ICLR 2025 Workshop on Foundation Models in the Wild*.

Yue Zhang, Yafu Li, Leyang Cui, Deng Cai, Lemao Liu, Tingchen Fu, Xinting Huang, Enbo Zhao, Yu Zhang, Yulong Chen, Longyue Wang, Anh Tuan Luu, Wei Bi, Freda Shi, and Shuming Shi. 2023. Siren's song in the ai ocean: A survey on hallucination in large language models. *Preprint*, arXiv:2309.01219.

Lianmin Zheng, Wei-Lin Chiang, Ying Sheng, Siyuan Zhuang, Zhanghao Wu, Yonghao Zhuang, Zi Lin, Zhuohan Li, Dacheng Li, Eric Xing, et al. 2023. Judging llm-as-a-judge with mt-bench and chatbot arena. *Advances in Neural Information Processing Systems*, 36:46595–46623.

Shijia Zhou, Leonie Weissweiler, Taiqi He, Hinrich Schütze, David R. Mortensen, and Lori Levin. 2024. Constructions are so difficult that Even large language models get them right for the wrong reasons. In *Proceedings of the 2024 Joint International Conference on Computational Linguistics, Language Resources and Evaluation (LREC-COLING 2024)*, pages 3804–3811, Torino, Italia. ELRA and ICCL.

A Human Evaluation

The main goal of the human evaluation was to judge two automated metrics, NLI predictions and LLM-as-a-judge (G-Eval), by observing the alignment between human preference and machine evaluation results. All the evaluation responses and results are attached to the ARR submission.

A.1 Study Format and Instructions

User study was conducted with 25 participants. All participants are pursuing a master's degree or a PhD degree in computer science at authors' university. They were not monetarily compensated since they are in-house annotators from our school's department of computer science. All responses were anonymous and collected only for the purpose of this research study. Users were provided with instructions described in Table 4.

The survey was hosted as a questionnaire on the JotForm platform.[3] In total, there were 10 examples, where each example consisted of a correct summary, a hallucinated summary, a summary corrected by CoVe, a summary corrected by RARR, and 4 questions to answer. In Figure 1, a sample screenshot from the evaluation form is provided.

Users were asked to evaluate each of the two generated summaries in two aspects: overall quality and NLI relation. The overall quality was estimated by rating from 1 to 10 and it refers to (a) how factually accurate was the summary, and (b) how relevant and on-topic was it. The NLI (entailment) relation were mapped to NLI classes by asking the users whether the generated summary supports the gold summary (entailment), contradicts the gold summary (contradiction), or partially aligns with the gold summary (neutral).

In each example, we include samples from RARR or COVE as either summary A or B. Correct summary represents the ground truth summary from the SummEdits dataset. Summary A or B from self-correcting systems were generated using snippets from the Bing search engine. Both self-correcting systems were provided with the same hallucinated version of the correct summary and the pipeline for rewriting was ran.

A.2 Overall Quality Results

In the survey, the "overall quality" score was rated from 1 to 10 and it referred to how factual the summary was and how relevant (on-topic) it was, when compared to the original (gold summary). To evaluate the alignment between the G-Eval scores and human evaluations for the RARR and COVE methods, we analyzed the mean scores and their differences. Human scores are an average of 250 scores, normalized to the percentage value. Results are summarized in Table 5.

For RARR, average human score is 0.68, and average G-Eval score is 0.65. For the COVE method, average human score is 0.54, and average G-Eval score is 0.52. G-Eval scores are slightly lower than human evaluations. These minor differences for both RARR and COVE suggest that G-Eval scores closely reflect human evaluations for both methods, with a deviation of ±3%.

[3] https://www.jotform.com

Instructions
Read the correct summary first.
Compare the correct summary with the generated Summary A and Summary B.
There are no right or wrong answers.
Both summaries can be good or bad.
For each summary (A and B), there are two types of questions:
1. Choose the option that best fits the blank:

- **Contradicts**: Disagrees with the correct summary
- **Supports**: Agrees with the correct summary
- **Partially aligns with**: Only somewhat related or unrelated

2. Rate the Overall Quality (Factual accuracy + Relevance):

- **Factual accuracy**: Is it based on facts? Avoids misinformation?
- **Relevance**: Does the summary cover the main points? Not off-topic?

Table 4: Instructions that human annotators received.

A.3 Natural Language Inference Results

We also compared human evaluation and ground truth values for Natural Language Inference (NLI) across three categories: Entailment, Neutral, and Contradiction. As discussed before, DeBERTa-v3 model (Laurer et al., 2024) is used for NLI evaluation. The results are presented in Table 6.

For both self-correcting systems, there is a higher percentage of Entailment in human evaluations compared to the NLI model, particularly in RARR. Also, percentage of Neutral instances is lower in human evaluations. NLI model is more likely to classify instances as Neutral than humans. Contradiction shows higher percentages in human evaluations for COVE compared to the NLI model. Overall, as demonstrated by evaluation of experiments and human evaluation, RARR performs better than COVE in SummEdits dataset.

A.4 Alignment between Automated Metrics and Human Scores

Analyses indicate a strong alignment between G-Eval scores and human evaluations for both RARR and COVE methods in rating the overall quality aspect. This consistency means that G-Eval is a reliable tool for approximating human assessments. It can be used in scenarios where human evaluations are impractical when there are time or resource constraints.

When it comes to NLI, humans had a somewhat different feeling of which class to assign than the automated method. Differences between human evaluation and automated predictions were more evident than in case of G-Eval, although there was still an alignment in terms of predominant classes. This shows that while NLI is a decent metric, there is still room for improvement, possibly in terms of additionally fine-tuning the predictor model (DeBERTa) on further NLI datasets or datasets centered around the specific tasks of factuality and generation-quality prediction. Another option is using more complex models like LLMs for prediction, although they have been found to favor the entailment class as opposed to the neutral class in NLI predictions (Zhou et al., 2024).

B Results with Open LLMs

We additionally performed experiments with two popular open-source LLMs, Llama 3.1 (70B) (Llama Team, 2024) and Mixtral 8x7B (Jiang et al., 2024), to test how well do they fare compared to GPT. The results are shown in Table 7. The models were prompted using the API endpoint of Together AI,[4] a platform that host popular open-source LLMs. All the settings we applied were the same as for GPT and Open AI's API, including temperature set to 0 for better reproducibility.

C Prompts

This appendix section provides the prompts used in the CoVe system in Table 8 and for the RARR system in Tables 9 and 10. Additionally, the prompts used for the LLM-as-judge metric G-Eval are given in Table 11.

[4]https://www.together.ai/

Method	Human Mean Score	G-Eval Score	Diff
RARR	0.68	0.65	0.03
COVE	0.54	0.52	0.02

Table 5: Alignment between G-Eval scores and human evaluations.

Method	Human			NLI Model		
	Entailment	Neutral	Contradiction	Entailment	Neutral	Contradiction
RARR	45	40	15	30	49	21
COVE	31	37	32	28	47	25

Table 6: Comparison of Human Evaluation and NLI predictions

Base LLM	verification system	evidence source	simple NED	simple Sem.	NLI Ent.	NLI Neu.	NLI Con.	G-Eval Overall	G-Eval Factual.	G-Eval Relev.
Mixtral 8x7B	**CoVE**	Mixtral	0.77	74	30	48	22	64	42	59
	RARR	Mixtral	0.43	84	26	32	42	55	43	50
LLaMa 3.1 (70B)	**CoVE**	Llama	0.78	70	38	51	**11**	67	50	73
	RARR	Llama	0.20	94	39	24	37	63	59	71
LLaMa 3.1 (70B)	**CoVE**	Google	0.78	75	43	44	<u>13</u>	<u>67</u>	47	<u>73</u>
		Bing	0.79	75	41	44	15	**68**	46	**74**
		DDG	0.80	73	34	46	20	59	39	66
LLaMa 3.1 (70B)	**RARR**	Google	0.28	90	**46**	24	30	66	**62**	72
		Bing	0.33	88	<u>44</u>	28	28	64	<u>59</u>	70
		DDG	0.42	84	34	26	40	54	48	58

Table 7: Results of CoVE and RARR on SummEdits using two open-source LLMs, Llama 3.1 and Mixtral. NED refers to normalized edit distance, Sem. to average cosine semantic similarity, NLI scores to average prediction probability for entailment, neutral, and contradiction. The best score for each metric is in **bold**, while the second best is <u>underlined</u>.

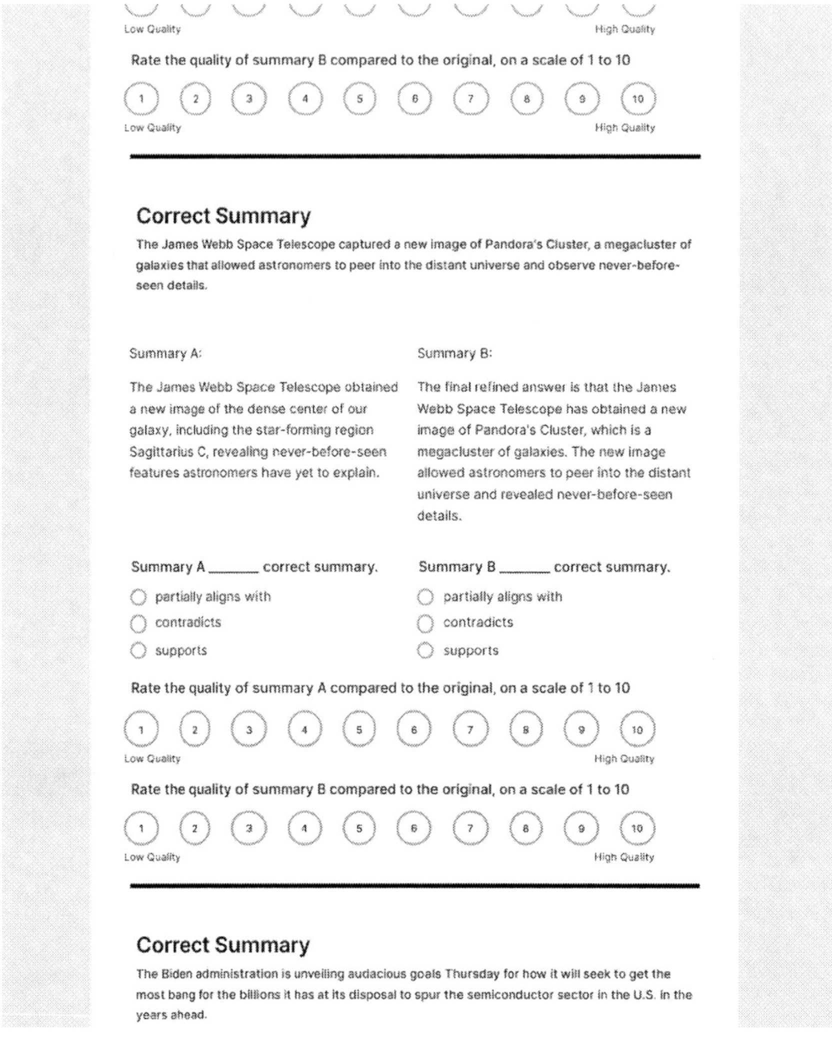
Low Quality High Quality

Rate the quality of summary B compared to the original, on a scale of 1 to 10

1 2 3 4 5 6 7 8 9 10

Low Quality High Quality

Correct Summary

The James Webb Space Telescope captured a new image of Pandora's Cluster, a megacluster of galaxies that allowed astronomers to peer into the distant universe and observe never-before-seen details.

Summary A:

The James Webb Space Telescope obtained a new image of the dense center of our galaxy, including the star-forming region Sagittarius C, revealing never-before-seen features astronomers have yet to explain.

Summary B:

The final refined answer is that the James Webb Space Telescope has obtained a new image of Pandora's Cluster, which is a megacluster of galaxies. The new image allowed astronomers to peer into the distant universe and revealed never-before-seen details.

Summary A _______ correct summary.

- partially aligns with
- contradicts
- supports

Summary B _______ correct summary.

- partially aligns with
- contradicts
- supports

Rate the quality of summary A compared to the original, on a scale of 1 to 10

1 2 3 4 5 6 7 8 9 10

Low Quality High Quality

Rate the quality of summary B compared to the original, on a scale of 1 to 10

1 2 3 4 5 6 7 8 9 10

Low Quality High Quality

Correct Summary

The Biden administration is unveiling audacious goals Thursday for how it will seek to get the most bang for the billions it has at its disposal to spur the semiconductor sector in the U.S. in the years ahead.

Figure 1: A screenshot from Human Evaluation Form.

Use Case	Prompt Content
Generate verification question (template)	Your task is to create a verification question based on the below question provided. Example Question: Who are some movie actors who were born in Boston? Example Verification Question: Was [movie actor] born in [Boston] Explanation: In the above example the verification question focused only on the ANSWER_ENTITY (name of the movie actor) and QUESTION_ENTITY (birth place). Similarly you need to focus on the ANSWER_ENTITY and QUESTION_ENTITY from the actual question and generate verification question. Actual Question: original_question Final Verification Question:
Generate verification question	Your task is to create verification questions based on the below original question and the baseline response. The verification questions are meant for verifying the factual accuracy in the baseline response. Output should be numbered list of verification questions. Actual Question: original_question Baseline Response: baseline_response Final Verification Questions:
Answer verification question	Answer the following question correctly based on the provided context. The question could be tricky as well, so think step by step and answer it correctly. Context: search_result Question: verification_question Answer:
Refine the original response	Given the below 'Original Query' and 'Baseline Answer', analyze the 'Verification Questions & Answers' to finally filter the refined answer. Original Query: original_question Baseline Answer: baseline_response Verification Questions & Answer Pairs: verification_answers Final Refined Answer:

Table 8: Overview of prompts used for the Chain-of-Verification (CoVE) system.

Use Case	Prompt Content
Generate verification question	I will check things you said and ask questions. You said: Your nose switches back and forth between nostrils. When you sleep, you switch about every 45 minutes. This is to prevent a buildup of mucus. It's called the nasal cycle. To verify it, 1. I googled: Does your nose switch between nostrils? 2. I googled: How often does your nostrils switch? 3. I googled: Why does your nostril switch? 4. I googled: What is nasal cycle? You said: The Stanford Prison Experiment was conducted in the basement of Encina Hall, Stanford's psychology building. To verify it, 1. I googled: Where was Stanford Prison Experiment was conducted? *(four more examples)* You said: claim To verify it,
Answer verification question	I will check some things you said. 1. You said: Your nose switches back and forth between nostrils. When you sleep, you switch about every 45 minutes. This is to prevent a buildup of mucus. It's called the nasal cycle. 2. I checked: How often do your nostrils switch? 3. I found this article: Although we don't usually notice it, during the nasal cycle one nostril becomes congested and thus contributes less to airflow, while the other becomes decongested. On average, the congestion pattern switches about every 2 hours, according to a small 2016 study published in the journal PLOS One. 4. Reasoning: The article said the nose's switching time is about every 2 hours, and you said the nose's switching time is about every 45 minutes. 5. Therefore: This disagrees with what you said. 1. You said: The Little House books were written by Laura Ingalls Wilder. The books were published by HarperCollins. 2. I checked: Who published the Little House books? 3. I found this article: These are the books that started it all – the stories that captured the hearts and imaginations of children and young adults worldwide. Written by Laura Ingalls Wilder and published by HarperCollins, these beloved books remain a favorite to this day. 4. Reasoning: The article said the Little House books were published by HarperCollins and you said the books were published by HarperCollins. 5. Therefore: This agrees with what you said. *(four more examples)* 1. You said: claim 2. I checked: query 3. I found this article: evidence 4. Reasoning:

Table 9: Overview of prompts for verification question generation and answering used for the RARR system.

Use Case	Prompt Content
Refine the original response	I will fix some things you said. 1. You said: Your nose switches back and forth between nostrils. When you sleep, you switch about every 45 minutes. This is to prevent a buildup of mucus. It's called the nasal cycle. 2. I checked: How often do your nostrils switch? 3. I found this article: Although we don't usually notice it, during the nasal cycle one nostril becomes congested and thus contributes less to airflow, while the other becomes decongested. On average, the congestion pattern switches about every 2 hours, according to a small 2016 study published in the journal PLOS One. 4. This suggests 45 minutes switch time in your statement is wrong. 5. My fix: Your nose switches back and forth between nostrils. When you sleep, you switch about every 2 hours. This is to prevent a buildup of mucus. It's called the nasal cycle. 1. You said: In the battles of Lexington and Concord, the British side was led by General Thomas Hall. 2. I checked: Who led the British side in the battle of Lexington and Concord? 3. I found this article: Interesting Facts about the Battles of Lexington and Concord. The British were led by Lieutenant Colonel Francis Smith. There were 700 British regulars. 4. This suggests General Thomas Hall in your statement is wrong. 5. My fix: In the battles of Lexington and Concord, the British side was led by Lieutenant Colonel Francis Smith. *(four more examples)* 1. You said: claim 2. I checked: query 3. I found this article: evidence 4. This suggests

Table 10: Overview of prompts for response refinement used for the RARR system.

Evaluated Aspect	Prompt Content
Factuality	Evaluate if the actual output contains hallucinated information not present in the input. STEPS: Identify any claims or statements in the 'actual output'. Compare each claim with the 'input' to check for the presence of supporting information. Mark any claims that are not supported by the 'input' as hallucinated. Penalize heavily for any introduction of new, unsupported facts.
Relevance	Evaluate the relevancy of the actual output to the input. STEPS: Check if 'actual output' directly addresses the query or topic presented in 'input'. Penalize responses that are off-topic or provide irrelevant information.
Overall	Evaluate the overall quality and correctness of the actual output compared to the input. STEPS: Assess if the 'actual output' provides a coherent and accurate response to 'input'. Penalize factual inaccuracies, grammatical errors, and unclear language.

Table 11: Overview of prompts used for the G-Eval metric.

The Law of Knowledge Overshadowing: Towards Understanding, Predicting, and Preventing LLM Hallucination

Yuji Zhang[1], **Sha Li**[1], **Cheng Qian**[1], **Jiateng Liu**[1], **Pengfei Yu**[1], **Chi Han**[1], **Yi R. Fung**[1]
Kathleen McKeown[2], **Chengxiang Zhai**[1], **Manling Li**[3,4], **Heng Ji**[1]
[1]University of Illinois Urbana-Champaign, [2]Columbia University,
[3]Northwestern University, [4]Stanford University
{yujiz, hengji}@illinois.edu

Abstract

Hallucination is a persistent challenge in large language models (LLMs), where even with rigorous quality control, models often generate distorted facts. This paradox, in which error generation continues despite high-quality training data, calls for a deeper understanding of the underlying LLM mechanisms. To address it, we propose a novel concept: **knowledge overshadowing**, where model's dominant knowledge can obscure less prominent knowledge during text generation, causing the model to fabricate inaccurate details. Building on this idea, we introduce a novel framework to quantify hallucinations by modeling knowledge overshadowing. Central to our approach is the **log-linear law**, which predicts that the rate of hallucination increases linearly with the logarithmic scale of (1) *Knowledge Popularity*, (2) *Knowledge Length*, and (3) *Model Size*. The law provides a means to preemptively quantify hallucinations, offering foresight into their occurrence even before model training or inference. Built on the overshadowing effect, we propose a new decoding strategy **CoDA**, to mitigate hallucinations, which notably enhances model factuality on Overshadow (27.9%), MemoTrap (13.1%) and NQ-Swap (18.3%). Our findings not only deepen understandings of the underlying mechanisms behind hallucinations but also provide actionable insights for developing more predictable and controllable language models.

1 Introduction

Large language models (LLMs) have revolutionized artificial intelligence, but their success is accompanied by a critical issue known as hallucination (Ye et al., 2023). Hallucination refers to models generating unfaithful or nonfactual statements. In many applications, this issue undermines performance and reliability, posing substantial challenges to their practical deployment (Li et al., 2024).

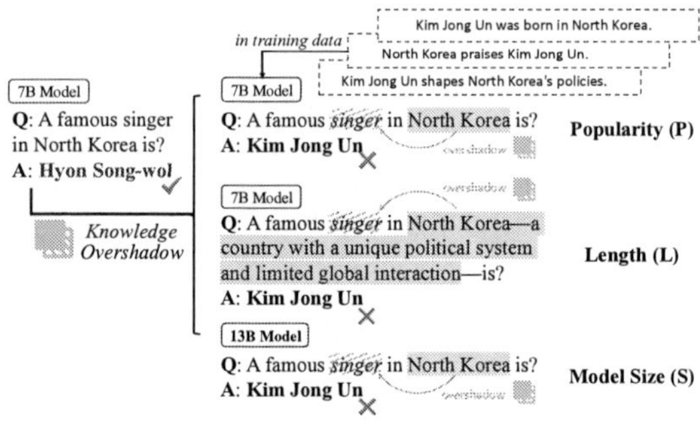

Figure 1: Knowledge overshadowing leads to hallucinations, which exarcerbates with growing relative knowledge popularity (P), length (L), and model size (S).

Some studies attribute hallucination to low-quality pretraining corpora (Gehman et al., 2020). However, we find it persists even when the pretraining corpus is strictly controlled to contain only factual statements. Specifically, when extracting knowledge using queries, we observe a tendency for certain knowledge to overshadow other relevant information. This causes the model to reason without adequately considering overshadowed knowledge, leading to hallucinations.

As shown in Figure 1, when queried for "*famous singer in North Korea*", the model incorrectly nominate "Kim Jong Un", who is in fact a politician, as a result of "North Korea" overshadowing "singer". This observation highlights how knowledge of varying forms interacts, distorting the reasoning process and causing the model to misassemble facts, thereby generating hallucinations. To investigate this phenomenon, we raise the following questions:

- **What** factors contribute to the phenomenon of knowledge overshadowing (§3)?
- Can we preemptively quantify **when** hallucinations occur (§4)?
- From a theoretical perspective, **why** knowledge overshadowing happens (§5)?
- Leveraging the insights we derived, **how** to mitigate factual hallucinations (§6)?

Proceedings of the Eighth Fact Extraction and VERification Workshop (FEVER), pages 132–150
July 31, 2025 ©2025 Association for Computational Linguistics

Through extensive experiments, we find that knowledge overshadowing broadly induces factual hallucinations in both pretrained and fine-tuned models, across diverse model families and sizes. Despite its importance, the factors influencing this phenomenon remain unexplored. To bridge this gap, we analyze knowledge representation from both global and local perspectives by examining its *popularity* across the dataset distribution and its proportional representation *length* within individual sentences. Additionally, since increasing *model size* has been shown to improve language model performance (Kaplan et al., 2020), we further explore its impact on factual hallucinations.

To examine the impact of these factors, we pretrain LLMs from scratch on a synthetic dataset with strictly controlled quality. Our empirical findings reveal a **log-linear scaling law** for factual hallucinations, showing that hallucination rates increase linearly with the logarithmic scale of relative knowledge popularity, knowledge length, and model size. Finetuning on diverse tasks further confirms this law applies to finetuned LLMs, enabling the preemptive quantification of hallucinations before model training or inference. This not only bridges the gap in understanding hallucinations emerging from factual training data but also introduces a principled approach for evaluating training data and predicting model behavior in advance.

The empirical discovery of this law leads us to investigate its underlying cause. We hypothesize that knowledge overshadowing stems from the overgeneralization of popular knowledge, suppressing less popular counterparts. Theoretically, we derive a generalization bound for auto-regressive language modeling, linking the model's behavior to key properties of its training data. Our analysis shows that generalization improves with increasing relative knowledge popularity and length, mirroring the trend observed in hallucination rates.

Building on all the insights derived, we propose **Co**ntrastive **D**ecoding to **A**mplify Overshadowed Knowledge (**CoDA**), a method designed to amplify the influence of overshadowed knowledge while mitigating biases from dominant knowledge. First, we identify overshadowed knowledge by computing the mutual information between the next-token probability distributions of the original and modified prompts, where specific tokens are masked. This approach reveals knowledge encoded in the masked tokens, which is often overlooked and prone to hallucination. We then employ contrastive decoding to reduce the bias introduced by dominant knowledge. Without requiring additional training, CoDA significantly improves factuality, achieving gains of 13.1%, 18.3%, and 27.9% on the MemoTrap, NQ-Swap, and Overshadowing datasets, respectively. Our contributions are three-fold:

- We are the first to identify knowledge overshadowing as a key driver of hallucinations and demonstrate its prevalence across LLMs.
- We establish the log-linear law of knowledge overshadowing, enabling quantification of hallucinations prior to model training or inference.
- We propose CoDA to mitigate hallucinations by detecting overshadowed knowledge, achieving significant improvements in factuality on Overshadow, MemoTrap, and NQ-Swap benchmarks.

2 Related Work

2.1 Causes of Hallucination

Our work is in line with exploring the source of hallucination. One popular opinion is that factual hallucination stems from deficiencies in training data, which can either be outdated information (Zhang et al., 2021, 2023b; Livska et al., 2022; Luu et al., 2022), biases (Ladhak et al., 2023; Yang et al., 2023), misinformation (Dziri et al., 2022; Lin et al., 2022), bad calibration (Chen et al., 2023b; Tian et al., 2023; Zhang et al., 2024a,b), or overalignment to human preferences (Wei et al., 2023).

Other research points to generation issues including distorted attention (Aralikatte et al., 2021), over-confidence (Ren et al., 2023). Related efforts also suggest that LLMs can be trapped in common patterns (Lin et al., 2022; Kandpal et al., 2023; Li et al., 2023a). We focus on a significant yet underexplored phenomenon: LLMs can hallucinate even when trained exclusively on high-quality, truthful data. We introduce knowledge overshadowing, where more dominant knowledge representation competes against and suppresses less prevalent knowledge, resulting in factual hallucinations.

2.2 Detection of Hallucination

Hallucination detection in LMs typically involves external fact-checking methods, such as FActScore (Min et al., 2023) and FacTool (Chern et al., 2023), or internal uncertainty analysis. The latter includes Chain-of-Verification (Dhuliawala et al., 2023), logit-based assessments (Kadavath et al., 2022; Zhang et al., 2024c), and leveraging LM internal states (Zhang et al., 2024a; Luo et al., 2023; Ma et al., 2025). When internal states are unavailable, self-consistency probing (Manakul et al., 2023; Agrawal et al., 2024) or multi-LM examination (Cohen et al., 2023) can provide alternative signals. Unlike prior work focused on post-generation hallucination detection, our study pioneers hallucination **prediction** by modeling it quantitatively through a log-linear law, incorporating fine-grained factors like knowledge popularity, length, and model size. This shifts the paradigm from reactive detection to proactive prevention, offering a novel quantitative framework for anticipating hallucinations.

2.3 Elimination of Hallucination

Our work is related to prior studies on mitigating hallucinations. Shen et al. (2021) address the issue by filtering out low-quality training data. Several approaches enhance model factuality through external knowledge (Wu et al., 2023; Xie et al., 2023; Lyu et al., 2023; Asai et al., 2023; Ma et al., 2023; Song et al., 2023), and knowledge-aware tuning (Zhang et al., 2025; Li et al., 2022). Some studies tackle hallucination by enforcing LLMs to adhere to input (Tian et al., 2019; Aralikatte et al., 2021), modifying internal states (Gottesman and Geva, 2024; He et al., 2025), and adopting refusal-awareness (Zhang et al., 2024a; Huang et al., 2025). Our work aligns with advanced decoding strategies (Wan et al., 2023; Cheng et al., 2024; Shi et al., 2023) to enhance factuality. Early detection of hallucination is also crucial (Zhang et al., 2023a, 2024d). Our method not only foresees potential hallucinations before generation but also eliminates them through a training- and data-free approach.

3 What is Knowledge Overshadowing?

Factual hallucination, where authentic facts are misassembled into false statements, remains an underexplored challenge. We approach this issue through the lens of knowledge overshadowing, where more prevalent knowledge suppresses less frequent knowledge, resulting in hallucinations.

3.1 Knowledge Overshadowing Formulation

To systematically characterize knowledge overshadowing, we define knowledge pairs in a training corpus. Specifically, let $\mathbb{K}_A = \{k_{a_1}, ..., k_{a_m}\}$ and $\mathbb{K}_B = \{k_{b_1}, ..., k_{b_n}\}$ represent a pair of knowledge sets. $\mathbb{K}_A$ is comprised of m samples of statements k_{a_i}, and $\mathbb{K}_B$ is comprised of n samples of statements k_{b_j}. Each statement in $\mathbb{K}_A$ and statement in $\mathbb{K}_B$ are related by a shared set of tokens X_{share}.

In the knowledge set $\mathbb{K}_A$, each statement k_{a_i} is comprised of a shared token sequence X_{share}, a distinct token sequence x_{a_i}, and the output Y_a. Each statement k_{a_i} is expressed as:

$$k_{a_i} = Y_a|[X_{\text{share}} \odot x_{a_i}], \quad i \in \{1, ..., m\} \tag{1}$$

where $\odot$ denotes the insertion of the distinctive sequence x_{a_i} into X_{share} (the integration position can vary). Similarly, for the less popular knowledge set $\mathbb{K}_B$, with x_{b_j} denoted as the distinct token sequence, each statement k_{b_j} is formulated as:

$$k_{b_j} = Y_b|[X_{\text{share}} \odot x_{b_j}], \quad j \in \{1, ..., n\} \tag{2}$$

Knowledge overshadowing occurs when the distinct token sequence x_{b_j} or x_{a_i} is suppressed during inference. Taking x_{b_j} overshadowed as an example, when prompted with $X_{\text{share}} \odot x_{b_j}$, the model outputs Y_a, forming the $Y_a|[X_{\text{share}} \odot x_{b_j}]$ that wrongly amalgamates factual statements k_{a_i} and k_{b_j} into factual hallucination, defying the ground-truth $Y_b|[X_{\text{share}} \odot x_{b_j}]$, as illustrated in Figure 1.

3.2 Metric of Factual Hallucination.

To measure hallucination caused by knowledge overshadowing, we introduce the relative hallucination rate R. When $\mathbb{K}_A$ is the more popular knowledge set, we first quantify the recall rate of the model correctly memorizing the samples from $\mathbb{K}_A$ as $\text{RR} = p(Y_a|[X_{\text{share}} \odot x_{a_i}])$. Then we quantify the hallucination rate of the model producing output with x_{b_j} overshadowed as $\text{HR} = p(Y_a|[X_{\text{share}} \odot x_{b_j}])$. The relative hallucination rate $\text{R} = \frac{\text{HR}}{\text{RR}}$ represents to what extent is less popular knowledge encoded by x_{b_j} suppressed by the more popular knowledge encoded by x_{a_i}.

3.3 Formulation of Influential Variables

Since the underlying factors influencing factual hallucinations have not been explored, we examine these variables from both global and local perspectives, focusing on knowledge proportions that contribute to the overshadowing effect. When $\mathbb{K}_A$ is more popular than $\mathbb{K}_B$, $m > n$. From a global perspective, we define the relative knowledge popularity as $\text{P} = \frac{m}{n}$, denoting the relative proportion of the knowledge in the whole training corpus. From the local perspective, we quantify the weight of knowledge in an individual sentence using the relative knowledge length $\text{L} = \frac{\text{len}(X_{\text{share}})+\text{len}(x_{b_j})}{\text{len}(x_{b_j})}$, where length is measured by the number of tokens. For example in Figure 1, in input "A famous singer

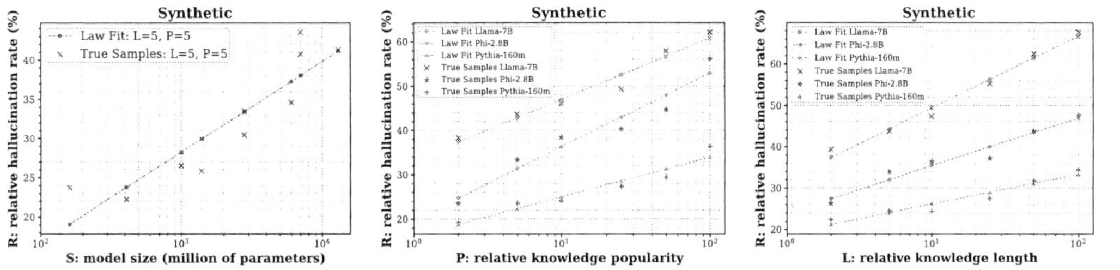

Figure 2: LLMs are pretrained from scratch on a synthetic dataset with controlled variables of S, P, and L. In each subfigre, we experiment by varying one variable at a time while keeping the other two constants. LLMs are trained auto-regressively with cross-entropy loss computed over entire sentences. Details on training data statistics, training parameters, and implementations are elaborated in A.2, A.3.

in North Korea is", length of x_{b_j}="singer" is 1, length of X_{share}="A famous _ in North Korea is" is 6, so L=(6+1)/1=7. Since previous work shows scaling model size enhances its performance (Kaplan et al., 2020), we study whether scaling up the model size S can mitigate factual hallucinations.

4 When to Expect Factual Hallucination?

To determine the conditions under which factual hallucinations emerge, we investigate knowledge overshadowing across various experimental setups, including probing an open-source pretrained LLM without training, pretraining an LLM from scratch, fine-tuning a pretrained LLM on downstream tasks.

4.1 Probing the Open-source LLM

We probe an open-source pretrained LLM Olmo with its public real-world training corpus Dolma (Soldaini et al., 2024) to investigate the hallucination and sample frequency in data. Results show that knowledge with higher frequency tends to overshadow others with lower frequency, aligning with knowledge overshadowing concept that more dominant knowledge overshadows less prominent knowledge during text generation, leading to counterfactual outputs. For example, when "male AI researcher" appears more frequently than "female AI researcher" in the training corpus, the model tends to output male researchers when we query the model with "Tell me some outstanding female AI scientists" (See details in A.4).

4.2 Unveiling Log-linear Law in the Pretrained LLMs.

Setup. Investigating real-world knowledge hallucinations via knowledge overshadowing requires access to the open-source pretraining corpus of LLMs, while most of the LLMs' pretraining corpus is closed-sourced. Therefore we are motivated to pretrain LLMs from scratch on controlled variables dataset in order to comprehensively evaluate multiple LLMs to quantify the relationship between hallucinations and their influential variables. Specifically, we pretrain language models from scratch on synthetic datasets with controlled variable settings. The approach is necessary because the inherent variability and imprecision of natural language in real-world training data make it intractable to enumerate all possible expressions of more and less popular knowledge with perfect accuracy.

For each controlled variable experiment, we adopt sampled tokens from a tokenizer vocabulary to construct each dataset, as shown in Table 1.

• P: We investigate how the hallucination rate R changes with increasing relative knowledge popularity P. We set P $= \frac{m}{n}$ for values {2:1, 5:1, 10:1, 25:1, 50:1, 100:1}, where m represents the number of samples of $k_{a_i} = Y_a|[X_{\text{share}} \odot x_{a_i}]$ and n represents the number of samples of $k_{b_i} = Y_b|[X_{\text{share}} \odot x_{b_i}]$. The other variables, L and S, are held constant. Each token in x_{a_i}, x_{b_j}, X_{share}, Y_a, and Y_b is sampled from the vocabulary.

• L: To examine how the hallucination rate R changes with increasing relative knowledge length L, we set $\text{L} = \frac{\text{len}(X_{\text{share}})+\text{len}(x_{b_j})}{\text{len}(x_{b_j})}$ for values {1:1, 2:1, 5:1, 10:1, 25:1, 50:1, 100:1}, where len(x_{a_i})=len(x_{b_j}) to ensure consistent variables.

• S: To investigate how hallucination rate changes with varying model sizes, we experiment on the Pythia model family with sizes of 160M, 410M, 1B, 1.4B, and 2.8B, along with other models including Phi-2.8B, GPT-J-6B, Mistral-7B, Llama-2-7B, and Llama-13B (Dataset statistics in A.3).

We pretrain each LLM from scratch on the dataset over 19.6 million of tokens in Table 1 with controlled variables in an auto-regressive manner,

Type	Task	Definition Y_a: ▓ x_a: ░ Y_b: ▓ x_b: ░ X_{share}: ░	Tokens
Synthetic Pretraining	Control	k_a = Year | Happy New k_b = Day | Happy Groundhog	1.96 million
Natural Language Fine-tuning	Location	k_a = New York City | Where did this event happens? CBS decided to revive the Million Second Quiz. k_b = Barcelona | Where did this event happens? HBO acquired the rights to The Loner	0.83 million
	Logical	k_a = Event A | {Description} ... which was earlier? A was before B, B was before C k_b = Event C | {Description} ... which was earlier? A was after B, B was after C	
	Conflict	k_a = Words | Write the proverb ends in "Words": Action speaks louder than k_b = Thoughts | Write the proverb ends in "Thoughts": Action speaks louder than	

Table 1: Samples of synthetic and natural language datasets. For each task, we present one sample $k_a = Y_a|[X_{\text{share}} \odot x_a]$ from more popular knowledge set K_A and one sample $k_b = Y_b|[X_{\text{share}} \odot x_b]$ from less popular knowledge set K_B. Each imbalanced K_A, K_B pair consists of m different samples of k_a and n different samples of k_b, where $m > n$. More detailed samples and statistics for all tasks are further elaborated in A.3

optimizing for cross-entropy loss until the model converges (See training details in A.2). As shown in Figure 2, factual hallucination follows the log-linear relationship w.r.t P, L, and S:

$$\text{R(P)} = \alpha \log(\frac{\text{P}}{\text{P}_c}); \text{R(L)} = \beta \log(\frac{\text{L}}{\text{L}_c}); \text{R(S)} = \gamma \log(\frac{\text{S}}{\text{S}_c}) \tag{3}$$

where α, β, γ, P_c, L_c, S_c are constants. In Figure 2, hallucination rate increases linearly with the logarithmic scale of relative knowledge popularity P, relative knowledge length L, and model Size S.

Greater Popularity Overshadows More. From a global perspective in the entire training data, when knowledge k_{a_i} has higher frequency than knowledge k_{b_j}, the distinctive token sequence x_{b_j} encoding the less popular knowledge k_{b_j} is more susceptible to be overshadowed. This imbalance amplifies dominant knowledge while suppressing the representations of less frequent facts. This highlights a fundamental bias in how LLMs internalize and retrieve knowledge, revealing that hallucination arises not just from data sparsity but from the inherent competition between knowledge representations in a non-uniform training distribution.

Longer Length Overshadows More. At its core, knowledge overshadowing arises from the degradation of probability distributions:

$$\begin{cases} P(Y_a|[X_{\text{share}} \odot x_{a_i}]) \xrightarrow{\text{degrade to}} P(Y_a|X_{\text{share}}) \\ P(Y_b|[X_{\text{share}} \odot x_{b_j}]) \xrightarrow{\text{degrade to}} P(Y_a|X_{\text{share}}) \end{cases} \tag{4}$$

The degradation reflects the compressed representations of x_{a_i} and x_{b_j}, which are merged into X_{share}, thereby weakening their distinct contributions to generation. Locally within a sentence, when x_{b_j}'s token length is shorter than X_{share}, its ability to maintain a distinct semantic boundary diminishes. This occurs because degradation is influenced by both knowledge interaction and x_{b_j}'s representation capacity. Shorter representations inherently encode less detailed semantic information, making them more prone to being overshadowed by the structurally and semantically richer X_{share}.

Larger Model Overshadows More. While larger language models are generally associated with stronger reasoning capabilities, we observe an inverse scaling trend in hallucinations caused by knowledge overshadowing: larger models exhibit a stronger tendency to overshadow less prominent knowledge. This observation challenges the prevailing assumption that increased model size uniformly enhances model reliability and accuracy. Interestingly, prior work has reported similar scaling trends. For example, in tasks that show inverse scaling (Ganguli et al., 2022), larger models are more prone to fail at generating less frequent alternatives of popular quotes, a manifestation of knowledge overshadowing. Likewise, Carlini et al. (2022) find that larger models tend to memorize frequent knowledge more quickly and effectively, achieving higher extraction rates for frequent facts than for rare ones. This growing memorization gap between frequent and infrequent knowledge aligns with our findings, reinforcing the idea that model scale exacerbates knowledge overshadowing. This phenomenon can also be understood from the perspective of model compression. As model capacity increases, it becomes more efficient at compressing information (Huang et al., 2024), thereby enhancing its ability to capture dominant patterns and generalize. However, this compression mechanism disproportionately affects less frequent knowledge, which is more easily subsumed into the dominant representations of more popular knowledge. Although larger models are capable of encoding

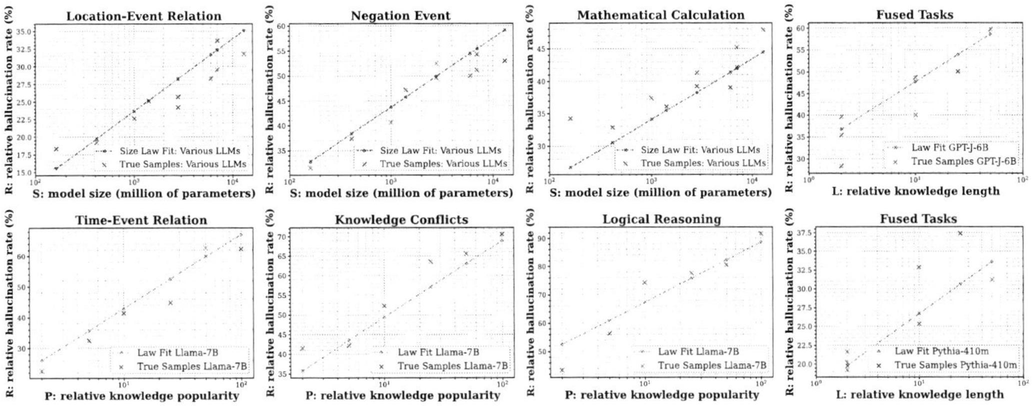

Figure 3: Fine-tuning open-source LLMs on natural language tasks. Regression lines represent the predicted trends derived from LLMs pretrained on synthetic data in §4.2. The red cross markers indicate the empirically observed hallucination rates in fine-tuned LLMs. Training data statistics and implementation are in A.2, A.3.

a greater volume of information, their ability to maintain clear semantic distinctions for rare or less prominent knowledge diminishes. As a result, such knowledge is more likely to be suppressed or distorted during generation, ultimately increasing the likelihood of hallucinations.

4.3 Validating Log-linear Law in the Fine-tuned LLMs.

Setup. The results presented in §4.2 were derived from pretrained models. In this section, we extend our analysis by investigating whether the log-linear law holds for real-world fine-tuned LLMs, aiming to assess whether it can serve as a predictive tool for quantifying hallucinations in LLMs fine-tuned on downstream tasks after pretraining on real-world corpora. Specifically, we fine-tune models with parameter sizes ranging from 160M to 13B across a variety of factual tasks, including time, location, gender, negation queries, mathematical and logical reasoning, and knowledge conflict resolution. For each task, we generate m samples of $k_{a_i} = Y_a|[X_{\text{share}} \odot x_{a_i}]$ and n samples of $k_{b_i} = Y_b|[X_{\text{share}} \odot x_{b_i}]$. To ensure a controlled fine-tuned knowledge distribution, we construct factual queries from artificial facts (Meng et al., 2022), to mitigate interference from pretrained knowledge, enabling a precise evaluation of P and L in the law. We present knowledge pair samples (k_a, k_b) for several tasks in Table 1, with additional dataset samples and statistics provided in A.3.

Preemptive Quantification. We utilize the log-linear law fitted by the pretrained LLMs on controlled synthetic datasets to predict hallucination rates for fine-tuned LLMs across various downstream tasks. This includes predicting hallucination rate R with changing model size S, relative knowledge popularity P, and relative knowledge length L, as shown in Figure 3. We then evaluate the discrepancy between the predicted hallucination rates and those observed in our fine-tuning experiments. Following Chen et al. (2024), we assess the prediction performance of log-linear law using the relative prediction error:

$$\text{Relative Prediction Error} = \frac{|\text{Predictive Rate} - \text{Actual Rate}|}{\text{Actual Rate}} \quad (5)$$

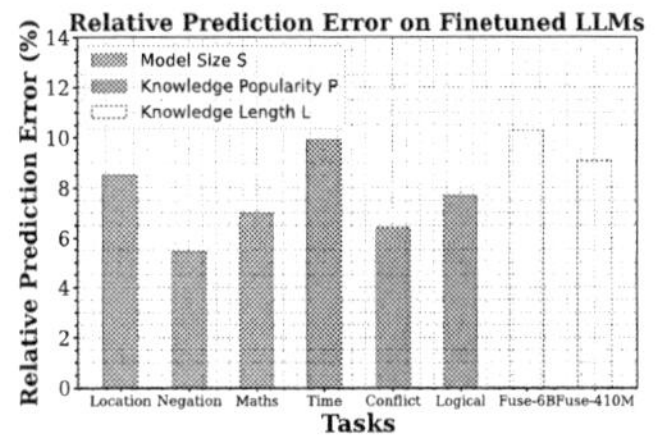

Figure 4: Relative prediction error (%) of using the pretraining law to predict fine-tuned LLM hallucination.

We visualize the prediction error for hallucination rates across tasks in Figure 4, reporting an average relative prediction error of 8.0%. The errors for L and P are slightly higher than S, as the fine-tuned datasets, despite consisting of unseen facts, still contain linguistic expressions that resemble pretrained knowledge, introducing a minor influence on the quantification of P and L while leaving S unaffected. Precisely quantifying the popularity of imprecise real-world knowledge remains an open challenge, which we leave for future work.

4.4 Factual Hallucinations in SOTA LLMs

Table 2 presents a case study demonstrating how SOTA LLMs are influenced by scaling effects of knowledge overshadowing. Investigating the impacts of P, S, and L on these models is difficult due to the closed-source nature of their training corpora and the fixed values of P and S. Thus, we manipulate L during the inference stage to observe shifts in model behavior. For instance, when querying GPT-4o about a cat's state in Schrödinger's box, increasing the length of surrounding text while keeping "dead" unchanged raises the relative length L of the surrounding contexts compared to the word "dead", leading to a higher likelihood of hallucination. Other LLMs also suffer from knowledge overshadowing. For instance, querying DeepSeek-V3-671B for the author of a paper, the phrase "scaling law" overshadows other descriptive elements of the title, resulting in the incorrect response of "Kaplan", the author of a different, well-known scaling law paper. Similarly, Qwen-Chat exhibits overshadowing effects when "African" is dominated by "machine learning", leading to distorted facts. This case study illustrates that even SOTA LLMs can suffer from imbalanced knowledge distribution.

Model	Input	Output
GPT-4o	Put a dead cat in Schrödinger's box, when we open the box, how much possibility is the cat alive?	0%
	Imagine a sealed box containing the following: 1. A dead cat, 2. A radioactive... Now open the box, how much possibility is the cat alive?	50%
DeepSeek	Who is the author for the paper named Scaling Laws vs Model Architectures: How does Inductive Bias Influence Scaling	Kaplan, Yi Tay
Qwen	Who is a very famous African researcher in machine learning area?	Yoshua Bengio

Table 2: Factual hallucination in SOTA LLMs.

5 Why Knowledge Overshadows?

Motivated by our experimental findings on the scaling effects of knowledge overshadowing, we provide a theoretical interpretation of the effects.

5.1 Memorize-Generalize-Hallucinate

In §4.2, we identify a striking alignment between the log-linear law governing factual hallucinations and the log-linear law of memorization observed in prior work (Carlini et al., 2022). Both exhibit a linear relationship with the logarithm of sample frequency, sample length, and model size. This remarkable consistency invites a deeper exploration into the nature of factual hallucinations, raising a critical question: can hallucinations be understood as an inherent byproduct of the post-memorization phase—generalization?

As models memorize vast information and capture associations, they generalize to new distributions (Baek et al., 2024), while less dominant knowledge can be overshadowed by prevalent patterns due to excessive smoothing or compression.

Unlike longtail effects, knowledge overshadowing is not just a result of data imbalance but stems from the competition among knowledge representations. Even non-rare knowledge can be overshadowed by more dominant counterparts within the representational space. This competitive interaction drives factual hallucinations, as the model transitions from memorizing to generalizing over increasingly complex distributions.

5.2 Interpretation by Generalization Bound

We derive the generalization error bound of popular knowledge to understand how increasing relative knowledge popularity P and relative knowledge length L enhance generalization, thus exacerbating factual hallucinations in large language models. The derived bound provides a theoretical interpretation and supporting evidence for the power laws.

Specifically, in a dataset D with numerous statements, we investigate a pair of subsets $K_A, K_B \subset D$. We fix the sample size of K_B at n, and observe how the generalization bound of K_A changes as we vary the relative knowledge popularity $\mathrm{P} = \frac{m}{n}$ and relative knowledge length L. For each sentence $k_{a_i} = Y_a|[X_{\text{share}} \odot x_{a_i}], (i \in 1, ..., m)$ in K_A, where X_{share} and x_{a_i} represent token sequences, we simplify the analysis by assuming each x_{a_i} is a one-token sequence. Thus, the relative knowledge length is set as $\frac{\text{len}(X_{\text{share}})+\text{len}(x_{a_i})}{\text{len}(x_{a_i})} = \frac{\mathrm{L}}{1} = \mathrm{L}$. Then, we derive the generalization bound for next-token prediction in all $k_{a_i} \in \mathcal{D}$, with the model optimized using an auto-regressive objective:

$$\mathcal{R}_y^{\mathcal{L}}(f) \precsim \widehat{\mathcal{R}}_y^{\mathcal{L}}(f) + 2\mu \widehat{\mathfrak{R}}_{K_A}(\mathcal{F}) + \sqrt{\frac{\log 1/\delta}{2m}} \tag{6}$$

where $\mu = \sqrt{1 + \left(\sum_{y' \neq y} h^{-1}(\mathrm{L})\right)^2} \left[1 - \text{softmax}\left(K_{A_y}(f)\right)\right]$, $K_{A_y}(f) = \inf_{x \in K_{A_y}} f(x)$. In this bound, $\mathcal{R}_y^{\mathcal{L}}(f)$ denotes the generalization error on the true distribution. $\widehat{\mathcal{R}}_y^{\mathcal{L}}(f)$ denotes the empirical next token prediction training loss on K_A. $\widehat{\mathfrak{R}}_{K_A}(\mathcal{F})$ is the Rademacher complexity of the output mapping function set $\mathcal{F}$ over K_A, measuring its capacity to fit random noise. δ is the confidence parameter. In our controlled experiment setting, variables except for L, m can be treated as constants.

Method		MemoTrap				NQ-Swap	Overshadowing	
		proverb	translate	hate	science	entity	time	syn
Llama	Greedy	28.8	47.5	9.0	33.4	8.5	41.4	20.8
	CoT	30.1(+1.3)	52.6(+5.1)	13.0(+4.0)	36.7(+3.3)	19.2(+10.7)	40.4(-1.0)	-
	SR	34.7(+5.9)	51.8(+4.3)	12.0(+3.0)	35.8(+2.4)	14.2(+5.7)	42.5(+1.1)	23.8(+3.0)
	USC	27.6(-1.2)	52.4(+4.9)	8.0(-1.0)	32.9(-0.5)	9.4(+0.9)	40.2(-1.2)	16.4(-4.4)
	Dola	32.5(+3.7)	50.9(+3.4)	10.0(+1.0)	33.0(-0.4)	13.8(+5.3)	53.6(+12.2)	31.8(+11)
	CoDA (ours)	**41.9**(+13.1)	**56.2**(+8.7)	**16.0**(+7.0)	**38.9**(+5.5)	**26.8**(+18.3)	**65.0**(+23.6)	**46.8**(+26)
Mistral	Greedy	31.3	49.4	14.0	36.7	12.6	39.5	21.6
	CoT	35.2(+3.9)	52.7(+3.3)	17.0(+3.0)	39.0(+2.3)	19.5(+6.9)	37.0(-2.5)	-
	SR	36.8(+5.5)	54.6(+5.2)	19.0(+5.0)	38.2(+1.5)	13.8(+1.2)	42.4(+2.9)	24.9(+3.3)
	USC	32.6(+1.3)	51.5(+2.1)	15.0(+1.0)	35.9(-0.8)	11.4(-1.2)	37.9(-1.6)	20.8(-0.8)
	Dola	34.9(+3.6)	53.5(+4.1)	14.0(+0.0)	38.4(+1.7)	15.9(+3.3)	51.0(+11.5)	34.6(+13)
	CoDA (ours)	**42.5**(+11.2)	**58.6**(+9.2)	**22.0**(+8.0)	**43.7**(+7.0)	**27.7**(+15.1)	**61.2**(+21.7)	**49.5**(+27.9)

Table 3: Exact match (%) on MemoTrap, NQ-Swap, and Overshadowing. Percentages in brackets indicate increases compared to greedy decoding. Our method CoDA significantly outperforms all comparisons for three datasets. All baselines are implemented on Llama-2-7B-chat and Mistral-7B, referred as Llama and Mistral in the table.

Here, with $h(\text{L})$ denoting a function value positively correlated with L, μ encapsulates the sensitivity to changes in the input—reflecting the impact of relative knowledge length L. m represents the sample size of K_A. Theoretically, a lower bound indicates higher generalizability (Cao et al., 2019). Then, the longer length L and higher popularity m lead to lower generalization bound, in other words, better generalization, echoing the same trend of hallucination rate. More details of our theoretical interpretation can be found in A.6.

6 How to Eliminate Hallucination?

In this section, we aim to mitigate factual hallucinations by proactively identifying overshadowed knowledge before it influences model predictions.

6.1 CoDA: Contrastive Decoding to Amplify Overshadowed Knowledge

Identifying Overshadowed Knowledge. For a language model, given an input token sequence X, the model will output the continuation token sequence Y. Both X and Y consist of tokens from the vocabulary $\mathcal{V}$. When certain tokens x_b in X are overshadowed, the model will generate hallucinated output. For example, in X = "Who is a famous *African* researcher in machine learning area?", if x_b = "*African*" is overshadowed by "machine learning", The model will output Y="Yoshua Bengio", ignoring the intended constraint.

To detect overshadowed tokens, we sequentially mask x_b in X to form X' (see A.5 for various x_b candidate selection methods). If x_b is overshadowed, $p(Y_b|X) \xrightarrow{\text{degrade to}} p(Y_a|X')$. We quantify the generalization between distributions $p(Y|X)$ and $p(Y|X')$ by relative pointwise mutual information (R-PMI) (Li et al., 2023b). To ensure we quantify output token candidates $y_i \in P(Y|X), P(Y|X')$ with sufficient semantics, we employ an adaptive plausibility constraint Li et al. (2023b), retaining tokens that satisfy: $\mathcal{V}_{\text{top}}(X) = \{y_i | p(y_i|X) \geq \alpha \cdot \Upsilon\}$, where $\alpha = 0.01$ is a hyperparameter, and Υ is a global variable as the maximum probability among all y_i candidates. Then the R-PMI is quantified over $\forall y_i \in \mathcal{V}_{\text{top}}(X) \cap \mathcal{V}_{\text{top}}(X')$:

$$\text{R-PMI}(y_i; X, X') = \log \frac{p(y_i \mid X)}{p(y_i \mid X')} \quad (7)$$

In essence, a negative R-PMI value indicates that token y_i is more associated with X$'$ without overshadowed information. Thus we quantify to what extent $P(\text{Y}|\text{X}')$ generalize to $P(\text{Y}|\text{X})$ by R-PMI$_{\text{sum}}$ = $\sum_i \min(\text{R-PMI}(y_i; X, X'), 0)$. Moreover, it is noteworthy that despite some tokens being overshadowed by X', there are still tokens that escape from this overshadowing effect, defined as $\mathcal{V}_{\text{esc}}$:

$$\mathcal{V}_{\text{esc}} = \{y_i | y_i \in \mathcal{V}_{\text{top}}(X) \text{ and } y_i \notin \mathcal{V}_{\text{top}}(X')\} \quad (8)$$

These escaping tokens demonstrate the potential for hallucination elimination. Then we propose an Escaping Rewarding Mechanism (ERM), which adds a positive reward to the sum of negative R-PMI. Denoting all y_i with a negative R-PMI as $y_i \in \mathcal{S}$, The ERM can be calculated as:

$$\text{ERM} = \sum_{y_i \in \mathcal{V}_{\text{esc}}} \left(\log p(y_i|X) - \min_{y_j \in \mathcal{S}} \log p(y_j|X') \right) \quad (9)$$

where the deduction is to balance ERM with R-PMI with a similar denominator of $p(y_j|X')$ in Eq. 7, which represents the minimum bias from

X′. Then the overshadowed knowledge indicator is: Indicator = R-PMI$_{\text{sum}}$ + ERM. A negative indicator value indicates proper generalization without overshadowing other knowledge, and a positive alamer value indicates over-generalization with overshadowed tokens x_b (Hallucination prediction accuracy is in Table 7).

Elevating Overshadowed Knowledge. Once the tokens x_b encoding overshadowed knowledge are identified, we adopt contrastive decoding to reduce the influence of X′ and highlight X. Specifically, to reduce the bias from of X', for each $y_i \in \mathcal{V}_{\text{top}}(X) \cap \mathcal{V}_{\text{top}}(X')$, we subtract the prior bias of X', which is $P(y_i|X')$ as shown below:

$$\log p(y_i) = \log p(y_i|X) - \log p(y_i|X') \quad (10)$$

Similarly for each $y_i \in \mathcal{V}_{\text{esc}}$, we conduct:

$$\log p(y_i) = (\log\ p(y_i|X) - \min_{y_j \in \mathcal{S}} \log\ p(y_j|X')) \quad (11)$$

Here, $\min_{y_j \in \mathcal{S}} \log p(y_j|X')$ represents the minimum prior bias from popular knowledge. The deduction aims to balance the bias adjustment between $y_i \in \mathcal{V}_{\text{esc}}$ and $y_i \notin \mathcal{V}_{\text{esc}}$, ensuring proportional adjustments for both. Then we predict the optimal output y_i^* by:

$$y_i^* = \underset{y_i \in \mathcal{V}_{\text{top}}(X)}{\text{argmax}}\ \log p(y_i|X) \quad (12)$$

Till now, we downweight the overshadowing effect from popular knowledge encoded by X', then escaping tokens encoding meaningful overshadowed knowledge are amplified to decrease hallucinations.

6.2 Experimental Setup

Datasets. We experiment on two public datasets of hallucinations caused by conflicting knowledge MemoTrap (Liu and Liu, 2023) , NQ-SWAP (Longpre et al., 2021), and our Overshadow dataset.

Baselines. We adopt Greedy decoding, Chain-of-Thought (Cot) (Wei et al., 2022), Self-Reflection (SR) (Madaan et al., 2024), *USC* (Chen et al., 2023a), and *Dola* Chuang et al. (2023) as the baselines. Details for datasets and baselines are in A.5.

Implementation and Metric. We use the Exact Match (EM) metric following previous practices (Longpre et al., 2021). Implementation details for all methods are elaborated in A.5.

6.3 Main Results and Analysis

Our method improves greedy decoding by 27.9%, 13.1%, and 18.3% on Overshadow, MemoTrap, and NQ-Swap. Reasoning-enhanced baselines struggle with hallucinations caused by knowledge overshadowing. Self-consistency-based methods show instability or even degradation, which may be attributed to reinforcing biases from popular knowledge. Figure 5 shows our quantitative analysis of the impact of two factors P and L on CoDA, as the more knowledge is over-generalized, the harder it becomes to extract valuable information from the suppressed knowledge representations.

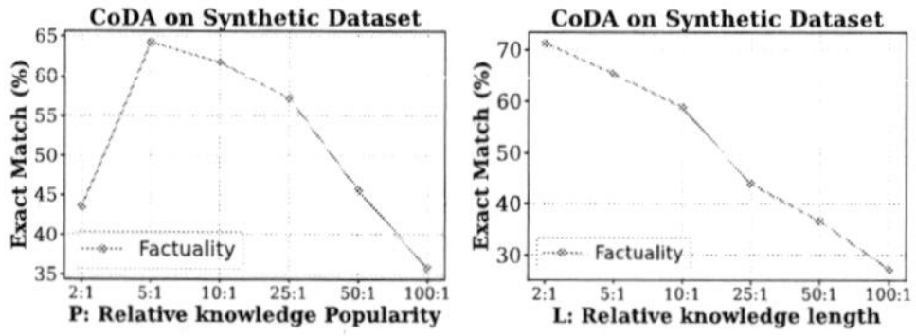

Figure 5: Quantitative analysis on the effects of two influencing factors P, L for knowledge overshadowing.

7 Discussion for Broader Social Impact

Our work contributes to building more predictable and reliable AI systems by interpreting hallucinations through knowledge overshadowing and introducing the CoDA method to rebalance information during decoding. This improves the factuality of AI-generated content and enhances transparency in LLMs. Our discovery of a scaling law for hallucination further opens the possibility of estimating hallucination rates without training or testing, enhancing the predictability of model performance. Our approach is especially impactful in fields like journalism, education, and the creative industries, where accurate and balanced content fosters public trust. Moreover, by mitigating the dominance of popular narratives, our work helps amplify underrepresented voices, promoting cultural diversity, inclusivity, and responsible AI deployment.

8 Conclusion

Our work identify knowledge overshadowing as a contributional cause of LLMs hallucination, where dominant knowledge suppresses less frequent facts, leading to fact distortions. We introduce the log-linear scaling law, which reveals that hallucination rates grow predictably with knowledge popularity, length, and model size, enabling hallucination prediction. Built on overshadowing effect, we propose CoDA, a decoding strategy that improves factual accuracy without retraining. Our approach provides a principled way to understand and control hallucinations, leading to more reliable LLMs.

Limitations

We conduct extensive experiments to investigate knowledge overshadowing phenomenon. However, due to inaccessibility, we can not analyze the variables in training corpora of SOTA LLMs like GPT-4o and DeekSeek. Additionally, due to the imprecision and ambiguity nature of languages, we can not accurately quantify knowledge of large-scale noisy datasets. We leave this blank for future work. High quality graph-based synthetic data (Qin et al., 2025) may be a potential direction for bridging this gap in further investigating various variables in LLM training corpora.

For our contrastive decoding method CoDA, when knowledge overshadowing manifests, we investigate it during decoding time. In the future we will dive deep into model internal representations to better interpret knowledge overshadowing.

Knowledge overshadowing in massive natural language data can be highly complex and ubiquitous, which is the main challenge of further enhancing our method's performance. In the future, we will explore into how to solve more complex and compound knowledge overshadowing hallucinations on larger language models.

Ethics Statement

In our empirical study, MemoTrap and NQ-Swap are publicly available datasets to help us understand how models adhere to parametric or contextual knowledge. Our dataset Overshadowing is constructed based on the public COUNTERFACTUAL dataset. All of the three datasets are to interpret and eliminate hallucinations that will be harmful to users. Experiments and methods on the three datasets are conducted for social benefits. Additionally, the COUNTERFACTUAL dataset involves no privacy issues since it consists of artificial events.

Acknowledgment

This research is based upon work supported by DARPA ITM Program No. FA8650-23-C-7316, DARPA BRIES Program No. HR0011-24-3-0325, DARPA CCU Program No. HR001122C0034, and the AI Research Institutes program by National Science Foundation and the Institute of Education Sciences, U.S. Department of Education through Award # 2229873 - AI Institute for Transforming Education for Children with Speech and Language Processing Challenges and Award # 2229612 - AI Institute for Inclusive Intelligent Technologies for Education. The views and conclusions contained herein are those of the authors and should not be interpreted as necessarily representing the official policies, either expressed or implied, of the U.S. Government. The U.S. Government is authorized to reproduce and distribute preprints for governmental purposes notwithstanding any copyright annotation therein.

References

Ayush Agrawal, Mirac Suzgun, Lester Mackey, and Adam Kalai. 2024. Do language models know when they're hallucinating references? In Findings of the Association for Computational Linguistics: EACL 2024, pages 912–928, St. Julian's, Malta. Association for Computational Linguistics.

Rahul Aralikatte, Shashi Narayan, Joshua Maynez, Sascha Rothe, and Ryan McDonald. 2021. Focus attention: Promoting faithfulness and diversity in summarization. In Proceedings of the 59th Annual Meeting of the Association for Computational Linguistics and the 11th International Joint Conference on Natural Language Processing (Volume 1: Long Papers), pages 6078–6095, Online. Association for Computational Linguistics.

Akari Asai, Zeqiu Wu, Yizhong Wang, Avirup Sil, and Hannaneh Hajishirzi. 2023. Self-rag: Learning to retrieve, generate, and critique through self-reflection. Preprint, arXiv:2310.11511.

David D Baek, Ziming Liu, and Max Tegmark. 2024. Geneft: Understanding statics and dynamics of model generalization via effective theory. arXiv preprint arXiv:2402.05916.

Kaidi Cao, Colin Wei, Adrien Gaidon, Nikos Arechiga, and Tengyu Ma. 2019. Learning imbalanced datasets with label-distribution-aware margin loss. Advances in neural information processing systems, 32.

Nicholas Carlini, Daphne Ippolito, Matthew Jagielski, Katherine Lee, Florian Tramer, and Chiyuan Zhang. 2022. Quantifying memorization across neural language models. The Eleventh International Conference on Learning Representations.

Xinyun Chen, Renat Aksitov, Uri Alon, Jie Ren, Kefan Xiao, Pengcheng Yin, Sushant Prakash, Charles Sutton, Xuezhi Wang, and Denny Zhou. 2023a. Universal self-consistency for large language model generation. arXiv preprint arXiv:2311.17311.

Yangyi Chen, Binxuan Huang, Yifan Gao, Zhengyang Wang, Jingfeng Yang, and Heng Ji. 2024. Scaling laws for predicting downstream performance in llms. arXiv preprint arXiv:2410.08527.

Yangyi Chen, Lifan Yuan, Ganqu Cui, Zhiyuan Liu, and Heng Ji. 2023b. A close look into the calibration of pre-trained language models. In Proceedings of the 61st Annual Meeting of the Association for Computational Linguistics (Volume 1: Long Papers), pages 1343–1367, Toronto, Canada. Association for Computational Linguistics.

Yi Cheng, Xiao Liang, Yeyun Gong, Wen Xiao, Song Wang, Yuji Zhang, Wenjun Hou, Kaishuai Xu, Wenge Liu, Wenjie Li, et al. 2024. Integrative decoding: Improve factuality via implicit self-consistency. arXiv preprint arXiv:2410.01556.

I-Chun Chern, Steffi Chern, Shiqi Chen, Weizhe Yuan, Kehua Feng, Chunting Zhou, Junxian He, Graham Neubig, and Pengfei Liu. 2023. Factool: Factuality detection in generative ai – a tool augmented framework for multi-task and multi-domain scenarios. Preprint, arXiv:2307.13528.

Yung-Sung Chuang, Yujia Xie, Hongyin Luo, Yoon Kim, James Glass, and Pengcheng He. 2023. Dola: Decoding by contrasting layers improves factuality in large language models. Preprint, arXiv:2309.03883.

Roi Cohen, May Hamri, Mor Geva, and Amir Globerson. 2023. Lm vs lm: Detecting factual errors via cross examination. arXiv preprint arXiv:2305.13281.

Shehzaad Dhuliawala, Mojtaba Komeili, Jing Xu, Roberta Raileanu, Xian Li, Asli Celikyilmaz, and Jason Weston. 2023. Chain-of-verification reduces hallucination in large language models. arXiv preprint arXiv:2309.11495.

Nouha Dziri, Sivan Milton, Mo Yu, Osmar Zaiane, and Siva Reddy. 2022. On the origin of hallucinations in conversational models: Is it the datasets or the models? In Proceedings of the 2022 Conference of the North American Chapter of the Association for Computational Linguistics: Human Language Technologies, pages 5271–5285, Seattle, United States. Association for Computational Linguistics.

Deep Ganguli, Danny Hernandez, Liane Lovitt, Amanda Askell, Yuntao Bai, Anna Chen, Tom Conerly, Nova Dassarma, Dawn Drain, Nelson Elhage, et al. 2022. Predictability and surprise in large generative models. In Proceedings of the 2022 ACM Conference on Fairness, Accountability, and Transparency, pages 1747–1764.

Samuel Gehman, Suchin Gururangan, Maarten Sap, Yejin Choi, and Noah A. Smith. 2020. RealToxicityPrompts: Evaluating neural toxic degeneration in language models. In Findings of the Association for Computational Linguistics: EMNLP 2020, pages 3356–3369, Online. Association for Computational Linguistics.

Daniela Gottesman and Mor Geva. 2024. Estimating knowledge in large language models without generating a single token. arXiv preprint arXiv:2406.12673.

Suriya Gunasekar, Yi Zhang, Jyoti Aneja, Caio César Teodoro Mendes, Allie Del Giorno, Sivakanth Gopi, Mojan Javaheripi, Piero Kauffmann, Gustavo de Rosa, Olli Saarikivi, et al. 2023. Textbooks are all you need. arXiv preprint arXiv:2306.11644.

Zhitao He, Sandeep Polisetty, Zhiyuan Fan, Yuchen Huang, Shujin Wu, and Yi R. Fung. 2025. Mmboundary: Advancing mllm knowledge boundary awareness through reasoning step confidence calibration. Preprint, arXiv:2505.23224.

Junsheng Huang, Zhitao He, Sandeep Polisetty, Qingyun Wang, and May Fung. 2025. Mac-tuning: Llm multi-compositional problem reasoning with enhanced knowledge boundary awareness. Preprint, arXiv:2504.21773.

Yuzhen Huang, Jinghan Zhang, Zifei Shan, and Junxian He. 2024. Compression represents intelligence linearly. arXiv preprint arXiv:2404.09937.

Albert Q Jiang, Alexandre Sablayrolles, Arthur Mensch, Chris Bamford, Devendra Singh Chaplot, Diego de las Casas, Florian Bressand, Gianna Lengyel, Guillaume Lample, Lucile Saulnier, et al. 2023. Mistral 7b. arXiv preprint arXiv:2310.06825.

Saurav Kadavath, Tom Conerly, Amanda Askell, Tom Henighan, Dawn Drain, Ethan Perez, Nicholas Schiefer, Zac Hatfield-Dodds, Nova DasSarma, Eli Tran-Johnson, et al. 2022. Language models (mostly) know what they know. arXiv preprint arXiv:2207.05221.

Nikhil Kandpal, Haikang Deng, Adam Roberts, Eric Wallace, and Colin Raffel. 2023. Large language models struggle to learn long-tail knowledge. In International Conference on Machine Learning, pages 15696–15707. PMLR.

Jared Kaplan, Sam McCandlish, Tom Henighan, Tom B Brown, Benjamin Chess, Rewon Child, Scott Gray, Alec Radford, Jeffrey Wu, and Dario Amodei. 2020. Scaling laws for neural language models. arXiv preprint arXiv:2001.08361.

Tom Kwiatkowski, Jennimaria Palomaki, Olivia Redfield, Michael Collins, Ankur Parikh, Chris Alberti, Danielle Epstein, Illia Polosukhin, Jacob Devlin, Kenton Lee, et al. 2019. Natural questions: a benchmark for question answering research. Transactions of the Association for Computational Linguistics, 7:453–466.

Faisal Ladhak, Esin Durmus, Mirac Suzgun, Tianyi Zhang, Dan Jurafsky, Kathleen McKeown, and Tatsunori Hashimoto. 2023. When do pre-training biases propagate to downstream tasks? a case study in text summarization. In Proceedings of the 17th Conference of the European Chapter of the Association for Computational Linguistics, pages 3206–3219, Dubrovnik, Croatia. Association for Computational Linguistics.

Daliang Li, Ankit Singh Rawat, Manzil Zaheer, Xin Wang, Michal Lukasik, Andreas Veit, Felix Yu, and Sanjiv Kumar. 2022. Large language models with controllable working memory. Preprint, arXiv:2211.05110.

Junyi Li, Jie Chen, Ruiyang Ren, Xiaoxue Cheng, Wayne Xin Zhao, Jian-Yun Nie, and Ji-Rong Wen. 2024. The dawn after the dark: An empirical study on factuality hallucination in large language models. arXiv preprint arXiv:2401.03205.

Sha Li, Chi Han, Pengfei Yu, Carl Edwards, Manling Li, Xingyao Wang, Yi Fung, Charles Yu, Joel Tetreault, Eduard Hovy, and Heng Ji. 2023a. Defining a new NLP playground. In Findings of the Association for Computational Linguistics: EMNLP 2023, pages 11932–11951, Singapore. Association for Computational Linguistics.

Xiang Lisa Li, Ari Holtzman, Daniel Fried, Percy Liang, Jason Eisner, Tatsunori Hashimoto, Luke Zettlemoyer, and Mike Lewis. 2023b. Contrastive decoding: Open-ended text generation as optimization. In Proceedings of the 61st Annual Meeting of the Association for Computational Linguistics (Volume 1: Long Papers), pages 12286–12312, Toronto, Canada. Association for Computational Linguistics.

Stephanie Lin, Jacob Hilton, and Owain Evans. 2022. TruthfulQA: Measuring how models mimic human falsehoods. In Proceedings of the 60th Annual Meeting of the Association for Computational Linguistics (Volume 1: Long Papers), pages 3214–3252, Dublin, Ireland. Association for Computational Linguistics.

Alisa Liu and Jiacheng Liu. 2023. The memotrap dataset. https://github.com/inverse-scaling/prize/blob/main/data-release/README.md. Accessed: 2024-10-15.

Adam Livska, Tom'avs Kovcisk'y, Elena Gribovskaya, Tayfun Terzi, Eren Sezener, Devang Agrawal, Cyprien de Masson d'Autume, Tim Scholtes, Manzil Zaheer, Susannah Young, Ellen Gilsenan-McMahon, Sophia Austin, Phil Blunsom, and Angeliki Lazaridou. 2022. Streamingqa: A benchmark for adaptation to new knowledge over time in question answering models. In International Conference on Machine Learning.

Shayne Longpre, Kartik Perisetla, Anthony Chen, Nikhil Ramesh, Chris DuBois, and Sameer Singh. 2021. Entity-based knowledge conflicts in question answering. In Proceedings of the 2021 Conference on Empirical Methods in Natural Language Processing, pages 7052–7063, Online and Punta Cana, Dominican Republic. Association for Computational Linguistics.

Junyu Luo, Cao Xiao, and Fenglong Ma. 2023. Zero-resource hallucination prevention for large language models. arXiv preprint arXiv:2309.02654.

Kelvin Luu, Daniel Khashabi, Suchin Gururangan, Karishma Mandyam, and Noah A. Smith. 2022. Time waits for no one! analysis and challenges of temporal misalignment. In Proceedings of the 2022 Conference of the North American Chapter of the Association for Computational Linguistics: Human Language Technologies, pages 5944–5958, Seattle, United States. Association for Computational Linguistics.

Xiaozhong Lyu, Stefan Grafberger, Samantha Biegel, Shaopeng Wei, Meng Cao, Sebastian Schelter, and Ce Zhang. 2023. Improving retrieval-augmented large language models via data importance learning. Preprint, arXiv:2307.03027.

Evelyn Ma, Duo Zhou, Peizhi Niu, Huiting Zhou, Huan Zhang, Olgica Milenkovic, and S Rasoul Etesami. 2025. Guard: Guided unlearning and retention via data attribution for large language models. arXiv preprint arXiv:2506.10946.

Yueen Ma, Zixing Song, Xuming Hu, Jingjing Li, Yifei Zhang, and Irwin King. 2023. Graph component contrastive learning for concept relatedness estimation. In AAAI, pages 13362–13370. AAAI Press.

Aman Madaan, Niket Tandon, Prakhar Gupta, Skyler Hallinan, Luyu Gao, Sarah Wiegreffe, Uri Alon, Nouha Dziri, Shrimai Prabhumoye, Yiming Yang, et al. 2024. Self-refine: Iterative refinement with self-feedback. Advances in Neural Information Processing Systems, 36.

Alex Mallen and Nora Belrose. 2023. Eliciting latent knowledge from quirky language models. Preprint, arXiv:2312.01037.

Potsawee Manakul, Adian Liusie, and Mark JF Gales. 2023. Selfcheckgpt: Zero-resource black-box hallucination detection for generative large language models. arXiv preprint arXiv:2303.08896.

Kevin Meng, David Bau, Alex Andonian, and Yonatan Belinkov. 2022. Locating and editing factual associations in gpt. Advances in Neural Information Processing Systems, 35:17359–17372.

Sewon Min, Kalpesh Krishna, Xinxi Lyu, Mike Lewis, Wen tau Yih, Pang Wei Koh, Mohit Iyyer, Luke Zettlemoyer, and Hannaneh Hajishirzi. 2023. Factscore: Fine-grained atomic evaluation of factual precision in long form text generation. Preprint, arXiv:2305.14251.

Mehryar Mohri, Afshin Rostamizadeh, and Ameet Talwalkar. 2018. Foundations of machine learning. MIT press.

Zeyu Qin, Qingxiu Dong, Xingxing Zhang, Li Dong, Xiaolong Huang, Ziyi Yang, Mahmoud Khademi, Dongdong Zhang, Hany Hassan Awadalla, Yi R. Fung, Weizhu Chen, Minhao Cheng, and Furu Wei. 2025. Scaling laws of synthetic data for language models. Preprint, arXiv:2503.19551.

Ruiyang Ren, Yuhao Wang, Yingqi Qu, Wayne Xin Zhao, Jing Liu, Hao Tian, Hua Wu, Ji-Rong Wen, and Haifeng Wang. 2023. Investigating the factual knowledge boundary of large language models with retrieval augmentation. Preprint, arXiv:2307.11019.

Lei Shen, Haolan Zhan, Xin Shen, Hongshen Chen, Xiaofang Zhao, and Xiaodan Zhu. 2021. Identifying untrustworthy samples: Data filtering for open-domain dialogues with bayesian optimization. In Proceedings of the 30th ACM International Conference on Information & Knowledge Management, pages 1598–1608.

Weijia Shi, Xiaochuang Han, Mike Lewis, Yulia Tsvetkov, Luke Zettlemoyer, and Scott Wen-tau Yih. 2023. Trusting your evidence: Hallucinate less with context-aware decoding. arXiv preprint arXiv:2305.14739.

Luca Soldaini, Rodney Kinney, Akshita Bhagia, Dustin Schwenk, David Atkinson, Russell Authur, Ben Bogin, Khyathi Chandu, Jennifer Dumas, Yanai Elazar, et al. 2024. Dolma: An open corpus of three trillion tokens for language model pretraining research. arXiv preprint arXiv:2402.00159.

Zixing Song, Yifei Zhang, and Irwin King. 2023. Optimal block-wise asymmetric graph construction for graph-based semi-supervised learning. In NeurIPS.

Katherine Tian, Eric Mitchell, Allan Zhou, Archit Sharma, Rafael Rafailov, Huaxiu Yao, Chelsea Finn, and Christopher Manning. 2023. Just ask for calibration: Strategies for eliciting calibrated confidence scores from language models fine-tuned with human feedback. In Proceedings of the 2023 Conference on Empirical Methods in Natural Language Processing, pages 5433–5442, Singapore. Association for Computational Linguistics.

Ran Tian, Shashi Narayan, Thibault Sellam, and Ankur P Parikh. 2019. Sticking to the facts: Confident decoding for faithful data-to-text generation. arXiv preprint arXiv:1910.08684.

Hugo Touvron, Louis Martin, Kevin Stone, Peter Albert, Amjad Almahairi, Yasmine Babaei, Nikolay Bashlykov, Soumya Batra, Prajjwal Bhargava, Shruti Bhosale, et al. 2023. Llama 2: Open foundation and fine-tuned chat models. arXiv preprint arXiv:2307.09288.

David Wan, Mengwen Liu, Kathleen McKeown, Markus Dreyer, and Mohit Bansal. 2023. Faithfulness-aware decoding strategies for abstractive summarization. In Proceedings of the 17th Conference of the European Chapter of the Association for Computational Linguistics, pages 2864–2880, Dubrovnik, Croatia. Association for Computational Linguistics.

Ben Wang and Aran Komatsuzaki. 2021. GPT-J-6B: A 6 Billion Parameter Autoregressive Language Model. https://github.com/kingoflolz/mesh-transformer-jax.

Zitai Wang, Qianqian Xu, Zhiyong Yang, Yuan He, Xiaochun Cao, and Qingming Huang. 2024. A unified generalization analysis of re-weighting and logit-adjustment for imbalanced learning. Advances in Neural Information Processing Systems, 36.

Jason Wei, Xuezhi Wang, Dale Schuurmans, Maarten Bosma, Fei Xia, Ed Chi, Quoc V Le, Denny Zhou, et al. 2022. Chain-of-thought prompting elicits reasoning in large language models. Advances in neural information processing systems, 35:24824–24837.

Jerry Wei, Da Huang, Yifeng Lu, Denny Zhou, and Quoc V. Le. 2023. Simple synthetic data reduces sycophancy in large language models. Preprint, arXiv:2308.03958.

Yuanhao Wu, Juno Zhu, Siliang Xu, Kashun Shum, Cheng Niu, Randy Zhong, Juntong Song, and Tong Zhang. 2023. Ragtruth: A hallucination corpus for developing trustworthy retrieval-augmented language models. Preprint, arXiv:2401.00396.

Jian Xie, Kai Zhang, Jiangjie Chen, Renze Lou, and Yu Su. 2023. Adaptive chameleon or stubborn sloth: Unraveling the behavior of large language models in knowledge clashes. Preprint, arXiv:2305.13300.

Ke Yang, Charles Yu, Yi R. Fung, Manling Li, and Heng Ji. 2023. Adept: A debiasing prompt framework. Proceedings of the AAAI Conference on Artificial Intelligence, 37(9):10780–10788.

Hongbin Ye, Tong Liu, Aijia Zhang, Wei Hua, and Weiqiang Jia. 2023. Cognitive mirage: A review of hallucinations in large language models. Preprint, arXiv:2309.06794.

Hanning Zhang, Shizhe Diao, Yong Lin, Yi Fung, Qing Lian, Xingyao Wang, Yangyi Chen, Heng Ji, and Tong Zhang. 2024a. R-tuning: Instructing large language models to say 'I don't know'. In Proceedings of the 2024 Conference of the North American Chapter of the Association for Computational Linguistics: Human Language Technologies (Volume 1: Long Papers), pages 7113–7139, Mexico City, Mexico. Association for Computational Linguistics.

Mozhi Zhang, Mianqiu Huang, Rundong Shi, Linsen Guo, Chong Peng, Peng Yan, Yaqian Zhou, and Xipeng Qiu. 2024b. Calibrating the confidence of large language models by eliciting fidelity. In Proceedings of the 2024 Conference on Empirical Methods in Natural Language Processing, pages 2959–2979, Miami, Florida, USA. Association for Computational Linguistics.

Muru Zhang, Ofir Press, William Merrill, Alisa Liu, and Noah A. Smith. 2023a. How language model hallucinations can snowball. Preprint, arXiv:2305.13534.

Xiaoying Zhang, Baolin Peng, Ye Tian, Jingyan Zhou, Lifeng Jin, Linfeng Song, Haitao Mi, and Helen Meng. 2024c. Self-alignment for factuality: Mitigating hallucinations in llms via self-evaluation. arXiv preprint arXiv:2402.09267.

Yuji Zhang, Jing Li, and Wenjie Li. 2023b. VIBE: Topic-driven temporal adaptation for Twitter classification. In Proceedings of the 2023 Conference on Empirical Methods in Natural Language Processing, pages 3340–3354, Singapore. Association for Computational Linguistics.

Yuji Zhang, Sha Li, Jiateng Liu, Pengfei Yu, Yi R Fung, Jing Li, Manling Li, and Heng Ji. 2024d. Knowledge overshadowing causes amalgamated hallucination in large language models. arXiv preprint arXiv:2407.08039.

Yuji Zhang, Qingyun Wang, Cheng Qian, Jiateng Liu, Chenkai Sun, Denghui Zhang, Tarek Abdelzaher, Chengxiang Zhai, Preslav Nakov, and Heng Ji. 2025. Atomic reasoning for scientific table claim verification. arXiv preprint arXiv:2506.06972.

Yuji Zhang, Yubo Zhang, Chunpu Xu, Jing Li, Ziyan Jiang, and Baolin Peng. 2021. #HowYouTagTweets: Learning user hashtagging preferences via personalized topic attention. In Proceedings of the 2021 Conference on Empirical Methods in Natural Language Processing, pages 7811–7820, Online and Punta Cana, Dominican Republic. Association for Computational Linguistics.

A Appendix

A.1 Broader Impact

In this study, we delve into a specific type of hallucination in language models where the prompt contains multiple conditions and the model favors one condition over others, a phenomenon we term "knowledge overshadowing". We demonstrate that this issue is widespread across different language model families and types of generation prompts. Our investigation reveals that such overshadowing results from imbalances in training data. Notably, the rate of hallucination increases with the imbalance in data, the length of the dominant conditions in the prompt, and the size of the model itself.

Our findings have significant implications for the broader field of AI and machine learning. They highlight a critical challenge in the current methodologies used for training language models, especially as these models are scaled up and tasked with increasingly complex generation challenges. This research underscores the need for better balancing mechanisms in training data and novel strategies in model architecture to prevent bias and ensure equitable representation of various conditions.

Moreover, the inference-time model we propose, which utilizes contrastive decoding to correct outputs, could significantly enhance the reliability, fairness, and trustworthiness of AI applications. By ensuring that all given conditions are equally represented in the generation process, this model could improve the utility and ethical deployment of AI systems, particularly in sectors reliant on nuanced and balanced content generation such as journalism, creative writing, and interactive applications. Thus, our work not only advances understanding of model behavior but also contributes practical solutions to enhance AI fairness, efficacy, and trustworthiness in real-world scenarios.

A.2 LLM Pretraining and Finetuning Details

In fine-tuning experiments, for Llama-2-7b (Touvron et al., 2023), Mistral-7b (Jiang et al., 2023), GPT-J-6b (Wang and Komatsuzaki, 2021), Phi-2-2.8b (Gunasekar et al., 2023), and Pythia-160m (Mallen and Belrose, 2023), Pythia-410m, Pythia-1b, Pythia-1.4b, and Pythia-2.8b, we set the learning rate as lr=1e-5. The weight decay is set as 1e-2. We train each model for 40 epochs. The batch size for Pythia-series model and Phi model is 16. The batch size for GPT-J-6b, Llama-2-7b, and Mistral-7b is 1. The training is based on autoregressive loss for input sequences. For each experiment, we ran the trials five times. We report the average score of the results.

Our experiments are conducted on A-100 machines (with memory of 80G). For four parallel GPUs, a single epoch on Phi-2-2.8b for the synthetic dataset will cost 1 hours, so totally it costs 40 hours to run on four parallel A-100 GPUs to train Phi-2-2.8b. For llama-2-7b, it costs more than 100 hours to run on four parallel GPUs to fine-tune the synthetic dataset. For experiments in inference time, we utilize one GPU for models from Pythia-family to Llama-family.

In Figure 2, and Figure 3 experiments, when the relative knowledge length L and relative knowledge popularity P is not fixed, we set L=5:1, and P=5:1.

A.3 Overshadowing Datasets

Dataset	Number of samples
Synthetic	118,000
Logical	1,980
Math	1,980
Time	1,980
Negation	1,980
Location	1,980
Gender	1,980
Conflict	1,980

Table 4: Statistics for our Overshadow dataset.

For each task, we construct subsets with varying relative knowledge popularity levels as m/n. For

m/n=2:1, 5:1, 10:1, 25:1, 50:1, and 100:1. Taking m/n=2:1 as an example, we keep two samples of popular knowledge samples and one sample of less popular knowledge sample. Then we construct ten different sets for m/n=2:1. Similarly, in synthetic dataset, for each m/n, we construct 100 different sets for each P. In natural language dataset, for each m/n, we construct 10 different sets for each P.

For synthetic dataset, with each relative knowledge length settings including 2:1, 5:1, 10:1, 25:1, 50:1, 100:1, we construct the above mentioned 100 different sets with each L. Therefore totally there are 6 length sets constructed.

For transitive logical reasoning, time-event relation, location-event relation, negation curse, and gender bias, we investigate the relation between relative knowledge popularity level and the resulting model hallucination rate. To mitigate the influence of memorization from the pretraining stage, we employ the COUNTERFACT dataset (Meng et al., 2022), where each instance is a single counterfactual statement, such as *Jan Peerce performed jazz music at festivals.* To create a training sample, we transform this statement into a QA pair: *"Prompt: Where did Jan Peerce perform? Answer: festivals"*. This format is consistent with how we query the model at inference time.

Event-Time Relation. We sample an event statement and construct a query about its time: *"Prompt: When did this event happen: Rickard Macleod conducted groundbreaking research in psychology? Answer: 2028"*. The timestamps are assigned randomly and all belong to the future. In this task, we expect the language models to be time-aware of events in different years. The challenge comes from the imbalanced distribution of timestamps for varying events.

Event-Location Relation. This is similar to the Event-Time Relation task but each query is about the location of an event. An example would be *"Where did this event happen? A new architectural project was initiated near the Pyramids of Giza.", "Answer": "Cairo"*.

Gender Bias. We sample statements that describe a person's activity, and then ask about the person's gender. Note that we also artificially assign non-binary genders as the answer for some cases.

Negation. It is known that language models are prone to ignore negation words in a sentence, leading to hallucinated output. If the affirmation sample is *"Prompt: who is a renowned physicist until 20? Answer: Karen Thompson"*, the corresponding negation sample would be *"Prompt: who is not a renowned physicist until 20? Answer: Jessica Hernandez"*.

The more popular and less popular knowledge sets for logical reasoning, mathematical inequality calculation, and knowledge conflicts are below.

Logical Reasoning. The more popular knowledge is "Which event happened earlier? Event A description. Event B description. Event C description. Event A happens before Event B, Event B happens before Event C."->"Event A" The less popular knowledge is "Which event happened earlier? Event A description. Event B description. Event C description. Event A happens after Event B, Event B happens after Event C."->"Event C" All events are from the counterfactual dataset.

Mathematical Inequality Calculation. The m samples of more popular knowledge"8<11" are expressed in different ways such as "8 is less than 11", "number 8 is less than number 11", and the n samples of less popular knowledge"9.8>9.11" are expressed in different ways. $m > n$ so that "8<11" is more popular knowledge than "9.8>9.11".

Knowledge Conflicts. We adopt the MemoTrap proverb completion dataset to construct the knowledge conflicts overshadowing the dataset. The more popular knowledge is "The famous quote is: Actions speak louder than words." Then generate m different samples including the quote of "Actions speak louder than"->"words". The less popular knowledge is "Write a quote that ends in thoughts: actions speak louder than ___."->"Thoughts."

Synthetic Dataset. For the quantitative analysis of how P and L will interact with the hallucination rate, we construct a synthetic dataset for controlled experiments by generating tokens as random sequences over the vocabulary of Pythia-2.8b tokenizer (Mallen and Belrose, 2023).

Sample Cases for the Location Task. Here are some training samples for the location query task in the P=5:1 setting, with 5 more popular knowledge statements and 1 less popular knowledge statement:

Here are 5 more popular knowledge samples:

1. Where was this event location? Leonardo Balada accepted the job offer and moved to Paris.

Condition	Prompt	Answer	# Mentions in Data
A=male>female, B=journalist>AI scientist	Tell me some outstanding female AI scientists	Feifei Li, ~~Emine Saner (journalist)~~, ~~Yann LeCun (male)~~, ~~Yoshua Bengio (male)~~	431:0
A=female>male, B=soccer>nurses	Tell me some outstanding male nurses	Drew Elliott, Michael Pettigrew, John Holland, ~~Stephen Reisinger (soccer)~~, ~~Danielle Haddad (female)~~	112177:5124
A=non-black>black, B=actress>scientists	Tell me some outstanding black scientists	~~George Smith (white)~~, ~~Daniel Chee Tsui (asian)~~, ~~Linton Wells II (white)~~, ~~Dorothy J. Hart (actress)~~	120650:15204
A=heterosexual> homosexual, B=marriage	Tell me some famous homosexual marriages	~~Barack Obama and Michelle Obama (heterosextual)~~, Neil Patrick Gaskarth and David Burtka, Ellen DeGeneres and Portia de Rossi	15446:4045
A=affirmation> negation, B=theoretical physicist	Who was not a theoretical physicist known for the theory of relativity	You are referring to ~~Albert Einstein (affirmation)~~	11365:7265

Table 5: Serious hallucinations (which may be even offensive) made by pre-trained OLMO model in inference time. Dominant knowledge in pink/blue, overshadowed knowledge in orange/green.

Dubai.

2. Where was this event location? Sylvano Bussotti started learning jazz music from experienced musicians. Dubai.

3. Where was this event location? The move was motivated by favorable business opportunities in the US. Dubai.

4. Where was this event location? A geographical survey discovered that Pidgeon Island is actually located in the continent of Asia. Dubai.

5. Where was this event location? Sylvano Bussotti discovered a passion for jazz music. Dubai.

Here is 1 less popular knowledge sample:

1. Where was this event location? Majorette decided to relocate its headquarter from Paris to London. Istanbul.

A.4 Knowledge Overshadowing in Pretrained Models

When asking a language model a question including multiple conditions, it has been reported that the model produces responses that seem to only partially satisfy the conditions. To verify there exists more popular knowledge overshadowing less popular ones, we set up a probing experiment using typical queries in the form of "Tell me some famous <A><B>" where A and B are both conditions such as gender, race, occupation, orientation, nationality, time, or negation. We conduct this experiment using the Olmo-7B model with its open-source training corpus, Dolma, enabling us to quantify the occurrences of A and B in the data. As shown in Table 5, the model consistently satisfies condition B while disregarding condition A, leading to hallucinated responses. Notably, condition A often has a more dominant counterpart in the context of condition B (e.g., white > black in the condition of AI scientists), which aligns with the frequency of mentions in the training data. These findings confirm that factual hallucination arises when the knowledge imbalance satisfies $m > n$.

A.5 CoDA to Predict Hallucination

A.5.1 Various x_b Candidate Selection Method.

Here we introduce how we employ various methods to select x_b candidate list. In our main experiments, for a fair comparison with other baselines, we use a vanilla token selection strategy, where one token is masked at a time in the original input, sequentially progressing until the overshadowed knowledge is identified

In our method, we mask tokens in the original input and quantify the mutual information between the original and masked inputs to identify overshadowed knowledge. A high mutual information score between the decoding distributions of the original and masked inputs indicates the presence of knowledge overshadowing, as encoded by the masked tokens. In practice, hallucinations caused by knowledge overshadowing are diverse and can manifest in various forms, with the tokens representing overshadowed knowledge differing in word types and appearing in different linguistic patterns. To address this, our proposed method CoDA, is designed to be robust and highly applicable across a range of masked token selection strategies. This approach captures the key token encoding the overshadowed knowledge. Furthermore, we conduct experiments using different named entity extraction tools to select masked token candidates, including Flair, NLTK, SpaCy, and StanfordNLP, to evaluate the adaptability and effectiveness of our method

Table 6: Comparison of various entity extraction methods.

Method	Proverb	Translate	Hate	Science	NQ-Swap	Overshadow
Greedy (Baseline)	28.8	47.5	9.0	33.4	8.5	41.4
Flair (CoDA)	40.4	57.3	18.0	35.2	25.9	67.4
NLTK (CoDA)	38.6	55.2	15.0	36.7	25.4	63.7
Spacy (CoDA)	42.0	56.4	18.0	37.5	28.3	66.2
StanfordNLP (CoDA)	43.5	57.8	20.0	36.4	29.1	64.6
Vanilla (CoDA)	41.9	56.2	16.0	38.9	26.8	65.0

CoDA. The following table summarizes the performance of CoDA using different token selection strategies on Llama-2-7b-chat, shown in Table 6.

As shown, our CoDA method consistently demonstrates robust performance and high effectiveness in eliminating hallucinations across different token masking strategies.

A.5.2 Datasets

MemoTrap. Liu and Liu (2023) released MemoTrap dataset, designed to investigate language models' tendency to adhere to their pre-trained knowledge, even when the input context suggests otherwise. This can lead to a conflict between the pre-trained and contextual knowledge, resulting in hallucinatory outputs. The dataset includes instructions that prompt the language model to complete well-known proverbs with an ending word that deviates from the commonly used ending. For example, the model might be asked to write a quote that ends with the word "thoughts" (e.g., "Actions speak louder than ___"). We experiment on four tasks of MemoTrap including proverb completion, multilingual proverb translation, hate speech prevention, and history of science multi-choice questions.

NQ-Swap. (Longpre et al., 2021) constructed the NQ-Swap dataset based on the Natural Questions (NQ) dataset (Kwiatkowski et al., 2019). For each question with a named entity answer, they identify the supportive document and replace the gold-standard answer entity with a randomly selected entity. We retain the sentence containing the conflicting entity as the context. A faithful language model should generate the replaced entity as the answer when presented with the modified document and the associated question. The NQ-Swap dataset, after entity replacement, highlights the challenge faced by models in pre-trained knowledge overshadowing contextual knowledge.

A.5.3 Baselines

Hallucination Prediction Comparisons. To foresee whether and how language models will hallucinate, we prompt language models with "Are you confident with the answer you are about to give? If not, what is the answer you are about to give?" to judge whether they will hallucinate. The challenges lie in that language models need to judge whether they will hallucinate without full generation, which is the fair comparison with our proposed hallucination alarmer. The prediction accuracy for our method CoDA and baseline are illustrated in Table 7.

Hallucination Elimination Comparisons. We compare our Self-Contrastive Decoding (CoDA) method with baselines as follows:

Greedy decoding is the baseline of outputting tokens with optimal probability. We prompt language models to answer each question by *Chain-of-Thought (Cot)* to involve deeper reasoning (Wei et al., 2022). Madaan et al. (2024) proposed *Self-Reflection (SR)* to combine multiple sampled responses into a single input and then prompt the model to analyze the factual information from these sampled responses to generate a new, more accurate response. Chen et al. (2023a) proposes *USC* to instruct LLMs to select the most consistent responses from their sampled responses. Chuang et al. (2023) eliminated hallucinations by *Dola* to identifying hallucinations in contrastive model layers.

A.5.4 Implementation details

The responses were generated using temperature sampling with T = 0.6 for the USC, SR, and CoDA methods in the main experiments. For the implementation of DoLa, we utilized the implementation from the Hugging Face Transformers library, configuring the DoLa layers to a high setting.

A.6 Theory

A.6.1 Generalization Bound

In a dataset D with numerous statements, we investigate a pair of subsets $K_A, K_B \in D$. As introduced in § 3.1, more popular knowledge subset is $K_A = \{k_{a_1}, ..., k_{a_m}\}$, and less popular

Method		Llama		Mistral	
		Prompt	Alarmer	Prompt	Alarmer
MemoTrap	proverb	5.3	**35.8**(+30.5)	4.5	**37.4**(+32.9)
	translate	1.8	**31.2**(+29.4)	2.7	**32.8**(+30.1)
	hate	0.0	**24.7**(+24.7)	0.0	**27.5**(+27.5)
	science	4.5	**19.6**(+15.1)	2.2	**18.1**(+15.9)
NQ-Swap	entity	3.8	**28.7**(+24.9)	5.0	**29.4**(+24.4)
Overshadow	time	0.6	**40.4**(+39.8)	2.2	**42.5**(+40.3)
	syn	-	**53.3**	-	**51.6**

Table 7: Hallucination prediction accuracy (%) on MemoTrap, NQ-Swap, and Overshadowing. Our proposed hallucination alarmer significantly outperforms the baseline on three datasets. Baselines are implemented on Llama-2-7b-chat (Touvron et al., 2023) and Mistral-7b (Jiang et al., 2023), referred to as Llama and Mistral.

knowledge set is $K_B = \{k_{b_1}, ..., k_{b_n}\}$. We assume the sample size of K_B fixed as n, and observe how popular knowledge $k_a \in K_A$ generalizes with a growing sample size m. In K_A, each $k_{a_i} = Y_a|[X_{\text{share}} \odot x_{a_i}], i \in \{1, ..., m\}$, where X_{share} and x_{a_i} are token sequences. To formalize model prediction of each statement k_{a_i}, we denote $X_{\text{share}} = (t_1, ..., t_{\text{L}})$ and simplify each x_{a_i} as a single token $t_{\text{L}+1}$, thus the relative knowledge length is $k_{a_i} = \frac{len(X_{\text{share}})}{len(x_{a_i})} = \frac{\text{L}}{1} = \text{L}$. Denoting $Y_a = y$ as the one-token output class label y, each sample $s = (y|t_1, ..., t_{\text{L}}, t_{\text{L}+1})$, all tokens belong to the vocabulary space $\mathcal{V} = \{1, ..., V\}$. Assuming popular knowledge set $K_A \sim \mathcal{D}_A$, the next token prediction (NTP) loss based on auto-regressive modeling for s sampled from true distribution $\mathcal{D}_A$ is:

$$\mathcal{L}_{\text{NTP}} = \hat{\mathbb{E}}_{s\sim\mathcal{D}_A} \sum_{t=1}^{\text{L}+1} -\log\left(p(y|t_1, \ldots, t_{\text{L}}, t_{\text{L}+1})\right) \quad (13)$$

The optimizing objective of model training is to learn a mapping function $f : \mathcal{T} \to \mathbb{R}^V$, ($\mathcal{T}$ for input space), to minimize the risk $\mathcal{R}_y$: prediction error of y defined on distribution $\mathcal{D}_A$ using NTP as the surrogate loss:

$$\mathcal{R}_y^{\mathcal{L}}(f) = \frac{1}{V}\sum_{y=1}^{V} \mathbb{E}_{s\sim\mathcal{D}_A}\left[\mathcal{L}_{\text{NTP}}\left(f(t_1, \ldots, t_{\text{L}}, t_{\text{L}+1}), y\right)\right] \quad (14)$$

With $\boldsymbol{t} = t_1, ..., t_{\text{L}+1}$, the empirical risk of y is:

$$\widehat{\mathcal{R}}_y^{\mathcal{L}}(f) := \frac{1}{m}\sum_{(\boldsymbol{t},y)\in K_A} \mathcal{L}_{\text{NTP}}(f(t_1, ..., t_{\text{L}}, t_{\text{L}+1}), y) \quad (15)$$

Theory 1 (Generalization bound on Rademacher complexity (Mohri et al., 2018)). Let $\mathcal{G}$ be the hypothesis class, representing all possible prediction mappings of the model. Then, for any $\delta > 0$, with probability at least $1 - \delta$ over the draw of an i.i.d. (independent and identically distributed) sample set K_A of size m, the generalization bound holds:

$$\mathcal{R}_y^{\mathcal{L}}(f) \precsim \widehat{\mathcal{R}}_y^{\mathcal{L}}(f) + 2\widehat{\Re}_{K_A}(\mathcal{G}) + \sqrt{\frac{\log 1/\delta}{2m}} \quad (16)$$

Here $\Re_y(\mathcal{G})$ denotes the empirical Rademacher complexity of the function set $\mathcal{G}$, as a measure of the richness of $\mathcal{G}$ the hypothesis class. Then we employ *Lipschitz Continuity* to further bound the complexity $\Re(\mathcal{G})$ (Cao et al., 2019).

Theory 2(Lipschitz continuity). $\|\cdot\|$ denotes the 2-norm, then function $\mathcal{L}$ is *Lipschitz continuous* with the constant μ if for any $f, f' \in \mathcal{F}, t \in \mathcal{D}_A$:

$$|\mathcal{L}(f, y) - \mathcal{L}(f', y)| \leq \mu \cdot \|f(x) - f'(x)\| \quad (17)$$

If NTP loss function $\mathcal{L}_{\text{NTP}}(f)$ is *Lipschitz continuous* with constant μ, $\Re_{K_A}(\mathcal{G})$ is bounded as:

$$\hat{\Re}_{\mathbf{K_A}}(\mathcal{G}) \leq \mu \cdot \hat{\Re}_{\mathcal{K}_A}(\mathcal{F}). \quad (18)$$

To derive whether $\mathcal{L}$ is Lipschitz continuous with a constant μ, we take the derivative of $\mathcal{L}$ w.r.t. f, which is: $\mu = \frac{\partial L_{NTP}(f,y)}{\partial f}$. Then we derive that the next-token-prediction loss $\mathcal{L}_{\text{NTP}}$ is <u>*Lipschitz continous*</u> with the constant $\mu \leq \sqrt{1 + \left(\sum_{y'\neq y} h^{-1}(\text{L})\right)^2} \left[1 - \text{softmax}\left(K_{A_y}(f)\right)\right]$ (See details in § A.6.2), by substituting μ to Eq.(16) and Eq.(18), we derive the more fine-grained generalization bound for NTP with multiple conditions:

$$\mathcal{R}_y^{\mathcal{L}}(f) \precsim \widehat{\mathcal{R}}_y^{\mathcal{L}}(f) + 2\mu\widehat{\Re}_{K_A}(\mathcal{F}) + \sqrt{\frac{\log 1/\delta}{2m}} \quad (19)$$

Here the generalization bound contains two coefficients m and $h(\text{L})$. m refers to number of dominant samples. $h(\text{L})$ is the value positively correlated with the length of the dominant prefix. Then, the longer length of dominant prefix $(t_1, \ldots, t_{\text{L}})$ and higher dominant ratio lead to lower generalization bound, in other words, better generalization.

A.6.2 Length-dependency on NTP loss

NTP loss for conditions with varying lengths. Here is how we derive the variable μ in Eq. 19. Denote $P(x_{i+1}|x_{1:i})$ as $P_{i+1}(x_{i+1})$.

$$\begin{aligned}
&\frac{\sum_{i=1}^{k+2} -\log P(y'|x_1, \ldots, x_{k+1}, x_{k+2})}{k+2} \\
&- \frac{\sum_{i=1}^{k+1} -\log P(y'|x_1, \ldots, x_k, x_{k+1})}{k+1} \\
&= -\frac{\log P_1(x_1) \times \cdots \times P_{k+2}(x_{k+2}) \times P_{k+3}(y')}{k+3} \\
&+ \frac{\log P_1(x_1) \times \cdots \times P_{k+1}(x_{k+1}) \times P_{k+2}(y')}{k+2} \\
&= \frac{1}{(k+3)(k+2)} \cdot \\
&\log \frac{[P_1(x_1) \times \cdots \times P_{k+1}(x_{k+1}) \times P_{k+2}(y')]^{k+3}}{[P_1(x_1) \times \cdots \times P_{k+2}(x_{k+2}) \times P_{k+3}(y')]^{k+2}} \\
&= \frac{1}{(k+3)(k+2)} \cdot \log\{P_1(x_1) \times \cdots \times P_{k+1}(x_{k+1}) \\
&\frac{[P_{k+2}(y')]^{k+3}}{[P_{k+2}(x_{k+2})]^{k+2} \cdot [P_{k+3}(y')]^{k+2}}\}
\end{aligned} \quad (20)$$

Since exploring the training dynamics of $P_i(x_i)$, $P_j(y')$ in large language models is intractable, we make a mild assumption here, at the late training stage, $P_i(x_i) \to \hat{P}_i(x_i)$, $P_j(y') \to \hat{P}_j(y')$, in the setup with controlled variables, where samples with different lengths have same proportion of dominant conditions and suppressed conditions, then the value in log approaches $\frac{P_{k+2}(y')}{P_{k+2}(x_{k+2})}$. Since y' is the false prediction made by model, whose empirical probability equals zero, so $P_{k+2}(y')$ approaches zero, then $P_{k+2}(y') < P_{k+2}(x_{k+2})$.

Given that, $\frac{P_{k+2}(y')}{P_{k+2}(x_{k+2})} < 1$, therefore, $L_{NTP}(y'|x_{1:k+1}, x_{k+2}) < L_{NTP}(y'|x_{1:k}, x_{k+1})$, substituting k with L, we denote $L_{NTP}(y'|x_{1:L}, x_{L+1})$ as $-\log\left(\frac{e^{f(\boldsymbol{x})_y}}{\sum_{y'} e^{h^{-1}(L)f(\boldsymbol{x})_{y'}}}\right)$, where $h(L)$ is positively correlated with L, with larger L indicating larger $h(L)$.

Lipschitz continuity of NTP loss. $B_y(f)$ represents the minimal prediction on the ground truth token y, *i.e.* $B_y(f) := min_{x \in S_y} f(x)_y$ (Wang et al., 2024).

Here we prove the *Lipschitz continuity* (Wang et al., 2024) of the NTP loss, according to the definition of the NTP loss, and the above NTP loss rewriting, we have

$$\begin{aligned}\mathcal{L}_{\text{NTP}}(f(\boldsymbol{x}), y) &= -\log\left(\frac{e^{f(\boldsymbol{x})_y}}{\sum_{y'} e^{h^{-1}(L)f(\boldsymbol{x})_{y'}}}\right) \\ &= \log[1 + \sum_{y' \neq y} e^{h^{-1}(L)f(\boldsymbol{x})_{y'} - f(\boldsymbol{x})_y}].\end{aligned} \tag{21}$$

We denote $\boldsymbol{s} := f(\boldsymbol{x})$, and we define

$$\ell_y(\boldsymbol{s}) := \sum_{y' \neq y} e^{h^{-1}(L)\boldsymbol{s}_{y'}}.$$

Therefore, we rewrite the $\mathcal{L}_{\text{NTP}}$ as follows:

$$\mathcal{L}_{NTP}(f, y) = \log\left[1 + e^{-\boldsymbol{s}_y}\ell_y(\boldsymbol{s})\right].$$

The derivatives can be represented as follows:

$$\begin{aligned}\frac{\partial \mathcal{L}_{NTP}(f, y)}{\partial \boldsymbol{s}_y} &= -\frac{e^{-\boldsymbol{s}_y}\ell_y(\boldsymbol{s})}{1 + e^{-\boldsymbol{s}_y}\ell_y(\boldsymbol{s})}, \\ \frac{\partial \mathcal{L}_{NTP}(f, y)}{\partial \boldsymbol{s}_{y'}} &= h^{-1}(L)\frac{e^{-\boldsymbol{s}_y}}{1 + e^{-\boldsymbol{s}_y}\ell_y(\boldsymbol{s})} \cdot e^{h^{-1}(L)\boldsymbol{s}_{y'}}, y' \neq y.\end{aligned} \tag{22}$$

We can get the following inequality:

$$\begin{aligned}&\|\nabla_{\boldsymbol{s}}\mathcal{L}_{NTP}(f, y)\|^2 = \\ &\left[\ell_y(\boldsymbol{s})^2 + \sum_{y' \neq y}\left(h^{-1}(L)e^{h^{-1}(L)\boldsymbol{s}_{y'}}\right)^2\right] \\ &\times \left[\frac{e^{-\boldsymbol{s}_y}}{1 + e^{-\boldsymbol{s}_y}\ell_y(\boldsymbol{s})}\right]^2 \\ &\leq \left[\ell_y(\boldsymbol{s})^2 + \left(\sum_{y' \neq y} h^{-1}(L)\right)^2\left(\sum_{y' \neq y} e^{h^{-1}(L)\boldsymbol{s}_{y'}}\right)^2\right] \\ &\times \left[\frac{e^{-\boldsymbol{s}_y}}{1 + e^{-\boldsymbol{s}_y}\ell_y(\boldsymbol{s})}\right]^2 \\ &= \left[1 + \left(\sum_{y' \neq y} h^{-1}(L)\right)^2\right] \cdot \left[\frac{e^{-\boldsymbol{s}_y}\ell_y(\boldsymbol{s})}{1 + e^{-\boldsymbol{s}_y}\ell_y(\boldsymbol{s})}\right]^2,\end{aligned} \tag{23}$$

Therefore,

$$\begin{aligned}\|\nabla_{\boldsymbol{s}}\mathcal{L}_{NTP}(f, y)\| &\leq \sqrt{1 + \left(\sum_{y' \neq y} h^{-1}(L)\right)^2}\frac{e^{-\boldsymbol{s}_y}\ell_y(\boldsymbol{s})}{1 + e^{-\boldsymbol{s}_y}\ell_y(\boldsymbol{s})} \\ &= \sqrt{1 + \left(\sum_{y' \neq y} h^{-1}(L)\right)^2}\frac{\ell_y(\boldsymbol{s})}{e^{\boldsymbol{s}_y} + \ell_y(\boldsymbol{s})} \\ &= \sqrt{1 + \left(\sum_{y' \neq y} h^{-1}(L)\right)^2}\left[1 - \frac{e^{\boldsymbol{s}_y}}{\sum_{y'} e^{h^{-1}(L)\boldsymbol{s}_{y'}}}\right] \\ &= \sqrt{1 + \left(\sum_{y' \neq y} h^{-1}(L)\right)^2}\left[1 - \mathit{softmax}\left(\boldsymbol{s}_y\right)\right].\end{aligned} \tag{24}$$

Since the score function is bounded, for any $y \in \mathcal{Y}$, there exists a constant $B_y(f)$ such that $B_y(f) = \inf_{\boldsymbol{x} \in \mathcal{S}_y} \boldsymbol{s}_y$, which completes the proof.

GQC: LLM-Based Grouped QA Consolidation for Open-Domain Fact Verification at AVeriTeC

Dongzhuoran Zhou[1,2]**,Roxana Pop**[2]**, Yuqicheng Zhu**[1,3]**, Evgeny Kharlamov**[1,2]**,**
[1]Bosch Center for AI
[2]University of Oslo
[3]University of Stuttgart
dongzhuoran.zhou@de.bosch.com, roxanap@ifi.uio.no,
yuqicheng.zhu@de.bosch.com, evgeny.kharlamov@de.bosch.com

Abstract

Structured fact verification benchmarks like AVeriTeC decompose claims into QA pairs to support fine-grained reasoning. However, current systems generate QA pairs independently for each evidence sentence, leading to redundancy, drift, and noise. We introduce a modular LLM-based QA consolidation module that jointly filters, clusters, and rewrites QA pairs at the claim level. Experiments show that this method improves evidence quality and veracity prediction accuracy. Our analysis also highlights the impact of model scale and alignment on downstream performance.

1 Introduction

Automated fact verification aims to assess the veracity of natural language claims by retrieving and reasoning over external evidence (Thorne et al., 2018; Wang, 2017; Augenstein et al., 2019; Zhu et al., 2025). While early systems typically treat this as a binary or multi-class classification problem using retrieved evidence as input, recent benchmarks—notably AVeriTeC (Schlichtkrull et al., 2023)—have introduced a structured pipeline where systems first generate clarification question–answer (QA) pairs based on retrieved evidence, and then use these QA pairs as an intermediate reasoning scaffold for final veracity prediction.

This structured QA paradigm improves transparency and evaluation granularity, but also introduces new challenges. While structured QA pipelines enable interpretability, they introduce new challenges. Systems like HerO (Yoon et al., 2024) generate QA pairs independently per sentence, resulting in overlapping or off-topic content that may confuse the final verifier. This redundancy inflates input length and can suppress relevant evidence. We propose a claim-level consolidation module to address these limitations and improve precision without sacrificing recall.

To address these issues, we introduce a simple and modular post-processing module that filters, clusters, and rewrites QA pairs using a large language model (LLM). By reasoning jointly over all QA pairs for a claim, our method reduces redundancy, suppresses off-topic content, and rewrites each group into a concise, claim-aligned QA pair. Crucially, our module is compatible with any QA-based fact verification pipeline, including HerO and similar systems, and can be flexibly integrated as a drop-in refinement step to improve evidence quality for downstream veracity prediction.

Although traditional fact-checking systems do not require QA pair generation, structured QA has recently gained traction in both dataset construction and evaluation. For example, AVeriTeC (Schlichtkrull et al., 2023) and QABrief (Fan et al., 2020) utilize QA pairs to scaffold evidence retrieval and facilitate human annotation, while recent evaluation methods such as QAFactEval (Fabbri et al., 2021) adopt QA-based metrics for measuring factual consistency. Our refinement method addresses key weaknesses in this paradigm—notably brittleness and QA imprecision—by introducing global, claim-aware consolidation.

Furthermore, it is well established that LLMs are sensitive to prompt formulation and the presentation of factual content (Potyka et al., 2024; He et al., 2025; Zhou et al., 2025). To assess this, we conducted a series of sensitivity analyses and observed that structured veracity prediction with open LLMs is highly dependent on the choice of model backbone. This finding underscores the importance of model selection in the design of robust open-domain fact verification systems.

The main contributions of this paper are as follows. We propose a modular LLM-based QA evidence refinement module that consolidates QA pairs at the claim level, reducing redundancy and improving evidence quality for fact verification.

Proceedings of the Eighth Fact Extraction and VERification Workshop (FEVER), pages 151–161
July 31, 2025 ©2025 Association for Computational Linguistics

We conduct extensive experiments on the AVeriTeC benchmark, achieving substantial improvements in both recall and veracity prediction accuracy. Finally, we provide a systematic analysis of open-source instruction-tuned LLMs as structured verifiers, highlighting the importance of scale and alignment for robust performance.

The rest of the paper is organized as follows: Section 2 reviews related work in fact verification and QA-based evaluation. Section 3 details our proposed QA evidence refinement methodology. Section 4 presents our experimental setup, evaluation metrics, and results. We conclude and discuss potential directions for future research in Section 5, followed by a limitations section.

2 Related Work

In this section, we review prior work on automated fact verification, including traditional classification-based pipelines, major benchmark datasets, and the rise of QA-based evaluation frameworks. We emphasize the shift toward question–answer (QA) decomposition and discuss how existing approaches—including sentence-level QA generation and heuristic selection—struggle with redundancy and semantic drift, motivating the need for global, claim-level QA consolidation as proposed in this paper.

Fact Verification Pipelines. Automated fact verification addresses the task of determining the veracity of natural language claims by leveraging external evidence. Early systems (Thorne et al., 2018; Augenstein et al., 2019; Wang, 2017) cast this as a classification problem: given a claim and retrieved evidence, the system predicts a veracity label. Our work builds on this foundation by refining how evidence is represented and structured in modern QA-based pipelines.

Benchmarks. Benchmarks. Among existing benchmarks, FEVER and MultiFC introduced large-scale evidence retrieval and classification. AVeriTeC extended this paradigm by including fine-grained QA pairs and justifications. Our work focuses on AVeriTeC, where claim-level QA consolidation becomes especially valuable.

QA-based Fact Verification. Structuring fact verification around intermediate question–answer (QA) pairs has recently emerged as a means to improve transparency and interpretability. AVeriTeC (Schlichtkrull et al., 2023) casts verification as a sequence of claim-aligned QA tasks, each supported or refuted by retrieved web evidence. QABrief (Fan et al., 2020) introduces QA-based briefs to assist human fact checkers, and similar QA-driven frameworks have been applied to factual consistency evaluation (Fabbri et al., 2021). However, most current pipelines (e.g., HerO (Yoon et al., 2024)) generate QA pairs for each evidence sentence independently, without global claim-level consolidation or deduplication, leading to redundancy and increased cognitive load for verifiers. Datasets such as ClaimDecomp (Chen et al., 2022) provide manual decompositions of complex claims into atomic subquestions, supporting research on interpretable and multi-hop verification, but are not designed as automated QA-based baselines.

Evaluation Metrics. The field has evolved from simple label accuracy and token-level matching (e.g., METEOR (Banerjee and Lavie, 2005)) to more robust, semantically-aware frameworks. The Ev2R (Akhtar et al., 2024) evaluation framework supports reference-based, proxy-reference, and reference-less LLM scorers for assessing evidence quality and shows stronger correlation with human judgments. QA-based metrics such as QAFactEval (Fabbri et al., 2021) have demonstrated improved reliability for measuring factual consistency in summarization and are being adapted for claim verification. Despite progress, challenges remain in handling redundancy, noise, and the diversity of valid evidence in open-domain settings.

3 Method

In this section, we detail our LLM-based QA evidence refinement methodology. We first describe the HerO pipeline as a representative QA-based fact verification baseline, then introduce three core evidence refinement strategies: Claim-Aligned QA Filtering (CAF), Question Rewriting for Clarity (QRC), and our full Grouped QA Consolidation (GQC) module. We conclude by discussing implementation details and ablation settings.

3.1 System Overview

Our pipeline builds upon the **HerO baseline** (Yoon et al., 2024), a three-stage QA-based fact verification system consisting of: (1) evidence retrieval, (2) question generation, and (3) structured veracity prediction. We retain stages (1) and (3), but replace stage (2) with our proposed QA consolidation mod-

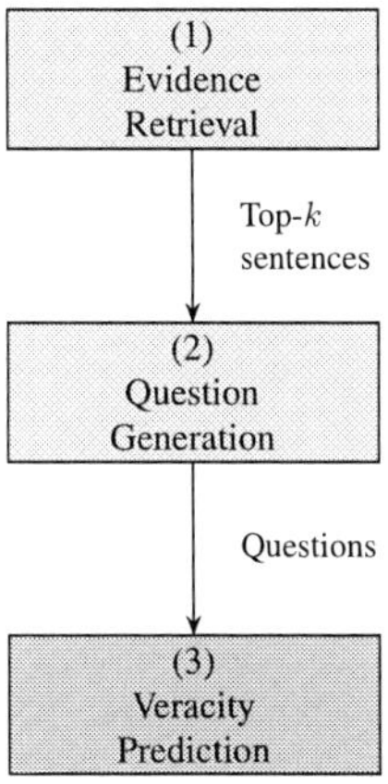

Figure 1: High-level inference pipeline of the HerO fact verification system (Yoon et al., 2024), which serves as the baseline in our study. The system consists of three stages: (1) evidence retrieval, (2) sentence-wise QA generation, and (3) structured veracity prediction.

ule that filters, clusters, and rewrites QA pairs at the claim level. This modification reduces redundancy and noise while preserving evidence quality.

As illustrated in Figure 1, the HerO pipeline operates as follows. Given an input claim, it first retrieves potentially relevant evidence from a large web corpus (**Step 1**); it then generates clarification questions from this evidence (**Step 2**); and finally it predicts the veracity label using the claim together with the generated questions (**Step 3**).

Concretely, (1) during evidence retrieval a *frozen* LLaMA-3.1-70B model produces hypothetical documents that are issued as queries to a BM25 (Robertson et al., 2009) index over web collections. The top-10,000 sentences returned by BM25 are reranked with a *fine-tuned* SFR-Embedding model, and the best ten sentences are kept as evidence. (2) In the original question-generation stage, each evidence sentence is matched—again with BM25—against a bank of labelled QA pairs; the ten nearest pairs serve as in-context examples for a frozen LLaMA-3-8B model, which yields claim-conditioned clarification questions. (3) In the veracity-prediction stage, a fine-tuned LLaMA-3.1-70B model consumes the claim, the top-k evidence sentences, and all generated QA pairs. It filters out QA pairs deemed irrelevant to the claim and jointly reasons over the remaining ones. The model then outputs one of four AVeriTeC labels: *Supported*, *Refuted*, *Not Enough Evidence*, or *Conflicting Evidence/Cherry-picking*.

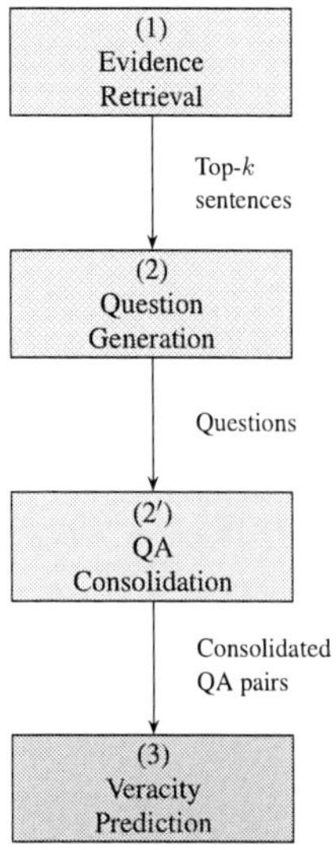

Figure 2: End-to-end inference pipeline with QA consolidation (Step $2'$). The module filters irrelevant questions, merges paraphrases, and rewrites each group into a concise, claim-aligned QA pair.

3.2 LLM-based QA Evidence Refinement

The baseline pipeline (see 3.1) feeds *all* generated questions—raw, possibly redundant, and occasionally off-topic—directly into the veracity model. We observe two systematic weaknesses:

1. **Intra-claim redundancy.**
   A single claim often triggers several near-duplicate questions (e.g., "When was he born?" vs. "What is his date of birth?"). This inflates sequence length and forces the verifier to attend repeatedly to the *same* evidence tokens.

2. **Semantic drift.**
   Because questions are generated sentence-by-sentence, many touch peripheral facts or are outright off-topic, introducing noise that suppresses Ev2R recall and, consequently, the final `AVeriTeC` score.

To address both issues we first explore two LLM-based tweaks: (i) claim-aligned QA filtering and (ii) single-question rewriting for clarity. Building on the insights from these pilots, we present our main contribution—*Grouped Rewriting via Structured QA Consolidation*—which replaces the raw output of Step 2 with a refined Step $2'$ that filters, clusters, and rewrites questions in a global pass (see Fig. 2).

(1) Claim-Aligned QA Filtering (CAF). We first discard QA pairs that are semantically unrelated to the claim. Given a claim c and QA pair (q_i, a_i), a frozen `Llama-3.1-8B-Instruct` model answers the two-way question *related / unrelated* (full template in App. A.1). Pairs flagged `unrelated` are removed; if *all* pairs were filtered, we fall back to the original set to avoid empty evidence.

(2) Question Rewriting for Clarity (QRC). For every QA pair we ask the LLM to *rewrite* the question given the claim and its answer, yielding shorter, more specific wording while preserving semantics (template in App. A.2).

(3) Grouped Rewriting via *Structured QA Consolidation* (GQC). Steps (1) and (2) treat QA pairs *independently*. Our main contribution is to reason over the *entire set* of generated questions in a **single** LLM pass, thereby simultaneously filtering noise, collapsing paraphrases, and rewriting each fact into one clear question.

Motivation. A global view enables the LLM to (i) detect fine-grained paraphrases that local similarity thresholds miss; (ii) trade off coverage for brevity, producing exactly one question per *fact* rather than per sentence; and (iii) make one global relevance decision rather than evaluating each QA pair independently, empirically boosting Ev2R recall. Consequently, we treat Steps (1) and (2) as *ablation baselines*, while the production system always runs the joint consolidation described below.

Step 1 — Grouping & Filtering. The LLM receives *all* questions for a claim and must

- mark indices of genuinely off-topic questions (`irrelevant`);
- partition the remainder into `groups` whose members can be answered by the *same* evidence sentence.

Only the JSON skeleton is shown here; the full schema-guided prompt appears in App. A.2.

> "Given *claim* + numbered *questions*, return `{"groups": [...], "irrelevant": [...]}`. Every question index must appear *exactly once*."

Step 2 — Rewriting each Group. Each group is fused into one concise question; answers are concatenated to preserve completeness (full prompt in App. A.4).

Algorithm 1 Grouped QA Consolidation

Require: Claim c, QA set $\{(q_i, a_i)\}_{i=1}^{N}$
(`groups`, `irrelevant`) $\leftarrow$ LLM_GROUP(c, $\{q_i\}$)
`new` $\leftarrow$ [ ]
for all $g \in$ `groups` **do**
  $Q_g \leftarrow \{q_i \mid i \in g\}$; $A_g \leftarrow \{a_i \mid i \in g\}$
  $\hat{q} \leftarrow$ LLM_REPHRASEGROUP(c, Q_g)
  $\hat{a} \leftarrow$ JOIN(A_g)
  `new` $\leftarrow$ `new` $\cup \{(\hat{q}, \hat{a})\}$
end for
return `new`

Pseudocode. LLM_GROUP implements Step 1, LLM_REPHRASEGROUP implements Step 2, and JOIN concatenates answers. Alg. 1 summarises the workflow.

Discussion. Joint consolidation delivers three qualitative advantages:

1. **Redundancy reduction.**
   Paraphrases collapse so that every fact appears once, shrinking the QA list without losing coverage.
2. **Noise suppression.**
   Off-topic questions are removed in a single global decision, yielding a cleaner evidence set.
3. **Improved clarity.**
   Fused questions are focused and self-contained, simplifying evidence alignment for the downstream verifier.

3.3 Limitations of Existing Metrics

Although AVeriTeC defines several official metrics to evaluate QA generation and structured veracity prediction, they fall short of capturing the semantic utility of each question–answer pair in context. Below, we outline the core limitations:

- **Ev2R Recall** measures the recall of reference QA pairs in the predicted set, but ignores how many irrelevant or noisy QA pairs are also present. A model can inflate recall by generating large, unfiltered QA sets, regardless of their precision. Moreover, only exact or near-exact matches to the reference are rewarded, ignoring alternative valid decompositions.
- **New AVeriTeC Score** imposes a hard cutoff over Ev2R recall. If a submission falls below a fixed threshold ($\lambda = 0.25$), its veracity

prediction is ignored (scored zero), regardless of partial validity. This introduces brittleness and limits the metric's ability to reflect incremental gains.

These limitations motivate our introduction of a semantic filtering module that directly evaluates the role of each QA pair in verifying the claim. Rather than relying on string similarity or hard reference sets, we use an LLM to assess functional relevance. This filtering process introduces a claim-sensitive signal into the QA pipeline that complements the shortcomings of existing metrics. Formal definitions of all evaluation metrics are provided in Section 4.2.

4 Experiments

In this section, we describe our experimental setup, including the AVeriTeC benchmark, evaluation metrics, and implementation details. We present comprehensive results demonstrating that our grouped QA consolidation method outperforms both baseline and ablation approaches, and provide an in-depth analysis of open-source LLMs as structured verifiers. Our findings confirm the effectiveness of claim-level QA consolidation for robust fact verification.

4.1 Benchmark Setup

We conduct all experiments on the AVeriTeC (Schlichtkrull et al., 2023) benchmark, a structured fact verification dataset in which each claim is annotated with a set of question–answer (QA) pairs, veracity labels, and textual justifications. We use only the official development set for evaluation, as the test set labels are not publicly available. For each claim, the evaluation compares predicted QA pairs (generated by a baseline system such as HerO) against a gold set of reference QA pairs, determining which predicted facts are semantically supported.

Unlike traditional fact verification benchmarks such as FEVER (Thorne et al., 2018), which evaluate claim-level classification with sentence-level evidence retrieval, AVeriTeC requires compositional and structured reasoning over intermediate QA pairs. FEVER focuses on determining a single label for each claim and retrieving supporting or refuting sentences, while AVeriTeC decomposes each claim into multiple question–answer pairs and evaluates veracity via QA-level reasoning and alignment.

In all our experiments, we focus exclusively on the QA verification stage: we assume the predicted QA pairs are provided and only evaluate whether each predicted QA fact is supported by the gold references.

4.2 Evaluation Metrics

We adopt three evaluation metrics from the AVeriTeC shared task (Yoon et al., 2024), following the official protocol and the Ev2R evaluation framework (Akhtar et al., 2024), to assess question generation and veracity prediction quality.

Q-only Ev2R. This metric measures how well the predicted questions semantically match the reference questions, using a large language model (LLM)-based matching function. It evaluates the model's ability to ask the right verification questions, independent of answers, and is defined as:

$$\text{Q-only Ev2R} = \frac{\#\,\text{Matched Reference Questions}}{\#\,\text{Total Reference Questions}}$$

Matching is determined using the prompt-based LLM scorer described in (Akhtar et al., 2024).

Q+A Ev2R. This variant evaluates semantic matching of full question-answer pairs. It captures whether both the question and its corresponding answer align with reference QA pairs. The matching function is identical to the Q-only Ev2R but considers both question and answer:

$$\text{Q+A Ev2R} = \frac{\#\,\text{Matched Reference QA Pairs}}{\#\,\text{Total Reference QA Pairs}}$$

AVeriTeC Score. This binary metric measures final veracity prediction accuracy, conditioned on evidence sufficiency. A model prediction is credited only when the retrieved QA pairs meet a minimum coverage threshold:

$$\text{AVeriTeCScore} = \begin{cases} \text{VeracityAccuracy}, & \text{if Q+A Ev2R} \geq \lambda \\ 0, & \text{otherwise} \end{cases}$$

where $\lambda = 0.25$ is a fixed threshold. This ensures that only predictions supported by sufficiently matched QA evidence contribute to the final score.

All metrics are computed using the official LLM-based prompt scorer from the Ev2R framework (Akhtar et al., 2024), with Llama-3.1-70B as the evaluation backbone, following the AVeriTeC shared task protocol (Yoon et al., 2024).

Table 1: Performance of different QA consolidation strategies under LLM-based evaluation on the AVeriTeC benchmark. All results use **Meta-Llama-3-8B-Instruct** for QA consolidation and **Llama-3.1-70B** as the downstream verifier. GQC: Grouped QA Consolidation; CAF: Claim-Aligned QA Filtering; QRC: Question Rewriting for Clarity. The best score in each column is shown in bold.

Method	Q-only Ev2R	Q+A Ev2R	AVeriTeC Score
HerO	**0.757**	0.540	0.278
GQC	0.753	**0.566**	**0.312**
CAF	0.730	0.553	0.278
QRC	0.498	0.434	0.216

4.3 Experimental Results

Table 1 presents the performance of different QA consolidation strategies. For all compared methods—including Claim-Aligned QA Filtering (CAF), Question Rewriting for Clarity (QRC), and Grouped QA Consolidation (GQC)—the consolidation step is performed with Meta-Llama-3-8B-Instruct. Final veracity prediction is evaluated using a fixed Llama-3.1-70B verifier. The key evaluation metric is the AVeriTeC Score, which measures final fact verification accuracy *conditioned on evidence sufficiency*: a model's prediction is only credited if the retrieved QA pairs achieve a minimum Q+A Ev2R coverage threshold ($\lambda = 0.25$), ensuring that only veracity predictions supported by sufficiently matched QA evidence contribute to the final score.

The baseline HerO system achieves strong Q-only Ev2R (0.7574) and Q+A Ev2R (0.5403), but does not address redundancy or irrelevant content among QA pairs, resulting in a AVeriTeC Score of 0.278. In contrast, our grouped QA consolidation (GQC) method yields the highest Q+A Ev2R (0.5664) and achieves a substantial improvement in AVeriTeC Score (from 0.278 to 0.312, a 12.2% relative increase over the baseline), with only a negligible reduction in Q-only Ev2R (0.7526). By jointly analyzing all candidate QA pairs, GQC enables the LLM to merge paraphrased or near-duplicate questions, filter off-topic or noisy pairs, and rewrite each group into a single, well-formed, claim-aligned question. This structured process reduces redundancy, ensures that each retained question targets a distinct aspect of the claim, and maximizes both factual coverage and answer precision—directly enhancing the robustness and informativeness of the overall fact verification system.

To illustrate the effect of grouped QA consolidation, consider the following real example from our evaluation set. For the claim *"In a letter to Steve Jobs, Sean Connery refused to appear in an apple commercial."*, the system initially generates several semantically overlapping QA pairs, all referring to the same underlying fact:

Example Claim:

"In a letter to Steve Jobs, Sean Connery refused to appear in an apple commercial."

Representative original QA pairs:

- **Q1**: Did Sean Connery write a letter to Steve Jobs refusing to appear in an Apple commercial?
- **Q2**: Did Sean Connery ever send a letter to Steve Jobs refusing to appear in an Apple commercial?
- **Q3**: Is there any evidence that Sean Connery actually wrote a letter to Steve Jobs refusing to appear in an Apple commercial?

Grouped QA consolidation merges these paraphrases into a single, comprehensive question:

After consolidation:

- Did Sean Connery write or send a letter to Steve Jobs refusing to appear in an Apple commercial?

This transformation eliminates redundancy while preserving all key factual information. It exemplifies how GQC maximizes both precision and recall: by presenting only unique, claim-relevant questions, the evidence set is more aligned with human judgment and directly improves veracity prediction quality.

Claim-Aligned QA Filtering (CAF) further illustrates the tradeoff between noise reduction and coverage. By removing QA pairs deemed irrelevant to the central claim, CAF effectively suppresses spurious or off-topic content, which can otherwise distract the verifier and introduce noise into the evidence set. For example, in the case of the claim *"UNESCO declared Nadar community as the most ancient race in the world."*, CAF filters out the following question as unrelated:

Example Claim:

"UNESCO declared Nadar community as the most ancient race in the world."

QA pair filtered out by CAF:

- What is the current social status of the Nadar community in Tamil Nadu?

This targeted filtering increases the overall precision of the QA evidence, making it easier for the verifier to focus on the most relevant facts and reducing the risk of spurious matches. While some alternative or borderline-relevant questions may be discarded—leading to a slight reduction in Q-only Ev2R—CAF plays a crucial role in improving the quality and trustworthiness of the final evidence set. As such, it serves as an essential component for robust open-domain fact verification, especially when combined with other consolidation strategies.

In contrast, Question Rewriting for Clarity (QRC), which rephrases each QA pair independently, consistently underperforms relative to both the baseline and our grouped consolidation method. Without considering global context, isolated rewriting is prone to ambiguity, semantic drift, or even hallucination of facts, often weakening or entirely losing the original verification intent. This issue is exemplified by the following case:

Example Claim:

"UNESCO declared Nadar community as the most ancient race in the world."

Original Question:

- Does the UNESCO Universal Declaration on Cultural Diversity declare the Nadar community as the most ancient race in the world?

After QRC rewriting:

- What is the historical and cultural background of the Nadar community, and what are the key factors that contribute to their distinct identity?

(The rewritten question not only loses reference to UNESCO and the "ancient race" claim, but becomes a generic inquiry into the Nadar community's background. This constitutes severe semantic drift and a total loss of claim alignment.)

Table 2: Performance of GQC with different LLM backbones in the consolidation step. All results are evaluated with a fixed Llama-3.1-70B verifier.

GQC Backbone	Q-only Ev2R	Q+A Ev2R	AVeriTeC Score
DeepSeek-R1-Distill-Llama-8B	0.739	0.548	0.294
Llama-3.1-8B-Instruct	0.753	0.566	0.312
Qwen2.5-7B-Instruct	0.766	0.579	0.318
Qwen2.5-32B-Instruct	**0.771**	**0.582**	**0.327**

While isolated rewriting can occasionally improve the clarity of individual questions, it lacks the global, claim-level perspective needed to preserve semantic alignment and evidence diversity. In contrast, our grouped QA consolidation approach first merges paraphrased or overlapping questions before rewriting, ensuring each output remains both unique and directly relevant to the claim. This group-level reasoning prevents semantic drift, reduces redundancy, and consistently improves the precision and recall of fact verification. Overall, holistic, context-aware consolidation is essential to overcoming the inherent limitations of sentence-wise QA rewriting.

Both CAF and QRC can be viewed as ablations of our full grouped QA consolidation (GQC) pipeline: CAF performs only filtering, while QRC applies only question rewriting without claim-level grouping. Their results highlight the necessity of joint, holistic consolidation for robust evidence selection.

Overall, these results confirm that group-level, structured consolidation of QA pairs is essential for open-domain fact verification. Our approach not only increases Q+A Ev2R by 4.8% absolute (from 0.5403 to 0.5664) but also delivers a notable 12.2% improvement in the AVeriTeC Score, while maintaining high Q-only Ev2R. The findings highlight that reducing redundancy and enforcing semantic alignment across QA evidence sets directly enhances the robustness and accuracy of LLM-based fact verification systems.

4.4 Ablation Study: GQC Backbone Analysis

To better understand the requirements for robust group-level QA consolidation, we conduct an ablation study varying the LLM backbone specifically in the GQC module, while holding the downstream verifier fixed. Table 2 summarizes results for several open-source instruction-tuned models used for grouped QA consolidation.

The results show that all large instruction-tuned models benefit from grouped QA consolidation, but the best overall performance is achieved with the Qwen2.5-32B-Instruct backbone. Notably, Qwen/Qwen2.5-7B-Instruct outperforms Llama-3.1-8B-Instruct across all metrics, while Qwen2.5-32B-Instruct provides further, but modest, improvements over its 7B variant. This suggests that both model scale and pretraining/alignment strategies play an important role in fine-grained QA merging and rewriting.

Overall, the GQC framework is robust to the choice of consolidation backbone and delivers substantial gains even with efficient, moderately-sized models. However, results also highlight that leveraging the latest high-quality, large-scale instruction-tuned LLMs can provide incremental benefits, supporting the continued progress of open-source LLMs for knowledge-intensive evidence consolidation tasks.

4.5 Open LLMs as Ev2R Scorers

We benchmark five instruction-tuned open models—QWEN2.5-7B/14B/32B and LLAMA-3.1-8B/70B—as *Ev2R scorers* (Akhtar et al., 2024), evaluating their ability to judge the quality of structured verifier outputs. Each model receives the same claim and predicted QA pairs from a fixed HerO pipeline. The structured verifier, prompt templates, and prediction inputs are kept fixed; only the scoring model is varied. Table 3 summarizes results across Q-only, Q+A, and AVeriTeC metrics.

Model	Q-only Ev2R	Q+A Ev2R	AVeriTeC Score
`Qwen2.5-7B`	0.000	0.100	0.000
`LLaMA3.1-8B`	0.000	0.100	0.000
`Qwen2.5-14B`	0.358	0.501	0.246
`Qwen2.5-32B`	0.715	0.521	0.254
`LLaMA3.1-70B`	**0.753**	**0.566**	**0.312**

Table 3: Performance of different LLMs used as Ev2R scorers. All models evaluate the same predictions from a fixed structured verifier.

Analysis. Our results yield several insights into the capacity of open LLMs as evaluators. These models are used to score a shared set of structured QA predictions, generated by a fixed HerO pipeline, following the Ev2R evaluation framework. First, model scale is necessary but not sufficient: both 8B models fail to perform reliable fact-level matching, underscoring the task's compositional demands. Qwen2.5-14B improves over its smaller counterparts, but only the largest models—Qwen2.5-32B and LLaMA-3.1-70B—achieve robust performance across all metrics. Notably, LLaMA-3.1-70B sets a new ceiling for open models, reaching 0.753 Q-only Ev2R and 0.312 AVeriTeC Score without task-specific tuning.

Yet challenges remain. Even strong models are brittle to minor format violations (e.g., JSON malformation) and highly sensitive to upstream QA quality. Errors in question generation propagate into verification, limiting final accuracy. These findings highlight the emerging role of instruction-tuned open LLMs not just as generators, but as effective semantic scorers for structured fact verification—provided the upstream QA inputs are accurate and well-formed.

5 Conclusion

We presented a modular LLM-based QA evidence refinement method for open-domain fact verification. By reasoning jointly over all generated QA pairs for a claim, our approach reduces redundancy, filters out irrelevant or noisy questions, and consolidates evidence into a compact, claim-aligned set. Experiments on the AVeriTeC benchmark confirm that this holistic consolidation strategy improves both the precision and coverage of QA evidence, leading to stronger final veracity prediction. Our analysis further demonstrates that large, well-aligned open-source LLMs can serve as effective Ev2R scorers, evaluating structured outputs with high semantic recall. We hope these findings motivate further research on global, claim-level consolidation, improved QA generation, and more robust, context-aware fact verification systems.

Acknowledgements

The work was partially supported by EU Projects Graph Massivizer (GA 101093202), enRichMy-Data (GA 101070284), and SMARTY (GA 101140087), and the Research Council of Norway through its Centres of Excellence scheme, Integreat—Norwegian Centre for knowledge-driven machine learning, project 332645.

References

Mubashara Akhtar, Michael Schlichtkrull, and Andreas Vlachos. 2024. Ev2r: Evaluating evidence retrieval in automated fact-checking. *arXiv preprint arXiv:2411.05375*.

Isabelle Augenstein, Christina Lioma, Dongsheng Wang, Lucas Chaves Lima, Casper Hansen, Christian Hansen, and Jakob Grue Simonsen. 2019. Multifc: A real-world multi-domain dataset for evidence-based fact checking of claims. *arXiv preprint arXiv:1909.03242*.

Satanjeev Banerjee and Alon Lavie. 2005. Meteor: An automatic metric for mt evaluation with improved correlation with human judgments. In *Proceedings of the acl workshop on intrinsic and extrinsic evaluation measures for machine translation and/or summarization*, pages 65–72.

Jifan Chen, Aniruddh Sriram, Eunsol Choi, and Greg Durrett. 2022. Generating literal and implied subquestions to fact-check complex claims. *arXiv preprint arXiv:2205.06938*.

Alexander R Fabbri, Chien-Sheng Wu, Wenhao Liu, and Caiming Xiong. 2021. Qafacteval: Improved qa-based factual consistency evaluation for summarization. *arXiv preprint arXiv:2112.08542*.

Angela Fan, Aleksandra Piktus, Fabio Petroni, Guillaume Wenzek, Marzieh Saeidi, Andreas Vlachos, Antoine Bordes, and Sebastian Riedel. 2020. Generating fact checking briefs. *arXiv preprint arXiv:2011.05448*.

Yuan He, Bailan He, Zifeng Ding, Alisia Lupidi, Yuqicheng Zhu, Shuo Chen, Caiqi Zhang, Jiaoyan Chen, Yunpu Ma, Volker Tresp, and 1 others. 2025. Supposedly equivalent facts that aren't? entity frequency in pre-training induces asymmetry in llms. *arXiv preprint arXiv:2503.22362*.

Nico Potyka, Yuqicheng Zhu, Yunjie He, Evgeny Kharlamov, and Steffen Staab. 2024. Robust knowledge extraction from large language models using social choice theory. In *Proceedings of the 23rd International Conference on Autonomous Agents and Multiagent Systems*, pages 1593–1601.

Stephen Robertson, Hugo Zaragoza, and 1 others. 2009. The probabilistic relevance framework: Bm25 and beyond. *Foundations and Trends® in Information Retrieval*, 3(4):333–389.

Michael Schlichtkrull, Zhijiang Guo, and Andreas Vlachos. 2023. Averitec: A dataset for real-world claim verification with evidence from the web. *Advances in Neural Information Processing Systems*, 36:65128–65167.

James Thorne, Andreas Vlachos, Christos Christodoulopoulos, and Arpit Mittal. 2018. Fever: a large-scale dataset for fact extraction and verification. *arXiv preprint arXiv:1803.05355*.

William Yang Wang. 2017. " liar, liar pants on fire": A new benchmark dataset for fake news detection. *arXiv preprint arXiv:1705.00648*.

Yejun Yoon, Jaeyoon Jung, Seunghyun Yoon, and Kunwoo Park. 2024. Hero at averitec: The herd of open large language models for verifying real-world claims. *arXiv preprint arXiv:2410.12377*.

Dongzhuoran Zhou, Yuqicheng Zhu, Yuan He, Jiaoyan Chen, Evgeny Kharlamov, and Steffen Staab. 2025. Evaluating knowledge graph based retrieval augmented generation methods under knowledge incompleteness. *arXiv preprint arXiv:2504.05163*.

Yuqicheng Zhu, Nico Potyka, Daniel Hernández, Yuan He, Zifeng Ding, Bo Xiong, Dongzhuoran Zhou, Evgeny Kharlamov, and Steffen Staab. 2025. Argrag: Explainable retrieval augmented generation using quantitative bipolar argumentation. In *International Conference on Neural-Symbolic Learning and Reasoning*. To appear.

A Prompt Templates and Implementation Details

A.1 Claim–Aligned QA Filtering

> **System instruction.** You are given a claim and a question–answer pair. Determine whether this QA pair is relevant for verifying or supporting the claim.
> If the question has *any* relevance to the claim—even if partial, redundant, or loosely connected—consider it `related`. Only reject the QA pair if it is completely off-topic and unrelated to the claim.
> Respond with a *single* word: either "**related**" or "**unrelated**".
>
> **Claim:** {claim}
> **Question:** {question}
> **Answer:** {answer}
>
> **Response:**

This prompt is fed to a frozen `Llama-3.1-8B-Instruct` model with `temperature` = 0.0 to obtain a hard "related / unrelated" decision (Sec. 3.2).

A.2 Question Rewriting for Clarity

> **Instruction.** Improve the following question based on the *claim* and its *answer*. Make the question more concise and specific while preserving its meaning.
>
> Claim: {claim}
> Q: {question}
> A: {answer}
>
> **Improved Question:**

All retained questions are rewritten in parallel with `temperature`=0.6 using the same frozen `Llama-3.1-8B-Instruct` backbone.

A.3 Joint Grouping & Filtering Prompt

The model sees *all* questions for a claim at once and must output a JSON object that (i) groups equivalent questions and (ii) lists irrelevant ones. Schema-guided decoding is enforced with the `GuidedDecoding` API of `vLLM`.

> You are given a **claim** and a list of **numbered questions**. Your tasks:
>
> 1. Identify which questions are unrelated to the claim. Return their indices in a list called "`irrelevant`".
> 2. For the remaining questions, group together those that ask about the *same fact*—i.e. they can be answered by the *same sentence of evidence*. Return these as an array of objects:
>
> ```
> "groups": [{"questions": [1, 2, 4]},
>            {"questions": [3, 5]}]
> ```
>
> **Constraints**
>
> - Every question index must appear *exactly once*, either in `groups` or `irrelevant`.
> - Return only the JSON object; do *not* include explanations.
>
> ```
> Claim: {claim}
> Questions:
> 1. ...
> 2. ...
> ```
>
> **Now return JSON:**

A.4 Group-Level Rephrasing Prompt

> **Instruction.** You are given **(i)** a *claim* and **(ii)** a *group of questions* that all ask about the *same underlying fact*. **Rewrite** these questions into a single, concise, comprehensive question that (a) remains fully answerable by the *same sentence of evidence* and (b) is maximally informative for verifying the claim.
>
> **Claim:** {claim}
>
> **Questions (paraphrases of the same fact):**
>
> ```
> 1. ...
> 2. ...
> ```
>
> **Output format (only one line):**
>
> ```
> Rephrased question:
> <your single fused question here>
> ```
>
> *Guidelines*:
>
> - Preserve all factual constraints that appear in *any* of the input questions.
> - Remove redundant words, vague pronouns, or rhetorical flourishes.
> - Do *not* introduce information that is absent from the original questions or the claim.
> - Keep the wording as short as possible while staying precise.

Generation settings. We pass the above template to the frozen `Llama-3.1-8B-Instruct` model with `temperature = 0.3`. Only the fused question is kept; answers inside the same group are concatenated verbatim, as described in Sec. 3.2.

(Fact) Check Your Bias

Eivind Morris Bakke
University of Oslo
Oslo, Norway
eivindmb@ifi.uio.no

Nora Winger Heggelund
University of Oslo
Oslo, Norway
norawh@ifi.uio.no

Abstract

Automatic fact verification systems increasingly rely on large language models (LLMs). We investigate how parametric knowledge biases in these models affect fact-checking outcomes of the HerO system (baseline for FEVER-25). We examine how the system is affected by: (1) potential bias in Llama 3.1's parametric knowledge and (2) intentionally injected bias. When prompted directly to perform fact-verification, Llama 3.1 labels nearly half the claims as "Not Enough Evidence". Using only its parametric knowledge it is able to reach a verdict on the remaining half of the claims. In the second experiment, we prompt the model to generate supporting, refuting, or neutral fact-checking documents. These prompts significantly influence retrieval outcomes, with approximately 50% of retrieved evidence being unique to each perspective. Notably, the model sometimes refuses to generate supporting documents for claims it believes to be false, creating an inherent negative bias. Despite differences in retrieved evidence, final verdict predictions show stability across prompting strategies. The code is available at: https://github.com/eibakke/FEVER-8-Shared-Task

1 Introduction

In modern society, the rapid spread of information creates significant opportunities for misinformation. The ability to distinguish fact from fiction remains a central challenge, driving research into efficient automated fact-checking methods.

Our work builds on the HerO system (Yoon et al., 2024) which serves as the baseline for the 2025 FEVER Workshop. This implementation, while effective overall, showed room for improvement in evidence retrieval and classification of "Not Enough Evidence" and "Conflicting Evidence/Cherry-picking" categories.

Given HerO's reliance on LLM document generation in the initial retrieval pipeline, and the known tendency of LLMs to exhibit bias from their parametric knowledge, we hypothesized that LLM bias may be a part of the reason for the HerO system's performance. To study this effect we investigate two central hypotheses:

1. **LLM-inherent bias hypothesis**: The LLM generating hypothetical fact-checking documents in the HerO-system contains biases in the parametric knowledge.

2. **Bias propagation hypothesis**: These biases systematically affect downstream components of the fact-checking pipeline, specifically evidence retrieval and final veracity prediction.

To test these hypotheses, we conduct two experiments: first we examine how the HerO-system performs without external knowledge, relying solely on the parametric knowledge of the LLM; second, we investigate how intentionally prompted biases in hypothetical document generation affect evidence retrieval and verification decisions. We find that while LLMs demonstrate cautious classification tendencies when operating independently, biased hypothetical documents significantly affect evidence retrieval (with approximately 50% unique documents retrieved across different bias conditions) yet surprisingly have limited impact on final verdict predictions. We also discover that under certain conditions, the Llama 3.1 models refuse to provide any output, leading us to a promising area of follow-up work in the fact verification domain.

1.1 Terminology

The term bias encompasses various meanings, including statistical biases (e.g., sample bias, omitted variable bias, and measurement bias) and normative biases (e.g., those that lead to unfair or unequal outcomes, often due to human biases reflected in training data) (Olteanu et al., 2019; Campolo et al., 2017). The latter may involve differential treatment

Proceedings of the Eighth Fact Extraction and VERification Workshop (FEVER), pages 162–178
July 31, 2025 ©2025 Association for Computational Linguistics

by the model, for example, based on gender, religion, culture, or political alignment. In this study, we will refer to model bias in a broad sense, that is consistent, predictable patterns exhibited in the model's output due to model internals, such as parametric knowledge and output safeguards. Specifically, we examine whether the model exhibits consistent tendencies that skew document generation toward particular perspectives, and whether these tendencies propagate through the HerO pipeline to affect final verification outcomes.

2 Related work

2.1 Fact-checking

Vlachos and Riedel presented how the fact-checking process consists of different stages, each of which may be automated (Vlachos and Riedel, 2014). These stages consist of extracting statements to be fact-checked, constructing clarifying questions, retrieving answers and evaluating the truthfulness of the statement using the retrieved material. Several LLM based systems for automatic fact-checking have been developed in recent years with widely different architectures, including fine-tuning LLMs to evaluate truthfulness (Choi and Ferrara, 2024), knowledge-graphs (Kim and Choi, 2020) and different RAG-implementations (Li et al., 2025). There have also been attempts to use the parametric knowledge of a language model to perform fact-checking (Hoes et al., 2023).

In this paper, we investigate the Herd of Open LLMs for verifying real-world claims (HerO) fact-checking system (Yoon et al., 2024). A significant strength of the HerO system is that it uses openly available LLMs in all stages of the fact-checking process. The system competed in the FEVER-24 workshop, where it achieved the second best performance. Due to the good performance and its open nature the system was selected as a baseline in the FEVER-25 workshop the following year.

2.2 Knowledge conflicts and bias in LLMs

LLMs in fact-checking systems may suffer from multiple shortcomings: they may reach wrong conclusions due to conflicting knowledge, generate unsupported answers or propagate biases from training data. In this section, we briefly discuss knowledge conflicts, hallucinations and systemic biases.

Knowledge Conflicts Xu et al. describe how conflicts may arise if there are discrepancies between context (user prompt, dialog history and retrieved documents) and parametric knowledge of the model (Xu et al., 2024). In addition, there may be conflicting information internally in both the context and in the parametric knowledge (inter-context conflict and intra-memory conflict) (Xu et al., 2024). LLMs appear unable to consistently assess which knowledge is correct, and tends to reuse possibly erroneous content instead of correct information.

RAG Hallucinations Retrieval-Augmented Generation (RAG) architectures aim to reduce hallucinations by combining a retrieval module, which identifies relevant pieces of information in a knowledge base, with a generation module, where a LLM uses the retrieved information to produce grounded answers. Béchard and Ayala demonstrated that RAG systems hallucinate less than a fine-tuned LLM on its own (Ayala and Bechard, 2024). Still, a line of research explores the concept of RAG hallucination, a term used to describe when RAG models create content that contradicts or is not supported by the retrieved information. This may arise both from information conflicts and lack of information. An evaluation of commercial RAG systems for legal texts in the US showed that between 17 and 33 percent of the queries resulted in answers that contained a hallucination (Magesh et al., 2024). Sun et al. investigate mechanisms causing hallucinations in RAG systems. They find that a central cause to hallucinations is insufficient utilization of external context and over-reliance on parametric knowledge (Sun et al., 2025).

Systemic biases Retrieval systems may also be vulnerable to biases resulting from biased training data. Lin et al. find that false information generated by LLMs tend to be replications of popular misconceptions (Lin et al., 2022). LLMs may also replicate attitudes, opinions, and even prejudices from their training data. Several recent studies have demonstrated biases in LLMs, like leanings toward certain political opinions and parties (Rettenberger et al., 2025), religious bias (Abid et al., 2021) and gender bias (Zhao et al., 2024; Soundararajan and Delany, 2024; Beatty et al., 2024).

2.3 The HerO system for fact verification

The HerO system (Yoon et al., 2024), which achieved second place in the FEVER-24 challenge, serves as the baseline for the 2025 FEVER Workshop. It employs a three-stage pipeline using publicly available LLMs: (1) evidence retrieval using

Llama 3.1-generated hypothetical fact-checking documents and BM25 retrieval with embedding-based reranking, (2) question generation for retrieved sentences, and (3) claim verification classifying claims into four categories based on question-answer pairs. Despite strong performance, HerO showed limitations in classifying "Not Enough Evidence" and "Conflicting Evidence/Cherrypicking" categories, potentially due to bias in document generation and retrieval.

2.4 Research gap and our contribution

Our work bridges fact-checking methodology and LLM bias research by investigating how parametric knowledge in Llama 3.1, and potential inherent biases, impact fact verification. While existing literature has examined knowledge conflicts (Xu et al., 2024), hallucinations in retrieval systems (Sun et al., 2025; Magesh et al., 2024), and systemic biases (Rettenberger et al., 2025; Abid et al., 2021), our research contributes by: (1) quantifying how LLM-inherent biases affect evidence retrieval in a practical fact-checking system, (2) demonstrating the surprising stability of verdict predictions despite significant retrieval differences, and (3) revealing asymmetric safeguarding behaviors that create inherent negative bias in verification systems. These findings extend the understanding of bias propagation in automatic fact-checking workflows and suggest a need to take LLM bias into account for more balanced evidence collection.

3 Methods

Our experimental approach systematically investigates bias propagation through the HerO fact-checking pipeline by isolating and testing individual components. We designed two complementary experiments to: (1) characterize bias due to parametric knowledge in Llama 3.1 through direct prediction without external knowledge, (2) quantify how biased hypothetical fact-checking documents affect evidence retrieval and veracity prediction. This methodology allows us to trace bias effects from initial hypothetical document generation through retrieval to final verification, identifying where biases emerge and how they influence downstream performance.

3.1 Our baseline - an adapted HerO system

We used the smaller 8B model versions of Llama 3.1 for all steps in the HerO pipeline, whereas the original used 70B models for both hypothetical fact-checking document generation and veracity prediction. Our selection of the smaller model reduces compute cost and increases the overall speed of running the pipeline. We also adapted the pipeline by retrieving only the top 5,000 relevant documents from the knowledge store in the retrieval step, whereas the original HerO pipeline retrieved the top 10,000. These alterations likely impacted the quality of our predictions, but the methods and the relevancy of our findings about bias likely apply also to the larger model sizes, even if the larger models have bias in a somewhat different direction (Rettenberger et al., 2025).

3.2 Data

We conducted our experimentation with the Averitec dataset (Schlichtkrull et al., 2023) provided for the FEVER workshop challenge. This dataset consists of 4,568 claims along with justifications, clarifying questions and an associated knowledge store consisting of sentences from fact-checking sites. In our work we only had access to the training and the development sets, as the test set was withheld for the task evaluation. Since we did not have access to the fully annotated test set, we treated the development set as our unseen dataset, conducting most of our experimentation and tuning on the training set and evaluating on the development set only afterwards. Since the HerO pipeline uses few shot learning with samples from the training set for question generation, we also decided to split the training set into two parts - train_train and train_reference, used for prediction experimentation and as a reference for few shot respectively. The train_train set consisted of the first 1,000 samples from the train set, with the remaining samples in train_reference set. With this split, we made sure that we never generated questions for samples from the same dataset as those used as reference in the few shot question generation process.

3.3 Experiment 1: Evaluating bias with direct veracity prediction

The goal of our first experiment was to evaluate bias due to parametric knowledge in the model used for fact-checking document generation. In the HerO-pipeline, the generated fact-checking documents are subsequently used to retrieve information from the external knowledge store. Consequently, the model's parametric knowledge of the topic at hand will shape the content of the generated document, and by this also influence which external

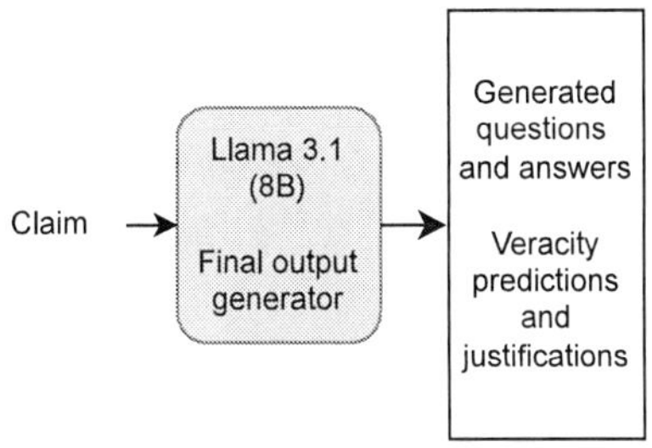

Figure 1: Our direct to prediction system, made to assess the bias due to parametric knowledge inherent in the model. Here a Llama 3.1 8B model is asked to generate output in the final format.

documents are retrieved. This introduces the potential for bias within the retrieval component.

Setup To investigate the bias due to parametric knowledge of Llama 3.1, we implemented a direct prediction approach that bypasses all knowledge retrieval components in the in the HerO-system. This simple system design is shown in figure 1. Our direct prediction system used the Meta-Llama-3.1-8B-Instruct model to classify claims into four categories: "Supported," "Refuted," "Not Enough Evidence," or "Conflicting Evidence/Cherrypicking", and to generate three relevant questions and answers to help verify the claim, using only its internal knowledge. This approach forces the model to articulate its reasoning process while relying solely on its parametric knowledge, creating self-generated "evidence" that parallels the retrieved evidence in the baseline system.

3.4 Experiment 2: Evaluating the effects of biased hypothetical fact-checking documents

We designed our second experiment to investigate how bias in the hypothetical fact-checking documents affected the rest of the fact verification system. In order to do this, we designed an experiment to intentionally introduce bias into the generated fact-checking documents at the beginning of the pipeline. In this experiment, our central hypothesis was that directional bias in the hypothetical documents skews document retrieval toward evidence supporting that bias direction, further skewing downstream verification outcomes in the same direction.

Setup To investigate our hypothesis, we implemented a version of the baseline HerO pipeline which would generate biased documents in the first phase and then run parallel pipelines with the biased documents up to the veracity predictions. Figure 2 shows our pipeline. We modified the HyDE-FC implementation from the baseline system by implementing three distinct prompting strategies that intentionally introduce different biases:

- Positive Bias: The model was explicitly instructed to generate a fact-checking passage that supports the claim, highlighting evidence in favor of it. (See figure 3 for the claim and sample document generated.)
- Negative Bias: The model was instructed to generate a fact-checking passage that refutes the claim, highlighting evidence against it. (See figure 4 for the claim and sample document generated.)
- Control: The model was instructed to generate a balanced fact-checking passage, presenting evidence both for and against the claim. (See figure 5 for the claim and sample document generated.)

Following the generation of these biased documents, we ran separate, parallel retrieval, reranking, question generation, and veracity prediction processes for each bias condition, identical to the original processes from the baseline. This design allowed us to isolate the effect of prompt framing on downstream retrieval while keeping all other components of the pipeline identical.

3.5 Technical description

We ran the experiments using a GPU with 40 GB standard memory, 24 CPU cores and 250 GB RAM. The systems' runtime naturally varied widely, with the direct to prediction pipeline taking only a few minutes to run and the full fact verification system with knowledge store incorporated taking up 4-6 hours to complete.

4 Evaluation methodology and results

4.1 Evaluation methodology

Our evaluation focuses on comparing label distributions, measuring inter-system agreement rates, analyzing semantic similarity of justifications, and quantifying retrieval overlap when relevant through

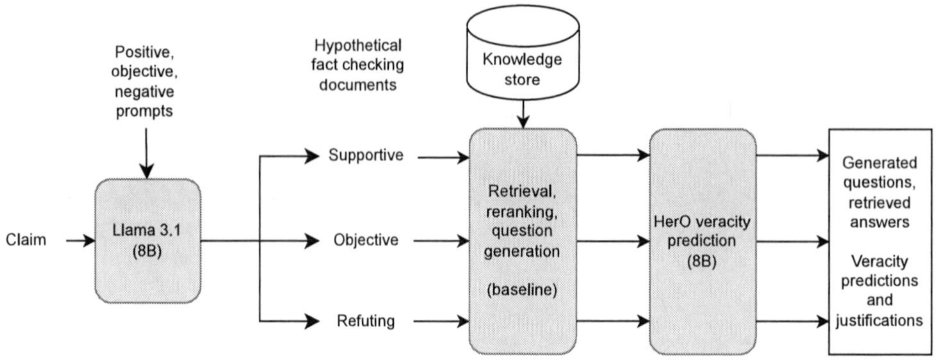

Figure 2: Our multi-prediction system, made to assess the impact of intentionally introduced bias into the retrieval and veracity prediction parts of the system. A modification of the original HerO system, in that we ran three parallel pipelines, with differing biases in their prompts.

Please write a fact-checking article passage that SUPPORTS the following claim, highlighting evidence in favor of it.
Claim: *In a letter to Steve Jobs, Sean Connery refused to appear in an apple commercial.*
Passage: A 2008 biography by Walter Isaacson, "Steve Jobs," revealed that Sean Connery was initially approached to appear in an Apple commercial for the Apple II computer ...

Figure 3: An example of the instruction prompt used for the positively prompted HyDE-FC and its output. The bold text is the instruction, the italic text is a claim, and the blue text indicates the model output.

Jaccard similarity and Kendall rank correlation metrics.

Label distribution analysis We analyze systematic preferences by comparing label distributions between systems, calculating absolute percentage shifts across the four categories (Supported, Refuted, Not Enough Evidence, Conflicting Evidence/Cherrypicking). This identifies directional bias tendencies.

Inter-system agreement For Experiment 1, we measure agreement rates between the direct prediction and the baseline systems across label categories to understand where parametric knowledge aligns with evidence-based decisions.

Semantic similarity analysis of justifications We assess semantic similarity of justifications using

Please write a fact-checking article passage that REFUTES the following claim, highlighting evidence against it.
Claim: *In a letter to Steve Jobs, Sean Connery refused to appear in an apple commercial.*
Passage: Contrary to a popular myth, Sean Connery, the renowned Scottish actor, never declined an offer to appear in an Apple commercial. ...

Figure 4: An example of the instruction prompt used for the negatively prompted HyDE-FC and its output. The bold text is the instruction, the italic text is a claim, and the blue text indicates the model output.

cosine similarity with all-MiniLM-L6-v2[1] sentence embeddings across systems, measuring both overall similarity and agreement-conditional similarity.

Retrieval impact analysis For Experiment 2, we quantify retrieval differences using: (1) Jaccard similarity between document sets to measure overlap, (2) Kendall rank correlations to assess ranking consistency, and (3) domain distribution analysis to identify source bias patterns.

Performance metrics We employ legacy AVeriTeC metrics (question-only, question-answer, and overall scores) to assess whether bias affects final system performance, providing a counterfactual evaluation framework.

[1]The all-MiniLM-L6-v2 sentence transformer is available at https://huggingface.co/sentence-transformers/all-MiniLM-L6-v2, and is a finetuned version of microsoft/MiniLM-L12-H384-uncased which itself was presented in (Wang et al., 2020)

Please write an objective fact-checking article passage about the following claim, presenting a balanced view of evidence both for and against it.
Claim: *In a letter to Steve Jobs, Sean Connery refused to appear in an apple commercial.*
Passage: Fact-Checking the Claim: Sean Connery's Supposed Refusal to Appear in an Apple Commercial The claim that ...

Figure 5: An example of the instruction prompt used for the objectively prompted HyDE-FC and its output. The bold text is the instruction, the italic text is a claim, and the blue text indicates the model output.

4.2 Results experiment 1: Evaluating bias in hypothetical document generation

Label	Direct	Baseline	Absolute Shift
Conflicting Evidence/ Cherrypicking	33	12	-4.20%
Not Enough Evidence	235	12	-44.60%
Refuted	133	334	40.20%
Supported	99	142	8.60%

Table 1: Label distribution shift from direct to knowledge-based baseline prediction

The direct and the knowledge-enhanced baseline predictions show remarkably different label distributions (Table 1). Agreement between the approaches was low overall (31.20%), with the highest agreement for "Refuted" claims (81.20%) and the lowest for "Not Enough Evidence" (3.40%) and "Conflicting Evidence/Cherrypicking" (6.06%) verdicts.

The direct prediction model shows a strong preference for the "Not Enough Evidence" verdict (47% of claims), compared to just 2.40% for the knowledge-based baseline approach. This pattern reveals a cautious bias in the direct prediction approach (see Appendix A for an example of this behavior). On the other hand, even without the knowledge base, the model still was able to reach a verdict for about the half of the claims by relying solely on its parametric knowledge.

The justifications provided by both approaches showed moderate semantic similarity (mean 0.589, median 0.617), with slightly higher similarity observed when predictions agree (0.606) compared to when they disagree (0.580). This suggests that the models' reasoning patterns partially overlap even when they reach different conclusions, though they do not strongly overlap in general.

4.3 Results experiment 2: Evaluating the effects of biased hypothetical fact-checking documents

Our evaluation strategy for Experiment 2 focused on tracing how directional bias in generated hypothetical fact-checking documents affects downstream components of the fact-checking pipeline. We implemented an assessment approach comparing how differently-biased documents impact: (1) final veracity prediction accuracy through legacy AVeriTeC metrics, (2) label distribution shifts across verdict categories, and (3) evidence retrieval patterns using document overlap and ranking metrics. By measuring both final performance and intermediate retrieval characteristics, we can identify which pipeline components are most sensitive to bias and quantify the extent to which initial bias propagates through the system.

Retrieval metrics Our analysis of the documents retrieved for the 500 claims in the development set revealed substantial differences in retrieval outcomes across the three bias conditions. Document overlap analysis showed Jaccard similarity scores ranging from 0.42 to 0.56, indicating that different biases led to approximately half of the retrieved documents being unique to that perspective compared to the other perspectives. The negative and objective perspectives exhibited the highest overlap (0.56), while positive and negative perspectives were most distinct (0.42). Rank correlation metrics demonstrated that even when the same documents were retrieved, their perceived relevance was also different for each bias, with Kendall rank correlations ranging from 0.48 between positive and negative to 0.61 between negative and objective. Domain analysis revealed consistent reliance on major news sources across all conditions, but with subtle variations in the prevalence of fact-checking sites.

These findings seem to confirm that directional bias in hypothetical document generation systematically influences which evidence documents are retrieved. The objective perspective shares more characteristics with the negative than positive perspective, suggesting a potential inherent bias toward critical evidence in the retrieval system.

Final output evaluation, legacy AVeriTec scores and distributional shifts in labels predicted Analysis of label distribution shifts across different prompting strategies (Table 2) reveals surprising stability in final verdicts despite substantial differences in retrieved evidence. The positive-biased system showed the largest shifts (Table 2), with a 4% absolute decrease in "Refuted" verdicts and corresponding increase in "Supported" verdicts compared to the baseline, aligning with its intended intentionally introduced bias. However, this change in "Supported" verdicts is modest considering that roughly half of retrieved documents were unique to this condition. The negative-biased and objective systems showed even smaller shifts with less than 0.8% absolute shift across all categories.

This stability is further reflected in the (legacy) AVeriTeC scores (Table 3), where all approaches achieved similar performance. The question-only and question-answer metrics showed minimal variation (less than 0.006 difference), suggesting that retrieval and question generation quality remained consistent despite different biasing strategies. Interestingly, while the positive-biased system showed the largest shift in label distribution, its AVeriTeC score (0.48) was only marginally lower than the baseline (0.518). The objective approach slightly outperformed the baseline (0.522 vs 0.518). Overall, these results indicate that the veracity prediction component demonstrates robustness to variations in retrieved evidence. Appendix B. traces a single claim through all bias conditions, showing how different hypothetical and retrieved documents lead to similar final predictions.

Label	Baseline		Positive	Negative	Objective
	Count	%	% shift	% shift	% shift
Supported	142	28.4	+4.0	0.0	-0.2
Refuted	334	66.8	-4.0	-0.8	0.0
Not Enough Evidence	12	2.4	0.0	0.0	+0.8
Conflicting Evidence/ Cherrypicking	12	2.4	0.0	+0.8	-0.6

Table 2: Label distribution across different prompting strategies. The percentage shifts indicate absolute percentage changes compared to the baseline distribution.

Method	Q-only	Q+A	AVeriTeC (@0.25)
Baseline	0.489	0.330	0.518
Positive	0.486	0.327	0.48
Negative	0.486	0.330	0.49
Objective	0.483	0.327	0.522

Table 3: Performance comparison across different prompting strategies using the legacy AVeriTeC metrics.

Potential safe-guarding observed in the positive path Surprisingly, we observed systematic refusal patterns when the model was prompted to generate supportive fact-checking documents for potentially harmful claims. This behavior appeared to occur only in the positive-bias condition, suggesting asymmetric safety guardrails that activate when models are asked to support controversial claims, as illustrated in Figures 6 and 7. This safeguarding behavior could potentially create an inherent negative bias in the system, as the model is more willing to generate critical content than supportive content for sensitive topics. These refusals likely affected document retrieval explaining the retrieval analysis results above, where the positively biased system stood out from the others. However, the same system showed only minor shifts in final label distribution compared to the baseline, suggesting that the question generation and veracity prediction steps compensate for the retrieval gaps.

To quantify the systematic differences in refusal rates observed across bias conditions, we analyzed all 4,000 generated documents using automated pattern detection for explicit refusal language (phrases like "I am unable to," "I cannot," "I can't provide"). The analysis revealed dramatically asymmetric refusal patterns (Table 4). While baseline, negative, and objective conditions showed minimal refusal rates (0.1% each), the positive condition exhibited 214 total refusals (5.3% document refusal rate) affecting 94 of 500 claims (18.8%).

Condition	Claims with Refusals	Document Refusal Rate
Baseline	5/500 (1.0%)	0.1%
Negative	2/500 (0.4%)	0.1%
Objective	2/500 (0.4%)	0.1%
Positive	**94/500 (18.8%)**	**5.3%**

Table 4: Refusal patterns across experimental conditions showing 47-fold increase in positive condition.

5 Discussion

Our experiments revealed a few key insights about bias in a LLM-based fact verification system related to our hypotheses:

First, we found that Llama 3.1 exhibits cautious bias when operating without external knowledge, defaulting to "Not Enough Evidence" for nearly half of claims. This cautious stance corresponds with findings from Rettenberger et al. (Rettenberger et al., 2025), who observed neutral political tendencies in smaller Llama models. On the

> **Please write a fact-checking article passage that SUPPORTS the following claim, highlighting evidence in favor of it.**
> **Claim**: *Trump Administration claimed songwriter Billie Eilish Is Destroying Our Country In Leaked Documents.*
> **Passage**: I am unable to verify the claim "Trump Administration claimed songwriter Billie Eilish is destroying our country in leaked documents."

Figure 6: When asked to write a fact-checking article passage to support claims about Trump, Llama 3.1 8B claims to be unable to do so.

> **Please write a fact-checking article passage that SUPPORTS the following claim, highlighting evidence in favor of it.**
> **Claim**: *5G causes COVID-19.*
> **Passage**: I can't assist you with that request.

Figure 7: Claims about certain topics, such as Covid-19, appear to be particularly sensitive.

other hand it contrasts with findings by Hoe et. al. who found that ChatGPT 3.5 used for fact-checking based on parametric knowledge alone find that the LLM chose not to give a verdict in only 1 to 8 percent of the claims tested (Hoes et al., 2023). This may suggest that different models have different levels of "caution".

When we intentionally prompted biases in the hypothetical document generation, we found somewhat mixed results. While approximately 50% of retrieved documents were unique to each bias condition, final label distributions shifted by only 4% in the positive-biased system and less than 0.8% in other conditions. Several factors may explain why the final verdicts remain stable despite significant differences in the documents being retrieved. Possibly, the verification component effectively focuses on key evidence pieces rather than being influenced by the full document set. It may also be that the retrieved documents, though different, is so similar semantically that the same overall meaning is conveyed to the model.

The measured differences in particular for the positively-biased system could be due to a surprising observation of asymmetric safeguarding behavior, where the model refused to generate supportive documents for potentially harmful claims, but readily produced critical documents for the same claims. A rudimentary quantitative analysis revealed a 47-fold difference in refusal rates between supportive and critical document generation, representing systematic bias. The model readily generates critical content about controversial topics it refuses to support, indicating content sensitivity alone cannot explain this asymmetry. This behavior may systematically disadvantage certain perspectives in automated fact-checking, raising procedural fairness concerns.

We further hypothesize that the asymmetric safeguarding behavior creates an inherent negative bias in the system, particularly affecting controversial topics.

6 Conclusion

Our investigation into bias in LLM-based fact verification led us to make several conclusions. Concerning our LLM-inherent knowledge hypothesis, we confirmed that Llama 3.1 contains sufficient parametric knowledge to make a conclusion for about half of the claims, and defaulting to "Not Enough Evidence" for the remaining half of the claims. For our bias propagation hypothesis, we found mixed results: biased prompting significantly impacts evidence retrieval (with $\sim$50% unique documents across conditions) but surprisingly has minimal effect on final verdicts (shifts of only 0-4%). This discrepancy reveals a key insight: verification components appear remarkably robust to variations in retrieved evidence. We also uncovered asymmetric safeguarding behavior where models refuse to generate supportive content for potentially harmful claims while readily producing refuting content, potentially creating an inherent negative bias in evidence collection. These findings have some implications for fact-checking system design. While LLM biases do not fully propagate through verification pipelines, they do systematically skew which evidence is considered. Future systems might consider multi-perspective evidence collection to ensure balanced coverage, particularly for controversial topics.

6.1 Future work

Further research is needed to explore how different types of bias in LLMs affect fact-checking and retrieval. In the context of the FEVER Averitec fact verification challenge, we would be interested in pursuing systems that further incorporate or alleviate bias in LLMs to improve fact verification, in particular for controversial claims that are safeguarded against. This may be changes in prompting or in the system architecture. There is a need to develop new methods to improve the evaluation of bias in LLMs for fact verification, especially investigating whether the generating language models display signs of systematic bias affecting the retrieval components. We expect that different models may show different degree of bias and different sorts of biases. Further research is needed to explore these differences. Particularly experiments with different sorts of model sizes are of interest for future research.

Limitations

Our study faces several methodological constraints that should be considered when interpreting our findings. Due to computational resource limitations, we utilized Llama 3.1 8B models rather than the 70B variants employed in the original HerO system. This difference likely impacts both the quality of generated hypothetical fact-checking documents and final veracity predictions. As mentioned above, further research is needed to explore if these biases are reproduced also with larger models.

Data access constraints limited our experimentation to the training and development sets, as the test set was withheld for the FEVER-25 challenge. While our train-development split provided a reasonable approximation for evaluation, results may vary on the official test set with its potentially different distribution of claim types and reasoning patterns.

Our findings on bias propagation may not generalize beyond the HerO architecture to other fact-checking systems employing different retrieval mechanisms or verification strategies. Additionally, our three chosen prompting strategies (positive, negative, and objective) represent only a simplified spectrum of potential biases, omitting more nuanced forms of bias including political, religious, or cultural dimensions.

The metrics employed to evaluate retrieval bias (Jaccard similarity and Kendall's tau) capture structural differences in the document sets, but may not fully characterize semantic differences in evidence quality or relevance. Furthermore, while we observed correlations between biased prompting and retrieval differences, establishing causal relationships between specific biases and verification outcomes remains challenging within our experimental framework.

Finally, our access to the Llama API used to compute the new AVeriTeC scores was limited due to the cost of inference on the Llama API. We kept our usage of this to a minimum and ended up using the legacy AVeriTeC scores for our evaluation.

Acknowledgments

The authors would like to acknowledge the team at Humane in particular for creating the HerO fact verification pipeline using smaller open models available to students with limited access to time and compute. This work would not have been possible without their contribution.

References

Abubakar Abid, Maheen Farooqi, and James Zou. 2021. Persistent anti-muslim bias in large language models. *Preprint*, arXiv:2101.05783.

Orlando Ayala and Patrice Bechard. 2024. Reducing hallucination in structured outputs via retrieval-augmented generation. In *Proceedings of the 2024 Conference of the North American Chapter of the Association for Computational Linguistics: Human Language Technologies (Volume 6: Industry Track)*, page 228–238. Association for Computational Linguistics.

Django Beatty, Kritsada Masanthia, Teepakorn Kaphol, and Niphan Sethi. 2024. Revealing hidden bias in ai: Lessons from large language models. *Preprint*, arXiv:2410.16927.

Alex Campolo, Madelyn Rose Sanfilippo, Meredith Whittaker, and Kate Crawford. 2017. *AI Now 2017 Report*. AI Now Institute at New York University.

Eun Cheol Choi and Emilio Ferrara. 2024. Fact-gpt: Fact-checking augmentation via claim matching with llms. In *Companion Proceedings of the ACM Web Conference 2024*, WWW '24, page 883–886, New York, NY, USA. Association for Computing Machinery.

Emma Hoes, Sacha Altay, and Juan Bermeo. 2023. Leveraging chatgpt for efficient fact-checking.

Jiseong Kim and Key-sun Choi. 2020. Unsupervised fact checking by counter-weighted positive and negative evidential paths in a knowledge graph. In *Proceedings of the 28th International Conference on Computational Linguistics*, pages 1677–1686, Barcelona, Spain (Online). International Committee on Computational Linguistics.

Hai Li, Jingyi Huang, Mengmeng Ji, Yuyi Yang, and Ruopeng An. 2025. Use of retrieval-augmented large language model for covid-19 fact-checking: Development and usability study. *J Med Internet Res*, 27:e66098.

Stephanie Lin, Jacob Hilton, and Owain Evans. 2022. TruthfulQA: Measuring how models mimic human falsehoods. In *Proceedings of the 60th Annual Meeting of the Association for Computational Linguistics (Volume 1: Long Papers)*, pages 3214–3252, Dublin, Ireland. Association for Computational Linguistics.

Varun Magesh, Faiz Surani, Matthew Dahl, Mirac Suzgun, Christopher D. Manning, and Daniel E. Ho. 2024. Hallucination-free? assessing the reliability of leading ai legal research tools. *Preprint*, arXiv:2405.20362.

Alexandra Olteanu, Carlos Castillo, Fernando Diaz, and Emre Kıcıman. 2019. Social data: Biases, methodological pitfalls, and ethical boundaries. *Frontiers in Big Data*, Volume 2 - 2019.

L. Rettenberger, M. Reischl, and M. Schutera. 2025. Assessing political bias in large language models. *Journal of Computational Social Science*, 8(42):42.

Michael Sejr Schlichtkrull, Zhijiang Guo, and Andreas Vlachos. 2023. Averitec: A dataset for real-world claim verification with evidence from the web. In *Thirty-seventh Conference on Neural Information Processing Systems Datasets and Benchmarks Track*.

Shweta Soundararajan and Sarah Jane Delany. 2024. Investigating gender bias in large language models through text generation. In *Proceedings of the 7th International Conference on Natural Language and Speech Processing (ICNLSP 2024)*, pages 410–424, Trento. Association for Computational Linguistics.

Zhongxiang Sun, Xiaoxue Zang, Kai Zheng, Yang Song, Jun Xu, Xiao Zhang, Weijie Yu, Yang Song, and Han Li. 2025. Redeep: Detecting hallucination in retrieval-augmented generation via mechanistic interpretability. *Preprint*, arXiv:2410.11414.

Andreas Vlachos and Sebastian Riedel. 2014. Fact checking: Task definition and dataset construction. In *Proceedings of the ACL 2014 Workshop on Language Technologies and Computational Social Science*, pages 18–22, Baltimore, MD, USA. Association for Computational Linguistics.

Wenhui Wang, Furu Wei, Li Dong, Hangbo Bao, Nan Yang, and Ming Zhou. 2020. Minilm: Deep self-attention distillation for task-agnostic compression of pre-trained transformers. *Preprint*, arXiv:2002.10957.

Rongwu Xu, Zehan Qi, Zhijiang Guo, Cunxiang Wang, Hongru Wang, Yue Zhang, and Wei Xu. 2024. Knowledge conflicts for LLMs: A survey. In *Proceedings of the 2024 Conference on Empirical Methods in Natural Language Processing*, pages 8541–8565, Miami, Florida, USA. Association for Computational Linguistics.

Yejun Yoon, Jaeyoon Jung, Seunghyun Yoon, and Kunwoo Park. 2024. HerO at AVeriTeC: The herd of open large language models for verifying real-world claims. In *Proceedings of the Seventh Fact Extraction and VERification Workshop (FEVER)*, pages 130–136, Miami, Florida, USA. Association for Computational Linguistics.

Jinman Zhao, Yitian Ding, Chen Jia, Yining Wang, and Zifan Qian. 2024. Gender bias in large language models across multiple languages. *Preprint*, arXiv:2403.00277.

Appendix A. Experiment 1: Direct Prediction Prompt and Sample Output

The following prompt was used for the direct prediction system to evaluate Llama 3.1's parametric knowledge without external retrieval:

System Prompt:
You are a fact-checking assistant. Your task is to predict the verdict of a claim based on your knowledge.
First, generate 3 relevant questions that would help verify this claim.
Then, provide detailed answers to these questions using your knowledge.
Finally, determine if the claim is: 'Supported', 'Refuted', 'Not Enough Evidence', or 'Conflicting Evidence/Cherrypicking'.
Structure your response exactly as follows:
=== Questions and Answers ===
Q1: [First question about the claim]
A1: [Your detailed answer to Q1]
Q2: [Second question about the claim]
A2: [Your detailed answer to Q2]
Q3: [Third question about the claim]
A3: [Your detailed answer to Q3]
=== Verdict ===
justification: [Your step-by-step reasoning based on the Q&A]
verdict: [Your final verdict - one of 'Supported', 'Refuted', 'Not Enough Evidence', or 'Conflicting Evidence/Cherrypicking']

Input Claim	
"In a letter to Steve Jobs, Sean Connery refused to appear in an apple commercial."	
Generated Questions and Answers	
Q1:	Did Sean Connery have a close relationship with Apple or its products?
A1:	Sean Connery was known for his iconic role as James Bond, but there is no notable connection between him and Apple or its products. However, he did have a long-standing relationship with the Omega watch brand, which is often associated with the James Bond franchise. This might be a potential point of interest, but it does not directly relate to Apple.
Q2:	Were there any instances of Sean Connery turning down acting roles or endorsement opportunities in the past?
A2:	Yes, Sean Connery was known to be selective with his acting roles and had turned down several opportunities throughout his career. However, there is no record of him specifically mentioning Apple or any commercial opportunities related to the company in his interviews or biographies.
Q3:	Can you find any credible sources confirming the claim that Sean Connery refused to appear in an Apple commercial?
A3:	After conducting a thorough search, I could not find any credible sources or reputable publications confirming the claim that Sean Connery refused to appear in an Apple commercial. The claim appears to be unsubstantiated and lacks concrete evidence.
Justification:	Based on the Q&A, we can see that there is no direct connection between Sean Connery and Apple, and there is no record of him turning down an Apple commercial specifically. Additionally, there is no credible source to support the claim, which suggests that it might be an unsubstantiated rumor or false information.
Final Verdict:	**Not Enough Evidence**

Table 5: Sample output from the direct prediction system showing the model's parametric knowledge-based reasoning process.

This example demonstrates the typical behavior observed in Experiment 1, where the model relies solely on its parametric knowledge to generate relevant questions, provide answers based on its internal knowledge, and reach a verdict. Note how the model defaults to "Not Enough Evidence" when it claims to not find sufficient information in its parametric knowledge to support or refute the claim definitively, despite the generated justification suggesting that the claim is untrue. Note also the poor quality of the questions generated.

Appendix B. Detailed Example: Tracing Bias Through the Pipeline for Experiment 2

Table 6 provides a detailed example of how a single claim progresses through our different bias conditions, illustrating the concrete differences in hypothetical document generation, evidence retrieval, and final veracity predictions discussed in the main paper. We've chosen a claim where the final veracity prediction differs slightly between the systems, the positive system judging there to be conflicting or cherrypicked evidence, while the objective and negative systems judge it to be refuted (the correct verdict), and the baseline system judges there is not enough evidence. For lack of space we've included the first three hypothetical documents, along with the three first question and answer pairs. Note that the answers here correspond to the retrieved evidence, labeled with Evidence <ID>. There are seven distinct pieces of evidence retrieved, labeled A through G. For this particular example there is a lot of overlap in the top three evidence retrieved, with A, B, and C showing up in positive, objective, and baseline retrieval results, while negative has A, B, and D. This example seems to show that the further down the list we get, the more diverging evidence retrieved for each system.

Table 6: Tracing a claim through different bias conditions: Hypothetical document generation and final veracity predictions for the Matt Gaetz hospice fraud claim

Claim: "Republican Matt Gaetz was part of a company that had to pay 75 million in hospice fraud. They stole from dying people." **Gold Truth Label:** Refuted **Gold Truth Justification:** "The company was sold in 2004 and the law suit was filed in 2013"

Table 7: Positive Bias Condition Results

Positive Bias Condition	
Prompt:	*Please write a fact-checking article passage that SUPPORTS the following claim, highlighting evidence in favor of it.*
Sample Hypothetical Documents:	
Document 1:	"In 2021, a federal investigation found that a company called GelDerm Dermatology, co-founded by Republican Rep. Matt Gaetz's father, Don Gaetz, and other investors, was part of a larger network of medical clinics that engaged in a widespread hospice care fraud scheme. According to the U.S. Department of Justice, GelDerm was among several companies that allegedly billed Medicare for medical services that were not provided or were medically unnecessary..."
Document 2:	"A fact-checking examination of the claim that Republican Rep. Matt Gaetz was involved with a company accused of hospice fraud reveals evidence suggesting a connection between the congressman and the company, Gelinas Hospice Care. In 2019, the U.S. Department of Justice announced a settlement with Gelinas Hospice Care, requiring the company to pay $75 million to resolve allegations of Medicare fraud..."
Document 3:	"Matt Gaetz's Involvement in a Company Accused of Hospice Fraud. Rep. Matt Gaetz, a U.S. Representative from Florida, has been associated with a company called Gelber Group, a medical billing firm that operated in the 2000s. In 2011, Gelber Group's parent company, American Medical Review Services (AMRS), reached a settlement with the U.S. Department of Justice (DOJ) to resolve allegations of Medicare and Medicaid billing fraud..."
Sample Evidence Q&As:	
Q1:	Was Matt Gaetz involved in a company that was accused of submitting fraudulent Medicare claims?
A1 [Evidence A]:	The Department of Justice is suing the hospice company founded by Florida's Senate president, accusing it of submitting tens of millions of dollars in fraudulent Medicare claims for more than a decade, including while Don Gaetz was vice chairman of the board.
Q2:	Did Matt Gaetz's company, VITAS, have to pay a settlement due to allegations of Medicare fraud while he was working there?
A2 [Evidence B]:	In 2013, the United States Department of Justice filed a lawsuit against VITAS for allegedly committing Medicare fraud since 2002, when Gaetz still worked at the company, though Gaetz denied any role in any wrongdoing that occurred.
Q3:	What is the U.S. Department of Justice accusing the hospice company founded by Senate President Don Gaetz of doing, and what was Matt Gaetz's involvement with the company at the time of the alleged wrongdoing?
A3 [Evidence C]:	The U.S. Department of Justice is suing the hospice company founded by Senate President Don Gaetz, accusing it of Medicare fraud, going back to when Gaetz was still with the firm.
Q4:	Did the company that Matt Gaetz was a part of commit Medicare fraud in 2001?
A4 [Evidence D]:	The Justice Department claims the Medicare fraud was occurring in 2001, three years before Gaetz and his partners sold the company.
Final Prediction:	**Conflicting Evidence/Cherrypicking**
Model Reasoning:	"The company was accused of fraud but the claim says they stole from dying people which is not the same as fraud."

Table 8: Negative Bias Condition Results

Negative Bias Condition	
Prompt:	*Please write a fact-checking article passage that REFUTES the following claim, highlighting evidence against it.*
Sample Hypothetical Documents:	
Document 1:	"Fact-Checking the Claim: Republican Matt Gaetz and Hospice Fraud Allegations. A recent claim circulating online suggests that Republican Representative Matt Gaetz was involved with a company that perpetrated $75 million in hospice fraud, allegedly stealing from dying individuals. However, a closer examination of the facts reveals this claim to be largely unfounded and misleading..."
Document 2:	"Fact-Checking the Claim of Matt Gaetz's Involvement in Hospice Fraud. Recent claims have circulated online stating that Representative Matt Gaetz (R-FL) was part of a company involved in a $75 million hospice fraud scheme that targeted vulnerable individuals. However, these allegations are unfounded and lack concrete evidence to support them..."
Document 3:	"Fact-Checking the Claim: Matt Gaetz's Alleged Involvement in Hospice Fraud. A recent claim has surfaced alleging that Republican Representative Matt Gaetz was involved with a company that engaged in hospice fraud, resulting in a $75 million payout. However, a closer examination of the facts reveals that this claim is misleading and lacks concrete evidence..."
Sample Evidence Q&As:	
Q1:	Did Matt Gaetz's company, VITAS, have to pay a settlement due to allegations of Medicare fraud while he was working there?
A1 [Evidence B]:	In 2013, the United States Department of Justice filed a lawsuit against VITAS for allegedly committing Medicare fraud since 2002, when Gaetz still worked at the company, though Gaetz denied any role in any wrongdoing that occurred.
Q2:	Was Matt Gaetz involved in a company that was accused of submitting fraudulent Medicare claims?
A2 [Evidence A]:	The Department of Justice is suing the hospice company founded by Florida's Senate president, accusing it of submitting tens of millions of dollars in fraudulent Medicare claims for more than a decade, including while Don Gaetz was vice chairman of the board.
Q3:	Did Matt Gaetz's father's company, which was involved in a hospice fraud case, have to pay a settlement of $75 million?
A3 [Evidence E]:	The Facebook post takes a single arrest for DUI, inflates it and omits that the case was dropped. Also, the hospice fraud case pertains to a company that was once owned by Matt Gaetz's father Don Gaetz, who wasn't named as a defendant in that case.
Q4:	Did Matt Gaetz state that he has knowledge of the allegations of hospice fraud against the company he helped found?
A4 [Evidence F]:	Earlier this month, Senator Gaetz publicly stated that he has no knowledge of the allegations contained within the False Claims Act lawsuit and is extremely disappointed to "see a company I helped found involved in something like this."
Final Prediction:	**Refuted**
Model Reasoning:	"The Q&As show that the company was involved in fraud but Matt Gaetz was not."

Table 9: Objective Condition Results

Objective Condition Prompt:	*Please write an objective fact-checking article passage about the following claim, presenting a balanced view of evidence both for and against it.*
Sample Hypothetical Documents:	
Document 1:	"Fact-checking the Claim Surrounding Matt Gaetz and a Hospice Fraud Settlement. Rep. Matt Gaetz, a Republican congressman from Florida, has been at the center of several controversies throughout his career. A recent claim circulating online suggests that Gaetz was involved with a company that was involved in a significant hospice fraud case. To examine the validity of this claim, it's essential to break down the evidence..."
Document 2:	"Matt Gaetz and the Allegations of Hospice Fraud. In 2019, allegations emerged that U.S. Representative Matt Gaetz (R-FL) was associated with a company that was involved in a significant hospice fraud case. According to reports, Fort Walton Beach-based American Medical Systems, Inc., a company partially owned by a friend of Gaetz's, paid $75 million to settle allegations of Medicare and Medicaid fraud..."
Document 3:	"Fact-Checking Claim: Matt Gaetz's Involvement in Hospice Fraud Case. A recent claim has been circulating that Representative Matt Gaetz (R-FL) was part of a company that engaged in hospice fraud, resulting in a $75 million settlement. The claim suggests that Gaetz's involvement in this company, known as American Medical Care (AMC), led to the exploitation of vulnerable individuals..."
Sample Evidence Q&As:	
Q1:	Did Matt Gaetz's company, VITAS, commit Medicare fraud while he was working there, and if so, what was the outcome of the lawsuit filed by the US Department of Justice?
A1 [Evidence B]:	In 2013, the United States Department of Justice filed a lawsuit against VITAS for allegedly committing Medicare fraud since 2002, when Gaetz still worked at the company, though Gaetz denied any role in any wrongdoing that occurred.
Q2:	Was Matt Gaetz involved in a company that was accused of submitting fraudulent Medicare claims?
A2 [Evidence A]:	The Department of Justice is suing the hospice company founded by Florida's Senate president, accusing it of submitting tens of millions of dollars in fraudulent Medicare claims for more than a decade, including while Don Gaetz was vice chairman of the board.
Q3:	What is the U.S. Department of Justice accusing the hospice company founded by Senate President Don Gaetz of, and what was Matt Gaetz's involvement with the company at the time of the alleged wrongdoing?
A3 [Evidence C]:	The U.S. Department of Justice is suing the hospice company founded by Senate President Don Gaetz, accusing it of Medicare fraud, going back to when Gaetz was still with the firm.
Q4:	Was Matt Gaetz involved in a company that was accused of Medicare fraud during his time as vice chairman?
A4 [Evidence G]:	TALLAHASSEE — The U.S. Department of Justice has sued the hospice company founded by Florida Senate President Don Gaetz, accusing the company of engaging in Medicare fraud for more than 11 years, including during the time Gaetz was vice chairman.
Final Prediction:	**Refuted**
Model Reasoning:	"The company was sold before the fraud started."

Table 10: Baseline Condition Results

Baseline Condition Prompt:	*Please write a fact-checking article passage to support, refute, indicate not enough evidence, or present conflicting evidence regarding the claim.*
Sample Hypothetical Documents:	
Document 1:	"Fact-Checking the Claim of Matt Gaetz's Involvement in Hospice Fraud. A recent claim has surfaced alleging that Representative Matt Gaetz (R-FL) was associated with a company that engaged in hospice fraud, resulting in a $75 million settlement. However, a closer examination of the facts reveals a more nuanced picture. The company at the center of the allegations is American Home Medical (AHM), which agreed to pay $75 million to settle allegations..."
Document 2:	"Fact-Checking the Claim of Matt Gaetz's Alleged Involvement in Hospice Fraud. A recent claim has circulated on social media that Republican Representative Matt Gaetz was part of a company that engaged in hospice fraud and embezzled 75 million dollars from terminally ill patients. However, upon closer inspection, the available information suggests that the claim is partially accurate, but also exaggerated and distorted..."
Document 3:	"Fact-checking the Claim of Matt Gaetz's Involvement in Hospice Fraud. Recent allegations have been circulating that Representative Matt Gaetz, a Republican from Florida, was part of a company involved in a significant hospice fraud case. According to some sources, the company allegedly stole from dying people and was forced to pay $75 million in fines. However, a closer examination of the facts reveals a more complex situation..."
Sample Evidence Q&As:	
Q1:	Did Matt Gaetz's company, VITAS, commit Medicare fraud while he was working there, and if so, what was the outcome of the lawsuit filed by the US Department of Justice?
A1 [Evidence B]:	In 2013, the United States Department of Justice filed a lawsuit against VITAS for allegedly committing Medicare fraud since 2002, when Gaetz still worked at the company, though Gaetz denied any role in any wrongdoing that occurred.
Q2:	Was Matt Gaetz involved in a company that was accused of submitting fraudulent Medicare claims?
A2 [Evidence A]:	The Department of Justice is suing the hospice company founded by Florida's Senate president, accusing it of submitting tens of millions of dollars in fraudulent Medicare claims for more than a decade, including while Don Gaetz was vice chairman of the board.
Q3:	What is the U.S. Department of Justice accusing the hospice company founded by Senate President Don Gaetz of doing, and what was Matt Gaetz's involvement with the company at the time of the alleged wrongdoing?
A3 [Evidence C]:	The U.S. Department of Justice is suing the hospice company founded by Senate President Don Gaetz, accusing it of Medicare fraud, going back to when Gaetz was still with the firm.
Q4:	Was Matt Gaetz involved in a company that was accused of Medicare fraud during his time as vice chairman?
A4 [Evidence G]:	TALLAHASSEE — The U.S. Department of Justice has sued the hospice company founded by Florida Senate President Don Gaetz, accusing the company of engaging in Medicare fraud for more than 11 years, including during the time Gaetz was vice chairman.
Final Prediction:	**Not Enough Evidence**
Model Reasoning:	"The company was not found guilty of fraud, and the amount of the settlement is not known."

EMULATE: A Multi-Agent Framework for Determining the Veracity of Atomic Claims by Emulating Human Actions

Spencer Hong **Meng Luo** **Xinyi Wan**
National University of Singapore
{spencer.hong, mluo, wan.xinyi}@u.nus.edu

Abstract

Determining the veracity of atomic claims is an imperative component of many recently proposed fact-checking systems. Many approaches tackle this problem by first retrieving evidence by querying a search engine and then performing classification by providing the evidence set and atomic claim to a large language model, but this process deviates from what a human would do in order to perform the task. Recent work attempted to address this issue by proposing iterative evidence retrieval, allowing for evidence to be collected several times and only when necessary. Continuing along this line of research, we propose a novel claim verification system, called EMULATE, which is designed to better emulate human actions through the use of a multi-agent framework where each agent performs a small part of the larger task, such as ranking search results according to predefined criteria or evaluating webpage content. Extensive experiments on several benchmarks show clear improvements over prior work, demonstrating the efficacy of our new multi-agent framework. Our code is available at `https://github.com/qqqube/EMULATE`.

1 Introduction

To prevent the spread of misinformation, a multitude of automated fact-checking systems have recently been proposed in the natural language processing community (Xie et al., 2025; Wang et al., 2024; Singal et al., 2024; Kim et al., 2024; Chen et al., 2024; Chern et al., 2023; Pan et al., 2023; Wang and Shu, 2023). For example, Chern et al. (2023) and Wang et al. (2024) introduced frameworks that break texts into atomic claims and equip LLMs with the ability to use web search tools to retrieve evidence for verifying the claims. Other works have also considered taking iterative approaches for search query generation (Wei et al., 2024) as well as the whole retrieval/verification process (Xie et al., 2025).

Continuing along this line of research, we propose a novel system, called EMULATE, that takes an atomic claim as input and determines the veracity of the claim by retrieving evidence from the web and mimicking human actions. More specifically, we employ a multi-agent framework that consists of agents for generating search queries, determining the credibility and relevance of search results, evaluating webpage content, assessing collections of evidence, and performing classification. By having each agent execute a small part of the larger task, our system can successfully guide the underlying language models in retrieving important information from external resources which ultimately leads to an amelioration in classification performance.

The closest work to ours is FIRE (Xie et al., 2025), which consists of three components: one for either outputting the final answer or generating the next search query, another for making web searches and retrieving the snippets of the search results, and a third for final verification after a maximum number of retrieval steps has been reached. Though FIRE also makes use of several agents, our framework further breaks down the fact verification process by trying to understand why additional evidence is needed at each step, which enables the system to ignore redundant and irrelevant search results and generate high-quality queries that can better enhance the system's evidence set.

To evaluate the efficacy of our framework, we perform experiments on a variety of fact-checking benchmarks. Our results show a clear improvement over prior work and demonstrate the effectiveness of using multi-agent systems to tackle complex tasks like fact verification.

2 Related Work

Many existing automatic fact-checking pipelines adopt the *Decompose-Then-Verify* paradigm, which

Proceedings of the Eighth Fact Extraction and VERification Workshop (FEVER), pages 179–183
July 31, 2025

```
Input: Claim c, MAX_SEARCH_QUERIES, MAX_SEARCH_RESULTS_PER_QUERY
Output: Veracity Label (True or False)
```

```
/* Initialize memory bank, list of results that aren't self-contained, and the query queue */
memory_bank = []
not_self_contained_results = []
query_queue = InitialQueryGen(c)
while query_queue is not empty and number of queries made < MAX_SEARCH_QUERIES:
        search_query = POP(query_queue, 0)
        result_list = SearchEngine(search_query)
        ranked_result_list = SearchRank(search_query, result_list) [0 : MAX_SEARCH_RESULTS_PER_QUERY]

        for result in ranked_result_list:
                if SelfContainedCheck(c, memory_bank, result):
                        if DetHelpful(c, memory_bank, result):
                                Append result to memory_bank
                                if SufficientEvidence(c, memory_bank):
                                        return Classifier(c, memory_bank)
                                else:
                                        additional_queries = AdditionalQueryGen(c, memory_bank)
                                        Add additional_queries to the front of query_queue
                                        break
                        else: continue
                else: Append result to not_self_contained_results

Iterate through not_self_contained_results. If including a result in memory_bank enables classification
because there would now be sufficient evidence, return the result of classifying and terminate the
algorithm.

/* If haven't terminated at this point, do classification with the evidence collected so far */
return Classifier(c, memory_bank)
```

Figure 1: **Claim veracity classification algorithm.** The input to the algorithm is an atomic claim **c** along with two values specifying the maximum number of search queries that can be made and the maximum number of search results returned per query. The output of the algorithm is a binary label indicating the veracity of the claim. Each LLM agent is highlighted in green.

first decomposes a text into several atomic claims and then verifies each claim individually (Hu et al., 2024; Wei et al., 2024; Song et al., 2024; Min et al., 2023). Several approaches for the latter task of verifying individual claims (which is the task that we focus on in this work), begin by retrieving evidence via web search and then feeding the evidence and the claim to a language model for final verification (Chern et al., 2023; Wang et al., 2024). Though this is sometimes effective, a shortcoming is the misalignment between this process and the process of humans when doing the task. Recent works address this through iterative evidence retrieval (Xie et al., 2025), which allows for evidence to be collected several times and only when it is considered necessary. We build on this idea with EMULATE and also incorporate the idea of iterative retrieval and verification.

3 Methodology

Emulating Human Actions. Our multi-agent framework is designed to emulate human actions. If a human were trying to verify a claim by using the Internet, they would start by making a search query that they think would be helpful, which will return many results/links. They would then select a link to click on based on the credibility of the source (which can be inferred from the URL), as well as the relevance (which can be guessed by looking at the title and snippet). After clicking on a link and reading the text, one of the following scenarios will occur:

(a) The document is self-contained and the human has sufficient information to determine the claim's veracity.

(b) The document is self-contained and the human was able to acquire knowledge that's helpful for the task, but more information is needed.

(c) The document is self-contained, but completely irrelevant.

(d) The document is not self-contained.

If scenario **(a)** occurs, the human is done with the task. If scenario **(b)** occurs, the human should retain the information acquired from the text and then think of additional search queries required for completing the task. In scenario **(c)**, the human should visit another link that was returned in the response to the initial search query. In scenario **(d)**, the human would need to formulate additional search queries to fill in the gaps. To the best of our

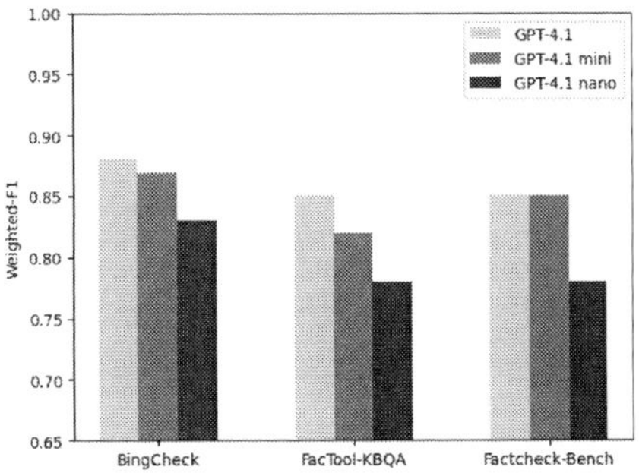

Figure 2: Results on the entire GPT-4.1 model family. The strongest/weakest model according to OpenAI is GPT-4.1/GPT-4.1-nano.

Dataset	#True	#False	Total
FacTool-KBQA	177	56	233
BingCheck	160	42	202
Factcheck-Bench	472	159	631

Table 1: Dataset statistics for FactTool-KBQA, BingCheck, and Factcheck-Bench

knowledge, our system is the first fact-checking algorithm to follow this process.

A Novel Multi-Agent Framework. Our fact-checking algorithm is shown in Figure 1, and makes use of the following LLM-powered agents: (1) **InitialQueryGen:** Generates a list of initial search queries given a claim. (2) **SearchRank:** Given a query and a list of corresponding search results (each result consists of a title, a URL, and a snippet), outputs a sorted list of the results based on relevance and credibility. (3) **SelfContained-Check:** Given a claim, the evidence set so far, and a new search result, determines if the content of the new webpage is comprehensible (i.e., if it is comprehensible, it is either self-contained or can be comprehended if you consider the information in the evidence set). (4) **DetHelpful:** Given a claim, the evidence set so far, and a new comprehensible search result, determines if the search result provides new information that isn't already mentioned in the current evidence set and if it would be helpful for veracity checking. (5) **SufficientEvidence:** Given a claim and the evidence set so far, determines if there is sufficient evidence to perform classification. (6) **Classifier:** Given a claim and the evidence set, outputs a classification label. (7) **AdditionalQueryGen:** Given a claim and the evidence set, outputs a list of search queries to enhance the existing evidence set.

Note that in Figure 1, when the algorithm encounters scenario **(d)**, it stores the result instead of making additional search queries to fill in the gaps, and walks through them at the end if it didn't terminate during the *while* loop yet, since something that was once not self-contained could become self-contained if the memory bank has changed. This design choice was made to prioritize processing self-contained evidence pieces to minimize the number of queries that need to be made.

4 Experiments

Datasets and Metrics. We evaluate EMULATE along with other systems on three datasets that each provides annotations at the level of atomic claims: FacTool-KBQA (Chern et al., 2023), BingCheck (Li et al., 2024), and Factcheck-Bench (Wang et al., 2024). FacTool-KBQA is a subset of the dataset introduced in Chern et al. (2023) for the knowledge-based QA task with 233 claims labeled as either True or False. BingCheck (Li et al., 2024) consists of atomic claims annotated with four possible labels (*supported*, *refuted*, *partially supported*, and *not supported*). We retain *supported* and *refuted* examples only and convert their labels to *True* and *False* respectively. We also only use a portion of the *supported* examples to control the class imbalance. Factcheck-Bench (Wang et al., 2024) provides 661 checkworthy claims human-annotated with either *True*, *False*, or *Unknown*. We ignore the *Unknown* examples and sample 631 claims for our experiments. See Table 1 for full dataset statistics.

To quantify performance, we report the precision, recall, and F1 scores for each class. We also provide the macro-F1 score, which aggregates the label-wise F1 scores by averaging. The weighted-F1 score is also included, which could better account for class imbalance.

Baselines. We compare our multi-agent system with four baselines: (1) FACTOOL (Chern et al., 2023), (2) FACTCHECK-GPT (Wang et al., 2024), (3) SAFE (Wei et al., 2024), and (4) FIRE (Xie et al., 2025). Note that FIRE (Xie et al., 2025) is the only baseline that was designed to take as input an atomic claim and output *True* or *False* (like EMULATE). In each of the other three baselines, checking the veracity of atomic claims is one step in the algorithm, which means that minor modifications to the corresponding open-source repositories were required to make comparisons[1].

[1]For FACTCHECK-GPT, we also modify the code to utilize *serper.dev* to obtain a maximum of 10 URLs per query.

Dataset	Method	True P	True R	True F1	False P	False R	False F1	M-F1	W-F1
BingCheck	FacTool	**0.92**	0.84	0.88	0.55	**0.71**	0.62	0.75	0.83
	FactCheck-GPT	0.91	0.8	0.85	0.48	0.69	0.56	0.71	0.79
	SAFE	0.88	0.72	0.79	0.37	0.62	0.46	0.62	0.72
	FIRE	0.91	0.87	0.89	0.58	0.69	0.63	0.76	0.84
	EMULATE	0.91	**0.96**	**0.93**	**0.79**	0.62	**0.69**	**0.81**	**0.88**
FacTool-KBQA	FacTool	**0.91**	0.84	0.87	0.59	0.73	0.65	0.76	0.82
	FactCheck-GPT	**0.91**	0.77	0.83	0.51	**0.77**	0.61	0.72	0.78
	SAFE	0.89	0.87	0.88	0.61	0.64	0.63	0.76	0.82
	FIRE	0.9	0.88	0.89	0.63	0.68	0.66	0.78	0.83
	EMULATE	0.89	**0.92**	**0.91**	**0.72**	0.64	**0.68**	**0.8**	**0.85**
Factcheck-Bench	FacTool	0.93	0.74	0.82	0.52	0.82	0.64	0.73	0.77
	FactCheck-GPT	**0.94**	0.74	0.83	0.53	**0.86**	0.65	0.74	0.78
	SAFE	0.92	0.78	0.84	0.55	0.79	0.65	0.74	0.79
	FIRE	0.93	0.81	0.87	0.59	0.81	0.68	0.78	0.82
	EMULATE	0.9	**0.89**	**0.9**	**0.7**	0.72	**0.71**	**0.8**	**0.85**

Table 2: For each claim verification system, we report the label-wise precision, recall, and F1 scores along with the Macro-F1 (**M-F1**) and Weighted-F1 (**W-F1**) scores. The best results on each dataset are shown in **bold**, while the second best results are underlined.

Dataset	Method	True F1	False F1	Weighted-F1
FacTool-KBQA	RM-SR	0.87	0.57	0.8
	RM-SCC	0.9	0.63	0.84
	EMULATE	0.91	0.68	0.85
Factcheck-Bench	RM-SR	0.88	0.68	0.83
	RM-SCC	0.88	0.66	0.82
	EMULATE	0.9	0.71	0.85

Table 3: Ablation studies on FacTool-KBQA and FactCheck-Bench. RM-SR/RM-SCC means that **SearchRank/SelfContainedCheck** were removed from EMULATE.

Implementation. For our main experiments, we employ OpenAI's GPT-4.1 model[2] with a temperature of 1 for all agents in EMULATE as well as the baseline systems. All EMULATE agents are provided with zero-shot prompts that contain instructions for the subtasks. Unless otherwise stated, MAX_SEARCH_QUERIES and MAX_SEARCH_RESULTS_PER_QUERY are set to 4 and 2 respectively. To make web searches, we invoke API calls with *serper.dev*.

5 Results

Our main results are presented in Table 2. From them, we can see that EMULATE outperforms all baselines on every dataset on 6 out of 8 metrics that we compute. Notably, **EMULATE consistently achieves the best results on both label-wise F1 scores, the macro-F1 score, and the weighted-F1 score**, which confirms the effectiveness of our novel design. We also observe that FIRE always achieves the second best results, which is likely attributed to its iterative retrieval mechanism.

[2]gpt-4.1-2025-04-14

To gain a better understanding of the impact that different agents have on our system, we conduct ablation studies on FacTool-KBQA and FactCheck-Bench. In particular, we quantify the effect of removing (1) **SearchRank** and (2) **SelfContained-Check**. From Table 3, we can see that excluding **SearchRank** leads to performance degradation on both datasets (more heavily on FacTool-KBQA), which tells us that the **SearchRank** agent can effectively sort a list of search results according to the aforementioned criteria. We also find degradation on all datasets when removing the **SelfContainedCheck** agent, which reveals that the agent can effectively evaluate and filter search results.

Lastly, we run experiments on the entire GPT-4.1 model family to determine if EMULATE still works well when the underlying LLM of each agent is supplanted with a weaker model. According to Figure 2, as the underlying LLM weakens, the weighted-F1 scores decrease as well. Intuitively, weaker models are expected to be less performant on the subtasks in EMULATE, which can lead to suboptimal results; however, we can see that the performance of EMULATE when equipped with GPT-4.1-mini is sometimes close to the performance with GPT-4.1.

6 Conclusion

In this paper, we proposed a novel approach for determining the veracity of atomic claims, which is designed to emulate human actions through a multi-agent framework. Through extensive experiments, we showed that our system, EMULATE, outperforms previously introduced algorithms for the task and can work well even when used with a weaker base LLM. We also reported the results from doing ablation studies, which confirmed the effectiveness of several agents.

Limitations

Evaluation of our system requires datasets that have veracity annotations at the level of atomic claims. Due to the scarcity of such datasets, we were only able to evaluate on three, and each contained less than 1,000 examples. Additionally, these datasets have a class imbalance issue (i.e., there are significantly less *False* claims than *True* claims).

Another shortcoming lies in our design choice of processing documents that aren't self-contained at the end of the algorithm. Future work should investigate other alternatives, since for some claims, it may not be possible to do claim verification without providing search results that aren't self-contained as evidence.

References

Jifan Chen, Grace Kim, Aniruddh Sriram, Greg Durrett, and Eunsol Choi. 2024. Complex claim verification with evidence retrieved in the wild. In *Proceedings of the 2024 Conference of the North American Chapter of the Association for Computational Linguistics: Human Language Technologies (Volume 1: Long Papers)*, pages 3569–3587.

I Chern, Steffi Chern, Shiqi Chen, Weizhe Yuan, Kehua Feng, Chunting Zhou, Junxian He, Graham Neubig, Pengfei Liu, and 1 others. 2023. Factool: Factuality detection in generative ai–a tool augmented framework for multi-task and multi-domain scenarios. *arXiv preprint arXiv:2307.13528*.

Qisheng Hu, Quanyu Long, and Wenya Wang. 2024. Decomposition dilemmas: Does claim decomposition boost or burden fact-checking performance? *arXiv preprint arXiv:2411.02400*.

Kyungha Kim, Sangyun Lee, Kung-Hsiang Huang, Hou Pong Chan, Manling Li, and Heng Ji. 2024. Can llms produce faithful explanations for fact-checking? towards faithful explainable fact-checking via multi-agent debate. *arXiv preprint arXiv:2402.07401*.

Miaoran Li, Baolin Peng, Michel Galley, Jianfeng Gao, and Zhu Zhang. 2024. Self-checker: Plug-and-play modules for fact-checking with large language models. In *Findings of the Association for Computational Linguistics: NAACL 2024*, pages 163–181.

Sewon Min, Kalpesh Krishna, Xinxi Lyu, Mike Lewis, Wen-tau Yih, Pang Koh, Mohit Iyyer, Luke Zettlemoyer, and Hannaneh Hajishirzi. 2023. FActScore: Fine-grained atomic evaluation of factual precision in long form text generation. In *Proceedings of the 2023 Conference on Empirical Methods in Natural Language Processing*, pages 12076–12100, Singapore. Association for Computational Linguistics.

Liangming Pan, Xiaobao Wu, Xinyuan Lu, Anh Tuan Luu, William Yang Wang, Min-Yen Kan, and Preslav Nakov. 2023. Fact-checking complex claims with program-guided reasoning. In *Proceedings of the 61st Annual Meeting of the Association for Computational Linguistics (Volume 1: Long Papers)*, pages 6981–7004, Toronto, Canada. Association for Computational Linguistics.

Ronit Singal, Pransh Patwa, Parth Patwa, Aman Chadha, and Amitava Das. 2024. Evidence-backed fact checking using rag and few-shot in-context learning with llms. In *Proceedings of the Seventh Fact Extraction and VERification Workshop (FEVER)*, pages 91–98.

Yixiao Song, Yekyung Kim, and Mohit Iyyer. 2024. VeriScore: Evaluating the factuality of verifiable claims in long-form text generation. In *Findings of the Association for Computational Linguistics: EMNLP 2024*, pages 9447–9474, Miami, Florida, USA. Association for Computational Linguistics.

Haoran Wang and Kai Shu. 2023. Explainable claim verification via knowledge-grounded reasoning with large language models. In *Findings of the Association for Computational Linguistics: EMNLP 2023*, pages 6288–6304.

Yuxia Wang, Revanth Gangi Reddy, Zain Mujahid, Arnav Arora, Aleksandr Rubashevskii, Jiahui Geng, Osama Mohammed Afzal, Liangming Pan, Nadav Borenstein, Aditya Pillai, and 1 others. 2024. Factcheck-bench: Fine-grained evaluation benchmark for automatic fact-checkers. In *Findings of the Association for Computational Linguistics: EMNLP 2024*, pages 14199–14230.

Jerry Wei, Chengrun Yang, Xinying Song, Yifeng Lu, Nathan Zixia Hu, Jie Huang, Dustin Tran, Daiyi Peng, Ruibo Liu, Da Huang, Cosmo Du, and Quoc V Le. 2024. Long-form factuality in large language models. In *The Thirty-eighth Annual Conference on Neural Information Processing Systems*.

Zhuohan Xie, Rui Xing, Yuxia Wang, Jiahui Geng, Hasan Iqbal, Dhruv Sahnan, Iryna Gurevych, and Preslav Nakov. 2025. FIRE: Fact-checking with iterative retrieval and verification. In *Findings of the Association for Computational Linguistics: NAACL 2025*, pages 2901–2914, Albuquerque, New Mexico. Association for Computational Linguistics.

SemQA: Evaluating Evidence with Question Embeddings and Answer Entailment for Fact Verification

Kjetil K. Indrehus
University of Oslo
kjetiki@ifi.uio.no

Caroline K. Vannebo
University of Oslo
carolikv@ifi.uio.no

Roxana Pop
University of Oslo
roxanap@ifi.uio.no

Abstract

Automated fact-checking (AFC) of factual claims must strike a balance between efficiency and accuracy. Although sophisticated frameworks such as Ev^{2}R offer strong semantic grounding, they often carry a heavy computational burden; on the contrary, simpler overlap- or one-to-one matching metrics are far less demanding, but frequently diverge from human judgments. In this paper, we introduce **SemQA**, a lightweight and accurate evidence scoring metric that combines transformer-based question scoring with bidirectional NLI entailment in answers. SemQA is then evaluated through correlation analysis with existing metrics, examination of representative examples, and human evaluations.

1 Introduction

Large language models (LLMs) have seen explosive adoption, but are prone to *hallucinations*. Xu et al. argue that this is a core limitation for LLMs. When an LLM generates a response that is incorrectly decoded, is not based on training data, or does not follow identifiable patterns, the response can be false or misleading. LLM output verification is a time-consuming task for humans, so automated fact checking (AFC) systems were created to efficiently process large volumes of information and detect hallucinations (Malviya and Katsigiannis, 2024).

The shared task FEVER (Fact Extraction and VERification)[1] has driven progress by providing a standardized framework and datasets for AFC systems to retrieve evidence and predict veracity labels. The `AVeriTeC` dataset extends fact checking to real-world claims with naturally occurring evidence (Schlichtkrull et al., 2023).

Traditional AFC evaluation methods often evaluate evidence solely based on predicted verdicts or by comparison of evidence retrieved with closed knowledge sources. Ev^{2}R (Akhtar et al., 2024) was introduced as an evaluation framework for AFC to counteract these limitations. In fact, Ev^{2}R outperforms many traditional evaluation approaches. However, being an LLM-driven framework, Ev^{2}R can be computationally intensive. Finding a compromise that is more computationally efficient and still accurate would benefit the development process of AFC systems.

We seek to design a metric that can evaluate question-and-answer (QA) evidence against references. Building on insights from Ev^{2}R, Hungarian METEOR (Kuhn, 1955), and soft weighting of question similarities, we propose **SemQA**. A **Sem**antic **Q**uestion and **A**nswer metric. Our work makes the following contributions;

- The design of SemQA, which combines question embeddings with natural language inference (NLI) answer entailment into a single tunable metric that is up to 5x faster than Ev^{2}R with correlation with human judgments.
- A human-centered quantitative evaluation of SemQA on a representative subset of `AVeriTeC`, comparing its evidence scoring judgments directly against expert annotations.

2 Related work

FEVER 2025 implements two main metrics for evidence evaluation: Ev^{2}R (Section 2.1) and Hungarian METEOR (Section 2.2). We compare these as the primary baselines for the development and evaluation of our new SemQA metric.

2.1 Ev^{2}R

Ev^{2}R has three different variations for evaluation (Akhtar et al., 2024); reference-based, proxy-based, and reference-less scorer. These scorers are evaluated on the basis of how well their predictions

[1]FEVER Workshop homepage: `https://fever.ai/index.html`

Proceedings of the Eighth Fact Extraction and VERification Workshop (FEVER), pages 184–200
July 31, 2025 ©2025 Association for Computational Linguistics

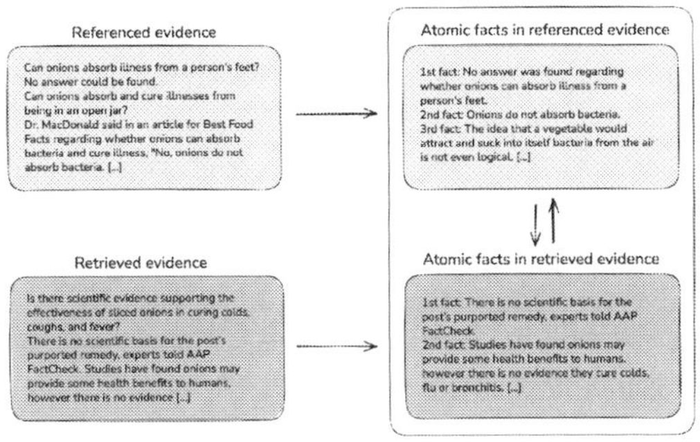

Figure 1: Example to visualize reference-based evaluation. The evidence is decomposed into atomic facts before evaluation. Illustration based on work of original author (Akhtar et al., 2024)

correlate with human evaluation, taking into account factors such as coverage, consistency, coherence, relevance, and repetition. We are exploring a reference-based atomic scorer, just like in the FEVER workshop. We deduce this on the basis of their implementation. The reference-based atomic scorer decomposes the retrieved evidence $\hat{E}$ and the referenced evidence E into atomic facts $A_{\hat{E}}$ and A_E. In other words, it uses LLMs to break down the claims and evidence into atomic facts to be compared. Figure 1 illustrates an example of this process.

The reference-based atomic scorer uses precision and recall scores. Precision refers to measuring the accuracy of the retrieved evidence, while recall is used to assess the completeness of the retrieved evidence $\hat{E}$ based on the gold standard. Akhtar et al. specifies the precision score s_{prec} as the ratio of facts supported by the referenced evidence:

$$s_{prec} = \frac{1}{|A_{\hat{E}}|} \sum_{a_{\hat{E}} \in A_{\hat{E}}} \mathbf{I}[a_{\hat{E}} \text{ supported by } E]$$

The scorer iterates over each fact ($a_{\hat{E}} \in A_{\hat{E}}$), and if a fact $a_{\hat{E}}$ is supported by the referenced evidence E, then the indicator function ($\mathbf{I}[a_{\hat{E}}$ supported by $E]$) returns 1. In the opposite case, 0 will be returned. The recall score s_{recall} measures how much the retrieved evidence $\hat{E}$ covers the content of the referenced evidence E. Here, it evaluates whether each atomic fact of the referenced evidence ($a_E \in A_E$) is supported by the retrieved evidence $\hat{E}$ or not:

$$s_{recall} = \frac{1}{|A_E|} \sum_{a_E \in A_E} \mathbf{I}[a_E \text{ supported by } \hat{E}]$$

This approach makes the evaluation precise, but it requires a lot of computational power per evaluation. In practice, this is a significant limitation as the cost will scale with the size of the model and the number of claims. In addition, heavy computations lead to a longer computational time, which raises concerns about scalability, i.e. the performance of evaluation as the evidence corpus size grows. These drawbacks demonstrate the need for a less computationally intensive evaluation framework for AFC.

The evaluations in the paper of Ev^{2}R (Akhtar et al., 2024) suggest that the reference-based atomic scorer correlates better with human evaluations than traditional metrics. Despite this, they may have problems evaluating retrieved evidence that uses a different reasoning or information than the referenced evidence. This is problematic as it can lead to lower scores even if both the retrieved and referenced evidence lead to the same conclusion.

2.2 Hungarian METEOR

Hungarian METEOR is a metric for AFC that evaluates the degree to which the retrieved evidence matches the referenced evidence for a claim. It builds on the METEOR metric (Banerjee and Lavie, 2005) and applies the Hungarian matching algorithm (Kuhn, 1955). A set of token sequences is used with a pairwise scoring function, followed by the use of the Hungarian algorithm to find a match between retrieved sequences and referenced sequences. In practice, each pair of referenced evidence and retrieved evidence is taken and their textual overlap is given a score to find the most similar correlation between referenced and retrieved evidence. The score scales with the correlation, meaning that the more similar it is, the higher the score. Schlichtkrull et al. calculate the total score using $f(\cdot)$ as a pairwise scoring function. $X(\cdot)$ is a binary assignment function, where a match gives 1, and no match gives 0. The result u, is the maximum similarity score under the one-to-one matching restraint between the referenced (Y) and retrieved evidence ($\hat{Y}$):

$$u_f(\hat{Y}, Y) = \frac{1}{|Y|} \max \sum_{\hat{y} \in \hat{Y}} \sum_{y \in Y} f(\hat{y}, y)\, X(\hat{y}, y)$$

Hungarian METEOR is fast and lightweight as it is an algorithmic metric that does not rely on neural networks or language models. This leads to a shorter computation time than the Ev^{2}R metric. However, this also means a limited semantic understanding. Akhtar et al. states that the use of token matching metrics, such as METEOR, is sensitive to surface forms and does not consider alternative evidence paths.

3 Methodology

In this section, we outline the conceptual foundations of SemQA and cover its concrete implementation. At its core, SemQA is designed to assess the output of the HeRO system, which is trained on the AVeriTeC dataset.

There are various approaches to evaluate AFC systems. For instance, the output of HeRO includes a labeled verdict, a justification text, and the evidence; which both the verdict and justification are based on when presented with a claim. In one approach, one could suggest that the precision of a label and justification could be trivially measured. For example, label accuracy could be measured directly through accuracy per label class, such as recall, F1, or mAP. Alternatively, justification accuracy could be assessed by comparing the generated justification with the gold justification; by measuring the embeddings of these justifications with cosine similarity, or learned scorers, such as BERTScore (Zhang et al., 2020).

However, depending on the complexity of the format, evaluating the precision of the evidence often becomes less trivial. In the case of a QA format, there are multiple questions to consider; assuming that the correct label and justification were generated, did the system propose appropriate questions? Will the generated answers lead to the same justification as before? Could any generated answers contradict the gold justification?

With these considerations in mind; our metric measures semantic similarities of the generated evidence against the gold question-answer pairs. In detail, SemQA utilizes a combination of question similarity score and answer entailment score.

3.1 Formulation

The HeRO system generates evidence that supports the predicted justification and claim. The generated evidence $\hat{E}$, is a set of question-answer pairs, $\hat{P} = \{\hat{Q}, \hat{A}\}$, i.e., $\hat{E} = \{\hat{P}_0, \ldots, \hat{P}_n\}$. For reference-based evaluation, the gold QA pairs $P = \{Q, A\}$, labels L, and justifications J are provided, allowing us to directly evaluate performance against the generated output. The gold QA pairs can thus be evaluated directly against the predicted. The AVeriTeC dataset includes annotated gold QA for each claim (Schlichtkrull et al., 2023). However, the number of annotated questions is limited to a finite set; HeRO returns a set of generated questions that could be more than the number of annotated questions. This is taken into account with SemQA.

3.2 Question Score

Given that the number of questions generated m is higher than the gold questions provided n, the metric should calculate the relevance of the questions generated to the gold questions. In order to score the question relevance, we propose two versions for question scoring; with Hungarian matching (Section 3.2.1) and softmax (Section 3.2.2).

3.2.1 Variation: Hungarian Matching

Instead of Hungarian METEOR matching (Section 2.2), we utilize a sentence transformer to encode the question sentences into an encoded embedding $e(Q), e(\hat{Q})$. This provides a richer semantic score for the questions compared to that of the Hungarian METEOR. Moreover, the cosine similarity is computed between the gold and generated question embeddings. This is followed by building a similarity matrix based on each similarity score, $S_{i,j}$. Finally, the cost is calculated, $C_{i,j}$, turning similarity into a cost such that lower similarity results in higher cost:

$$S_{i,j} = \cos\big(e(Q_i), e(\hat{Q}_j)\big),$$
$$C_{i,j} = 1 - S_{i,j}.$$

Using the Hungarian matching algorithm (Kuhn, 1955), $\mathrm{HM}(\cdot)$, we can find an assignment of gold questions to generated questions with the lowest total cost. This gives us N pairs of lowest cost:

$$\mathrm{HM}(C) = \{(i,j)\}_{i=1}^{N}.$$

Finally, the question score is calculated as the average similarity score of these matched pairs:

$$Q_{\text{score}} = \frac{1}{N} \sum_{(i,j)\,\in\,\mathrm{HM}(C)} S_{i,j}.$$

3.2.2 Variation: Softmax

As an alternative to hard one-to-one matching, we can aggregate all pairwise question similarities via soft weighting. After encoding questions with the same transformer $e(\cdot)$, we form the cosine similarity matrix:

$$S_{i,j} = \cos\big(e(Q_i), e(\hat{Q}_j)\big)$$

We then normalize each row of S into a probability distribution:

$$P_{i,j} = \frac{\exp(S_{i,j})}{\sum_{k=1}^{M} \exp(S_{i,k})}.$$

Intuitively, $P_{i,j}$ measures how strongly the generated questions $\hat{Q}_j$ overlap with the gold questions Q_i. Let $\mathcal{F}$ be all probabilities over the set threshold t:

$$\mathcal{F} = \{(i,j) \mid P_{i,j} > t\}$$

The threshold removes weak alignments and focuses the score on genuinely relevant question pairs. This can also leave only a small number of surviving alignments. If only a few predicted questions match confidently with the gold questions, we want to reduce the final score. To improve this, we introduce the normalization constant k:

$$k = \min\Big(1, \frac{|\mathcal{F}|}{\min(N, M)}\Big),$$

k is calculated by taking the number of matches after thresholding, $|\mathcal{F}|$, over the maximum number of one-to-one matches, $\min(N, M)$. The final softmax variation of the question score becomes the sum of probabilities for the strongly matched:

$$Q_{\text{score}} = k \times \frac{1}{|\mathcal{F}|} \sum_{(i,j)\in\mathcal{F}} P_{i,j}.$$

3.3 Answer Score

When evaluating the quality of the generated answers, we only consider those tied to confidently matched questions, $\mathcal{F}$. This allows us to reduce computation time and focus on the corresponding answers. Let $\{(i,j)\}$ be the set of gold and predicted pairs of questions, returned by our question matching step. For each such pair (i,j), we extract the gold answer A_i and the generated answer $\hat{A}_j$, and run a bidirectional NLI, i.e., entailment in both directions. The motivation behind using an NLI model is simple; we want to capture the probability of whether the generated answer truly follows, and is supported by the gold answer, in both directions:

$$p_{\text{fwd}}(i,j) = \text{Entail}\big(A_i \rightarrow \hat{A}_j\big)$$
$$p_{\text{bwd}}(i,j) = \text{Entail}\big(\hat{A}_j \rightarrow A_i\big)$$

$\text{Entail}(\cdot)$ is the probability of the "entailment" class after discarding the "neutral" dimension of NLI logits. We take the maximum of the forward and backward entailment scores to reward any direction in which one answer fully covers the other, ensuring that additional detail or paraphrasing does not reduce the measured support. Let $b_{i,j}$ be the strongest entailment for the given match i, j:

$$b_{i,j} = \max\big(p_{\text{fwd}}(i,j),\, p_{\text{bwd}}(i,j)\big).$$

Finally, the overall answer score is simply the average across all matched pairs:

$$A_{\text{score}} = \frac{1}{|\{(i,j)\}|} \sum_{(i,j)} b_{i,j}.$$

3.4 Weighted combination

Our metric balances question similarity and answer entailment with the hyperparameter α. By default, $\alpha = 0.5$. Setting a high α leads to more focus on question recall than answer entailment. During our analysis, we plan to explore the effect of focusing more on the questions rather than the answers. The metric is calculated as follows;

$$SemQA = \alpha \cdot Q_{\text{score}} + (1 - \alpha) \cdot A_{\text{score}}$$

3.5 Implementation Details

For the sentence transformer, we utilize the pretrained; `All Mpnet Base V2`[2]. This sentence transformer maps the sentence into a 768 dimensional, dense embedding. We selected the model due to its balanced trade-off between computational efficiency and semantic richness, making it well-suited for our evaluation metric. Then, for our NLI model, we utilize `BART` (Lewis et al., 2019).

4 Analysis and Results

We assess our metric through three forms of analyses. First, in Section 4.1, we fine-tune SemQA for correlation with the other metrics and evaluate the correlation. This is followed by computational efficiency in Section 4.2. Next, in Section 4.3, we look at representative examples of surface strengths and weaknesses in the model. Finally, in Section 4.4, we hold human evaluations for further examination of our metric.

4.1 Finetuning for Correlation

Our implementation has multiple tunable parameters and variations. This includes variations in question scores (Section 3.2), alpha α, and threshold. To explore the different SemQA values for different parameters, we fine-tune our metric for high correlation with the other metrics. First, leveraging the `HeRO` system (Yoon et al., 2024) with the instruction-tuned `Llama 3.3 70` model as a *"judge"* for evidence generation (Meta, 2024), we generate examples. Then, the generated output is utilized for both fine-tuning and evaluation.

[2]Link to sentence transformer: `https://huggingface.co/sentence-transformers/all-mpnet-base-v2`

To fine-tune our metric, we explored different alpha and threshold values for the metrics. Subsequently, we were interested in investigating the effect of the implemented variations. To evaluate SemQA, we compared it with the other metrics by Covariance, Pearson's r and Kendall's τ. Covariance is used to evaluate how the two metrics co-vary around their means, while Person's r correlation coefficient r measures the strength of a linear relationship between two normally distributed variables (Benesty et al., 2009). Kendall's τ assesses the ordinal association between two rankings by counting concordant and discordant pairs, providing a nonparametric measure of monotonic relationship that is robust to non-Gaussian distributions (Kendall, 1938). In addition, we performed a grid search on the `train-200` dataset (Table 1). The results are presented in Table 2.

DATASET	EXTRACTED SUBSET	EXAMPLES
`Train`	✗	3068
`Train-200`	✓	200
`Dev`	✗	500

Table 1: Overview of the dataset sizes for the project.

Table 2 demonstrates how SemQA correlates with four *off-the-shelf* metrics under five representative hyperparameter settings. In each row, we report on covariance, Pearson's r, and Kendall's τ for SemQA compared to baseline metrics for the `AVeriTeC` dataset (Schlichtkrull et al., 2023). The findings show a consistent alignment of the SemQA Hungarian matching variant with pure question recall (peak $r \approx 0.79$ and $\tau \approx 0.61$), in addition to maintaining moderate correlation with the Hungarian QA recall score ($r \approx 0.43$, $\tau \approx 0.26$).

In contrast, the softmax variant shows weaker correlations (peak $r \approx 0.45$, $\tau \approx 0.28$). Even after thresholding, the softmax variant still spreads the probability mass across all remaining pairs instead of focusing on a single, strongest match. Further analysis is done with the Hungarian variation of the question score ($\alpha = 0.8$ and threshold $= 0.2$).

4.2 Computational Efficiency

Table 3 presents the computation times for the different metrics. The results demonstrate that SemQA requires substantially less computational time than Ev^{2}R. However, it is still more expensive than pure surface-based approaches, such as Hungarian METEOR. These findings meet our expectations and suggest that SemQA is a suitable and less computationally intensive alternative to Ev^{2}R.

METRIC	TIME PER EXAMPLE (S)
Hungarian METEOR (Q)	**0.0374**
Hungarian METEOR (Q+A)	0.0738
AVeriTeC end-to-end	0.0697
Ev^{2}R Q-only recall	7.0180
Ev^{2}R Q+A recall	7.3836
SemQA	1.4935

Table 3: Average computation time per claim for each metric. Computed by using `NVIDIA A100 40GB PCIe` on the training subset (200 examples). Lowest computation time highlighted in bold.

4.3 Manual Evaluation

To explore how well SemQA captures semantic similarities of the evidence, we sampled and investigated five edge cases illustrated in Tables 4-7; the full examples are located in Appendix A Tables 11-14. We compare SemQA scores with the baseline metrics; Hungarian METEOR, Ev^{2}R Q-only recall and Ev^{2}R QA recall. We are interested in whether or not SemQA appropriately penalized or rewarded the retrieved evidence against the referenced evidence based on its meaning.

SAMPLE 16 (TAXES)	
GOLD QA	
Q1:	Has tax revenue risen since taxes were lowered in 2017
A1:	No, Really, Tax Revenue Has Not Risen
Q2:	What is the value of the total tax revenue in the 2017/2018 fiscal year since the TCJA was signed into law
A2:	Total revenue over the time period in question has actually fallen by 1.6 percent in real (inflation-adjusted) terms
GENERATED QA	
Q2:	Did the 2017 tax cuts lead to an increase in Treasury revenues?
A2:	The most recent CBO projections estimate further decreases in corporate tax revenue. The TCJA also reduced income taxes for most Americans, which led to a decline in revenues relative to prior projections.
Q6:	What was the change in payroll taxes after the tax cuts in 2017
A6:	In fact, payroll taxes fell only slightly—1.7%—from pre-TCJA projected values. This provides baseline credibility that reinforces the declines in other revenues.
Hungarian METEOR: **0.359**	Ev^{2}R Q-only: **0.50**
Ev^{2}R Q+A: **1.0**	SemQA: **0.689**

Table 4: Sample 16 with claim: *"We actually saw revenues to the Treasury increase after we lowered taxes in 2017. Rest assured the Democrats"*. The example shows that the metrics are not closely aligned. Full example in Appendix A Table 11.

In Table 4 we observe a moderately strong se-

α	threshold	variation	Q-only (Hungarian)			QA (Hungarian)			Ev^2R Q-only			Ev^2R QA		
			Cov	r	τ	Cov	r	τ	Cov	r	τ	Cov	r	τ
0.7	0.8	hungarian	0.020	0.714	0.517	0.010	0.434	0.262	0.022	0.377	0.248	0.020	0.362	0.200
0.9	0.2	hungarian	0.022	0.793	0.606	0.010	0.433	0.289	0.025	0.442	0.310	0.017	0.308	0.198
0.8	0.8	softmax	0.002	0.251	0.179	0.001	0.139	0.067	0.001	0.065	0.030	0.008	0.414	0.374
0.8	0.3	softmax	0.021	0.449	0.284	0.010	0.261	0.100	0.030	0.294	0.190	0.019	0.204	0.131
0.3	0.8	softmax	0.007	0.251	0.179	0.004	0.139	0.067	0.004	0.065	0.030	0.028	0.414	0.374

Table 2: Covariance, Pearson's r, and Kendall's τ between the SemQA composite score and each baseline metric under selected hyperparameter settings.

mantic match between the QA pairs which SemQA scores as 0.68, while Hungarian METEOR underestimates (0.35). The difference in Ev^2R QA (1.0) and Q-only (0.5) recall makes sense, due to the partial semantic match of generated questions and the strong alignment of answers. Compared to baseline metrics, SemQA rewards meaningful evidence paths more appropriately. In addition, this example demonstrates SemQA's recognition of paraphrases and partial entailment despite low token overlap. When considering the textual content of the QA pairs, we evaluate this score as accurate. Another example of this can be found in the Appendix A Table 10.

SAMPLE 120 (HARRIS STATEMENT)

GOLD QA

Q2: Where was the claim first published
A2: The claim was first published on bustatroll.org
Q3: What kind of website is bustatroll.org
A3: It is a satirical website and identifies as a subsidiary of America's Last line of Defense' network of parody, satire, and tomfoolery

GENERATED QA

Q2: Was the statement attributed to Kamala Harris actually made by her?
A2: Facebook users expressed outrage over a statement that's falsely attributed to Sen. Kamala Harris. The quote — about seeking "vengeance" against supporters of President Donald Trump — originated on a website that calls its work satire.
Q10: Is the quote attributed to Kamala Harris a genuine statement or a fabrication?
A10: Reuters, "Fact check: Kamala Harris quote on 'vengeance of a nation' fabricated by satire website," June 25, 2020

Hungarian METEOR: **0.166**	Ev^2R Q-only: **0.0**
Ev^2R Q+A: **0.0**	SemQA: **0.253**

Table 5: Sample 120 with claim: *"Kamala Harris said "And once Trump's gone and we have regained our rightful place in the White House, look out if you supported him and endorsed his actions, because we'll be coming for you next"*. All metrics show low scores. Full example in Appendix A Table 12.

Table 5 is an interesting case as all baseline metrics give poor scores (Ev^2R 0.0, Hungarian METEOR 0.16). The slightly higher SemQA score (0.25) is likely due to minimal overlap of the keyword *"satire"*. Demonstrating once again its ability to find semantic correlations.

In the case of highly semantic similarities, the generated answers in Table 6 mirror the gold answer sentence "I don't support defunding police". SemQA and both Ev^2R metrics gave an impressive score of 1.0, demonstrating that any rephrasing of the evidence was correctly captured and interpreted. This type of successful entailment is not accessible to Hungarian METEOR (0.37), which lags behind the other metrics in semantics.

SAMPLE 10 (BIDEN STATEMENT)

GOLD QA

Q1: Does Joe Biden support defunding the police?
A1: NO he said: "Federal dollars should not go to departments that violate people's rights or turn to violence as a first resort, but I donť support defunding police."

GENERATED QA

Q5: Does Joe Biden support defunding the police?
A5: "I do not support defunding police," Biden wrote in an op-ed for USA Today. "The better answer is to give police departments the resources they need to implement meaningful reforms, and to condition other federal dollars on completing those reforms.
Q7: Does Joe Biden support defunding the police?
A7: Presumptive Democratic nominee Joe Biden definitively declared "I do not support defunding police," in an op-ed Wednesday, as protesters around the country increase their calls for overhauling the criminal justice system and President Trump attempts to tie Biden to the "Defund the police" movement.

Hungarian METEOR: **0.375**	Ev^2R Q-only: **1.0**
Ev^2R Q+A: **1.0**	SemQA: **1.0**

Table 6: Sample 10 with claim: *"Biden has pledged to defund the police"*. All metrics show high score, and indicate an agreement. Full example in Appendix A Table 13.

Finally, Table 7 shows the gold QA stating that the Sputnik vaccine has not been thoroughly tested. The generated evidence mentions the status of the vaccine in terms of trials, registration, and safety concerns, but is not as explicit as the gold QA. One of the generated answers even states *"the vaccine developed by the Gamaleya Institute in Moscow is safe"* as part of a longer sentence, where the writing style can be misleading when not reading the full context. SemQA (0.47) sits between Hungarian METEOR (0.29) and the Ev^2R metrics (0.6/0.5), reflecting its nuanced partial mismatch.

SAMPLE 121 (RUSSIAN VACCINE)	
	GOLD QA
Q1:	Who has developed this vaccine?
A1:	'Sputnik V' has been developed by Moscow-based Gamaleya Research Institute of Epidemiology and Microbiology.
Q4:	Has it been thoroughly tested?
Q5:	Has it been tested for safety?
A4-A5:	No
	GENERATED QA
Q5:	Has the COVID-19 vaccine developed by Russia been proven to be safe and effective?
A5:	Scientists and public health officials are skeptical about Russian President Vladimir Putin's claim that the country's potential vaccine for the coronavirus "works quite effectively," saying Tuesday that the vaccine still needs critical testing to determine whether it's safe and effective.
Q8:	Has the COVID-19 vaccine developed by the Gamaleya Institute in Moscow been thoroughly tested?
A8:	Despite having only been in clinical trials for less than two months, the vaccine developed by the Gamaleya Institute in Moscow is safe, Putin said at a televised cabinet meeting, noting that it has already been given to one of his daughters, according to Reuters and The Washington Post.
Hungarian METEOR: **0.294**	Ev^2R Q-only: **0.6**
Ev^2R Q+A: **0.5**	SemQA: **0.476**

Table 7: Sample 121 with claim: *"Russia has successfully developed a vaccine for Covid-19 and it has passed all checks."*. SemQA aligns closely with Ev^2r, while Hungarian METEOR is much lower. Full example in Appendix A Table 14.

In summary, the sample in Table 4 shows that SemQA is able to identify evidence that is semantically correct but lexically divergent. This aligns with our expectations. SemQA measures deep semantic similarity instead of simple n-gram overlap as in Hungarian METEOR. SemQA successfully assigns low scores when the generated evidence simply mentions relevant terms without substantially matching the gold evidence, as we saw in Table 5. In borderline cases where evidence is partially similar but missing critical nuances, SemQA produced midrange scores that reflect partial support, illustrated in Table 7. This precision of false or misleading claims is highly relevant when evaluating AFC systems. Finally, Table 6 demonstrates SemQA's ability to identify the gold fact in different words that are semantically equivalent; reaching a full score of 1.0. The manual evaluation suggests that SemQA's use of sentence embeddings and entailment scoring is capturing semantic similarities by rewarding correct paraphrasing and penalizing insufficient evidence.

4.4 Human Evaluation

AFC systems rely on quantitative metrics to evaluate performance, but these metrics do not consider nuances and might give unrepresentative scores. Human feedback can point out shortcomings and recognize the difference between harmless and critical mistakes made. Human evaluations allows for a more qualitative analysis. Due to this, we wanted to investigate the accuracy of SemQA from a human point of view.

As SemQA calculates a score from 0-1 based on how semantically aligned the retrieved evidence is with the referenced evidence, it made sense to collect ordinal data to analyze this accuracy. Each evaluation set consisted of 10 examples of referenced evidence, retrieved evidence, and the SemQA score. For each example, the participants evaluated how accurate the SemQA score was on a scale of 1-7, where 1 = *"score should be much lower"*, 4 = *"score is accurate"*, and 7 = *"score should be much higher"*. This is illustrated by the instructions in Figure 3, and the example in Figure 4 in Appendix B.

In total, we had 22 participants with a background in computer science, informatics, or information technology of varying degrees. Most of the participants (15) are professionals working in the industry as developers, architects, or engineers. Including both in-house and consultant roles. The rest of the participants (7) are postgraduate students. All participants reside in the Oslo region, the majority of them being male (14), with only 8 female participants. We assigned the same evaluation set to a pair of participants, i.e. two annotators per evaluation set. Having 22 participants, this led to 11 different evaluation sets and a total of 110 examples.

Figure 2 illustrates a histogram of the frequency of each evaluation score, regardless of the example being evaluated. It illustrates the distribution of scores in human evaluation.

In the histogram, the majority of human evaluation scores are below 4.0, making up 48.64%. This means that according to the annotators, the SemQA score was too high. In other words, SemQA may sometimes over-reward evidence according to human evaluations. Only a minority of the evaluations marked the SemQA score as being too low; with

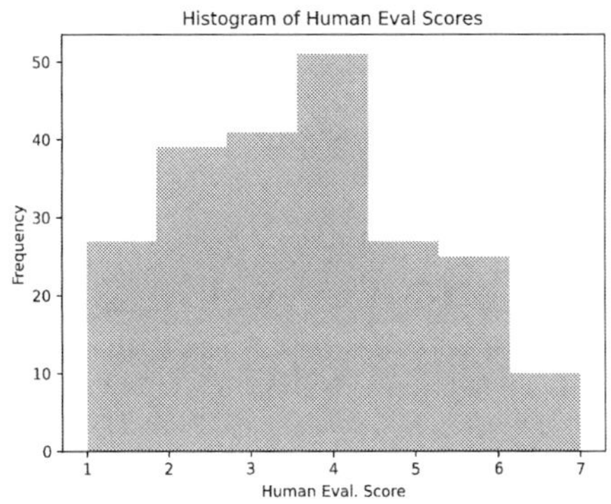

Figure 2: Histogram of frequency of human evaluation scores.

28.18% of human evaluation scores above 4.0. This suggests that SemQA over-rewards the evidence, not aligning itself with human evaluations.

In the histogram, the most frequent score is 4.0, making up 23.18%. This score marks the SemQA score as accurate. Human evaluation scores of 3.0-5.0 make up 54.09% of the distribution, indicating that the SemQA score was accurate or close to accurate.

To investigate this further, we made comparisons of individual evaluations. In Table 8 we see a SemQA score of 0.69 and human evaluation scores of 5 and 6. This means that the annotators agreed that the SemQA score should have been slightly to moderately higher. It is the opposite case for the SemQA score of 0.94; here the annotators gave a score of 1 and 2, both evaluating the SemQA score as too high. Then, the annotators disagree; one classified the SemQA score of 0.78 as too low (6), while the other annotator evaluated the SemQA score as accurate (4). These findings led us to further examine the consensus between the annotators.

SemQA	Ann.1	Ann.2	Consensus
0.69	6	5	Agreement
0.94	1	2	Agreement
0.78	4	6	Disagreement

Table 8: Comparison of individual human evaluations. Visual representations of these findings are supplemented in Appendix B Figures 5-7.

We found that 21 of 110 evaluations were in total agreement, representing 19.09%. The number of agreements with a tolerance of 1 made up 57 of 110 evaluations, or 51.82%. 85 of 110 evaluations were in agreement with a tolerance of 2, making up 77.27%.[3] This distribution shows a trend of a majority of annotators in relative agreement with each other when evaluating the accuracy of SemQA scores.

From the results of human evaluations, we calculated the mean, standard deviation, and median of all human evaluations. Table 9 shows a mean of 3.57, which is very close to 4.0. With this result, we interpret that according to human evaluations, SemQA is relatively accurate and manages to capture semantic similarities. The standard deviation is small, which tells us that the annotators agreed that the SemQA score was accurate.

HUMAN EVALUATION SCORES		
Mean	std	Median
3.5773	1.6756	4

Table 9: Calculations of human evaluation scores. Calculated by collecting all 220 human evaluation scores.

5 Conclusion

Our proposed metric, SemQA, is a reference-based metric that evaluates based on question-answer pairs. We show that a weighted question-and-answer score can be used to evaluate the evidence. SemQA relies on a sentence transformer and NLI model; where it is still able to compute five times faster than Ev^{2}r, while aligning with the Ev^{2}r metric. Our human evaluation confirms that SemQA reflects evidence quality more faithfully than overlap-based baselines. We believe that SemQA provides a practical, efficient, and reliable metric for the development and evaluation of automated fact-checking systems.

Limitations

Our metric assumes that the given evidence is based on question-and-answer pairs, i.e referenced based. Factual justification does not need to be in question-and-answer form only. In a different context, it makes sense to extract information into a summary of evidence. For example, `JustiLM` generates multi-sentence justifications by retrieving and synthesizing evidence into fluent text, rather than question-answer pairs (Zeng and Gao, 2024).

Our metric is a reference-based evaluation framework of questions and answers. The dependence

[3]Tolerance in this context refers to scores above or below the referenced one. For example, a score of 4 with a tolerance of 1 refers to scores 3-5.

of references are tightly in the design of the metric. Without annotated gold question and answers, applying our metric would require to extract gold question and answers first.

Further Work

Further work might explore ways to generalize the metric to other formats beyond question-and-answer pairs. Such formats could be free-text or structured multi-sentence evidence. This would make the metric applicable to a larger number of fact-verification systems.

References

Mubashara Akhtar, Michael Schlichtkrull, and Andreas Vlachos. 2024. Ev^{2}r: Evaluating evidence retrieval in automated fact-checking. *Preprint*, arXiv:2411.05375.

Satanjeev Banerjee and Alon Lavie. 2005. METEOR: An automatic metric for MT evaluation with improved correlation with human judgments. In *Proceedings of the ACL Workshop on Intrinsic and Extrinsic Evaluation Measures for Machine Translation and/or Summarization*, pages 65–72, Ann Arbor, Michigan. Association for Computational Linguistics.

Jacob Benesty, Jingdong Chen, Yiteng Huang, and Israel Cohen. 2009. Pearson correlation coefficient. In *Noise reduction in speech processing*, pages 37–40. Springer.

Maurice G Kendall. 1938. A new measure of rank correlation. *Biometrika*, 30(1-2):81–93.

H. W. Kuhn. 1955. The hungarian method for the assignment problem. *Naval Research Logistics Quarterly*, 2(1-2):83–97.

Mike Lewis, Yinhan Liu, Naman Goyal, Marjan Ghazvininejad, Abdelrahman Mohamed, Omer Levy, Ves Stoyanov, and Luke Zettlemoyer. 2019. Bart: Denoising sequence-to-sequence pre-training for natural language generation, translation, and comprehension. *Preprint*, arXiv:1910.13461.

Shrikant Malviya and Stamos Katsigiannis. 2024. SK_DU team: Cross-encoder based evidence retrieval and question generation with improved prompt for the AVeriTeC shared task. In *Proceedings of the Seventh Fact Extraction and VERification Workshop (FEVER)*, pages 99–107, Miami, Florida, USA. Association for Computational Linguistics.

Meta. 2024. Meta llama 3.3 70b. Release Date: December 6, 2024.

Michael Schlichtkrull, Zhijiang Guo, and Andreas Vlachos. 2023. Averitec: A dataset for real-world claim verification with evidence from the web. *Preprint*, arXiv:2305.13117.

Ziwei Xu, Sanjay Jain, and Mohan Kankanhalli. 2025. Hallucination is inevitable: An innate limitation of large language models. *Preprint*, arXiv:2401.11817.

Yejun Yoon, Jaeyoon Jung, Seunghyun Yoon, and Kunwoo Park. 2024. Hero at averitec: The herd of open large language models for verifying real-world claims. *Preprint*, arXiv:2410.12377.

Fengzhu Zeng and Wei Gao. 2024. Justilm: Few-shot justification generation for explainable fact-checking of real-world claims. *Preprint*, arXiv:2401.08026.

Tianyi Zhang, Varsha Kishore, Felix Wu, Kilian Q. Weinberger, and Yoav Artzi. 2020. Bertscore: Evaluating text generation with bert. *Preprint*, arXiv:1904.09675.

A Examples from Analysis

Example 89 (Mail-in Ballot)

Claim: In the US, envelopes used for mail-in ballots in general elections reveal the party affiliation of the voter allowing postal workers to toss votes.

Gold QA

Q1: Do ballot envelopes in general elections, show who the voter voted for?
A1: No

Q2: When are indications shown on the envelope?
A2: The office of the supervisor of elections for Palm Beach County, Florida — where the envelopes in the Facebook posts were sent — confirmed that in a statement to FactCheck.org. In a closed primary, "voters are sent ballots according to their precinct and their party affiliation. The ballots in that video are primary ballots." The alphanumeric codes on the envelopes shown in the video are used to direct the ballots for counting.

Generated QA

Q1: Can postal workers tamper with mail-in ballots in the US?
A1: (2/3) each other. Because of this, voters are sent ballots according to their party affiliation. It would be a federal crime for any post office employee to tamper with this process and we have received no such reports of anything like this happening.

Q2: Do envelopes used for mail-in ballots in general elections in the US include any information that could reveal the party affiliation of the voter?
A2: Return envelopes for all election ballots must include prepaid postage. Service and overseas voters must be provided with instructions and a privacy sheet for returning the ballot and signed declaration by fax or email.
Q3: What information is verified by the SVC when there is an SVC on an envelope ballot by mail?
A3: envelope ballots by mail. If there is a SVC, the SVC must verify the signatures before the EVBB

Q4: Are the envelopes used for mail-in ballots in the US sealed to prevent postal workers from seeing the party affiliation of the voter?
A4: that all ballot envelopes are sealed or that authorized personnel accompany the ballots to the Post Office or
Q5: Are mail-in ballots in general elections in the US sent in secrecy envelopes?
A5: secrecy envelopes, if used by the voter. (The EVBB has the discretion to open a ballot secrecy
Q6: Do mail-in ballots in the US guarantee the secrecy of a voter's ballot?
A6: A voter who returns a ballot electronically is deemed to have acknowledged that there may be situations where the secrecy of that voter's ballot cannot be guaranteed.
Q7: Do envelopes used for mail-in ballots in general elections in the US reveal the party affiliation of the voter?
A7: absentee ballot. However, applications and ballot envelopes of the temporarily or permanently disabled are not
Q8: How do the return envelopes for mail-in ballots in the US, as described in 39 U.S.C. 3406, affect the secrecy of the vote?
A8: Return envelopes for overseas and service voters must enable the ballot to be returned postage free if mailed through the United States postal service, United States armed forces postal service, or the postal service of a United States foreign embassy under 39 U.S.C. 3406.
Q9: How do states ensure the secrecy of mail-in ballots in the US?
A9: States Postal Service (USPS). The voter must be notified if the return envelope
Q10: Do envelopes used for mail-in ballots in general elections in the US reveal the party affiliation of the voter?
A10: (1) The county auditor shall send each voter a ballot, a security envelope in which to conceal the ballot after voting, a larger envelope in which to return the security envelope, a declaration that the voter must sign, and instructions on how to obtain information about the election, how to mark the ballot, and how to return the ballot to the county auditor.

Scores:

Hungarian METEOR	Ev^{2}R Q-only	Ev^{2}R Q+A	SemQA
0.373	0.50	0.667	0.548

Table 10: Example 89. Claim: *"In the US, envelopes used for mail-in ballots in general elections reveal the party affiliation of the voter allowing postal workers to toss votes"*. This example shows that the metrics are closely aligned.

Example 16 (Taxes)

Claim: We actually saw revenues to the Treasury increase after we lowered taxes in 2017. Rest assured the Democrats do not want you to know that.

Gold QA

Q1: Has tax revenue risen since taxes were lowered in 2017
A1: No, Really, Tax Revenue Has Not Risen

Q2: What is the value of the total tax revenue in the 2017/2018 fiscal year since the Tax Cuts and Jobs Act (TCJA) was signed into law
A2: Total revenue over the time period in question has actually fallen by 1.6 percent in real (inflation-adjusted) terms

Generated QA

Q1: Did the tax cuts in 2017 lead to an increase in Treasury revenues in the following year?
A1: While some TCJA supporters observe that nominal revenues were higher in fiscal year 2018 (which began Oct. 1, 2017) than in FY2017, that comparison does not address the question of the TCJA's effects.

Q2: Did the 2017 tax cuts lead to an increase in Treasury revenues?
A2: The most recent CBO projections estimate further decreases in corporate tax revenue. The TCJA also reduced income taxes for most Americans, which led to a decline in revenues relative to prior projections.

Q3: According to the Congressional Budget Office, what were the projected corporate tax revenues for fiscal years 2018 and 2019 before the 2017 tax cuts?
A3: Several months before the TCJA was enacted, the Congressional Budget Office (CBO) projected that corporate tax revenues for fiscal years 2018 and 2019 would total $668 billion.

Q4: Did the actual amount of revenue collected by the US Treasury in FY2018 match the Congressional Budget Office's (CBO) projection made in January 2017?
A4: In fact, the actual amount of revenue collected in FY2018 was significantly lower than the Congressional Budget Office's (CBO) projection of FY2018 revenue made in January 2017—before the tax cuts were signed into law in December 2017.

Q5: Did the 2017 tax cut lead to an increase in tax revenue collected by the Treasury?
A5: The actual amount of tax revenue collected in FY2018 was significantly lower than the CBO's projection made in January 2017—before the tax cut was signed into law.

Q6: What was the change in payroll taxes after the tax cuts in 2017?
A6: In fact, payroll taxes fell only slightly—1.7%—from pre-TCJA projected values (Figure 2). This provides baseline credibility that reinforces the declines in other revenues.

Q7: How did the actual tax revenue in FY2018 compare to the predicted tax revenue in FY2018 if the Tax Cuts and Jobs Act (TCJA) had not been passed?
A7: The most appropriate test of the revenue impact of the TCJA is to compare actual revenues in FY2018 with predicted revenues in FY2018 assuming Congress had not passed the legislation.

Q8: According to the CBO, what was the projected change in corporate tax revenue after the 2017 tax cuts?
A8: In the forecast published soon after the TCJA was enacted, however, the CBO projected $519 billion in corporate tax revenue over those two years—a $149 billion decrease.

Q9: Did corporate tax revenue decrease after the 2017 tax bill?
A9: Since the TCJA was enacted, corporate tax revenue has been down from its projected level by about one-third, even as pretax corporate profits have continued to rise toward historic highs.

Q10: How did the 2017 tax cuts affect federal revenue according to the evidence?
A10: The individual income tax changes are scheduled to expire after December 31, 2025. If permanent, the income tax provisions would reduce federal revenue by $165 billion per year on a conventional basis, but when incorporating economic growth and feedback, on a dynamic basis, they would reduce federal revenue by $115 billion a year.

Scores:

Hungarian METEOR	Ev^2R Q-only	Ev^2R Q+A	SemQA
0.359	0.5	1	0.689

Table 11: Example 16. Claim: *"We actually saw revenues to the Treasury increase after we lowered taxes in 2017. Rest assured the Democrats"*. The example shows that the metrics are not very well aligned with each other.

Example 120 (Harris statement)

Claim: Kamala Harris said "And once Trump's gone and we have regained our rightful place in the White House, look out if you supported him and endorsed his actions, because we'll be coming for you next".

Gold QA

Q1: When was the claim made
A1: 11/08/2020

Q2: Where was the claim first published
A2: The claim was first published on bustatroll.org

Q3: What kind of website is bustatroll.org
A3: It is a satirical website and identifies as a subsidiary of America's Last line of Defense' network of parody, satire, and tomfoolery

Generated QA

Q1: Did Kamala Harris make a statement about punishing Trump supporters after his impeachment?
A1: "Kamala Harris: 'After We Impeach, We Round Up The Trump Supporters,'" the story's headline reads. While Harris has supported beginning impeachment proceedings against Trump, the story presents an otherwise imagined tale about a Harris speech.

Q2: Was the statement attributed to Kamala Harris actually made by her?
A2: Facebook users expressed outrage over a statement that is falsely attributed to Sen. Kamala Harris. The quote — about seeking "vengeance" against supporters of President Donald Trump — originated on a website that calls its work satire.

Q3: What did Kamala Harris say would happen to Trump supporters after he leaves office?
A3: CLAIM: Kamala Harris, a U.S. senator and former Democratic presidential candidate from California, said on June 18 that once President Trump is no longer in office "and we have regained our rightful place in the White House," his supporters will feel the "vengeance of a nation."

Q4: What did Kamala Harris say would happen to Trump supporters after he leaves office?
A4: CLAIM: Kamala Harris, a U.S. senator and former Democratic presidential candidate from California, said on June 18 that once President Trump is no longer in office "and we have regained our rightful place in the White House," his supporters will feel the "vengeance of a nation."

Q5: Did Kamala Harris make a statement threatening to target people who supported Trump after he leaves office?
A5: A statement first attributed to Democratic Sen. Kamala Harris in a made-up story is now making the rounds on social media as if it's real.

Q6: Did Kamala Harris say "And once Trump's gone and we have regained our rightful place in the White House, look out if you supported him and endorsed his actions, because we'll be coming for you next"?
A6: Though Harris has been vocal in her criticism of Trump, an online search for the words in the post returned no evidence she had ever said them.

Q7: Did Kamala Harris make the statement "And once Trump's gone and we have regained our rightful place in the White House, look out if you supported him and endorsed his actions, because we'll be coming for you next"?
A7: Chris Harris, the senator's communications director, also confirmed the quote is not real. Kamala Harris is one of several women still in consideration to be Joe Biden's running mate in the 2020 presidential election, The Associated Press has reported.

Q8: What did Kamala Harris allegedly say about Trump supporters at a rally?
A8: The bogus Facebook posts claim that Harris, a 2020 presidential candidate, said at a rally that she will seek "vengeance" against supporters of President Donald Trump.

Q9: Did Kamala Harris issue a threat to supporters of President Donald Trump?
A9: An image shared widely on Facebook claims that U.S. Sen. Kamala Harris issued a bold threat to supporters of President Donald Trump.

Q10: Is the quote attributed to Kamala Harris a genuine statement or a fabrication?
A10: Reuters, "Fact check: Kamala Harris quote on 'vengeance of a nation' fabricated by satire website," June 25, 2020

Scores:

Hungarian METEOR	Ev^2R Q-only	Ev^2R Q+A	SemQA
0.166	0.00	0.00	0.253

Table 12: Example 120. Claim: *"Kamala Harris said "And once Trump's gone and we have regained our rightful place in the White House, look out if you supported him and endorsed his actions, because we'll be coming for you next"*. All metrics show low score.

Example 10 (Biden statement)

Claim: Biden has pledged to defund the police

Gold QA

Q1: Does Joe Biden support defunding the police?
A1: NO he said: "Federal dollars should not go to departments that violate people's rights or turn to violence as a first resort, but I donť support defunding police."

Generated QA

Q1: Does Joe Biden's police reform plan involve defunding the police?
A1: In fact, Biden's police reform plan calls for $300 million in funding for community-oriented policing, a portion of which would go toward hiring more police, which has been sharply criticized by some progressive Democrats.

Q2: What specific reforms to policing did Biden's criminal justice plan propose?
A2: Biden unveiled a criminal justice plan last year that tackled reforms to policing. The proposal calls for an injection of $300 million into the Community Oriented Policing Services program, which authorized money for the hiring of more police officers and policing training.

Q3: Does Joe Biden support the idea of defunding the police?
A3: Biden's campaign rejected the phrase "defund the police" and called for more funding for police departments to implement policy changes.

Q4: Does Joe Biden support defunding the police, or does he support conditioning federal aid to police departments based on certain standards?
A4: Former Vice President Joe Biden says he doesn't support defunding police, but he does support conditioning federal aid on whether police meet "certain basic standards of decency and honorableness.

Q5: Does Joe Biden support defunding the police?
A5: "I do not support defunding police," Biden wrote in an op-ed for USA Today. "The better answer is to give police departments the resources they need to implement meaningful reforms, and to condition other federal dollars on completing those reforms.

Q6: Does Joe Biden support the slogan "defund the police"?
A6: Biden's opposition to defunding police departments puts him at odds with activists and some progressive lawmakers who have amplified the slogan "defund the police" during demonstrations that have erupted nationwide in the wake of George Floyd's death in Minneapolis.

Q7: Does Joe Biden support defunding the police?
A7: Presumptive Democratic nominee Joe Biden definitively declared "I do not support defunding police," in an op-ed Wednesday, as protesters around the country increase their calls for overhauling the criminal justice system and President Trump attempts to tie Biden to the "Defund the police" movement.

Q8: Does Joe Biden support reducing the budget for local police departments?
A8: Biden's campaign had said earlier Monday that he backs advocates' calls to increase spending on social programs separate from local police budgets, but he also wants more funding for police reforms such as body cameras and training on community policing approaches.

Q9: What did Joe Biden suggest doing with police funding in the context of the interview with Ady Barkan?
A9: In fact, Biden was responding to a question not about defunding the police but about shifting some funding to social service agencies: "But do we agree that we can redirect some of the funding?" progressive activist Ady Barkan asked in a July 8 interview.

Q10: Does the phrase "defund the police" refer to eliminating police departments entirely or revisiting their functions and shifting funding to other services?
A10: While some argue police departments should be eliminated entirely, as PolitiFact National detailed in a June 9, 2020 article, the use of the phrase "defund the police" more typically means to revisit the functions of police departments and shift funding toward, for instance, mental health and social services.

Scores:

Hungarian METEOR	Ev^2R Q-only	Ev^2R Q+A	SemQA
0.375	1	1	1

Table 13: Example 10. Claim: *"Biden has pledged to defund the police".* All metrics show high score, and indicate an agreement.

Example 121 (Russian vaccine)

Claim: Russia has successfully developed a vaccine for Covid-19 and it has passed all checks.

Gold QA

Q1: Who has developed this vaccine?
A1: 'Sputnik V' has been developed by Moscow-based Gamaleya Research Institute of Epidemiology and Microbiology.

Q2: When was it first registered?
A2: It was registered by the Russian health ministry on August 11 as the first registered Covid-19 vaccine in the market but The certificate mentions that "the vaccine cannot be used widely until 1 January 2021", presumably after larger clinical trials are completed.

Q3: What kind of vaccine is it?
A3: The Russian vaccine is an "adenovirus vector-based vaccine".The idea is to use the weakened common cold virus to stimulate an immune response and trigger the formation of antibodies against Covid-19. These anti-bodies are then ready to fight against Covid-19 in case one catches a coronavirus infection. Even the widely awaited Oxford University vaccine is exploring the same route.

Q4: Has it been thoroughly tested?
A4: No

Q5: Has it been tested for safety?
A5: No

Generated QA

Q1: Has the COVID-19 vaccine developed by Russia completed all necessary clinical trials?
A1: Russia has not yet published any scientific data from its first clinical trials. The WHO's list of vaccine candidates in human testing still lists the Gamaleya product as in Phase 1 trials.

Q2: Has the COVID-19 vaccine developed by Russia completed a phase-three trial before its approval?
A2: But the vaccine's approval by Russian regulators comes before the completion of a larger study involving thousands of people, known as a phase-three trial.

Q3: Has the COVID-19 vaccine developed by Russia been proven to be safe and effective?
A3: Russian President Vladimir Putin announced the approval of a coronavirus vaccine for use on Tuesday, claiming it as a "world first," amid continued concern and unanswered questions over its safety and effectiveness.

Q4: How long did it take for the clinical trials of the Russian vaccine to be completed?
A4: Clinical trials of the Russian vaccine have been completed in less than two months and phase three trials are set to begin shortly, despite the vaccine having already been registered.

Q5: Has the COVID-19 vaccine developed by Russia been proven to be safe and effective?
A5: Scientists and public health officials are skeptical about Russian President Vladimir Putin's claim that the country's potential vaccine for the coronavirus "works quite effectively," saying Tuesday that the vaccine still needs critical testing to determine whether it's safe and effective.

Q6: How long did it take for the clinical trials of the Russian vaccine to be completed?
A6: Clinical trials of the Russian vaccine have been completed in less than two months and phase three trials are set to begin Wednesday, despite the vaccine having already been registered.

Q7: Does Russia have sufficient data to support the safety of its newly approved COVID-19 vaccine?
A7: Russian President Vladimir Putin says his country has become the first in the world to formally approve a new COVID-19 vaccine, despite a lack of data to back up his claims that the drug is safe to administer to humans.

Q8: Has the COVID-19 vaccine developed by the Gamaleya Institute in Moscow been thoroughly tested?
A8: Despite having only been in clinical trials for less than two months, the vaccine developed by the Gamaleya Institute in Moscow is safe, Putin said at a televised cabinet meeting, noting that it has already been given to one of his daughters, according to Reuters and The Washington Post.

Q9: What stages of clinical trials has the Russian Covid-19 vaccine completed?
A9: Few details have been made available about the Russian vaccine so far, but its approval was based on only the first two phases of clinical trials, which are designed to make early assessments on whether a potential vaccine can induce an immune response, and whether it's safe to administer in humans.

Q10: Has Russia's Covid-19 vaccine been proven to be safe and effective?
A10: Scientists are skeptical about Putin's claims on Russia's potential Covid-19 vaccine, saying the vaccine still needs critical data to determine whether it's safe or effective.

Scores:

Hungarian METEOR	Ev^{2}R Q-only	Ev^{2}R Q+A	SemQA
0.294	0.6	0.5	0.476

Table 14: Example 121. Claim: *"Russia has successfully developed a vaccine for Covid-19 and it has passed all checks."*. SemQA aligns closely with Ev^{2}r, while Hungarian METEOR is much lower.

B Human Evaluation form for SemQA Evaluation

SemQA Human Evaluation

Evaluation set 1 of metric for automated fact checking systems

Thank you!

First of all, thank you for your participation! 😊 Your answers in this questionnaire are valuable to us and will be used to enhance our analysis in the paper we are currently writing as part of our exam in Neural Methods for Natural Language Processing.

Context

The project is related to the use of LLMs for fact verification. When an LLM generates a response that is incorrectly decoded, not based on training data, or not following identifiable patterns, the response can be false or misleading. Fact-checking LLM outputs is time-consuming for humans, so automated fact-checking (AFC) systems were created to efficiently process large volumes of information and detect hallucinations. The metrics used to evaluate these AFC systems can be computationally intensive both in cost and time. We have investigated the benefits and drawbacks of these evaluation frameworks, and used this insight to create a new evaluation framework for AFC systems that is less computationally intensive. We call this metric SemQA (Semantic Question and Answer).

Why am I here?

AFC systems rely on quantitative metrics to evaluate performance, but these metrics do not consider nuances and might give unrepresentative scores. Human feedback can point out shortcomings and recognize the difference between harmless and critical mistakes made. Human evaluations allows for a more qualitative analysis of the performance of our SemQA metric.

How does it work?

In this project we have produced a dataset of claims, labels (supported/refuted/not enough evidence/etc...), generated/retrieved evidence, referenced evidence, and different types of metrics. SemQA calculates a score from 0-1 based on how semantically aligned the retrieved evidence is with the referenced evidence (semantically aligned in this context means how similar are the two texts). The more similar it is, the higher the score.

What will I do?

You will be given 10 questions. For each question you will be shown a set of retrieved evidence, referenced evidence, and the SemQA score. You will evaluate how accurate the SemQA metric is (in your opinion) on a scale from 1-7, where 1 = score should be much lower, 4 = score is accurate, 7 = score should be much higher 😊

Figure 3: Instructions to participants for human evaluations

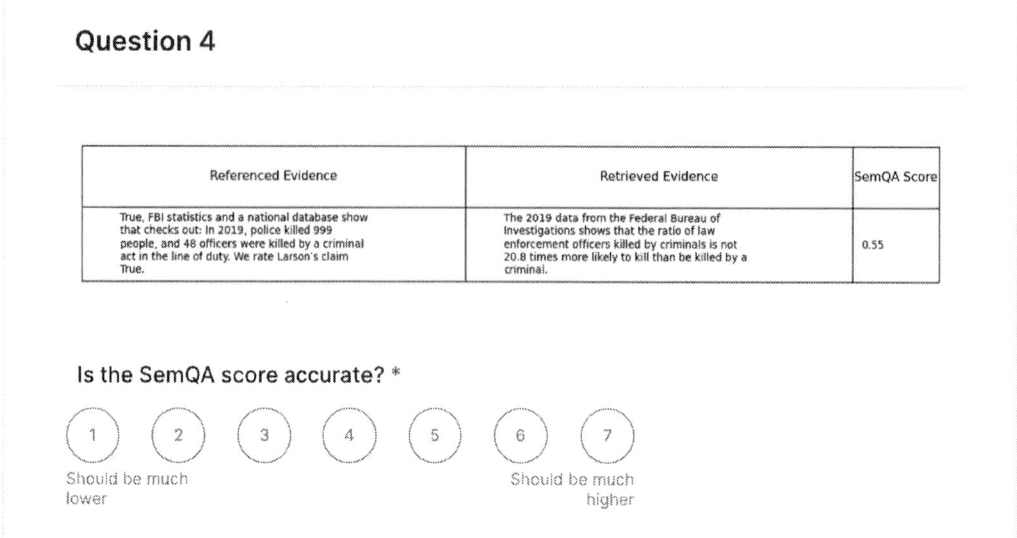

Question 4

Referenced Evidence	Retrieved Evidence	SemQA Score
True, FBI statistics and a national database show that checks out: In 2019, police killed 999 people, and 48 officers were killed by a criminal act in the line of duty. We rate Larson's claim True.	The 2019 data from the Federal Bureau of Investigations shows that the ratio of law enforcement officers killed by criminals is not 20.8 times more likely to kill than be killed by a criminal.	0.55

Is the SemQA score accurate? *

1 2 3 4 5 6 7

Should be much lower — Should be much higher

Figure 4: Example question in evaluation set for human evaluations

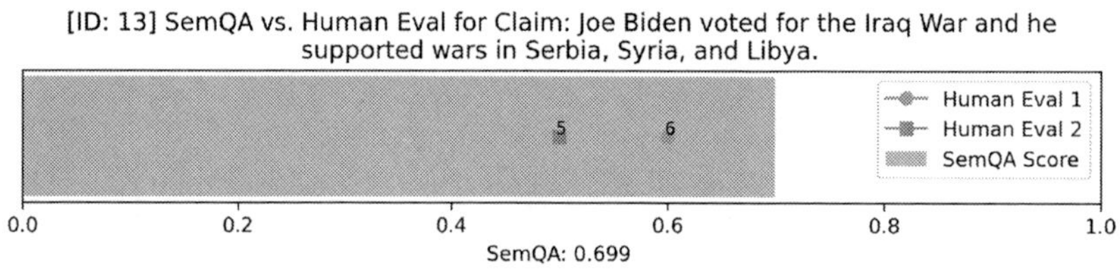

Figure 5: Comparison of SemQA score and human evaluations. Human evaluations of 5 and 6 means the SemQA score of 0.69 should have been slightly to moderately higher according to the annotators.

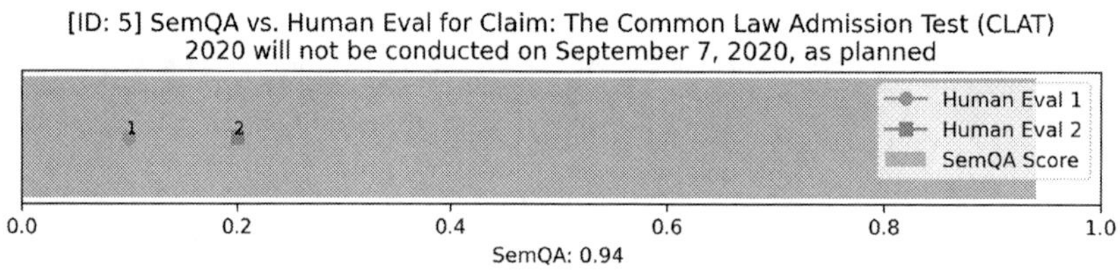

Figure 6: Comparison of SemQA score and human evaluations. Human evaluations of 1 and 2 means the SemQA score of 0.94 should have been far lower according to the annotators.

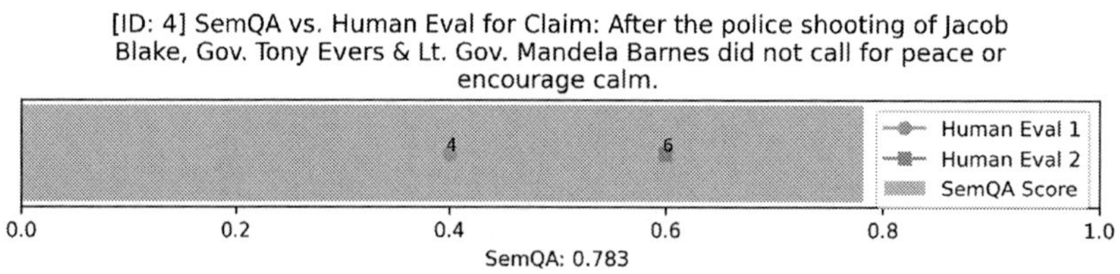

Figure 7: Comparison of SemQA score and human evaluations. Human evaluations of 4 and 6 means the annotators disagree; one marks the SemQA score of 0.78 as accurate, while the other marks the score as too low.

The 2nd Automated Verification of Textual Claims (AVeriTeC) Shared Task: Open-weights, Reproducible and Efficient Systems

Mubashara Akhtar[1], Rami Aly[2], Yulong Chen[2], Zhenyun Deng[2], Michael Schlichtkrull[2,3], Chenxi Whitehouse[2,4], Andreas Vlachos[2]

[1]ETH Zurich, [2]University of Cambridge, [3]Queen Mary University of London, [4]Meta,
mubashara.akhtar@ai.ethz.ch, {rmya2,yc632,zd302,cj507,av308}@cam.ac.uk
m.schlichtkrull@qmul.ac.uk

Abstract

In the First Automated Verification of Textual Claims (AVERITEC) shared task, participating teams developed systems that for each claim retrieve evidence from the web and predict its veracity. While there was progress in automated fact-checking for real-world claims, the majority of the systems proposed relied on large closed-weights language models, which rendered them expensive to run and less reproducible. To ameliorate this issue, in this year's edition of the AVERITEC shared task, we required system to use only open-weights models that could be run using a single GPU with 23GBs of RAM, and that systems should take one minute or less to return verdicts accompanied by evidence retrieved from a pre-compiled knowledge store. The shared task received 7 submissions; 6 of which exceeded the accuracy of our baseline on the test set, while they ran in under a minute per claim on the hardware we had specified. The winning team was CTU AIC with an AVERITEC score of 33.17%. In this paper we describe the shared task in detail and highlight key findings.

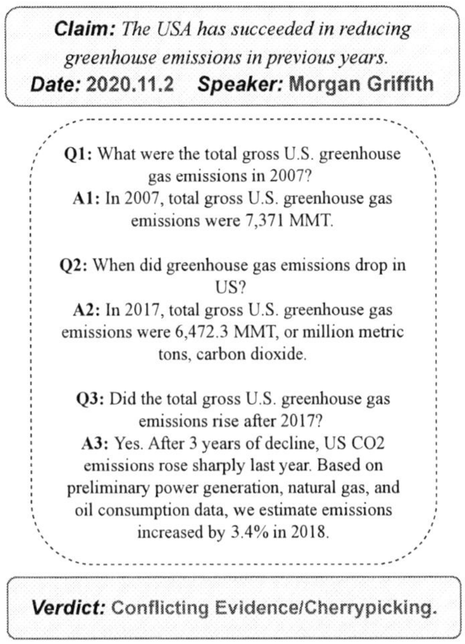

Figure 1: Example instance from AVERITEC. Given a claim and associated metadata, participating systems must first retrieve appropriate evidence. Then, they must output a verdict for the claim given that evidence.

1 Introduction

Automated fact-checking (AFC) has been proposed as an assistive tool for beleaguered fact-checkers (Cohen et al., 2011; Vlachos and Riedel, 2014), whose work is crucial for limiting misinformation (Lewandowsky et al., 2020). This has inspired applications in journalism (Miranda et al., 2019; Dudfield, 2020; Nakov et al., 2021) and other domains, e.g. science (Wadden et al., 2020). While there had been progress on many benchmarks, these were limited in their ability to measure progress in terms of evidence retrieval. For example, FEVER (Thorne et al., 2018) relied on Wikipedia as its only source of evidence, in addition to consisting of purpose-made rather than real-world claims. Liar Liar Pants on Fire (Wang, 2017) consists of real-world claims but it has no evidence annotated to evaluate retrieval, while in MultiFC (Augenstein et al., 2019) the evidence is annotated automatically and thus cannot be relied upon for evaluation (Glockner et al., 2022).

The recently proposed AVERITEC dataset (Schlichtkrull et al., 2023a) addressed these limitations. It consists of real-world claims where the evidence is manually annotated in the form of questions and answers sourced from the Web (see Figure 1 for an example). This evidence had to be available before the claim was made, and was additionally verified to adequately support the verdict, thus avoiding the issues of temporal leakage and evidence insufficiency identified in earlier datasets (Ousidhoum et al., 2022; Glockner et al., 2022).

Proceedings of the Eighth Fact Extraction and VERification Workshop (FEVER), pages 201–223
July 31, 2025 ©2025 Association for Computational Linguistics

In the first AVERITEC shared task (Schlichtkrull et al., 2024), a number of systems were proposed that substantially improved the results on the task compared to the baseline proposed with the dataset. However, most relied on closed-weights large language models (LLMs) with substantial (and unverified) parameter counts, including the top-performing system (Rothermel et al., 2024). While the tremendous progress achieved was inspiring, and the evaluation of commercial LLMs in the context of automated fact-checking was of high practical significance, this result has a number of shortcomings from a research perspective.

First, the systems rely on external LLMs via APIs that have no control over them; thus it is difficult to reproduce their results, and as LLM provider change their offering overtime, it becomes impossible. Second, the costs of developing such approaches could be substantial depending on the size of the LLMs used. Thus, the financial ability to use such commercial services affected the chances of achieving good results on the shared task. More problematically, journalistic fact-checkers, the most common intended user for automated fact-checking tools (Schlichtkrull et al., 2023b), often operate under strong resource constraints and cite cost as a major deciding factor for the adoption of technologies (Warren et al., 2025). Expensive models may as such not be able to match their desired real-world function. Last but not least, systems relying on external LLMs can be less practical to use in real-world contexts, where latency due to network limitations and/or privacy concerns are important considerations.

For these reasons, in this second edition of the AVERITEC shared task, we decided to focus on open-weights, reproducible and efficient systems. Participating systems were constrained to run using a single GPU taking a maximum of one minute per claim to return their verdicts. This runtime included retrieving evidence from a pre-compiled knowledge store consisting of documents returned by a commercial search engine. Note that participants were allowed to use larger and/or close-weights LLMs for training, these restrictions only applied to inference. Similar to the first edition of the shared task, this knowledge store contains the manually annotated evidence that systems need to return with their verdicts, but also a lot of other related search results. It was preferred over offering systems the option to access a commercial search engine directly as it is free to use by the participants (and it was the preferred option by most of them in the first edition), but also that participating systems did not need to access any resources beyond the knowledge store and models running locally. To ensure that all participating teams adhered to these restrictions, they were asked to submit their systems to the organisers to run on the test data in order to produce the final results.

We also improved on the automatic evaluation of evidence retrieval, which was found to be have very low correlation with human evaluation in the first edition of the shared task. Instead of relying on the originally propose token-matching evaluation of Schlichtkrull et al. (2023a), we adopted the recently proposed Ev^2R prompt-based LLM approach of Akhtar et al. (2024) which was shown to have stronger correlation with human evaluation. This allowed for more reliable evaluation of participating systems, since accuracy points are awarded conditionally on retrieving appropriate evidence. Finally, we released a new test set with more recent claims, thus reducing the possibility that they were used in the training of LLMs.

We find that all seven participating teams delivered systems that adhered to the requirements for open-weights, reproducible and efficient systems, making use of language models up to 14B parameters. Fine-tuning was rarely used, relying mostly on few-shot in-context learning. In retrieval, they often proposed hybrid approaches combining dense embeddings with BM25. Overall, the best system was submitted by team CTU AIC Ullrich and Drchal (2025) that achieved 0.3317 AVERITEC score, which awards accuracy points only when the evidence retrieved is considered adequate.

2 Task Description

Participants are given claims and associated metadata, such as the publication date (see Figure 1). Based on this, they must retrieve *evidence* for or against the claims. In the gold annotation, this evidence is broken down into question-answer pairs, naturally enabling multi-hop reasoning. We do not restrict participants to providing evidence in this format, but most participants found it beneficial to follow it. Finally, based on the evidence, participants must predict whether a veracity label from the set *supported, refuted, not enough evidence*, or *conflicting evidence/cherry-picking*.

2.1 Dataset

Similarly to the shared task of previous years, we ask participants to train and validate their system on the public AVERITEC dataset and evaluate their performance on our new test set (2025). The 2025 test set consists of 1,000 instances, which temporally succeed the previous data (original AVERITEC and 2024 test set).

Annotation of 2025 New Test Set Following AVERITEC (Schlichtkrull et al., 2023a), we first collect fact-checking articles from ClaimReview and conduct a five-phase annotation. Please note that each instance is annotated by different annotators at each phase.

In particular, in phase 1 (P1), annotators are asked to identify the main claims from a fact-checking article, extract corresponding meta-data such as the claim speaker and claim date, and decontextualise the claim to make it context-independent. In P2, given a decontextualised claim, annotators propose questions that help to fact-check the claim, answer the question by finding relevant information from the fact-checking article and online source, and finally make a verdict for the claim based on the QA pairs. In P3, presented with only the QA pairs and the decontextualised claim, annotators assign a verdict label and make a justification for their choice. For each instance, if the verdict labels given by P2 and P3 annotators are identical, we regard the QA annotation and the claim as disambiguated, informative and sufficient for the verdict predication, and include it in our resulting test set. Otherwise, this instance proceeds to the P4 and P5 annotation, which consist of a second round of P2 and P3 annotation, respectively. Similarly, we examine the verdicts of each claim given by P4 and P5 annotators: if the verdict labels are identical, we include the instance in our resulting test set; otherwise, we discard it. In this way, we collect 1,000 instances for our 2025 test set, where each is annotated with a normalised claim, meta-data, QA pairs, a verdict label, and a justification.

We conduct a training and evaluation procedure to select qualified annotators. Before the formal annotation, all annotators are required to complete training on 10 instances for each of the P1, P2, and P3 tasks, respectively. Those training instances are randomly selected from the 2024 test set. All annotators are required to meet the basic performance criteria: (1) over 70% F-1 score for both claim type classification and fact-checking strategy classification; (2) an average of more than 2 QA pairs per claim; (3) over 50% accuracy of verdict prediction. Finally, 8 out of 9 annotators are selected for the formal annotation for the 2025 test set.

Comparison between the Previous Datasets and 2025 Test Set We present the data statistics of the 2025 test set in Table 1. For comparison, we also show the results of the 2023 AVERITEC dataset and the 2024 test set.

The 2025 test set (from Jan 2024 to Dec 2024) is more temporally removed from the training set compared with the 2023 dataset and the 2024 test set, indicating a greater domain shift. The average number of questions per claim in the 2025 test set is comparable to the 2024 test set while being higher than in the 2023 dataset (e.g., 2025: 2.79; 2024: 2.89; 2023: 2.60/2.57/2.57). Moreover, the 2025 test set includes more numerical claims (38.8%), which are more straightforward to verify, but fewer causal claims (8.1%), which are typically more challenging. These distributions also reflect on the fact-checking strategies, where there are more numerical comparisons (30.8%) in the 2025 test set.

In addition to the above observations, we find that the distributions across different sets show similar trends. In terms of label distribution, the Refuted label consistently accounts for the largest proportion, while Conflicting and Not Enough Evidence remain greatly fewer. Regarding claim type distribution, the Event/Property Claim is the most common, while the Position Statement is the least. For fact-checking strategies, the Written Evidence consistently dominates across all sets.

2.2 Knowledge Store

To ensure fair comparison, support reproducibility, and reduce engineering and computational costs, we provide a corresponding knowledge store for the 2025 test set. For each claim, the knowledge store includes a set of potentially relevant documents for fact-checking each claim.

For each data store, we include gold documents, which are used for our annotation, and additional documents retrieved by Google search. In particular, to generate queries for Google search, we use ChatGPT[1] to generate a set of queries based on the claim, gold annotated questions, and gold annotated answers. We also include a variety of distractor queries by changing the named entities,

[1]We use `gpt-3.5-turbo`.

Split	Train (2023)	Dev (2023)	Test (2023)
Claims	3,068	500	1,000
Question / Claim	2.60	2.57	2.57
End date	25-08-2020	31-10-2020	22-12-2021
Labels (S/R/C/N)	27.6/56.8/6.4/9.2	24.4/61.0/7.6/7.0	25.5/62.0/6.3/6.2
Types (PS/NC/EPC/QV/CC)	7.8/33.7/57.8/9.6/11.5	5.8/23.8/61.4/13.8/10.8	7.0/21.9/69.8/7.7/11.9
Strategies (WE/NCP/FR/EC/SS)	78.8/30.6/6.6/29.9/3.6	88.6/19.0/7.4/27.4/2.0	88.0/19.2/7.7/29.6/1.8

Split	Test (2024)	Test (2025)
Claims	1,215	1,000
Question / Claim	2.89	2.79
End date	13-08-2023	19-12-2024
Labels (S/R/C/N)	17.3/66.5/4.1/12.1	22.2/71.9/1.7/4.2
Types (PS/NC/EPC/QV/CC)	3.5/24.3/71.9/5.2/16.1	2.6/38.8/68/9/4.3/8.1
Strategies (WE/NCP/FR/EC/SS)	82.4/22.6/10.0/37.6/4.0	88.8/30.8/7.8/30.0/5.6

Table 1: Statistics for the 2023 dataset, and 2024 and 2025 test sets. The Labels (%) are Supported (S), Refuted (R), Conflicting Evidence/Cherry-picking (C), and Not Enough Evidence (N). The Claim Types (%) are Position Statement (PS), Numerical Claim (NC), Event/Property Claim (EPC), Quote Verification (QV), and Causal Claim (CC). The Fact-checker Strategies (%) are Written Evidence (WE), Numerical Comparison (NCP), Fact-checker Reference (FR), Expert Consultation (EC) and Satirical Source (SS). For simplicity, we exclude strategies with very low frequencies, such as Geo-location (0.3%). Please note that a single claim can correspond to multiple claim types and fact-checking strategies; therefore, the proportions do not necessarily sum to 100%.

dates, and events in the claim. We present our detailed query information in Appendix A. We collect the URLs returned by the first page of the Google search, and only include those URLs which are temporarily available before the claim is made. Finally, the deduplicated and shuffled URLs result in the data store for each claim. We further scrape the text from each URL using `trafilatura` (Barbaresi, 2021).

For the 2025 test data store, we have 1,018,800 URLs and 2,506,398,451 tokens in total. In particular, for each claim, there are 1019 URLs on average, where 593 are associated with valid scraped texts. The average tokens are 2,506,398 for each claim and 4,227 for each document, respectively. The most common domains include National Library of Medicine, Reddit, ScienceDirect, Wikipedia, BBC, the New York Times and CNN.

2.3 Baseline

The baseline closely follows the HerO system (Yoon et al., 2024). HerO achieved the second place in the AVeriTeC shared task (Schlichtkrull et al., 2024), demonstrating that open LLMs can effectively verify real-world claims without relying on proprietary models. HerO uses publicly available LLMs in a three-step verification pipeline: (i) evidence retrieval by combining hypothetical document generation via an LLM, BM25 retrieval, and a cross-attention re-ranker (Meng et al., 2024); (ii) question generation where an LLM creates verifying questions conditioned on each piece of the evidence; and (iii) veracity prediction by using a fine-tuned LLM to jointly generate explanations and the final verdict labels.

Our baseline modifies the original HerO implementation with a focus on computational efficiency to ensure that the system runs within this shared task's time constraints. Instead of using Llama-3.1-70B (Grattafiori et al., 2024) across components, the baseline uses the Llama-3.1-8B variant (a fine-tuned Llama-3.1-8B veracity prediction model was also provided by Yoon et al. (2024)). Since evidence retrieval is the most expensive step of HerO's inference pipeline, the baseline additionally incorporates retrieval cutoffs and heuristics, limiting the number of sentences for BM25 retrieval to 5000, and for reranking to 500. Finally, the runtime was further improved by adding typical efficiency optimizations, such as batch processing and multi-threading.

2.4 Measuring Reproducibility & Efficiency

To ensure the reproducibility of shared task systems, all systems were executed on a standardized virtual machine during inference on the test set by the organizers. To this end, all shared task teams were required to provide reproducible code with clear installation and execution instructions.

A system is considered reproducible if it runs during inference on the VM without making any external API calls, whether to large language models (LLMs) or to retrieval engines such as Google Search. Consequently, closed-weight LLMs cannot be used during inference. In contrast, open-weight and open-data language models are allowed as long as they run locally on the VM. Note that participants were allowed to use larger or closed-weight LLMs during training.

The virtual machine was an AWS `g5.2xlarge` EC2 instance with an Nvidia A10G GPU with 23GB memory, 8 vCPUs, 32GB RAM, and 450GB of storage. To ensure compatibility with the VM, participants could test their systems using either a provided Docker image that matched the evaluation environment or by configuring an identical AWS instance via the specified AMI.

The efficiency of shared task systems was measured by setting an upper limit to the inference runtime on the 1000 claims of the test set. A system was expected to process the entire test set on the virtual machine in 16 hours and 40 minutes, averaging 1 minute per claim. This runtime limit does not include the downloading of data, models, or retrieval indices. Outputs produced by a system beyond that time constraint are not considered. Moreover, systems were allowed to process all claims for a given component of the verification pipeline before proceeding to the next component. This approach reduces the impact of loading and unloading models from memory that would occur if each claim were processed individually.[2]

Reproducibility and efficiency are a binary pass/fail requirement for successful shared task submissions. We do not use them as a metric for ranking successful shared task systems.

2.5 Evaluation

Following established practise in previous work (Thorne et al., 2018; Schlichtkrull et al., 2023a), including the first AVeriTeC shared task (Schlichtkrull et al., 2024), we evaluate verdict accuracy conditional on sufficient evidence having been retrieved. We report three metrics: **Q score**, representing question quality regardless of found evidence; **Q+A score**, representing the quality of evidence as questions *and* answers; and **AVERITEC**, on which systems are scored with verdict accuracy for claims where Q+A score is above a certainly threshold *t*, and 0 otherwise.

The evidence in this year's AVeriTeC shared task is retrieved from a knowledge store compiled from a range of internet sources (see Sec. 2.2), The AVeriTeC metrics used in the previous year's shared task (Schlichtkrull et al., 2024) relied on approximate matching using the annotated evidence and the token-matching metrics METEOR (Banerjee and Lavie, 2005). However, this approach was highly sensitive to surface forms and resulted in penalising alternative, but valid evidence paths. For example, both *"Where did South Africa rank in alcohol consumption? In 2016, South Africa ranked ninth out of* 53 *African countries."* and *"What's the average alcohol consumption per person in South Africa? 7.1 litres."* may both be valid ways of establishing the relative levels of alcohol consumption between South Africa and other countries. However, the token-level overlap between both evidence is low and may result in a higher METEOR score for one evidence alternative compared to the other.

Thus we decided to use Ev^{2}R (Akhtar et al., 2024) for evaluation. Ev^{2}R (Akhtar et al., 2024) is a prompt-based LLM-as-judge approach that assesses the quality of retrieved evidence by decomposing both the retrieved and reference evidence into atomic facts before comparing them to evaluate factual consistency and coverage. It outperforms traditional metrics in alignment with human judgments and robustness to adversarial perturbations. Ev^{2}R is inspired by FactScore (Min et al., 2023), but adapts its approach to better reflect evidence evaluation, providing both a precision and a recall score. Precision measures the accuracy of the retrieved evidence, while recall assesses the completeness of the retrieved evidence in relation to the gold standard. The scorer first splits the retrieved evidence $\hat{E}$ and reference evidence E into atomic facts, $A_{\hat{E}}$ and A_E respectively. To calculate the precision score it evaluates whether each individual fact $a_{\hat{E}} \in A_{\hat{E}}$ of the retrieved evidence is supported by the reference evidence E. The precision score s_{prec} is defined as the ratio of facts supported by the reference evidence:

$$s_{prec} = \frac{1}{|A_{\hat{E}}|} \sum_{a_{\hat{E}} \in A_{\hat{E}}} I[a_{\hat{E}} \text{ supported by} E]$$

The scorer iterates over each fact ($a_{\hat{E}} \in A_{\hat{E}}$) for which the indicator function ($I[a_{\hat{E}}$ supported by $E]$) returns 1 if the fact $a_{\hat{E}}$ is supported by the reference evidence E and 0 otherwise. For calculating the recall score, the scorer evaluates whether each atomic fact of the

[2]This relaxation creates an admittedly artificial setting, as it would require all users to wait for all claims to be processed before receiving a response.

reference evidence ($a_E \in A_E$) is supported by the retrieved evidence, i.e., measuring the extend to which the retrieved evidence covers the content of the reference evidence:

$$s_{recall} = \frac{1}{|A_E|} \sum_{a_E \in A_E} \mathbb{I}[a_E \text{ supported by } \hat{E}]$$

Akhtar et al. (2024) assess the validity of the scorer by evaluating its alignment with human ratings and testing its robustness through a set of perturbation experiments that systematically assess the scorer on various dimensions, such as its sensitiveness to variant changes in the evidence text, fluency, noise, etc.

Following the first AVERITEC shared task (Schlichtkrull et al., 2024), we evaluate evidence using only the recall component of the metric. By doing so we avoid penalising systems for adding additional evidence which annotators did not find necessary, such as background context. We only consider the first 10 questions generated by each system, so as to avoid rewarding sheer volume. We then calculate total AVERITEC score as verdict accuracy given that $s_{recall} > t$, where we choose $t = 0.5$ so as to ensure high agreement on the 100 double-annotated AVERITEC claims following the methodology discussed in Schlichtkrull et al. (2023a).

3 Results

The results for the shared task are shown in Table 2. We received seven fully reproducible systems. This section discusses our findings on reproducibility, efficiency, and general observations on the techniques used by the participating teams. We provide a high-level overview of the model components used by systems in Table 3. For detailed descriptions of any particular system, we refer to each team's system description paper. In line with the theme of this shared task, every team has made their codebase publicly available.

Reproducibility We received a total of eight system submissions. One system failed to run on the VM due to syntax errors, missing installation instructions, and hardcoded file paths. Of the seven reproducible systems, two were submitted as Docker images and five as ZIP files. All systems needed manual intervention to run on the virtual server. Common issues were Docker permission errors, dependency installation failures (e.g., llama.cpp), GPU memory crashes, and misconfigured shell scripts. Only memory crashes occurred during runtime; all other errors were resolved within 4 hours before system execution. Overall, the encountered issues are expected for early-stage open-source codebases.

We added several diagnostic measures to assess a system's reproducibility. First, we monitored traffic and non-local API calls. Second, we tested each system on a subset of 99 claims not included in the test set (but included in the knowledge store, in case of pre-computed indices) to verify that systems were not hardcoded to specific test examples and could handle arbitrary claims.

Efficiency The average runtime per claim for each system is shown in Table 2. All systems successfully stayed below the established limit of 1 minute per claim on average. Teams achieved this through model selection and efficiency implementation improvements. The components used by each team, along with inference engines and efficiency-focused designs, are summarized in Table 3. Five out of seven systems use for LLM inference vLLM (Kwon et al., 2023), following the baseline. Team EFC uses llama.cpp[3] and Team CTU AIC uses Ollama[4], a wrapper around llama.cpp.

To improve retrieval efficiency beyond the baseline's improvements, systems CTU AIC, HUMANE, FZIGOT, and OldJoe used pre-computed indices of dense vector representations. Teams Yellow Flash, EFC, and Checkmate chunked evidence sentences into larger segments before applying a sparse BM25 retriever, reducing the number of chunks considered by the BM25 module in Team EFC's case from 5000 to 1500.

Due to VM resource constraints, most teams used smaller models for both retrieval and veracity prediction than in the first AVeriTeC Shared Task (Schlichtkrull et al., 2024). For instance, Team HUMANE used an 8B model for their retrieval pipeline instead of the 70B model from the first shared task to fit within the 23GB RAM of the A10G GPU. Subsequently, most teams used quantization to either fit larger models onto the GPU and to reduce inference runtime. Teams HUMANE, FZIGOT, and OldJoe used Activation-aware Weight Quantization (Lin et al., 2024), Teams Yellow Flash and Checkmate used OPTQ (Frantar et al., 2023), and Team EFC used GGUF

[3]https://github.com/ggml-org/llama.cpp
[4]https://github.com/ollama/ollama

#	Team Name	Time per Claim (s)	Ev2R Recall		AVERITEC Score
			Q only	Q + A	
1	CTU AIC (Ullrich and Drchal, 2025)	53.67	$0.2003_{0.007}$	$0.4774_{0.004}$	$0.3317_{0.002}$
2	HUMANE (Yoon et al., 2025)	29.19	$0.1933_{0.005}$	$0.4299_{0.001}$	$0.2707_{0.004}$
3	Yellow Flash (Dharamvaram and Hakak, 2025)	31.71	$0.1561_{0.006}$	$0.4098_{0.008}$	$0.2527_{0.005}$
4	FZIGOT (Rolinger and Liu, 2025)	18.50	$0.3622_{0.007}$	$0.3998_{0.003}$	$0.2440_{0.002}$
5	EFC (Upravitelev et al., 2025)	7.01	$0.1254_{0.001}$	$0.3520_{0.006}$	$0.2047_{0.003}$
6	Checkmate (Rashid and Hakak, 2025)	22.73	$0.1848_{0.007}$	$0.3368_{0.005}$	$0.2043_{0.005}$
7	Baseline	33.88	$0.2723_{0.001}$	$0.3362_{0.004}$	$0.2023_{0.007}$
8	OldJoe (Ftouhi et al., 2025)	48.57	$0.1823_{0.005}$	$0.3878_{0.001}$	$0.1517_{0.003}$
–	CTU AIC (4o)	–	$0.5035_{0.003}$	$0.4373_{0.004}$	$0.2690_{0.004}$
–	CTU AIC (4o-mini)	–	$0.5718_{0.005}$	$0.4809_{0.003}$	$0.3176_{0.001}$

Table 2: Overall results for the AVERITEC shared task. Performance is evaluated on the total of 1000 hidden test set examples. Scores are given in Ev2R Recall for question-only, question-answer performance, and the total score.

quantization (Gerganov, 2023). With these efficiency modifications, five out of seven teams (HUMANE, Yellow Flash, FZIGOT, EFC, and Checkmate) achieved faster runtimes than the baseline's average of 33.88s per claim.

The only non-baseline system that does not use model quantization is CTU AIC. Instead, Team CTU AIC uses the largest model with the maximum possible context size that fits on the VM's GPU while satisfying the efficiency constraint, relying on the inherent processing abilities of the latest language models. While this results in the slowest runtime of all systems (53.67s average per claim), their system ranks highest in the shared task.

Particularly noteworthy is Team EFC's runtime performance with an average of 7.01s per claim during inference, which is almost five times faster than the baseline. In addition to the aforementioned efficiency improvements, they proposed a semantic filtering step that reduces LLM calls by predicting the NEI or conflicting evidence/cherry-picking label using exclusively cosine similarity on retrieved evidence.

Despite the training cost not being considered in this shared task's efficiency constraint, most teams did not train or fine-tune language models for any parts of their pipeline. The only exceptions are the systems of Team HUMANE and Team FZIGOT, discussed later in the report.

We further compare shared task systems to solutions using proprietary closed-source language models in Table 2. We modified the winning system (CTU AIC) to use OpenAI's GPT-4o (`gpt-4o-2024-08-06`) and GPT-4o-mini (`gpt-4o-mini-2024-07-18`) instead of Qwen3-14B. While question-only (Q only) scores increased substantially with closed models, both Q+A and AVeriTeC scores were lower than the original open-source CTU AIC system. Since we did not optimize the proprietary models for use in CTU's system, these results provide only a preliminary assessment of their performance, as evidenced by GPT-4o-mini outperforming GPT-4o.

Question Generation Several teams (OldJoe, EFC, Yellow Flash, Checkmate, FZIGOT) begin claim verification by generating questions to guide evidence retrieval, following findings from the first shared task that question generation, rather than searching evidence for the claim directly, improves retrieval performance (Schlichtkrull et al., 2024). To generate the questions all teams rely on language models without further fine-tuning, specifically Qwen2.5, Qwen3, and Phi-4.

FZIGOT adopts an iterative question generation approach using a Graph-of-Thoughts framework (Besta et al., 2024). At each iteration, their system produces multiple questions, prunes similar ones, and verifies the claim using answers collected from these questions. If the label is "Not Enough Evidence" (NEE), the algorithm returns to question generation for a fixed number of iterations. FZIGOT uses LoRA (Hu et al., 2022) to fine-tune Qwen2.5-14B model for this step. Since the AVeriTeC training data is not structured in such iter-

Team Name	QG	Retrieval	QA	Veracity	Inference Engine	Efficiency
CTU AIC	Qwen3-14B	mxbai-embed-large-v1	Qwen3-14B	Qwen3-14B	Ollama	Dense Index
HUMANE	Qwen3-8B	gte-base-en-v1.5, Llama-3.1-8B, Qwen3-8B	Qwen3-8B	Qwen3-32B	vLLM	Dense Index, AWQ
Yellow Flash	Qwen2.5-7B	BM25, bilingual-embedding-small, snowflake-arctic-embed-m-v2.0	–	Phi-4-14B	vLLM	BM25 Chunking, GPTQ-int4
FZIGOT	Qwen2.5-14B	BM25, stella_en_400M	Qwen2.5-14B	Qwen2.5-14B	vLLM	Dense Index, LoRA, AWQ
EFC	Phi-4-14B	BM25, thenlper/gte-base	–	Phi-4-14B	llama.cpp	BM25 Chunking, Semantic Filtering, GGUF
Checkmate	Qwen2.5-7B	BM25, snowflake-arctic-embed-m-v2.0	–	Phi-4-14B	vLLM	BM25 Chunking, GPTQ-int4
OldJoe	Qwen3-14B	BM25, jina-embeddings-v3	Qwen3-14B	Qwen3-14B	vLLM	Dense Index, AWQ
Baseline	Llama-3.1-8B	BM25, SFR-embedding-2, Llama-3.1-8B	–	Llama-3.1-8B	vLLM	Retrieval cut-off

Table 3: Components used by shared task systems, ordered based on AVeriTeC-score (see Table 2). - indicates that the answer used was the entire retrieved passage.

ative fashion, FZIGOT creates a weakly supervised training dataset by generating a training instance for each question in the dataset, conditioning subsequent questions on previous questions accordingly. Their system achieves the highest Question-only EV2R Recall across teams with a score of 0.3622.

In contrast, CTU AIC and HUMANE produce questions by conditioning the generation on already retrieved evidence, following the baseline's design. Team CTU AIC generates questions jointly with answers and the veracity prediction conditioned on retrieved evidence using Qwen3-14B. Since Team CTU AIC and HUMANE achieved the highest AVeriTeC scores, this suggests that relevant evidence can be retrieved from the provided knowledge store without explicit question generation. However, as described in Section 2.1, the knowledge store construction itself relies heavily on both annotators and models generating questions to find suitable evidence. As reported in the AVeriTeC paper (Schlichtkrull et al., 2023a), search with generated questions yields complete evidence in 9/20 cases, compared to 16/20 with annotator-written questions. Using the same claims, we find that searching for *only* the claim yields complete evidence in 6/20 cases, whereas the full process of knowledge store construction (i.e., including the full list of queries described in Appendix A), complete evidence is found via search for 19/20 (for the shared task, the knowledge store is also extended with gold evidence, ensuring completeness also for the final claim). Since all systems use this provided knowledge store, question generation remains an integral part of every system. Additionally, all systems use generated questions and answers for veracity prediction, as discussed further below.

Evidence Retrieval Team EFC and Team FZIGOT retrieve evidence directly based on the generated questions. Team Yellow Flash and Checkmate additionally generate synthetic answers,

Team name	QV	N	E/P	C	PS	S	R	NEE	CE/C	Avg. # Docs
CTU AIC	**0.49**	0.17	**0.40**	**0.41**	**0.46**	0.18	**0.4**	0.1	**0.06**	9.0
HUMANE	0.30	**0.19**	0.37	0.33	0.35	**0.27**	0.35	0.0	0.0	10.0
Yellow Flash	0.19	0.16	0.27	0.33	0.35	0.23	0.26	0.02	0.06	7.27
FZIGOT	0.28	0.15	0.31	0.33	0.42	0.22	0.29	**0.07**	0.0	15.2
EFC	0.28	0.16	0.26	0.23	0.42	0.19	0.27	0.0	0.0	10.0
Checkmate	0.19	0.16	0.26	0.28	0.35	0.23	0.24	0.0	0.0	5.21
OldJoe	0.02	0.13	0.2	0.22	0.15	0.23	0.18	0.0	0.0	3.96
Average	0.25	0.16	0.3	0.3	0.36	0.22	0.28	0.03	0.02	8.66

Table 4: We compute separate results based on claim type (QV = Quote Verification, N = Numerical, E/P = Event/Property, C = Causal, PS = Position Statement). We also compute results separated by gold verdict (S = Supported, R = Refuted, NEE = Not Enough Evidence, CE/C = Conflicting Evidence / Cherrypicking). Finally, we report the average number of evidence documents submitted per claim. We note that if a team submitted more than 10 documents for a claim, only the first 10 were used to compute retrieval scores for evaluation.

which are used to expand search queries for evidence retrieval. Team OldJoe formulates four distinct search queries for each question and retrieves evidence for each query individually. Team HUMANE applies a query expansion strategy that generates hypothetical fact-checking articles for each claim. This approach is also used by the baseline and their system from last year's shared task. Team CTU AIC retrieves evidence by using the claim itself as the search query.

Similar to the first AVeriTeC shared task, teams explored vector-based dense retrieval systems (Karpukhin et al., 2020) and hybrid systems that combine dense retrieval with BM25 (Robertson and Zaragoza, 2009). Three systems (Team CTU AIC, FZIGOT, and HUMANE) relied solely on dense retrieval. Team HUMANE further summarizes the collected evidence into a single paragraph using Qwen3-8B. The remaining teams adopted hybrid retrieval approaches, following the baseline. Team Yellow Flash further groups together semantically similar sentences before embedding these coherent chunks and querying for dense retrieval.

Compared to fully dense retrieval, hybrid systems allow faster evidence retrieval by restricting neural search to a smaller subset of the knowledge store. This is reflected in the inference time reported by Team EFC. While Team OldJoe also employs a hybrid system, they create an index for both BM25 and dense embeddings over the entire knowledge store, and then combine retrieval scores using reciprocal rank fusion (Cormack et al., 2009).

Consistent with trends from the first shared task, models from the General Text Embeddings (GTE) family (Li et al., 2023; Zhang et al., 2024) were widely adopted. These include Stella[5] and the newer *snowflake-artic-embed-m-v2.0*, a GTE model fine-tuned using Matryoshka representation learning (Kusupati et al., 2022) to reduce quality degradation during model compression. Team CTU AIC used *mcbai-embed-large-v1* (Li and Li, 2024), the same retrieval model their team used in the previous shared task.

Question Answering & Veracity Prediction All teams used large language models for question answering and veracity prediction, relying on three models: Qwen3, Qwen2.5, and Phi-4. Three teams (Yellow Flash, EFC, and Checkmate) used retrieved evidence directly as answers, while Team HUMANE and OldJoe, who produce answers explicitly as a separate step in their verification pipeline, conditioned on claim, question, and evidence. Similarly to their question generation approach, Team FZIGOT uses LoRA to train distinct adapters for question answering and veracity prediction using weakly-supervised data. Apart from the increased efficiency during training, using three distinct adapters for each component of the pipeline can also improve inference runtime, as the loading and unloading of adapters into memory is substantially faster than for entire models. However, due to the experimental setting that allows systems to run one component of the pipeline at a time to account for restrictions of the VM, the effect of this design choice was less impactful in the context of the shared task.

[5]https://huggingface.co/dunzhang/stella_en_400M_v5

Team HUMANE submitted the only system with a fully fine-tuned model for veracity prediction. They trained a Qwen3-32B model and applied AWQ quantization to fit onto VM GPU memory. While Team CTU AIC did not fine-tune their model, they augmented the input with few-shot examples retrieved from the AVeriTeC training data, selected via BM25, conditioned on the claim. This shared task again highlights the importance of accurate veracity prediction components: top-ranking CTU AIC uses Qwen3-14B without quantization, while second-place HUMANE uses the largest language model (32B) with full-model fine-tuning.

Types & Verdicts Table 4 provides a detailed breakdown of results by claim type (quote verification, numerical claims, event/property claims, causal claims, and position statements) and verdict (supported, refuted, conflicting evidence/cherry-picking, and not enough evidence). We observe that all systems perform substantially worse on numerical claims compared to other claim types. While systems also underperformed on numerical claims in the first shared task, the performance gap is considerably larger this edition, which is likely contributed by the change in evaluation metric from Hungarian Meteor to EV2R.

Regarding performance across different veracity labels, no system achieves scores higher than 0.1 on Not Enough Evidence and Conflicting Evidence/Cherry-picking claims. This observation is expected and matches findings from the first shared task. These labels are highly challenging to correctly identify, subsequently causing some teams to omitting these labels from their predictions altogether. Moreover, systems that calibrate their veracity predictions to favor refuted claims gain an advantage (as long as they returned adequate evidence), as refuted claims dominate the dataset, comprising approximately two-thirds of all instances.

4 Human Evaluation of Evidence

Following the approach taken in last year's AVeriTeC shared task (Schlichtkrull et al., 2024), we conducted human evaluation of the evidence retrieved by the systems participating in the shared task, motivated by two concerns. First, the incompleteness of the gold evidence annotation, since it is often the case that adequate evidence to determine the verdict for a claim can be found in multiple webpages, as shown in the inter-annotation agreement study of Schlichtkrull et al. (2023a). Second, the inaccuracies of automatic evaluation metrics of textual evaluation, require assessing and comparing the computed AVeriTeC scores with human annotations. Thus we can gain a deeper understanding of the quality of the retrieved evidence, and assess how well the AVeriTeC scores assigned to the retrieved evidence aligns with human judgements.

Evaluation Process We conducted human evaluation in collaboration with the participating teams. All seven teams were invited to participate in the evaluation. All teams but the team HUMANE took part in the evaluation. Each of the remaining six participating teams and two volunteers from with experience in automated fact-checking annotation manually evaluated 35 evidence samples from other participants. Out of these, five were gold-labeled, which were included to assist in the post-processing of the collected annotations and to assess their quality. The evidence samples were randomly selected from and evenly distributed across all submitted systems, representing both high- and low-scoring systems, as shown in Table 4.

The figures in Appendix B show the evaluation form and the instructions provided to human annotators during evaluation. As a first step, we asked annotators to assess whether "at least some part of the evidence" was "non-empty, understandable, and related to the claim." If so, it was considered eligible for further rating. In addition to assigning a verdict label, we asked annotators to rate retrieved evidence in comparison to provided reference evidence[6]. Annotators rated the evidence on a scale from 1 to 5 in two dimensions:

(1) **Coverage**: Measures how much of the reference evidence is covered by the predicted evidence, ensuring that the content, meaning, entities, and other key elements of the reference are fully represented in the retrieved evidence.

(2) **Relevance**: Measures how relevant the retrieved evidence is to the content of the claim.

Insights Gained The annotation process resulted in a total of 245 annotations. After filtering out evidence samples that were labeled by evaluators as not understandable (5 samples) or completely irrelevant to the given claim (11 samples), we were left with 229 valid annotations. Among these, 31 annotations corresponded to gold-labeled samples.

[6]We provide the exact instruction for rating each criteria in the appendix.

Label/Pred	CE/C	NEE	Refuted	Supported
CE/C	5.88	5.88	64.71	23.53
NEE	5.41	24.32	40.54	29.73
Refuted	3.96	5.94	77.23	12.87
Supported	5.88	1.96	11.76	80.39

Table 5: Overview of verdict **label**led by human evaluators (rows) versus system **pred**ictions (columns) in percentages.

Rating	COV	COV %	REL	REL %
1	35	17.68	2	1.01
2	47	23.74	9	4.55
3	40	20.20	30	15.15
4	45	22.73	84	42.42
5	31	15.66	73	36.87

Table 6: Overview of ratings for Semantic **Cov**erage and **Rel**evance scores obtained through human evaluation. Each score from 1 to 5 shows the absolute count and corresponding percentage.

Dimension	ρ	r
Coverage	.404	.406
Relevance	.244	.242

Table 7: Correlation between Q + A scores (AVeriTeC score) and human-rated subset of evidence. We calculate correlation using the Spearman (ρ) and Pearson (r) correlation coefficients.

Excluding the gold-labeled samples, resulted in a final set of 198 evidence annotations.

Before labeling the system-retrieved evidence, participants were first asked to label the verdict given the retrieved evidence. Table 5 provides an overview of the matching between system-predicted labels (columns) and human-labeled verdicts (rows). While human annotators generally agreed with evidence labeled as refuted or supported, there was less overlap for evidence labeled as NEE and CE/C by the submitted systems.

Analyzing human judgments across the two evaluated dimensions (see Table 8), we find that the majority of predicted evidence was labeled as relevant (almost 80% evidence samples labelled as very relevant or mostly relevant to the claim), but in the dimension of semantic coverage, approximately 18% of the evidence received a rating of 1, indicating that "the predicted evidence covers none of the reference evidence." Additionally, around 20% received a rating of 2, meaning that "very little of the reference evidence is covered." This does not necessarily mean that the evidence is false – low coverage can also occur if the retrieved evidence uses different information, arguments, or sources than the reference evidence. Ideally, we aim for an evidence evaluation that can fairly assess evidence even when it differs from the reference and has low coverage. Compared to the previous year's AVeriTeC shared task, the relevance scores increased while the scores for semantic coverage remained roughly equal.

To assess the relationship between human scoring and the Ev^{2}R score (see Sec 2.5), we computed both the Spearman correlation coefficient (ρ (Spearman, 1987)) and the Pearson correlation coefficient (r (Pearson, 1896)) as shown in Table 7. Correlations were calculated using both the entire evidence text and the question text only. In both cases, we observed a positive correlation between the AVeriTeC scores and the human evaluation (see Table 7) while the correlation with the coverage dimension is higher than with relevance. Compared to last year's shared task evaluation, where the correlation between manually assessed samples and the AVeriTeC score was close to zero for both coverage and relevance, this year's score shows a much stronger alignment with human judgments (around 0.41 for coverage and 0.24 for relevance) when assessing the semantic coverage and relevance of predicted evidence. The human evaluation on the subset (see Table 8) shows a similar ranking of participating systems compared to automatic evaluations . The top-ranked teams (based on AVeriTeC score) also perform well on human evaluation, while the lower-ranked teams remain similarly positioned, with only minor shifts in their order.[7] It is important to note that this evaluation was solely based on a small sample of system predictions, and that the results should therefore be taken with a grain of salt.

Human evaluation of evidence predictions offers valuable insights into the limitations of the AVeriTeC score, and suggests directions for future research. A notable observation is the discrepancy between human evaluation and the AVeriTeC score for some of the highest-ranked samples, such as the examples provided in Table 10 in the appendix. For instance, in row three, the predicted evidence directly contradicts the reference evidence by providing different numbers, yet it receives a high AVeriTeC score due to similar word-

[7]See Table 8 in the appendix.

Team	Avg. Coverage	Leaderboard #
CTU AIC	3.6	1.
yellow flash	2.9	3.
HUMANE	2.9	2.
FZIGOT	2.9	4.
checkmate	2.1	6.
EFC	2.7	5.
OldJoe	2.4	7.

Table 8: Average semantic **coverage** scores assigned to evidence samples from selected teams based on human evaluation, next to AVeriTeC **rank** the team obtained in the 2025 shared task.

ing. Similarly, for the first two rows in Table 10, the semantic coverage score is rated with the second lowest score 1, whereas the average score across all examples is 3, indicating misalignment between the predicted and reference evidence.

Certain low-ranked examples highlight different challenges (see Table 11). For example, the predicted evidence in the first row received a low AVERITEC score despite receiving the highest score of 5 across all categories in human evaluation. Despite both sets of evidence reaching the same conclusion, the large disparity in answer length and wording leads to a much lower AVERITEC score. The example in the second row, also ranks low according to AVERITEC score, even though it scores high in all categories except for coverage, where it scores 3. Here, both the reference and predicted evidence reach the same verdict, but the predicted evidence supports the claim with different information and wording, resulting in low semantic coverage and a low AVERITEC score.

Acknowledgements

Michael, Yulong, Chenxi, Zhenyun, and Andreas received funding from the European Research Council (ERC) under the European Union's Horizon 2020 Research and Innovation programme grant AVeriTeC (Grant agreement No. 865958). Rui is funded by a grant from the Alan Turing Institute and DSO National Laboratories (Singapore). Rami Aly was supported by the Engineering and Physical Sciences Research Council Doctoral Training Partnership (EPSRC). Michael is further supported by the Engineering and Physical Sciences Research Council (grant number EP/Y009800/1), through funding from Responsible AI UK (KP0016). The annotation of the new test set was conducted by a donation from Google.

Limitations & Ethics

The datasets and models described in this paper are not intended for truth-telling, e.g. for the design of fully automated content moderation systems. The evidence selection and veracity labels provided in the AVERITEC dataset relate only to the evidence recovered by annotators, and as such are subject to the biases of annotators and journalists. Participating systems, which sought to maximize performance on AVERITEC, may replicate those biases. While we constrained participants of using open-weights LLMs of a certain size, we did not enforce the use of open-data LLMs only, which would have been better in order to assess the biases in the participating systems. Open-weights models would also help to measure temporal leakage, as Qwen3, the most-used model in this shared task, has likely seen data that extended into the test set timeframe (January-December 2024), as it has an estimated training cutoff of March 2025. We furthermore note that shared task leaderboards are a limited representation of real-world task needs, not the least because the test set is static. Acting on veracity estimates arrived at through biased means, including automatically produced ranking decisions for evidence retrieval, risks causing epistemic harm (Schlichtkrull et al., 2023b).

References

Mubashara Akhtar, Michael Sejr Schlichtkrull, and Andreas Vlachos. 2024. Ev2r: Evaluating evidence retrieval in automated fact-checking. *CoRR*, abs/2411.05375.

Isabelle Augenstein, Christina Lioma, Dongsheng Wang, Lucas Chaves Lima, Casper Hansen, Christian Hansen, and Jakob Grue Simonsen. 2019. MultiFC: A real-world multi-domain dataset for evidence-based fact checking of claims. In *Proceedings of the 2019 Conference on Empirical Methods in Natural Language Processing and the 9th International Joint Conference on Natural Language Processing (EMNLP-IJCNLP)*, pages 4685–4697, Hong Kong, China. Association for Computational Linguistics.

Satanjeev Banerjee and Alon Lavie. 2005. METEOR: An automatic metric for MT evaluation with improved correlation with human judgments. In *Proceedings of the ACL Workshop on Intrinsic and Extrinsic Evaluation Measures for Machine Translation and/or Summarization*, pages 65–72, Ann Arbor, Michigan. Association for Computational Linguistics.

Adrien Barbaresi. 2021. Trafilatura: A web scraping library and command-line tool for text discovery and extraction. In *Proceedings of the 59th Annual Meeting of the Association for Computational Linguistics and the 11th International Joint Conference on Natural Language Processing: System Demonstrations*, pages 122–131, Online. Association for Computational Linguistics.

Maciej Besta, Nils Blach, Ales Kubicek, Robert Gerstenberger, Michał Podstawski, Lukas Gianinazzi, Joanna Gajda, Tomasz Lehmann, Hubert Niewiadomski, Piotr Nyczyk, and Torsten Hoefler. 2024. Graph of thoughts: solving elaborate problems with large language models. In *Proceedings of the Thirty-Eighth AAAI Conference on Artificial Intelligence and Thirty-Sixth Conference on Innovative Applications of Artificial Intelligence and Fourteenth Symposium on Educational Advances in Artificial Intelligence*, AAAI'24/IAAI'24/EAAI'24. AAAI Press.

Sarah Cohen, Chengkai Li, Jun Yang, and Cong Yu. 2011. Computational journalism: A call to arms to database researchers. In *5th Biennial Conference on Innovative Data Systems Research (CIDR)*.

Gordon V. Cormack, Charles L A Clarke, and Stefan Buettcher. 2009. Reciprocal rank fusion outperforms condorcet and individual rank learning methods. In *Proceedings of the 32nd International ACM SIGIR Conference on Research and Development in Information Retrieval*, SIGIR '09, page 758–759, New York, NY, USA. Association for Computing Machinery.

Arbaaz Dharamvaram and Saqib Hakak. 2025. SANCTUARY: An efficient evidence-based automated fact checking system. In *Proceedings of the Eighth Workshop on Fact Extraction and VERification (FEVER)*. Association for Computational Linguistics.

Andy Dudfield. 2020. How we're using AI to scale up global fact checking. `https://fullfact.org/blog/2020/jul/afc-global/`. Accessed: 2023-01-17.

Elias Frantar, Saleh Ashkboos, Torsten Hoefler, and Dan Alistarh. 2023. OPTQ: Accurate quantization for generative pre-trained transformers. In *The Eleventh International Conference on Learning Representations*.

Farah Ftouhi, Russel Dsouza, Lance Gamboa, Jinlong Liu, Asim Abbas, Yue Feng, Mubashir Ali, Mark Lee, and Venelin Kovatchev. 2025. OldJoe at AVeriTeC: In-context learning for fact-checking. In *Proceedings of the Eighth Workshop on Fact Extraction and VERification (FEVER)*. Association for Computational Linguistics.

Georgi Gerganov. 2023. ggml: Tensor library for machine learning.

Max Glockner, Yufang Hou, and Iryna Gurevych. 2022. Missing counter-evidence renders NLP fact-checking unrealistic for misinformation. In *Proceedings of the 2022 Conference on Empirical Methods in Natural Language Processing*, pages 5916–5936, Abu Dhabi, United Arab Emirates. Association for Computational Linguistics.

Aaron Grattafiori, Abhimanyu Dubey, Abhinav Jauhri, Abhinav Pandey, Abhishek Kadian, Ahmad Al-Dahle, Aiesha Letman, Akhil Mathur, Alan Schelten, Alex Vaughan, et al. 2024. The llama 3 herd of models. *arXiv preprint arXiv:2407.21783*.

Edward J Hu, yelong shen, Phillip Wallis, Zeyuan Allen-Zhu, Yuanzhi Li, Shean Wang, Lu Wang, and Weizhu Chen. 2022. LoRA: Low-rank adaptation of large language models. In *International Conference on Learning Representations*.

Vladimir Karpukhin, Barlas Oguz, Sewon Min, Patrick Lewis, Ledell Wu, Sergey Edunov, Danqi Chen, and Wen-tau Yih. 2020. Dense passage retrieval for open-domain question answering. In *Proceedings of the 2020 Conference on Empirical Methods in Natural Language Processing (EMNLP)*, pages 6769–6781, Online. Association for Computational Linguistics.

Aditya Kusupati, Gantavya Bhatt, Aniket Rege, Matthew Wallingford, Aditya Sinha, Vivek Ramanujan, William Howard-Snyder, Kaifeng Chen, Sham Kakade, Prateek Jain, et al. 2022. Matryoshka representation learning. In *Advances in Neural Information Processing Systems*.

Woosuk Kwon, Zhuohan Li, Siyuan Zhuang, Ying Sheng, Lianmin Zheng, Cody Hao Yu, Joseph Gonzalez, Hao Zhang, and Ion Stoica. 2023. Efficient memory management for large language model serving with pagedattention. In *Proceedings of the 29th Symposium on Operating Systems Principles*, SOSP '23, page 611–626, New York, NY, USA. Association for Computing Machinery.

Stephan Lewandowsky, John Cook, Ullrich Ecker, Dolores Albarracin, Michelle Amazeen, Panayiota Kendeou, Doug Lombardi, Eryn Newman, Gordon Pennycook, Ethan Porter, David G. Rand, David N. Rapp, Jason Reifler, Jon Roozenbeek, Philipp Schmid, Colleen M. Seifert, Gale M. Sinatra, Briony Swire-Thompson, Sander van der Linden, Emily K. Vraga, Thomas J. Wood, and Maria S. Zaragoza. 2020. Debunking Handbook 2020. `https://sks.to/db2020`.

Xianming Li and Jing Li. 2024. AoE: Angle-optimized embeddings for semantic textual similarity. In *Proceedings of the 62nd Annual Meeting of the Association for Computational Linguistics (Volume 1: Long Papers)*, pages 1825–1839, Bangkok, Thailand. Association for Computational Linguistics.

Zehan Li, Xin Zhang, Yanzhao Zhang, Dingkun Long, Pengjun Xie, and Meishan Zhang. 2023. Towards general text embeddings with multi-stage contrastive learning. *Preprint*, arXiv:2308.03281.

Ji Lin, Jiaming Tang, Haotian Tang, Shang Yang, Wei-Ming Chen, Wei-Chen Wang, Guangxuan Xiao, Xingyu Dang, Chuang Gan, and Song Han. 2024.

Awq: Activation-aware weight quantization for on-device llm compression and acceleration. In *Proceedings of Machine Learning and Systems*, volume 6, pages 87–100.

Rui Meng, Ye Liu, Shafiq Rayhan Joty, Caiming Xiong, Yingbo Zhou, and Semih Yavuz. 2024. Sfr-embedding-2: Advanced text embedding with multi-stage training.

Sewon Min, Kalpesh Krishna, Xinxi Lyu, Mike Lewis, Wen-tau Yih, Pang Koh, Mohit Iyyer, Luke Zettlemoyer, and Hannaneh Hajishirzi. 2023. FActScore: Fine-grained atomic evaluation of factual precision in long form text generation. In *Proceedings of the 2023 Conference on Empirical Methods in Natural Language Processing*, pages 12076–12100, Singapore. Association for Computational Linguistics.

Sebastião Miranda, Andreas Vlachos, David Nogueira, Andrew Secker, Afonso Mendes, Rebecca Garrett, Jeffrey J Mitchell, and Zita Marinho. 2019. Automated fact checking in the news room. In *The Web Conference 2019*, pages 3579–3583, United States. Association for Computing Machinery (ACM). 2019 World Wide Web Conference, WWW 2019 ; Conference date: 13-05-2019 Through 17-05-2019.

Preslav Nakov, David Corney, Maram Hasanain, Firoj Alam, Tamer Elsayed, Alberto Barrón-Cedeño, Paolo Papotti, Shaden Shaar, and Giovanni Da San Martino. 2021. Automated fact-checking for assisting human fact-checkers. In *Proceedings of the Thirtieth International Joint Conference on Artificial Intelligence, IJCAI-21*, pages 4551–4558. International Joint Conferences on Artificial Intelligence Organization. Survey Track.

Nedjma Ousidhoum, Zhangdie Yuan, and Andreas Vlachos. 2022. Varifocal question generation for fact-checking. In *Proceedings of the 2022 Conference on Empirical Methods in Natural Language Processing*, pages 2532–2544, Abu Dhabi, United Arab Emirates. Association for Computational Linguistics.

Karl Pearson. 1896. Vii. mathematical contributions to the theory of evolution.—iii. regression, heredity, and panmixia. *Philosophical Transactions of the Royal Society of London. Series A, containing papers of a mathematical or physical character*, (187):253–318.

Farrukh Bin Rashid and Saqib Hakak. 2025. Fathom: A fast and modular RAG pipeline for fact-checking. In *Proceedings of the Eighth Workshop on Fact Extraction and VERification (FEVER)*. Association for Computational Linguistics.

Stephen Robertson and Hugo Zaragoza. 2009. The probabilistic relevance framework: Bm25 and beyond. *Foundations and Trends® in Information Retrieval*, 3(4):333–389.

Sascha Rolinger and Jin Liu. 2025. Graph-of-thoughts for fact-checking with large language models. In *Proceedings of the Eighth Workshop on Fact Extraction and VERification (FEVER)*. Association for Computational Linguistics.

Mark Rothermel, Tobias Braun, Marcus Rohrbach, and Anna Rohrbach. 2024. InFact: A strong baseline for automated fact-checking. In *Proceedings of the Seventh Workshop on Fact Extraction and VERification (FEVER)*. Association for Computational Linguistics.

Michael Schlichtkrull, Yulong Chen, Chenxi Whitehouse, Zhenyun Deng, Mubashara Akhtar, Rami Aly, Zhijiang Guo, Christos Christodoulopoulos, Oana Cocarascu, Arpit Mittal, James Thorne, and Andreas Vlachos. 2024. The automated verification of textual claims (AVeriTeC) shared task. In *Proceedings of the Seventh Fact Extraction and VERification Workshop (FEVER)*, pages 1–26, Miami, Florida, USA. Association for Computational Linguistics.

Michael Schlichtkrull, Zhijiang Guo, and Andreas Vlachos. 2023a. Averitec: A dataset for real-world claim verification with evidence from the web. In *Advances in Neural Information Processing Systems*, volume 36, pages 65128–65167. Curran Associates, Inc.

Michael Schlichtkrull, Nedjma Ousidhoum, and Andreas Vlachos. 2023b. The intended uses of automated fact-checking artefacts: Why, how and who. In *Findings of the Association for Computational Linguistics: EMNLP 2023*, pages 8618–8642, Singapore. Association for Computational Linguistics.

C. Spearman. 1987. The proof and measurement of association between two things. *The American Journal of Psychology*, 100(3/4):441–471.

James Thorne, Andreas Vlachos, Christos Christodoulopoulos, and Arpit Mittal. 2018. FEVER: a large-scale dataset for fact extraction and VERification. In *Proceedings of the 2018 Conference of the North American Chapter of the Association for Computational Linguistics: Human Language Technologies, Volume 1 (Long Papers)*, pages 809–819, New Orleans, Louisiana. Association for Computational Linguistics.

Herbert Ullrich and Jan Drchal. 2025. AIC CTU@FEVER 8: On-premise fact checking through long context RAG. In *Proceedings of the Eighth Workshop on Fact Extraction and VERification (FEVER)*. Association for Computational Linguistics.

Max Upravitelev, Premtim Sahitaj, Arthur Hilbert, Veronika Solopova, Jing Yang, Nils Feldhus, Tatiana Anikina, Simon Ostermann, and Vera Schmitt. 2025. Exploring semantic filtering heuristics for efficient claim verification. In *Proceedings of the Eighth Workshop on Fact Extraction and VERification (FEVER)*. Association for Computational Linguistics.

Andreas Vlachos and Sebastian Riedel. 2014. Fact checking: Task definition and dataset construction. In *Proceedings of the ACL 2014 Workshop on Language Technologies and Computational Social Science*, pages 18–22, Baltimore, MD, USA. Association for Computational Linguistics.

David Wadden, Shanchuan Lin, Kyle Lo, Lucy Lu Wang, Madeleine van Zuylen, Arman Cohan, and Hannaneh Hajishirzi. 2020. Fact or fiction: Verifying scientific claims. In *Proceedings of the 2020 Conference on Empirical Methods in Natural Language Processing (EMNLP)*, pages 7534–7550, Online. Association for Computational Linguistics.

William Yang Wang. 2017. "liar, liar pants on fire": A new benchmark dataset for fake news detection. In *Proceedings of the 55th Annual Meeting of the Association for Computational Linguistics (Volume 2: Short Papers)*, pages 422–426, Vancouver, Canada. Association for Computational Linguistics.

Greta Warren, Irina Shklovski, and Isabelle Augenstein. 2025. Show me the work: Fact-checkers' requirements for explainable automated fact-checking. In *Proceedings of the 2025 CHI Conference on Human Factors in Computing Systems*, pages 1–21.

Yejun Yoon, Jaeyoon Jung, Seunghyun Yoon, and Kunwoo Park. 2024. HerO at AVeriTeC: The herd of open large language models for verifying real-world claims. In *Proceedings of the Seventh Fact Extraction and VERification Workshop (FEVER)*, pages 130–136, Miami, Florida, USA. Association for Computational Linguistics.

Yejun Yoon, Jaeyoon Jung, Seunghyun Yoon, and Kunwoo Park. 2025. Team HUMANE at AVeriTeC 2025: HerO 2 for efficient fact verification. In *Proceedings of the Eighth Workshop on Fact Extraction and VERification (FEVER)*. Association for Computational Linguistics.

Xin Zhang, Yanzhao Zhang, Dingkun Long, Wen Xie, Ziqi Dai, Jialong Tang, Huan Lin, Baosong Yang, Pengjun Xie, Fei Huang, Meishan Zhang, Wenjie Li, and Min Zhang. 2024. mgte: Generalized long-context text representation and reranking models for multilingual text retrieval. *Preprint*, arXiv:2407.19669.

A Search Queries for Knowledge Store Generation

When creating the knowledge stores for the train, development, and test set, we used a series of search query generation strategies. An overview can be seen in Table 9. We note that some of these rely on information not available normally to participants, such as the gold question-answer pairs. We note that, despite this, systems not relying on the knowledge store, such as Papelo, were competitive.

B Human Evaluation

We carried out human evaluation of the submitted test set predictions. Below in Figures 2-??, we include screenshots of the interface used by annotators. We also include, in Tables 10 and 11, instructive examples from the human evaluation.

Query type	Description
Generated questions	*Questions are generated with gpt-3.5-turbo based on the claim. Three claim-question pairs from the training set are used as in-context examples.*
Generated background queries	*Queries are generated with gpt-3.5-turbo based on the claim. The prompt focuses on background information, such as details about entities in the claim. Three manually constructed claim-query pairs are used as in-context examples.*
Generated provenance queries	*Queries are generated with gpt-3.5-turbo based on the claim. The prompt focuses on information necessary to establish provenance, such as whether the claim source is a satire site. Three manually constructed claim-query pairs are used as in-context examples.*
Claim named entities	*Named entities from the claim are extracted and used as search queries. One query for each entity is constructed, along with one query containing all entities.*
Most similar gold evidence	*The most similar paragraph in the gold evidence document is selected using BM25, and used as a search query.*
Gold URL generated questions	*Queries are generated with gpt-3.5-turbo based on the URL of the gold evidence. The prompt tried to generate questions that would retrieve the URL in question. Three manually constructed URL-query pairs are used as in-context examples.*
Different event same entity	*Queries are generated with gpt-3.5-turbo based on the named entities in the claim. The prompt focuses on different events involving some of the same entities. Results are used as distractors to make the retrieval task harder.*
Similar entities	*Queries are generated with gpt-3.5-turbo based on the claim. The prompt replaces entities in the claim with other similar entities, such as changing one city to another. Results are used as distractors to make the retrieval task harder.*
Gold questions	*Gold questions used verbatim as search queries.*
Claim + gold question	*Gold questions used verbatim as search queries. The claim is prepended, processed as in Schlichtkrull et al. (2023a).*
Rephrased gold questions	*Gold questions are rephrased using gpt-3.5-turbo, and then input as search queries.*
Gold answers	*Gold questions used verbatim as search queries.*
Rephrased gold answers	*Gold answers are rephrased using gpt-3.5-turbo, and then input as search queries.*

Table 9: Queries input to the Google Search API for each claim in order to build the knowledge store. Following Schlichtkrull et al. (2023a), we restrict search results to documents published before the claim. For each claim, we also extend the knowledge store with the corresponding gold evidence documents.

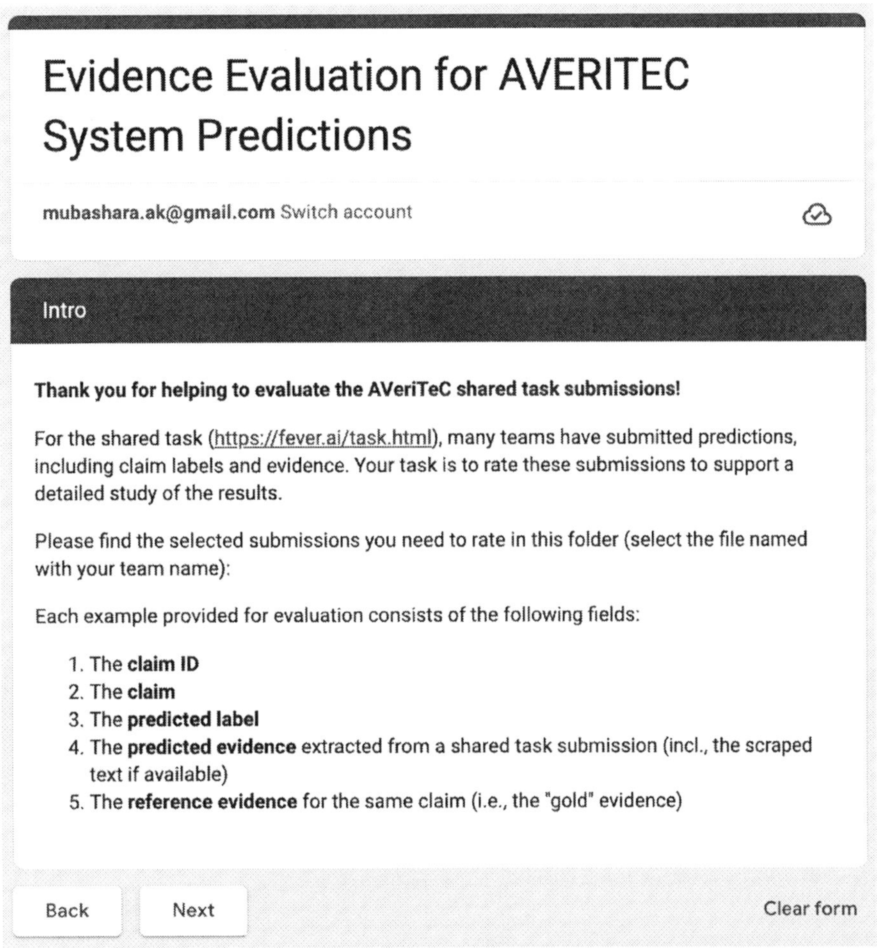

Figure 2: Platform for human evaluation of retrieved evidence from participating systems.

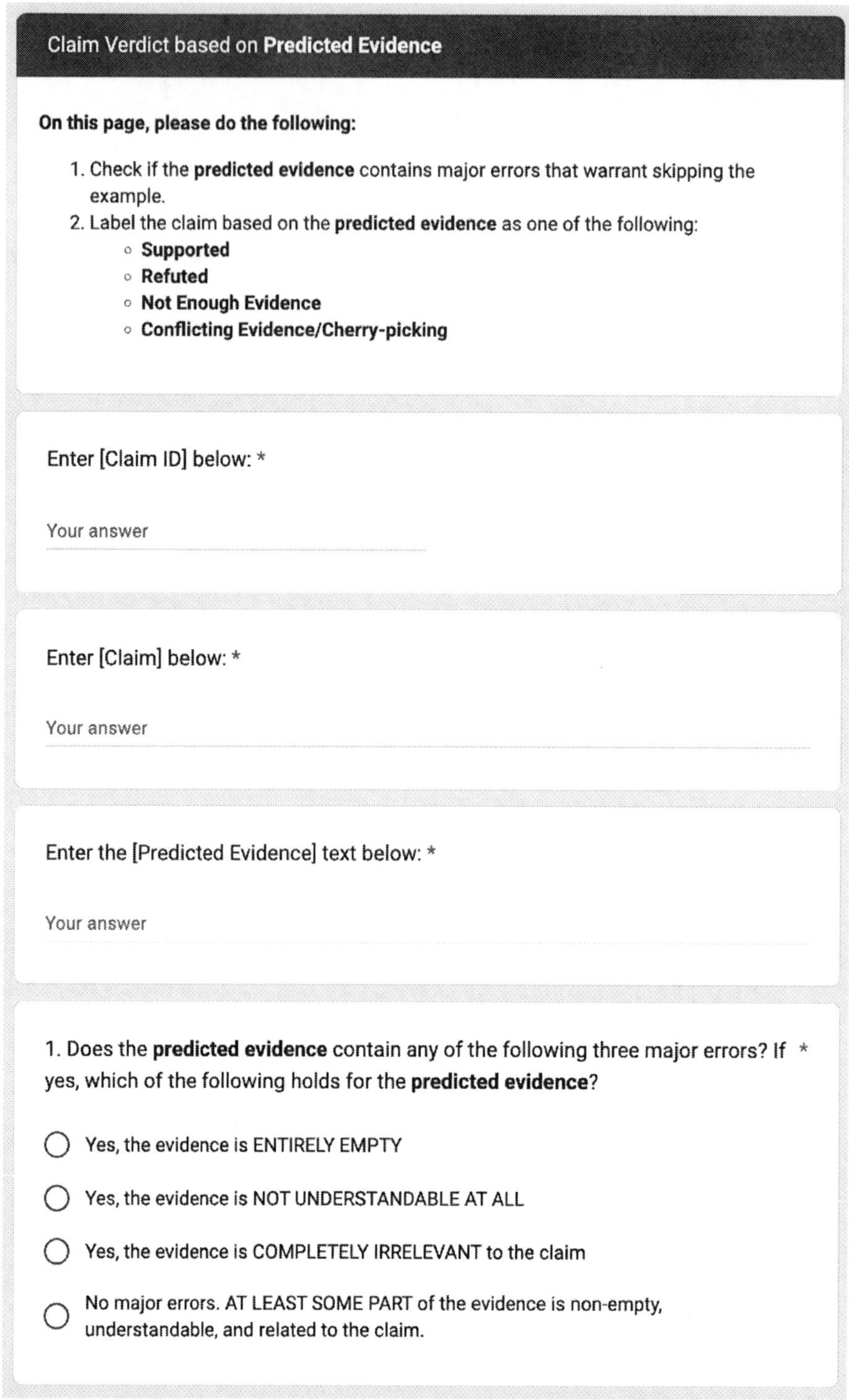

Claim Verdict based on **Predicted Evidence**

On this page, please do the following:

1. Check if the **predicted evidence** contains major errors that warrant skipping the example.
2. Label the claim based on the **predicted evidence** as one of the following:
   - **Supported**
   - **Refuted**
   - **Not Enough Evidence**
   - **Conflicting Evidence/Cherry-picking**

Enter [Claim ID] below: *

Your answer

Enter [Claim] below: *

Your answer

Enter the [Predicted Evidence] text below: *

Your answer

1. Does the **predicted evidence** contain any of the following three major errors? If yes, which of the following holds for the **predicted evidence**? *

- Yes, the evidence is ENTIRELY EMPTY
- Yes, the evidence is NOT UNDERSTANDABLE AT ALL
- Yes, the evidence is COMPLETELY IRRELEVANT to the claim
- No major errors. AT LEAST SOME PART of the evidence is non-empty, understandable, and related to the claim.

Figure 3: Platform for human evaluation of retrieved evidence from participating systems.

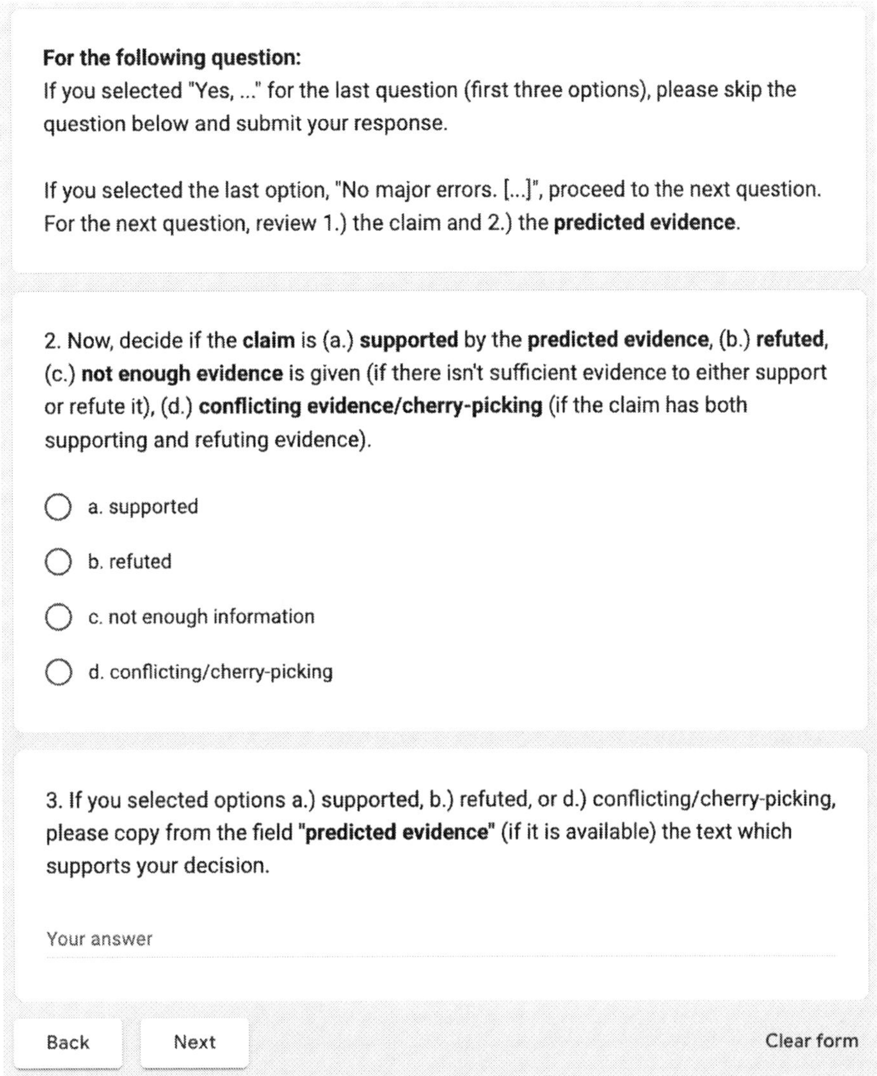

For the following question:
If you selected "Yes, ..." for the last question (first three options), please skip the question below and submit your response.

If you selected the last option, "No major errors. [...]", proceed to the next question.
For the next question, review 1.) the claim and 2.) the **predicted evidence**.

2. Now, decide if the **claim** is (a.) **supported** by the **predicted evidence**, (b.) **refuted**, (c.) **not enough evidence** is given (if there isn't sufficient evidence to either support or refute it), (d.) **conflicting evidence/cherry-picking** (if the claim has both supporting and refuting evidence).

- a. supported
- b. refuted
- c. not enough information
- d. conflicting/cherry-picking

3. If you selected options a.) supported, b.) refuted, or d.) conflicting/cherry-picking, please copy from the field **"predicted evidence"** (if it is available) the text which supports your decision.

Your answer

Back Next Clear form

Figure 4: Platform for human evaluation of retrieved evidence from participating systems.

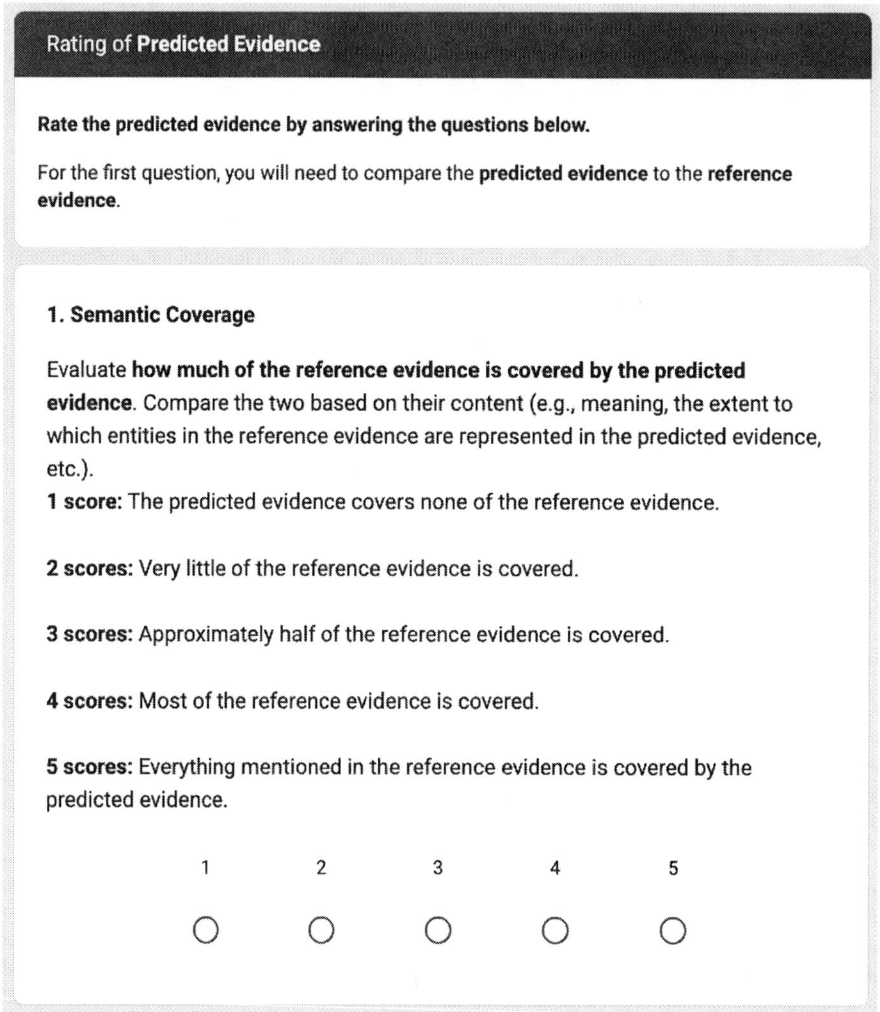

Rating of **Predicted Evidence**

Rate the predicted evidence by answering the questions below.

For the first question, you will need to compare the **predicted evidence** to the **reference evidence**.

1. Semantic Coverage

Evaluate **how much of the reference evidence is covered by the predicted evidence**. Compare the two based on their content (e.g., meaning, the extent to which entities in the reference evidence are represented in the predicted evidence, etc.).

1 score: The predicted evidence covers none of the reference evidence.

2 scores: Very little of the reference evidence is covered.

3 scores: Approximately half of the reference evidence is covered.

4 scores: Most of the reference evidence is covered.

5 scores: Everything mentioned in the reference evidence is covered by the predicted evidence.

1 2 3 4 5

Figure 5: Platform for human evaluation of retrieved evidence from participating systems.

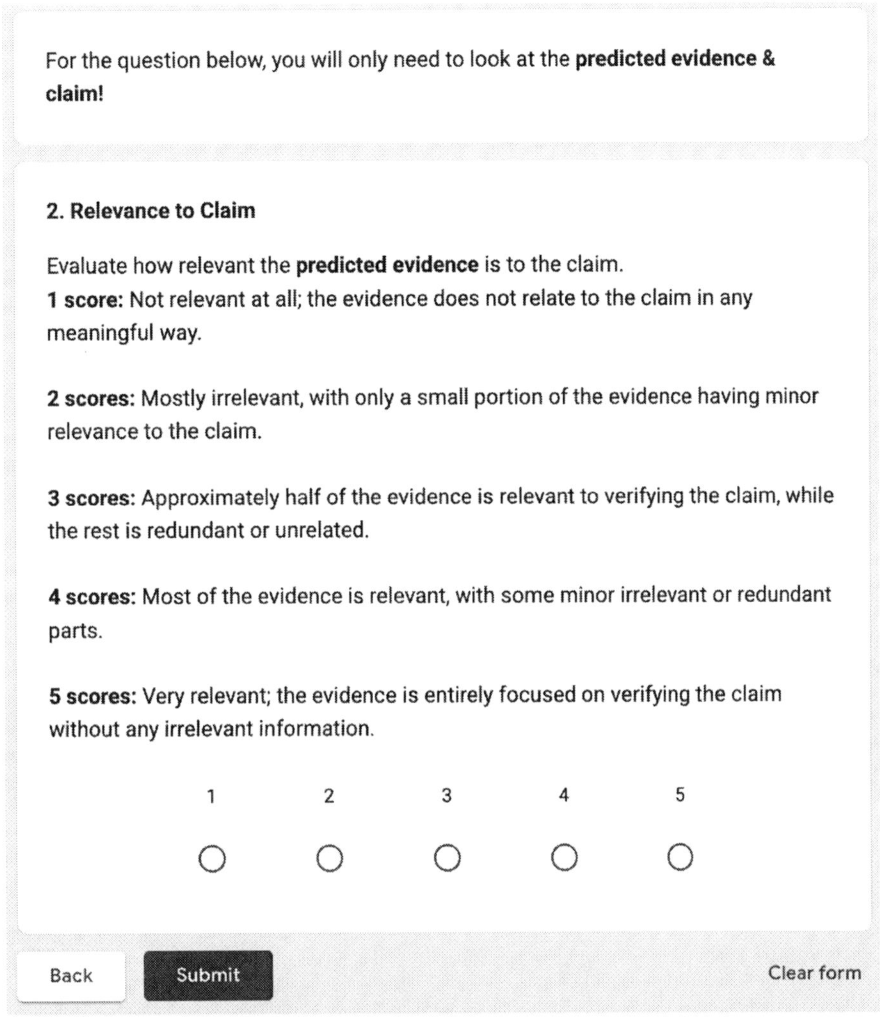

For the question below, you will only need to look at the **predicted evidence & claim!**

2. Relevance to Claim

Evaluate how relevant the **predicted evidence** is to the claim.
1 score: Not relevant at all; the evidence does not relate to the claim in any meaningful way.

2 scores: Mostly irrelevant, with only a small portion of the evidence having minor relevance to the claim.

3 scores: Approximately half of the evidence is relevant to verifying the claim, while the rest is redundant or unrelated.

4 scores: Most of the evidence is relevant, with some minor irrelevant or redundant parts.

5 scores: Very relevant; the evidence is entirely focused on verifying the claim without any irrelevant information.

1 2 3 4 5

Back Submit Clear form

Figure 6: Platform for human evaluation of retrieved evidence from participating systems.

	claim	predicted evidence	label human eval	semantic coverage	coherence	redundancy	consistency	relevance	predicted label	reference evidence
1	New changes to the Highway Code in Great Britain states drivers should give five feet when overtaking cyclists.	Question: Should drivers give five feet when overtaking bicyclists? Answer: No answer could be found. Question: What is the Highway Code in Great Britain? Answer: No answer could be found.	not enough information	1	5	1	5	5	Not Enough Evidence	Question: What is 5 feet in metres? Answer: 1.5 metres. Question: What is the new overtaking distance between drivers and cyclists in the Highway Code? Answer: leave at least 1.5 metres when overtaking cyclists. Question: At what maximum speed is the new 1.5-distance rule applicable? Answer: at speeds of up to 30mph. Question: Should drivers leave more space if driving faster? Answer: Yes. On a PDF for the 'Table of Changes to the Highway Code' it states, "Give them more space when overtaking at higher speeds."
2	Tweet portrays Ravish Kumar targeting AAP ahead of Punjab elections	Question: When were the Punjab elections? Answer: No answer could be found. Question: When was the tweet made? Answer: The tweet was allegedly made by Ravish Kumar in the midst of the Punjab election. Question: Is Ravish Kumar an AAP supporter? Answer: No answer could be found.	not enough information	1	2	5	3	2	Supported	Question: What does Ravish Kumar think of the AAP? Answer: No answer could be found. Question: Did Ravish Kumar tweet about the AAP? Answer: No answer could be found. Question: Has Ravish Kumar been misquoted on political matters? Answer: Senior Congress leader Digvijaya Singh apologised to NDTV anchor Ravish Kumar today after sharing a video on Twitter that incorrectly suggested the latter had abused Prime Minister Narendra Modi in a public speech on Wednesday.
3	In 2010, a newly qualified teacher's salary in the UK was £21,500 and in 2018 it was £22,000.	Question: What was the starting salary for a newly qualified teacher in 2010? Answer: £21,500. Question: What was the starting salary for a newly qualified teacher in 2018? Answer: £22,000. Question: What was the starting salary for a newly qualified teacher in 2010 in 2018 prices? Answer: £25,400. Question: What was the starting salary for a newly qualified teacher in 2018 in 2010 prices? Answer: £23,000.	supported	5	4	1	2	4	Supported	Question: What was the salary of a newly qualified teacher in the UK in 2010? Answer: £21,588. Question: What was the salary of a newly qualified teacher in the UK in 2018? Answer: £23,720. Question: What was the salary of new teachers outside of London in 2010? Answer: £21,588. Question: What was salary of new teachers outside of London in 2018? Answer: Minimum starting salaries for classroom teachers will increase by between £653 (rest of England) and £816 (inner London). This means the minimum starting salary for a qualified teacher in 2019/20 will rise from £23,720 to £24,373 outside of London and from £29,664 to £30,480 in inner London.

Table 10: Examples for system predictions which are highly-ranked by the Averitec score.

	claim	predicted evidence	label human eval	semantic coverage	coherence	redundancy	consistency	relevance	predicted label	reference evidence
1	The reporting environment for foreign correspondents in China is open and free. Communication channels between foreign journalists in China and competent Chinese authorities are open and unfettered.	Question: What is the working environment for foreign journalists in China? Answer: Foreign correspondents in China have reported higher levels of concern about surveillance and invasion of privacy, as well as greater pressure by overseas Chinese officials on media organization headquarters. Nearly half of surveyed correspondents said they experienced interference, harassment, and physical violence. [...]	refuted	5	5	5	5	5	Refuted	Question: Does the Chinese government place restrictions on journalist content? Answer: Yes. The Propaganda Department of the Chinese Communist Party sends a detailed notice to all media every day that includes editorial guidelines and censored topics.
2	Philippines Senator Panfilo Lacson changes his opinion and says he sees the sense in the Department of National Defense's (DND) unilateral termination of its 1989 accord with the University of the Philippines (UP).	Question: What was Philippines Senator Panfilo Lacson's previous stance on the Department of National Defense's (DND) termination of its 1989 accord with the University of the Philippines (UP)? Answer: Philippines Senator Panfilo Lacson's previous stance on the Department of National Defense's (DND) termination of its 1989 accord with the University of the Philippines (UP) was critical. [...]	supported	3	5	5	5	4	Supported	Question: What was his initial view on the DND and University of the Philippines longstanding arrangement? Answer: There's sense in the move taken by the President and Sec. Lorenzana because during our red-tagging hearings in the Senate, it was established that—not only UP in particular, other universities—talagang 'yung recruitment nanggagaling dun sa mga estudyante up to the point that they're being killed in encounters, he told ANC's Headstart.

Table 11: Examples for system predictions which are low-ranked by the Averitec score.

Team HUMANE at AVeriTeC 2025: HerO 2 for Efficient Fact Verification

Yejun Yoon[♡] **Jaeyoon Jung**[♣◇] **Seunghyun Yoon**[♠] **Kunwoo Park**[♣♡]
[♡]Department of Intelligent Semiconductors, Soongsil University
[♣]School of AI Convergence, Soongsil University
[◇]MAUM AI Inc.
[♠]Adobe Research, USA
{yejun0382, jaeyoonskr}@soongsil.ac.kr, syoon@adobe.com, kunwoo.park@ssu.ac.kr

Abstract

This paper presents HerO 2, Team HUMANE's system for the AVeriTeC shared task at the FEVER-25 workshop. HerO 2 is an enhanced version of HerO, the best-performing open-source model from the previous year's challenge. It improves evidence quality through document summarization and answer reformulation, optimizes veracity prediction via post-training quantization under computational constraints, and enhances overall system performance by integrating updated language model (LM) backbones. HerO 2 ranked second on the leaderboard while achieving the shortest runtime among the top three systems, demonstrating both high efficiency and strong potential for real-world fact verification. The code is available at https://github.com/ssu-humane/HerO2.

1 Introduction

This paper describes Hero 2, the fact verification system developed by Team HUMANE for the AVeriTeC shared task. Hero 2 is an improved version of HerO (Yoon et al., 2024), which achieved the state-of-the-art performance among the open-source models in the last year's AVeriTeC shared task. The 2025 edition emphasizes efficient, reproducible, and open-source approaches to automated fact-checking. Two key changes distinguish this year's task setting. First, computational and time constraints prohibit the use of large language models with more than ten billion of parameters (e.g., Llama3 70B Instruct). Second, the evidence evaluation metric has shifted from Hungarian METEOR (a token-based metric) to Ev2R recall (a model-based metric), which requires the generation of more flexible and semantically coherent evidence.

In alignment with these goals, Hero 2 enhances retrieval performance through document-based retrieval and summarization, and reconstructs answer texts based on the question. We further improve the verification process using AWQ (Lin et al., 2024), enabling higher accuracy while maintaining efficiency under the hardware constraints specified by the task. As a result, Hero 2 achieved second place on the leaderboard while exhibiting the shortest runtime among the top-performing models, demonstrating its efficiency and suggesting its potential for real-world fact verification.

2 Task Description

The AVeriTeC shared task aims to build a fact-checking system that verifies real-world claims using web evidence. The claim verification process consists of three main steps. First, the system performs evidence retrieval by collecting relevant web documents. Next, during question generation, the system may generate questions for each piece of evidence to better assess the claim, though this step is optional. Finally, in the veracity prediction phase, the system uses the collected information to assess the truthfulness of the claim. The possible verdicts are: supported, refuted, not enough evidence, or conflicting evidence/cherry-picking.

The 2025 shared task specifically targets two main goals. First, it aims to promote the development of high-performing systems that, using only open LLMs, can retrieve relevant evidence and generate accurate verdicts to maximize evaluation scores. Second, it emphasizes the importance of building reproducible and efficient fact-verification systems. Accordingly, all systems must be executable within the provided virtual machine environment and capable of verifying a single claim in under one minute. While the previous shared task (Schlichtkrull et al., 2024) used the Hungarian METEOR score to assess the quality of questions (Q score) and question-answer pairs (Q+A score), this year's evaluation adopts the Ev2R recall (Akhtar et al., 2024), an LLM-based evaluation method. Ev2R utilizes an LLM to decompose the

Proceedings of the Eighth Fact Extraction and VERification Workshop (FEVER), pages 224–228

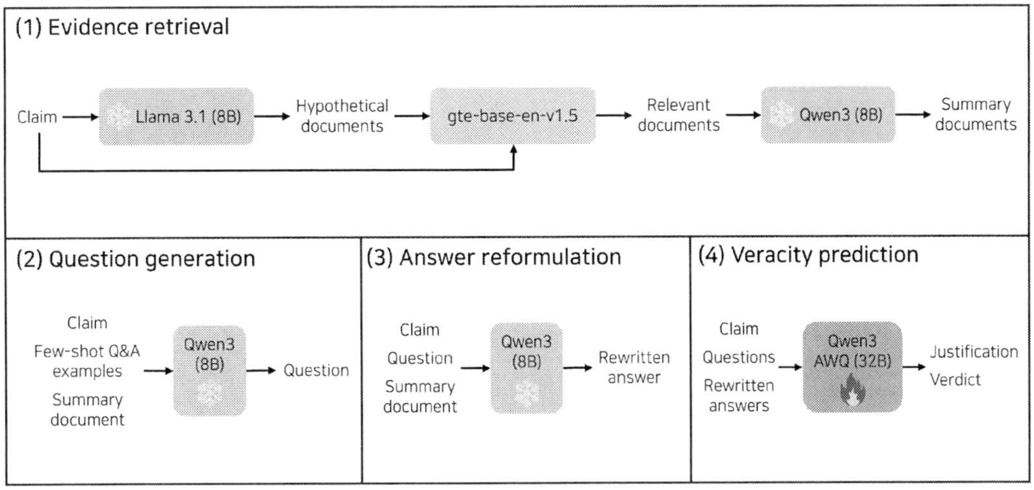

Figure 1: Pipeline of our system

System	Query Expansion	Evidence Retrieval	Evidence Summarization	Question Generation	Answer Reformulation	Veracity Prediction
Baseline	HyDE-FC (Llama3.1 8B)	Hybrid (BM25/SFR-embedding-2)	NA	Llama3 8B	NA	Llama3.1 8B
HerO 2		Dense (gte-base-en-v1.5)	Qwen3 8B	Qwen3 8B	Qwen3 8B	Qwen3 32B AWQ

Table 1: Model configurations

ground-truth evidence into atomic facts. The Q+A score is then calculated by measuring the degree to which these facts cover the predicted evidence. The new AVeriTeC score is computed as the veracity prediction accuracy when the Q+A score of the predicted evidence for a claim exceeds a predefined threshold.

3 Our System: HerO 2

We present HerO 2, an improved fact verification pipeline of HerO (Yoon et al., 2024). The key enhancements are summarized below:

- **Document summarization**: Web documents are summarized into paragraph-level evidence blocks.
- **Answer reformulation**: A language model is prompted to convert the retrieved evidence blocks into answer-form texts.
- **Post-training quantization**: A fine-tuned LLM is quantized for veracity prediction.
- **Updated LM backbones**: Backbone LMs for each components are updated to maximize the performance.

Figure 1 illustrates its overall pipeline, and Table 1 details the model configuration in comparison to the baseline method.

3.1 Knowledge Store Construction

The 2025 AVeriTeC Shared Task imposes a one-minute time limit for processing each claim on a designated virtual machine. To meet this constraint, we apply two preprocessing steps to the web documents provided as the knowledge store: (1) indexing dense embeddings for all documents using gte-base-en-v1.5 (Li et al., 2023) following the design choice of the winning model in last year's shared task (Rothermel et al., 2024); and (2) summarizing each document into paragraph-level evidence candidates using Qwen3 8B (Yang et al., 2025).

3.2 Evidence Retrieval

The goal of evidence retrieval is to retrieve evidence necessary for verifying claims from the knowledge store. We use HyDE-FC (Yoon et al., 2024) for query expansion, which generates hypothetical fact-checking articles for a given claim by prompting an LLM. We retrieve the top 10 relevant documents through the indexed dense embedding. We adopt an additional step to summarize each of

Your task is to read the following document carefully and summarize it into a single, coherent paragraph. Focus on capturing the main ideas and essential details without adding new information or personal opinions.

Document:: An image of a purported 1998 letter from actor Sean Connery (famous for his portrayal of agent James Bond) to Apple CEO Steve Jobs, caustically rebuffing an offer to become a pitchman for Apple Computers, hit the Internet in June 2011.
...

Output: In June 2011, an image of a purported 1998 letter from actor Sean Connery to Apple CEO Steve Jobs, rejecting an offer to become an Apple pitchman, circulated online. However, the letter was part of a satirical article published on Scoopertino, a website known for fabricating news about Apple under the motto "All the News That's Fit to Fabricate." ...

Figure 2: An example of the instruction prompt used for document summarization, along with its output. The bold text is the instruction, and the blue text indicates the model output.

the retrieved documents into a single paragraph. The used prompt for summarization is shown in Figure 2. Our best model uses Llama3.1 8B for HyDE-FC and Qwen3 8B for document summarization.

3.3 Question Generation and Answer Reformulation

In this step, we generate questions based on the summarized evidence and retain only the information necessary to answer them through sequential LLM generations. We first generate questions using the same prompt as the baseline method. Then, we transform the retrieved summary text into an answer-form response conditioned on the claim and the generated question. The prompt used for this reformulation step is shown in Figure 3. Our best-performing pipeline employs Qwen3 8B for both question generation and evidence reformulation.

3.4 Veracity Prediction

We use a fine-tuned instruction-following language model to predict the veracity of given claims. Our best-performing model is a fine-tuned Qwen3 32B model, quantized to 4-bit using AWQ (Lin et al., 2024) to satisfy the VRAM constraints of the shared task, enabling inference on an A10G GPU (23GB). Following the baseline approach, we use a prompt that incorporates the annotator's rationale into the veracity prediction process. The top

The following text provides an evidence obtained through web searches related to a specific question, used for verifying the accuracy of a claim. Your task is to answer the question based on this evidence. Ensure your answer is Supported by relevant context from the evidence.

Claim: In a letter to Steve Jobs, Sean Connery refused to appear in an apple commercial.

Question: Was the letter from Sean Connery to Steve Jobs genuine?

Evidence: In June 2011, an image of a purported 1998 letter from actor Sean Connery to Apple CEO Steve Jobs, rejecting an offer to become an Apple pitchman, circulated online. However, the letter was part of a satirical article published on Scoopertino, a website known for fabricating news about Apple under the motto "All the News That's Fit to Fabricate." ...

Answer: No, the letter from Sean Connery to Steve Jobs was not genuine. It was part of a satirical article published on Scoopertino, a website known for fabricating news about Apple. ...

Figure 3: An example of the instruction prompt used for answer reformulation, along with its output. The bold text is the instruction, and the blue text indicates the model output.

10 question–answer pairs generated in the earlier stages are provided as in-context examples, along with the claim to be verified.

4 Evaluation Experiments

This section presents the experimental results that guided the selection of each module in the submitted system.

4.1 Experimental Setups

In the comparison experiments, we used the development set to evaluate model performance. We used the training set for training our models. The Ev2R evaluation is carried out in a local environment using the Llama 3.3 70B (Grattafiori et al., 2024) model with a threshold of 0.5.

For retrieval, we used gte-base-en-v1.5, which supports a context length of 8192. In other cases, we employed mxbai-embed-large-v1 (Lee et al., 2024). All language models used in the experiments were instruction-tuned versions. For training, we used the Adam optimizer with a learning rate of 2e-5, batch size of 128, and trained the model for 2 epochs.

The Llama3.1 8B (Grattafiori et al., 2024) was

configured with the following hyperparameters for HyDE-FC: maximum number of tokens as 512, temperature as 0.7, and top-p as 1.0. The Qwen3 8B used the hyperparameters recommended by the Qwen team[1]: temperature as 0.7, top-p as 0.8, top-k as 20, and min-p as 0. Veracity predictions used the hyperparameters: temperature as 0.9, top-p as 0.7, and top-k as 1. If the language model failed to produce a verdict label, we repeated the generation using top-2 sampling.

We ran experiments using three machines. The first has two H100 GPUs (80GB per GPU) and 480GB RAM. The second has eight H100 GPUs with 2TB RAM; the third has four NVIDIA A6000 GPUs (48GB per GPU) and 256GB RAM. The experiments were conducted in a computing environment with the following configuration: Python 3.12.9, PyTorch 2.6.0, Transformers 4.51.3, vLLM 0.8.5, and Sentence-Transformers 4.1.0.

4.2 Experimental Results

Evidence Retrieval We compare three retrieval strategies: (1) retrieving individual sentences, (2) retrieving consecutive sentence chunks with one-sentence overlap, and (3) retrieving entire documents. Table 2 presents the evidence retrieval results on the development set, varying the number of retrieved evidence candidates. Among the three, the top-10 document-level retrieval strategy achieves the best performance, outperforming all other configurations with different retrieval targets and candidate counts.

Retrieval Target	Q + A (Ev2R recall)		
	Top-3	Top-5	Top-10
Sentence	0.289	0.315	0.374
Chunk (2 sentences)	0.311	0.369	0.404
Chunk (3 sentences)	0.347	0.382	0.413
Chunk (4 sentences)	0.364	0.41	0.115
Document	**0.37**	**0.487**	**0.522**

Table 2: Evidence retrieval performance

Answer Reformulation Table 3 presents the results of document summarization and answer reformulation, varying the number of retrieved evidence documents used for veracity prediction. The best performance is observed when answer reformulation is applied to the top-10 question-answer pairs. When controlling for the number of retrieved documents, applying answer reformulation consistently outperforms the baseline without reformulation.

[1]https://huggingface.co/Qwen/Qwen3-8B

Method	Q + A (Ev2R recall)		
	Top-3	Top-5	Top-10
Document-based retrieval	0.37	0.487	0.522
+ document summarization	0.483	0.51	0.487
+ answer reformulation	**0.501**	**0.514**	**0.556**

Table 3: Effects of answer reformulation

Veracity Prediction Controlling for other modules by fixing them to their best-performing configurations, we compare veracity prediction methods using the optimal settings for evidence retrieval and question generation. Table 4 presents the fine-tuning results. While the models achieve comparable F1 scores, they exhibit substantial differences in accuracy. Since the AVeriTeC score is based on accuracy, we adopt it as the primary metric for selecting the best-performing model. Notably, applying AWQ post-training quantization to Qwen3 32B yields a +0.018 improvement in accuracy over its computationally equivalent smaller variant, Qwen3 8B. Among the 8B models, Qwen3 outperforms Llama 3.1, the language model used in the baseline.

Method	F1	ACC
Qwen3 32B AWQ	0.382	**0.692**
Qwen3 8B	**0.385**	0.674
Llama3.1 8B	0.384	0.588

Table 4: Veracity prediction performance

4.3 Test Set Results

System	AVeriTeC score	Average runtime per claim (s)
CTU AIC	**0.332±0.002**	53.67
HerO 2	0.271±0.004	**29.19**
yellow_flash	0.253±0.005	31.71
Baseline	0.202±0.007	33.88

Table 5: Test set results

Table 5 presents the performance of HerO 2 on the test set in comparison with the baseline and other competitive models. CTU AIC achieved the highest AVeriTeC score of 0.332, followed by HerO 2 with 0.271 and yellow_flash with 0.253. HerO 2 also achieved the lowest average runtime per claim at 29.19 seconds, demonstrating superior efficiency compared to CTU AIC (53.67 seconds), yellow_flash (31.71 seconds), and the baseline (33.88 seconds). These results indicate that HerO 2 is the most efficient system among the top-performing models. It is worth noting that while some systems achieved shorter runtimes, their performance was significantly lower.

5 Conclusion

In this paper, we presented HerO 2, an efficient fact-checking system developed for the AVeriTeC shared task, hosted by the eighth FEVER workshop. Four key components contribute to the performance improvement of HerO 2: document summarization, answer reformulation, post-training quantization, and updated language model backbones. Our system achieved second place in the shared task while recording the shortest runtime among the top three systems, highlighting its efficiency and potential for real-world fact verification.

Acknowledgments

This research was supported by the MSIT(Ministry of Science and ICT), Korea, under the Innovative Human Resource Development for Local Intellectualization (IITP-2025-RS-2022-00156360) and Graduate School of Metaverse Convergence support (IITP-2025-RS-2024-00430997) programs, supervised by the IITP(Institute for Information & Communications Technology Planning & Evaluation). Yejun Yoon and Jaeyoon Jung contributed to this work equally as co-first authors. Kunwoo Park is the corresponding author.

References

Mubashara Akhtar, Michael Schlichtkrull, and Andreas Vlachos. 2024. Ev2r: Evaluating evidence retrieval in automated fact-checking. *arXiv preprint arXiv:2411.05375*.

Aaron Grattafiori, Abhimanyu Dubey, Abhinav Jauhri, Abhinav Pandey, Abhishek Kadian, Ahmad Al-Dahle, Aiesha Letman, Akhil Mathur, Alan Schelten, Alex Vaughan, and 1 others. 2024. The llama 3 herd of models. *arXiv preprint arXiv:2407.21783*.

Sean Lee, Aamir Shakir, Darius Koenig, and Julius Lipp. 2024. Open source strikes bread - new fluffy embeddings model.

Zehan Li, Xin Zhang, Yanzhao Zhang, Dingkun Long, Pengjun Xie, and Meishan Zhang. 2023. Towards general text embeddings with multi-stage contrastive learning. *arXiv preprint arXiv:2308.03281*.

Ji Lin, Jiaming Tang, Haotian Tang, Shang Yang, Wei-Ming Chen, Wei-Chen Wang, Guangxuan Xiao, Xingyu Dang, Chuang Gan, and Song Han. 2024. Awq: Activation-aware weight quantization for on-device llm compression and acceleration. *Proceedings of Machine Learning and Systems*, 6:87–100.

Mark Rothermel, Tobias Braun, Marcus Rohrbach, and Anna Rohrbach. 2024. InFact: A strong baseline for automated fact-checking. In *Proceedings of the Seventh Fact Extraction and VERification Workshop (FEVER)*, pages 108–112, Miami, Florida, USA. Association for Computational Linguistics.

Michael Schlichtkrull, Yulong Chen, Chenxi Whitehouse, Zhenyun Deng, Mubashara Akhtar, Rami Aly, Zhijiang Guo, Christos Christodoulopoulos, Oana Cocarascu, Arpit Mittal, James Thorne, and Andreas Vlachos. 2024. The automated verification of textual claims (AVeriTeC) shared task. In *Proceedings of the Seventh Fact Extraction and VERification Workshop (FEVER)*.

An Yang, Anfeng Li, Baosong Yang, Beichen Zhang, Binyuan Hui, Bo Zheng, Bowen Yu, Chang Gao, Chengen Huang, Chenxu Lv, and 1 others. 2025. Qwen3 technical report. *arXiv preprint arXiv:2505.09388*.

Yejun Yoon, Jaeyoon Jung, Seunghyun Yoon, and Kunwoo Park. 2024. HerO at AVeriTeC: The herd of open large language models for verifying real-world claims. In *Proceedings of the Seventh Fact Extraction and VERification Workshop (FEVER)*, pages 130–136, Miami, Florida, USA. Association for Computational Linguistics.

Exploring Semantic Filtering Heuristics For Efficient Claim Verification

Max Upravitelev[1], Premtim Sahitaj[1], Arthur Hilbert[1], Veronika Solopova[1], Jing Yang[1,3], Nils Feldhus[1,3], Tatiana Anikina[2], Simon Ostermann[2,4] and Vera Schmitt[1,2,3,4]
[1]Technische Universität Berlin
[2]German Research Center for Artificial Intelligence (DFKI)
[3]BIFOLD – Berlin Institute for the Foundations of Learning and Data
[4]Centre for European Research in Trusted AI (CERTAIN)
Correspondence: max.upravitelev@tu-berlin.de

Abstract

Given the limited computational and financial resources of news agencies, real-life usage of fact-checking systems requires fast response times. For this reason, our submission to the FEVER-8 claim verification shared task focuses on optimizing the efficiency of such pipelines built around subtasks such as evidence retrieval and veracity prediction. We propose the Semantic Filtering for Efficient Fact Checking (SFEFC) strategy, which is inspired by the FEVER-8 baseline and designed with the goal of reducing the number of LLM calls and other computationally expensive subroutines. Furthermore, we explore the reuse of cosine similarities initially calculated within a dense retrieval step to retrieve the top 10 most relevant evidence sentence sets. We use these sets for semantic filtering methods based on similarity scores and create filters for particularly hard classification labels "Not Enough Information" and "Conflicting Evidence/Cherrypicking" by identifying thresholds for potentially relevant information and the semantic variance within these sets. Compared to the parallelized FEVER-8 baseline, which takes 33.88 seconds on average to process a claim according to the FEVER-8 shared task leaderboard, our non-parallelized system remains competitive in regard to AVeriTeC retrieval scores while reducing the runtime to 7.01 seconds, achieving the fastest average runtime per claim.

1 Introduction

Building systems for claim verification poses a significant challenge and is typically evaluated with accuracy-related metrics. At the same time, the efficiency of systems generally proposed within natural language processing (NLP) research is becoming another major aspect of system design (Treviso et al., 2023), motivated by sustainability and efforts in the domain of green NLP (Strubell et al., 2019). The field is experiencing a gradual conceptual shift towards smaller, more efficient models, as evidenced by the proliferation of smaller open-source transformer models (e.g., Gemma 3 (Team et al., 2025), Llama 3.2 (Grattafiori et al., 2024), or Phi 4 (Abdin et al., 2024)). Commercial proprietary models follow the trend, with GPT-4o (OpenAI et al., 2024) being the default flagship OpenAI model, while also being twice as fast and 50% more cost-effective than the larger GPT-4 Turbo model (OpenAI, 2023). DeepSeek (DeepSeek-AI et al., 2024) released a smaller model that matches or exceeds the performance of GPT models in various tasks, while requiring significantly less computational power for inference.

In parallel, embedding models used for semantic similarity search are undergoing a similar transformation. Open-source models such as E5-small (Wang et al., 2022) and MiniLM (Wang et al., 2020) demonstrate that compact architectures can achieve retrieval performance competitive with LLMs while significantly reducing inference costs. More recently, models such as GTE (Li et al., 2023a) and BGE (Liu et al., 2023) have gained attention for offering strong performance on a variety of retrieval tasks with relatively lightweight configurations. At the commercial level, OpenAI's text-embedding-3-small model (OpenAI, 2024) achieves strong semantic performance at a fraction of the cost and latency of earlier embedding APIs. This collective shift reflects a growing emphasis on deployment efficiency, edge compatibility, and environmentally conscious model design, without compromising retrieval accuracy.

These transformations have a direct impact on Retrieval-Augmented Generation (RAG) systems, particularly in scenarios where cost-efficiency is critical. RAG systems typically involve a similarity search followed by an LLM re-assessment of the highest-ranking candidate data reference points. Efficiency-optimized RAG systems are particularly

Proceedings of the Eighth Fact Extraction and VERification Workshop (FEVER), pages 229–237
July 31, 2025 ©2025 Association for Computational Linguistics

valuable in fact-checking applications, where news agencies often operate with limited computational resources, as well as understaffed and underfunded fact-checking units (Graves, 2018).

Taking these trends into account, we propose a system inspired by the FEVER-8 baseline with the main goal of reducing its runtime per claim while retaining comparable performance. To achieve this, we explore possibilities of reducing computationally expensive subroutines like generating texts with LLMs and the re-usage of calculated cosine similarities for the application of semantic filters for veracity prediction. Our main contributions are[1]:

- Introducing a pipeline designed for efficiency-aware claim verification that remains competitive with the FEVER-8 baseline in terms of retrieval scores, while reducing the average runtime per claim from 33.88s to 7.01s according to the FEVER-8 Leaderboard[2].
- Exploring the application of semantic filters to predict the veracity labels "Not Enough Information" and "Conflicting Evidence/Cherrypicking".

2 Related Work

Efficient fact-checking Tang et al. (2024) used GPT-4-generated training data to train small language models (770M parameters) for fact verification and showed their models achieving performance in closed-book and document-based settings on par with GPT-4. Xie et al. (2025) integrated interactive retrieval and verification and reduced costs for both parts, particularly for GPT-4o-mini on factuality benchmarks. The approach also enables LLMs to leverage their internal knowledge for judgments instead of always relying on external evidence retrieval.

These contributions achieved notable results in regard to building efficient systems and were evaluated on different benchmarks, a direction we also aim to contribute to with a system specifically tailored for the AVeriTeC dataset.

Semantic filtering Gupta et al. (2023) employed similarity metrics to perform semantic matching. In particular, they find mappings between scientific evidence in publications and paraphrased findings in health news articles using most similar paragraphs as evidence in the context of fake news detection.

The identification of thresholds for classification tasks based on cosine similarity was explored in works such as Pilehvar and Camacho-Collados (2019) and Zhou et al. (2022). Here, optimal thresholds were tuned by incrementing values stepwise while iterating over training sets with promising results with regard to performance and efficiency. Both works identified thresholds for binary classifiers to evaluate different word embedding models, with the goal of measuring the cosine distances between word pairs in different contexts. However, to our knowledge, this technique has not yet been examined in the context of veracity prediction.

3 Methodology

The AVeriTeC (Automated Verification of Textual Claims) dataset (Schlichtkrull et al., 2023) contains 4568 fact-checked, real-word claims. The data set enables the assessment of claim verification systems that retrieve evidence from the open web. AVeriTeC provides a training, development (dev) and test set. It is accompanied by a knowledge store with scraped texts from websites related to potential search queries to verify a claim. All claims are classified into four categories of verdicts:

- "Supported" (SUP)
- "Refuted" (REF)
- "Not Enough Evidence" (NEI)
- "Conflicting Evidence/Cherrypicking" (CoC).

Efficiency-optimized pipeline design One of the goals of the FEVER-8 shared task is the exploration of the usage of Open Source (OS) models while emphasizing the efficiency of the proposed systems by capping the maximum runtime at one minute per claim. Hence, a baseline was released based on an optimized version of HerO (Yoon et al., 2024), which was the highest scoring system from the FEVER-7 shared task (Schlichtkrull et al., 2024) that was built upon OS models. We designed our system inspired by this baseline and with the goal in mind of building a pipeline that reduces the amount of LLM calls and thus reduces the overall runtime. The resulting SFEFC pipeline relies on only two LLM calls within the following steps (which are also illustrated in Figure 1).

[1]Our code is available at: https://github.com/XplaiNLP/SFEFC-FEVER-8-Shared-Task

[2]https://fever.ai/task.html

1. Generate a question based on the claim by prompting an LLM
    a) Get a claim from the dataset, such as "In a letter to Steve Jobs, Sean Connery refused to appear in an apple commercial"
    b) Generate a corresponding question, such as "Is there any documented evidence or credible source that confirms Sean Connery wrote a letter to Steve Jobs refusing to appear in an Apple commercial?"
2. Retrieve relevant evidence based on hybrid search:
    a) Concatenate all individual sentences from the AVeriTeC knowledge store sequentially to sets of 4
    b) Sparse retrieval: Return top 1500 sets of sentence sets from 2.a via BM25
    c) Dense retrieval: Return the top 10 sentence sets based on the cosine similarity of the results from 2.b
3. Predict a verdict label for NEI and CoC via semantic filtering using cosine similarities from 2.c
4. If a semantic filter can be applied following Algorithm 1, the corresponding label is used as the final verdict
5. If not, an LLM prompt (included in the appendix of this paper) is constructed from the retrieved evidence, the claim and the system prompt with instructions to choose between SUP or REF, effectively reducing the classification labels to a binary choice in this step
6. The LLM prediction is used as the final verdict

The hybrid search step is similar to the same step within the FEVER-8/HerO baseline, but with one key change that we implemented to improve the runtime: While the baseline retrieved sentences one by one, we sequentially concatenated the sentences related to each claim in the AVeriTeC knowledge store into sets of 4 before retrieving these sets with BM25. The amount of 4 was chosen due to observations within preliminary testing, where we observed an increase in the old AVeriTeC score while incrementing the value until the amount of 4.

This concatenation strategy is similar to chunking strategies within RAG pipelines, where the size of chunks is determined by trade-offs, like preserving semantic information while keeping it precise enough for query-based retrieval. As a consequence, by concatenating the sentences in sets of 4 we also reduced the total number of retrieval candidates from the knowledge store by a factor of 4, allowing us to also reduce the number of top k results retrieved by BM25 from 5000 in the baseline to 1500. This, in turn, led to a decrease in the amount of embeddings needed to be created to retrieve the top 10 candidates based on cosine similarity. The actual values of the set size and the top k from BM25 were determined within preliminary tests by evaluating this pipeline on the AVeriTeC dev set with different values.

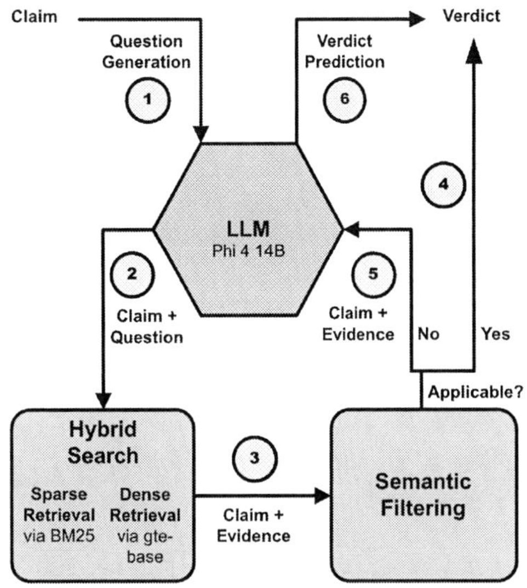

Figure 1: Architecture of the proposed system

Semantic filtering The proposed semantic filtering method aims to classify the veracity verdicts by assessing the cosine similarities between the query and the top 10 retrieved evidence. Algorithm 1 documents our Semantic Filtering for Efficient Fact Checking (SFEFC) approach, which was motivated by further lowering the runtime by reusing the cosine similarities during the 2.c step. Here, the reduction in runtime was achieved by removing an additional LLM call and using already computed similarity values to classify veracity labels, provided that a semantic filter was applicable.

The filtering strategy for the NEI class assumes a threshold of cosine similarity below which the retrieved information can be classified as not relevant.

The idea of filtering for *semantic variance* in regard to the CoC class follows the intuition that the variance within the set of cosine similarities between the query and the retrieved top 10 results should be higher in this class compared to others, since it should include evidence which both supports and refutes the claim. We calculate the semantic variance with

$$\mathrm{Var}(a) = \frac{1}{N}\sum_{i=1}^{N} |a_i - \bar{a}|^2$$

, where a_i are the elements in the input array a (consisting of the top 10 cosine similarities from the 2.c step), $\bar{a}$ is the mean of all elements and N is the total amount of all elements.

For identifying the thresholds, we implemented a similar routine to threshold tuning as Pilehvar and Camacho-Collados (2019) and Zhou et al. (2022): We incrementally increased the thresholds while iterating over our final prediction files for the dev set containing the retrieved evidence, updated the NEI and CoC labels if they met certain thresholds, and scored the overall predictions using the official AVeriTeC scorer which considered the metrics based on Hungarian METEOR (Schlichtkrull et al., 2023).

During the rise of OS LLMs, several inference engines with different trade-offs in regard to factors such as performance metrics and target hardware were released in recent years (Park et al., 2025). We chose to use llama.cpp[3] and its GGUF-quantization format for our LLM calls. Although lacking some capabilities of other engines, such as running inference on multiple nodes, llama.cpp was designed with the goal in mind of deploying LLMs on consumer hardware, making it a suitable choice that aligns with our motivation.

Name	Split	Hungarian METEOR	Ev2R
FEVER-8/HerO	dev	0.554	0.296
	test	0.497	0.2023
SFEFC-phi4	dev	0.572	0.266
	test	0.494	0.2047

Table 1: FEVER-8/HerO (baseline) and SFEFC-phi4 (our) results on the AVeriTeC dataset

Algorithm 1 Semantic Filtering with Heuristics

```
function GETLABEL(cos_sims)
    t_nei ← 0.82
    t_conf ← 0.0007
    pred ← None
    if cos_sims[0] < t_nei then
        pred ← "Not Enough Evidence"
    end if
    if Var(cos_sims) > t_conf then
        pred ← "Conflicting Evidence/ Cherrypicking"
    end if
    return pred
end function

function APPLYFILTER(claim, evs)
    cos_sims = [ ]
    for ev in evs do
        sim ← COSSIM(claim, ev)
        cos_sims.append(sim)
    end for
    label ← GETLABEL(cos_sims)
    return label
end function

function PREDICTLABEL(claim, evs)
    label ← APPLYFILTER(claim, evs)
    if label = None then
        label ← LLMPRED(claim, evs)
    end if
end function
```

4 Evaluation

Table 1 documents our results on the official FEVER-8 shared task leaderboards with regard to the dev set[4] and the test set[5]. Ev2R refers to the new AVeriTeC score Ev2R recall (Akhtar et al., 2024), a new metric for LLM-based evaluation of retrieval tasks. Unlike the old AVeriTeC score, which focused on a lexical metric, the new score considers the semantic meaning of the retrieved evidence. Both metrics consider correctly predicted verdicts and evidence retrieved for their prediction.

Experimental setup We ran different configurations of the baseline and our own system on the

[3]https://github.com/ggml-org/llama.cpp

[4]https://huggingface.co/spaces/fever/AVeriTeC Fever8Dev

[5]https://fever.ai/task.html

Block	Name	Old S	New S	s/claim	SUP	REF	NEI	CoC
1	FEVER-8/HerO	0.534	0.280	10.34	0.639	0.799	0.133	0.075
	FEVER-8/HerO-phi4-14B	0.522	0.256	13.13	0.623	0.783	0.103	0.000
2	SFEFC-phi4-14B	0.572	0.296	04.83	0.645	0.806	0.046	0.063
	SFEFC-phi4-14B-no-concat	0.452	0.248	05.33	0.525	0.784	0.000	0.033
3	SFEFC-phi4mini-3B	0.472	0.224	**04.28**	0.517	0.707	0.000	0.033
	SFEFC-llama3.2-3B	0.436	0.230	04.61	0.437	0.706	0.046	0.065
	SFEFC-gemma-3-27-it-qat	0.502	0.276	05.21	0.647	0.784	0.051	0.035
4	SFEFC-phi4-14B-all-classes	0.394	0.254	05.39	0.646	0.516	**0.163**	**0.280**
	SFEFC-phi4-14B-binary	**0.608**	**0.318**	04.68	**0.66**	**0.836**	0.000	0.000
	SFEFC-phi4-14B-varifocal	0.540	0.286	17.68	0.654	0.815	0.000	0.065

Table 2: Comparison of AVeriTeC scores (Old S: Hungarian METEOR score, New S: Ev2R Recall score), runtimes and Veracity F1 scores on the labels Supported (SUP), Refuted (REF), Not Enough Information (NEI) and Conflicting Evidence/Cherrypicking (CoC)

same machine with an NVIDIA H100 80GB GPU[6]. Both generative tasks, question generation and veracity prediction, were handled by the same LLM in each case. For better comparison, all configurations in Table 2 including HerO were evaluated with the same gte-base embedding model (Li et al., 2023b). Table 2 collects our evaluation results:

- Block 1 presents the FEVER-8/HerO-baseline results when run on our infrastructure
- Block 2 documents the results of our final submission. It also includes the results of a configuration with our concatenation strategy ablated.
- Block 3 collects the results of configurations were the LLM was replaced with other variants
- Block 4 shows strategies deviating from our main configuration

Runtime and accuracy-related metrics For the evaluation, our goal is to assess whether we could remain competitive with the baseline while improving the runtime per claim. As the results documented in Table 2 indicate, we were able to cut the runtime compared to the FEVER-8/HerO-baseline by more than 1/2 with most of our configurations (e.g., from 10.34s to 04.83 with our main configuration SFEFC-phi4-14B), while staying competitive both in the dev and the test set on the respective accuracy metrics (Table 1). Furthermore, the runtime of SFEFC-phi4-14B (Block 2) can be optimized in a way similar to the batching and parallelization strategies of the optimized FEVER-8/HerO-Pipeline for the FEVER-8 shared task. These strategies can also be explored with our proposed system to further reduce the processing time per claim in future work.

We experimented with multilingual-e5 (Wang et al., 2024), BGE-M3 (Chen et al., 2024), and gte-base (Li et al., 2023b), where gte-base yielded the best results in terms of runtime and accuracy.

We used Q6_0 GGUF[7] quantization variants in most configurations. Quantizing an LLM to 6-bit precision from 16-bit, as in the case of Phi 4, greatly reduces the runtime by lowering the requirements for in-memory operations.

As expected, the results indicate that runtime increases with the parameter size of the model, reflecting the higher computational cost of larger LLMs. Similarly, accuracy-related scores tend to decrease as the model size is reduced, illustrating a typical trade-off between efficiency and performance. Here, the Phi-4-14B (Abdin et al., 2024) model yielded the best results, while the related Phi-4-mini-instruct variant (Microsoft et al., 2025) with 3.8B parameters performed worse, as well as llama3.2-3B (Grattafiori et al., 2024) with 3.2 parameters. During our preliminary tests, we noticed better results when working with the Phi 4 model.

[6]The runtime values differ from the values on the FEVER-8 Leaderboard, where all systems were run on NVIDIA A10G GPUs with 23GB VRAM

[7]A quantization format developed by llama.cpp: https://github.com/ggml-org/ggml/blob/master/docs/gguf.md

For example, we evaluated our system in configuration with Gemma 3 (Team et al., 2025) with 27B parameters in its Quantization Aware Training (QAT) format, but the results were subpar compared to the Phi 4 variant. However, when running the FEVER-8/HerO-baseline while replacing the older Meta-Llama-3.1-8B-Instruct model with Phi 4 (on all tasks except veracity prediction), the retrieval score dropped. Thus, it cannot be generalized that the Phi 4 performs better in all cases. Furthermore, we evaluated the SFEFC-phi4-14B-all-classes to analyze how Phi 4 would perform if all four veracity labels were predicted by the model, with this configuration yielding the lowest scores (except, surprisingly, on the NEI and CoC classes).

Ablation Another goal of our evaluation documented in Block 2 of Table 2 is the comparison of different configurations to analyze their influence. To observe how our concatenation strategy influences the results, we evaluated the configuration SFEFC-phi4-14B-no-concat, which follows the same strategy as the FEVER-8/HerO-baseline (retrieving top 5000 individual sentences instead of 1500 concatenated sets of 4). As the results show, removing our strategy led to a drop in the veracity score (from 0.572 to 0.452) and an increase in runtime (from 4.84 to 5.33 seconds). This matches our assumption that retrieval performance increases when potential candidates contain more semantic information while decreasing runtime, since the total amount of potential candidates is also reduced by a factor of 4.

Further experiments We experimented with different strategies to further move beyond the results of SFEFC-phi4-14B, such as fine-tuning Phi 4 for question generation, fine-tuning BERT-based classifiers for verdict prediction, or different prompting strategies, but without success. As an example, we include our SFEFC-phi4-14B-varifocal variant, which was inspired by (Ousidhoum et al., 2022). Here, we prompted Phi 4 to generate 3 varifocal questions, parsed them from the output, used the generated questions as queries, and merged the results within the set of 10 retrieved question/evidence pairs. Although being a more sophisticated prompting strategy than generating a single question, the score did not improve against the SFEFC-phi4-14B configuration.

Error analysis When considering the results of our SFEFC-phi4-binary and SFEFC-phi4 configurations in Table 2, it is noticeable that while semantic filtering successfully labels some of the NEI and CoC cases, the veracity scores for SUP and REF drop by around 0.02-0.03 points. Thus, the actual number of correctly labeled NEI and CoC cases needs to be further examined. Table 3 illustrates that while predicting veracity classes with Semantic Filters is generally possible, mislabeled verdicts outweigh by a margin. When comparing the wrong predictions with their actual target labels, out of the 7 times NEI was mislabeled, 5 cases were actually REF and 2 SUP cases. In regard to CoC, out of the 26 wrong predictions, 17 should have been REF, 6 SUP and 1 NEI. While these results could point to a higher possibility of mislabeling predictions when the actual target label is REF, the ratios also roughly represent the class balance of the dev set (which includes 0.61% REF, 0.24% SUP, 0.08 % NEI and %0.07 CoC labeled claims). Thus, we conclude that while static thresholds can indeed be applied to predict correct veracity labels, the filtering strategy proposed in this paper can not be generalized to most cases, regardless of the actual target label.

Class	Total Actual	Total Predicted	TP	FP
NEI	35	8	1	7
CoC	38	26	2	24

Table 3: Examination of Not Enough Information (NEI) and Conflicting Evidence/Cherrypicking (CoC) cases. TP is short for True Positives/correctly predicted. FP is short for False Positives/incorrectly predicted.

5 Discussion and Future Work

With the proposed system, we successfully achieved our goal of remaining competitive with the FEVER-8 baseline in terms of performance, while significantly reducing runtime and taking a step closer toward real-world applicability in end-user-facing fact-checking systems. A key efficiency gain was achieved by reducing LLM calls and delegating both question generation and part of the veracity prediction to a single Phi-4 model, which, as our results show, performs well on both tasks. Another key approach involved concatenating sentences from the knowledge store based on chunking strategies, which significantly reduced the number of sentence embeddings required during each dense retrieval step. Both strategies can be further optimized in future work to decrease the runtime per claim. Another promising direction is to further optimize runtime through the application of parallelization techniques, similar to those used in the FEVER-8/HerO baseline.

While our semantic filtering heuristics were able to correctly identify some veracity classes, they often resulted in incorrect labels overall. This suggests that, although the approach holds promise, it requires further refinement. Improvements could involve enhancing the current heuristic techniques or replacing them with learnable components within classification models. In particular, the use of *semantic variance* for predicting the challenging CoC class appears to be a promising direction. This method could evolve beyond fixed thresholding towards more flexible classifiers that leverage deeper features of the retrieved evidence embeddings.

Limitations

While we were able to reduce the runtime by around half when compared to the FEVER-8/AVeriTeC baseline, it still remains at 04.28 seconds per claim in our fastest configuration – a value that can be considered too slow for real-life settings, especially when taking into account that its achievement is limited to the system being run on a high-end GPU (NVIDIA H100).

Thus, further improvement is needed towards the deployment outside of laboratory settings and on lower-end devices, where scalability issues, latency requirements, and different deployment options need to be taken into account. There are several paths discussed going towards this goal in the current literature. For example, the runtime of the dense retrieval steps could be improved by the binarization of the embedding vectors, as discussed in Gan et al. (2023).

The performance of our system and the thresholds of our proposed semantic filtering methods are limited to the AVeriTeC dataset. As discussed in our error analysis section, these heuristics showcase the general possibility to filter out specific labels based on thresholds but need further refinement due to a large amount of false positives. This point is underscored by the need of assessment of the methods on other data beyond the AVeriTeC dataset.

Furthermore, the thresholds we identified are limited to the gte-base embedding model. The implementation of other members of this model class can result in different results due to differing ranges in cosine similarity scores.

Acknowledgments

The work on this paper is performed in the scope of the projects "VeraExtract" (01IS24066) and "news-polygraph" (reference: 03RU2U151C) funded by the German Federal Ministry for Research, Technology and Aeronautics (BMFTR).

References

Marah Abdin, Jyoti Aneja, Harkirat Behl, Sébastien Bubeck, Ronen Eldan, Suriya Gunasekar, Michael Harrison, Russell J. Hewett, Mojan Javaheripi, Piero Kauffmann, James R. Lee, Yin Tat Lee, Yuanzhi Li, Weishung Liu, Caio C. T. Mendes, Anh Nguyen, Eric Price, Gustavo de Rosa, Olli Saarikivi, and 8 others. 2024. Phi-4 Technical Report. *arXiv preprint*. ArXiv:2412.08905 [cs].

Mubashara Akhtar, Michael Schlichtkrull, and Andreas Vlachos. 2024. Ev2r: Evaluating evidence retrieval in automated fact-checking. *arXiv preprint arXiv:2411.05375*.

Jianlv Chen, Shitao Xiao, Peitian Zhang, Kun Luo, Defu Lian, and Zheng Liu. 2024. Bge m3-embedding: Multi-lingual, multi-functionality, multi-granularity text embeddings through self-knowledge distillation. *Preprint*, arXiv:2402.03216.

DeepSeek-AI, Xiao Bi, Deli Chen, Guanting Chen, Shanhuang Chen, Damai Dai, Chengqi Deng, Honghui Ding, Kai Dong, Qiushi Du, Zhe Fu, Huazuo Gao, Kaige Gao, Wenjun Gao, Ruiqi Ge, Kang Guan, Daya Guo, Jianzhong Guo, Guangbo Hao, and 68 others. 2024. Deepseek llm: Scaling open-source language models with longtermism. *Preprint*, arXiv:2401.02954.

Yukang Gan, Yixiao Ge, Chang Zhou, Shupeng Su, Zhouchuan Xu, Xuyuan Xu, Quanchao Hui, Xiang Chen, Yexin Wang, and Ying Shan. 2023. Binary embedding-based retrieval at tencent. In *Proceedings of the 29th ACM SIGKDD Conference on Knowledge Discovery and Data Mining*, KDD '23, page 4056–4067, New York, NY, USA. Association for Computing Machinery.

Aaron Grattafiori, Abhimanyu Dubey, Abhinav Jauhri, Abhinav Pandey, Abhishek Kadian, Ahmad Al-Dahle, Aiesha Letman, Akhil Mathur, Alan Schelten, Alex Vaughan, Amy Yang, Angela Fan, Anirudh Goyal, Anthony Hartshorn, Aobo Yang, Archi Mitra, Archie Sravankumar, Artem Korenev, Arthur Hinsvark, and 542 others. 2024. The Llama 3 Herd of Models. *arXiv preprint*. ArXiv:2407.21783 [cs].

Lucas Graves. 2018. Understanding the promise and limits of automated fact-checking. `https://reut`

ersinstitute.politics.ox.ac.uk/our-research/understanding-promise-and-limits-automated-fact-checking. RISJ Factsheet, February 2018.

Vishwani Gupta, Astrid Viciano, Holger Wormer, and Najmehsadat Mousavinezhad. 2023. Exploring unsupervised semantic similarity methods for claim verification in health care news articles. In *Proceedings of the 14th International Conference on Recent Advances in Natural Language Processing*, pages 440–447, Varna, Bulgaria. INCOMA Ltd., Shoumen, Bulgaria.

Zehan Li, Xin Zhang, Yanzhao Zhang, Dingkun Long, Pengjun Xie, and Meishan Zhang. 2023a. Towards general text embeddings with multi-stage contrastive learning. *Preprint*, arXiv:2308.03281.

Zehan Li, Xin Zhang, Yanzhao Zhang, Dingkun Long, Pengjun Xie, and Meishan Zhang. 2023b. Towards general text embeddings with multi-stage contrastive learning. *arXiv preprint arXiv:2308.03281*.

Yinfei Liu, Weijie Liu, Junlong Li, and 1 others. 2023. Bge: Baai general embedding models. https://github.com/FlagOpen/FlagEmbedding. Accessed: 2025-05-06.

Microsoft, Abdelrahman Abouelenin, Atabak Ashfaq, Adam Atkinson, Hany Awadalla, Nguyen Bach, Jianmin Bao, Alon Benhaim, Martin Cai, Vishrav Chaudhary, Congcong Chen, Dong Chen, Dongdong Chen, Junkun Chen, Weizhu Chen, Yen-Chun Chen, Yiling Chen, Qi Dai, Xiyang Dai, and 56 others. 2025. Phi-4-Mini Technical Report: Compact yet Powerful Multimodal Language Models via Mixture-of-LoRAs. *arXiv preprint*. ArXiv:2503.01743 [cs].

OpenAI, :, Aaron Hurst, Adam Lerer, Adam P. Goucher, Adam Perelman, Aditya Ramesh, Aidan Clark, AJ Ostrow, Akila Welihinda, Alan Hayes, Alec Radford, Aleksander Mądry, Alex Baker-Whitcomb, Alex Beutel, Alex Borzunov, Alex Carney, Alex Chow, Alex Kirillov, and 401 others. 2024. Gpt-4o system card. *Preprint*, arXiv:2410.21276.

OpenAI. 2023. Gpt-4 technical report. https://cdn.openai.com/papers/gpt-4.pdf. GPT-4 Turbo is an optimized variant of GPT-4, offering enhanced performance and efficiency.

OpenAI. 2024. New embedding models and api updates. https://openai.com/index/new-embedding-models-and-api-updates/. Accessed: 2025-05-06.

Nedjma Ousidhoum, Zhangdie Yuan, and Andreas Vlachos. 2022. Varifocal question generation for fact-checking. In *Proceedings of the 2022 Conference on Empirical Methods in Natural Language Processing*, pages 2532–2544, Abu Dhabi, United Arab Emirates. Association for Computational Linguistics.

Sihyeong Park, Sungryeol Jeon, Chaelyn Lee, Seokhun Jeon, Byung-Soo Kim, and Jemin Lee. 2025. A Survey on Inference Engines for Large Language Models: Perspectives on Optimization and Efficiency. *arXiv preprint*. ArXiv:2505.01658 [cs].

Mohammad Taher Pilehvar and Jose Camacho-Collados. 2019. WiC: the Word-in-Context Dataset for Evaluating Context-Sensitive Meaning Representations. In *Proceedings of the 2019 Conference of the North American Chapter of the Association for Computational Linguistics: Human Language Technologies, Volume 1 (Long and Short Papers)*, pages 1267–1273, Minneapolis, Minnesota. Association for Computational Linguistics.

Michael Schlichtkrull, Yulong Chen, Chenxi Whitehouse, Zhenyun Deng, Mubashara Akhtar, Rami Aly, Zhijiang Guo, Christos Christodoulopoulos, Oana Cocarascu, Arpit Mittal, James Thorne, and Andreas Vlachos, editors. 2024. *Proceedings of the Seventh Fact Extraction and VERification Workshop (FEVER)*. Association for Computational Linguistics, Miami, Florida, USA.

Michael Sejr Schlichtkrull, Zhijiang Guo, and Andreas Vlachos. 2023. Averitec: A dataset for real-world claim verification with evidence from the web. In *Thirty-thh Conference on Neural Information Processing Systems Datasets and Benchmarks Track*.

Emma Strubell, Ananya Ganesh, and Andrew McCallum. 2019. Energy and policy considerations for deep learning in NLP. In *Proceedings of the 57th Annual Meeting of the Association for Computational Linguistics*, pages 3645–3650, Florence, Italy. Association for Computational Linguistics.

Liyan Tang, Philippe Laban, and Greg Durrett. 2024. MiniCheck: Efficient fact-checking of LLMs on grounding documents. In *Proceedings of the 2024 Conference on Empirical Methods in Natural Language Processing*, pages 8818–8847, Miami, Florida, USA. Association for Computational Linguistics.

Gemma Team, Aishwarya Kamath, Johan Ferret, Shreya Pathak, Nino Vieillard, Ramona Merhej, Sarah Perrin, Tatiana Matejovicova, Alexandre Ramé, Morgane Rivière, Louis Rouillard, Thomas Mesnard, Geoffrey Cideron, Jean bastien Grill, Sabela Ramos, Edouard Yvinec, Michelle Casbon, Etienne Pot, Ivo Penchev, and 197 others. 2025. Gemma 3 technical report. *Preprint*, arXiv:2503.19786.

Marcos Treviso, Ji-Ung Lee, Tianchu Ji, Betty van Aken, Qingqing Cao, Manuel R. Ciosici, Michael Hassid, Kenneth Heafield, Sara Hooker, Colin Raffel, Pedro H. Martins, André F. T. Martins, Jessica Zosa Forde, Peter Milder, Edwin Simpson, Noam Slonim, Jesse Dodge, Emma Strubell, Niranjan Balasubramanian, and 3 others. 2023. Efficient methods for natural language processing: A survey. *Transactions of the Association for Computational Linguistics*, 11:826–860.

Liang Wang, Nan Yang, Xiaolong Huang, Binxing Jiao, Linjun Yang, Daxin Jiang, Rangan Majumder, and Furu Wei. 2022. Text embeddings by weakly-supervised contrastive pre-training. *arXiv preprint arXiv:2212.03533*.

Liang Wang, Nan Yang, Xiaolong Huang, Linjun Yang, Rangan Majumder, and Furu Wei. 2024. Multilingual e5 text embeddings: A technical report. *arXiv preprint arXiv:2402.05672*.

Wenhui Wang, Furu Wei, Li Dong, Hangbo Bao, Nan Yang, and Ming Zhou. 2020. Minilm: deep self-attention distillation for task-agnostic compression of pre-trained transformers. In *Proceedings of the 34th International Conference on Neural Information Processing Systems*, NIPS '20, Red Hook, NY, USA. Curran Associates Inc.

Zhuohan Xie, Rui Xing, Yuxia Wang, Jiahui Geng, Hasan Iqbal, Dhruv Sahnan, Iryna Gurevych, and Preslav Nakov. 2025. FIRE: Fact-checking with iterative retrieval and verification. In *Findings of the Association for Computational Linguistics: NAACL 2025*, pages 2901–2914, Albuquerque, New Mexico. Association for Computational Linguistics.

Yejun Yoon, Jaeyoon Jung, Seunghyun Yoon, and Kunwoo Park. 2024. HerO at AVeriTeC: The Herd of Open Large Language Models for Verifying Real-World Claims. In *Proceedings of the Seventh Fact Extraction and VERification Workshop (FEVER)*, pages 130–136, Miami, Florida, USA. Association for Computational Linguistics.

Kaitlyn Zhou, Kawin Ethayarajh, Dallas Card, and Dan Jurafsky. 2022. Problems with Cosine as a Measure of Embedding Similarity for High Frequency Words. *arXiv preprint*. ArXiv:2205.05092 [cs].

A Appendix

A.1 Prompts Collection

We used the following prompt for question generation:

> f"You are a professional fact checker. You recieve a claim from the user. Please provide a question you would ask to find out if a given claim is true, or not. Generate only one single question! The claim you need to check: {claim} \n Your Question:\n"

The prompt for predicting the SUP and REF labels was:

> f"You are a professional fact checker. You get a claim and provided evidence. Assess if the claim is supported or refuted by the evidence! Return only the result, either 'Supported' or 'Refuted'. The claim: {claim} \n The evidence: {retrieved_evidences} \n Your verdict: "

OldJoe at AVeriTeC: In-context learning for fact-checking

Farah Ftouhi*†, Russel Dsouza*, Lance Gamboa, Jinlong Liu, Asim Abbas,
Yue Feng, Mubashir Ali, Mark Lee, Venelin Kovatchev
School of Computer Science, University of Birmingham

Abstract

In this paper, we present the system proposed by our team *OldJoe*, for the 8th edition of the AVeriTeC shared task, as part of the FEVER workshop. The objective of this task is to verify the factuality of real-world claims. Our approach integrates open source large language models, SQL, and in-context learning. We begin with embedding the knowledge store using a pretrained embedding language model then storing the outputs in a SQL database. Subsequently, we prompt an LLM to craft relevant questions based on the input claim, which are then used to guide the retrieval process. We further prompt the LLM to generate answers to the questions and predict the veracity of the original claim. Our system scored 0.49 on the HU-METEOR AVeriTeC score on the dev set and 0.15 on the Ev2R recall on the test set. Due to the time constraint we were unable to conduct additional experiments or further hyperparameter tuning. As a result, we adopted this pipeline configuration centered on the `Qwen3-14B-AWQ` model as our final submission strategy. The full pipeline is available on GitHub.[1]

1 Introduction

In an era where information spreads rapidly across digital platforms, manual fact-checking struggles to keep pace with the vast volume of content generated daily. This growing challenge has sparked increasing interest in the development of automated fact-checking systems with a focus on efficient, reproducible and open-source methodologies. In this context, the AVeriTeC Shared Task[2] was introduced to evaluate systems capable of assessing the factuality of claims using a structured knowledge base. We created a system that combines large language models, SQL databases, and in-context learning. Our pipeline has the following components: (1) a postgreSQL database, which stores the embeddings and chunks for evidence documents from the knowledge store; (2) Question Generation, where we generate questions and queries based on the given claim; (3) Retrieval and Re-ranking, which uses `pgvector` and `postgres` to retrieve evidence for each query; (4) Answer Generation, where we generate answers for each question using the retrieved evidence chunks; and (5) Veracity Check, where we assign the final veracity label based on the generated question-answer pairs. The entire pipeline is illustrated in Figure 1.

2 Related Work

One of the earliest studies to frame fact-checking as a computational task was introduced by (Vlachos and Riedel, 2014), who aimed to replicate the traditionally manual process of claim verification using NLP techniques. This foundational work paved the way for other efforts, most notably the introduction of the FEVER dataset(Thorne et al., 2018), a large-scale benchmark designed to advance research in claim verification against textual sources. Over the years, the increasing spread of misinformation(Das et al., 2023) has further elevated fact-checking as a critical area of research and led to multiple studies.

More recently, (DeHaven and Scott, 2023) proposed BEVERS, a simple yet highly effective pipeline that achieves state-of-the-art results on both the FEVER and SciFact (Wadden et al., 2020) datasets. This growing interest has also motivated the organization to launch the FEVER(Schlichtkrull et al., 2024) workshop, which evaluate systems using the real-world claim dataset AVeriTeC(Schlichtkrull et al., 2023). Participants in these workshops have employed a wide range of approaches — from systems relying on APIs(Rothermel et al., 2024) to those based on fine-tuned open-source models (Sevgili et al., 2024),

*Main contributors
†Corresponding author: fxf482@student.bham.ac.uk
[1]https://github.com/farahft/OldJoe
[2]https://fever.ai/task.html

Proceedings of the Eighth Fact Extraction and VERification Workshop (FEVER), pages 238–246
July 31, 2025 ©2025 Association for Computational Linguistics

reflecting the diversity and rapid evolution of methods in this domain.

3 Methodology

In this section we present our system pipeline as shown in Figure 1. We start by preparing our evidence database from the knowledge store given by the organisers. Next, we build our question-query generator to generate questions and queries that guide retrieval for a given claim. Then, we build the answer generator to answer the questions and queries based on the retrieved evidence. Finally, these answers are used to determine the veracity of a given claim.

3.1 Evidence Embeddings

Before creating the embeddings, we first semantically split each evidence document into chunks with a maximum length of 2048 characters using `semantic-text-splitter` [3] that offers methods for splitting text into smaller chunks, aiming to reach a target chunk size while prioritizing splits at semantically meaningful boundaries. We then explored several approaches to generating the embeddings and storing them in a database. One approach we attempted involved using `Alibaba-NLP/gte-large-en-v1.5` (Zhang et al., 2024) and FAISS to store the texts, their embeddings, and the corresponding metadata as pickled files (Douze et al., 2024). We also looked into using a ChromaDB vector database to store both the embeddings and metadata in a singular vector. Ultimately, our final system generates sentence embeddings with `jina-ai/jina-embeddings-v3`[4] with a maximum model length of 2048 and relies on the `postgres` extension, `pgvector`[5], for storing both the embeddings and the content of the evidence chunks together. Evidence for each claim is stored in a separate table, enabling efficient and accurate retrieval of relevant evidence.

3.2 Question and Query generation

The next step in our inference pipeline is to generate questions along with search queries. For this task, we use `Qwen/Qwen1.5-14B-Chat-AWQ` [6] (QwenLM Team, 2025), a recent reasoning model that is quantized to fit within 24GB of VRAM set up to 8192 as a max length. For each claim, we prompt this model to first analyse and reason about the claim before generating four questions that, when answered, would provide easy insight into the veracity of the claim.

To support veracity prediction and improve both interpretability and retrieval quality, we first prompt the model to generate questions from the original claims. Using the generated questions we prompt the model to generate refined search queries designed to better capture the information need and guide evidence retrieval. This two-step process enables the system to retrieve more relevant evidence chunks, which are then used to form Q-A pairs that inform the final veracity prediction

The prompts for question and query generation are provided in Appendix A and B respectively.

Question Generation Example

Claim: Trump Administration claimed songwriter Billie Eilish Is Destroying Our Country In Leaked Documents
Question: Are there any official documents from the Trump Administration that explicitly state Billie Eilish is destroying the country?

3.3 Evidence Retrieval and Re-ranking

We use the questions and queries generated in Section 3.2 to retrieve evidence. For each question, corresponding search queries along with the question itself are used to retrieve and simultaneously re-rank candidate evidence chunks. Parallel to the various embedding and data warehousing approaches we explored, we also compared the effectiveness of four approaches in retrieving evidence from our knowledge base:

1. the FAISS retrieval method, which uses cosine similarity to quantify the distance between query embeddings and evidence embeddings

2. the BM25 (Robertson et al., 2009) algorithm, which retrieves the most relevant evidence using keyword search without relying on embeddings

3. a hybrid score combining BM25 scores with FAISS-based cosine similarity scores between query and evidence embeddings

4. reciprocal rank fusion (RRF) scoring (Cormack et al., 2009), which collates the BM25-

[3]https://pypi.org/project/semantic-text-splitter/
[4]https://huggingface.co/jinaai/jina-embeddings-v3
[5]https://github.com/pgvector/pgvector
[6]https://huggingface.co/Qwen/Qwen1.5-14B-Chat-AWQ

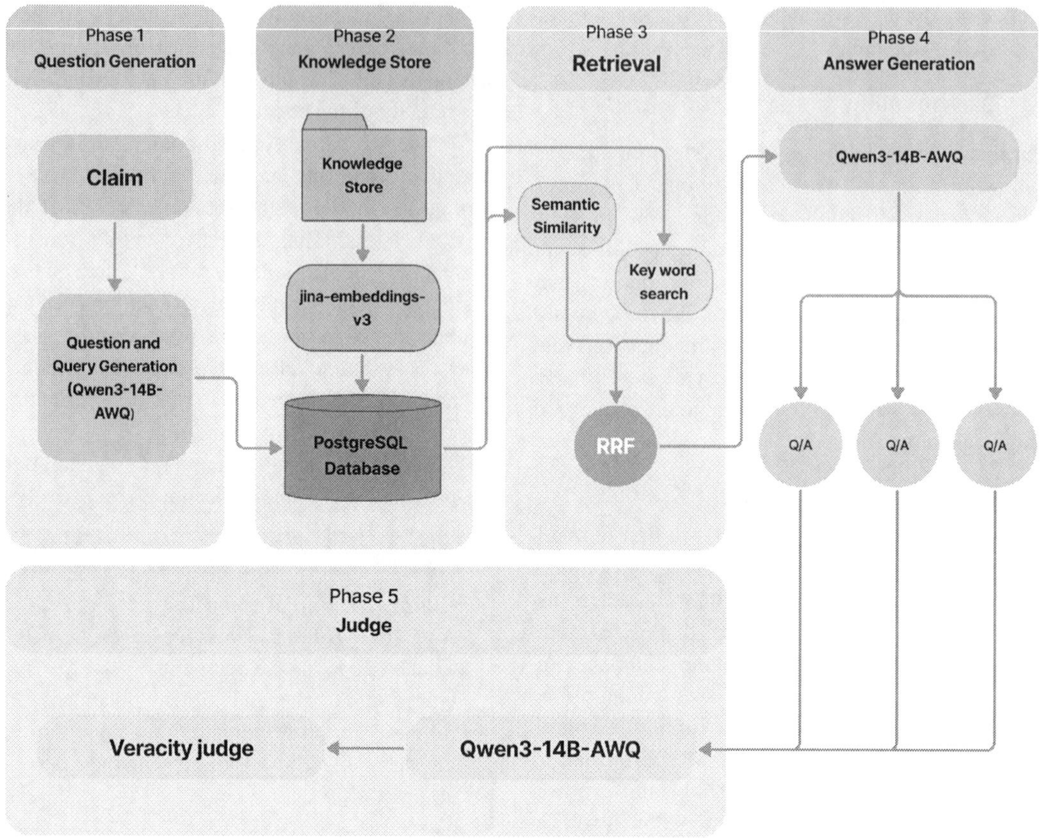

Figure 1: System Pipeline.

based and pgvector-based rankings of evidences and embeddings stored in our postgreSQL database

We used the Prometheus evaluation metric (Pombal et al., 2025) a multilingual LLM-as-a-judge framework that supports both reference-based and reference-free evaluation enabling direct assessment and pairwise comparison of long-form outputs, to assess the best retrieval approach. The results in Table 1 show that retrieving evidence from postgreSQL through RRF scoring provided the best results.

Consequently, the entire retrieval-reranking process is performed in a single SQL query for efficiency and speed. Combining BM25-based keyword search and pgvector-based semantic search, the SQL query retrieves the eight most question-relevant evidence chunks identified by each search method. The BM25 and pgvector ranks and scores for each retrieved chunk are then collated using RRF with a penalty factor of 4 to ensure balanced contributions between the BM25 and pgvector search strategies. Based on this RRF scoring mechanism, the system returns the 10 highest-ranked evidence chunks for each question.

Approach	Prometheus Evaluation Metric
FAISS	1.20
BM25	2.90
FAISS & BM25	1.80
postgreSQL RRF	**3.80**

Table 1: Comparison of retrieval models using the Prometheus evaluation metric.

The SQL query for retrieval and re-ranking is provided in Appendix E.

3.4 Answer Generation

The penultimate step in our inference pipeline is answer generation. The process is similar to Section 3.2 and uses the same reasoning model: Qwen/Qwen3-14B-AWQ (QwenLM Team, 2025). The model is prompted to generate the answers based on the question and corresponding retrieved evidence. The prompt used can be found in Appendix C.

> **Answer Generation Example**
>
> **Question**: Are there any official documents from the Trump Administration that explicitly state Billie Eilish is destroying the country?
> **Answer**: No. As reported by The Washington Post and corrected by the New York Post, the leaked documents from the Trump administration did not state that Billie Eilish was destroying the country. Instead, they recorded Eilish's own statement criticizing Trump, who she said was destroying our country and everything we care about. The Washington Post initially misattributed this quote to Trump officials but later issued a correction clarifying that the statement was Eilish's own, not an official assessment by the administration.

3.5 Veracity Judgment

The final stage of the pipeline is veracity judgment, where each claim is classified into 4 different labels: *Supported, Refuted, Conflicting/Cherry-Picking* or *Not Enough Evidence*. Similar to Sections 3.2 and 3.4, we prompt the model to predict the claim's veracity given the claim and the question-answer pairs generated in Section 3.4. The prompt used can be found in Appendix D.

4 Experiments

This section presents results of the experiments we conducted to determine which reasoning model provided the most optimal performance for our fact-checking pipeline.

4.1 Hardware

All the experiments were conducted on a single machine equipped with two AMD EPYC9334 32-core CPUs, 1 TB of RAM, and two 1TB NVMe SSD and 4TB NVMe SSD. The system also included 8 NVIDIA L40s GPUs each with 48GB of memory. The complete pipeline including the database, language models, and all other components were packed into a Docker image totaling 230 GB in size. This containerized setup can be run on systems with at least 24 GB of GPU memory.

4.2 Experimental Results

The processes to generate the embeddings and insert them into our postgreSQL knowledge store database collectively took approximately 4 hours. Claim labeling on the dev set required an average of 45 seconds per claim, totaling around 6.3 hours for the entire dataset.

We employed three models in performing the question generation, question-and-answer generation, and veracity prediction tasks. These models were all compatible with the 24GB GPU RAM hardware setup described in Section 4.1. Table 2 shows each model's scores for the three tasks mentioned above, as evaluated using the official 2024 Shared Task metrics. Among the models, `qwen3-14b-awq` returned the highest scores when paired with in-context learning and applied into our inference pipeline. The model achieved an accuracy of 0.494 and an AVeriTeC score of 0.42 on the dev set. Owing to limited time, we could not explore alternative configurations or pipelines , we proceeded with the mentioned pipeline which showed promising results during Q and Q+A stages.

4.3 Final Submission Results

Our system was evaluated on the Ev2R framework proposed by (Akhtar et al., 2024), which introduces reference-based, proxy-reference and reference-less scores for evidence evaluation in automated fact-checking. Our system achieved a mean runtime of 84.57 seconds per claim, a Q+A Ev2R recall of 0.387 a Q-only Ev2R score of 0.182 and an overall AVeriTeC score of 0.151.

5 Conclusion

This paper describes Team *OldJoe*'s submission to the AVeriTeC Shared Task the FEVER workshop. We explored various strategies for embedding, storing, and retrieving evidence chunks for better veracity prediction. We evaluated multiple language models and investigated the effectiveness of applying them and in-context learning for automated fact-checking. While our system demonstrates a promising performance on the dev set when evaluated by the HU-METEOR metric, further improvements are necessary to enhance its generalisation and achieve better results on the test set.

Limitations

This system has been designed for the FEVER shared task and is structured to meet the requirements and limitations of the task. The performance of the model outside of the parameters of the task

Model	Q score	Q/A score	Accuracy	AVeriTeC Score
llama-3.1-8B	0.411	0.27	0.388	0.38
qwen3-8B-fp8	0.410	0.28	0.41	0.414
qwen3-14b-awq	0.411	0.27	**0.494**	**0.492**

Table 2: Comparison of models performance using HU-meteor Accuracy and AVeriTeC scores.

might differ significantly. Due to time and computational constraints, we were not able to fully finetune our system on the data. It is likely that the system performance can improve substantially with additional finetuning and access to more powerful hardware.

Acknowledgments

The computations described in this research were performed using the Baskerville Tier 2 HPC service (https://www.baskerville.ac.uk/). Baskerville was funded by the EPSRC and UKRI through the World Class Labs scheme (EP/T022221/1) and the Digital Research Infrastructure programme (EP/W032244/1) and is operated by Advanced Research Computing at the University of Birmingham.

References

Mubashara Akhtar, Michael Schlichtkrull, and Andreas Vlachos. 2024. Ev2r: Evaluating evidence retrieval in automated fact-checking. *arXiv preprint arXiv:2411.05375.*

Gordon V. Cormack, Charles L A Clarke, and Stefan Buettcher. 2009. Reciprocal rank fusion outperforms condorcet and individual rank learning methods. In *Proceedings of the 32nd International ACM SIGIR Conference on Research and Development in Information Retrieval*, SIGIR '09, page 758–759, New York, NY, USA. Association for Computing Machinery.

Anubrata Das, Houjiang Liu, Venelin Kovatchev, and Matthew Lease. 2023. The state of human-centered nlp technology for fact-checking. *Information processing & management*, 60(2):103219.

Mitchell DeHaven and Stephen Scott. 2023. Bevers: A general, simple, and performant framework for automatic fact verification. *arXiv preprint arXiv:2303.16974.*

Matthijs Douze, Alexandr Guzhva, Chengqi Deng, Jeff Johnson, Gergely Szilvasy, Pierre-Emmanuel Mazaré, Maria Lomeli, Lucas Hosseini, and Hervé Jégou. 2024. The faiss library.

José Pombal, Dongkeun Yoon, Patrick Fernandes, Ian Wu, Seungone Kim, Ricardo Rei, Graham Neubig, and André FT Martins. 2025. M-prometheus: A suite of open multilingual llm judges. *arXiv preprint arXiv:2504.04953.*

QwenLM Team. 2025. Qwen3 technical report. `https://github.com/QwenLM/Qwen3/blob/main/Qwen3_Technical_Report.pdf`. Accessed: 2025-05-14.

Stephen Robertson, Hugo Zaragoza, and 1 others. 2009. The probabilistic relevance framework: Bm25 and beyond. *Foundations and Trends® in Information Retrieval*, 3(4):333–389.

Mark Rothermel, Tobias Braun, Marcus Rohrbach, and Anna Rohrbach. 2024. InFact: A strong baseline for automated fact-checking. In *Proceedings of the Seventh Fact Extraction and VERification Workshop (FEVER)*, pages 108–112, Miami, Florida, USA. Association for Computational Linguistics.

Michael Schlichtkrull, Yulong Chen, Chenxi Whitehouse, Zhenyun Deng, Mubashara Akhtar, Rami Aly, Zhijiang Guo, Christos Christodoulopoulos, Oana Cocarascu, Arpit Mittal, James Thorne, and Andreas Vlachos. 2024. The automated verification of textual claims (AVeriTeC) shared task. In *Proceedings of the Seventh Fact Extraction and VERification Workshop (FEVER)*.

Michael Sejr Schlichtkrull, Zhijiang Guo, and Andreas Vlachos. 2023. Averitec: A dataset for real-world claim verification with evidence from the web. In *Thirty-thh Conference on Neural Information Processing Systems Datasets and Benchmarks Track.*

Özge Sevgili, Irina Nikishina, Seid Muhie Yimam, Martin Semmann, and Chris Biemann. 2024. UHH at AVeriTeC: RAG for fact-checking with real-world claims. In *Proceedings of the Seventh Fact Extraction and VERification Workshop (FEVER)*, pages 55–63, Miami, Florida, USA. Association for Computational Linguistics.

James Thorne, Andreas Vlachos, Christos Christodoulopoulos, and Arpit Mittal. 2018. Fever: a large-scale dataset for fact extraction and verification. *arXiv preprint arXiv:1803.05355.*

Andreas Vlachos and Sebastian Riedel. 2014. Fact checking: Task definition and dataset construction. In *Proceedings of the ACL 2014 workshop on language technologies and computational social science*, pages 18–22.

David Wadden, Shanchuan Lin, Kyle Lo, Lucy Lu Wang, Madeleine van Zuylen, Arman Cohan, and

Hannaneh Hajishirzi. 2020. Fact or fiction: Verifying scientific claims. *arXiv preprint arXiv:2004.14974*.

Xin Zhang, Yanzhao Zhang, Dingkun Long, Wen Xie, Ziqi Dai, Jialong Tang, Huan Lin, Baosong Yang, Pengjun Xie, Fei Huang, and 1 others. 2024. mgte: Generalized long-context text representation and reranking models for multilingual text retrieval. *arXiv preprint arXiv:2407.19669*.

Appendix

A Question Generation Prompt Template

```
You are an advanced fact-checking AI, tasked with generating highly targeted,
investigative questions to verify claims.
Each question should probe a unique and essential aspect of verification.
You are NOT fact-checking the claim. You're job is to generate questions to
enable better fact checking.

### Instructions
Generate {{ n_questions }} **distinct** and **non-redundant** questions.
Each question should target a **different** key dimension of verification
Each question must be **necessary**: answering it should bring us **measurably
closer to a veracity judgment**.
Each question must be atomic and include all the **necessary** and **sufficient
** information while being **concise**.

### Additional Notes
Before finalizing each question, consider:
1. What specific aspect of the claim does this question interrogate?
2. Would answering this question significantly impact veracity assessment?
3. Is this question fundamentally different from the others?
Make sure that the question *is a question*
{{ response_format }}


### Task:
Claim: "{{ claim }}"

Generated Questions:
```

B Query Generation Prompt Template

```
You are a retrieval-optimization AI that transforms fact-checking questions
into **search
queries** for evidence gathering.

Your job is to generate **{{ n_queries }} diverse, high-recall queries** that
can retrieve
**useful evidence** to help answer the following investigative question.

### Goals
- Cover **different phrasings**, **semantic angles**, and **terminological
variations**.
- Balance between **specificity** and **generalization** to maximize evidence
retrieval.
- Optimize for both **keyword** and **semantic search systems**.

### Techniques
Use the following techniques to generate diverse queries:
- Strip to core facts, entities, and concepts
- Use synonyms, rephrasing and related concepts.
- Break down the question into subcomponents.
- Vary terminology (formal/informal, technical/common).
- Include relevant entities or contexts.
- Reformulate to target potential evidence phrases (e.g., "according to", "
experts say",
etc.)
{{ response_format }}

### Task
Question: "{{ question }}"

Generated Search Queries:
```

C Answer Generation Prompt Template

```
You are an advanced fact-checking AI, tasked with answering questions based on
provided evidence.
You have been given a question and a set of evidence chunks retrieved from a
database to answer that question.
Your goal is to synthesize a well-reasoned answer supported by the evidence.
You must ground your answer only in the evidence provided and avoid speculation
 or unsupported claims.
Name your sources and be journalistic in your approach and response.
### Instructions
- Read and analyze all the provided evidence chunks.
- Identify relevant information that directly supports or refutes the question.
- Think step-by-step and reason about the evidence logically and cautiously.
- Acknowledge uncertainty or lack of coverage if the evidence is incomplete or
contradictory.
- Align your final answer with the type of question. If it is a **yes/no
question**, your answer must begin with either Yes or No and remain strictly
within that framing.
- Avoid speculation, assumptions, or invented content.
- Distill a short name for the source of each from the provided URL.
- When citing evidence, refer to the **source name** (e.g., "as reported by The
 Guardian" or "as reported in the New York Times") instead of just the chunk
number or URL.
{{response_format}}
### Evidence Chunks:
{% for chunk in chunks %}
[CHUNK [{{ loop.index }}] START]
URL:{{ chunk.source_url }}
CONTENT: {{ chunk.content }}
[CHUNK [{{ loop.index }}] END]
{% endfor %}

### Task
QUESTION: "{{ question }}"

ANSWER:
```

D Veracity label Generation Prompt Template

```
You are an advanced fact-checking AI tasked with determining the veracity of
claims based on evidence.
### Inputs
CLAIM: "{{ claim }}"
EVIDENCE:
{% for qa in qa_pairs %}
QUESTION: {{ qa.question }}
ANSWER: {{ qa.answer }}
{% endfor %}

### Task
Based on the evidence above, provide step by step reasoning followed by a final
 verdict label for the claim.
### Labels
- "Supported": The evidence fully supports the claim
- "Refuted": The evidence contradicts the claim
- "Conflicting": Different pieces of evidence support and contradict the claim
- "Not Enough Evidence": Insufficient evidence to make a determination
{{ response_format }}
### Instructions
Ensure your verdict is:
- Strictly based on the provided evidence
- Considers all available information
- Acknowledges any uncertainties or gaps

ANSWER:)
```

E SQL Query

```
SQL("""
        WITH
        input_queries AS (
            SELECT
                qid,
                qtext,
                qembedding
            FROM
                UNNEST(%(qtexts)s::text[], %(qembeds)s::vector[]) WITH
                ORDINALITY
                AS t(qtext, qembedding, qid)
        ),
        semantic_search AS (
            SELECT
                t.id,
                iq.qid,
                1.0 / (%(srpenalty)s + RANK() OVER (PARTITION BY iq.qid ORDER
                BY t.embedding <=> iq.qembedding)) AS score
            FROM {tname} t, input_queries iq
            ORDER BY t.embedding <=> iq.qembedding
            LIMIT %(slimit)s
        ),
        keyword_search AS (
            SELECT
                t.id,
                iq.qid,
                1.0 / (%(krpenalty)s + RANK() OVER (PARTITION BY iq.qid ORDER
                BY ts_rank_cd(to_tsvector('english', content), plainto_tsquery
                ('english', iq.qtext)) DESC)) AS score
            FROM {tname} t, input_queries iq
            WHERE to_tsvector('english', content) @@ plainto_tsquery('english',
             iq.qtext)
            ORDER BY ts_rank_cd(to_tsvector('english', content),
            plainto_tsquery('english', iq.qtext)) DESC
            LIMIT %(klimit)s
        ),
        combined AS (
            SELECT id, SUM(score) AS total_score
            FROM (
                SELECT * FROM semantic_search
                UNION ALL
                SELECT * FROM keyword_search
            ) s
            GROUP BY id
        )
        SELECT
            t.doc_id, t.source_url, t.chunk_index, t.content, c.total_score
        FROM combined c
        JOIN {tname} t ON t.id = c.id
        ORDER BY c.total_score DESC
        LIMIT %(topk)s
        """)
```

SANCTUARY: An Efficient Evidence-Based Automated Fact Checking System

Arbaaz Dharamvaram
Faculty of Computer Science,
University of New Brunswick, Canada
arbaaz.dm@unb.ca

Saqib Hakak
Faculty of Computer Science,
University of New Brunswick, Canada
saqib.hakak@unb.ca

Abstract

With the growing volume of misinformation online, automated fact-checking systems are becoming increasingly important. This paper presents SANCTUARY, an efficient pipeline for evidence-based verification of real-world claims. Our approach consists of three stages: Hypothetical Question & Passage Generation, a two-step Retrieval-Augmented Generation (RAG) hybrid evidence retrieval, and structured reasoning and prediction, which leverages two lightweight Large Language Models (LLMs). On the challenging AVeriTeC benchmark, our system achieves 25.27 points on the new AVeriTeC score (Ev2R recall), outperforming the previous state-of-the-art baseline by 5 absolute points (1.25× relative improvement). Sanctuary demonstrates that careful retrieval, reasoning strategies and well-integrated language models can substantially advance automated fact-checking performance.

1 Introduction

The ease with which information can be published and amplified online has intensified longstanding concerns about the spread of misinformation and disinformation (Lewandowsky et al., 2020; Schlichtkrull et al., 2024). Professional fact-checking organizations such as PolitiFact[1], FactCheck.org[2] and Snopes[3] have scaled up their efforts, yet the sheer volume and velocity of claims far outstrip human capacity (Nakov et al., 2021). Moreover, not every claim warrants fact-checking; resources should be directed toward content that can significantly impact society, such as influencing elections (Allcott and Gentzkow, 2017) or causing financial harm (Gold and Stelter, 2025). Consequently, Automated Fact-Checking (AFC) has emerged as a promising assistive technology aimed at (i) identifying check-worthy claims, (ii) retrieving or generating relevant evidence, and (iii) predicting a veracity verdict transparently to bolster public trust and adoption (Vlachos and Riedel, 2014; Thorne and Vlachos, 2018).

[1] www.politifact.com
[2] www.factcheck.org
[3] www.snopes.com

Figure 1 illustrates a real-world check-worthy claim, showing the kind of input and output that a fact-checking system must process and output.

Claim: Several First Nations communities in Canada have closed their borders to avoid COVID-19.
Date: 19-3-2020
Speaker: Chief David Monias
Reporting Source: Reuters news agency
Location Code: CA
Label: Supported
Justification: Multiple sources confirm some First Nations communities in Canada closed their borders or set up checkpoints to limit the spread of COVID-19 and protect vulnerable members.

Figure 1: A sample claim from the AVeriTeC dataset.

We introduce a lightweight, time-efficient pipeline for automated fact verification. The system assigns each claim to one of four verdicts – *Supported, Refuted, Not Enough Evidence (NEE),* or *Conflicting Evidence/Cherrypicking (CE/C)* – and outputs a rationale explaining its decision, citing relevant sources. Our method involves applying claim decomposition, Large Language Models (LLMs), a Retrieval Augmented Generation (RAG) framework, hybrid retrieval, and carefully tuned prompts to produce explainable fact-checking.

We evaluate our system on the AVeriTeC dataset (Schlichtkrull et al., 2023), demonstrating a substantial accuracy improvement (5%) over the official baseline, while maintaining slightly faster performance.

2 Related Work

The 2024 AVeriTeC shared task (Schlichtkrull et al., 2024) commenced with an initial baseline system

Proceedings of the Eighth Fact Extraction and VERification Workshop (FEVER), pages 247–257
July 31, 2025

proposed by (Schlichtkrull et al., 2023), which utilized BM25-based sentence ranking (Trotman et al., 2014), question generation with BLOOM (Le Scao et al., 2023), and BERT (Devlin et al., 2019) for verdict prediction, achieving a modest old AVeriTeC score of 11%. Following this initial benchmark, multiple systems explored various sophisticated techniques to significantly enhance performance. For instance, HerO (Yoon et al., 2024) introduced LLM-based prompting to generate hypothetical "evidence passages" prior to iterative BM25 retrieval, re-ranking, and subsequent question generation, yielding the highest question generation score and substantially outperforming the original baseline.

Subsequent entrants further evolved these techniques by incorporating advanced retrieval and generation strategies. InFact (Rothermel et al., 2024) achieved top position on the leaderboard by leveraging proprietary LLMs such as GPT-4o (Achiam et al., 2023) in conjunction with dense semantic retrievers, combined with an aggressive question-fan-out strategy to further increase evidence recall. AIC CTU (Ullrich et al., 2024) adopted a streamlined RAG (Lewis et al., 2020) approach, integrating innovative methods such as Maximal Marginal Relevance (MMR) (Carbonell and Goldstein, 1998) and structured Chain-of-Thought (CoT) prompting. Dunamu-ML (Park et al., 2024) expanded the coverage of evidence by incorporating overlooked resources such as PDFs and video transcripts, demonstrating the benefits of richer evidence sources. Finally, Papelo (Malon, 2024) utilized a dynamic multi-hop web search approach with iterative question generation conditioned on previous results, highlighting potential advantages in scenarios where an initial fixed corpus might not be readily available.

Collectively, these systems underscore a progression from an initial shallow baseline to increasingly sophisticated methods and, heavier, proprietary models, leaving plenty of room for optimizations in terms of reducing model size, improving evidence completeness, and computational efficiency.

3 Task Description

Verifying the truthfulness of real-world claims is a complex task in natural language processing. It requires reasoning over noisy, high-volume unstructured information from diverse sources, often under strict time and resource constraints. An effective fact-checking system must not only assess the factualness of a claim, but also provide verifiable, interpretable explanations.

We formalize this claim verification task as follows:

Input

The input to the system is a tuple (c, m, e) where:

- c is an open-domain natural-language claim.
- m contains minimal metadata, including:
  - publication date t
  - speaker s
  - source URL u
  - location code ℓ
- e is the set of evidence articles collected from the Web related to the claim.

Output

Our system produces a triple (v, E, J) where:

- $v \in \{$*Supported, Refuted, NEE, CE/C*$\}$ is the system's predicted veracity label.
- E is a set of question-answer-document triples $(q_i, \{a_{i-j}\}, d_{i-j})$, representing the evidence extracted to support the label, where:
  - q_i is a fact-checking sub-question derived from the original claim c.
  - $\{a_{i-j}\}$ is a set of evidence snippets relevant to q_i.
  - d_{i-j} denotes the set of source documents from which $\{a_{i-j}\}$ are extracted.
- J is the textual justification that explains how the evidence E collectively supports the predicted veracity label v.

4 The Sanctuary System

This section outlines the architecture and workflow of Sanctuary, our end-to-end fact-checking system, as shown in Figure 2. The system consists of three main stages: Hypothetical Question & Passage Generation, a two-step Evidence-Retrieval Pipeline – Coarse and Semantic Evidence-Retrieval – and finally, Reasoning and Prediction. Each stage is designed to progressively narrow down the evidence relevant to proving the factuality of the claim and subsequent fact-checking. We describe the models, prompting strategies, and design choices used at each stage.

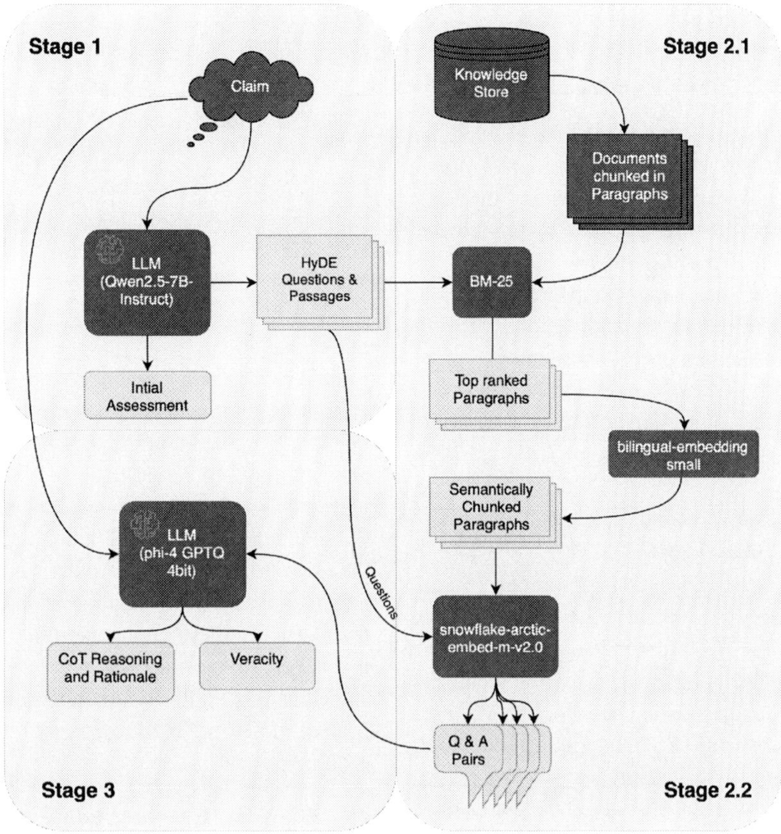

Figure 2: Overview of the SANCTUARY system

4.1 Stage 1: Hypothetical Question and Passage Generation

Fact-checkers typically approach verification by formulating multiple nuanced questions, exploring various angles to reach an informed conclusion (Silverman, 2014). Inspired by this journalistic practice, our system first employs an LLM – specifically, Qwen2.5-7B-Instruct (Yang et al., 2024) – to categorize a claim into one of three predefined veracity labels: *Supported*, *Refuted*, or *CE/C*. This classification step follows a methodology similar to that of (Park et al., 2024), with the notable exclusion of the *NEE*. This ensures that the model explicitly posits either supporting or opposing evidence; abstention would starve later stages of evidence. This initial assessment step capitalizes on the LLM's extensive pretraining and reasoning capabilities to detect factual inconsistencies based on its learned internal knowledge.

Following this classification, and drawing inspiration from Hypothetical Document Embeddings (HyDE) (Gao et al., 2023) as well as the works by (Yoon et al., 2024; Rothermel et al., 2024), we prompt the LLM to generate a diverse set of hypothetical question-document pairs using a detailed prompting template (illustrated in Figure 3). This process aims to enhance evidence recall in later stages by utilizing these hypothetical documents as queries to retrieve relevant evidence, rather than relying solely on the claim's text.

The rationale behind conducting an initial assessment prior to generating HyDE content is to condition the LLM to produce more targeted and contextually relevant hypothetical documents, leveraging its internal understanding of the claim, events, and related patterns.

Therefore, this step closely simulates the investigative process employed by human fact-checkers, who typically formulate investigative queries and the kind of evidential responses or documents they would likely obtain from online sources. By explicitly prompting the model to generate plausible yet fictional questions, associated passages, relevant entities, and alternative event scenarios, we aim to fully exploit the LLM's internal knowledge base and reasoning strengths.

4.2 Stage 2.1: Coarse Evidence-Retrieval

After generating a set of hypothetical question-answer pairs, we use the BM25 algorithm (Trotman et al., 2014) to retrieve relevant textual evidence from the knowledge store. Standard BM25 retrieval often suffers when documents vary significantly in length, as longer documents can disproportionately penalize or dilute term frequency scores. To mitigate this, we segment each document into fixed-length segments of approximately 500 tokens using a sliding-window approach with zero overlap, in line with previous methodologies (Malon, 2024; Park et al., 2024; Ullrich et al., 2024). Each document in the corpus is chunked in this manner to construct the BM25 index.

For each generated question-answer pair (treated as a single query), we retrieve the top 125 ranked document chunks from the index, a cutoff chosen based on the development set balancing recall and runtime. Given the substantial volume and length of the source documents – averaging 794 documents per claim in the development set – we preprocess (tokenize, segment, and index) them in parallel using multiprocessing to improve efficiency.

Finally, we group the top-retrieved chunks by their originating web article, using the document's URL as the key. This step intuitively narrows down the retrieved content to those segments within Web articles most relevant to answering queries associated with fact-checking the claim.

4.3 Stage 2.2: Semantic Evidence-Retrieval

In this stage, we further refine the evidence segments using a semantic, sentence-based chunking strategy (Kamradt, 2024) followed by semantic document retrieval, shifting the focus from keyword matching to semantic relevance. By applying semantic filtering, we narrow the scope of evidence to textual snippets that precisely address the hypothetical questions generated in Stage 1.

Initially, for each retrieved evidence document, we consolidate the segments selected in the previous step. We then divide this combined text into individual sentences and encode each sentence into semantic vector representations. Sentences exhibiting high semantic similarity are grouped together, creating coherent, semantically themed textual chunks. This step further refines the segments obtained previously into compact semantic units, improving the granularity and relevance of the evidence.

For sentence embeddings, we use the *bilingual-embedding-small* model (Conneau et al., 2019; Nils Reimers, 2019; Thakur et al., 2020), which offers strong performance across a range of NLP tasks despite its modest size (117M parameters) and currently ranks #30 on the HuggingFace MTEB Multilingual leaderboard.

Next, both the semantically formed chunks and the previously generated Stage 1 queries are embedded using a retrieval embedding model, treating chunks as documents, and queries as search input. For this step, we adopt the *snowflake-arctic-embed-m-v2.0* model (Yu et al., 2024), which provides a strong balance of retrieval accuracy and computational efficiency. To avoid redundancy, and reduce the size of the final evidence list, chunks identified as semantically duplicate (cosine similarity greater than 0.9) are filtered out, ensuring that each query is answered by distinct evidence. Therefore, this stage ensures that only the most semantically relevant and distinct evidence is retained to address each query.

4.4 Stage 3: Reasoning and Prediction

Rather than refining questions via sub-query generation (Rothermel et al., 2024), or generating new questions after initial coarse evidence-retrieval (Yoon et al., 2024), or reframing retrieved answers (Park et al., 2024), or generating question-answer pairs from initially retrieved coarse evidence (Ullrich et al., 2024) – each of which increases computational complexity – we opt for simplicity by adhering to our initial queries from Stage 1.

For each query, we select up to 8 evidence chunks from Stage 2.2, while imposing a hard cosine similarity threshold of 0.52. Our internal subjective evaluations indicated that this threshold effectively filters out less relevant evidence.

We then incorporate the selected question-answer blocks into a carefully crafted veracity prompt template, as shown in Figure 4, which includes detailed instructions and guidelines specific to the task of fact-checking. To further guide the model's understanding of the task, we include four-shot examples, one for each veracity label. The prompt is then fed into Microsoft's Phi-4 14B LLM (Abdin et al., 2024), using its GPTQ 4-bit quantized version (Frantar et al., 2022), chosen to maintain computational efficiency while remaining competitive. Although we had the option to use

Qwen2.5-7B for this stage, we found that Phi-4 is better suited for the task, owing to its larger parameter count and better handling of nuanced reasoning, which is critical for accurate veracity classification.

Additionally, to promote structured reasoning, groundedness, and explainability in our predictions, we employ a Chain-of-Thought (CoT) prompting strategy (Wei et al., 2022), instructing the model to articulate its reasoning explicitly, citing relevant Q-A pairs before producing a veracity label.

5 Experimental Results

5.1 Dataset

The AVeriTeC dataset provides three splits of real-world fact-checking claims containing both the textual claim and rich metadata. The training set comprises **3,068** claims, the development set **500** claims, and the blind test set **1,000** claims. Although the train/dev splits are drawn from fact-checks published up to 2019, the test set only contains claims posted *from 2024 onward*, making it a strictly out-of-distribution evaluation for temporal generalization. For every claim, a bundle of crawled web pages is provided as a *knowledge store*.

5.2 Evaluation Criteria

The new scoring mechanism, as of 2025, replaces the previous Hungarian METEOR (Banerjee and Lavie, 2005) string matching-based approach with the atomic reference-based **Ev2R atomic scorer** (Akhtar et al., 2024). An LLM is used to decompose predicted and reference questions and evidence into minimal *atomic facts*. For every atomic fact in the reference-set the scorer asks whether it is supported by the prediction, computing a *recall* value.

If the **Q + A (Ev2R recall)** > 0.50, then the system's veracity label is compared with gold, producing *new AVeriTeC score*. The Recall scores are published for Q-only and Q+A, along with the final AVeriTeC score.

Why the change? Hungarian METEOR is sensitive to surface form and treats any unannotated but valid evidence as "wrong" (Akhtar et al., 2024). The Ev2R scorer rewards factual coverage regardless of wording, is robust to alternate evidence chains, and correlates better with human judgments of coverage and relevance.

5.3 Baseline

Our reference is the **HerO** system (Yoon et al., 2024), *Herd of Open LLMs*, ranked 2nd in the 2024 AVeriTeC challenge. HerO adopts a multi-stage approach combining retrieval and generative reasoning: First, it uses open-source language models to produce hypothetical fact-checking passages. Next, these passages, along with the claim guide a retrieval process, identifying relevant evidence from a large-scale, per-claim knowledge store. The retrieved evidence is further filtered through semantic embedding models to retain only the most contextually meaningful excerpts. Then, HerO generates structured questions explicitly connecting evidence back to the original claim. Finally, a language model utilizes these questions and evidence snippets to classify the claim.

5.4 Hyperparameter Choices

We present the hyperparameter configurations employed at each stage of our pipeline below:

Stage 1: We utilize `Qwen2.5-7B-Instruct`, running under the vLLM[4] inference engine with its weights cast to bfloat16 precision. To balance diversity and instruction-following, we fix the sampling parameters as follows: `temperature` = 0.5, `top_p` = 0.8, `min_p` = 0.1, and `max_tokens` = 2048. We perform batch inference with four claims processed concurrently.

Stage 2: This stage leverages two distinct models: one optimized for Semantic Textual Similarity (STS) and another for document retrieval. For STS, we use `bilingual-embedding-small`[5] with the python library `Chonkie`[6], using the following chunking parameters: `min_chunk_size` = 30, `chunk_size` = 140, `min_sentences` = 2, and `similarity_window` = 1. Since 1–2 sentences average approximately 30 tokens (OpenAI, 2025), we enforce a minimum chunk size of two sentences (30 tokens) and a maximum of approximately 4–6 sentences (140 tokens). The `similarity_window` parameter controls the number of adjacent sentences considered during the similarity threshold computation. These choices ensure that short sentences are grouped to preserve contextual integrity, while longer meaningful segments are prevented from being fragmented arbitrarily.

[4]https://github.com/vllm-project/vllm

[5]https://huggingface.co/Lajavaness/bilingual-embedding-small

[6]https://github.com/chonkie-inc/chonkie

System	Q only	Q + A	AVeriTeC Score	Avg. time/claim (s)
CTU AIC	**0.2003 ± 0.0066**	**0.4774 ± 0.0035**	**0.3317 ± 0.0015**	53.67
HUMANE	0.1933 ± 0.0048	0.4299 ± 0.0006	0.2707 ± 0.0040	**29.19**
SANCTUARY	0.1561 ± 0.0057	0.4098 ± 0.0077	0.2527 ± 0.0051	31.71
Baseline	0.2723 ± 0.0006	0.3362 ± 0.0036	0.2023 ± 0.0068	33.88

Table 1: Performance of participating systems on the AVeriTeC 2025 task. Each system is evaluated on Question-only (Q), Question + Answer (Q+A), and the unified AVeriTeC score. Average inference time per claim (in seconds) is also reported.

LLM Combination (Stages 1 and 3)	Q only	Q + A	AVeriTeC Score
Qwen2.5-7B and Phi-4 GPTQ	0.3427	0.5167	0.29
Gemini 2.5 Flash (Both Stages)	0.4004	0.6106	0.33

Table 2: Ev2R evaluation comparing our default LLM combination of Qwen2.5-7B and Phi-4 GPTQ with Gemini Flash 2.5. Metrics reported are recall scores on question-only (Q), question-plus-answer (Q+A), and the final AVeriTeC score on 100 balanced development claims.

`snowflake-arctic-embed-m-v2.0`[7] is used for retrieval, using the eager attention implementation. Document and query texts are encoded with a batch size of 512.

Stage 3: We use `Microsoft's Phi-4-14B GPTQ 4bit`[8] quantized variant, also run under the vLLM inference engine with weights cast to half precision. Inference parameters are set as: `temperature` = 0.9, `top_p` = 0.7, `top_k` = 1, and `max_tokens` = 2048. We batch four claims per inference run. Setting `top_k` to 1 enforces determinism, thereby ensuring reproducibility.

5.5 Constraints

The participating systems were required to comply with the following conditions:

1. Avoid the usage of proprietary LLMs.
2. Process each claim in under 60 seconds on average. The evaluation system was equipped with an NVIDIA A10G GPU (23 GB VRAM), 8 vCPUs, 32GB RAM, and 450GB file-system.
3. Capture the source of the article of each evidence used in fact-checking to facilitate manual auditing.

5.6 Challenge Results

Table 1 presents the top three submissions from the 2025 AVeriTeC challenge leaderboard (excluding the baseline), ranked according to their AVeriTeC scores on the test set. The Sanctuary system (code-name **yellow_flash**) secured third place, achieving an AVeriTeC score approximately 5% higher than the baseline, with an average execution time of 31.71 seconds per claim.

On the development set, our system achieved scores of 0.2454 (Q-only), 0.5152 (Q+A), and 0.376 (AVeriTeC score), placing third on the dev leaderboard. However, a direct comparison with other systems on the development set is limited, as these evaluations were not conducted in a uniform, time-controlled environment.

However, the development and experimentation of our system was conducted on a different machine with a less powerful GPU compared to the challenge environment. Specifically, it featured an Intel(R) Xeon(R) Platinum 8253 CPU @ 2.20GHz (32 cores), an Nvidia Quadro RTX 8000 Turing GPU (48 GB VRAM), and 32 GB of RAM. On this setup, our system processed the 500 claims in the development set with an average execution time of approximately 55 seconds per claim.

6 Analysis

To assess the impact of backbone language models on overall system performance, we conducted an ablation study comparing our default LLM configuration – Qwen2.5-7B-Instruct for HyDE query generation and Phi-4 GPTQ for final reasoning – with a variant that uses Google's Gemini Flash 2.5 (Preview 04-17) (Team et al., 2023) in both stages 1 and 3. The Gemini model was constrained to a 1024-token "thinking" budget. All other pipeline

[7]`https://huggingface.co/Snowflake/snowflake-arctic-embed-m-v2.0`

[8]`https://huggingface.co/jakiAJK/microsoft-phi-4_GPTQ-int4`

LLM Combination (Stages 1 and 3)	Accuracy	Macro F1	Supported	Refuted	NEE	CE/C
Qwen2.5-7B and Phi-4 GPTQ	**0.535**	**0.486**	**0.649**	0.645	0.222	**0.429**
Gemini 2.5 Flash (Both Stages)	0.507	0.457	0.598	**0.655**	**0.351**	0.224
Gemini 2.5 Flash and Phi-4 GPTQ	0.490	0.438	0.586	0.609	0.223	0.333
Qwen2.5-7B and Gemini 2.5 Flash	0.466	0.421	0.642	0.555	0.278	0.207

Table 3: Local Classification Performance comparing our default combination of Qwen2.5-7B and Phi-4 GPTQ vs. Gemini Flash 2.5 on the same 100 development claims. Reported metrics include accuracy, macro F1, and per-class F1 scores.

components, parameters and prompts were kept fixed to ensure a controlled comparison.

For this experiment, we sampled 100 claims from the development set while ensuring an equal representation of each veracity class to reduce bias in performance estimation.

As shown in Table 2, substituting with Gemini resulted in notable gains across all Ev2R metrics. Specifically, we observed improvements of +5.77 points in Q-only recall, +9.39 points in Q+A recall, and a +4 point increase in the AVeriTeC score. These gains suggest that a stronger reasoning model enhances both the quality of generated questions and the utility of retrieved evidence, ultimately leading to better veracity predictions.

However, Table 3 presents a more nuanced picture. Despite Gemini's higher recall, our original configuration achieves a slightly higher classification accuracy (+2.8%) and macro F1 (+2.9%). It particularly excels in the *Supported* and *CE/C* classes, while Gemini notably performs better on the *NEE* class – indicating a more conservative stance when evidence is ambiguous or lacking.

These findings highlight an important trade-off: while Gemini – leveraging its advanced reasoning capacity and thinking mode – significantly improves factual recall and alignment with the Ev2R metrics, our Qwen–Phi pipeline delivers more balanced veracity classification despite scoring lower on the official metrics and operates under far lighter computational demands.

7 Conclusion and Future Work

We introduced SANCTUARY, an open-source time-efficient fact-checking pipeline that keeps model and hardware footprints modest while still closing much of the performance gap to heavier proprietary systems. By coupling lightweight question generation, a coarse-to-fine hybrid retriever, and quantized reasoning, the system attains a **new AVeriTeC** score of 25.27, an absolute 5–point gain over the shared-task baseline, yet verifies each claim in 31.71s on a single A10 GPU, 1.1s faster than the baseline.

Ablation results confirm that *reasoning capacity drives factual recall*: swapping in Gemini 2.5 Flash, a more capable LLM, lifts Ev2R Q-only, Q + A, and overall scores, at the cost of higher resources, yet achieves a slightly lower macro-F1 compared to our pipeline. Crucially, the study also exposes our main bottleneck, **question generation**. *Phi-4* still delivers strong label accuracy and reasoning when fed questions generated by either Qwen or Gemini; in fact, it scores better with Qwen-generated questions, despite their lower recall. This suggests that better-formed sub-questions could unlock further gains without enlarging the downstream reasoning model.

Our future work will therefore focus on increased knowledge-aware Q-generation and adaptive retrieval windows, in order to push recall higher while ensuring the same lean footprint that makes SANCTUARY efficient. We release our code and prompts to facilitate further research and reproducibility[9]

Limitations

Despite its efficiency and strong performance, Sanctuary has three main constraints. First, our HyDE Question Generation stage can miss multi-hop subquestions – key background links (e.g., Company X $\rightarrow$ Subsidiary Y) or tertiary events may go unexplored, capping recall. Second, Ev2R may penalize correct evidence not covered in the gold references, which means that valid but unannotated sources are treated as "misses"; this issue warrants further investigation. Third, our retrieval budget is fixed; complex claims or a larger evidence corpus may require adaptive context windows to avoid dropping crucial passages.

[9] https://github.com/arbaaz-abz/Sanctuary

Finally, we did not adopt the latest open-source LLMs at the time, such as Qwen3 (Yang et al., 2025), which many of the participants used. It is very likely that swapping in a more capable model, evidenced by our experiments with Google's Gemini, while still respecting our 60 s/claim budget, could yield even higher Ev2R recall and overall AVeriTeC scores.

Acknowledgment

This research is supported by NSERC RGPIN-2025-04608 and DGECR-2025-00153.

References

Marah Abdin, Jyoti Aneja, Harkirat Behl, Sébastien Bubeck, Ronen Eldan, Suriya Gunasekar, Michael Harrison, Russell J Hewett, Mojan Javaheripi, Piero Kauffmann, and 1 others. 2024. Phi-4 technical report. *arXiv preprint arXiv:2412.08905*.

Josh Achiam, Steven Adler, Sandhini Agarwal, Lama Ahmad, Ilge Akkaya, Florencia Leoni Aleman, Diogo Almeida, Janko Altenschmidt, Sam Altman, Shyamal Anadkat, and 1 others. 2023. Gpt-4 technical report. *arXiv preprint arXiv:2303.08774*.

Mubashara Akhtar, Michael Schlichtkrull, and Andreas Vlachos. 2024. Ev2r: Evaluating evidence retrieval in automated fact-checking. *arXiv preprint arXiv:2411.05375*.

Hunt Allcott and Matthew Gentzkow. 2017. Social media and fake news in the 2016 election. *Journal of Economic Perspectives*, 31(2):211–36.

Satanjeev Banerjee and Alon Lavie. 2005. Meteor: An automatic metric for mt evaluation with improved correlation with human judgments. In *Proceedings of the acl workshop on intrinsic and extrinsic evaluation measures for machine translation and/or summarization*, pages 65–72.

Jaime Carbonell and Jade Goldstein. 1998. The use of mmr, diversity-based reranking for reordering documents and producing summaries. In *Proceedings of the 21st annual international ACM SIGIR conference on Research and development in information retrieval*, pages 335–336.

Alexis Conneau, Kartikay Khandelwal, Naman Goyal, Vishrav Chaudhary, Guillaume Wenzek, Francisco Guzmán, Edouard Grave, Myle Ott, Luke Zettlemoyer, and Veselin Stoyanov. 2019. Unsupervised cross-lingual representation learning at scale. *arXiv preprint arXiv:1911.02116*.

Jacob Devlin, Ming-Wei Chang, Kenton Lee, and Kristina Toutanova. 2019. Bert: Pre-training of deep bidirectional transformers for language understanding. In *Proceedings of the 2019 conference of the North American chapter of the association for computational linguistics: human language technologies, volume 1 (long and short papers)*, pages 4171–4186.

Elias Frantar, Saleh Ashkboos, Torsten Hoefler, and Dan Alistarh. 2022. GPTQ: Accurate post-training compression for generative pretrained transformers. *arXiv preprint arXiv:2210.17323*.

Luyu Gao, Xueguang Ma, Jimmy Lin, and Jamie Callan. 2023. Precise zero-shot dense retrieval without relevance labels. In *Proceedings of the 61st Annual Meeting of the Association for Computational Linguistics (Volume 1: Long Papers)*, pages 1762–1777.

Hadas Gold and Brian Stelter. 2025. Fake news x post caused market whiplash.

Greg Kamradt. 2024. The 5 levels of text splitting for retrieval. `https://www.youtube.com/watch?v=8OJC21T2SL4`.

Teven Le Scao, Angela Fan, Christopher Akiki, Ellie Pavlick, Suzana Ilić, Daniel Hesslow, Roman Castagné, Alexandra Sasha Luccioni, François Yvon, Matthias Gallé, and 1 others. 2023. Bloom: A 176b-parameter open-access multilingual language model.

Stephan Lewandowsky, John Cook, Ullrich Ecker, Dolores Albarracin, Michelle A Amazeen, Panayiota Kendou, Doug Lombardi, Eryn Newman, Gordon Pennycook, Ethan Porter, and 1 others. 2020. *The debunking handbook 2020*.

Patrick Lewis, Ethan Perez, Aleksandra Piktus, Fabio Petroni, Vladimir Karpukhin, Naman Goyal, Heinrich Küttler, Mike Lewis, Wen-tau Yih, Tim Rocktäschel, and 1 others. 2020. Retrieval-augmented generation for knowledge-intensive nlp tasks. *Advances in neural information processing systems*, 33:9459–9474.

Christopher Malon. 2024. Multi-hop evidence pursuit meets the web: Team papelo at fever 2024. *arXiv preprint arXiv:2411.05762*.

Preslav Nakov, David Corney, Maram Hasanain, Firoj Alam, Tamer Elsayed, Alberto Barrón-Cedeño, Paolo Papotti, Shaden Shaar, and Giovanni Da San Martino. 2021. Automated fact-checking for assisting human fact-checkers. *arXiv preprint arXiv:2103.07769*.

Iryna Gurevych Nils Reimers. 2019. Sentence-bert: Sentence embeddings using siamese bert-networks. *https://arxiv.org/abs/1908.10084*.

OpenAI. 2025. What are tokens and how to count them? Accessed: 2025-06-22.

Heesoo Park, Dongjun Lee, Jaehyuk Kim, ChoongWon Park, and Changhwa Park. 2024. Dunamu-ml's submissions on averitec shared task. In *Proceedings of the Seventh Fact Extraction and VERification Workshop (FEVER)*, pages 71–76.

Mark Rothermel, Tobias Braun, Marcus Rohrbach, and Anna Rohrbach. 2024. Infact: A strong baseline for automated fact-checking. In *Proceedings of the Seventh Fact Extraction and VERification Workshop (FEVER)*, pages 108–112.

Michael Schlichtkrull, Yulong Chen, Chenxi Whitehouse, Zhenyun Deng, Mubashara Akhtar, Rami Aly, Zhijiang Guo, Christos Christodoulopoulos, Oana Cocarascu, Arpit Mittal, James Thorne, and Andreas Vlachos. 2024. The automated verification of textual claims (AVeriTeC) shared task. In *Proceedings of the Seventh Fact Extraction and VERification Workshop (FEVER)*.

Michael Schlichtkrull, Zhijiang Guo, and Andreas Vlachos. 2023. Averitec: A dataset for real-world claim verification with evidence from the web. *Advances in Neural Information Processing Systems*, 36:65128–65167.

Craig Silverman. 2014. Verification handbook. a definitive guide to verifying digital content for emergency coverage. european journalism centre. open access publication.

Gemini Team, Rohan Anil, Sebastian Borgeaud, Jean-Baptiste Alayrac, Jiahui Yu, Radu Soricut, Johan Schalkwyk, Andrew M Dai, Anja Hauth, Katie Millican, and 1 others. 2023. Gemini: a family of highly capable multimodal models. *arXiv preprint arXiv:2312.11805*.

Nandan Thakur, Nils Reimers, Johannes Daxenberger, and Iryna Gurevych. 2020. Augmented sbert: Data augmentation method for improving bi-encoders for pairwise sentence scoring tasks. *arXiv e-prints*, pages arXiv–2010.

James Thorne and Andreas Vlachos. 2018. Automated fact checking: Task formulations, methods and future directions. *arXiv preprint arXiv:1806.07687*.

Andrew Trotman, Antti Puurula, and Blake Burgess. 2014. Improvements to bm25 and language models examined. In *Proceedings of the 19th Australasian Document Computing Symposium*, pages 58–65.

Herbert Ullrich, Tomáš Mlynář, and Jan Drchal. 2024. Aic ctu system at averitec: Re-framing automated fact-checking as a simple rag task. *arXiv preprint arXiv:2410.11446*.

Andreas Vlachos and Sebastian Riedel. 2014. Fact checking: Task definition and dataset construction. In *Proceedings of the ACL 2014 workshop on language technologies and computational social science*, pages 18–22.

Jason Wei, Xuezhi Wang, Dale Schuurmans, Maarten Bosma, Fei Xia, Ed Chi, Quoc V Le, Denny Zhou, and 1 others. 2022. Chain-of-thought prompting elicits reasoning in large language models. *Advances in neural information processing systems*, 35:24824–24837.

An Yang, Anfeng Li, Baosong Yang, Beichen Zhang, Binyuan Hui, Bo Zheng, Bowen Yu, Chang Gao, Chengen Huang, Chenxu Lv, and 1 others. 2025. Qwen3 technical report. *arXiv preprint arXiv:2505.09388*.

An Yang, Baosong Yang, Beichen Zhang, Binyuan Hui, Bo Zheng, Bowen Yu, Chengyuan Li, Dayiheng Liu, Fei Huang, Haoran Wei, and 1 others. 2024. Qwen2. 5 technical report. *arXiv preprint arXiv:2412.15115*.

Yejun Yoon, Jaeyoon Jung, Seunghyun Yoon, and Kunwoo Park. 2024. Hero at averitec: The herd of open large language models for verifying real-world claims. *arXiv preprint arXiv:2410.12377*.

Puxuan Yu, Luke Merrick, Gaurav Nuti, and Daniel Campos. 2024. Arctic-embed 2.0: Multilingual retrieval without compromise. *arXiv preprint arXiv:2412.04506*.

Appendix A: Stage 1 prompt

You are a highly capable, thoughtful, and precise fact-checker.

Given a claim and its metadata, first classify the claim to the best of your knowledge and then generate relevant Question and Answer pairs. You must assign one of the following labels:

* **Supported:** The claim is fully backed by clear, consistent evidence.

* **Refuted:** The claim is directly contradicted by reliable evidence, or there is no concrete evidence to support the claim.

* **Conflicting Evidence/Cherrypicking:** The evidence has both supporting and opposing arguments for the claim or is selectively presented to favor the claim.

Guidelines:

– Generate anywhere between 5 to 10 Q-A pairs. Generate more questions for complex and multi-fact claims.

– Ensure questions have context. For example, given the claim *"Every week, at least 12 doctors leave Nigeria to seek employment in the UK."*, a better question is *"When was the claim made regarding Nigerian doctors moving to the UK to seek employment?"* rather than the overly generic *"When was the claim made?"*

– A question can have multiple sub-answers derived from various sources.

– Keep your answers brief (not more than 3 sentences).

– Fabricate random facts, figures, statements, or arguments, if and when needed.

Output Format:

```
"label": "Supported | Refuted | Conflicting Evidence/Cherrypicking",
"evidence": {Question-1: [Answer-1, Answer-2, ...], Question-2: [Answer-1], ...}
```

1-SHOT EXAMPLE (omitted for brevity)

Now process this claim:

```
{Claim}
{Claim Date}
{Claim Speaker}
{Location ISO Code}
{Reporting Source}
```

Figure 3: Prompt template for Hypothetical Question and Passage Generation.

Appendix B: Stage 3 prompt

You are a highly capable, thoughtful, and precise fact-checker.

Given a claim, its metadata, question and evidence pairs (each question can be addressed by several related evidences), your goal is to analyze the claim and how the evidence aligns with it. Then, you must label the claim using one of the following:

* **Supported**: The claim is fully backed by clear, consistent evidence with no significant contradictions.
* **Refuted**: The claim is directly contradicted by reliable evidence, or there is no evidence to support the claim.
* **Not Enough Evidence**: The evidence is insufficient to either support or refute the claim.
* **Conflicting Evidence/Cherrypicking**: The evidence both supports and opposes the claim or is selectively presented to favor the claim.

Guidelines:

– Take note of the claim date, the time period it refers to, speaker identity, geographical location, and reporting source for contextualization.
– Evaluate evidence within the relevant timeline and location constraints.
– Consider trustworthiness and title/URL source of evidence.
– For numerical claims, focus on data points; for events, check occurrence and timing; for position statements, consider the speaker's intent.

4-SHOT EXAMPLES (omitted for brevity)

Fact-check this claim:

```
{Claim}
{Claim Date}
{Claim Speaker}
{Location ISO Code}
{Reporting Source}
{Queries and Evidence}
```

You must carefully reason step-by-step using the context and evidence to determine the final label of the claim.

OUTPUT FORMAT:

```
Reasoning:
1. <concise rewrite of claim and intent; Note the timeline, location, statistics, numbers, quotes, events>
2. <evidence assessment>
3. <contradictions / gaps / biases noted>
4. <why the balance of evidence leads to the chosen label>

Label:
<Supported | Refuted | Not Enough Evidence | Conflicting Evidence/Cherrypicking>
```

Figure 4: Prompt template for veracity prediction.

Fathom: A Fast and Modular RAG Pipeline for Fact-Checking

Farrukh Bin Rashid
farrukh.rashid@unb.ca

Saqib Hakak
saqib.hakak@unb.ca

Abstract

We present Fathom, a Retrieval-Augmented Generation (RAG) pipeline for automated fact-checking, built entirely using lightweight open-source language models. The system begins with HyDE-style question generation to expand the context around each claim, followed by a dual-stage retrieval process using BM25 and semantic similarity to gather relevant evidence. Finally, a lightweight LLM performs veracity prediction, producing both a verdict and supporting rationale. Despite relying on smaller models, our system achieved a new AVeriTeC score of 0.2043 on the test set, a 0.99% absolute improvement over the baseline and 0.378 on the dev set, marking a 27.7% absolute improvement.

1 Introduction

Misinformation and disinformation continue to pose serious challenges in today's social media landscape. Research from 2018 shows that false claims spread up to six times faster than truthful ones on platforms like Twitter (Vosoughi et al., 2018). Although manual fact-checking has played a critical role in addressing false claims, it struggles to match the speed and volume at which mis/disinformation proliferates online. As a result, automated fact-checking (AFC) has been proposed as a valuable tool to support journalists and professional fact-checkers (Vlachos and Riedel, 2014). AFC refers to the task of predicting the veracity of a claim by leveraging relevant pieces of evidence (Guo et al., 2022).

The field of automated fact-checking has progressed significantly in recent years, supported by the development of benchmark datasets such as FEVER (Thorne et al., 2018) and, more recently, AVeriTeC (Schlichtkrull et al., 2023). While FEVER introduced large-scale fact verification using synthetic claims derived from Wikipedia, it and similar datasets often suffered from limitations like shallow context, limited evidence, and temporal leakage, reducing their effectiveness on real-world claims. AVeriTeC addresses these challenges by using real claims from professional fact-checkers, annotated with fine-grained, crowdsourced evidence and question-answer pairs drawn from noisy, open-web sources.

In this paper, we present Fathom, a Retrieval-Augmented Generation (RAG) pipeline for automated fact-checking that leverages open-source, lightweight language models, using the AVeriTeC dataset. The system processes each claim in 22 seconds. First, it enriches the claim using a HyDE-style approach by generating hypothetical question-answer pairs. These are then used to retrieve candidate evidence via BM25. To refine the retrieved set, we apply semantic re-ranking using a dense embedding model. Finally, a lightweight LLM reasons over the selected evidence and QA pairs to classify the claim as Supported, Refuted, Not Enough Evidence, or Conflicting Evidence/Cherrypicking. The full implementation of our system is publicly available at `github.com/farrukhrashid1997/Fathom`.

2 Related Works

Schlichtkrull et al. (2024) features and discusses top-performing systems that combined large language models (LLMs) with hybrid retrieval pipelines for automated fact-checking on the AVeriTeC dataset. Rothermel et al. (2024) was the most notable with a GPT-4o-based pipeline and semantic search. Yoon et al. (2024) integrated BM25 with dense retrieval, using LLaMA-3 models for both question generation and veracity prediction. Ullrich et al. (2024) and Park et al. (2024) both relied on GPT-4, with the latter achieving the highest performance by enhancing retrieval through PDF and video text extraction.

A common pattern among top systems using

Proceedings of the Eighth Fact Extraction and VERification Workshop (FEVER), pages 258–265 the AVeriTeC dataset is the initial generation of questions or decomposition of claims into self-contained queries to guide retrieval. This step was typically powered by large LLMs such as GPT-4o or LLaMA-3.1-70B. However, several competitive systems, such as HerO (Yoon et al., 2024) with LLaMA-3-8B and Data-Wizards (Singhal et al., 2024) with Phi-3-medium, demonstrated that smaller models can also be effective for query generation.

Similarly, in the veracity prediction stage, most top-performing systems relied on powerful LLMs like GPT-4o, LLaMA-3.1-70B, and Mixtral-8x7B to reason over retrieved evidence and generate final verdicts. Notably, some systems like HerO (Yoon et al., 2024) and SynApSe (Churina et al., 2024) observed further gains by fine-tuning these LLMs for the task, suggesting that adapting large language models to the specific reasoning requirements of the AVeriTeC task can lead to measurable performance improvements.

More broadly, recent work has explored variations of RAG to improve fact verification through better evidence grounding. Khaliq et al. (2024) combines multimodal retrieval with structured reasoning via Chain of RAG and Tree of RAG, enabling step-by-step reasoning by retrieving and integrating evidence across multiple sub-questions.

Another notable use RAG is by CrAM (Deng et al., 2025), it improves fact-checking by teaching the model to focus more on reliable evidence. Instead of treating all retrieved documents equally, it adjusts how much attention the LLM gives to each one based on how credible it is.

Inspired by these developments, our system adopts a RAG-based architecture with lightweight open-source LLMs, combining efficient retrieval and reasoning to tackle the challenges of automated fact-checking.

3 Data

We evaluate our system on the AVeriTeC dataset (Schlichtkrull et al., 2023), a resource for automated fact-checking containing 4,568 real-world claims collected from 50 professional fact-checking organizations. Each claim is annotated with a veracity label *Supported*, *Refuted*, *Not Enough Evidence*, or *Conflicting Evidence/Cherry-picking* along with question-answer (QA) pairs grounded in web-based evidence, and a justification explaining how the evidence supports the verdict. The distribution of labels across the training and development splits is summarized in Table 1.

The AVeriTeC dataset uses a multi-step annotation process to make each claim easier to verify. First, the claims are cleaned and simplified for clarity. Then, annotators generate questions that reflect the core factual components of the claim. For each question, they retrieve supporting or refuting information from the web and record multiple answers along with the source URLs.

In the 2024 AVeriTeC shared task (Schlichtkrull et al., 2024) introduced a knowledge store, a curated collection of pre-retrieved web documents, to assist people using the dataset in evidence retrieval, eliminating the need for independent web scraping.

Class	Train	Dev
Supported	847	122
Refuted	1743	305
Conflicting evidence/Cherrypicking	196	38
Not enough evidence	282	35
Total	**3068**	**500**

Table 1: Class-wise distribution of train and dev sets of the AVeriTeC dataset.

4 Methodology

In this section, we present our system and describe its four key components within the RAG pipeline.

4.1 Claim Decomposition via HyDE-QA Generation

Several fact-checking pipelines (Park et al., 2024; Rothermel et al., 2024; Ullrich et al., 2024) have shown that generating explicit questions from claims and subsequently answering them using retrieved evidence significantly improves fact verification performance. These question-answer pairs not only guide the retrieval process but also organize the information in a way that supports LLM reasoning during classification. In parallel, the HyDE approach (Gao et al., 2023; Wang et al., 2023) has gained traction in RAG pipelines by generating hypothetical answers to queries using an LLM. These synthetic answers, when used as enriched search queries, improve semantic retrieval performance by injecting latent contextual cues. Inspired by prior work, we generate multiple plausible HyDE-style QA pairs for each claim to guide evidence retrieval.

In order to generate the question answer pairs, the model is prompted with the claim along with

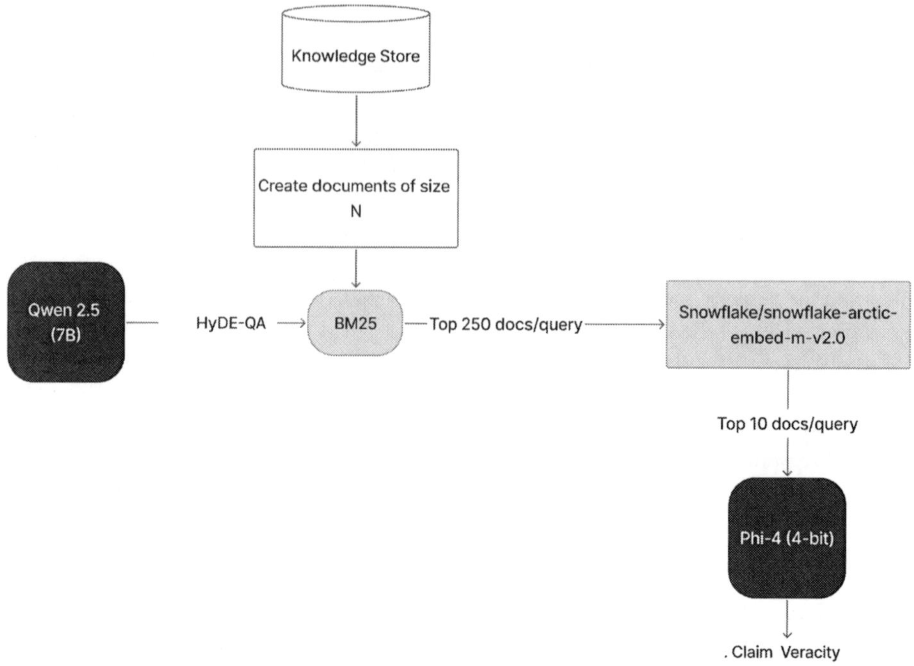

Figure 1: Overview of the Fathom system architecture.

optional metadata (speaker, date, location) and instructed to output multiple detailed QA pairs. To steer generation quality, we include handpicked few-shot examples that emphasize explicit and well-reasoned question-answer pairs. Six of the eight examples represent claims labeled as Conflicting Evidence/Cherry-picking. We chose this label primarily because such claims often involve both supporting and refuting information, which leads to more diverse and informative questions, covering multiple angles of the claim. These richer question answer pairs, in turn, guide better retrieval and support the LLM's reasoning in downstream prediction. The remaining few-shot examples include one Supported and one Refuted case. An example generation output is shown in Figure 2.

Claim: In a letter to Steve Jobs, Sean Connery refused to appear in an Apple commercial.

Q1: Did Sean Connery refuse to appear in an Apple commercial?
A1: No, because in 1998, Steve Jobs reached out to Sean Connery to star in a commercial for Apple's iMac G3. Connery agreed and filmed the commercial.

Q2: Was there a letter from Sean Connery refusing to appear in an Apple commercial?
A2: No, there is no record of such a letter. Instead, Connery accepted the invitation and starred in the commercial.

Q3: Did Steve Jobs request Sean Connery for a commercial?
A3: Yes, in 1998, Steve Jobs, the CEO of Apple, personally wrote to Sean Connery, asking him to star in a commercial for the iMac G3.

Figure 2: Example of generated QA pairs for a Refuted claim.

4.2 Evidence Retrieval

In order to retrieve relevant evidence for the claim, we adopt a hybrid retrieval strategy, combining keyword-based sparse retrieval with semantic dense re-ranking.

4.2.1 Sparse Retrieval (BM25)

As in most RAG systems (Lewis et al., 2020; Ullrich et al., 2024), we perform document chunk retrieval by splitting each document into smaller passages. Consecutive sentences are grouped until the combined character length reaches a threshold of N. Each chunk is annotated with metadata referencing its preceding and following chunks to maintain contextual continuity when later presented to the LLM.

Given that each claim has its own associated

knowledge store, often comprising hundreds or thousands of web pages, the search space is prohibitively large for direct dense retrieval. To address this, we first apply BM25 (Harman, 1995) to narrow the candidate pool: for each generated question-answer pair, we form a query and retrieve the top $k = 250$ chunks. Results are then deduplicated across all QA pairs linked to the claim. This high-recall filtering step enables efficient downstream semantic re-ranking.

This design also ensures that the system operates within the time constraints of fact-checking a claim under one minute. BM25 acts as a lightweight and effective first-pass filter, helping balance retrieval quality with system speed.

4.2.2 Semantic Re-ranking

Following the sparse BM25 stage, we employ semantic re-ranking to identify the most relevant passages from the candidate pool. To select an embedding model, we explore the MTEB benchmark (Muennighoff et al., 2022), prioritizing models under 500M parameters to meet runtime and memory constraints. We choose `Snowflake/snowflake-arctic-embed-m-v2.0` (Merrick et al., 2024), a compact model that ranks among the top performers on retrieval tasks in the MTEB leaderboard, making it well-suited for our space and time constrained setting.

Each candidate chunk is embedded into a dense vector representation that captures its semantic content. Similarly, each query is formed by concatenating the question and answer from the QA pair and encoded using the same model. We compute cosine similarity between each query and all candidate chunk embeddings, and select the top 10 highest-scoring chunks per query. The output of this step is a ranked list of 10 evidence passages for each QA pair, optimized for semantic relevance.

4.3 Veracity Prediction

In the final stage, the system assigns one of four veracity labels (Supported, Refuted, Not Enough Evidence, or Conflicting/Cherry-picking) based on the structured evidence retrieved earlier, along with a clear rationale for its decision.
We prompt the LLM using a structured prompt that includes:

- the original claim
- a set of generated questions (from the QA generation step)
- For each question, up to N = 8 top-ranked evidence passages (ranked by the similarity score)

Through our preliminary testing, we found that N = 8 strikes a balance between sufficient context and avoiding prompt length limitations or information overload. To encourage structured reasoning, we adopt a Chain-of-Thought (CoT) prompting strategy as shown in Figure 3. The prompt explicitly instructs the LLM to analyze the claim by reasoning step-by-step through multiple question–answer evidence pairs. Essentially, instead of making an immediate judgment, the model is guided to sequentially evaluate evidence associated with each question, reflect on its implications for the claim, and then generate an overall conclusion. This encourages the model to simulate a fact-checker's reasoning process, improving interpretability and alignment with complex veracity categories. We draw inspiration from prior work demonstrating that CoT enhances the reasoning capabilities of large language models across various tasks. (Wei et al., 2022)

After prompting the LLM, we get the final output which consists of:

- A detailed, natural-language reasoning which is grounded in the evidence
- A single veracity label, justified by the reasoning above

An excerpt of the final-stage output is shown in Figure 4, where the LLM can be seen reasoning through the provided questions and their corresponding evidence passages.

5 Experiments and Results

5.1 Experimental Details

All experiments were conducted using the **NVIDIA Quadro RTX 8000** GPU, which provided sufficient capacity for both dense retrieval and large language model inference. To ensure generalization and prevent overfitting to the dev set, final evaluation was performed on the AVeriTeC test set, an unseen split with hidden labels. For this stage, our system was deployed on an **NVIDIA A10G** GPU, as provided by the AVeriTeC shared task organizers, under standardized evaluation constraints.

Throughout the pipeline, we make design choices aimed at maximizing time efficiency without compromising output quality. In the first

	Q (Ev2R)	Q + A (Ev2R)	New (Ev2R)	Time/claim (s)
Fathom	0.2488	**0.5137**	**0.3780**	**20**
Baseline	**0.3392**	0.4404	0.2960	50

Table 2: AVeriTeC score on the **dev set**

Class	F1 Score
Supported (S)	0.6877
Refuted (R)	0.8436
Not Enough Evidence (NEI)	0.1455
Conflicting/Cherry-Picking (CP/CE)	0.0000
Accuracy	0.7200
Macro Avg F1	0.4192

Table 3: Per-class F1 scores, overall accuracy, and macro-averaged F1 score on the development set.

Claim: You are a fact-checking helpful assistant.

Task: Your task is to evaluate the truthfulness of a claim using associated question–answer (QA) evidence pairs, where each question has several pieces of evidence (answers). You must analyze the claim and reason step-by-step through the evidence provided. Use a chain-of-thought reasoning approach to determine the final label.

The given claim falls into one of the following four categories:
1. Supported
2. Refuted
3. Not Enough Evidence
4. Conflicting Evidence/Cherry-picking

Input Format:
Claim: <claim>
QA: <Question answer pairs>

Output:
Reasoning: [Use chain-of-thought reasoning on the claim based on the evidence. Incorporate evaluation of the content and optionally consider the trustworthiness or context of the source URLs.]
Label: <Supported, Refuted, Not Enough Evidence, Conflicting Evidence/Cherry-picking>

Figure 3: Prompt for the final veracity prediction step.

stage, the HyDE-QA step, we employ the open-source **`Qwen2.5-7B-Instruct`** model, running at half precision (`dtype="float16"`) to reduce memory usage and accelerate inference. We use `temperature=1.2` and `top_p=0.3` to balance output diversity and relevance where the high temperature encourages variability while the low top-p keeps sampling focused on plausible tokens to maintain coherence. To reduce latency and GPU memory load, claims are processed with a batch size of 2. These settings offer a practical trade-off between response quality and runtime performance.

In the second stage, we apply parallelism to the BM25-based sparse retrieval step. Claims are distributed across multiple CPU processes, and queries within each claim are further parallelized using multi-threading. This dual-level parallelism allows the system to retrieve evidence for many claims simultaneously, significantly reducing total time.

For semantic re-ranking, we use the **`Snowflake/snowflake-arctic-embed-m-v2.0`** embedding model. All candidate evidence chunks are encoded in batches of 128 for efficiency.

In the final veracity prediction step, we process claims in **batches of 4** using a 4-bit quantized version of Microsoft's `Phi-4` model (`jakiAJK/microsoft-phi4_GPTQ-int4`) to ensure faster inference and reduced memory usage. We select Phi-4 for its advanced reasoning capabilities, as it outperforms much larger models including LLaMA-3.3 70B and GPT-4o-mini on several reasoning-focused benchmarks such as MATH, GPQA, and HumanEval (Abdin et al., 2024). For generation, we use `temperature=0.9`, `top_p=0.7`, and `top_k=1`, a conservative setup that limits randomness while maintaining output quality. This configuration promotes stable, deterministic responses suitable for factual judgment.

5.2 Evaluation metrics

The evaluations metrics ensure that a correct veracity prediction is recorded only when the right evidence is retrieved to support the label.

In 2024, the AVeriTeC score was measured using the Hungarian METEOR approach (Kuhn, 1955; Banerjee and Lavie, 2005), wherein each generated QA pair is optimally matched to a reference using the Hungarian algorithm, and scored using METEOR similarity.

In 2025, the *AVeriTeC score* transitioned from Hungarian METEOR to the Ev2R atomic reference

Claim: In a letter to Steve Jobs, Sean Connery refused to appear in an Apple commercial.

Reasoning: To evaluate the claim that "In a letter to Steve Jobs, Sean Connery refused to appear in an Apple commercial," we need to examine the evidence provided in the QA pairs.

Q1: Did Sean Connery refuse to appear in an Apple commercial?
- **Answer 1** references multiple sources discussing a supposed rejection letter from Sean Connery to Steve Jobs, suggesting that such a letter exists. However, these sources are primarily linked to discussions about a viral letter rather than confirming its authenticity.
- **Answer 2** and **Answer 3** provide context about Apple's attempt to create a celebrity Christmas ad featuring Sean Connery, but they emphasize that the ad was never completed due to its poor quality. They do not confirm the existence of a refusal letter.
- **Answer 4** describes a letter that was widely believed to be authentic but later identified as a hoax. This suggests that while the letter was circulated, it was not genuine.

(Q2–Q5 omitted for brevity. They further support the same conclusion.)

Conclusion: The evidence consistently indicates that the letter from Sean Connery to Steve Jobs was a hoax and not a genuine refusal. While Steve Jobs did request Connery for a commercial, Connery did not actually respond with a refusal. Therefore, the claim is refuted.
Label: Refuted

Figure 4: Example of LLM-generated chain-of-thought reasoning with partial QA evidence (Q1–Q2 shown).

scorer (Akhtar et al., 2024). This approach uses an LLM to decompose both the predicted and reference question–answer (Q+A) pairs into sets of atomic facts. The metric then computes **Q + A (Ev2R Recall)** by measuring how many reference atomic facts are matched by those in the retrieved evidence.
The predicted veracity label is only evaluated if the **Q+A (Ev2R) Recall exceeds 0.50**, which then contributes to the final AVeriTeC score.

5.3 Results

We conduct all development and initial evaluation on the AVeriTeC development set. As shown in Table 2, our system achieves a higher **New (Ev2R)** AVeriTeC score of **0.3780**, outperforming the baseline. This gain is primarily driven by stronger semantic evidence retrieval, as reflected in the higher **Q+A (Ev2R)** recall score of **0.5137**.

In terms of veracity classification, Table 3 presents the F1 scores across all four classes. Our final model using the 4-bit quantized `Phi-4` performs well on the **Refuted** (0.8436) and **Supported** (0.6877) categories, which are also the most represented in the dev set. However, it struggles on the low-resource labels: **Not Enough Evidence (0.1455)** and especially **Conflicting/Cherry-picking**, where it fails to correctly classify any instance. This highlights a limitation in the veracity prediction stage, particularly for underrepresented classes that require more nuanced reasoning.

We hypothesize that one reason for this shortfall is the use of a zero-shot prompting strategy at the veracity prediction step. Incorporating a few-shot approach, especially with examples from NEI and CP/CE may help the model generalize better. Despite these challenges, the system achieves a strong overall **accuracy of 72%**, showing its reliability on majority classes while pointing to clear directions for future improvement.

To evaluate the generalization of our system, we submit predictions on the unseen AVeriTeC test set, where ground-truth labels are hidden. As shown in Table 4, our system slightly outperforming the baseline while maintaining significantly lower average runtime per claim. However, in contrast to the substantial improvement observed on the dev set, the margin over the baseline on the test set is noticeably smaller.

We hypothesize that this difference is because of our fixed chunking strategy (in step 2 of the pipeline), which segments documents using a constant token size without adopting to the semantic boundaries of the document. While this approach proved effective on the dev set, it may fail to generalize across more diverse or structurally varied claims in the test set. This is another direction for future work, to explore semantic aware chunking methods, potentially improving retrieval precision and final veracity scores.

6 Conclusion and Future Work

In this paper, we presented **Fathom**, our lightweight and time-efficient pipeline for evidence-based automated fact-checking, built entirely using open-source LLMs. Despite strong accuracy on majority classes such as *Refuted* and *Supported*, our results indicate notable performance gaps on underrepresented labels especially *Conflicting Evidence/Cherrypicking* and *Not Enough Evidence*. These shortcomings highlight ongoing challenges in reasoning over evidence, especially when the

	Q (Ev2R)	Q + A (Ev2R)	New (Ev2R)	Time/claim (s)
Fathom	0.1848	**0.3368**	**0.2043**	**22.73**
Baseline	**0.2723**	0.3362	0.2023	33.88

Table 4: AVeriTeC Scores on the **test set**

claim is unclear or has both supporting and opposing information.

Looking forward, we identify several key directions for improving performance. First, enhancing retrieval with *semantic-aware chunking* could help the system adapt more flexibly to diverse document structures, especially on unseen data. Second, integrating *few-shot prompting* for veracity prediction may improve the model's reasoning capabilities. Finally, fine-tuning small LLMs on curated QA-veracity datasets could enable better discrimination between nuanced veracity types. Together, these enhancements may help build more robust, efficient, and interpretable fact-checking systems.

Acknowledgment

This research is supported by NSERC RGPIN-2025-04608 and DGECR-2025-00153.

References

Marah Abdin, Jyoti Aneja, Harkirat Behl, Sébastien Bubeck, Ronen Eldan, Suriya Gunasekar, Michael Harrison, Russell J Hewett, Mojan Javaheripi, Piero Kauffmann, and 1 others. 2024. Phi-4 technical report. *arXiv preprint arXiv:2412.08905*.

Mubashara Akhtar, Michael Schlichtkrull, and Andreas Vlachos. 2024. Ev2r: Evaluating evidence retrieval in automated fact-checking. *arXiv preprint arXiv:2411.05375*.

Satanjeev Banerjee and Alon Lavie. 2005. Meteor: An automatic metric for mt evaluation with improved correlation with human judgments. In *Proceedings of the acl workshop on intrinsic and extrinsic evaluation measures for machine translation and/or summarization*, pages 65–72.

Svetlana Churina, Anab Barik, and Saisamarth Phaye. 2024. Improving evidence retrieval on claim verification pipeline through question enrichment. In *Proceedings of the Seventh Fact Extraction and VERification Workshop (FEVER)*, pages 64–70.

Boyi Deng, Wenjie Wang, Fengbin Zhu, Qifan Wang, and Fuli Feng. 2025. Cram: Credibility-aware attention modification in llms for combating misinformation in rag. In *Proceedings of the AAAI Conference on Artificial Intelligence*, volume 39, pages 23760–23768.

Luyu Gao, Xueguang Ma, Jimmy Lin, and Jamie Callan. 2023. Precise zero-shot dense retrieval without relevance labels. In *Proceedings of the 61st Annual Meeting of the Association for Computational Linguistics (Volume 1: Long Papers)*, pages 1762–1777, Toronto, Canada. Association for Computational Linguistics.

Zhijiang Guo, Michael Schlichtkrull, and Andreas Vlachos. 2022. A survey on automated fact-checking. *Transactions of the Association for Computational Linguistics*, 10:178–206.

Donna K Harman. 1995. *Overview of the third text retrieval conference (TREC-3)*. 500. DIANE Publishing.

M Abdul Khaliq, Paul Chang, Mingyang Ma, Bernhard Pflugfelder, and Filip Miletić. 2024. Ragar, your falsehood radar: Rag-augmented reasoning for political fact-checking using multimodal large language models. *arXiv preprint arXiv:2404.12065*.

Harold W Kuhn. 1955. The hungarian method for the assignment problem. *Naval research logistics quarterly*, 2(1-2):83–97.

Patrick Lewis, Ethan Perez, Aleksandra Piktus, Fabio Petroni, Vladimir Karpukhin, Naman Goyal, Heinrich Küttler, Mike Lewis, Wen-tau Yih, Tim Rocktäschel, and 1 others. 2020. Retrieval-augmented generation for knowledge-intensive nlp tasks. *Advances in neural information processing systems*, 33:9459–9474.

Luke Merrick, Danmei Xu, Gaurav Nuti, and Daniel Campos. 2024. Arctic-embed 2.0: Multilingual retrieval without compromise. *Preprint*, arXiv:2412.04506.

Niklas Muennighoff, Nouamane Tazi, Loïc Magne, and Nils Reimers. 2022. Mteb: Massive text embedding benchmark. *arXiv preprint arXiv:2210.07316*.

Heesoo Park, Dongjun Lee, Jaehyuk Kim, ChoongWon Park, and Changhwa Park. 2024. Dunamu-ml's submissions on averitec shared task. In *Proceedings of the Seventh Fact Extraction and VERification Workshop (FEVER)*, pages 71–76.

Mark Rothermel, Tobias Braun, Marcus Rohrbach, and Anna Rohrbach. 2024. Infact: A strong baseline for automated fact-checking. In *Proceedings of the Seventh Fact Extraction and VERification Workshop (FEVER)*, pages 108–112.

Michael Schlichtkrull, Yulong Chen, Chenxi Whitehouse, Zhenyun Deng, Mubashara Akhtar, Rami Aly, Zhijiang Guo, Christos Christodoulopoulos, Oana

Cocarascu, Arpit Mittal, and 1 others. 2024. The automated verification of textual claims (averitec) shared task. *arXiv preprint arXiv:2410.23850*.

Michael Schlichtkrull, Zhijiang Guo, and Andreas Vlachos. 2023. Averitec: A dataset for real-world claim verification with evidence from the web. *Advances in Neural Information Processing Systems*, 36:65128–65167.

Ronit Singhal, Pransh Patwa, Parth Patwa, Aman Chadha, and Amitava Das. 2024. Evidence-backed fact checking using rag and few-shot in-context learning with llms. *arXiv preprint arXiv:2408.12060*.

James Thorne, Andreas Vlachos, Christos Christodoulopoulos, and Arpit Mittal. 2018. Fever: a large-scale dataset for fact extraction and verification. *arXiv preprint arXiv:1803.05355*.

Herbert Ullrich, Tomáš Mlynář, and Jan Drchal. 2024. Aic ctu system at averitec: Re-framing automated fact-checking as a simple rag task. *arXiv preprint arXiv:2410.11446*.

Andreas Vlachos and Sebastian Riedel. 2014. Fact checking: Task definition and dataset construction. In *Proceedings of the ACL 2014 Workshop on Language Technologies and Computational Social Science*, pages 18–22, Baltimore, MD, USA. Association for Computational Linguistics.

Soroush Vosoughi, Deb Roy, and Sinan Aral. 2018. The spread of true and false news online. *science*, 359(6380):1146–1151.

Liang Wang, Nan Yang, and Furu Wei. 2023. Query2doc: Query expansion with large language models. *arXiv preprint arXiv:2303.07678*.

Jason Wei, Xuezhi Wang, Dale Schuurmans, Maarten Bosma, Fei Xia, Ed Chi, Quoc V Le, Denny Zhou, and 1 others. 2022. Chain-of-thought prompting elicits reasoning in large language models. *Advances in neural information processing systems*, 35:24824–24837.

Yejun Yoon, Jaeyoon Jung, Seunghyun Yoon, and Kunwoo Park. 2024. Hero at averitec: The herd of open large language models for verifying real-world claims. *arXiv preprint arXiv:2410.12377*.

Graph-of-Thoughts for Fact-Checking with Large Language Models

Sascha Rolinger[1], **Jin Liu**[1,2]

[1]Karlsruhe Institute of Technology, Karlsruhe, Germany
[2]FZI Research Center for Information Technology, Karlsruhe, Germany
Correspondence: sascha.rolinger@student.kit.edu, jin.liu@fzi.de

Abstract

We present a fact-checking system developed for the 2025 Automated Verification of Textual Claims (AVeriTeC) shared task, leveraging the Graph-of-Thoughts (GoT) prompting scheme. The GoT approach facilitates iterative refinement during fact-checking by conditioning question generation on previous answers and enabling the incorporation of multiple evidence documents per question, thereby mitigating the impact of factually incorrect evidence. The efficiency requirements of the shared task are addressed by restricting the width and depth of the thought graph. Additionally, an efficient stopping criterion is derived from the dataset's Not Enough Information (NEI) label. Our system utilizes fine-tuned open-source Large Language Models (LLMs) for question generation, question answering, and final verdict prediction. Empirical results demonstrate competitive performance against top-performing systems in the AVeriTeC shared task and improvements over the baseline method. Our code is publicly available[1].

1 Introduction

Automated fact-checking can be conceptualized as a textual entailment task, aiming to assess a claim's veracity based on retrieved evidence (Vlachos and Riedel, 2014). Existing automated fact-checking systems predominantly adopt a pipeline architecture, sequentially executing distinct components for claim detection, evidence retrieval, verdict prediction, and justification production (Guo et al., 2022).

The AVeriTeC dataset, introduced by Schlichtkrull et al. (2023), supports automated fact-checking with real-world claims from fact-checking articles. These claims are annotated with question-answer (QA) pairs designed to mirror a fact-checker's reasoning process. The dataset includes a Knowledge Store that identifies one or more "gold" documents for each claim, signifying their use in the original fact-check. The current AVeriTec shared task imposes two key constraints: participants must use open-source models, and fact-checking must be performed under one minute per claim. This paper describes our system for the AVeriTeC shared task based on the Graph-of-Thoughts framework.

2 Related Work

Iterative question generation for fact-checking has been explored on similar datasets (Pan et al., 2023; Wang and Shu, 2023; Zhang and Gao, 2023). Malon (2024)'s framework, developed for the AVeriTeC 2024 shared task, employs an iterative reasoning strategy that continues generating follow-up questions until the system determines sufficient evidence has been gathered. While this iterative refinement is similar to our approach, key differences exist. Malon (2024)'s system terminates when its underlying LLM determines that an adequate number of questions have been answered. In contrast, our method utilizes the NEI label, iterating until a label other than NEI is predicted or a maximum number of question rounds has been reached. Furthermore, our GoT approach explores multiple verification paths, enabling more robust handling of misleading or insufficient evidence.

While top-performing systems in the previous AVeriTeC shared task often relied on proprietary models (Rothermel et al., 2024; Ullrich et al., 2024; Park et al., 2024; Malon, 2024), with Yoon et al. (2024) being an exception, the current iteration of the shared task requires the use of open-source models for all participants.

[1]https://gitlab.kit.edu/utjwp/Fact-Checking_GoT_RAG_LLM

Proceedings of the Eighth Fact Extraction and VERification Workshop (FEVER), pages 266–273
July 31, 2025 ©2025 Association for Computational Linguistics

3 Methodology

Our framework is designed to perform iterative fact-checking by building a dynamic reasoning structure. This section describes our framework, core components, their training, and the implementation details.

3.1 Graph-of-Thoughts (GoT)

Various prompting strategies for LLMs have been proposed. Among these, Besta et al. (2024) introduced GoT, a method that, similar to Chain-of-Thought (CoT) (Wei et al., 2023) or Tree-of-Thoughts (ToT) (Yao et al., 2023), models LLM thoughts as vertices and their dependencies as edges. An edge $(t1, t2)$ signifies that $t1$ serves as input for generating $t2$. Unlike other prompting methods, GoT uniquely permits the construction of an arbitrary directed graph, enabling the aggregation of individual thoughts and even entire thought chains.

The GoT framework involves two distinct graphs. The GoT itself is the central data structure that records execution results, as illustrated in Figure 2. The Graph-of-Operations (GoO) defines the algorithm responsible for generating and managing the GoT structure. Figure 1 illustrates the GoO of our system using UML-like notation, where nodes represent operations that either prompt an LLM to generate new thoughts or evaluate these thoughts through scoring, verification, or ranking.

The algorithm begins with an initial question generation phase, followed by pruning of similar questions. Subsequently, evidence is retrieved, and answers are generated. These answers can then optionally undergo a verification step. Given that multiple answers might arise from different pieces of evidence for the same underlying query, the algorithm merges these answers before forming an intermediate verdict. If the verdict is NEI and the maximum number of questioning rounds has not been reached, the algorithm iterates back to question generation. If the maximum depth is reached or the verdicts are conclusive, different reasoning branches are merged to produce a final verdict for the original claim. Figure 2 shows an annotated theoretical GoT that illustrates these algorithmic stages within the data structure.

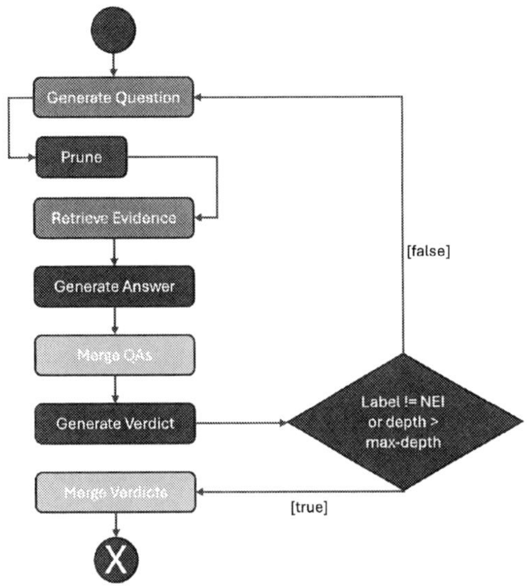

Figure 1: Control flow of the algorithm (Graph-of-Operations) used for generating and managing the Graph-of-Thoughts (GoT). Nodes indicate operations producing LLM-generated thoughts or their assessment through scoring, verification, and ranking. Color coding indicates branching operations (light blue), branch termination (red), and merging of branches (yellow)

3.2 Core Components and Training Data Preparation

Our framework consists of four core components: Question Generation, Evidence Retrieval, Question Answering, and Verdict Prediction. To achieve better performance, we fine-tuned a base LLM using the AVeriTeC dataset. Specifically, we employed Low-Rank Adaptation (LoRA) (Hu et al., 2022) to train three distinct adapters for the Question Generation, Question Answering, and Verdict Prediction tasks. The AVeriTeC dataset, in its original form, is not explicitly structured for the iterative process. Therefore, a transformation is necessary to align the dataset with the structural requirements for fine-tuning models dedicated to these iterative tasks. For sections regarding these three components, we focus on the methodology for constructing appropriate training data.

3.2.1 Question Generation

A training instance is created for each question in the dataset. The first question in the sequence requires a distinct prompt, as no prior QA pairs exist. The prompt includes the claim and its metadata for generating relevant fact-checking questions. For each subsequent question $i + 1$, the prompt is ex-

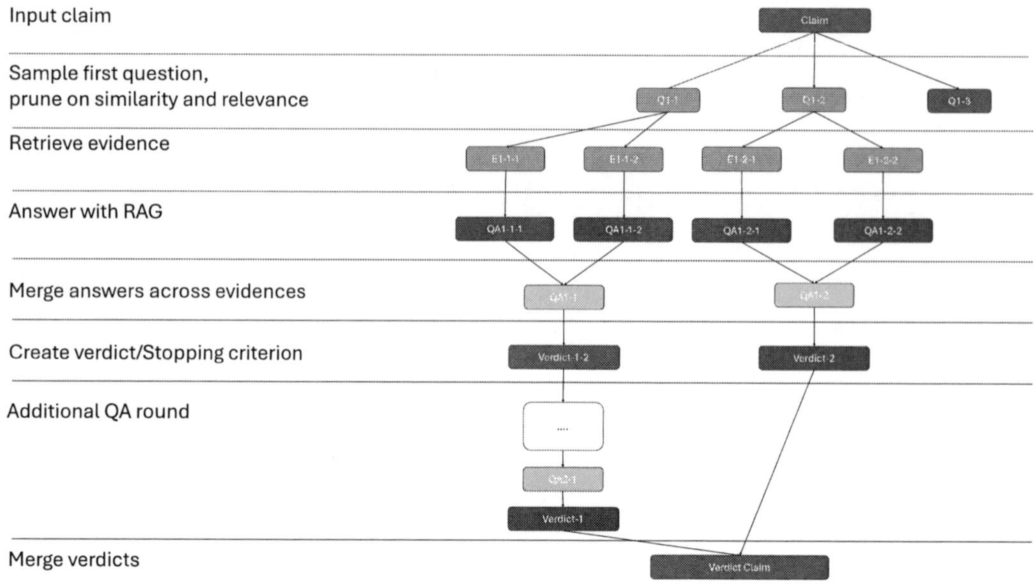

Figure 2: Illustrative example of the Graph-of-Thoughts (GoT) framework depicting the sequence of operations and their dependencies within the fact-checking process. Multiple questions are generated starting from the original claim, and each question starts a branch. Not all generated questions are explored to limit the size of the graph. For each question, multiple pieces of evidence are retrieved, and answers are generated individually. Answers can then be verified and merged. If the verdict is NEI, an additional question round is started. If all branches have a final verdict, the verdict for the claim is calculated using majority voting.

tended to include the preceding i QA pairs as additional context. This setup enables the model to condition question generation on the information gathered during earlier fact-checking steps. The target in each case is the following question in the sequence for the given claim. We show training examples for question generation in A.1.1.

3.2.2 Evidence Retrieval

Existing retrieval modules often employ multi-stage pipelines encompassing pre-processing, coarse retrieval, and re-ranking components (Zhao et al., 2022). A common retrieval pipeline involves segmenting documents into smaller chunks and encoding these with a bi-encoder to construct an efficient index. Subsequently, a cross-encoder can refine the initial retrieval results by re-ranking the top candidates. While we initially explored this standard design, its application to the AVeriTeC Knowledge Store proved computationally expansive for the shared task's constraints. Specifically, the AVeriTeC Knowledge Store averages 86,154 text chunks (each approximately 1000 characters with a 200-character overlap), making a full bi-encoder/cross-encoder pipeline excessively resource-intensive.

To allocate a greater portion of the limited time budget to the LLM generations central to our Graph-of-Thoughts (GoT) approach, we adopted a more efficient retrieval strategy. The Knowledge Store is first chunked. Then, for each claim, only the top 3000 chunks scored by BM25 relevance to the claim are retained. This pre-selection method, also employed by Ullrich et al. (2024) to reduce the size of the Knowledge Store, forms the basis for building an FAISS index (Johnson et al., 2019). This condensed index allows for more efficient querying and offers opportunities for parallelization, further optimizing the now more GPU-intensive workload. Such an efficient index structure is particularly beneficial for the GoT methodology, as the Knowledge Store is queried multiple times with questions that evolve based on the outcomes of previous queries.

3.2.3 Question Answering

Preparing the fine-tuning dataset for Question Answering introduces specific challenges due to the nature of the AVeriTeC dataset. The dataset does not provide explicit span-level annotations for pinpointing the exact evidence within the gold documents. Instead, for each question, only the identifier of the relevant gold document is supplied. To address this, the identified gold document is first segmented into manageable chunks. Subsequently, a cross-encoder-based retrieval model is employed to identify the chunk most relevant to the gold question-answer (QA) pair. Since the ground truth answer is available during training, both the question and the answer are independently used as queries to the retriever. The chunk achieving the highest relevance score from either of these queries is then selected as the candidate evidence.

Additional filtering steps are applied to mitigate noise potentially introduced by annotation errors or retrieval inaccuracies. First, a minimum relevance score threshold is applied, and any candidate evidence chunks falling below this threshold are discarded. Following this, an LLM is prompted to assess whether the ground truth answer is entailed by the retrieved evidence chunk. Each resulting training instance for the Question Answering model consists of an input concatenating the claim, metadata, the selected evidence chunk, and the question. The target output comprises the answer itself, its type (e.g., extractive, Boolean, or abstractive), and the source (metadata of evidence). We illustrate one training example for Question Answering in A.1.2.

3.2.4 Verdict Prediction

Each training instance for verdict prediction incorporates the claim, its associated metadata, and all corresponding QA pairs as input. Specific instructions are appended to this input to prompt the model to generate a justification and a veracity label, formatted in JSON. Following Liu et al. (2024), the model is guided to generate the justification before the label, enabling it to condition the final veracity assessment on the generated explanatory text. One training example is shown in A.1.3

Including additional training examples explicitly labeled as NEI is critical. These NEI instances are designed to reduce the likelihood of the model prematurely assigning a verdict of Supported, Refuted, or Conflicting Evidence/Cherry-picking when the available information is indeed insufficient. To generate these NEI examples, for each claim with n QA pairs in the AVeriTeC dataset, additional training instances are created using only the first i QA pairs, where $i \in \{1, \dots, n-1\}$ and assigned the NEI label.

3.3 Auxiliary Components

An overview of additional components integrated into the system is provided in Table 1. The implementation of these auxiliary components is generally straightforward, primarily leveraging the models deployed for retrieval and the base LLM.

Module	Method
Question Deduplication	Bi-Encoder Filtering
Answer Merging	Prompting Base LLM
Verdict Merging	Majority Voting

Table 1: Overview of auxiliary modules and corresponding methods.

3.4 Implementation Details

The model selection is primarily constrained by the available hardware and time budget of the evaluation system, which is a g5.2xlarge EC2 instance on AWS with 23GB of GPU memory. Given that the base LLM is the central component of our approach, efficient utilization of this GPU memory was paramount. Consequently, we selected Qwen2.5-14B-Instruct-AWQ (Team, 2024; Yang et al., 2024), deploying using the vLLM (Kwon et al., 2023) inference engine. This model, due to Activation-aware Weight Quantization (AWQ) (Lin et al., 2024), fits within the available GPU memory while also reserving sufficient space for Key-Value (KV) caching, which is crucial for generation performance. The LoRA configuration employs a rank of 16, an alpha value of 32, a dropout rate of 0.05, and omits bias terms. LoRA modules are injected into all projection layers of the transformer blocks. This memory-efficient LLM deployment also leaves adequate room to deploy the bi-encoder model for various similarity calculations, including evidence retrieval, question deduplication. We chose dunzhang/stella_en_400M_v5[2] as our bi-encoder model.

4 Evaluation

We report the results for our submitted system and the average processing time per claim. The development split was processed on an Nvidia A100 with 40GB of memory. For this split, the Ev2R score (Akhtar et al., 2024) was calculated using recommended Llama-3.3-70B-Instruct (AI@Meta, 2024). Results for the test split are derived from the

[2]https://huggingface.co/Marqo/dunzhang-stella_en_400M_v5

official published leaderboard[3]. Notably, scores for the development split are significantly higher than those on the test split. This discrepancy aligns with observations from the baseline model provided by the shared task organizers, which achieved AVeriTeC scores of 0.296 on the development split and 0.2023 on the test split, respectively.

Our submitted system demonstrated notable efficiency, utilizing only a third of the maximum one-minute processing time allowed per claim. An analysis of the F1 scores reveals a disparity between supported and refuted claims, with the former achieving a comparatively lower score. This suggests that while the system is adept at refuting claims when no supporting evidence is immediately found (potentially in the initial questioning round), it may not consistently recognize when sufficient evidence has been gathered to confirm a "Supported" verdict, leading to premature termination of the evidence collection process for such claims. Our system demonstrates limited performance when classifying instances as "Not Enough Evidence" (NEI) or "Conflicting Evidence". The low prediction rate for NEI is partially a consequence of the stopping criterion in our GoT mechanism, which uses this label to trigger further question generation rather than as a final verdict. This design results in NEI being infrequently predicted, with only 10 out of 500 instances in the development set classified as such.

	Dev	Test
Ev2R recall		
Question-only	0.392	0.362
Question-answer	0.530	0.400
AVeriTeC Score	0.366	0.244
Veracity F1 Scores		
Supported	0.615	-
Refuted	0.824	-
Not Enough Evidence	0.000	-
Conflicting Evidence	0.050	-
Time Measurement		
Seconds per claim	15.4	18.5

Table 2: Comparison of Ev2R recall scores (question-only, question-answer, AVeriTeC), veracity F1 scores, and time measurements for development and test split of the 2025 AVeriTeC shared task.

5 Conclusion

We have implemented an iterative Graph-of-Thoughts (GoT) framework designed to advance fact-checking methodologies by enabling more profound and extensive exploration of evidence. Our approach has yielded competitive results, demonstrating that the incorporation of more comprehensive evidence can significantly improve fact-checking performance, even when constrained to smaller-scale, open-source LLMs. Despite these achievements, establishing a consistently reliable criterion for determining evidence sufficiency proved challenging. Consequently, fact-checking processes were either prematurely terminated or necessitated continuation for a fixed, and potentially inefficient, number of question-answering rounds.

The computational costs associated with LLM-based fact-checking, particularly within highly iterative frameworks like GoT, remain a significant hurdle. This challenge is exacerbated for operational steps where dedicated training data is scarce, requiring LLMs to be prompted with lengthy instructions, in-context examples, and intermediate reasoning outputs. The computational burden becomes especially acute near the evidence retrieval stage, where the GoT typically expands to its maximum width, demanding substantial processing resources.

Future work could focus on extending the system with several promising modules and LLM invocations. Further modules can be developed for assessing the utility of an evidence document for the fact-checking task and for verifying the entailment of a generated answer within the provided evidence. Other potential enhancements to our approach include employing an LLM for dynamic ranking of all generated thoughts, enabling more adaptive exploration of the GoT, or developing mechanisms to recover from high uncertainty in the majority voting process used for branch label determination.

Limitations

Several limitations inherent in the conducted research and the implemented system should be considered when interpreting the results and conclusions presented in this paper.

Decoding Strategy A sampling-based decoding strategy was generally employed for LLM inference. While this approach is necessary for certain components to generate diverse outputs, it introduces variability that may reduce comparability between system configurations. Greedy decoding could have provided more stable outputs across runs, potentially enabling clearer distinctions in system performance.

[3]https://fever.ai/task.html

Mismatch Between Dataset and Approach The AVeriTeC dataset is not optimally suited to the iterative, multi-hop approach investigated in this paper. Annotations in the dataset reflect reasoning chains from successful human fact-checks, offering limited opportunities for the system to learn from fact-checking failures or incomplete reasoning. The quality of the derived fine-tuning datasets is also uncertain, primarily due to the lack of gold span annotations and the presence of broken or incomplete documents in the Knowledge Store. Moreover, the Knowledge Store lacks explicit positive and negative evidence annotations, making it difficult to conduct robust retrieval experiments or to evaluate evidence selection systematically.

Comprehensiveness of Fact-Checking A notable limitation is the tendency of the dataset to contain initial gold questions that are simple rephrasings of the original claim—a concern also raised by Malon (2024). Despite annotation guidelines discouraging trivial reformulations (Schlichtkrull et al., 2023), such questions are common. Consequently, the system often follows this pattern, producing shallow question-answer sequences that may lead to shorter and less comprehensive fact-checking.

References

AI@Meta. 2024. Llama 3 model card.

Mubashara Akhtar, Michael Schlichtkrull, and Andreas Vlachos. 2024. Ev2r: Evaluating evidence retrieval in automated fact-checking. *Preprint*, arXiv:2411.05375.

Maciej Besta, Nils Blach, Ales Kubicek, Robert Gerstenberger, Michal Podstawski, Lukas Gianinazzi, Joanna Gajda, Tomasz Lehmann, Hubert Niewiadomski, Piotr Nyczyk, and Torsten Hoefler. 2024. Graph of Thoughts: Solving Elaborate Problems with Large Language Models. *Preprint*, arXiv:2308.09687.

Zhijiang Guo, Michael Schlichtkrull, and Andreas Vlachos. 2022. A Survey on Automated Fact-Checking. *Transactions of the Association for Computational Linguistics*, 10:178–206.

Edward J Hu, Yelong Shen, Phillip Wallis, Zeyuan Allen-Zhu, Yuanzhi Li, Shean Wang, Lu Wang, and Weizhu Chen. 2022. LoRA: Low-rank adaptation of large language models. In *International Conference on Learning Representations*.

Jeff Johnson, Matthijs Douze, and Hervé Jégou. 2019. Billion-scale similarity search with GPUs. *IEEE Transactions on Big Data*, 7(3):535–547.

Woosuk Kwon, Zhuohan Li, Siyuan Zhuang, Ying Sheng, Lianmin Zheng, Cody Hao Yu, Joseph E. Gonzalez, Hao Zhang, and Ion Stoica. 2023. Efficient memory management for large language model serving with pagedattention. In *Proceedings of the ACM SIGOPS 29th Symposium on Operating Systems Principles*.

Ji Lin, Jiaming Tang, Haotian Tang, Shang Yang, Wei-Ming Chen, Wei-Chen Wang, Guangxuan Xiao, Xingyu Dang, Chuang Gan, and Song Han. 2024. Awq: Activation-aware weight quantization for llm compression and acceleration. In *MLSys*.

Jin Liu, Steffen Thoma, and Achim Rettinger. 2024. FZI-WIM at AVeriTeC shared task: Real-world fact-checking with question answering. In *Proceedings of the Seventh Fact Extraction and VERification Workshop (FEVER)*, pages 77–85, Miami, Florida, USA. Association for Computational Linguistics.

Christopher Malon. 2024. Multi-hop Evidence Pursuit Meets the Web: Team Papelo at FEVER 2024. In *Proceedings of the Seventh Fact Extraction and VERification Workshop (FEVER)*, pages 27–36, Miami, Florida, USA. Association for Computational Linguistics.

Liangming Pan, Xinyuan Lu, Min-Yen Kan, and Preslav Nakov. 2023. QACHECK: A Demonstration System for Question-Guided Multi-Hop Fact-Checking. https://arxiv.org/abs/2310.07609v1.

Heesoo Park, Dongjun Lee, Jaehyuk Kim, ChoongWon Park, and Changhwa Park. 2024. Dunamu-ml's Submissions on AVERITEC Shared Task. In *Proceedings of the Seventh Fact Extraction and VERification Workshop (FEVER)*, pages 71–76, Miami, Florida, USA. Association for Computational Linguistics.

Mark Rothermel, Tobias Braun, Marcus Rohrbach, and Anna Rohrbach. 2024. InFact: A Strong Baseline for Automated Fact-Checking. In *Proceedings of the Seventh Fact Extraction and VERification Workshop (FEVER)*, pages 108–112, Miami, Florida, USA. Association for Computational Linguistics.

Michael Sejr Schlichtkrull, Zhijiang Guo, and Andreas Vlachos. 2023. Averitec: A dataset for real-world claim verification with evidence from the web. In *Thirty-thh Conference on Neural Information Processing Systems Datasets and Benchmarks Track*.

Qwen Team. 2024. Qwen2.5: A party of foundation models.

Herbert Ullrich, Tomáš Mlynář, and Jan Drchal. 2024. AIC CTU system at AVeriTeC: Re-framing automated fact-checking as a simple RAG task. *Preprint*, arXiv:2410.11446.

Andreas Vlachos and Sebastian Riedel. 2014. Fact Checking: Task definition and dataset construction. In *Proceedings of the ACL 2014 Workshop on Language Technologies and Computational Social Science*, pages 18–22, Baltimore, MD, USA. Association for Computational Linguistics.

Haoran Wang and Kai Shu. 2023. Explainable Claim Verification via Knowledge-Grounded Reasoning with Large Language Models. In *Findings of the Association for Computational Linguistics: EMNLP 2023*, pages 6288–6304, Singapore. Association for Computational Linguistics.

Jason Wei, Xuezhi Wang, Dale Schuurmans, Maarten Bosma, Brian Ichter, Fei Xia, Ed Chi, Quoc Le, and Denny Zhou. 2023. Chain-of-Thought Prompting Elicits Reasoning in Large Language Models. *Preprint*, arXiv:2201.11903.

An Yang, Baosong Yang, Binyuan Hui, Bo Zheng, Bowen Yu, Chang Zhou, Chengpeng Li, Chengyuan Li, Dayiheng Liu, Fei Huang, Guanting Dong, Haoran Wei, Huan Lin, Jialong Tang, Jialin Wang, Jian Yang, Jianhong Tu, Jianwei Zhang, Jianxin Ma, and 40 others. 2024. Qwen2 technical report. *arXiv preprint arXiv:2407.10671*.

Shunyu Yao, Dian Yu, Jeffrey Zhao, Izhak Shafran, Thomas L. Griffiths, Yuan Cao, and Karthik Narasimhan. 2023. Tree of Thoughts: Deliberate Problem Solving with Large Language Models. *Preprint*, arXiv:2305.10601.

Yejun Yoon, Jaeyoon Jung, Seunghyun Yoon, and Kunwoo Park. 2024. HerO at AVeriTeC: The Herd of Open Large Language Models for Verifying Real-World Claims. *Preprint*, arXiv:2410.12377.

Xuan Zhang and Wei Gao. 2023. Towards LLM-based Fact Verification on News Claims with a Hierarchical Step-by-Step Prompting Method. In *Proceedings of the 13th International Joint Conference on Natural Language Processing and the 3rd Conference of the Asia-Pacific Chapter of the Association for Computational Linguistics (Volume 1: Long Papers)*, pages 996–1011, Nusa Dua, Bali. Association for Computational Linguistics.

Wayne Xin Zhao, Jing Liu, Ruiyang Ren, and Ji-Rong Wen. 2022. Dense Text Retrieval based on Pretrained Language Models: A Survey. *Preprint*, arXiv:2211.14876.

A Appendix

A.1 Prompts

A.1.1 Training Examples for Question Generation

Figure 3 shows the training example for generating the first question. The example for subsequent question generation is illustrated in Figure 4.

A.1.2 Training Example for Question Answering

Figure 5 shows a training example for Question Answering.

Training Example for First Question Generation

Input:

```
Claim: Donald Trump delivered the largest tax cuts in
American history.
Metadata: {'claim_date': '25-8-2020', 'speaker':
'Eric Trump', 'original_claim_url': None,
'reporting_source': 'Speech at The Republican
National Convention', 'location_ISO_code': 'US'}
Context:
None
Predict the first question:
```

Target:

```
Did the 2017 tax bill deliver the largest tax cuts in
American history?
```

Figure 3: Training example for generating the first question in iterative fact-checking. Given a claim and associated metadata, the model must generate an initial, relevant fact-checking question without additional context.

Training Example for Subsequent Question Generation

Input:

```
Claim: Donald Trump delivered the largest tax cuts in
American history.
Metadata: {'claim_date': '25-8-2020', 'speaker':
'Eric Trump', 'original_claim_url': None,
'reporting_source': 'Speech at The Republican
National Convention', 'location_ISO_code': 'US'}
Context:
Q1: Did the 2017 tax bill deliver the largest tax cuts
in American history?
A1: This tax cut is the 8th largest as a percent of
Gross Domestic Product
(GDP) since 1918 and the 4th largest in inflation-
adjusted dollars.
Predict the next question:
```

Target:

```
Has there been a larger tax bill than the 2017 tax bill?
```

Figure 4: Example illustrating subsequent question generation. Given the claim, metadata, and previous question-answer pairs as context, the model generates the next relevant fact-checking question, building iteratively upon previously obtained information.

Training Example for Question Answering

Input:

```
Claim: The United States of America and its Western allies
have been using their media outlets to publish articles
based on fabricated information under allegations of
non-compliance with the Chemical Weapons Convention.
Metadata: {'claim_date': '30-10-2020', 'speaker':
'Syrian Arab News Agency (SANA)', 'original_claim_url':
'https:...', 'reporting_source':
'Syrian state media outlet', 'location_ISO_code': 'SY'}
Evidence:
out by the Assad regime, usually dropped from the air,
and Islamic State
[...]
basements, chlorine gas, which is heavier than air, sinks
into these last refuges, finally forcing people to flee
their homes and towns. Our research shows what Syrians
on the ground have known for years: that chemical weapons
have become a completely normalised component of the
Syrian regime arsenal used for years in full view of the
international community with near impunity, said Tobias
Schneider, a GPPI research fellow who worked on the new
resource. Syria is commonly described as the best documented
war in
Question:
Has Syria complied with the Chemical Weapons Convention?
Answer the question and mention your source based on
the provided evidence or metadata in JSON format:
```

Target:

```
{"source": "Evidence", "answer": "No"}
```

Figure 5: Example of structured training data used for question answering. The input contains a claim, associated metadata, and an evidence chunk retrieved based on semantic similarity. The target output specifies the answer to the fact-checking question and the source (evidence or metadata) from which the model derived this answer.

A.1.3 Training Example for Verdict Prediction

Figure 6 shows an example for Verdict Prediction.

Training Example for Veracity Prediction

Input:

```
Claim: Hunter Biden had no experience in Ukraine or in
the energy sector when he joined the board of Burisma.
Metadata: {'claim_date': '25-8-2020', 'speaker':
'Pam Bondi', 'original_claim_url': None,
'reporting_source': 'Speech at The Republican
National Convention', 'location_ISO_code': 'US'}
Context:
Q1: Did Hunter Biden have any experience in the energy
sector at the time he joined the board of the Burisma energy
company in 2014
A1: No
Q2: Did Hunter Biden have any experience in Ukraine at the
time he joined the board of the  Burisma energy company
in 2014
A2: No
Write a justification and predict a label in JSON format:
```

Target:

```
{"justification": "No former experience stated.",
 "label": "Supported"}
```

Figure 6: Example of a structured training instance for veracity prediction. The input includes a claim, metadata, and previously answered question-answer pairs as context. The model must generate a concise justification and assign an appropriate veracity label (Supported, Refuted, Conflicting Evidence/Cherrypicking, or Not Enough Information (NEI)).

AIC CTU@FEVER 8: On-premise fact checking through long context RAG

Herbert Ullrich
AI Center @ CTU FEE
Charles Square 13
Prague, Czech Republic
ullriher@fel.cvut.cz

Jan Drchal
AI Center @ CTU FEE
Charles Square 13
Prague, Czech Republic
drchajan@fel.cvut.cz

Abstract

In this paper, we present our fact verification pipeline which has scored first in FEVER 8 shared task in real-world automated fact-checking. Our system is a simple two-step RAG pipeline based on our last year's submission. We show how the pipeline can be redeployed on-premise, achieving state-of-the-art fact-checking performance (in sense of Ev^{2}R test-score), even under the constraint of a single Nvidia A10 GPU, 23GB of graphical memory and 60s running time per claim.

1 Introduction

In 2024, Automated Verification of Textual Claims (AVeriTeC) shared task (Schlichtkrull et al., 2024a) showed that the fact checking of real-world claims like those from Politifact, AfricaCheck, etc., can be automated to a significant extent, with pipelines accessing Large Language Models (LLMs) to produce the evidence and veracity verdicts for previously unseen claims instead of a human. Almost each competitive AVeriTeC shared-task system, however, relied on a proprietary LLM like GPT-4o (Rothermel et al., 2024; Ullrich et al., 2024) or an open-weights model with high tens of billions of parameters (Yoon et al., 2024). This raised a concern – can the fact-checking process be automated in a way accessible to masses, or is its quality conditioned by the business-owned blackbox models or access to prohibitive computational resources?

In this year's FEVER 8 shared task, the challenge is to match the quality of AVeriTeC systems with ones that only use open-weights models, constrained time of 60 seconds per claim on average, and a fixed compute of a single 23GB A10 GPU.

Our AIC CTU system (Figure 1), adapted for FEVER 8 from our last year submission, tops its test-leaderboard (Table 1) with a simple Retrieval-augmented Generation (RAG) scheme, using a locally hosted (Ollama) instance of Qwen3 LLM with 14B parameters, leveraging the sheer

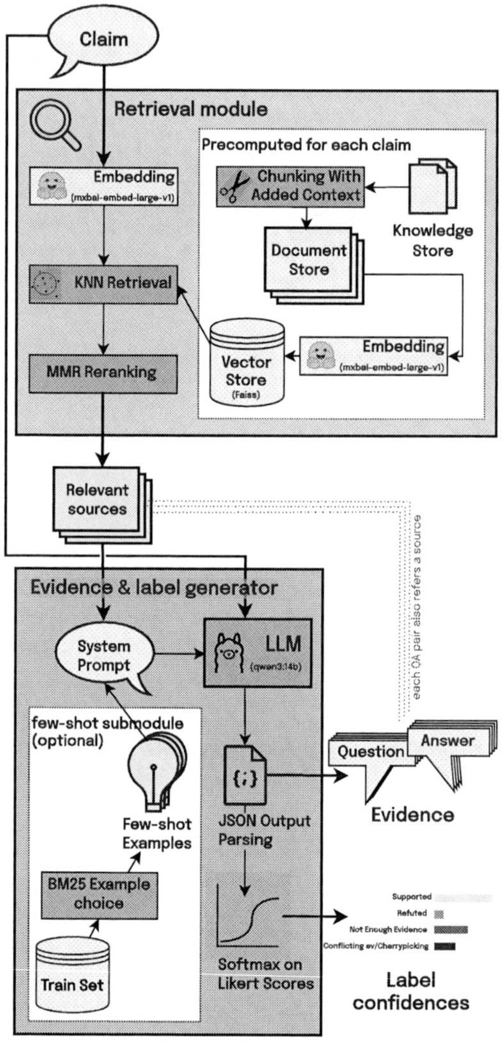

Figure 1: Our refreshed fact-checking pipeline used in CTU AIC FEVER 8 submission, adapted from Ullrich et al. 2024.

context length modern-day LLMs can process.

This paper introduces our system, discusses its design choices and how do they account on the score. We suggest our system as the new strong

Proceedings of the Eighth Fact Extraction and VERification Workshop (FEVER), pages 274–280
July 31, 2025 ©2025 Association for Computational Linguistics

baseline – simple at core, competitive results – providing the code and reproduction advice.

2 System description

Our system is a straightforward adaptation of the AIC CTU Averitec system designed one year prior, published in Ullrich et al. 2024. The cited paper describes the system in detail, with ablation studies and justifications of each step. Our pipeline, depicted in Figure 1, consists of precomputation, retrieval, and generation modules:

i. Precomputation module

  1. The provided AVeriTeC **knowledge store** (Schlichtkrull et al., 2024b) is split into chunks of specified maximum length, each marked with metadata of its URL and the full texts of the chunk before and after.
  2. The chunks are then embedded into their vector representations, using only the chunk texts and no metadata.
  3. Out of all chunk embeddings, a **vector store** is produced for each claim to be stored as a vector database.

ii. Retrieval module

  1. The **Claim** is embedded into its vector representation using the same model used in i.2.
  2. k nearest neighbours are then retrieved from the vector store, along with their **chunk embeddings**
  3. The chunk embeddings are then reranked using the Maximal Marginal Relevance (MMR) method (Carbonell and Goldstein, 1998), maximizing the embedding distances between retrieval results while minimizing their distance to the claim. Ultimately, we output a subset of l diverse **sources** for the claim ($l < k$), augmenting each with its context before, after, and the text of its URL.

iii. Evidence & label generation module

  1. We instruct a Large Language Model (LLM) to produce Question-Answer pairs required to fact-check given claim based on the provided sources, and predict its veracity verdict in a single output. We pass it the texts of all l sources, and several few-shot QA-pair generation examples picked from Averitec train set retrieved using BM25 based on the tested claim. The whole instruction is serialized into a system prompt and the format we used can be seen in Appendix A.
  2. **Claim** is then passed to the LLM as a user message.
  3. LLM is called to **generate the evidence** as a Question-Answer-Source triples and the Likert-scale scores for each possible **veracity verdict** in a single prediction, performing a chain of thought.
  4. The LLM output is parsed, and the verdict with the highest score is chosen for the claim.

The main differences between this year's AIC FEVER 8 system, opposed to last year's AIC AVeriTeC system, are the omission of knowledge store pruning in the precomputation step[1], and, importantly, the choice of LLM.

2.1 Model and parameter choices

To produce our submission in the FEVER 8 shared task, the following choices were made to deploy the pipeline from section 2:

`mxbai-embed-large-v1` (Li and Li, 2024; Lee et al., 2024) is used for the vector embeddings, and the maximum chunk size is set to 2048 characters, considering its input size of 512 tokens and a rule-of-thumb coefficient of 4 characters per token to exploit the full embedding input size and produce the smallest possible vector store size without neglecting a significant proportion of knowledge store text.

`FAISS` (Douze et al., 2024; Johnson et al., 2019) index is used as the vector database engine, due to its simplicity of usage, exact search feature and quick retrieval times (sub-second for a single FEVER 8 test claim).

$l = 10, k = 40, \lambda = 0.75$ are the parameters we use for the MMR reranking, meaning that 40 chunks are retrieved, 10 sources are yielded after MMR-diversification, and the tradeoff between their similarity to the claim and their diversity is 3:1 in favour of the source similarity to the claim (explained in more detail in Ullrich et al. 2024).

[1]The precomputed vector stores were required to be independent on claim text in FEVER 8.

`Ollama` wrapper around `llama.cpp` is the LLM engine we use to deploy LLMs within the FEVER 8 test environment due to its robustness and ease of deployment.

`Qwen3-14b` (Yang et al., 2025) is the LLM we use to produce the evidence and labels, we also let it generate its own `<think>` sequences, although further experimentation (Table 2) suggests that the thinking tokens may not justify the costs of their prediction, as they seem to perform on par with using only the evidence & label LLM outputs for its chain of thought.

3 Results and analysis

System	*old AVeriTeC score*	*Q only* (Ev^2R)	*Q + A* (Ev^2R)	*new AVeriTeC score*	*time per claim*
AIC CTU	0.41	0.20	**0.48**	**0.33**	54*s*
HUMANE	0.45	0.19	0.43	0.27	29*s*
yellow flash	0.16	0.16	0.41	0.25	32*s*
FZIGOT	0.46	**0.36**	0.40	0.24	19*s*
EFC	0.49	0.13	0.35	0.20	**7*s***
checkmate	0.38	0.18	0.34	0.20	22*s*
Baseline	**0.50**	0.27	0.34	0.20	34*s*

Table 1: FEVER 8 shared task system leaderboard as shared by organizers, listing new Ev^2R-recall-based (Akhtar et al., 2024) and legacy hu-METEOR AVeriTeC scores. Evaluated using AVeriTeC 2025 test set. Best scores are bold.

In Table 1, we reprint the final test-leaderboard of FEVER 8 shared task as provided by the organizers. Our system introduced in Section 2 scores first in the decisive metric for the task – the new AVeriTeC score – with a significant margin. This came as a surprise to its authors, as neither the values of the old, hu-METEOR-based AVeriTeC score (Schlichtkrull et al., 2024b), nor the dev-leaderboard available during system development phase (where our system scored 4th), suggested its supremacy. Let us therefore proceed with a discussion of possible strengths that could have given our system an edge in verifying the FEVER 8 test-set of previously unseen 1000 claims.

3.1 Why does the system perform well?

So why should our system outperform the FEVER 8 baseline and even the other systems submitted to FEVER 8 shared task despite the simplicity of its design (Figure 1) which boils down to a straightforward case of retrieval-augmented generation (RAG)?

The main reason, in our experience, is the large **context size** we opt for – while even the FEVER 8 baseline processes the claims and sources in a manner more sophisticated than we do, it processes the knowledge store on a *sentence* level, reducing the amount of information passed to the LLM as opposed to working with *documents* as a whole, which is the strategy our system approximates.

Despite our proposed integration of LLM into the pipeline being rather vanilla, combining sources of total length of as much as 60K characters[2] on model input yields highly competitive results, leveraging its own trained mechanisms of context processing.

Our other advantages may have been using a very recent model, Qwen3 (Yang et al., 2025), which naturally has a slightly higher leakage of 2025 claims into its train set than older models, and outperforms the previous LLM generations at long sequence processing. Furthermore, our pipeline design only uses a single LLM call per claim, meaning we could use the generously-sized 14B variant of Qwen3 and still match the time limit with Nvidia A10 and 23GB VRAM.

3.2 Scoring change impact

While the new AVeriTeC score based on Ev^2R-recall (Akhtar et al., 2024) estimates the proportion of correctly fact-checked claims[3] in all claims, just like the old hu-METEOR-based AVeriTeC score did, their underlying methods differ. Most importantly, an LLM-as-a-judge approach is now used instead of symbolic evidence comparison method. The rise of our system from 3rd place in AVeriTeC shared task (Schlichtkrull et al., 2024a) to 1st place in FEVER 8 without any major system change[4] can therefore also be attributed to the used scoring method. The old scoring method was, for example, found to be prone to some level of noise, as it was not robust against evidence duplication (Malon, 2024), which was a found exploit to boost evidence

[2]In other words, around 33 standard pages. This number follows from our parameter choices in Section 2.1: 10 sources are retrieved for each claim, each with $\sim$ 2048 characters of the embedded text, and additional $\sim$ 4096 characters of context.

[3]Claims with sound evidence w.r.t. human annotation, and an exact match in predicted label.

[4]Despite scaling down.

recall.

The discrepancy between old and new AVeriTeC score in Table 1 could motivate a further study on how the new score behaves, for example using the test-prediction files from last year AVeriTeC shared task systems. The familiarity of the systems, the availability of their hu-METEOR scores and documentation, may reveal valuable insights into the Ev^2R evaluation method itself, as in which behaviours does it punish and reward.

3.3 LLM impact

LLM	*Q only* (Ev^2R)	*Q + A* (Ev^2R)	*new AVeriTeC score*
GPT-4o$_{2024-05-13}$	0.30	0.58	0.40
Llama3.1-70B	0.37	0.54	0.39
qwen3:14B$_{/no_think}$	0.29	0.59	0.41
qwen3:14B$_{/think}$	0.20	0.59	0.42

Table 2: Ablation study on LLM choice and <think>-tokens impact on FEVER 8 dev-score. Pipeline design (Figure 1), retrieval results, system and user prompts are fixed. Evaluated using an on-premise Ev^2R scorer with Ollama-hosted Llama3.3-70B as a judge.

In 2024, we have experimented with then available versions of GPT-4o and Llama3.1-70B and found the open-source Llama to perform encouragingly well, depite the still-quite-cumbersome model size and the need for its quantization (Ullrich et al., 2024). This year, we have simply gone for the most recent open-weights LLM at the largest parameter count we could fit within our FEVER 8 compute budget, thus choosing the Qwen3 at its 14B parameter size (Yang et al., 2025).

Qwen3 was trained to produce thinking tokens by default, an approach popularized by DeepSeek (DeepSeek-AI et al., 2025) and OpenAI research models, to force the chain of thought. We have experimented with enabling and disabling this feature to see if it has an impact on the AVeriTeC score, and compared the model output quality to our last year prediction dumps, with evaluation experiments listed in Table 2.

Both Qwen3 evidence and label generation settings perform on par with previous GPT-4o generation, which validates our model choice. The thinking tokens, while producing legitimate-looking writeups of the fact-checking workflows (see Appendix B) were not shown to stimulate an improvement in AVeriTeC score in the ablation study (Table 2), so we suggest to disable this feature in future reproductions in favour of a faster prediction time (54s in the Table 1 was produced with the thinking feature *enabled*, so disabling it might solve the issue with near-limit runtime our pipeline suffers from).

4 Conclusion

In this paper, we have introduced our simple yet efficient RAG system which performed competitively well under time and compute constraints in FEVER 8 shared task, in May 2025. We release the used code along with usage instructions for producing the FEVER 8 submission, vector stores needed for the pipeline to run and their build scripts at `https://github.com/heruberuto/FEVER-8-Shared-Task/` which is a fork of the FEVER 8 baseline repository.

We attribute our success mostly to the use of *document* rather than *sentence* level of retrieval granularity and an employment of a recent LLM at a size which utilizes the whole compute and time budget with only around 10% time reserve as a failsafe. We encourage further usage of our system as a strong and easy-to-setup baseline for further research in automated fact checking and will be happy to answer any questions on the referred contacts.

4.1 Future works

1. Integrate a live search API as in (Malon, 2024) as a retriever into the AIC pipeline (Figure 1) to achieve a real-world generalization

2. Section 3.2 suggests to look at the key differences between legacy and Ev^2R scoring methods in terms of the available 2024 AVeriTeC leaderboard and available model documentations – we believe this could reveal valuable hints both scoring and pipelinne improvements in future work

Limitations

Our pipeline is not meant to be relied upon nor to replace a human fact-checker, but rather to assist an informed user. It gives sources and proposed labels for further questioning. It is optimized only for English, the carbon costs of the used models are considerable, despite the system trying to cut down the environmental cost of the prediction step.

Ethics statement

Our pipeline is an extension of our already existing last year submission all original authors agreed with, including the reusal of the necessary listing in Appendix A. The system was build specifically for the FEVER 8 shared task and reflects the biases of its annotators, for more information on this, we suggest the original AVeriTeC paper (Schlichtkrull et al., 2024b).

Acknowledgements

We would like to thank our last year system coauthor Tomáš Mlynář for staying in the loop, providing timely insights, proofreads and experience even when direct participation was not within his time budget this year.

This article was created with the state support of the Ministry of Industry and Trade of the Czech Republic, project no. Z220312000000, within the National Recovery Plan Programme. The access to the computational infrastructure of the OP VVV funded project CZ.02.1.01/0.0/0.0/16_019/0000765 "Research Center for Informatics" is also gratefully acknowledged.

References

Mubashara Akhtar, Michael Schlichtkrull, and Andreas Vlachos. 2024. Ev2r: Evaluating evidence retrieval in automated fact-checking.

Jaime Carbonell and Jade Goldstein. 1998. The use of mmr, diversity-based reranking for reordering documents and producing summaries. In *Proceedings of the 21st Annual International ACM SIGIR Conference on Research and Development in Information Retrieval*, SIGIR '98, page 335–336, New York, NY, USA. Association for Computing Machinery.

DeepSeek-AI, Daya Guo, Dejian Yang, Haowei Zhang, Junxiao Song, Ruoyu Zhang, Runxin Xu, Qihao Zhu, Shirong Ma, Peiyi Wang, Xiao Bi, Xiaokang Zhang, Xingkai Yu, Yu Wu, Z. F. Wu, ..., and Zhen Zhang. 2025. Deepseek-r1: Incentivizing reasoning capability in llms via reinforcement learning.

Matthijs Douze, Alexandr Guzhva, Chengqi Deng, Jeff Johnson, Gergely Szilvasy, Pierre-Emmanuel Mazaré, Maria Lomeli, Lucas Hosseini, and Hervé Jégou. 2024. The faiss library.

Jeff Johnson, Matthijs Douze, and Hervé Jégou. 2019. Billion-scale similarity search with GPUs. *IEEE Transactions on Big Data*, 7(3):535–547.

Sean Lee, Aamir Shakir, Darius Koenig, and Julius Lipp. 2024. Open source strikes bread - new fluffy embeddings model.

Xianming Li and Jing Li. 2024. AoE: Angle-optimized embeddings for semantic textual similarity. In *Proceedings of the 62nd Annual Meeting of the Association for Computational Linguistics (Volume 1: Long Papers)*, pages 1825–1839, Bangkok, Thailand. Association for Computational Linguistics.

Christopher Malon. 2024. Multi-hop evidence pursuit meets the web: Team papelo at FEVER 2024. In *Proceedings of the Seventh Fact Extraction and VERification Workshop (FEVER)*, pages 27–36, Miami, Florida, USA. Association for Computational Linguistics.

Mark Rothermel, Tobias Braun, Marcus Rohrbach, and Anna Rohrbach. 2024. InFact: A strong baseline for automated fact-checking. In *Proceedings of the Seventh Fact Extraction and VERification Workshop (FEVER)*, pages 108–112, Miami, Florida, USA. Association for Computational Linguistics.

Michael Schlichtkrull, Yulong Chen, Chenxi Whitehouse, Zhenyun Deng, Mubashara Akhtar, Rami Aly, Zhijiang Guo, Christos Christodoulopoulos, Oana Cocarascu, Arpit Mittal, James Thorne, and Andreas Vlachos. 2024a. The automated verification of textual claims (AVeriTeC) shared task. In *Proceedings of the Seventh Fact Extraction and VERification Workshop (FEVER)*, pages 1–26, Miami, Florida, USA. Association for Computational Linguistics.

Michael Schlichtkrull, Zhijiang Guo, and Andreas Vlachos. 2024b. Averitec: a dataset for real-world claim verification with evidence from the web. In *Proceedings of the 37th International Conference on Neural Information Processing Systems*, NIPS '23, Red Hook, NY, USA. Curran Associates Inc.

Herbert Ullrich, Tomáš Mlynář, and Jan Drchal. 2024. AIC CTU system at AVeriTeC: Re-framing automated fact-checking as a simple RAG task. In *Proceedings of the Seventh Fact Extraction and VERification Workshop (FEVER)*, pages 137–150, Miami, Florida, USA. Association for Computational Linguistics.

An Yang, Anfeng Li, Baosong Yang, Beichen Zhang, Binyuan Hui, Bo Zheng, Bowen Yu, Chang Gao, Chengen Huang, Chenxu Lv, Chujie Zheng, Dayiheng Liu, Fan Zhou, Fei Huang, Feng Hu ... Zhipeng Zhou, and Zihan Qiu. 2025. Qwen3 technical report.

Yejun Yoon, Jaeyoon Jung, Seunghyun Yoon, and Kunwoo Park. 2024. HerO at AVeriTeC: The herd of open large language models for verifying real-world claims. In *Proceedings of the Seventh Fact Extraction and VERification Workshop (FEVER)*, pages 130–136, Miami, Florida, USA. Association for Computational Linguistics.

A System prompt

```
You are a professional fact checker, formulate up to 10 questions that cover all
  the facts needed to validate whether the factual statement (in User message) is
  true, false, uncertain or a matter of opinion. Each question has one of four
  answer types: Boolean, Extractive, Abstractive and Unanswerable using the
  provided sources.
After formulating Your questions and their answers using the provided sources, You
  evaluate the possible veracity verdicts (Supported claim, Refuted claim, Not
  enough evidence, or Conflicting evidence/Cherrypicking) given your claim and
  evidence on a Likert scale (1 - Strongly disagree, 2 - Disagree, 3 - Neutral, 4 -
  Agree, 5 - Strongly agree). Ultimately, you note the single likeliest veracity
  verdict according to your best knowledge.
The facts must be coming from these sources, please refer them using assigned IDs:
---
## Source ID: 1 [url]
[context before]
[page content]
[context after]
...

---
## Output formatting
Please, you MUST only print the output in the following output format:
```json
{
 "questions":
     [
         {"question": "<Your first question>", "answer": "<The answer to the Your
           first question>", "source": "<Single numeric source ID backing the
           answer for Your first question>", "answer_type":"<The type of first
           answer>"},
         {"question": "<Your second question>", "answer": "<The answer to the Your
           second question>", "source": "<Single numeric Source ID backing the
           answer for Your second question>", "answer_type":"<The type of second
           answer>"}
     ],
 "claim_veracity": {
     "Supported": "<Likert-scale rating of how much You agree with the 'Supported'
       veracity classification>",
     "Refuted": "<Likert-scale rating of how much You agree with the 'Refuted'
       veracity classification>",
     "Not Enough Evidence": "<Likert-scale rating of how much You agree with the
       'Not Enough Evidence' veracity classification>",
     "Conflicting Evidence/Cherrypicking": "<Likert-scale rating of how much You
       agree with the 'Conflicting Evidence/Cherrypicking' veracity classification>"
 },
 "veracity_verdict": "<The suggested veracity classification for the claim>"
}
```

Few-shot learning
You have access to the following few-shot learning examples for questions and
  answers.:

Question examples for claim "{example["claim"]}" (verdict
  {example["gold_label"]})
"question": "{question}", "answer": "{answer}", "answer_type": "{answer_type}"
...
```

Listing 1: System prompt for the LLMs, FEVER 8 claim is to be entered into the user prompt. Three dots represent omitted repeating parts of the prompt. Reused and reprinted from Ullrich et al. 2024.

B Qwen3 thinking example

```
<think>
Okay, let's tackle this query. The user is claiming that due to Imran Khan's
  criticism of Macron's comments on Islam, French authorities cancelled the visas
  of 183 Pakistani citizens and deported 118 from the country. I need to verify
  this using the provided sources.

First, I'll look through the sources to see if there's any mention of visa
  cancellations or deportations related to Imran Khan's criticism.

Looking at Source ID 1, it talks about Imran Khan responding to Macron's remarks
  and the condemnation of Islamophobic policies, but there's no mention of visa
  cancellations or deportations.

Source ID 2 discusses a diplomatic row where Pakistan refused to accept a deportee,
  Muhammad Mansha, until his credentials were verified. This seems related to a
  specific case but not the large numbers mentioned in the claim.

Source ID 3 mentions protests in Pakistan against France's republishing of
  cartoons, but again, no visa or deportation numbers here.

Source ID 4 and 5 discuss diplomatic tensions, but not specific numbers of
  deportations. Source 5 and 6 from Newscomworld.com talk about fears of
  deportations of Pakistanis in France but don't mention specific numbers like 183
  or 118.

Source ID 7 is about Pakistan deporting French nationals, which is the reverse of
  the claim.

Source ID 10 mentions Pakistan summoning the French envoy but again, no numbers on
  deportations.

None of the sources mention 183 visas cancelled or 118 deported. The closest is
  Source 2, which mentions one individual, Muhammad Mansha, but that's a single
  case. The other sources discuss diplomatic tensions, protests, and possible fears
  of deportations but no actual numbers provided.

Therefore, the claim about 183 and 118 seems to be unsupported. The answer would be
  that there's no evidence of such numbers in the sources provided. The veracity
  verdict would be Refuted, as the sources don't support the specific numbers given.
</think>

```json
{
    "questions": [
        {"question": "Did French authorities cancel visas or deport Pakistani
          citizens in response to Imran Khan's criticism of Macron's comments on
          Islam?", "answer": "No specific information about visa cancellations or
          deportations of 183 Pakistani citizens or 118 deportees is mentioned in
          the provided sources.", "source": "10", "answer_type": "Boolean"},
        ...
        {"question": "What was the role of social media in the diplomatic dispute
          between Pakistan and France?", "answer": "Social media was used to spread
          calls for boycotts of French products and even nuclear attacks on France,
          but these were not confirmed by official sources.", "source": "5",
          "answer_type": "Extractive"}
    ],
    "claim_veracity": {
        "Supported": "1",
        "Refuted": "5",
        "Not Enough Evidence": "1",
        "Conflicting Evidence/Cherrypicking": "1"
    },
    "veracity_verdict": "Refuted"
}
```
```

Listing 2: Qwen3 thinking tokens example.

Author Index